Autodesk Maya 2017
A Comprehensive Guide

(9th Revised and Updated Edition)

Sham Tickoo
Professor
Purdue University Northwest
Hammond, Indiana, USA

Contributing Authors
Tickoo Institute of Emerging Technologies (TIET)
Gurgaon, India

CADCIM Technologies
Indiana, USA

BPB PUBLICATIONS

ISBN: 978-93-86551-14-6
9th Revised and Updated Edition
(For distribution in SAARC countries only)

Distributors

COMPUTER BOOK CENTRE
12, Shrungar Shopping Centre
M.G. Road
BENGALURU–560001
Ph: 25587923/25584641

BPB BOOK CENTRE
376 Old Lajpat Rai Market
DELHI-110006
Ph: 23861747

DECCAN AGENCIES
4-3-329, Bank Street
HYDERABAD-500195
Ph: 24756967/24756400

INFOTECH
G-2, Sidhartha Building, 96 Nehru Place
NEW DELHI-110019
Ph: 26438245

MICRO MEDIA
Shop No. 5, Mahendra Chambers
150 DN Rd. Next to Capital Cinema
V.T (C.S.T.) Station
MUMBAI-400001

BPB PUBLICATIONS
20, Ansari Road, Darya Ganj
New Delhi-110002
Ph: 23254990/23254991

Published by Manish Jain for BPB Publications, 20 Ansari Road, Darya Ganj
New Delhi-110002 and Printed Repro India Pvt. Ltd, Mumbai

DEDICATION

To teachers, who make it possible to disseminate knowledge to enlighten the young and curious minds of our future generations

To students, who are dedicated to learning new technologies and making the world a better place to live in

SPECIAL RECOGNITION

A special thanks to Mr. Denis Cadu and the ADN team of Autodesk Inc. for their valuable support and professional guidance to procure the software for writing this textbook

THANKS

To employees of CADCIM Technologies and Tickoo Institute of Emerging Technologies (TIET) for their valuable help

Note

If you are a faculty member, you can register by clicking on the following link to access the teaching resources: ***http://www.cadcim.com/Registration.aspx***. The student resources are available at ***http://www.cadcim.com***.

Table of Contents

Chapter 3: NURBS Curves and Surfaces

Chapter 4: NURBS Modeling

Chapter 5: UV Mapping

Chapter 6: Shading and Texturing

Chapter 8: Animation

Chapter 9: Rigging, Constraints, and Deformers

Chapter 10: Paint Effects

Chapter 11: Rendering

Chapter 12: Particle System

Chapter 13: Introduction to nParticles

Chapter 14: Fluids

Preface

Autodesk Maya 2017

Welcome to the world of Autodesk Maya 2017. Autodesk Maya 2017 is a powerful, integrated 3D modeling, animation, visual effects, and rendering software developed by Autodesk Inc. This integrated node-based 3D software finds its application in the development of films, games, and design projects. A wide range of 3D visual effects, computer graphics, and character animation tools make it an ideal platform for 3D artists. The intuitive user interface and workflow tools of Maya 2017 have made the job of design visualization specialists a lot easier.

Autodesk Maya 2017: A Comprehensive Guide textbook covers all features of Autodesk Maya 2017 in a simple, lucid, and comprehensive manner. It aims at harnessing the power of Autodesk Maya 2017 for 3D and visual effects artists, and designers. This textbook will help you transform your imagination into reality with ease. Also, it will unleash your creativity, thus helping you create realistic 3D models, animation, and visual effects. It caters to the needs of both the novice and advanced users of Maya 2017 and is ideally suited for learning at your convenience and at your pace.

The salient features of this textbook are as follows:

- **Tutorial Approach**
  The author has adopted the tutorial point-of-view and the learn-by-doing approach throughout the textbook. This approach will guide the users through the process of creating the models, adding textures, and animating them in the tutorials.

- **Real-World Models as Projects**
  The author has used about 37 real-world modeling and animation projects as tutorials in this textbook. This will enable the readers to relate the tutorials to the real-world models in the animation and visual effects industry. In addition, there are about 34 exercises that are also based on the real-world animation projects.

- **Tips and Notes**
  Additional information related to various topics is provided to the users in the form of tips and notes.

- **Learning Objectives**
  The first page of every chapter summarizes the topics that will be covered in that chapter.

- **Self-Evaluation Test, Review Questions, and Exercises**
  Each chapter ends with Self-Evaluation Test so that the users can assess their knowledge of the chapter. The answers to Self-Evaluation Test are given at the end of the chapter. Also, the Review Questions and Exercises are given at the end of each chapter and they can be used by the instructors as test questions and exercises.

- **Heavily Illustrated Text**
  The text in this book is heavily illustrated with about 550 diagrams and screen captures.

Symbols Used in the Textbook

Note

The author has provided additional information to the users about the topic being discussed in the form of notes.

Tip

Special information and techniques are provided in the form of tips that helps in increasing the efficiency of the users.

This symbol indicates that the command or tool being discussed is new in Autodesk Maya 2017.

This symbol indicates that the command or tool being discussed has been enhanced in Autodesk Maya 2017.

Formatting Conventions Used in the Textbook

Please refer to the following list for the formatting conventions used in this textbook.

- Names of tools, buttons, options, tabs, attributes, renderer, and toolbars are written in bold face

  Example: The **Unfold Selected UVs** tool, the **Apply and Close** button, the **Assign Material to Selection** option, the Maya Software renderer, the **Fill Style** attribute, and so on.

- Names of dialog boxes, drop-down lists, areas, edit boxes, check boxes, and radio buttons are written in boldface.

  Example: The **Save As** dialog box, the **Look In** drop-down list, the **Display** area, the **Particle name** edit box, the **Color feedback** check box, and the **Center** radio button.

- Values entered in edit boxes are written in boldface.

  Example: In the **Particle Size** area, enter the value **0.450** in the **Radius** edit box.

- Names of the files are italicized.

  Example: *c13tut2.mb*

- The methods of invoking a tool/option from menubar or the toolbar are given in a shaded box.

  Menubar: Edit Mesh > Components > Bridge
  UV Texture Editor Toolbar: Select > Polygons > Select Shortest Edge Path Tool

Naming Conventions Used in the Textbook

Tool

If you click on an item in a panel of the Tool Box and a command is invoked to create/edit an object or perform some action, then that item is termed as **tool**.

For example:
Select Tool, **Lasso Tool**, **Move Tool**, **Scale Tool**, **Rotate Tool**, **Show Manipulator Tool**

Flyout

A flyout is a menu that contains options with similar type of functions. Figure 1 shows the flyout displayed on pressing the right mouse button on the **Select Camera** tool.

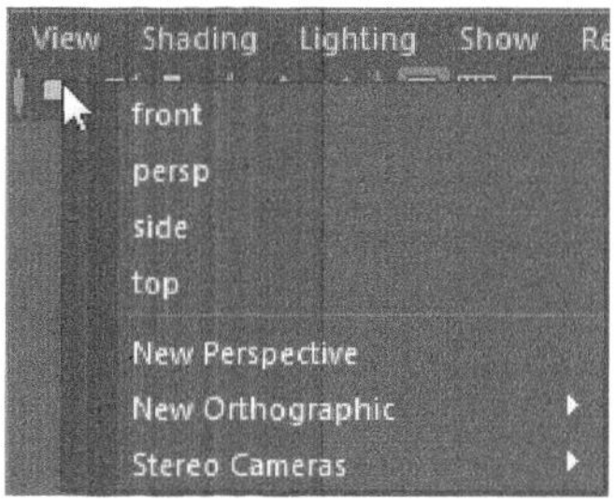

Figure 1 *The flyout displayed on clicking the right mouse button on the* ***Select Camera*** *tool*

Marking Menus

Marking menus are similar to shortcut menus that consist of almost all the tools required to perform an operation on an object. There are three types of marking menus in Maya.

The first type of marking menu is used to create default objects in the viewport. To create a default object, press and hold the SHIFT key and then right-click anywhere in the viewport; a marking menu will be displayed, as shown in Figure 2.

The second type of marking menu is used to switch among various components of an object such as vertices, faces, edges, and so on. To invoke this marking menu, select an object and right-click; a marking menu will be displayed, as shown in Figure 3.

The third type of marking menu is used to modify the components of an object. To invoke this marking menu, select a component, press and hold the SHIFT key, and then right-click on the selected object; a marking menu will be displayed, as shown in Figure 4.

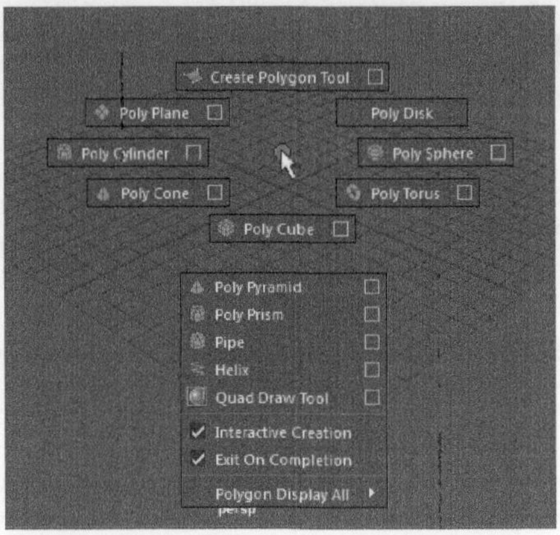

Figure 2 Marking menu displaying options for creating default objects

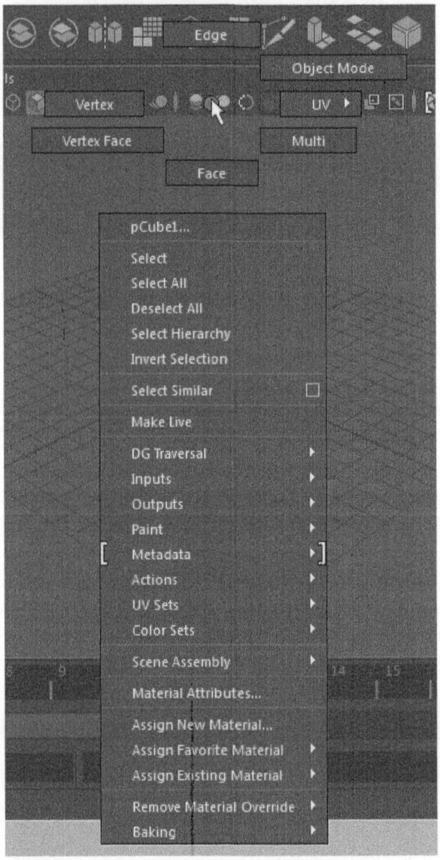

Figure 3 Marking menu displaying components of the selected object

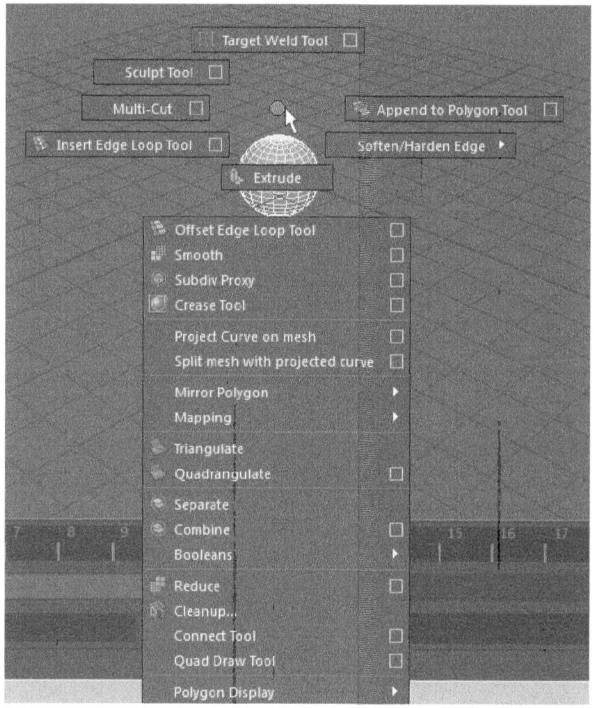

Figure 4 The marking menu displaying various tools for modifying the components of an object

Button

The item in a dialog box that has a 3D shape is termed as **Button**. For example, **Extrude** button, **Apply** button, **Close** button, and so on, refer to Figure 5.

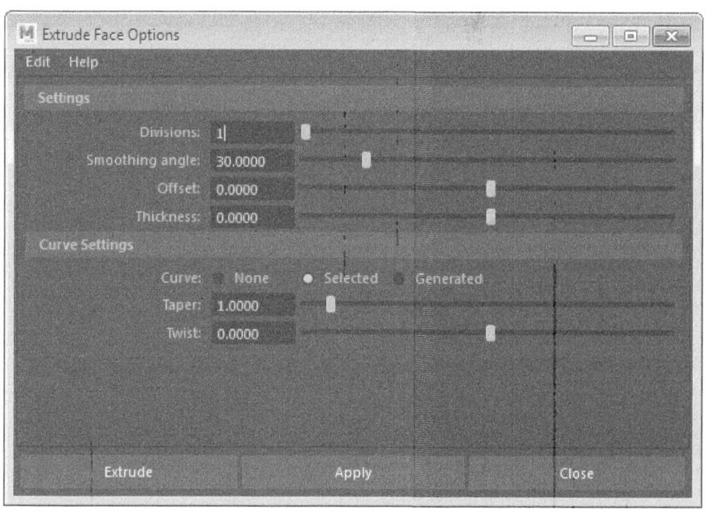

Figure 5 The **Extrude**, **Apply**, and **Close** buttons

Drop-down List

A drop-down list is the one in which a set of options are grouped together. You can set various parameters using these options. You can identify a drop-down list with a down arrow on it. For example, **Material Blend** drop-down list, refer to Figure 6.

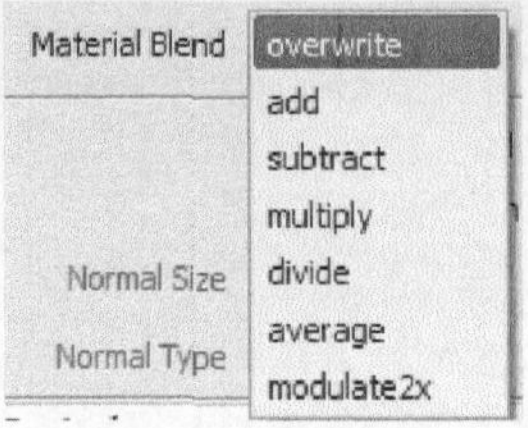

Figure 6 *The* ***Menuset*** *drop-down list*

Naming Convention Used for the Resources

You can access resource files related to this textbook by visiting *www.cadcim.com*. The path to access resources is as follows: *Textbooks > Animation and Visual Effects > Maya > Autodesk Maya 2017: A Comprehensive Guide.*

On this page, there are several drop-downs. You can download a resource file by first selecting it from the desired drop-down and then choosing the **Download** button corresponding to it. Table 1 shows the naming conventions in detail.

Table 1 *Naming conventions used for the resources in the textbook*

Drop-down	Convention
Evaluation Chapters	**Evaluation Chapters** *c01_maya_2017_eval.zip*, *c02_maya_2017_eval.zip*, and so on **TOC** *toc_maya_2017.zip*
Part Files	*c01_maya_2017_prt.zip*, *c02_maya_2017_prt.zip*, and so on
Tutorial Files	**Tutorials** *c01_maya_2017_tut.zip*, *c02_maya_2017_tut.zip*, and so on
Rendering/Media Files/ Data	**Rendered Output - Tutorials** *c01_maya_2017_rndr.zip*, *c02_maya_2017_rndr.zip*, and so on
PowerPoint Presentations (Faculty only)	*c01_maya_2017_ppt.zip*, *c02_maya_2017_ppt.zip*, and so on
IG (Faculty Only)	*ig_maya_2017.zip*

Free Companion Website

It has been our constant endeavor to provide you the best textbooks and services at affordable price. In this endeavor, we have come out with a free companion website that will facilitate the process of teaching and learning of Autodesk Maya 2017. If you purchase this textbook, you will get access to the companion website.

The following resources are available for faculty and students in this website:

Faculty Resources

- **Technical Support**
  You can get online technical support by contacting *techsupport@cadcim.com.*

- **Instructor Guide**
  Solutions to all review questions and exercises in the textbook are provided in this guide to help the faculty members test the skills of the students.

- **PowerPoint Presentations**
  The contents of the book are arranged in powerpoint slides that can be used by the faculty for their lectures.

- **Maya Files**
  The Maya files used in illustration, examples, and exercises are available for free download.

- **Rendered Images**
  If you do an exercise or tutorial, you can compare your rendered output with the one provided in the CADCIM website.

- **Additional Resources**
  You can access additional learning resources by visiting *http://mayaexperts.blogspot.com.*

Student Resources

- **Technical Support**
  You can get online technical support by contacting *techsupport@cadcim.com.*

- **Maya Files**
  The Maya files used in illustrations and examples are available for free download.

- **Rendered Images**
  If you do an exercise or tutorial, you can compare your rendered output with the one provided in the CADCIM website.

- **Additional Resources**
  You can access additional learning resources by visiting *http://mayaexperts.blogspot.com.*

If you face any problem in accessing these files, please contact the publisher at ***sales@cadcim.com*** or the author at ***stickoo@pnw.edu*** or ***tickoo525@gmail.com***.

Stay Connected

You can now stay connected with us through Facebook and Twitter to get the latest information about our textbooks, videos, and teaching/learning resources. To stay informed of such updates, follow us on Facebook ***(www.facebook.com/cadcim)*** and Twitter (**@cadcimtech**). You can also subscribe to our YouTube channel ***(www.youtube.com/cadcimtech)*** to get the information about our latest video tutorials.

Chapter 1

Exploring Maya Interface

Learning Objectives

After completing this chapter, you will be able to:

- *Start Autodesk Maya 2017*
- *Work with menusets in Autodesk Maya*
- *Understand various terms related to Maya interface*
- *Work with tools in Autodesk Maya 2017*

INTRODUCTION TO Autodesk Maya

Welcome to the world of Autodesk Maya 2017. Maya is a 3D software, developed by Autodesk Inc., which enables you to create realistic 3D models and visual effects with much ease. Although Maya is quite a vast software to deal with, yet all the major tools and features used in Autodesk Maya 2017 have been covered in this book.

STARTING Autodesk Maya 2017

To start Autodesk Maya 2017, choose **Start > All Programs > Autodesk > Autodesk Maya 2017 > Autodesk Maya 2017** from the taskbar, refer to Figure 1-1; the default interface of Maya will be displayed with its different components.

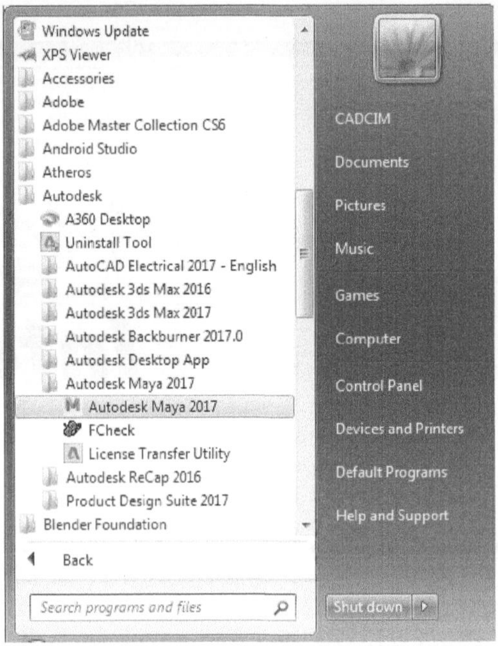

Figure 1-1 Starting Autodesk Maya 2017 using the taskbar

Alternatively, you can start Autodesk Maya 2017 by double-clicking on its shortcut icon displayed on the desktop of your computer. This icon is automatically created on installing Autodesk Maya 2017 on your computer. Double-click on the icon; three windows namely, the **Output Window**, the main **Autodesk Maya 2017** interface window, and the **What's New Highlight Settings** window will be displayed on the screen. The **Output Window** is shown in Figure 1-2. By default, all the new tools and icons are highlighted in green in Maya 2017. The **What's New Highlight Settings** window, as shown in Figure 1-3, is used to toggle the visibility of highlights.

Note

*The mental ray plugin does not get installed while installing Maya 2017. You can download this plugin from the following link: http://www.nvidia.com/object/nvidia-mental-ray-products.html. After installing the plugin, you need to activate it. To do so, choose **Window > Settings/Preferences > Plug-in Manager** from the main menubar; the **Plug-in Manager** dialog box will be displayed. Select the **Loaded** and **Auto load** check boxes on the right of the **Mayatomr.mll** entry and then choose the **Refresh** button followed by the **Close** button.*

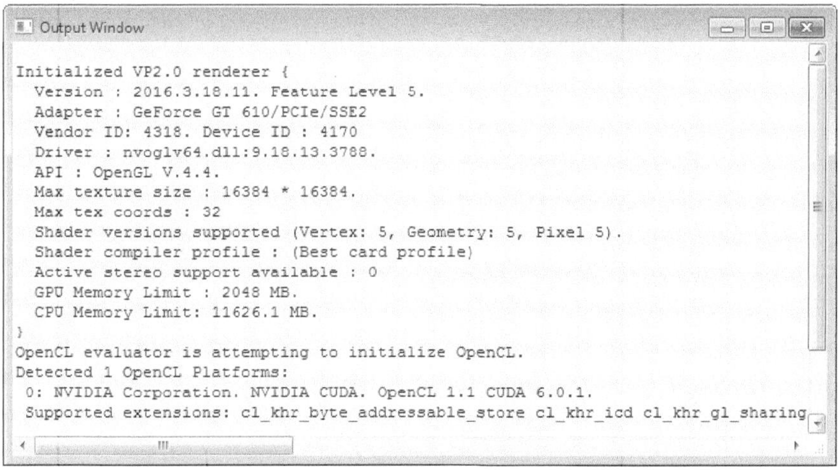

Figure 1-2 The ***Output Window***

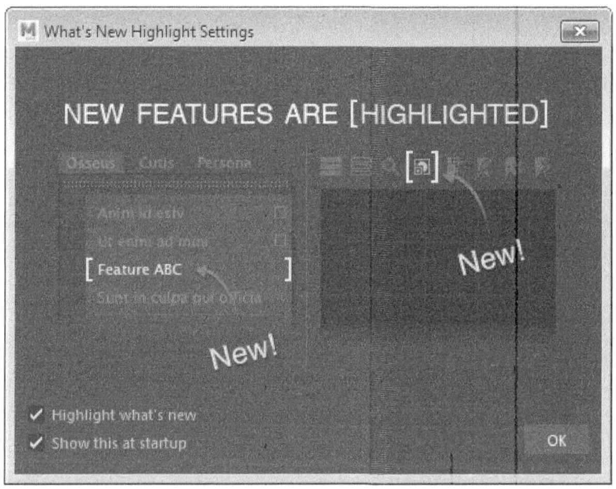

Figure 1-3 The ***What's New Highlight Settings*** *window*

Autodesk Maya 2017 SCREEN COMPONENTS

Autodesk Maya interface consists of viewports, title bar, menubar, Status Line, Shelf, Tool Box, and so on. All these components will be discussed later in this chapter. When you start Autodesk Maya 2017 for the first time, the persp viewport is displayed by default, refer to Figure 1-4.

Workspace is the part or the work area where you can create a 3D scene. Workspaces are also known as viewports or views. In this textbook, the workspaces will be referred to as viewports. Every viewport has a grid placed in the center. The grid acts as a reference that is used in aligning the 3D objects or 2D curves. A grid is a pattern of straight lines that intersect with each other to form squares. The center of the grid is intersected by two dark lines. The point of intersection of these two dark lines is known as the origin. The origin is an arbitrary point, which is used to determine the location of the objects. All the three coordinates, X, Y, and Z are set at 0 position on the origin. Note that in Maya, the X, Y, and Z axes are displayed in red, green, and blue colors, respectively.

***Figure 1-4** The default interface of Autodesk Maya 2017 with persp viewport displayed*

Autodesk Maya 2017 is divided into four viewports: top-Y, front-Z, side-X, and persp. These viewports are classified into two categories, orthographic, and isometric. The orthographic category comprises the top, front, and side viewports and the isometric category consists of the persp viewport. The orthographic viewport displays the 2-dimensional (2D) view of the objects created in it, whereas the isometric viewport displays the 3-dimensional (3D) view of the objects created. Every viewport can be recognized easily by its name, which is displayed at the bottom of each viewport. Figure 1-5 shows various components of the Maya interface.

Every viewport has its own **Panel** menu that allows you to access the tools related to that specific viewport. The Axis Direction Indicator located at the lower left corner of each viewport indicates about the X, Y, and Z axes. Similarly, every viewport in Maya has a default camera applied to it through which the viewport scene is visible. The name of the camera is displayed at the bottom of each viewport. In other words, the name of the viewport is actually the name of the camera of that particular viewport.

The title bar, which lies at the top of the screen, displays the name and version of the software, the name of the file, and the location where the file is saved. A Maya file is saved with the *.mb* or *.ma* extension. The three buttons on the extreme right of title bar are used to minimize, maximize, and close the Autodesk Maya 2017 window, respectively. Various interface components of the Autodesk Maya 2017 interface are discussed next.

Tip

To toggle between single viewport and four viewport views, hover the cursor over one of the viewports and press the SPACEBAR key.

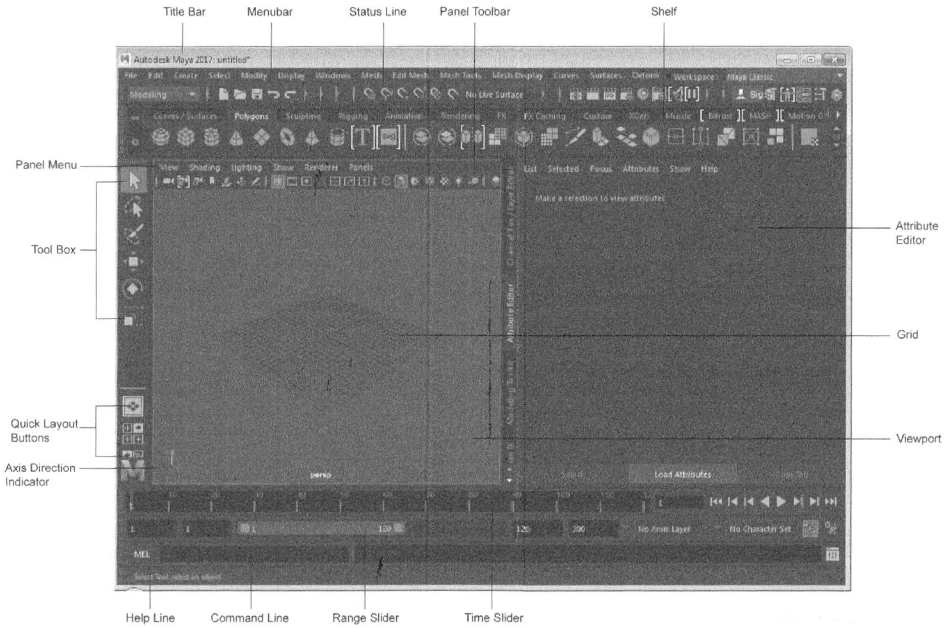

***Figure 1-5** Displaying various screen components of the Maya interface*

Menubar

The menubar is available just below the title bar. The type of menubar displayed depends on menusets. In Maya, there are different menusets namely, **Modeling**, **Rigging**, **Animation**, **FX**, and **Rendering**. These menusets are displayed in the **Menuset** drop-down list located on the extreme left of the Status Line. On selecting a particular menuset, the menus in the menubar change accordingly. However, there are nine common menus in Maya that remain constant irrespective of the menuset chosen. Figure 1-6 shows the menubar corresponding to the **Modeling** menuset.

***Figure 1-6** Menubar displayed on choosing the **Modeling** menuset*

On invoking a menu from the menubar, a pull-down menu is displayed. On the right of some of the options in these pull-down menus, there are two types of demarcations, arrows and option boxes. When you click on an option box, a dialog box will be displayed. You can use this dialog box to set the options for that particular tool or menu item. On clicking the arrow, the corresponding cascading menu will be displayed.

Tip

You can also select different menusets using the hotkeys that are assigned to them. The default hotkeys are F2 (Modeling), F3 (Rigging), F4 (Animation), F5 (FX), and F6 (Rendering).

Status Line

The Status Line is located below the menubar. The **Menuset** drop-down list is located at the left of the Status Line. The Status Line consists of different graphical icons. The graphical icons are further grouped and these groups are separated by vertical lines with either a box or an arrow symbol in the middle. These vertical lines are known as Show/Hide buttons, refer to Figure 1-7. You can click on a Show/Hide button with a box symbol to hide particular icons on the Status Line. On doing so, the corresponding icons will hide and the box will change into an arrow symbol. Similarly, if you click on a Show/Hide button that has an arrow symbol in the middle, the icons of the corresponding group will be displayed. Various groups separated by Show/Hide buttons are discussed next.

Figure 1-7 The Status Line

Menuset

As mentioned earlier, the **Menuset** drop-down list in the Status Line has different menusets such as **Modeling**, **Rigging**, **Animation**, **FX**, and **Rendering**, as shown in Figure 1-8. The options displayed in the menubar depend upon the menuset selected from this drop-down list. For example, if you select the **Rendering** menuset from the **Menuset** drop-down list, all the commands related to it will be displayed in the menus of the menubar. You can add a custom menuset by selecting the **Customize** option. On selecting it, the **Menu Set Editor** window will be displayed, as shown in Figure 1-9. To create a new menuset, choose the **New Menu Set** button from this dialog box; the **Create New Menu Set** dialog box will be displayed. Enter the menu name in **Enter name** edit box and then choose the **Create** button, the new menuset will be added in the **Menu sets** area of the dialog box. To add a menu in the **Menus in menu set** area; select the desired menu items from the **All menus** area and right-click on it and then choose **Add to Menu Set** from the shortcut menu displayed. The selected menu item will be added to the **Menus in menu set** area. Now, choose the **Close Window** button to close the dialog box.

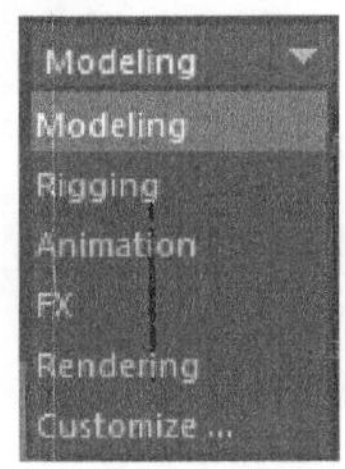

*Figure 1-8 The **Menuset** drop-down list*

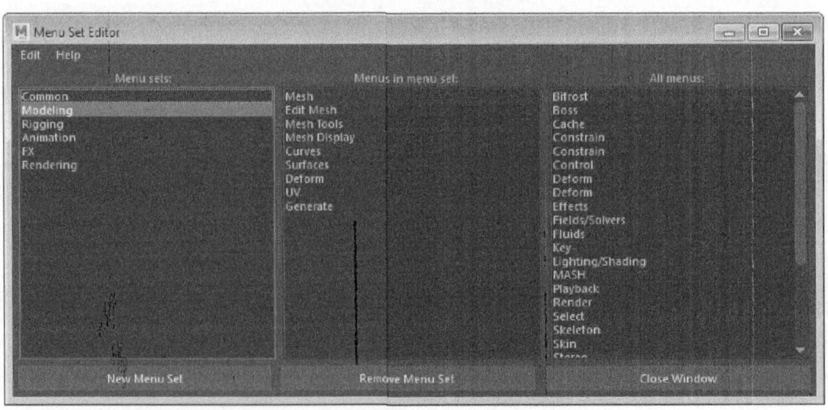

*Figure 1-9 The **Menu Set Editor** window*

File Buttons Group

The buttons in this group are used to perform different file related operations, refer to Figure 1-10. The tools in this group are discussed next.

Create a new scene

The **Create a new scene** button is used to create a new scene. To do so, choose the **New scene** button from the Status Line; the **Warning: Scene Not Saved** message box will be displayed with the **Save changes to untitled scene?** message, as shown in Figure 1-11. This warning message will only appear if the current scene is not saved. Choose the **Save** button to save the scene. Choose the **Don't Save** button to create a new scene without saving the changes made in the current scene. Choose the **Cancel** button to cancel the saving procedure.

Figure 1-10 The File Buttons group

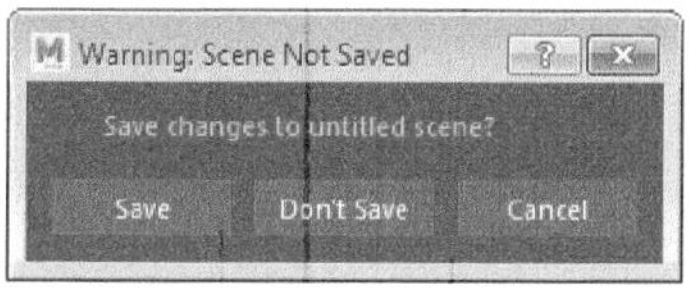

*Figure 1-11 The **Warning: Scene Not Saved** message box*

Open a scene

The **Open a scene** button is used to open a file created earlier. To do so, choose this button from the Status Line; the **Open** dialog box will be displayed, as shown in Figure 1-12. In this dialog box, specify the location of the file that you want to open and then choose the **Open** button; the selected file will open in the Maya interface. This dialog box is divided into different sections and some of them are discussed next.

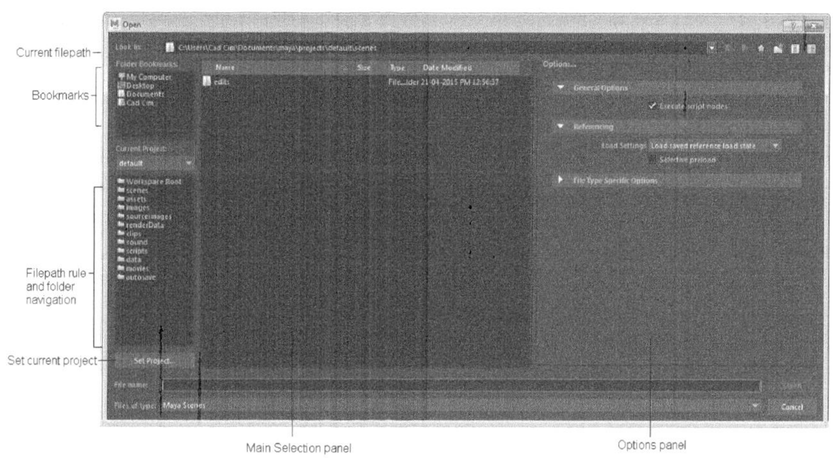

*Figure 1-12 The **Open** dialog box*

Folder Bookmarks

The bookmarks section is used to access the folders in your computer. You can also rearrange the default location of the folders in this section by dragging them up and down using the left mouse button.

Set project
This button is used to set a new project by replacing the current project. On choosing this button, a new window named **Set Project** will be displayed. You will learn about this window later in this book.

Save the current scene

The **Save the current scene** button is used to save the current scene. On choosing the **Save the current scene** button, the **Save As** dialog box will be displayed. Enter a name for the file in the **File name** text box, specify the location to save the current scene, and then choose the **Save As** button to save the current scene. Maya provides you with various options that can be used while saving a file. These options are given on the right side of the dialog box in the **Options** section.

Undo the last action/Redo the last undone action

The **Undo the last action** button is used to remove the last applied action and the **Redo the last undone action** button is used to apply the last undone action again.

Selection Set Icons Group

The Selection Set Icons group shown in Figure 1-13 is used to define the selection of objects or the components of objects from the viewport. This group comprises of three buttons that are discussed next.

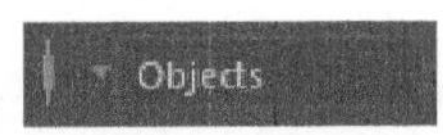

***Figure 1-13** The **Selection set icons** group*

Select by hierarchy and combinations

The **Select by hierarchy and combinations** button is used to select a group of objects in a scene in a hierarchical order. For example, if four objects are combined under a single group, clicking on a single object with this button chosen will select the entire group of objects.

Select by object type

The **Select by object type** button is used to select only a single object from a group of objects in a scene. For instance, if four objects are combined under a single group, this button will enable you to select only the desired object from the group, and not the entire group.

Select by component type

The **Select by component type** button is used to select the components of an object, such as vertices or faces. You can also select the control vertices of the NURBS surfaces using this button.

> **Tip**
> *To switch between the object and the component modes of the selection type, press the F8 key.*

Selection Mask Icons Group

The Selection Masks Icons group comprises of selection filters that help you in selecting objects or their components in the viewport. The selection mask helps you decide which filters/icons should be displayed in the viewport. The selection masks icons group depends on the selection mode button chosen. If the **Select by hierarchy and combinations** button is chosen, then the icons under this group will change, as shown in Figure 1-14.

*Figure 1-14 The **Selection Mask Icons** group displayed on choosing the **Select by hierarchy and combinations** button*

These icons represent the tools that enable you to select the objects based on their hierarchy. Similarly, on choosing the **Select by component type** button and the **Select by object type** button, the icons under these groups will change accordingly, and this will enable you to select either the entire object, or its components, refer to Figures 1-15 and 1-16. The most commonly used group is the icons group displayed on choosing the **Select by object type** button. Various buttons in this selection masks icons group are discussed next.

*Figure 1-15 The **Selection Mask Icons** group displayed on choosing the **Select by component type** button*

*Figure 1-16 The **Selection Mask Icons** group displayed on choosing the **Select by object type** button*

Set the object selection mask

The **Set the object selection mask** button is used to switch all the selection icons on or off. To do so, choose the **Set the object selection mask** button from the Status Line; a flyout will be displayed, as shown in Figure 1-17. Choose the **All objects on** option from the flyout to make all selection icons on or select the **All objects off** option to switch off all selection icons from the menu.

*Figure 1-17 Flyout displayed on choosing the **Set the object selection mask** button*

Note

*If the **All objects off** option is chosen, you cannot select any object in the viewport.*

Select handle objects

The **Select handle objects** button allows you to select IK handles and selection handles. You will learn more about this button in the later chapters.

Select joint objects

The **Select joint objects** button is used to select only the joints of the objects while animating or rigging them.

Select curve objects

The **Select curve objects** button is used to select the NURBS curves, curves on the surface, and paint effects strokes in the viewport.

Select surface objects

The **Select surface objects** button is used to select the NURBS surfaces, poly surfaces, planes, and GPU cache in the viewport.

Select deformations objects

The **Select deformations objects** button is used to select the lattices, clusters, nonlinear, and sculpt objects in the viewport.

Select dynamic objects

The **Select dynamic objects** button is used to select the dynamic objects in the viewport.

Select rendering objects

The **Select rendering objects** button is used to select the lights, cameras, and textures in the viewport.

Select miscellaneous objects

The **Select miscellaneous objects** button is used to select miscellaneous objects such as IK End Effectors, locators, and dimensions in the viewport.

Lock/Unlock current selection

The **Lock/Unlock current selection** button is used to lock the selection so that left mouse button acts on the manipulators instead of selecting objects. Select an object in the viewport and choose the **Lock/Unlock current selection** button from the Status Line; the tool manipulators will be locked to the object and no other object can be selected from the viewport.

Highlight Selection mode is on

The **Highlight Selection mode is on** button is used to turn off the automatic display of the components.

Snap Buttons Group

The Snap Buttons group comprises of different snap options, as shown in Figure 1-18. These options are used to snap the selected objects to specific points in a scene. The buttons in this group are discussed next.

***Figure 1-18** The **Snap Buttons** group*

Snap to grids

The **Snap to grids** button is used to snap an object to the closest grid intersection point. For example, to snap a sphere to the closest grid intersection point, choose **Create > Objects > NURBS Primitives > Sphere** from the menubar and then click in the viewport; a sphere will be created. Choose the **Snap to grids** tool from the Status Line and invoke **Move Tool** from the Tool Box. Next, press the middle mouse button over the sphere and drag it; the sphere will be snapped to the closest grid intersection point, refer to Figure 1-19.

Snap to curves

The **Snap to curves** button is used to snap an object to the curve in the viewport. For example, to snap a cube on a curve, choose **Create > Objects > NURBS Primitives >**

Cube from the menubar and then click in the viewport; a cube will be created. Next, choose **Create > Curve Tools > EP Curve Tool** from the menubar and then create a curve in the top viewport. Press ENTER to exit the **EP Curve Tool**. Next, choose **Move Tool** from the Tool Box and align the cube over the curve. Choose the **Snap to curves** button from the Status Line. Press the middle mouse button over the cube and drag it; the cube will move over the curve while remaining snapped to the curve, refer to Figure 1-20.

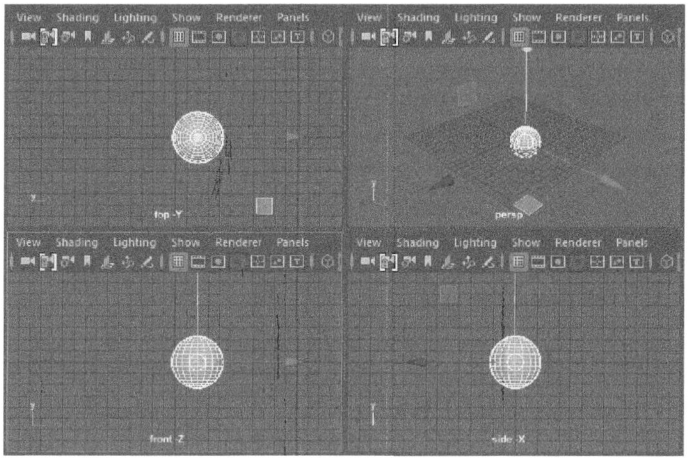

Figure 1-19 *The sphere snapped to the closest grid intersection point*

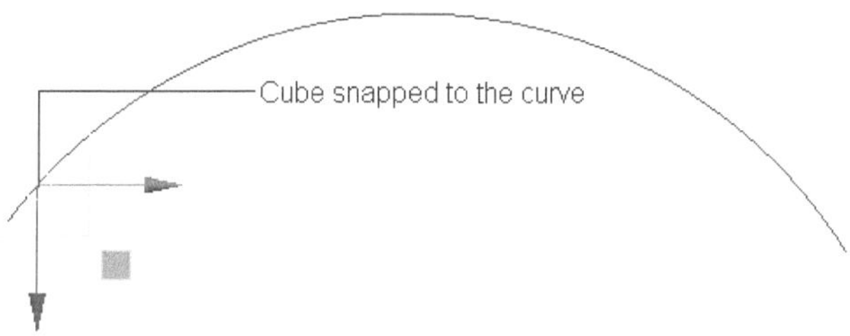

Figure 1-20 *The cube snapped to the curve*

Snap to points

The **Snap to points** button is used to snap the selected objects to the closest control vertex or pivot point. For example, to snap a cube to the vertices of a polygonal plane, choose **Create > Objects > Polygon Primitives > Plane > Option Box** from the menubar; the **Tool Settings** (**Polygon Plane Tool)** window will be displayed. Now, set the **Width divisions** and **Height divisions** to **10**, and then click in the viewport to make a plane. Next, create a cube in the viewport, as discussed earlier. Next, select the cube and choose the **Snap to points** button from the Status Line and drag the cube with the middle mouse button; the cube will snap to the closest control vertex of the polygonal plane.

Snap to Projected Center

The **Snap to Projected Center** button is used to snap an object (joint or locator) to the center of the other object. For example, to snap a locator to the center of a polygonal plane, choose **Create > Objects > Polygon Primitives > Plane** from the menubar and drag the cursor; a plane will be created. Next, choose **Create > Construction Aids > Locator** from the menubar; a locator will be created. Now, select the locator and choose the

Snap to Projected Center button from the Status Line; the locator will snap to the center of the polygonal plane.

Snap to view planes

The **Snap to view planes** button is used to snap the selected object to the view plane of the viewport.

> **Tip**
> *You can also use the shortcut keys to perform a particular snap functions. For example, press X for **Snap to grids**, C for **Snap to curves**, and V for the **Snap to points** tools.*

Make the selected object live

The **Make the selected object live** button is used to make the selected surface a live object. A live object is used to create objects or curves directly on its surface. For example, to snap a cube on the surface of a polygonal sphere, choose **Create > Objects > Polygon Primitives > Sphere** from the menubar and drag the cursor; a sphere will be created. To create a cube on the surface of the sphere, choose the **Make the selected object live** button from the Status Line; the sphere will appear in green wireframe. Now, choose **Create > Objects > Polygon Primitives > Cube** from the menubar and drag the cursor; a cube will be created on the surface of the sphere.

History Buttons Group

This group in the Status Line helps you control various objects. The objects with input connections are affected or controlled by other objects, whereas the objects with output connections affect or control other objects.

Inputs to the selected object

The **Inputs to the selected object** button is used to edit all input connections for the selected object such that the selected object gets influenced by another object.

Outputs from the selected object

The **Outputs from the selected object** button is used to select and edit the output operations of an object.

Construction history on/off

The **Construction history on/off** button is used to record the construction history. The construction history is used to track the changes made on an object at a later stage. Sometimes, the construction history may make a particular file size heavy. To decrease the file size, you can deactivate this option.

Render Tools Group

This group in the Status Line is used to access all render controls in Maya. The buttons in this group are discussed next.

Open Render View

The **Open Render View** button is used to open the **Render View** window.

Render the current frame

The **Render the current frame** button is used to render the selected viewport at the current frame using the **Maya Software** renderer. Choose the **Render the current frame** button from the Status Line; the **Render View** window will be displayed. The **Render View** window shows the rendered view of the selected scene, refer to Figure 1-21, whereas the **Output Window** will display all the rendering calculations made for rendering the active scene, refer to Figure 1-22.

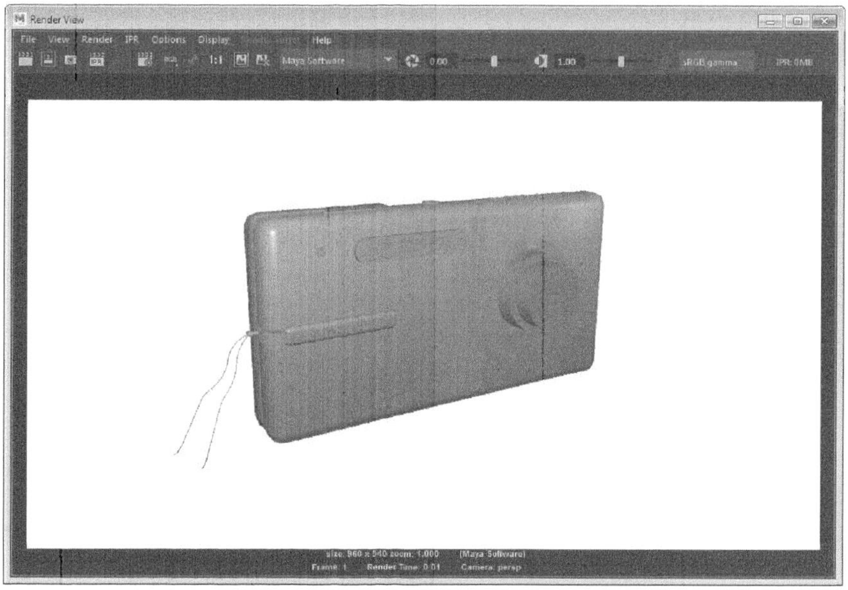

*Figure 1-21 The **Render View** window*

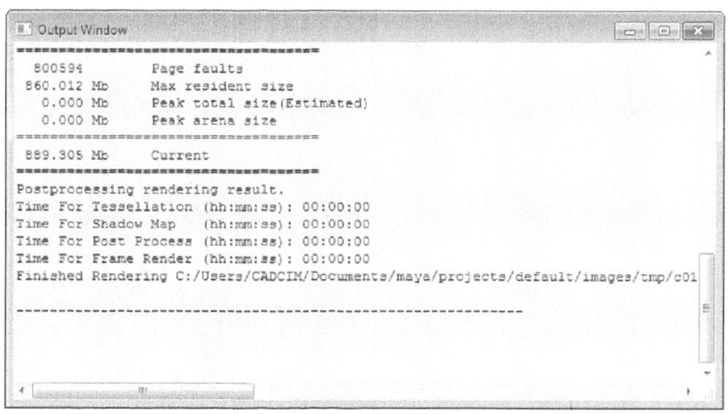

*Figure 1-22 The **Output Window***

IPR render the current frame

The **IPR render the current frame** button is used to perform an **IPR** render. Here, **IPR** stands for Interactive Photorealistic Rendering. This tool helps you to adjust the lighting or the shading attributes of the rendered scene and then update it as per the requirement. To render the current frame, choose this button from the Status Line; the **Render View** window will be displayed. Now, press the left mouse button and drag it in the **Render View** window to set the selection for IPR rendering. As a result, Maya will render the selected part only. In other words, it will help you visualize your scene dynamically. Now, if you make changes in the color or lighting attribute of the scene using the **Attribute Editor**, the selected part will be rendered automatically.

Display render settings window

On choosing the **Display render settings window** button, the **Render Settings** window will be displayed, as shown in Figure 1-23. This window comprises of all controls needed for rendering. These controls help you adjust the render settings such as resolution, file options, ray tracing quality, and so on.

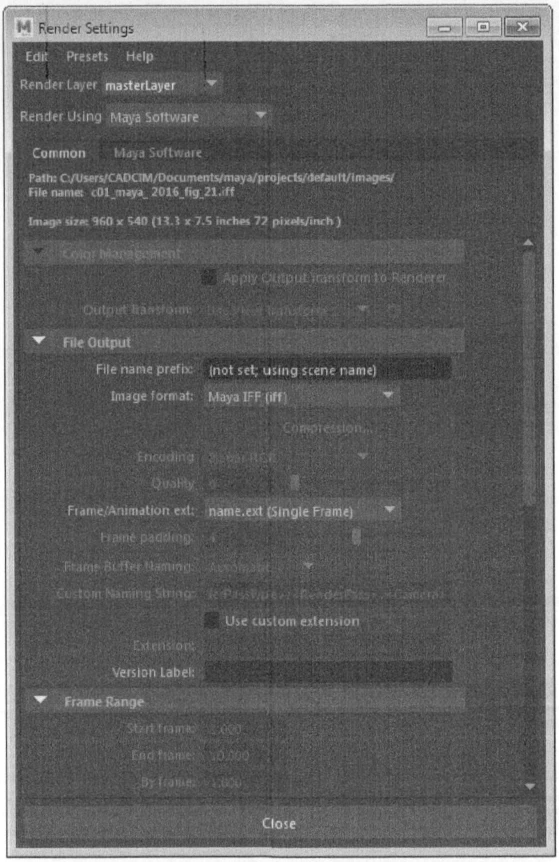

*Figure 1-23 The **Render Settings** window*

Display hypershade window

On choosing this button, the **Hypershade** window will be displayed. Using this window, you can create shading networks. The **Hypershde** window is discussed in detail in the later chapters.

Launch Render Setup Window

On choosing this button, the **Render Setup Editor** window will be displayed, with the **Render Setup** editor on the left and the **Property Editor** on the right. The **Render Setup** editor allows you to create layers, collections and overrides, whereas the **Property Editor** allows you to set their corresponding values.

Open the Light Editor

On choosing this button, the **Light Editor (Global Mode)** window will be displayed. This window lists all lights in the scene with commonly used attributes for each light.

Toggle pausing Viewport 2 display update

This button is used to pause Viewport 2 display update.

Input Line Operations Group

This group in the Status Line helps you quickly select, rename, and transform the objects that are created in the viewport. Some of the options in this group are in hidden modes. To view them, move the cursor over the arrow on the left of the input field and then press and hold the left mouse button on it; a flyout will be displayed. Now, select the required option from the flyout; the corresponding mode will be displayed. By default, the **Absolute transform** mode is active. The transform modes are discussed next.

Absolute transform

The **Absolute transform** area is used to move, rotate, or scale a selected object in the viewport. To do so, invoke the required transformation tool from the Tool Box and enter values in the **X**, **Y** and **Z** edit boxes in the **Absolute transform** area, refer to Figure 1-24. Now, press ENTER; the selected object will be moved, rotated, and scaled according to the values entered in the edit boxes.

Note

*The **Absolute transform** area takes the center of the viewport as a reference for transforming an object.*

Relative transform

The **Relative transform** area is also used to scale, rotate, or move a selected object in the viewport, refer to Figure 1-25. This area is similar to the **Absolute transform** area with the only difference that the **Relative transform** area takes the current position of the object as a reference point for transforming an object.

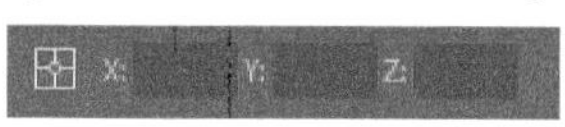

*Figure 1-24 The **Absolute transform** area*

*Figure 1-25 The **Relative transform** area*

Rename

The **Rename** area is used to change the name of a selected object. To rename an object, select the object from the viewport whose name you want to change; the default name of the selected object will be displayed in the text box in the **Rename** area, refer to Figure 1-26. Enter a new name for the object in the edit box and press ENTER.

Select by name

You can select an object in the viewport by entering its name in the text box in the **Select by name** area, refer to Figure 1-27.

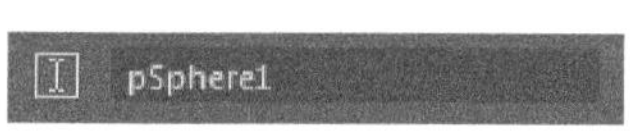

*Figure 1-26 The **Rename** area*

*Figure 1-27 The **Select by name** area*

Autodesk Store Group

There is a drop-down list in this group that has three options: **Sign In**, **Explore Purchase Options**, and **Manage License**. The **Sign In** option is used to sign in to the Autodesk account. On selecting **Explore Purchase Options** from this drop-down list, open the Autodesk Store web page from where you can buy various Autodesk products.

The **Manage License** option will open the **License Manager** that you can use to manage Maya license.

Sidebar Buttons Group

The toggle buttons in the Sidebar Buttons group are used to invoke tools, editors, and windows. The buttons in this group are discussed next.

Show/Hide Modeling Toolkit

The **Show/Hide Modeling Toolkit** button is used to open the **Modeling Toolkit** window, as shown in Figure 1-28. The **Modeling Toolkit** window is used to perform multiple modeling specific operations.

Show/Hide the Character Control Tool

The **Show/Hide the Character Control Tool** is used to open the **Human IK** window, as shown in Figure 1-29. The tools in this window allow you to define and control multiple character setups in a single window.

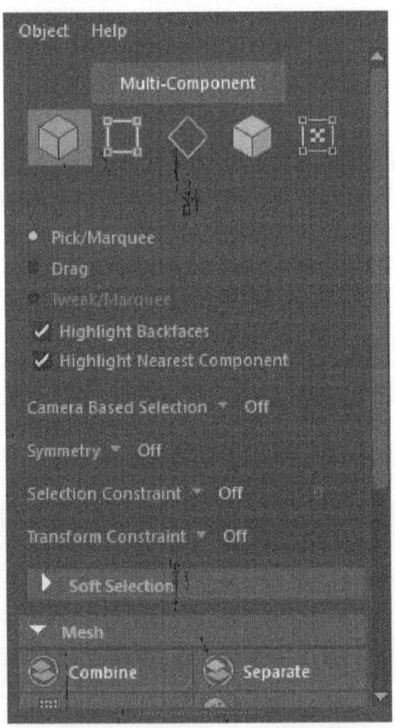

Figure 1-28 The ***Modeling Toolkit*** *window*

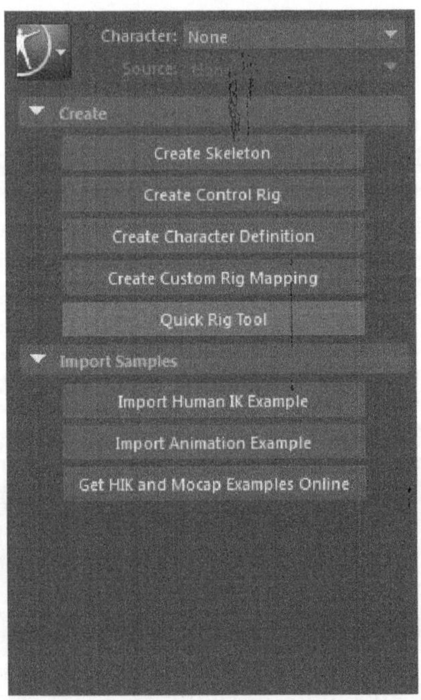

Figure 1-29 The ***Human IK*** *window*

Show/Hide the Attribute Editor

The **Show/Hide the Attribute Editor** button is used to toggle the visibility of the **Attribute Editor**, refer to Figure 1-30. The **Attribute Editor** is used to control different properties of the selected object.

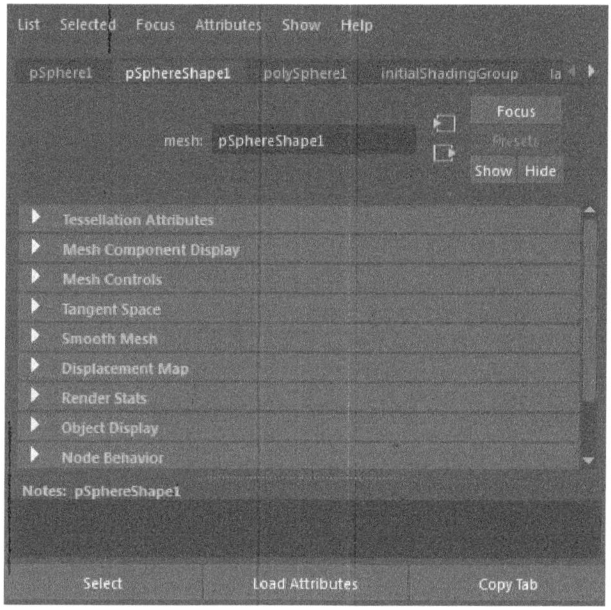

Figure 1-30 *The* ***Attribute Editor***

Show/Hide the Tool Settings

The **Show/Hide the Tool Settings** button is used to display the options for selected tool in the **Tool Settings** window. On choosing this button, the **Tool Settings** window of the selected tool will be displayed. For example, if you have chosen **Move Tool** from the Tool Box, then you can control its settings by using the **Tool Settings (Move Tool)** window, as shown in Figure 1-31.

Show/Hide the Channel Box

The **Show/Hide the Channel Box** button is used to toggle the visibility of the **Channel Box / Layer Editor**. This button is similar to the **Show/Hide the Attribute Editor** button. On choosing this button, the **Channel Box / Layer Editor** will be displayed on the right of the viewport, as shown in Figure 1-32. The **Channel Box** is used to control the transformation and the geometrical structure of the selected object. The **Layer Editor** is used to organize the objects in a scene when there are many objects in the viewport. Multiple objects can be arranged in the layer editor to simplify the scene.

Note

By default, the keyable attributes of selected object(s) are displayed in the ***Channel Box****. To add more attributes to it, choose* ***Windows > Editors > General Editors > Channel Control*** *from the menubar; the* ***Channel Control*** *window will be displayed. In this window, three areas will be displayed in the* ***Keyable*** *tab:* ***Keyable****,* ***Nonkeyable Hidden****, and* ***Nonkeyable Displayed****. To add attributes, select them from the* ***Nonkeyable Hidden*** *area and then choose the* ***Move >>*** *button. Next, choose the* ***Close*** *button.*

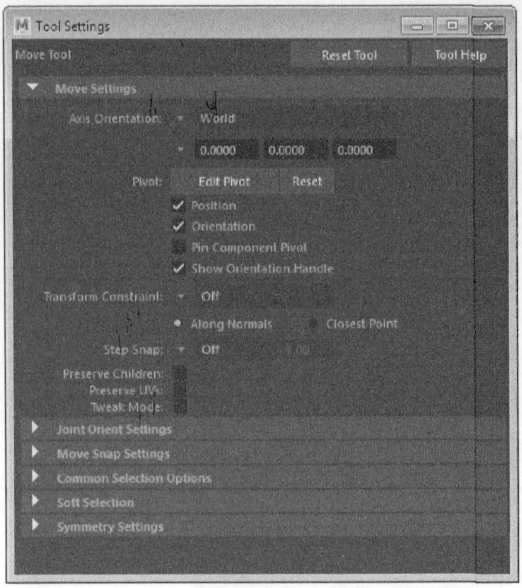

Figure 1-31 The ***Tool Settings (Move Tool)*** *window*

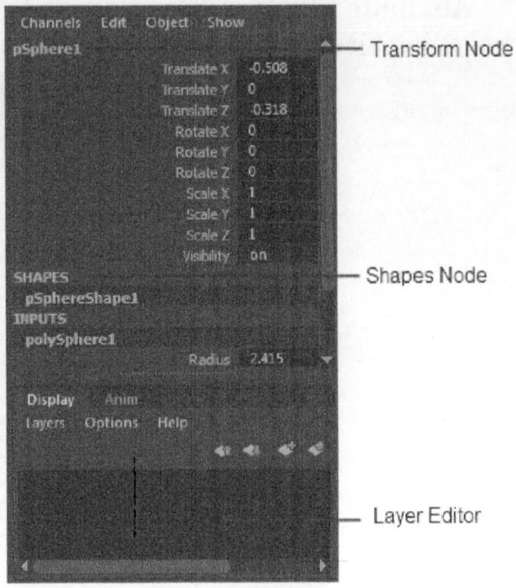

Figure 1-32 The ***Channel Box / Layer Editor***

Shelf

The Shelf is located below the Status Line, as shown in Figure 1-33. The Shelf is divided into two parts. The upper part in the Shelf consists of different Shelf tabs and lower part displays the icons of different tools. The icons displayed in this area depend on the tab chosen, refer to Figure 1-33.

Figure 1-33 The Shelf

You can also customize the Shelf as per your requirement. To do so, press and hold the left mouse button over the **Menu of items to modify the shelf** button, refer to Figure 1-34; a flyout will be displayed, as shown in Figure 1-34. Various options in this flyout are discussed next.

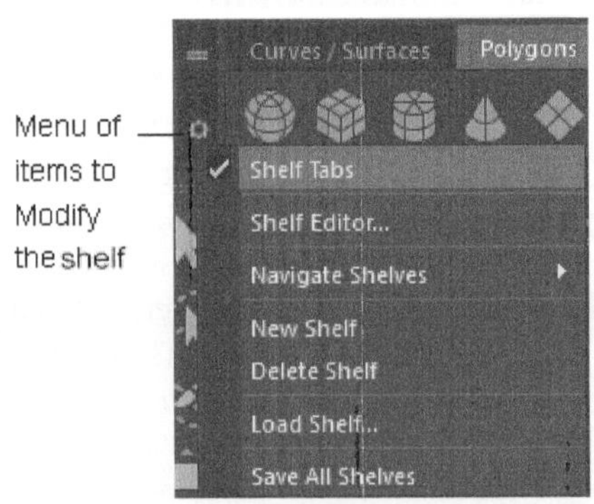

Figure 1-34 Flyout displayed on choosing the ***Menu of items to modify the shelf*** *button*

Shelf Tabs

The **Shelf Tabs** option is used to toggle the visibility of the Shelf tabs. On choosing this option, the Shelfs tabs will disappear, and only the tool icons corresponding to the selected tab will be visible.

Shelf Editor

The **Shelf Editor** option is used to create a Shelf and edit the properties of an existing Shelf. When this option is chosen, the **Shelf Editor** will be displayed in the viewport, as shown in Figure 1-35. Alternatively, you can choose **Windows > Editors > Settings/Preferences > Shelf Editor** from the menubar to display the **Shelf Editor**. In the **Shelf Editor**, you can change the name and position of shelves and their contents. You can also create a new shelf and its contents using the **Shelf Editor**.

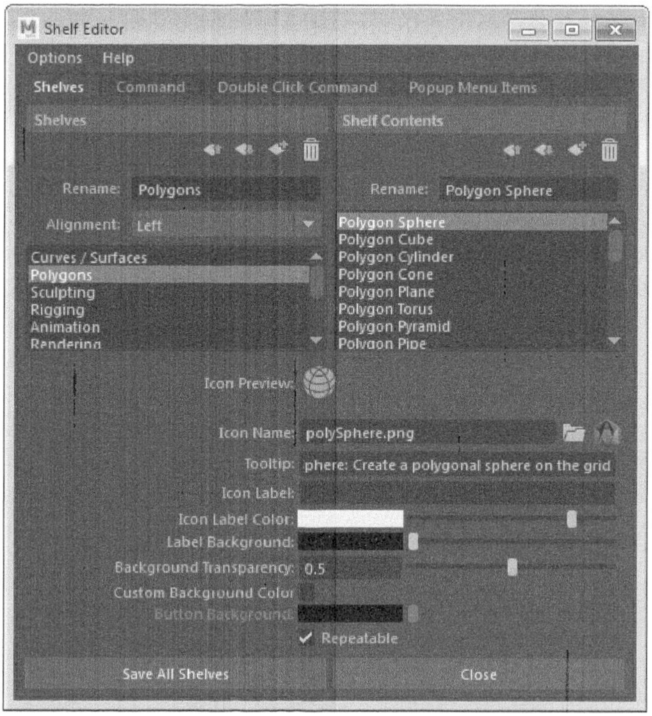

*Figure 1-35 The **Shelf Editor***

Navigate Shelves

The **Navigate Shelves** option is used to choose the previous or next Shelf of the currently chosen Shelf. On choosing this option, a cascading menu will be displayed, as shown in Figure 1-36. The options in the cascading menu are discussed next.

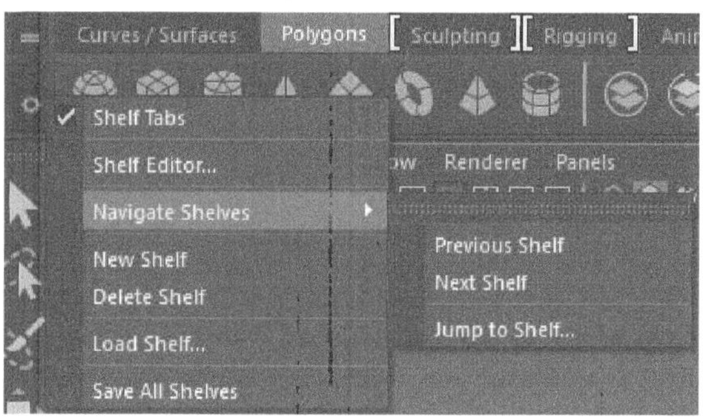

*Figure 1-36 Cascading menu displayed on choosing the **Navigate Shelves** option*

Previous Shelf

The **Previous Shelf** option is used to choose the Shelf that comes before the currently chosen Shelf. For example, choose the **Rendering** tab; the rendering specific icons will be displayed. Next, press and hold the left mouse button over the **Menu of items to modify the shelf** option; a flyout will be displayed. Choose **Navigate Shelves** from the flyout; a cascading menu is displayed. From the cascading menu, choose **Previous Shelf**; the **Animation** tab is chosen displaying the dynamic specific icons.

Next Shelf

The **Next Shelf** option is used to choose the shelf that comes after the currently chosen Shelf.

Jump to Shelf

The **Jump to Shelf** option is used to choose the specific Shelf by entering its name. On choosing this option, the **Jump to Shelf** dialog box will be displayed, as shown in Figure 1-37. Enter the name of the shelf in the **Shelf Name** text box and choose the **OK** button; the **Shelf** tab with icons specific to the corresponding shelf are displayed.

New Shelf

The **New Shelf** option is used to add a new Shelf tab to the existing Shelf. On choosing this option, the **Create New Shelf** dialog box will be displayed, as shown in Figure 1-38. Enter a name for the new Shelf and choose the **OK** button; a new Shelf will be created, as shown in Figure 1-39. For adding different tools in the tools area corresponding to the new Shelf created, press and hold CTRL+SHIFT and then select the desired tools from the pull-down menus.

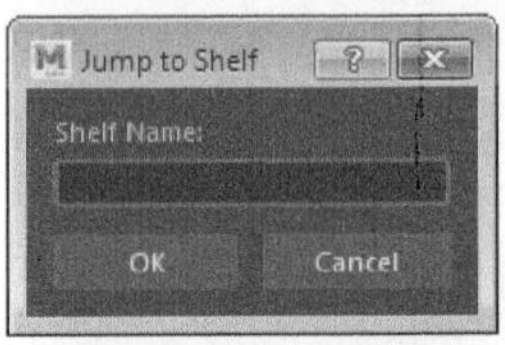

*Figure 1-37 The **Jump to Shelf** dialog box*

*Figure 1-38 The **Create New Shelf** dialog box*

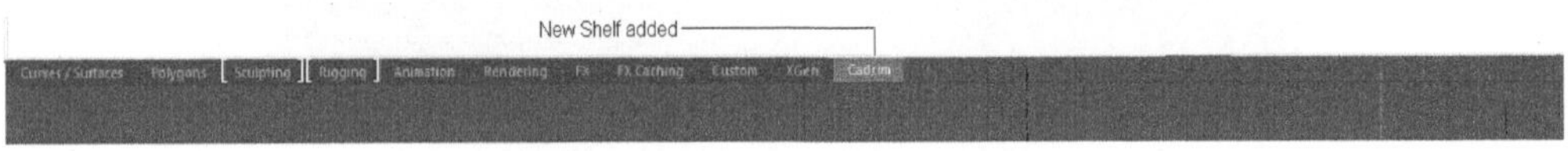

Figure 1-39 A new Shelf added

Delete Shelf

The **Delete Shelf** option is used to delete a shelf. On choosing this option, the **Confirm** message box will be displayed, as shown in Figure 1-40. Choose the **OK** button to delete the selected Shelf.

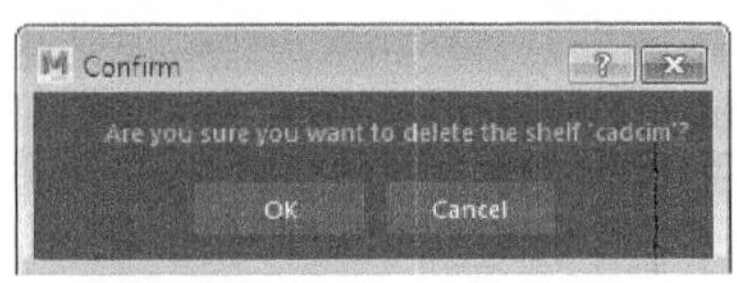

*Figure 1-40 The **Confirm** message box*

Load Shelf

The **Load Shelf** option is used to load the shelf that was saved previously. When this option is chosen, the **Load Shelf** dialog box will be displayed. You can choose the previously saved shelf from this dialog box; the desired **Shelf** tab will be displayed in the shelf.

Save all Shelves

The **Save all Shelves** option is used to save the shelves, so that you can use them later while working in Maya.

Tool Box

The Tool Box is located on the left side of the workspace. It comprises of the most commonly used tools in Maya. In addition to the commonly used tools, the Tool Box has several other options or commands that help you change the layout of the interface. Various tools in the Tool Box are discussed next.

Select Tool

The **Select Tool** is used to select the objects created in the viewport. To select an object, invoke the **Select Tool** from the Tool Box and click on an object in the viewport; the object will be selected. On invoking this tool, the manipulators will not be activated.

Lasso Tool

The **Lasso Tool** is used to select an object by using a free hand marquee selection. This tool is very much similar to the **Select Tool**. To select an object, invoke the **Lasso Tool**; the cursor will change to a rope knot. Next, press and hold the left mouse button and drag the cursor in the viewport to create a selection area around the object. Then, release the left mouse button; the object inside the selection area will be selected. To adjust the properties of the **Lasso Tool**, make sure that the **Lasso Tool** is invoked, and then choose the **Show/Hide the Tool Settings** button from the Status Line; the **Tool Settings (Lasso Tool)** window will be displayed. Adjust the **Lasso Tool** properties from the **Tool Settings (Lasso Tool)** window as per your requirement.

Paint Selection Tool

The **Paint Selection Tool** is used to select various components of an object. To select various components of an object, invoke the **Select Tool** from the Tool Box and select an object in the viewport. Next, press and hold the right mouse button over the selected object; a marking menu will be displayed. Choose **Vertex** from the marking menu to make the vertex selection mode active. Now, choose the **Paint Selection Tool** from the Tool Box; the cursor will change to the paint brush. Next, press and hold the left mouse button and drag the cursor over the object to select the desired vertices. To go back to the object mode, invoke the **Select Tool** and then press and hold the right mouse button; a marking menu will be displayed. Choose **Object Mode** from the marking menu to make the vertex selection mode inactive.

You can also increase the size of the **Paint Selection Tool** cursor. To do so, press and hold the B key on the keyboard. Next, press and hold the left mouse button in the viewport and drag the cursor to adjust the size of the brush.

Move Tool

The **Move Tool** is used to move an object from one place to another in the viewport. To do so, invoke **Move Tool** from the Tool Box; the cursor will change to an arrow with a box at its tip. Select the object in the workspace that you want to move. You can move the selected object in the X, Y, and Z directions by using the handles/manipulators over the object. You can also adjust the properties of the **Move Tool** by choosing the **Show or Hide the Tool Settings** button from the Status Line or by double-clicking on the **Move Tool** itself. To use the **Move Tool**, you need to create an object in the viewport. To do so, create a sphere by choosing **Create > Objects > Polygon Primitives > Sphere** from the menubar.

A sphere will be created. Now, invoke the **Move Tool** from the Tool Box and select the object created by clicking on it; the **Move Tool** manipulator will be displayed on the selected object with three color handles, as shown in Figure 1-41. These three color handles are used to move the object in the X, Y, or Z direction. The colors of the handles represent three axes; red represents the X-axis, green represents the Y-axis, and blue represents the Z-axis. At the intersection point of these handles, a box will be displayed that can be used to move the object proportionately in all the three directions. Press and hold the left mouse button over the box and drag the cursor to move the object freely in the viewport. To adjust the default settings of the **Move Tool**, double-click on it in the Tool Box; the **Tool Settings (Move Tool)** window will be displayed, as shown in Figure 1-42. Change the settings as per your requirement in this window.

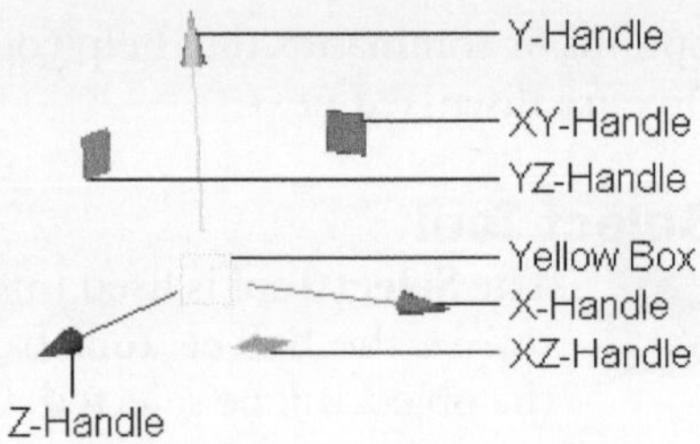

*Figure 1-41 The **Move Tool** manipulator*

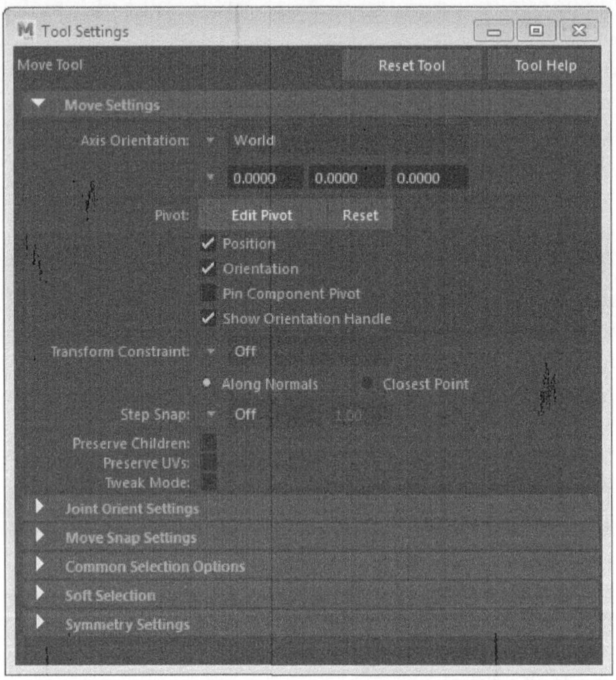

*Figure 1-42 The **Tool Settings (Move Tool)** window*

By default, the pivot point is located at the center of the object. To change the pivot point, make sure that the **Move Tool** is invoked and then press the INSERT key; the pivot point will be displayed in the viewport, as shown in Figure 1-43. Move the pivot point to adjust its position. You can also put the pivot at the center of the object. To do so, choose **Modify > Pivot > Center Pivot** from the menubar; the pivot point will be adjusted to the center of the object. You can also adjust the pivot point by pressing and holding the D key and moving the manipulator.

Note

A pivot is a point in 3D space that is used as a reference point for the transformation of objects.

Rotate Tool

The **Rotate Tool** is used to rotate an object along the X, Y, or Z axis. To rotate an object in the viewport, select the object and invoke the **Rotate Tool** from the Tool Box; the **Rotate**

Tool manipulator will be displayed on the object, as shown in Figure 1-44. The **Rotate Tool** manipulator consists of three colored rings. The red ring represents the X axis, whereas the green and blue rings represent the Y and Z axes, respectively. Moreover, the yellow ring around the selected object helps you rotate the selected object in the view axis. On selecting a particular ring, its color changes to yellow. You can change the default settings of the **Rotate Tool** by double-clicking on it in the Tool Box. On doing so, the **Tool Settings (Rotate Tool)** window will be displayed, as shown in Figure 1-45. This window contains various options for rotation. You can change the settings in this window as required.

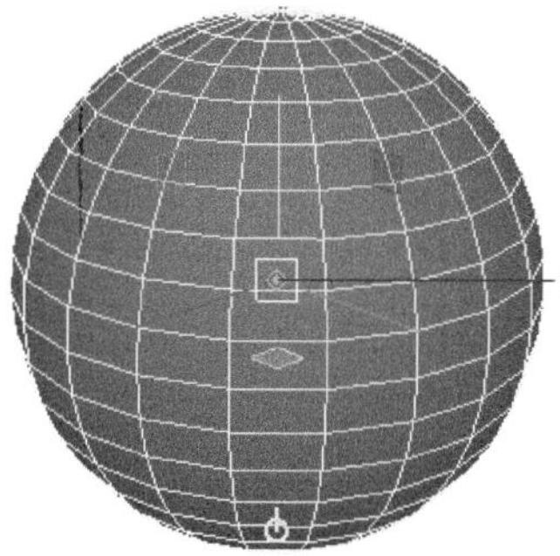

Figure 1-43 The pivot point

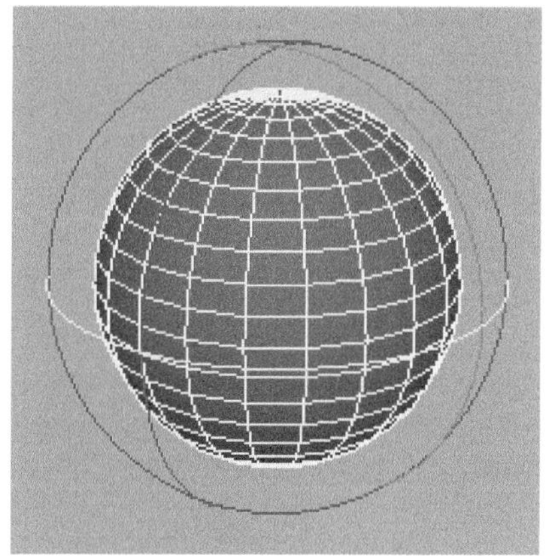

*Figure 1-44 The **Rotate Tool** manipulator*

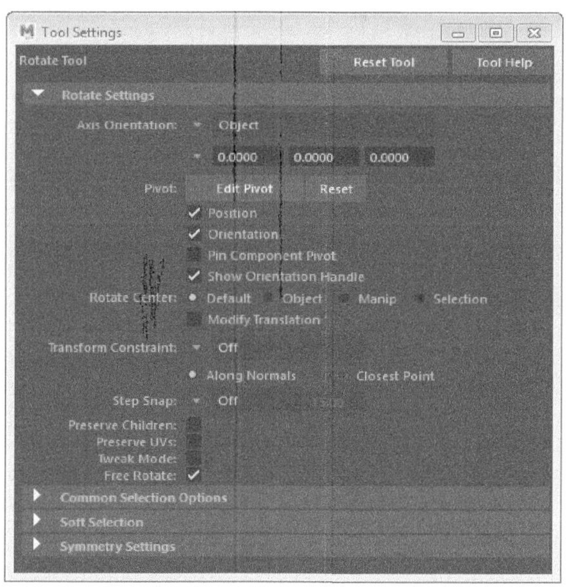

*Figure 1-45 Partial view of the **Tool Settings (Rotate Tool)** window*

Scale Tool

The **Scale Tool** is used to scale an object along the X, Y, or Z-axis. To scale an object in the viewport, select the object and invoke **Scale Tool** from the Tool Box; **Scale Tool**

manipulator will be displayed on the object, as shown in Figure 1-46.

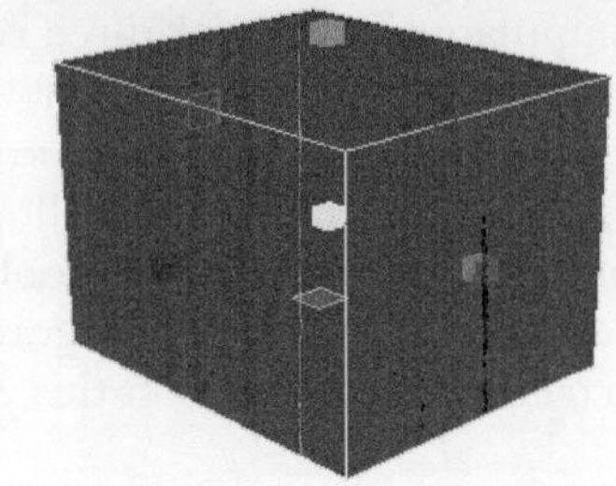

*Figure 1-46 The **Scale Tool** manipulator*

The **Scale Tool** manipulator consists of three boxes. The redbox represents the X axis, whereas the green and blue boxes represent the Y and Z axes, respectively. Moreover, the yellow colored box in the center lets you scale the selected object uniformly in all axes. On selecting any one of these colored scale boxes, the default color of the box changes to yellow. You can also adjust the default settings of **Scale Tool** by double-clicking on it in the Tool Box. On doing so, the **Tool Settings (Scale Tool)** window will be displayed, as shown in Figure 1-47. Make the required changes in the **Tool Settings (Scale Tool)** window to adjust the basic attributes of **Scale Tool**.

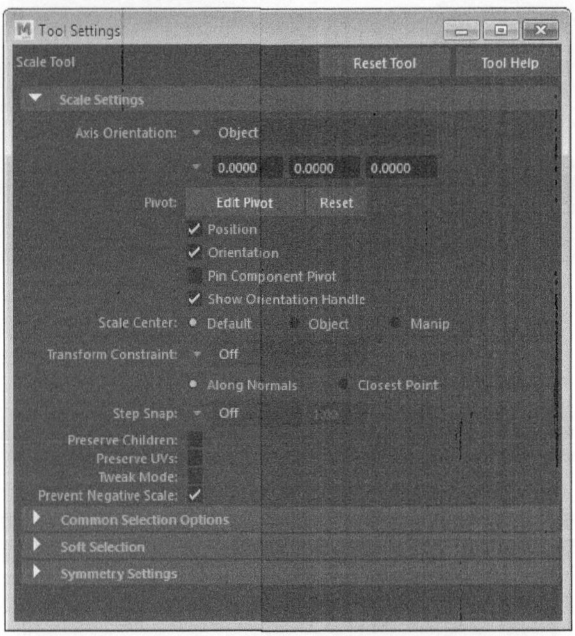

*Figure 1-47 The partial view of the **Tool Settings (Scale Tool)** window*

Note

While rotating, moving, or scaling an object, different colored handles are displayed. These handles indicate different axes. You can use this color scheme while working with three transform tools as well. The red, green, and blue colors represent the X, Y, and Z axes, respectively.

Last Tool Used

The **Last Tool Used** tool is used to invoke the last used or the currently selected tool. This tool displays the icon of the last used tool or currently active tool.

Quick Layout Buttons

Using the buttons in the Quick Layout buttons area, refer to Figure 1-5, you can the toggle the display of layouts as required. You can also change the display of layout buttons. To do so, right-click on one of the Quick Layout buttons; a shortcut menu with various layout options will be displayed, as shown in Figure 1-48. Next, choose any of the layout from the shortcut menu as per your need; the current layout will be replaced by the chosen layout. Using these buttons, you can also edit the current layout. To do so, right-click on the Quick Layout buttons; a shortcut menu will be displayed. Choose **Edit Layouts** from the shortcut menu; the **Panels** window will be displayed, as shown in Figure 1-49.

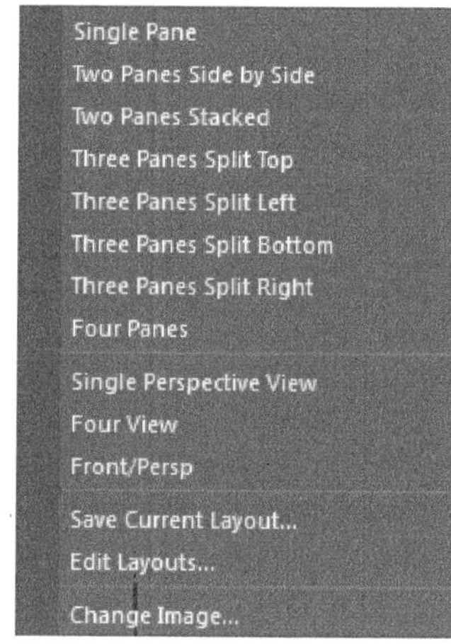

***Figure 1-48** Shortcut menu displayed on right-clicking on the Quick Layout button*

Time Slider and Range Slider

The Time Slider and the Range Slider, as shown in Figure 1-50, are located at the bottom of the viewport. These two sliders are used to control the frames in animation. The Time Slider comprises of the frames that are used for animation. There is an input box on the Time Slider called **Set the current time**, which indicates the current frame of animation. The keys in the Time Slider are displayed as red lines.

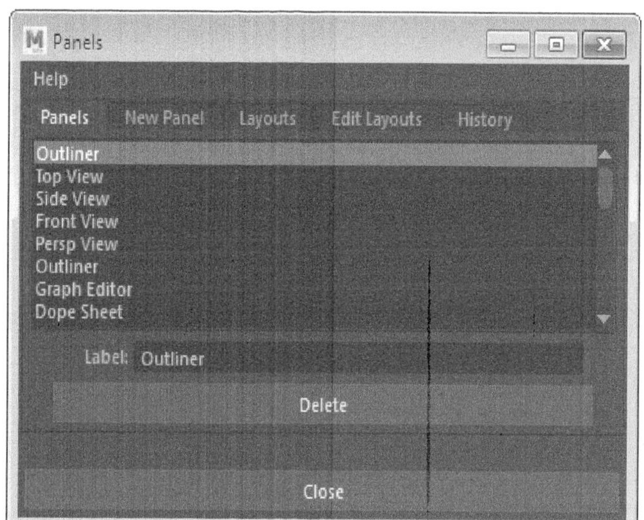

***Figure 1-49** The **Panels** window*

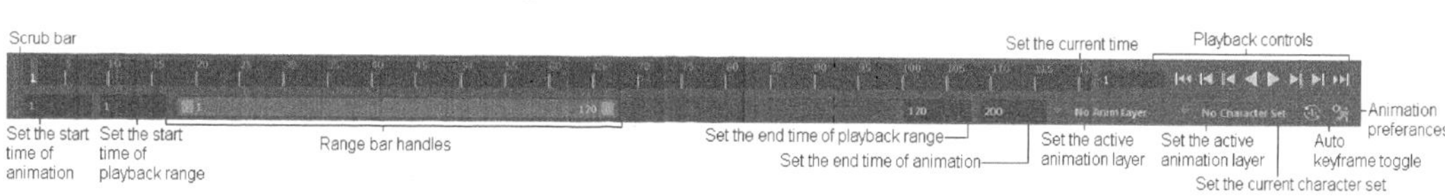

***Figure 1-50** The Time Slider and the Range Slider*

The Time Slider displays the range of frames available in your animation. In the Time Slider, the grey box, known as scrub bar, is used to move back and forth in the active range of frames available for animation. The Playback Controls at the extreme right of the current frame help you to play and stop the animation. The Range Slider located below the Time Slider is used to adjust the range of animation playback. The Range Slider shows the start and end time of the active animation. The edit boxes both on the left and right of the Range Slider direct you to the start and end frames of the selected range. The length of the Range Slider can be altered using these edit boxes. At the right of the **Set the end time of the animation** input box is the **Set the active animation layer** button. This feature gives you access to all the options needed to create and manipulate the animation layers. This option helps you to blend multiple animations in a scene. The **Set the current character set** is located on the right of the Range Slider. It is used to gain automatic control over the character animated object. There are two buttons on the extreme right of the Range Slider: **Auto keyframe toggle** and **Animation preferences**. These buttons are discussed next.

Tip
*You can also set the keys for animation by choosing **Key > Set > Set key** from the menubar or by pressing the 's' key. Ensure that you have selected the **Animation** menuset.*

Auto keyframe toggle

The **Auto keyframe toggle** button is used to set the keyframes. This button sets the keyframe automatically whenever an animated value is changed. Its color turns blue when it is activated.

Animation preferences

The **Animation preferences** button is used to modify the animation controls. On choosing this button, the **Preferences** dialog box will be displayed, as shown in Figure 1-51. In the **Preferences** dialog box, the **Time Slider** option is selected by default in the **Categories** area. You can set the animation controls in the **Time Slider** and **Playback** area of the **Preferences** window. Choose the **Save** button to save the changes and close the dialog box.

Command Line

The Command Line is located below the Range Slider. It works in Maya interface by using the MEL script or the Python script. The MEL and Python are the scripting languages used in Maya. Choose the **MEL** button to switch between the two scripts. The **MEL** button is located above the Help Line.

The Command Line also displays messages from the program in a grey box on the right. At the extreme right of the Command Line, there is an icon for the **Script Editor**. The **Script Editor** is used to enter complex and complicated MEL and Python scripts into the scene.

Note
*MEL stands for MAYA Embedded Language. The **MEL** command is a group of text strings that are used to perform various functions in Maya.*

Help Line

The Help Line is located at the bottom of the Command Line. It provides a brief description about the selected tool or the active area in the Maya interface.

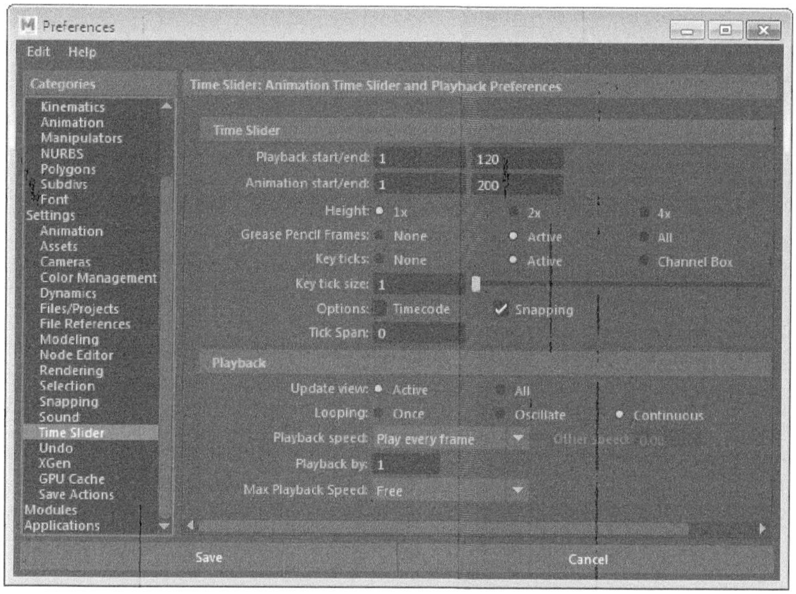

Figure 1-51 *The **Preferences** dialog box*

Panel Menu

The **Panel** menu is available in every viewport, as shown in Figure 1-52. The commands or options in the **Panel** menu controls all the actions performed in the workspace. The **Panel** menu comprises of six menus, which are discussed next.

Figure 1-52 *The **Panel** menu*

View

The **View** menu is used to view the object in the viewport from different angles using different camera views.

Shading

The **Shading** menu is used to view the object in various shading modes such as **Wireframe**, **Smooth Shade All**, **Flat Shade All**, **X-Ray**, and so on. You can also use the **Wireframe on Shaded** option in this menu for working comfortably in the shaded mode.

Lighting

The **Lighting** menu helps you use different presets of lights that help in illuminating objects in the viewport.

Show

The **Show** menu is used to hide or unhide a particular group of objects in the viewport.

Renderer

The **Renderer** menu is used to set the quality of rendering in the viewport. You can also set the color texture resolution and the bump texture resolution for high quality rendering using the options in this menu.

Panels

The **Panels** menu is used to switch the active viewport to a different view.

Panel Toolbar

The **Panel** toolbar, as shown in Figure 1-53, is located just below the **Panel** menu of all viewports. This toolbar consists of the most commonly used tools present in the **Panel** menu. These tools are discussed next.

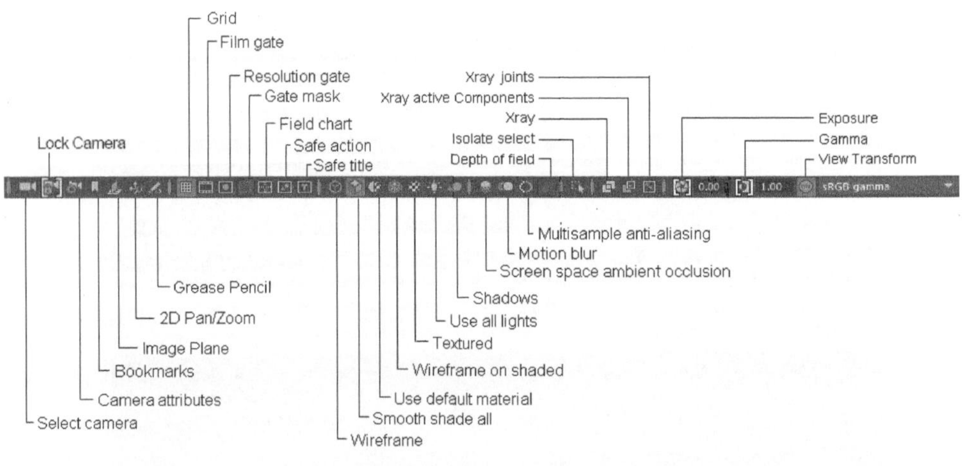

***Figure 1-53** The **Panel** toolbar*

Select camera

The **Select camera** tool is used to select the active camera in the selected viewport. You can also select the current camera in a scene by choosing **View > Select Camera** from the **Panel** menu. To switch between different camera views, right-click on the **Select camera** tool; a shortcut menu will be displayed, as shown in Figure 1-54. Now, you can switch to the desired camera views by choosing the corresponding option from the shortcut menu.

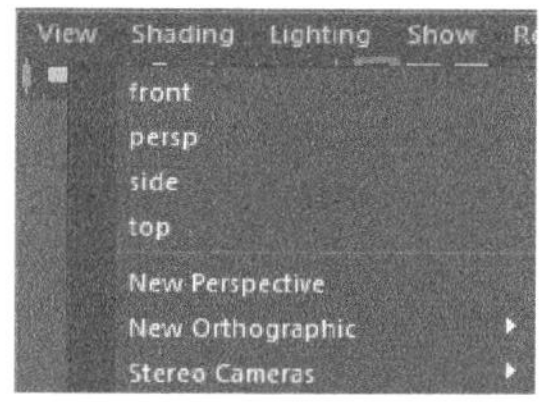

***Figure 1-54** The shortcut menu displayed on right-clicking on the **Select camera** tool*

Lock Camera

The **Lock Camera** tool is used to lock the active camera in a viewport. When camera is locked, you can not change its transform properties such as translate and rotation. To unlock the camera, choose the **Lock Camera** tool again.

Camera attributes

The **Camera attributes** tool is used to display the attributes of the active camera in the **Attribute Editor**. The attributes are displayed on the right of the viewport in the Attribute Editor. You can also view the attributes by choosing **View > Camera Attribute Editor** from the **Panel** menu.

Bookmarks

The **Bookmarks** tool is used to set the current view as a bookmark. To set a bookmark, you can set a view in the viewport and then invoke the **Bookmarks** tool; the set view is bookmarked for further reference. You can also edit an existing bookmark. To do so, press and hold the right mouse button over the **Bookmark** tool; a shortcut menu with a list of bookmarks created will be displayed in the Panel toolbar. Choose the **Edit 2D Bookmarks** option from this shortcut menu. On doing so, the **Bookmark Editor (persp)** dialog box will be displayed, as shown in Figure 1-55. You can change the name and other attributes of the selected bookmark from this dialog box.

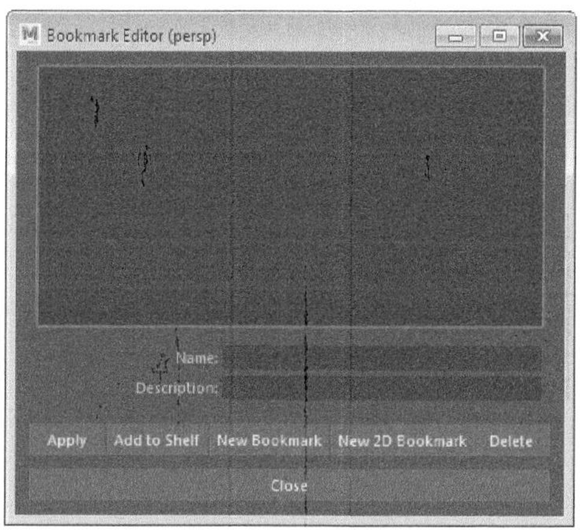

***Figure 1-55** The **Bookmark Editor (persp)** dialog box*

Image Plane

The **Image Plane** tool is used to import an image to the active viewport. On choosing the **Image Plane** tool, the **Open** dialog box will be displayed. In the **Open** dialog box, choose the image that you want to insert in the active viewport; the image plane will be inserted in the viewport. You can also set the image to the active viewport by choosing **View > Image Plane > Import Image** from the **Panel** menu.

2D Pan/Zoom

The **2D Pan/Zoom** tool is used to toggle the 2D pan/zoom mode on or off.

Grease Pencil

The **Grease Pencil** tool is used to draw 2D sketches in the viewport. On invoking this tool, the **Grease Pencil** window will be displayed, as shown in Figure 1-56. You can also invoke this tool by choosing **View > Camera Tools > Grease Pencil Tool** from the **Panel** menu.

*Figure 1-56 The **Grease Pencil** window*

Grid

The **Grid** tool is used to toggle the visibility of the grid in the viewport. You can also invoke this tool by choosing **Show > Grid** from the **Panel** menu. In addition, you can set the attributes for the grid in the viewport by using this tool. To set the grid attributes, press and hold the right mouse button on the **Grid** tool in the **Panel** toolbar; a flyout will be displayed. Choose **Grid Options** from the flyout; the **Grid Options** dialog box will be displayed, as shown in Figure 1-57. Next, you can set the grid attributes in this dialog box as per your requirement.

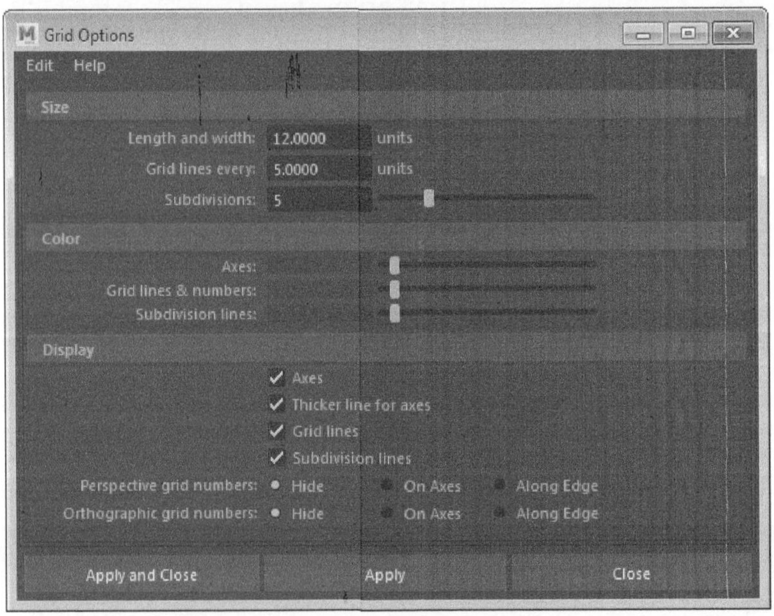

*Figure 1-57 The **Grid Options** dialog box*

Film gate

The **Film gate** tool is used to toggle the visibility of **Film gate** border on or off in the active viewport. You can also choose **View > Camera Settings > Film Gate** from the **Panel** menu to display the **Film gate** border in the active viewport.

Resolution gate

The **Resolution gate** tool is used to toggle the display of the **Resolution gate** border on or off in the active viewport. The resolution gate sets the area in the viewport that will be rendered. You can also choose **View > Camera Settings > Resolution Gate** from the **Panel** menu to set the resolution gate in the active viewport.

Gate mask

The **Gate mask** tool is used to turn on the display of the **Gate Mask** border. It changes the color and opacity of the area that lies outside the **Film gate** or the **Resolution gate**. The gate mask will only work when you have the **Film gate** or the **Resolution gate** applied to the active viewport. You can also choose **View > Camera Settings > Gate Mask** from the **Panel** menu to display the gate mask in the active viewport.

Field chart

The **Field chart** tool is used to turn on the display of the field chart border. On choosing the **Field chart** tool, a grid is displayed, representing twelve standard cell animation field sizes. The **Field chart** tool should be used only when the render resolution is set to NTSC dimensions. You can also invoke this tool by choosing **View > Camera Settings > Field Chart** from the **Panel** menu.

Safe action

The **Safe action** tool is used to turn on the display of the **Safe action** border. It is used to set the region in the active viewport for TV production. You can also invoke this tool by choosing **View > Camera Settings > Safe Action** from the **Panel** menu.

Safe title

The **Safe title** tool is used to turn on the display of the safe title border. It is also used to set the region for TV production in the active viewport. This tool should be used only when the render resolution is set to NTSC or PAL. You can also invoke this tool by choosing **View > Camera Settings > Safe Title** from the **Panel** menu.

Wireframe

The **Wireframe** tool is used to toggle the wireframe display on or off. You can also choose **Shading > Wireframe** from the **Panel** menu to switch to the wireframe mode. Alternatively, press 4 from the keyboard to turn on the **Wireframe** mode.

Smooth shade all

The **Smooth shade all** tool is used to set the display to smooth shade. You can also choose **Shading > Smooth Shade All** from the **Panel** menu to switch to smooth shade mode. Alternatively, press 5 from the keyboard to turn on the **Smooth Shade All** mode.

Use default material

The **Use default material** tool is used to display the default material on the objects, when they are in the smooth shaded mode.

Wireframe on shaded

The **Wireframe on shaded** tool is used to draw wireframes over the smooth shaded objects. You can also invoke this tool by choosing **Shading > Wireframe on Shaded** from the **Panel** menu.

Textured

The **Textured** tool is used to set the hardware texturing display of the objects in the viewport. Alternatively, press 6 from the keyboard to switch to the textured mode.

Use all lights

The **Use all lights** tool is used to illuminate objects by using all lights in the viewport. Alternatively, choose **Lighting > Use All Lights** from the **Panel** menu or press 7.

Shadows

The **Shadows** tool is used to display the hardware shadow maps. Alternatively, choose **Lighting > Shadows** from the **Panel** menu. This tool is only activated when the **Use All Lights** tool is selected in the **Panel** menu.

Screen space ambient occlusion

The **Screen space ambient occlusion** tool is used to toggle the display of the ambient occlusion in the viewport. This tool is enabled only when **Viewport 2.0** is active.

Motion blur

The **Motion blur** tool is used to toggle the display of motion blur in the viewport itself. This tool is enabled only when **Viewport 2.0** is active.

Multisample anti-aliasing

The **Multisample anti-aliasing** tool is used to toggle the display of multisample anti-aliasing in the viewport itself. This tool is enabled only when **Viewport 2.0** is active.

Depth of field

The **Depth of field** tool is used to toggle the display of depth of field in the viewport itself. This tool is enabled only when **Viewport 2.0** is active.

Isolate select

The **Isolate select** tool is used to display only the selected object in the viewport. To do so, select an object in the viewport and choose the **Isolate select** button from the **Panel** toolbar. Alternatively, choose **Show > Isolate Select** from the **Panel** menu or press SHIFT + I.

XRay

The **XRay** tool is used to make the objects semi-transparent in the viewport. You can also choose **Shading > X-Ray** from the **Panel** menu to switch to the **XRay** mode.

XRay active components

The **XRay active components** tool is used to display the active components over the top of other shaded objects. You can also invoke this tool by choosing **Shading > X-Ray active components** from the **Panel** menu.

XRay joints

The **XRay joints** tool is used to display the skeleton joints over the top of other objects in the shaded mode. You can also choose this tool by choosing **Shading > X-Ray joints** from the **Panel** menu.

Exposure

The **Exposure** tool is used to adjust the brightness of the display.

Gamma

The **Gamma** tool is used to adjust the contrast or brightness of the midtones in the image.

View Transform

The **View Transform** tool is used to change the working color space to display. To do so, choose color space use the drop-down list and choose a difference view transform.

Note

Your system should have a good quality graphic card to support high quality settings.

Channel Box / Layer Editor

The **Channel Box** and the **Layer Editor** are used to edit the attributes of an object. The **Channel Box** consists of all object attributes used for editing, and the **Layer Editor** is used for creating layers for objects in the scene. To display the **Channel Box / Layer Editor**, choose **Windows > Editors > General Editors > Channel Box / Layer Editor** from the menubar. Alternatively, press the CTRL +A keys to open the **Channel Box / Layer Editor**, if it is not already displayed. Select an object; the attributes of the selected object will be displayed in the **Channel Box / Layer Editor**, refer to Figure 1-58. The **Channel Box** is further divided into three parts, which are discussed next.

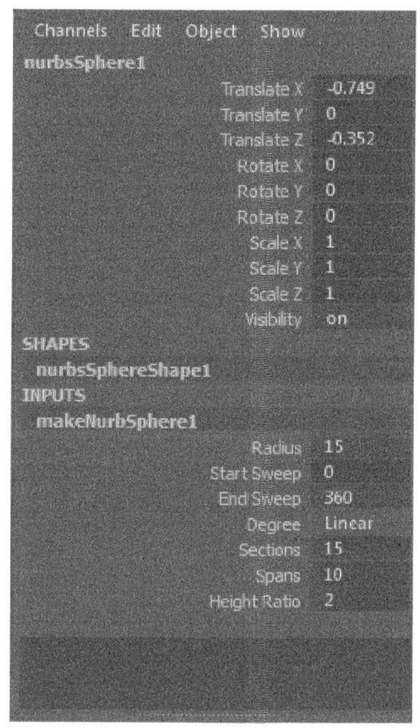

Figure 1-58** The **Channel Box /Layer Editor

Transform node

The Transform node contains the transformation attributes of the selected object. Select an object from the viewport; the Transform node will become active. In Figure 1-58, **nurbsSphere1** is the Transform node of a NURBS sphere. Enter the transform values in different transform parameters to transform the object in the viewport. Alternatively, click on an attribute name in the Transform node; the background of the attribute will change to blue color. Now, move the cursor to the viewport, press and hold the middle mouse button and drag it to make changes in the parameters of the selected attribute. You can also adjust the values of more than one attribute at a time. To do so, press and hold the SHIFT key and select the attributes that you want to adjust and then place the cursor in the viewport. Now, press and hold the middle mouse button and drag the cursor to make changes in the selected attributes. Choose the **Visibility** attribute to set the visibility of the object. Enter **0** in the **Visibility** edit box to make the visibility of the selected object off, and enter **1** in the **Visibility** edit box to set the visibility on.

SHAPES node

The **SHAPES** node provides a brief information about an object. It displays the shape name of the selected object, refer to Figure 1-58. For example, when you create a NURBS sphere in the viewport, it is named as **nurbsSphereShape1**. Here, NURBS indicates that the object has been created using the NURBS primitives; **Sphere** indicates that a sphere has been created; and **Shape1** indicates that this is the first sphere shape created in the viewport.

INPUTS node

The **INPUTS** node is used to modify the geometric structure of an object. To do so, create a sphere in the viewport and make sure that it is selected in the viewport. Next, select the **makeNurbSphere1** in the **INPUTS** node of the **Channel Box**; the geometric attributes of the sphere will be displayed, refer to Figure 1-58. Now, you can adjust the geometric values of the sphere as required.

The **Layer Editor** is located below the **Channel Box**. To create a new layer in the **Layer Editor**, choose **Layers > Create Empty Layer** from the **Layer Editor**, refer to Figure 1-59; a new layer will be created. To add an object to the layer, select the object in the viewport and then press and hold the right mouse button over the empty layer; a flyout will be displayed. Choose **Add Selected Objects** from the flyout; the selected object will be added to the layer.

The **Layer Editor** is mainly used when there are multiple objects in a scene. You can also change the name and color of layers by using the **Layer Editor**. To do so, double-click on the name of a layer; the **Edit Layer** dialog box will be displayed, as shown in Figure 1-60. Enter the name of the layer in the **Name** text box. You can select the display option of the object from the **Display type** drop-down list. If you select the **Normal** option from this list, the object will be displayed in its object mode and will be selectable. If you select the **Template** option from the drop-down list, the object will be displayed in the wireframe mode and the object will not be selectable. Similarly, if you select the **Reference** option, the object will be displayed in the shaded mode and will not be selectable. You can also set the visibility of an object by selecting the **Visible** check box. The **Color** swatches located at the bottom of the dialog box enables you to select a color for the layer to give it a distinct identity as compared to other layers.

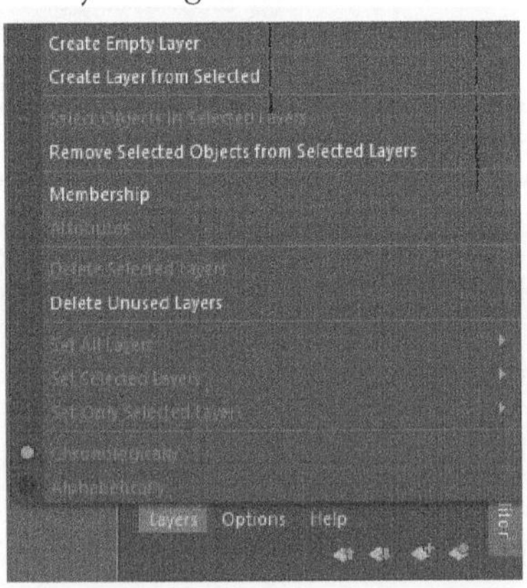

*Figure 1-59 Creating a new layer in the **Layer Editor***

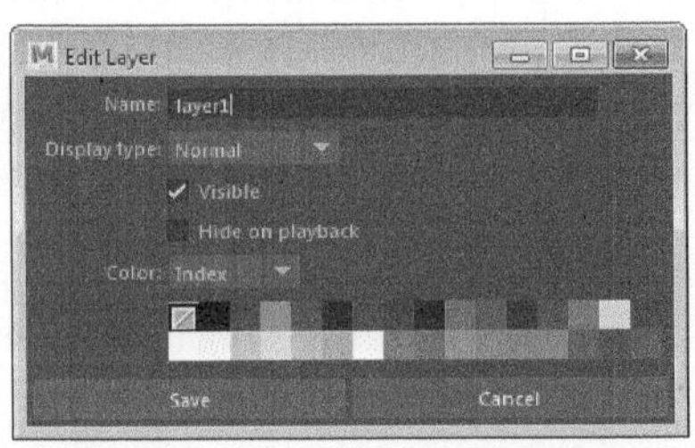

*Figure 1-60 The **Edit Layer** dialog box*

Attribute Editor

The Attribute Editor provides information about various attributes of a selected object, tool, or the material applied to the selected object. It is also used to make changes in the attributes of the selected object. Choose **Windows > Editors > General Editors > Attribute Editor** from the menubar; the **Attribute Editor** will be displayed on the right of the viewport, refer to Figure 1-61. The **Attribute Editor** comprises of a number of attribute tabs that help you modify an object.

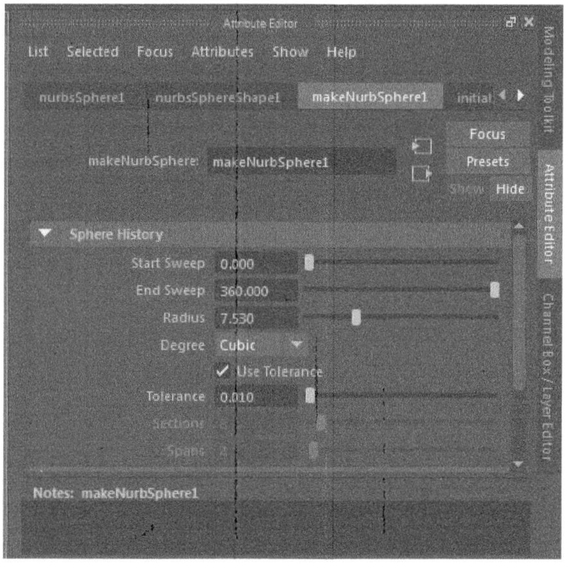

Figure 1-61 The ***Attribute Editor***

HOTKEYS

In Maya 2017, you can create your own shortcut keys or even change default shortcuts. To do so, choose **Window > Editors > Settings/Preferences > Hotkey Editor** from the menubar; the **Hotkey Editor** will be displayed, as shown in Figure 1-62. To edit hotkeys, select a hotkey category from the **Edit Hotkeys For** drop-down list. Now, find the desired command from the list displayed below the **Edit Hotkeys For** drop-down list. Click on the command and then enter a keyboard shortcut.

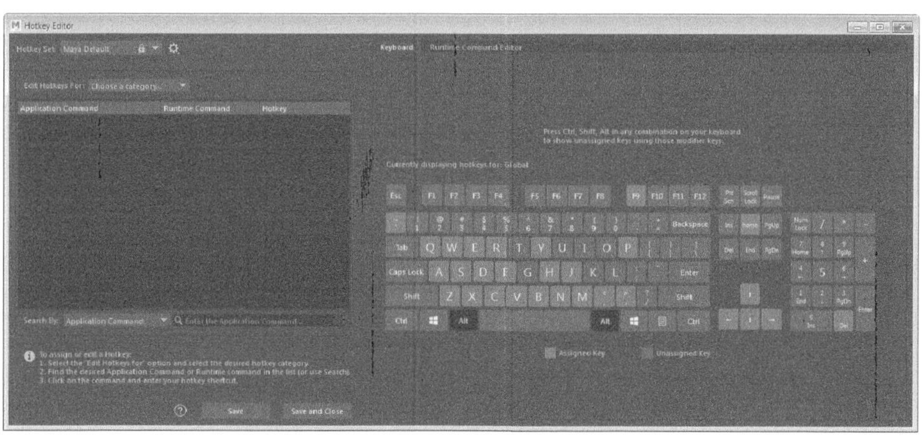

Figure 1-62 The ***Hotkey Editor***

You can search an application command by choosing the **Search By** text box. Enter the application command name in the search bar; filtered items will be displayed as shown in Figure 1-63. At the right side of the **Hotkey Editor**, the **Keyboard** tab will be displayed. In this tab the unassigned keys are highlighted in cyan color.

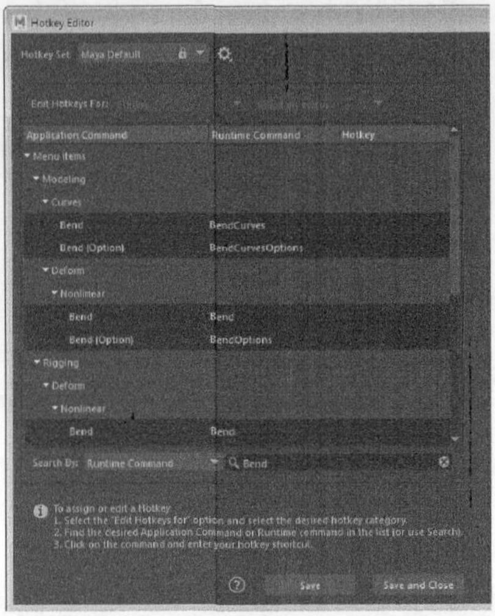

*Figure 1-63 Using the **Search By** filter*

HOTBOX

Hotbox, as shown in Figure 1-64, helps you access menu items in a viewport. The Hotbox is very useful, when you work in the expert mode or the full screen mode. It helps you access the menu items and tools by using cursor in the workspace. To access a command, press and hold the SPACEBAR key; the Hotbox will be displayed. Now, you can choose the option that you need to work from the Hotbox. The Hotbox is divided into five distinct zones, East, West, North, South, and Center, refer to Figure 1-64.

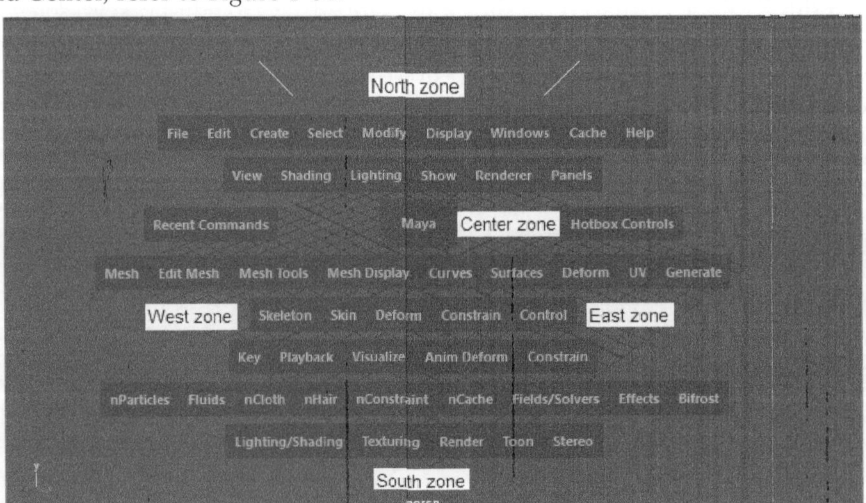

Figure 1-64 The Hotbox

Note

You can turn off various UI elements in the Maya interface to get more space and then use the Hotbox to access various commands and tools. But you should do it only after you have established a workflow for yourself. In the beginning, you should use the menubar at the top of the screen instead of using the Hotbox as it reduces the possibility of confusion in finding a command at a later stage

OUTLINER

The **Outliner** window is used to display all the objects of a scene in a hierarchical manner, as shown in Figure 1-65. An object in the scene can be selected by simply clicking on its name in the **Outliner** window. In the **Outliner** window, the objects are placed in the order of their creation in the viewport. For example, if you create a cube in the viewport followed by a sphere and a cylinder, then all these objects will be placed in a sequential manner in the **Outliner** window, which means the object (cube) created first will be placed first and the object created last (cylinder) will be placed at the last. To organize the sequence manually, choose the MMB and then drag and drop one object below another object. To rename an object, double-click on the name of the object. At the top of the **Outliner** window, there is an text box known as the **Text Filter Box**. You can use this box to select objects with a particular name. For example, enter ***front*** in the box and press ENTER; all the objects having the word 'front' in their name will be selected in the viewport. By default, there are four cameras in the **Outliner** window that represent four default viewports in Maya. As discussed earlier, everything that you see in the viewport is seen through the camera view. These cameras are visible in the **Outliner** window by default. Each object in the **Outliner** window has an icon of its own. When you double-click on any of these icons, the **Attribute Editor** will be displayed, where you can change the properties of various objects.

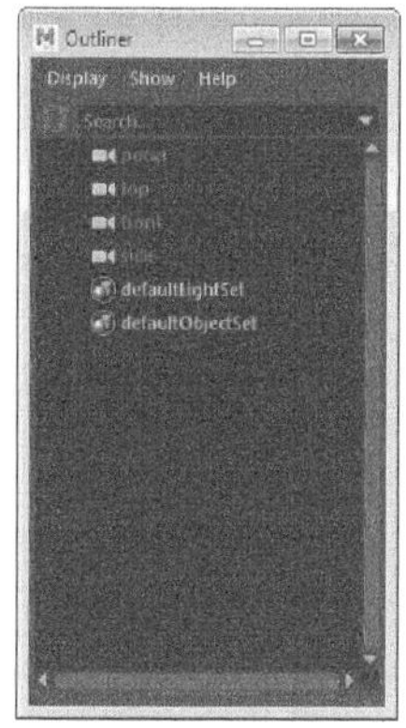

***Figure 1-65** Objects displayed in the **Outliner** window*

MARKING MENUS

Marking menus are similar to shortcut menus that consist of almost all the tools required to perform an operation on an object. There are three types of marking menus in Maya. The first type of marking menu is used to create default objects in the viewport. To create a default object, press and hold the SHIFT key and then right-click anywhere in the viewport; a marking menu will be displayed, as shown in Figure 1-66. In this marking menu, choose the object that you want to create.

The second type of marking menu is used to switch amongst various components of an object such as vertices, faces, edges, and so on. To invoke this marking menu, select an object and right-click; the marking menu will be displayed, as shown in Figure 1-67. Now, you can select the desired component of the selected object. This marking menu can also be used to apply material to an object. To do so, choose the **Assign New Material** option from this marking menu; the **Assign New Material** window will be displayed. Next, choose the required material; the material will be applied to the selected object. This method will be discussed in detail in later chapters.

The third type of marking menu is used to modify the components of an object. To invoke this marking menu, select a component, press and hold the SHIFT key, and then right-click on the selected object; the marking menu will be displayed, refer to Figure 1-68. After invoking this marking menu, you can choose the desired option to perform the corresponding function.

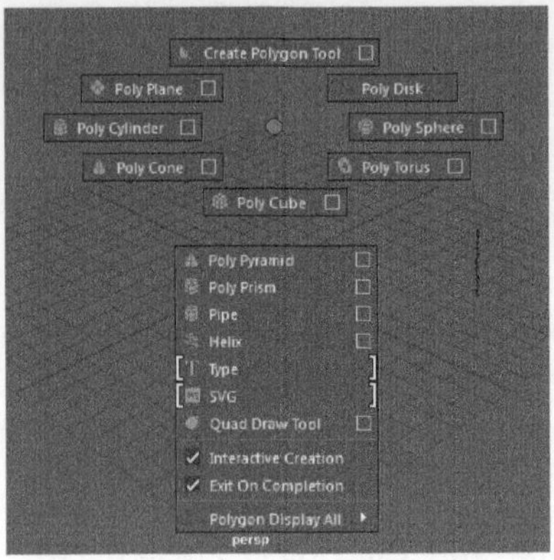

Figure 1-66 Marking menu displaying options used for creating default objects

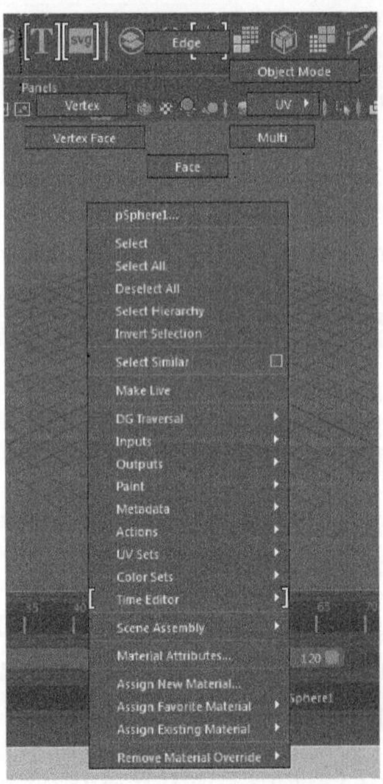

Figure 1-67 Marking menu displaying components of the selected object

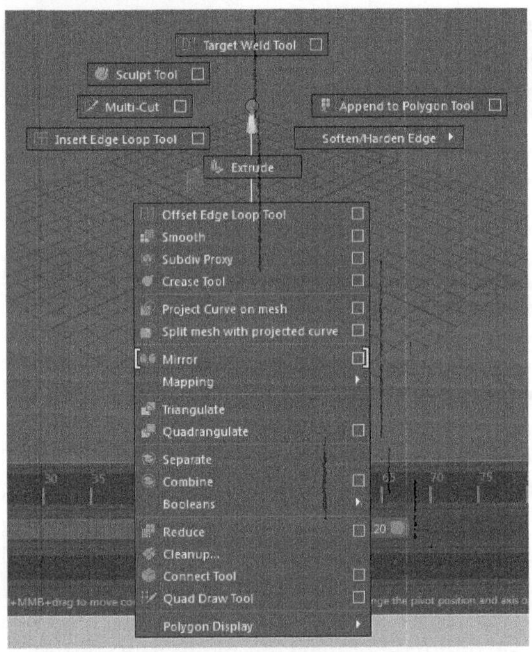

Figure 1-68 The marking menu displaying various tools for modifying an object

PIPELINE CACHING

In Maya, you can reduce the render time of a complex scene with the help of pipeline cache tools. Using these tools, you can also increase the loading speed of large 3D scenes. The two types of caching tools available in Maya are discussed next.

Alembic Cache

The enables you to save and export complex Maya scenes in alembic file format. The alembic file format has been developed to represent a complex 3D geometry as a simple geometry. The exported alembic files can then be re-imported into Maya to improve playback performance and reduce memory usage. In order to access this tool, choose **Cache > Alembic Cache** from the menubar; a flyout will be displayed, as shown in Figure 1-69. Various options in this flyout are discussed next.

Note

*The **Alembic Cache** tool not available by default. To invoke this tool, run the following script in Command Line: global proc perFrameCallback(int $frame){print $frame;}*

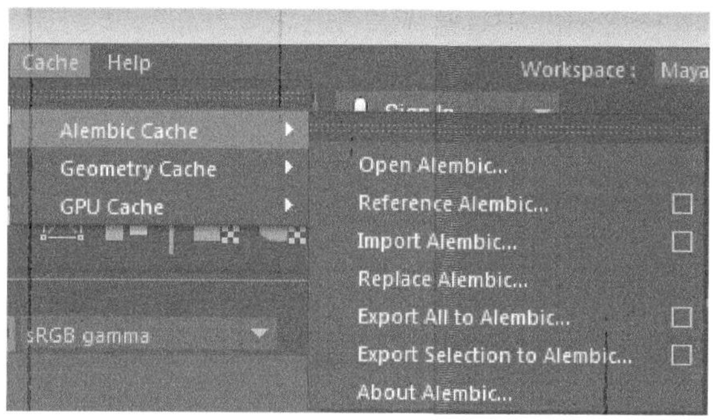

***Figure 1-69** Flyout displayed on choosing the **Alembic Cache** tool from the menubar*

Open Alembic

The **Open Alembic** option is used to open an alembic file in Maya. When you choose this option, the **Import Alembic** dialog box will be displayed. In this dialog box, you can browse to the location, where the required alembic file has been saved, and then you can open the file in Maya using the **Import** button.

Reference Alembic

The **Reference Alembic** option is used to import the contents of a scene, including objects, animation, and shaders into your currently opened scene without importing the files into the scene.

Import Alembic

The **Import Alembic** option is used to import an alembic file in Maya. When you choose this option, the **Import Alembic** dialog box will be displayed. You can set various options in this dialog box for the file to be imported.

Replace Alembic

The **Replace Alembic** option is used to replace the selected 3D object with the alembic object contained in the selected alembic file.

Export All to Alembic

The **Export All to Alembic** option is used to export all objects in Maya scene as an alembic cache file. By default, alembic cache files are saved in the **cache > alembic** folder of the current Maya project folder.

Export Selection to Alembic

The **Export Selection to Alembic** option is used to export the selected objects in the Maya scene as alembic objects.

INTEROPERABILITY OPTIONS IN MAYA

Autodesk Maya enables you to exchange data between Maya and different softwares such as 3ds Max, After Effects, and Print Studio. However, for exchanging data, the same version of the software must be available on your system. The **Send to 3ds Max**, **Send to After Effects**, and **Send to Print Studio** options located in the **File** menu of the menubar are used to send a Maya file to any of the above mentioned software.

Note

*The **Send to 3ds Max** option located in the **File** menu of the menubar will be displayed only if you have matching versions installed on your system. For example, 3ds Max 2017 and Maya 2017 are considered to be the matching versions.*

NAVIGATING THE VIEWPORTS

The persp view is the default camera view in Maya. To look around in a scene, you can move the virtual camera associated with the viewport. You can use the following shortcut keys while navigating the viewport.

Keyboard Shortcut	Function
ALT+MMB+Drag	Helps to pan the viewport
ALT+RMB+Drag	Helps to dolly in and out the viewport. You can also use the scroll wheel to dolly in and out.
ALT +LMB+Drag	Rotates or orbits the camera around in the persp window

WORKSPACES

In this version of Maya, workspaces are introduced. Workspaces are arrangement of windows, panels, and other interface elements. Maya comes with several predefined workspaces that you can access from the **Workspaces** drop-down list available on the far right of the menubar, as shown in Figure 1-70.

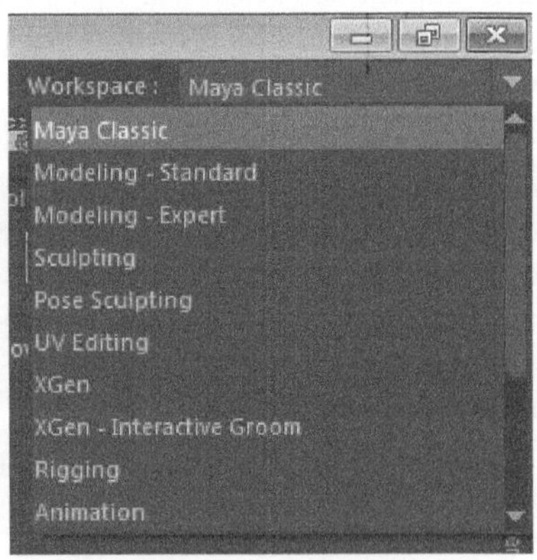

*Figure 1-70 The **Workspace** drop-down list*

You can also save your own workspaces or reset the factory workspaces. To do so, choose the options available in the **Windows > Workspaces** menu.

Self-Evaluation Test

Answer the following questions and then compare them to those given at the end of this chapter:

1. Which of the following windows is used to toggle the display of highlights of all menu items and tool icons?

   (a) **1-Minute Startup Movies** (b) The **Output window**
   (c) **What's New Highlight Settings** (d) None of these

2. Which of the following tools is used to adjust contrast or brightness of an image?

   (a) **Exposure** (b) **Gamma**
   (c) Display settings (d) Both (a) and (b)

3. The __________ button is used to snap the selected object to the center of the other object.

4. The __________ option helps you select an object by entering its name in the **Name Selection** area.

5. The **Show/Hide the Modeling Toolkit** button is used to toggle the __________ window.

6. The **Panel** menu has a set of __________ menus.

7. The keys set for animation are always displayed in red color. (T/F)

8. The MEL command is a group of text strings used for performing various actions in Maya. (T/F)

9. The Hotbox is used to assign the shortcut keys to the commands. (T/F)

Review Questions

Answer the following questions:

1. Which of the following tools helps you move the selected objects in a workspace from one place to another?

   (a) **Translate Tool** (b) **Paint Selection Tool**
   (c) **Move Tool** (d) **Scale Tool**

2. Which of the following combination of shortcut keys is used to toggle between **Attribute Editor** and **Channel Box/Layer Editor** ?

   (a) SHIFT+M (b) CTRL+ SHIFT+M
   (c) SHIFT+N (d) CTRL+A

3. Which of the following shortcut keys is used to invoke the Hotbox?

   (a) SPACEBAR (b) BACKSPACE
   (c) INSERT (d) ESC

4. Hotkeys are also known as __________ keys.

5. The __________ button helps you set keyframes in animation.

6. The user-defined shortcuts can be created by using the __________ .

7. The ___________ is an arbitrary point which is used to determine the location of objects.

8. MEL stands for __________ .

9. The options in the **Animation Preferences** dialog box are used to modify the animation controls. (T/F)

10. The **Absolute transform** mode is used to move, rotate, and scale a selected object in the viewport. (T/F)

Answers to Self-Evaluation Test

1. c, **2.** d, **3. Snap to Projected Center**, **4. Select by name**, **5. Modeling Toolkit**, **6.** six, **7.** T, **8.** T, **9.** F

Chapter 2

Polygon Modeling

Learning Objectives

After completing this chapter, you will be able to:

- *Create polygon primitives*
- *Edit polygon primitives*
- *Modify the components of polygon primitives*
- *Create models using polygon primitives*

INTRODUCTION

In this chapter, you will learn to create and edit polygon shapes using polygon modeling techniques. A polygon is made up of different closed planar shapes having straight sides. The most commonly used shapes in 3D polygons are triangles and quadrilaterals. These shapes are formed by vertices, edges, and faces. An edge is a straight line formed by joining two vertices. In a polygon, three vertices join to each other by three edges to form a triangle and four vertices join to each other by four edges to form a quadrilateral. By modifying faces, edges, and vertices of an object, you can create a polygon model as per your requirement.

POLYGON PRIMITIVES

In Maya, you can create objects interactively. By default, the **Interactive Creation** option is turned off. To enable the **Interactive creation** option, choose **Create > Objects > Polygon Primitives > Interactive Creation** from the menubar. When the **Interactive Creation** option is turned on, multiple click drag operations can be performed in the viewport. The number of click drag operations vary depending on the type of the primitive object you are creating. If the **Interactive Creation** option is turned off, Maya creates objects at the center of the grid.

Creating a Sphere

Menubar:	Create > Objects > Polygon Primitives > Sphere
Shelf:	Polygons > Polygon Sphere

A sphere is a solid object in which every point on its surface is equidistant from its center, as shown in Figure 2-1. The sphere can be created dynamically, or by entering the values using the keyboard. Both the methods are discussed next.

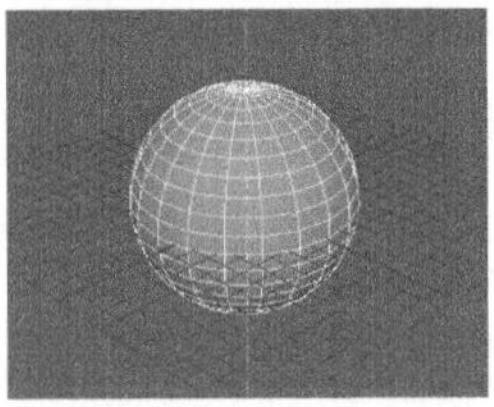

Figure 2-1 *A polygon sphere*

Creating a Sphere Dynamically

To create a sphere dynamically, choose **Create > Objects > Polygon Primitives > Sphere** from the menubar; you will be prompted to drag the cursor on the grid to draw the sphere in the viewport. Press and hold the left mouse button, and drag the cursor up or down to define the radius of the sphere. Now, release the left mouse button to get the desired radius; the sphere will be created and is visible in the **Smooth Shade All** mode.

Note

By default, polygon primitives are displayed in the ***Smooth Shade All*** *mode. Press 4 to change the display to* ***Wireframe****. Alternatively, choose* ***Shading > Wireframe*** *from the* ***Panel*** *menu. You can also switch back to the* ***Smooth Shade All*** *mode by pressing 5 or by choosing* ***Shading > Smooth Shade All*** *from the* ***Panel*** *menu.*

Creating a Sphere by Using the Keyboard

To create a sphere by using the keyboard, choose **Create > Objects > Polygon Primitives > Sphere > Option Box** from the menubar; the **Tool Settings (Polygon Sphere Tool)** window will be displayed, as shown in Figure 2-2. In this window, set the properties of the sphere using the keyboard and then click in the viewport; the sphere will be created. Choose **Reset Tool** at the top of the **Tool Settings (Polygon Sphere Tool)** window to reset the default values of the sphere.

It is recommended that you reset the values while creating a new polygon primitive.

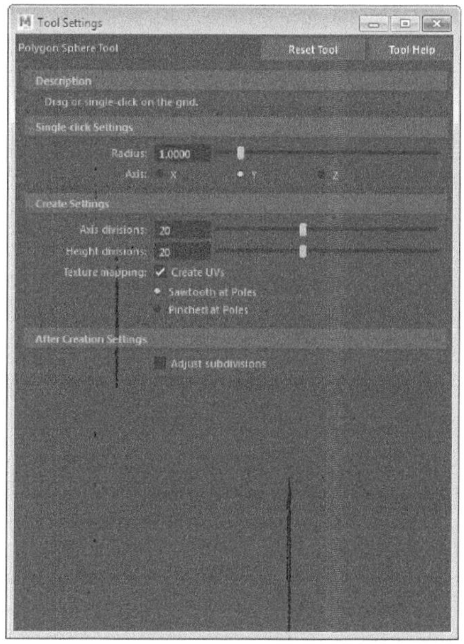

***Figure 2-2** The **Tool Settings (Polygon Sphere Tool)** window*

Modifying the Name and other Parameters of a Sphere

You can modify the name and other parameters of a sphere. To do so, select the sphere; the **Channel Box / Layer Editor** is displayed on the right of the viewport, refer to Figure 2-3. If the **Attribute Editor** is displayed on the right of the viewport, press **Ctrl+A** to switch to the **Channel Box / Layer Editor**. Now, click on the **pSphere1** label in the **Channel Box / Layer Editor**; the **pSphere1** label is converted into an edit box. Next, enter the desired name in the edit box and press ENTER. To modify the properties of the sphere, expand the **polySphere1** node in the **INPUTS** area; various options will be displayed. Enter the required values in the edit boxes; the changes will be dynamically reflected on the sphere in the viewport. Alternatively, select the label of the parameter of the sphere that you want to change; the corresponding label of the parameter will be highlighted in the **Channel Box / Layer Editor**. Now, press and hold the middle mouse button and drag the cursor horizontally in the viewport to change that particular value of the corresponding parameter.

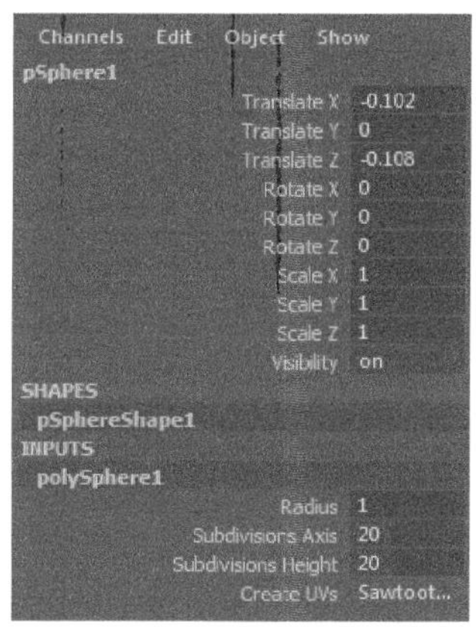

Figure 2-3** The **Channel Box / Layer Editor

Creating a Cube

Menubar:	Create > Objects > Polygon Primitives > Cube
Shelf:	Polygons > Polygon Cube

A cube is a three-dimensional shape with six sides or rectangular faces, as shown in Figure 2-4. A cube can be created dynamically or by entering values using the keyboard. Both these methods are discussed next.

Creating a Cube Dynamically

To create a cube dynamically, choose **Create > Objects > Polygon Primitives > Cube** from the menubar; you will be prompted to drag the cursor on the grid to draw the cube in the viewport. Press and hold the left mouse button, and drag the cursor on the grid to define the base of the cube. Next, release the left mouse button to get the desired base. Now, press and hold the left mouse button again and drag the cursor up to set the height of the cube and then release the left mouse button; the cube will be created.

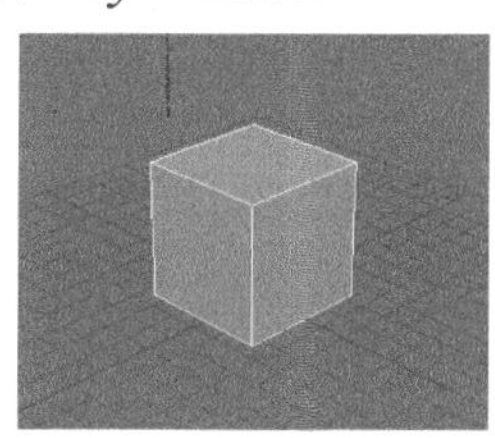

***Figure 2-4** A polygon cube*

Creating a Cube by Using the Keyboard

To create a cube by the using the keyboard, choose **Create > Objects > Polygon Primitives > Cube > Option Box** from the menubar; the **Tool Settings (Polygon Cube Tool)** window will be displayed, as shown in Figure 2-5.

In this window, set the properties of the cube by using the keyboard and then click in the viewport; the cube will be created in all viewports. Choose **Reset Tool** at the top of the **Tool Settings (Polygon Cube Tool)** window to reset the settings of the cube to their default values.

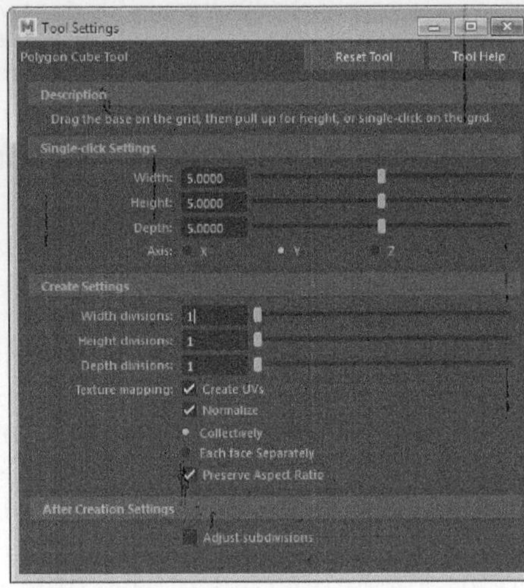

Figure 2-5 The ***Tool Settings (Polygon Cube Tool)*** *window*

Creating a Prism

Menubar:	Create > Objects > Polygon Primitives > Prism

A prism is a polyhedron that has two polygonal faces lying in parallel planes as bases and the other faces as parallelograms, as shown in Figure 2-6. You can create a prism dynamically or by using the keyboard. Both these methods are discussed next.

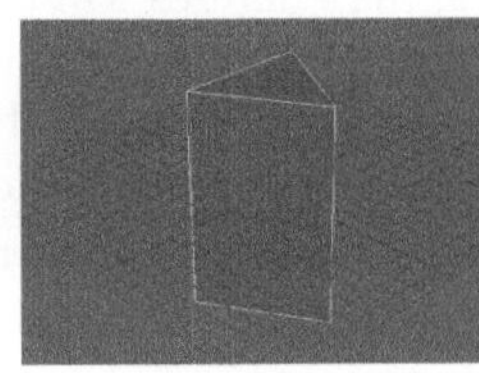

Figure 2-6 A polygon prism

Creating a Prism Dynamically

To create a prism dynamically, choose **Create >Objects > Polygon Primitives > Prism** from the menubar; you will be prompted to drag the cursor on the grid to draw the prism in the viewport. Press and hold the left mouse button and drag the cursor; the base of the prism is created.

Now, release the left mouse button to get the desired base. Again, press and hold the left mouse button and drag the cursor up to set the height of the prism. Next, release the left mouse button; the polygon prism will be created.

Creating a Prism by Using the Keyboard

To create a prism by using the keyboard, choose **Create > Objects > Polygon Primitives > Prism > Option Box** from the menubar; the **Tool Settings (Polygon Prism Tool)** window will be displayed, as shown in Figure 2-7.

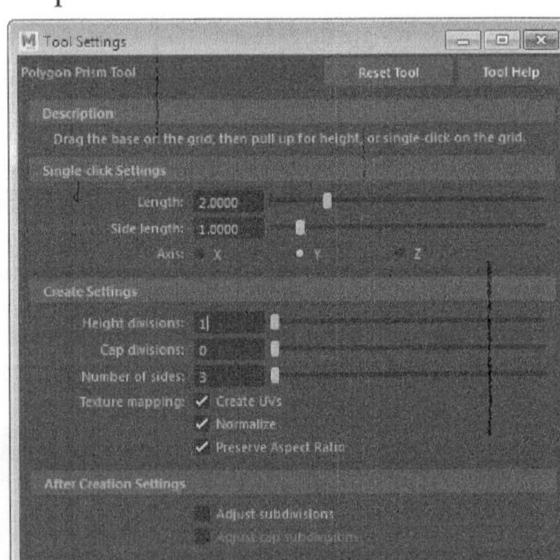

Figure 2-7 The ***Tool Settings (Polygon Prism Tool)*** *window*

In this window, set the properties of the prism by using the keyboard and then click in the viewport; the prism will be created in all viewports. Choose the **Reset Tool** button at the top of the **Tool Settings (Polygon Prism Tool)** window to reset the settings of the prism to their default values.

Creating a Pyramid

Menubar:	Create > Objects > Polygon Primitives > Pyramid
Shelf:	Polygons > Polygon Pyramid

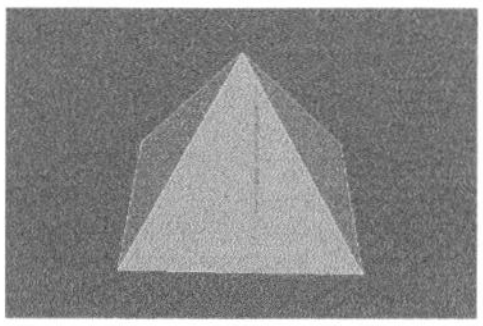

Figure 2-8 A polygon pyramid

A pyramid is a geometric shape with a polygonal base and a point called apex. The base and the apex are connected through triangular faces, as shown in Figure 2-8. You can create a pyramid dynamically or by entering values using the keyboard. Both these methods are discussed next.

Creating a Pyramid Dynamically

To create a pyramid dynamically, choose **Create > Objects >Polygon Primitives > Pyramid** from the menubar; you will be prompted to drag the cursor on the grid to draw the pyramid in the viewport. Press and hold the left mouse button, and drag the cursor up or down to define the shape of the pyramid, and then release the left mouse button; the pyramid will be created.

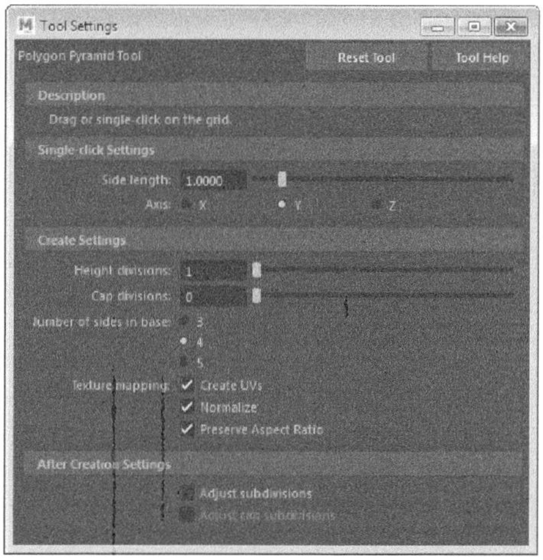

Figure 2-9 The ***Tool Settings (Polygon Pyramid Tool)*** *window*

Creating a Pyramid by Using the Keyboard

To create a pyramid by using the keyboard, choose **Create > Objects > Polygon Primitives > Pyramid > Option Box** from the menubar; the **Tool Settings** (**Polygon Pyramid Tool)** window will be displayed, as shown in Figure 2-9. In this window, set the properties of the pyramid by using the keyboard and then click in the viewport; the pyramid will be created in all viewports. Choose **Reset Tool** at the top of the **Tool Settings** (**Polygon Pyramid Tool)** window to reset the settings to default values.

Creating a Pipe

Menubar:	Create > Objects > Polygon Primitives > Pipe
Shelf:	Polygons > Polygon Pipe

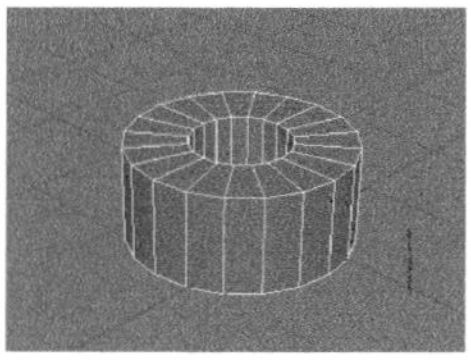

Figure 2-10 A polygon pipe

A pipe is similar to a cylinder polygonal shape with thickness, as shown in Figure 2-10. You can create a pipe either dynamically or by entering values using the keyboard. Both these methods are discussed next.

Creating a Pipe Dynamically

To create a pipe dynamically, choose **Create > Objects > Polygon Primitives > Pipe** from the menubar; you will be prompted to drag the cursor on the grid to draw the pipe in the viewport. Press and hold the left mouse button and drag the cursor; the base of the pipe is created. Next, release the left mouse button to get the desired base. Now, press and hold the left mouse button and drag the cursor up to set the height of the pipe. Next, release the left mouse button. Again, press and hold the left mouse button to set the thickness of the polygon pipe; the polygon pipe will be created.

Creating a Pipe by Using the Keyboard

To create a pipe by using the keyboard, choose **Create > Objects > Polygon Primitives > Pipe > Option Box** from the menubar; the **Tool Settings** (**Polygon Pipe Tool**) window will be displayed, as shown in Figure 2-11.

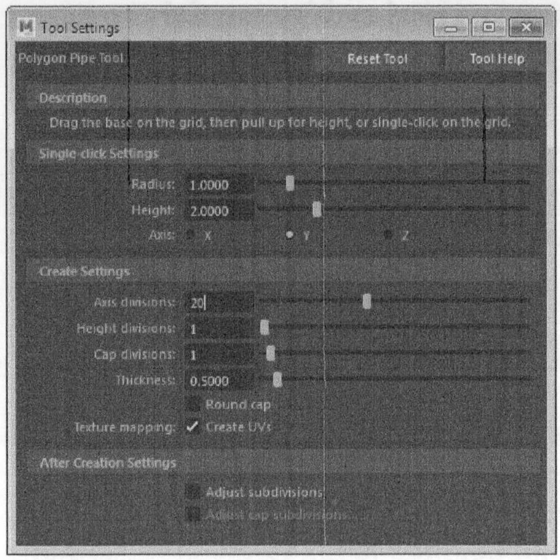

*Figure 2-11 The **Tool Settings (Polygon Pipe Tool)** window*

In this window, set the properties of the pipe by using the keyboard and then click in the viewport; the pipe will be created in all viewports. Choose the **Reset Tool** button at the top of the **Tool Settings** (**Polygon Pipe Tool**) window to reset the settings to default values.

Creating a Helix

Menubar:	Create > Objects > Polygon Primitives > Helix

A helix is a geometry in three dimensional space that lies on a cylinder and subtends a constant angle to a plane perpendicular to its axis, as shown in Figure 2-12. You can create a helix dynamically or by entering values using the keyboard. Both these methods are discussed next.

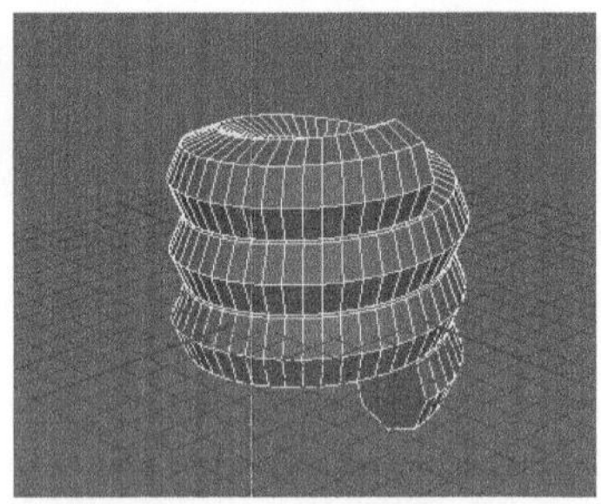

***Figure 2-12** A polygon helix*

Creating a Helix Dynamically

To create a helix dynamically, choose **Create > Objects > Polygon Primitives > Helix** from the menubar; you will be prompted to drag the cursor on the grid. Press and hold the left mouse button and drag the cursor on the grid to define the diameter of the helix and then release the left mouse button. Again, press and hold the left mouse button and drag the cursor up to set the height of the helix, and then release the left mouse button. Next, press and hold the left mouse button and drag the cursor to set the number of coils in the helix and then release the left mouse button. Again, press and hold the left mouse button and drag the cursor to set the section radius; the helix will be created.

Creating a Helix by Using the Keyboard

To create a helix by using the keyboard, choose **Create > Objects > Polygon Primitives > Helix > Option Box** from the menubar; the **Tool Settings (Polygon Helix Tool)** window will be displayed, as shown in Figure 2-13. In this window, set the properties of the helix by using the keyboard and then click in the viewport; the helix will be created in all viewports. Choose **Reset Tool** at the top of the **Tool Settings (Polygon Helix Tool)** window to reset the settings to their default values.

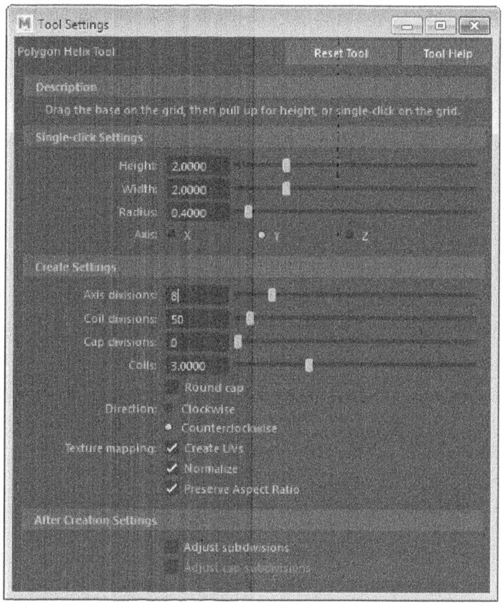

Figure 2-13 *The* ***Tool Settings (Polygon Helix Tool)*** *window*

Creating a Soccer Ball

Menubar: Create > Objects > Polygon Primitives > Soccer ball

A soccer ball polygon primitive created in Maya is very much similar to a real-world soccer ball, as shown in Figure 2-14. A soccer ball is formed by an alternate arrangement of hexagons and pentagons. It has total thirty two faces. You can create a soccer ball dynamically or by entering values using the keyboard. Both these methods are discussed next.

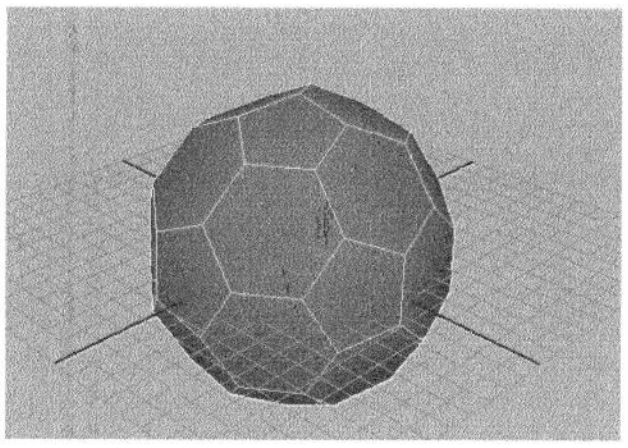

Figure 2-14 *A soccer ball*

Creating a Soccer Ball Dynamically

To create a soccer ball dynamically, choose **Create > Objects > Polygon Primitives > Soccer Ball** from the menubar; you will be prompted to drag the cursor on the grid to draw the soccer ball in the viewport. Press and hold the left mouse button and drag the cursor on the grid; the soccer ball will be created.

Tip

By default, the ***Polygon Helix Tool*** *is not available in the shelf. To add it to the shelf, choose the* ***Custom*** *shelf tab from the Shelf. By default, the* ***Custom*** *shelf tab is empty. This tab can be used to add tools that are frequently used. Press and hold the SHIFT and CTRL keys and choose* ***Create > Objects > Polygon Primitives > Helix*** *from the main menubar; a helix icon is formed in the* ***Custom*** *shelf. Similarly, you can add other tools to the* ***Custom*** *shelf tab for quick access.*

Creating a Soccer Ball by Using the Keyboard

To create a soccer ball by using the keyboard, choose **Create > Objects > Polygon Primitives > Soccer Ball > Option Box** from the menubar; the **Tool Settings (Polygon Soccer Ball Tool)** window will be displayed, as shown in Figure 2-15. In this window, set the properties of the soccer ball by using the keyboard and then click in the viewport; the soccer ball will be created. Choose **Reset Tool** at the top of the **Tool Settings (Polygon Soccer Ball Tool)** window to reset the settings to their default values.

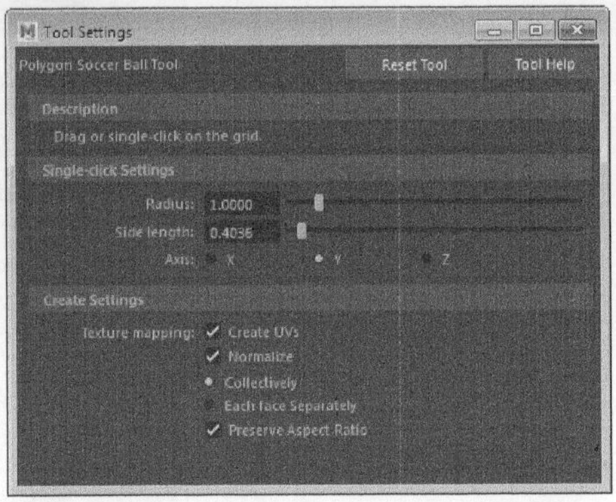

Figure 2-15 The ***Tool Stttings (Polygon Soccer Ball Tool)*** *window*

Creating a Platonic Solid

Menubar:	Create > Objects > Polygon Primitives > Platonic Solids

You can create various types of platonic solids such as tetrahedron, octahedron, dodecahedron, and icosehedron. Platonic solids have identical faces and its all sides are equal, refer to Figure 2-16. You can create a platonic solid dynamically or by entering values using the keyboard. Boththese methods are discussed next.

Creating a Platonic Solid Dynamically

To create a platonic solid dynamically, choose **Create > Objects > Polygon Primitives > Platonic Solids** from the menubar; you will be prompted to drag the cursor on the grid to draw the platonic solid in the viewport. Press and hold the left mouse button and drag the cursor on the grid; the platonic solid will be created.

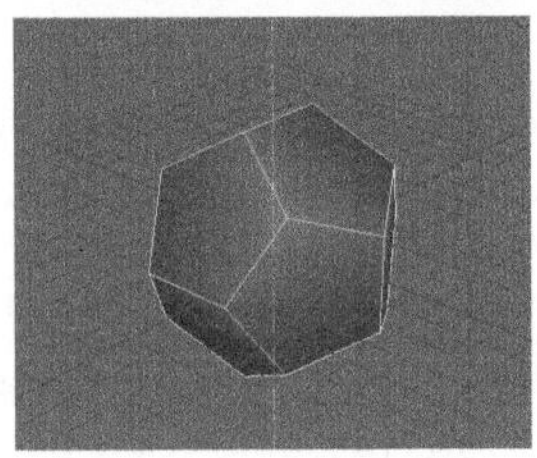

Figure 2-16 A platonic solid

Creating a Platonic Solid by Using the Keyboard

To create a platonic solid by using the keyboard, choose **Create > Objects > Polygon Primitives > Platonic Solids > Option Box** from the menubar; the **Tool Settings (Polygon Platonic Solid Tool)** window will be displayed. In this window, set the properties of the platonic solid by using the keyboard and then click in the viewport; the platonic solid will be created. Choose the **Reset Tool** button at the top of the **Tool Settings (Polygon Platonic Solid Tool)** window to reset the settings of the platonic solid, to their default values.

Creating a Type Tool Mesh

New

Menubar:	Create > Objects > Type
Shelf:	Polygons > Polygon Type

The **Polygon Type** tool is used to create polygon 3D text in the viewport. To create 3D text, choose **Create > Type** from the menubar; the **Loading Fonts** window will be displayed with a progress bar, as shown in Figure 2-17. Once the loading process is complete, **3D Type** text will be displayed in the viewport, as shown in Figure 2-18.

To change the appearance of the text, choose the **type1** tab in the **Attribute Editor**, refer to Figure 2-19. Using the options in this tab, you can change text, font, font size, and so on. You can apply various operations, such as **Extrude** and **Bevel**, on the text using the **typeExtrude1** tab of the **Attribute Editor**.

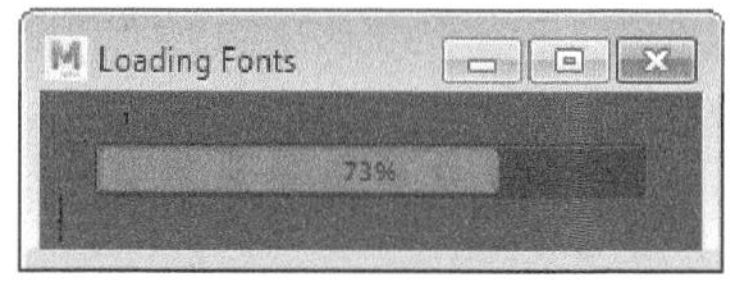

*Figure 2-17 The **Loading Fonts** window*

*Figure 2-18 The text **3D Type** displayed*

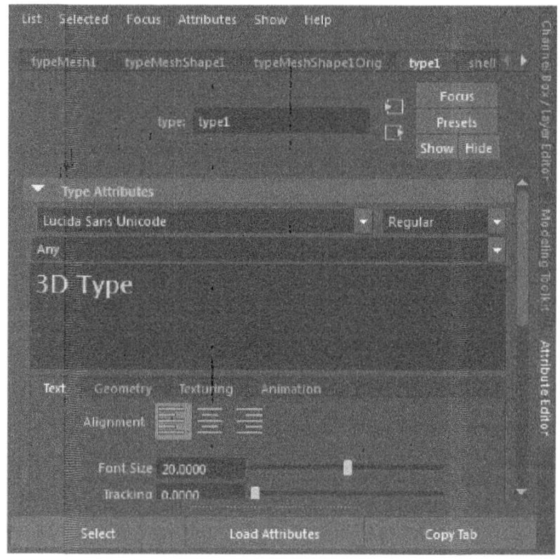

*Figure 2-19 The **type1** tab in **Attribute Editor***

Creating an SVG Mesh

Menubar:	Create > Objects > SVG
Shelf:	Polygons > SVG

This tool is used to create polygon text from an SVG file. To create an SVG mesh, make sure you have an SVG file or SVG content copied to the clapboard. Choose **Create > SVG** from the menubar; the default SVG mesh with the name **svg1** is displayed in the viewport, as shown in Figure 2-20. Now, in the **svg1** tab of the **Attribute Editor**, choose the **Import** button from the **SVG Attributes** area; the **Open** dialog box will be displayed. Navigate to the location where you saved the SVG file, select it, and then choose the **Open** button; the SVG mesh will be displayed in the viewport, refer to the Figure 2-21.

Figure 2-20 The default SVG mesh displayed

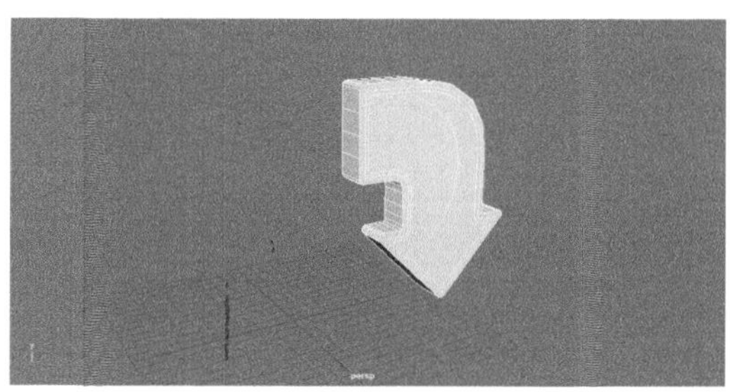

Figure 2-21 The SVG mesh displayed

Now, you can manipulate the shape as per the paths of the embedded SVG file. For example, if you want to offset the meshes, select the desired path from the **Path** drop-down list of the **Manipulations** area and then use the **Position Z Offset** attribute to offset the mesh, refer to Figure 2-22. Figure 2-23 shows the arrow shaped SVG used in the example.

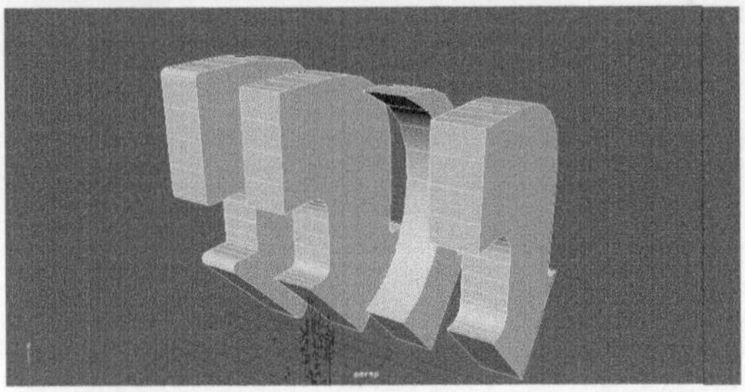

Figure 2-22 *The separated SVG mesh*

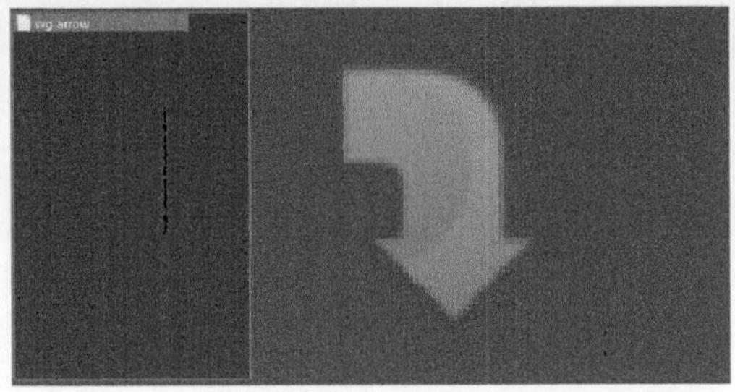

Figure 2-23 *The arrow shaped SVG file*

POLYGON EDITING TOOLS

In Maya 2017, the tools are grouped according to the function they perform. For example, the **Boolean**, **Combine**, and **Separate** tools are combined in the **Combine** group, refer to Figure 2-24. The polygon editing tools are used to perform different operations on the polygon objects. These editing tools are available in the **Mesh**, **Edit Mesh**, and **Mesh Tools** menus of the **Modeling** menu set. Figure 2-24 displays different tools in the **Mesh** menu. The most commonly used tools under this menu are discussed next.

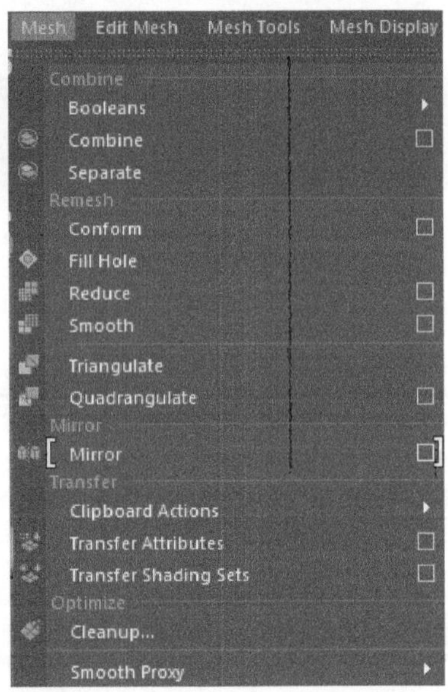

Figure 2-24 *The* ***Mesh*** *menu*

Booleans

Menubar: Mesh > Combine > Booleans

The booleans tools are used to combine the polygon objects to create a new object. Using these tools, you can perform three different operations to modify the shape of the new object. The booleans tools are show in Figure 2-25. The three options of this tool are discussed next.

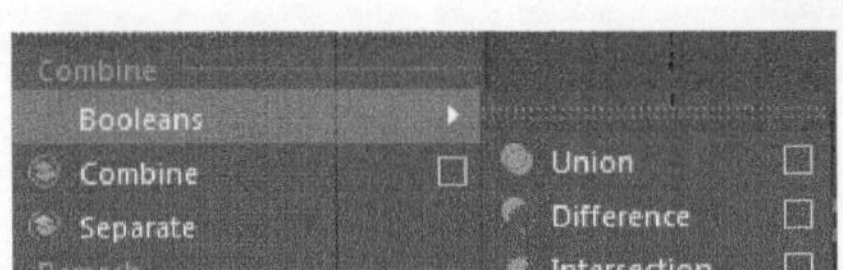

Figure 2-25 *The* ***Booleans*** *tools*

Union

Menubar: Mesh > Combine > Booleans > Union

The **Union** tool is used to combine the volume of two polygon meshes. To understand the function of this tool, create a sphere and torus and place them in the viewport, as shown in Figure 2-26.

Using the SHIFT key, select the torus and then the sphere. Next, choose **Mesh > Combine > Booleans > Union** from the menubar; both the objects will get merged and the intersecting geometry between them will be deleted, refer to Figure 2-27.

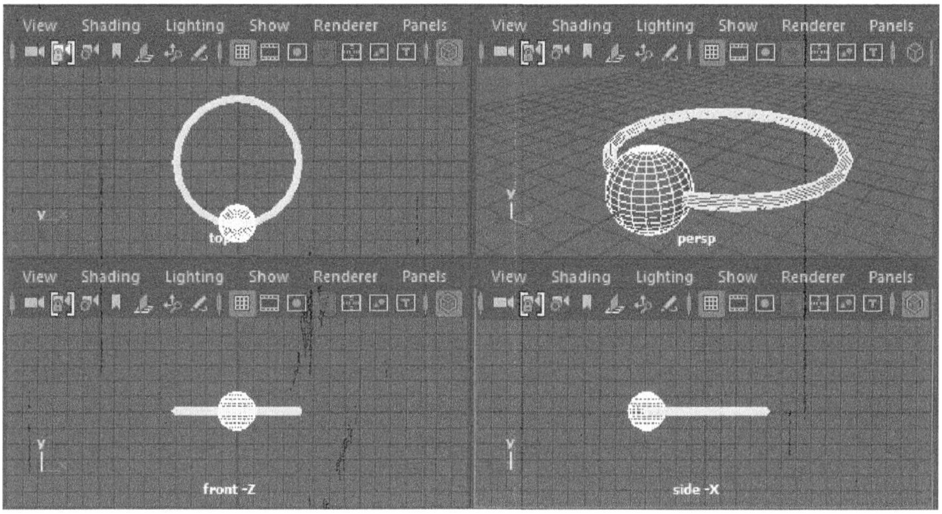

Figure 2-26 A torus and a sphere placed in the viewports

Difference

Menubar: Mesh > Combine > Booleans > Difference

The **Difference** tool is used to subtract the last selected geometry from the geometry that was selected first. To understand the function of this tool, create a sphere and a torus and place them in the viewport, refer to Figure 2-27. Using the SHIFT key, select the torus and then the sphere. Next, choose **Mesh > Combine > Booleans > Difference** from the menubar; the geometry will be deleted, as shown in Figure 2-28.

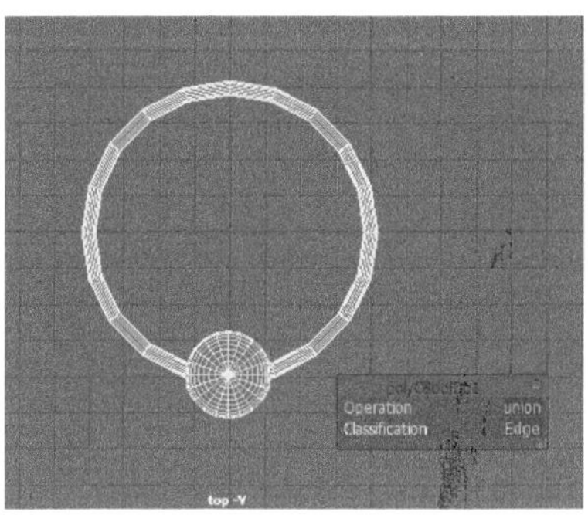

Figure 2-27 The Union operation carried out on the torus and the sphere

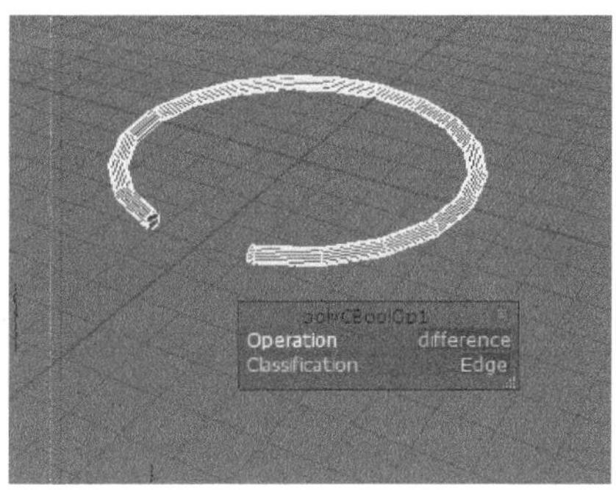

Figure 2-28 The Difference operation carried out on the torus and the sphere

Intersection

Menubar: Mesh > Combine > Booleans > Intersection

The **Intersection** tool is used to keep the intersecting geometry between two objects and delete the remaining geometry. To understand the function of this tool, create a sphere and torus and place them in the viewport, refer to Figure 2-26.

Using the SHIFT key, select the torus and the sphere. Next, choose **Mesh > Combine > Booleans > Intersection** from the menubar; the intersecting geometry will be displayed and the remaining parts will be deleted, as shown in Figure 2-29.

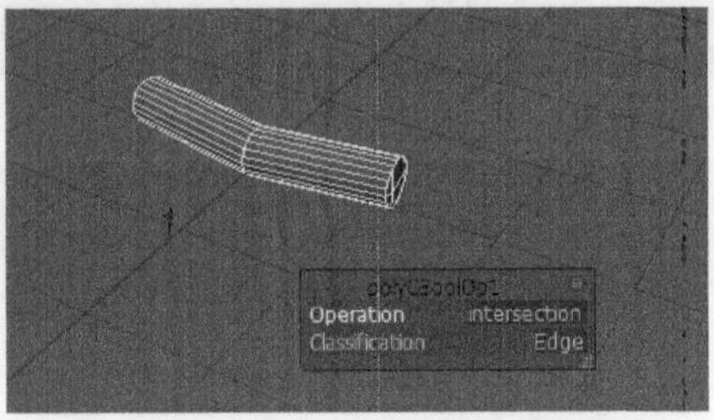

Figure 2-29 *The Intersection operation carried out on the torus and the sphere*

Note

When you choose any booleans operation, the ***polyCBoolOp1*** *In-View Editor will be displayed in the viewport. You can change any applied operation by choosing an option from the* ***Operation*** *flyout.*

Combine

Menubar: Mesh > Combine > Combine

The **Combine** tool is used to group two or more polygon objects into a single polygon object. To do so, select the polygon objects to be combined in the viewport and then choose **Mesh > Combine > Combine** from the menubar; the selected polygon objects are combined into a single polygon object.

Separate

Menubar: Mesh > Combine > Separate

The **Separate** tool is used to ungroup the combined polygon objects into separate polygon objects. To do so, select the group in the viewport and then choose **Mesh > Combine > Separate** from the menubar; the selected group of polygon objects are separated, refer to Figure 2-30.

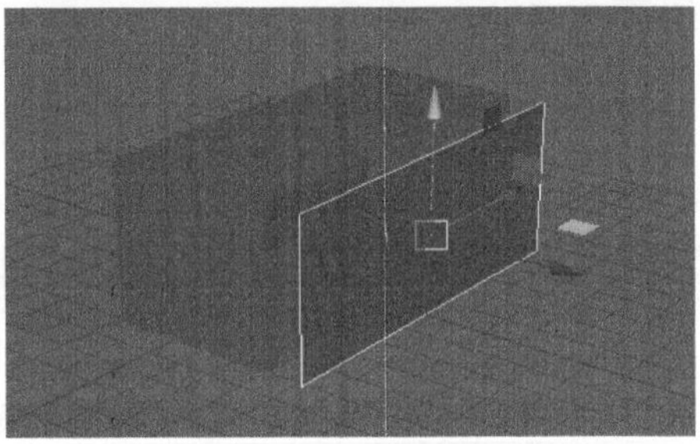

Figure 2-30 *The selected face separated from the polygon object*

Conform

Menubar: Mesh > Remesh > Conform

The **Conform** tool is used to wrap the vertices of an objects onto the surface of another object. To understand the function of this tool, you need at least two wrap polygon objects, refer to Figure 2-31. Next, select the object on which you want to wrap the vertices and then choose **Modify > Objects > Make Live** from the menubar to make the selected object live. Now, select the geometry that you want to wrap and then choose **Mesh > Remesh > Conform** from the menubar; the wrapper mesh will automatically wrap around the target geometry, refer to Figure 2-32.

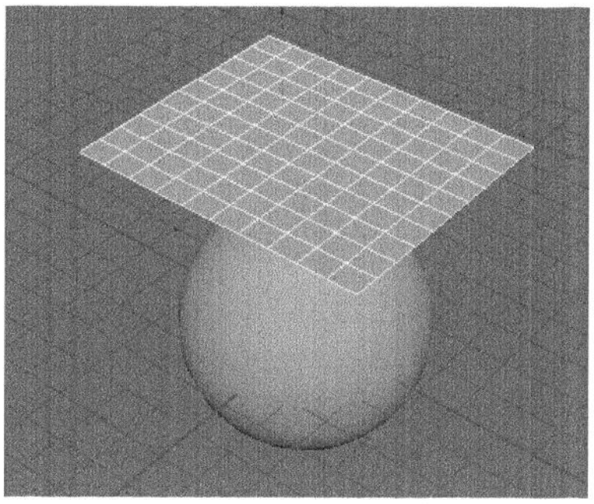

Figure 2-31 The polygon objects

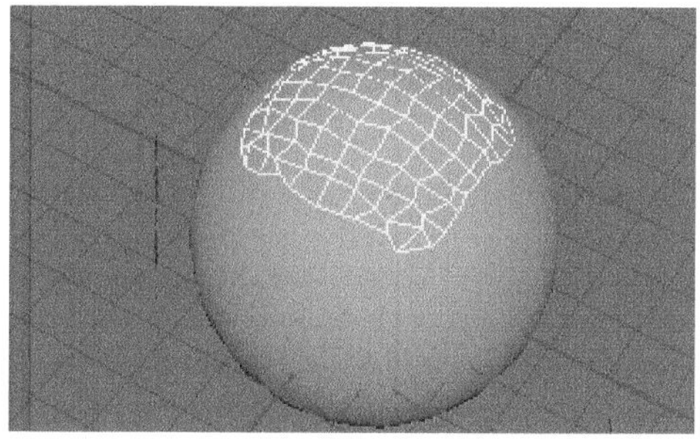

Figure 2-32 The plane wrapped onto the polygon sphere

Fill Hole

Menubar: Mesh > Remesh > Fill Hole

The **Fill Hole** tool is used to fill a hole in an object by adding a face to it. To understand the function of this tool, press and hold the right mouse button over an object with a hole; a marking menu will be displayed. Next, choose **Edge** from the marking menu. Now, select the boundary edge, refer to Figure 2-33. Next, choose **Mesh > Remesh > Fill Hole** from the menubar; the empty space will be filled, as shown in Figure 2-34.

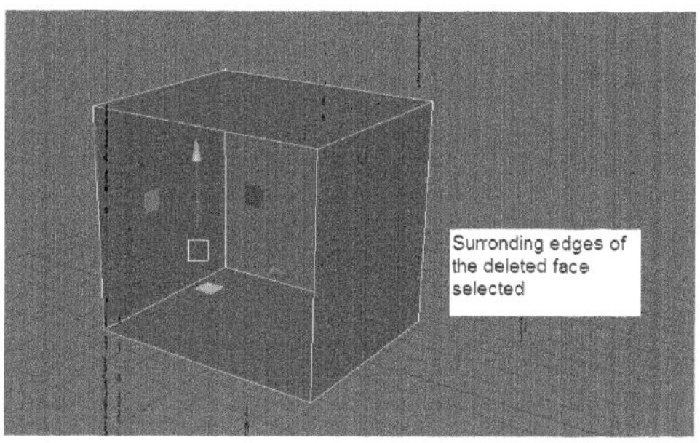

Figure 2-33 Edges of the deleted face selected

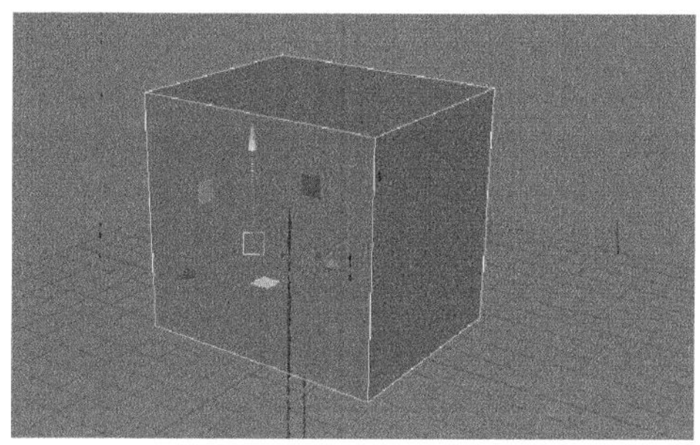

Figure 2-34 Filled hole of the cube

Tip

1. You can use the shortcut keys for displaying or activating various components of an object. For example, press F8 for object mode, F9 for vertices, F10 for edges, and F11 for faces.

2. To select the four surrounding edges of a deleted face, choose one of the edges and then press the right arrow key on your keyboard; all the four edges will be selected.

Reduce

Menubar: Mesh > Remesh > Reduce

The **Reduce** tool is particularly useful in reducing the number of polygons in a particular area of the mesh. You can also use the UVs or vertex colors to select an area on the mesh. To reduce polygons, select an area and then choose **Mesh > Remesh > Reduce** from the menubar; the **polyReduce1** In-View Editor will be displayed in the viewport. Enter the value in the **Percentage** edit box. You can change reduction method by clicking on the **Reduction Method** attribute. The other two methods are **Vertex Count** and **Triangle Count**.

Smooth

Menubar:	Mesh > Remesh > Smooth

The **Smooth** tool is used to make a polygon object smooth by adding divisions to it. To do so, create a polygonal object in the viewport and then choose **Mesh > Remesh > Smooth** from the menubar; the **polySmoothFace1** In-View Editor will be displayed in the viewport. Set the desired smoothing level by entering a value in the **Divisions** edit box. The default subdivision level is 1.

Triangulate

Menubar:	Mesh > Remesh > Triangulate

The **Triangulate** tool is used to convert the polygon faces into triangles.

Quadrangulate

Menubar:	Mesh > Remesh >Quadrangulate

The **Quadrangulate** tool is used to convert the polygon faces into quadrangles.

Mirror

New

Menubar:	Mesh > Mirror >Mirror

The **Mirror** tool is used to create duplicate of a selected object across an invisible mirror plane. To create a mirror object, select the object that you want to mirror and then choose **Mesh > Mirror > Mirror** from the menubar; the **polyMirror1** In-View Editor will be displayed in the viewport. Select the desired mirror axis using the **Axis** attribute. Now, use the **Offset** attribute to adjust the spacing between the objects. You can also change the offset by dragging the directional arrow of the gizmo in the viewport.

EDITING THE POLYGON COMPONENTS

In the previous section, you learned to modify simple polygon primitives. In this section, you will learn to edit the components of polygon primitives to create complex objects from it. To do so, select a polygon object in the viewport and then press and hold the right mouse button over it; the marking menu of the corresponding object will display various components of the object such as vertex, edge, face, and UV, refer to Figures 2-35 to 2-38.

To access various tools for editing the polygon primitives, select **Modeling** from the **Menuset** drop-down list in Status Line. Next, choose the **Edit Mesh** menu from the menubar. The most commonly used component editing tools are discussed next.

Note

1. The face selection mode in the marking menu allows you to select the faces of the active object. When you move the cursor on a face, the face will be highlighted in red. Next, when you click on the highlighted face, its color will change to green indicating that it is now selected. In this way, you can identify the selected and unselected faces.

*2. The **Multi** option allows you to select all components at a time without switching between the components. To select all components, press and hold the right mouse button on the already selected component, and then choose the **Multi** option from the marking menu. Next, select a face on the object, press and hold the SHIFT key, and then select the next required component.*

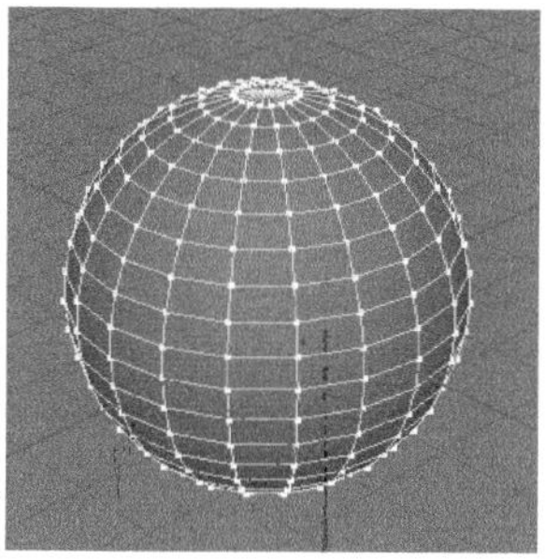

Figure 2-35 *Vertices of the sphere*

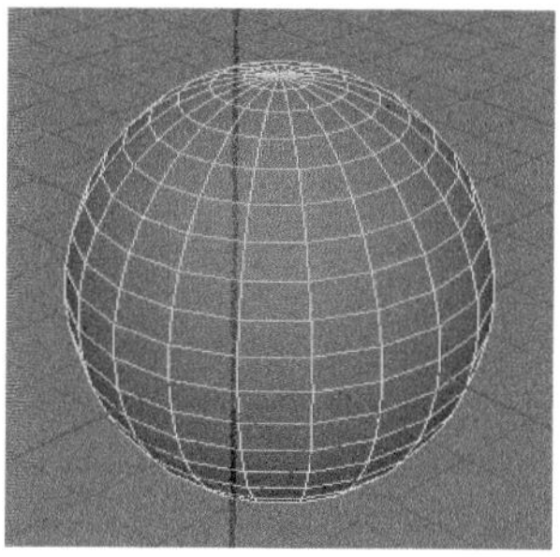

Figure 2-36 *Edges of the sphere*

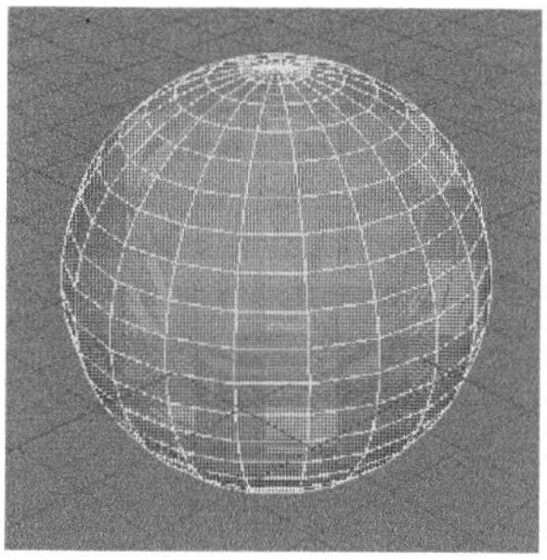

Figure 2-37 *Faces of the sphere*

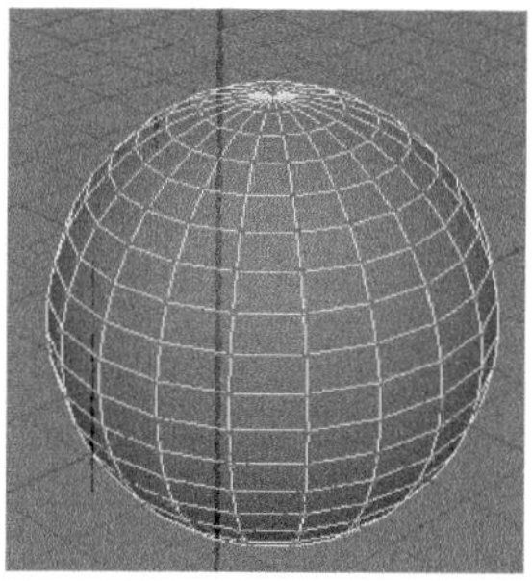

Figure 2-38 *UVs of the sphere*

Add Divisions

The **Add Divisions** tool is used to subdivide the edges or faces of a polygon object to smaller components. To add divisions, select that edges or faces that you wan to divide and then choose **Edit Mesh > Components > Add Divisions > Option Box** from the menubar; the **Add Divisions to Face Options** dialog box will be displayed. Set the required attributes in this dialog box and then choose the **Add Divisions** button to subdivide the selected area. You can also change the number of divisions by using the **Divisions** attribute in the **polySubFace1** In-View Editor.

Bevel

Menubar: Edit Mesh > Components > Bevel

The **Bevel** tool is used to expand the vertex or the face of a polygon object. This adds smoothness to a sharp object by adding fillets on the edges. The bevel operation adds fillet to the edges by creating new faces on the selected polygon object. To do so, create a polygon object in the viewport and select it. Next, choose **Edit Mesh > Components > Bevel** from the menubar; the selected polygon object will be beveled, as shown in Figure 2-39.

The **Bevel** tool is also used to bevel the components such as face, vertex, and edge of a polygon object individually. Create a polygon object in the viewport and right-click on it; the marking menu will be displayed. Next, choose **Edge** from the marking menu; the edge selection mode will be activated. Now, select any edge of the object and then choose **Edit Mesh > Components > Bevel** from the menubar; the selected edge will be beveled, refer to Figure 2-40.

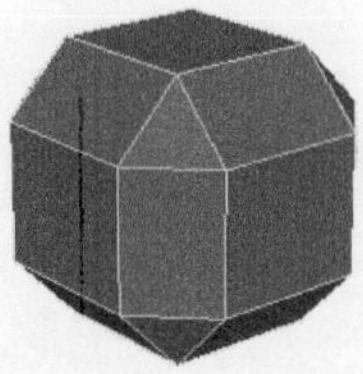

Figure 2-39 *Selected polygon object beveled*

Figure 2-40 *Selected edge beveled*

To adjust the bevel parameters, select the object in the viewport; the **Channel Box / Layer Editor** is displayed on the right of the viewport. Next, expand **polyBevel1** in the **INPUTS** area of the **Channel Box / Layer Editor** and then set the bevel parameters; the changes will be reflected on the selected object in the viewport.

You can also change the bevel parameters from the **Attribute Editor**. Press Ctrl+A to open the **Attribute Editor** and then choose the **polyBevel1** tab from the **Attribute Editor**; the bevel parameters will be displayed in the **Attribute Editor**, as shown in Figure 2-41. Set the parameters as per your requirement.

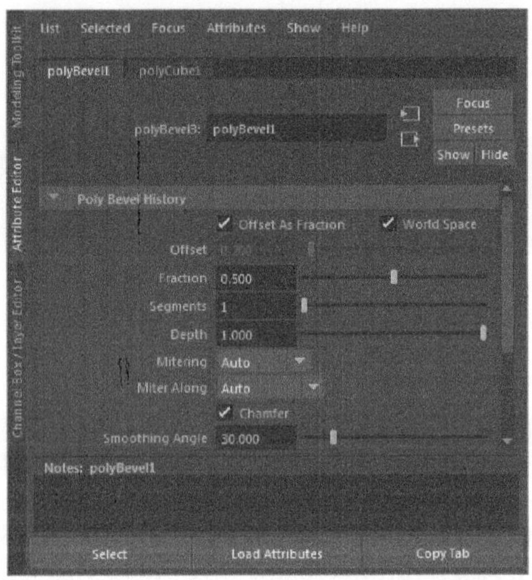

Figure 2-41 *Various bevel attributes in the* ***Attribute Editor***

Note

*Choose the **Show/Hide Channel Box** button from the Status Line, if the **Channel Box / Layer Editor** is not displayed in the viewport. Alternatively, you can press Ctrl+A.*

Bridge

The **Bridge** tool is used to construct faces between pair of the border edges. The connection between the edges or faces can be straight or curved, depending on the options, you choose from the **Bridge Options** dialog box.

To create a bridge between the border edges of an object, select the edges and then choose **Edit Mesh > Components > Bridge > Option Box** from the menubar; the **Bridge Options** dialog box will be displayed. In this dialog box, choose the type of bridge you want to create by selecting the a radio button corresponding to the Bridge type attribute and then choose the **Bridge** or **Apply** button; a bridge will be created, as shown in Figure 2-42.

Note

*To create a bridge between two separate objects, you need to combine the two objects by choosing **Mesh > Combine > Combine** from the menubar.*

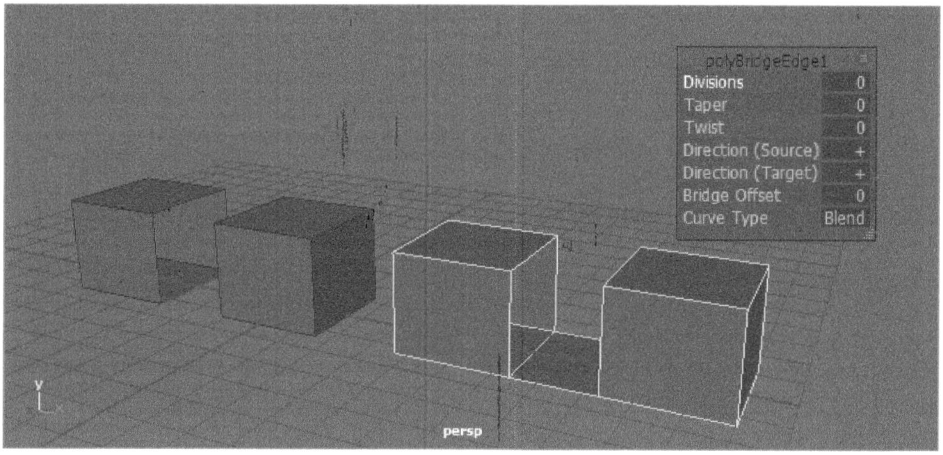

Figure 2-42 *The* ***Bridge*** *connection between two edges*

Collapse

Menubar: Edit Mesh > Components > Collapse

The **Collapse** tool use to collapse edges on a component and component basis and then it merges the associated vertices for each collapsed edge separately. To collapse the edges of an object, select the required edges and then choose **Edit Mesh > Components > Collapse** from the menubar; the selected edges will be collapsed and their vertices will be merged.

Note

This tool also works on faces. But it generates unpredictable results. If you want to merge the faces, use the ***Merge to Center option*** *which is available in the* ***Edit Mesh*** *menu.*

Connect

Menubar: Edit Mesh > Components > Connect

The **Connect** tool is used to connect the selected vertices or faces via edges. To use this tool, select faces or edges on an object and then choose **Edit Mesh > Components > Connect** from the menu bar to connect the selected component, refer to Figure 2-43.

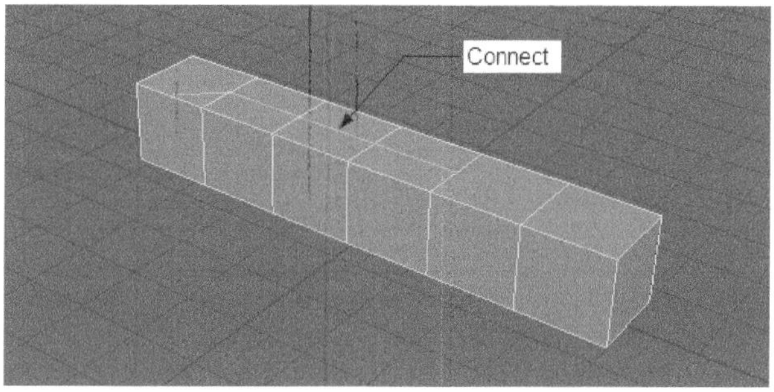

Figure 2-43 *The connected edge displayed*

Detach

Menubar: Edit Mesh > Components > Detach

The **Detach** tool is used to split a vertex into multiple vertices. To understand working of this tool, create a polygon object in the viewport and press and hold the right mouse button over it; a marking menu will be displayed. Choose **Vertex** from the marking menu; the vertex selection mode will be activated. Select a vertex of the object that needs to be split. Next, choose **Edit Mesh > Components > Detach** from the menubar; the selected vertex gets split into multiple vertices, refer to Figure 2-44. This tool also detaches the faces. When faces of an object are selected and you use this tool, it detaches the face selection along its perimeter edges.

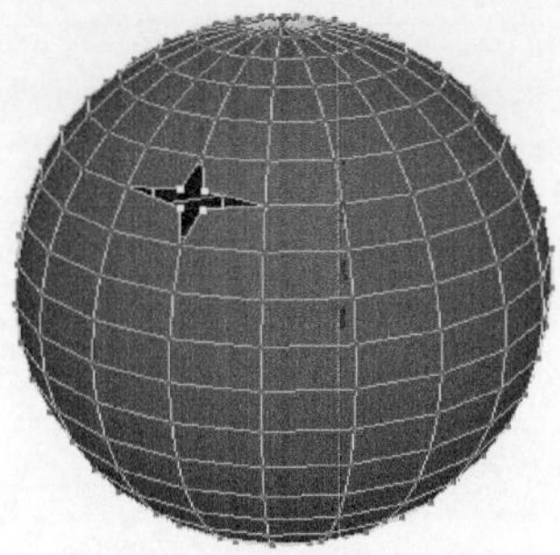

Figure 2-44 *Selected vertex gets split into multiple vertices*

Extrude

Menubar: Edit Mesh > Components > Extrude

The **Extrude** tool is used to extrude various components such as vertex, face, or an edge of a polygon object inward or outward.

To extrude a vertex, select the vertex that needs to be extruded. Next, choose **Edit Mesh > Components > Extrude** from the menubar; the selected vertex will be extruded and the **polyExtendedVertex#** In-View Editor will be displayed. You can change the width, length, and, division of the extruded vertex by entering the values in the **Width**, **Length**, and **Divisions** edit boxes, as shown in Figure 2-45.

To extrude an edge, select it and then choose **Edit Mesh > Components > Extrude** from the menubar; the **polyExtendedEdge#** In-View Editor will be displayed. Enter the desired value in the **Thickness** edit box of the **polyExtendedEdge#** In-View Editor. If the value in the edit box is negative, the face will be extruded inward and for a positive value, it will be extruded outward, refer to Figure 2-46.

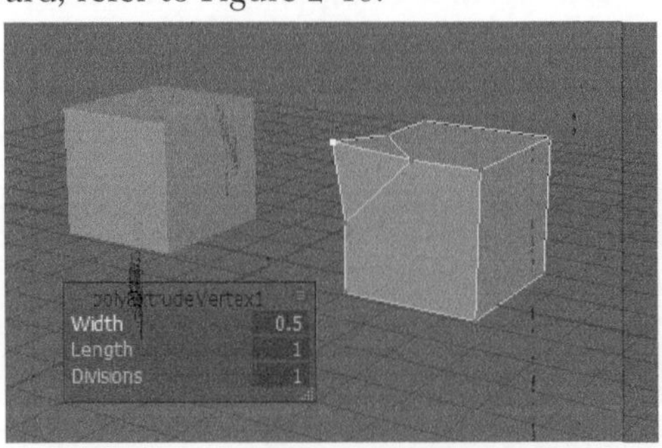

Figure 2-45 *The extruded vertex*

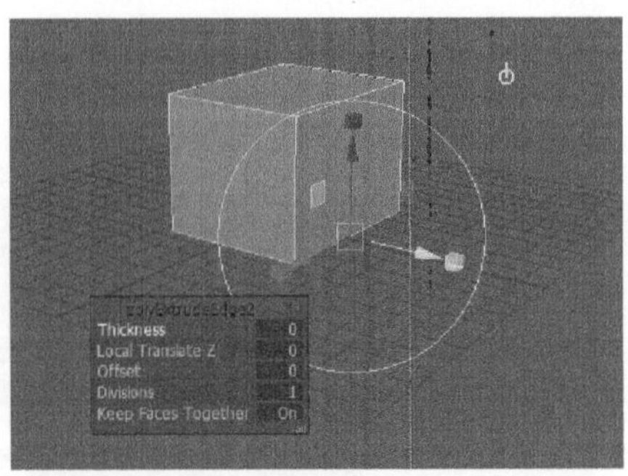

Figure 2-46 *The extruded edge*

To extrude a face, select it and then choose **Edit Mesh > Components > Extrude** from the menubar; the **polyExtrudeFace#** In-View Editor will be displayed. Enter the desired value in the **Thickness** edit box of the **polyExtrudeFace#** In-View Editor. If the value in the edit box is negative, the face will be extruded inward and for a positive values, it will be extruded outward, as shown in Figure 2-47.

Merge

Menubar: Edit Mesh > Components > Merge

The **Merge** tool is used to merge two vertices. To merge two vertices, select a object in the viewport and press and hold the right mouse button over it; a marking menu will be displayed. Choose **Vertex** from the marking menu; the vertex selection mode will be activated. Next, choose **Edit Mesh > Components > Merge > Option Box** from the menubar; the **Merge Vertices Options** will be activated. Now, select four vertices of top polygon, choose Merge from the displayed dialog box; the selected vertex is merged, refer to Figure 2-48.

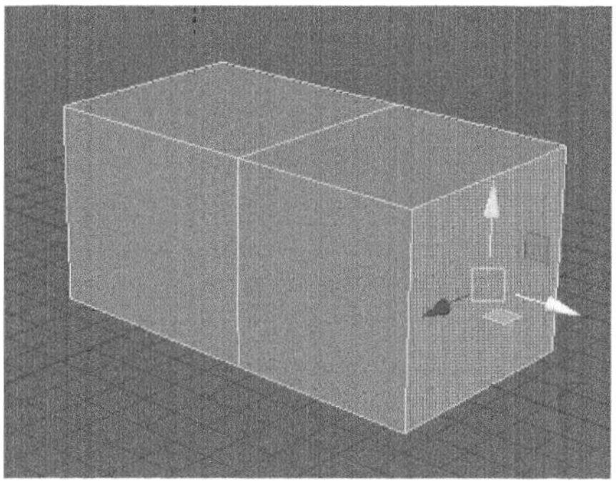

Figure 2-47 *The extruded face*

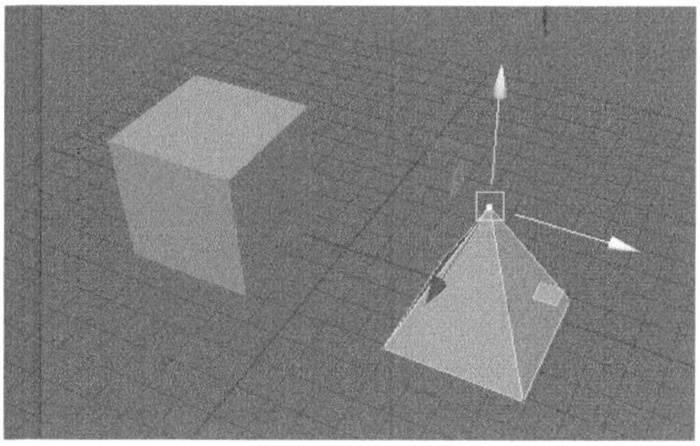

Figure 2-48 *Top vertices to be merged*

You can also use the **Merge to Center** tool for merging the selected vertices. To do so, choose **Edit Mesh > Components > Merge to Center**; the vertices will be merged to the center of the two vertices, refer to Figure 2-49.

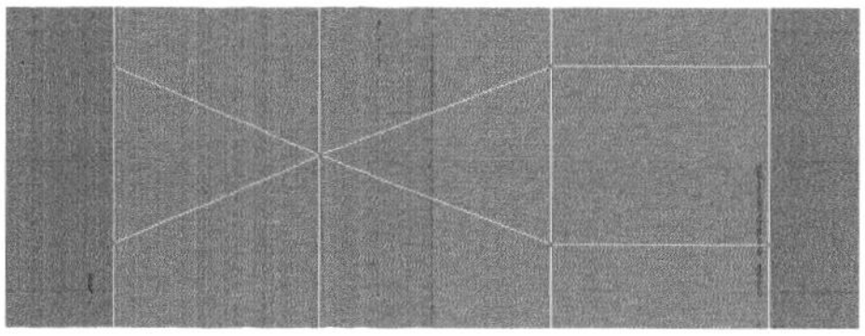

Figure 2-49 *Center vertices to be merged*

Average Vertices

Menubar: Edit Mesh > Vertex > Average Vertices

The **Average Vertices** tool is used to control the level of smoothing applied to the selection, refer to Figure 2-50. You can set the amount of smoothing in the **Iternation** edit box of the **polyAverageVertex1** In-View Editor.

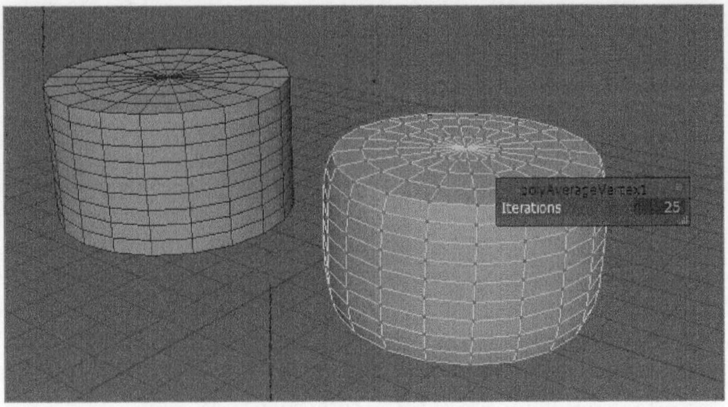

Figure 2-50 Selected vertices smoothend

Chamfer Vertices

Menubar:	Edit Mesh > Vertex > Chamfer Vertices

The **Chamfer Vertices** tool is used to replace a vertex to create a chamfered corner. To use this tool, create a polygon object in the viewport and press and hold the right mouse button over it; a marking menu will be displayed. Choose **Vertex** from the marking menu; the vertex selection mode will be activated. Select a vertex (or vertices) of the object. Next, choose **Edit Mesh > Vertex > Chamfer Vertices** from the menubar; a new polygon faces will be created, refer to Figure 2-51.

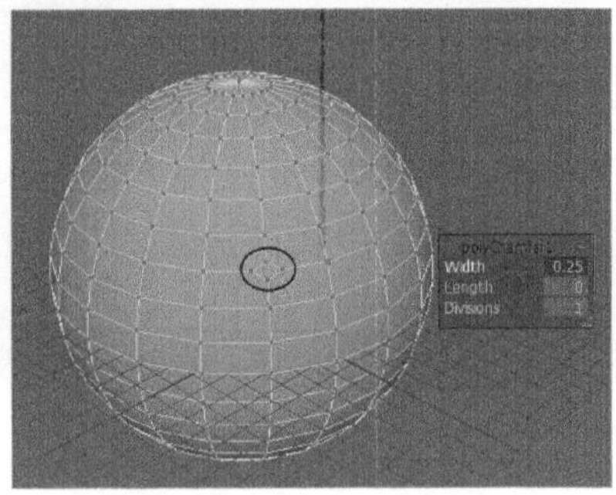

Figure 2-51 A new polygon face created using the ***Chamfer Vertices*** *tool*

Delete Edge/Vertex

Menubar:	Edit Mesh > Edge > Delete Edge/Vertex

The **Delete Edge/Vertex** tool is used to delete the selected edges or vertices of a polygon object. To do so, select vertices of an object that you want to delete and then choose **Edit Mesh > Edge > Delete Edge/Vertex** from the menubar; the selected vertices will be deleted. Similarly, using the **Delete Edge/Vertex** tool, you can delete the selected edges of the polygon object.

> **Tip**
> *You can also delete the selection using the DEL key. However, you can not delete a vertex when it shares more than two edges.*

Edit Edge Flow

Menubar:	Edit Mesh > Edge > Edit Edge Flow

The **Edit Edge Flow** tool is used to modify the position of edges along the curve of the surrounding mesh. To do so, select the two non-adjacent edges of an object and choose **Edit Mesh > Edge > Edit Edge Flow** from the menubar; the edges move along the curvature of the object. Now, to see the duplicate face, move it away from the centre using **Move** tool.

Duplicate

Menubar: Edit Mesh > Face > Duplicate

The **Duplicate** tool is used to create the duplicate copies of the selected faces. To use this tool, create a cube in the viewport. Select the polygon cube created and then press and hold the right mouse button on it; a marking menu will be displayed. Next, choose **Face** from the marking menu; the face selection mode will be activated. Choose **Move Tool** from the Tool Box. Next, select a face on the polygon cube and choose **Edit Mesh > Face > Duplicate** from the menubar; a duplicate copy of the selected face will be created in the viewport. Now, to see the duplicate face, move it away from the centre using **Move** tool.

EDITING THE POLYGON COMPONENTS USING MESH TOOLS

In the previous section, you learned to modify simple polygon primitives. In this section, you will learn to edit the polygon objects using the polygon components such as face, vertex, and edge. To access various tools for editing the polygon components, select **Modeling** from the **Menuset** drop-down list in Status Line. Next, choose the **Mesh Tools** menu from the menubar. The most commonly used tools under this menu are discussed next.

Create Polygon

Menubar: Mesh Tools > Tools > Create Polygon

The **Create Polygon** tool is used to create polygons by placing vertices in the viewport. To do so, choose **Mesh Tools > Tools > Create Polygon** tool from the menubar. Next, click in the viewport; a vertex point will be created in the viewport.

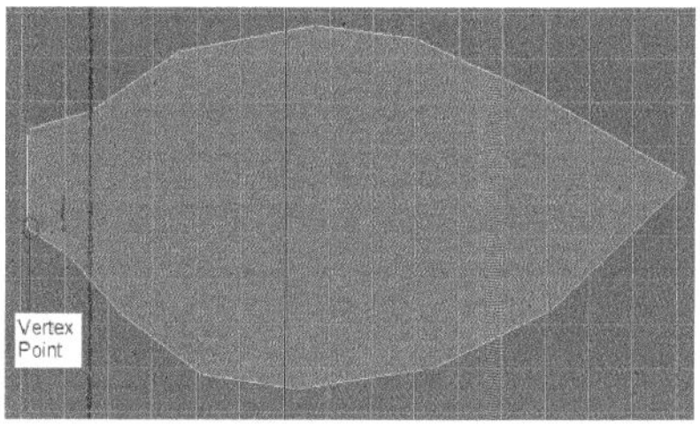

***Figure 2-52** A shape created using the **Create Polygon** tool*

Next, depending on the shape required, keep on clicking in the viewport to connect the points; a shape will be created, refer to Figure 2-52.

Insert Edge Loop

Menubar: Mesh Tools > Tools > Insert Edge Loop

The **Insert Edge Loop** tool is used to add segments to the selected object. The segment created by using this tool ends at the same point from where it starts, thus forming a loop. To use this tool, create a polygon object in the viewport and choose **Mesh Tools > Tools > Insert Edge Loop** tool from the menubar; the edges of the object will turn blue. Next, click on an edge; a new segment will be created on the selected object, as shown in Figure 2-53. Note that the **Insert Edge Loop** tool works only with objects that have quads (quads are faces with four sides). If the sides of a face are more or less than four, then this tool will not work. To set the properties of this tool, choose **Mesh Tools > Insert Edge Loop > Option Box** from the menubar; the **Tool Settings (Insert Edge Loop tool)** window will be displayed, refer to Figure 2-54.

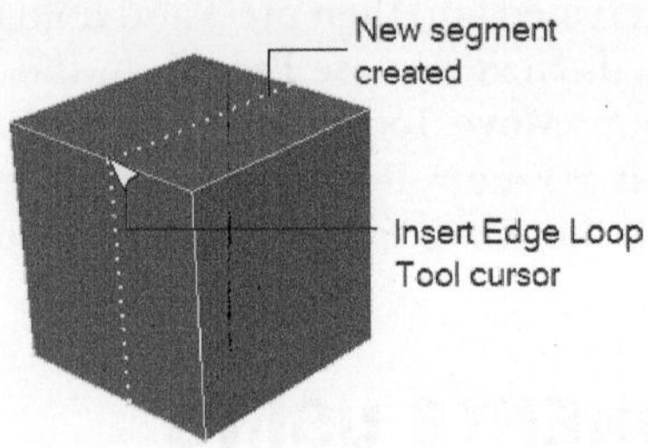

*Figure 2-53 A new segment created using the **Insert Edge Loop***

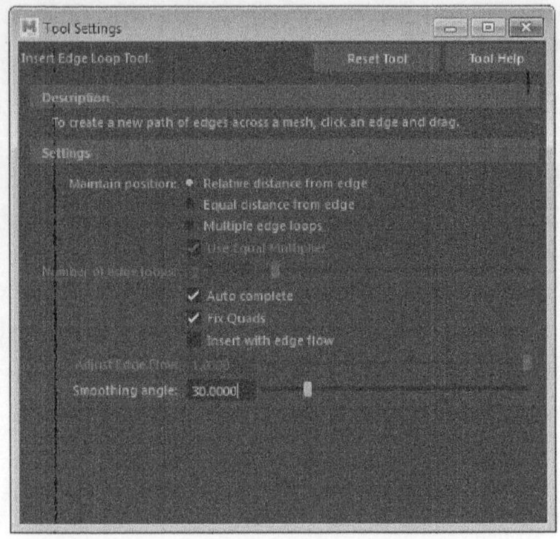

*Figure 2-54 The **Tool Settings (Insert Edge Loop tool)** window*

Multi-Cut

Menubar:	Mesh Tools > Tools > Multi-Cut

The **Multi-Cut** tool is used to manually add segments between two edges of an object. To add segments between two edges, select the polygon object and then choose **Mesh Tools > Tools > Multi-Cut** from the menubar.

Click on the edge to choose the starting point of the segment. Next, click on the edge where you want to end the segment and press ENTER; a segment will be added between the two edges, refer to Figure 2-55.

You can also make a cut in loop by using the **Multi-Cut** tool. To do so, choose the **Multi-Cut** tool from the **Mesh Tools** menubar, press CTRL key and then click on edge; A new segment will be created on the selected object.

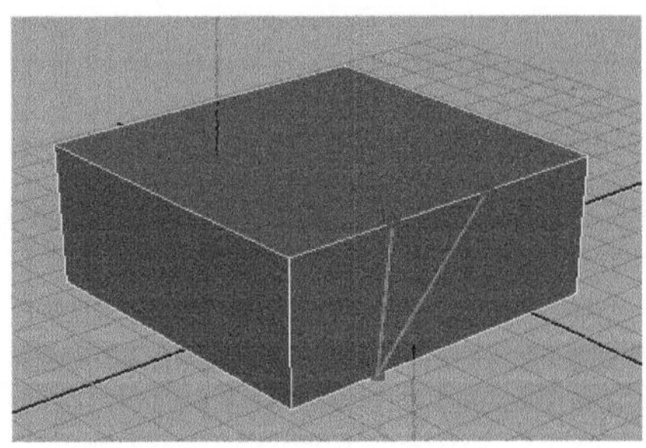

*Figure 2-55 Segments added using the **Multi-Cut** tool*

Offset Edge Loop

Menubar:	Mesh Tools > Tools > Offset Edge Loop

The **Offset Edge Loop** tool works similar to **Insert Edge Loop** tool with the only difference that it creates segments on both sides of the selected edges. To use this tool, create a polygon object in the viewport and choose **Mesh Tools > Tools > Offset Edge Loop** tool from the menubar. Next, click and drag the cursor to the already existing edges to create new segments on both sides of the selected object, as shown in Figure 2-56.

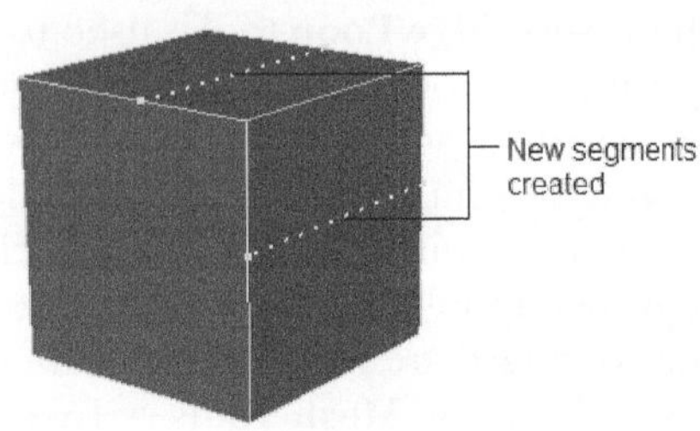

*Figure 2-56 New segments created using the **Offset Edge Loop** tool*

TUTORIALS

Tutorial 1

In this tutorial, you will create the model of a coffee mug, as shown in Figure 2-57, using the polygon modeling techniques. **(Expected time: 20 min)**

Figure 2-57 *The model of a coffee mug*

The following steps are required to complete this tutorial:

a. Create a project folder.
b. Create the basic shape of the mug.
c. Create the handle of the mug.
d. Change the background color of the scene.
e. Save and render the scene.

Creating a Project Folder

Before starting a new scene, it is recommended that you create a project folder. It helps you keep all the files of a project in an organized manner. Open Windows Explorer and browse to the *Documents* folder. In this folder, create a new folder with the name *maya2017*. The *maya2017* folder will be the main folder and it will contain all the projects folders that you will create while doing tutorials of this textbook. Now, you will create a project folder for Tutorial 1 of this chapter. To do so, you need to follow the steps given next.

1. Start Autodesk Maya 2017 by double-clicking on its icon on the desktop.

2. Choose **File > Project Window** from the menubar; the **Project Window** is displayed. Choose the **New** button; the **Current Project** and **Location** text boxes are enabled. Now, enter **c02_tut1** in the **Current Project** text box.

3. Click on the folder icon next to the **Location** text box; the **Select Location** dialog box is displayed. In this dialog box, browse to the *\Documents\maya2017* folder and choose the **Select** button to close the dialog box. Next, choose the **Accept** button in the **Project Window** dialog box; the *\Documents\maya2017\c02_tut1* folder will become the current project folder.

4. Choose **Save Scene** from the **File** menu; the **Save File As** dialog box is displayed.

Note

*The scenes created in Maya are saved with the .ma or .mb extension. As the project folder is already created, the path \Documents\maya2017\c02_tut1\scenes is displayed in the **Look in** drop-down list of the **Save As** dialog box.*

Tip

After setting the project folder when you open or save a scene, Maya uses the scenes folder inside the project folder by default.

5. Enter **c02tut1** in the **File name** edit box and then choose the **Save As** button to close the dialog box.

Note

It is recommended that you frequently save the file while you are working on it by pressing the CTRL+S keys.

Creating the Basic Shape of the Mug

In this section, you will use the **Cylinder** polygon primitive to create the basic shape of the mug.

1. Choose **Create > Objects >Polygon Primitives > Cylinder > Option Box** from the menubar; the **Tool Settings (Polygon Cylinder Tool)** window is displayed in the viewport. Enter the values in the **Tool Settings (Polygon Cylinder Tool)** window, as shown in Figure 2-58.

2. Click in the persp viewport; a cylinder is created, refer to Figure 2-59.

3. In the **Channel Box / Layer Editor**, click on the **pCylinder1** tab; a text box is activated. Next, type **mug** in the text box and press ENTER; the **pCylinder1** tab is renamed as *mug*.

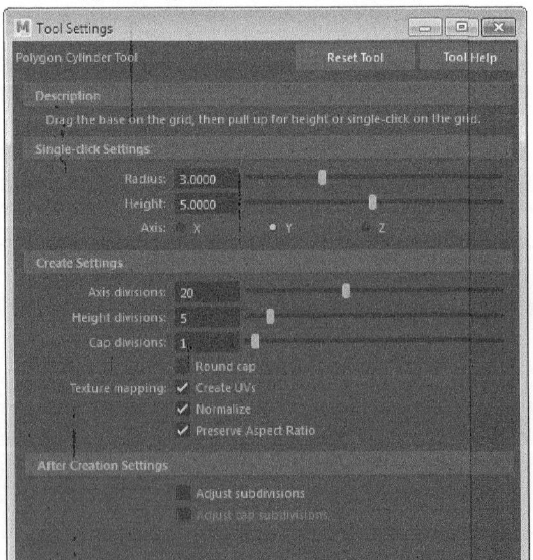

***Figure 2-58** The **Tool Settings (Polygon Cylinder Tool)** window*

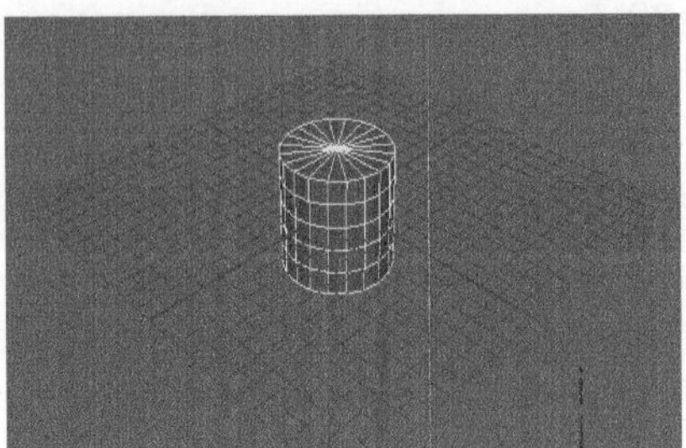

***Figure 2-59** Cylinder created in the viewport*

4. Hover the cursor in the persp viewport and press SPACEBAR; the four viewports are displayed. Next, hover the cursor on the front-Z viewport and press SPACEBAR; the front-Z viewport is maximized.

   Select *mug* if it is not selected and then press and hold the right mouse button; a marking menu is displayed.

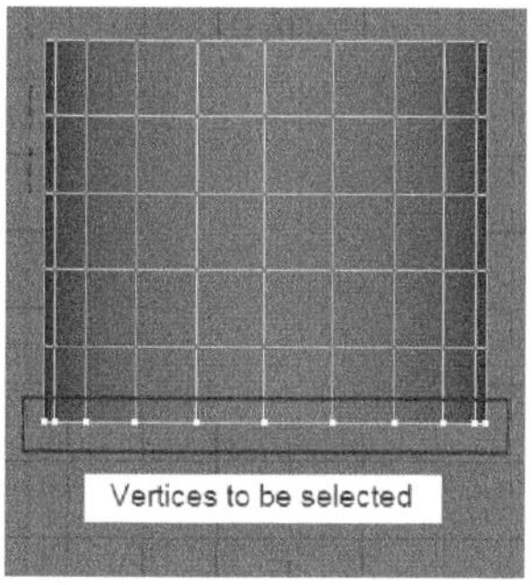

Figure 2-60 *Bottom vertices of the cylinder selected*

5. Choose **Vertex** from the marking menu; the vertex selection mode is activated.
6. Select the vertices at the bottom of *mug*, refer to Figure 2-60. Next, invoke **Scale Tool** by pressing the R key.
7. Scale down the selected vertices of *mug* inward uniformly, as shown in Figure 2-61. Similarly, select the top vertices and scale the vertices to form the shape of a mug, refer to Figure 2-62.

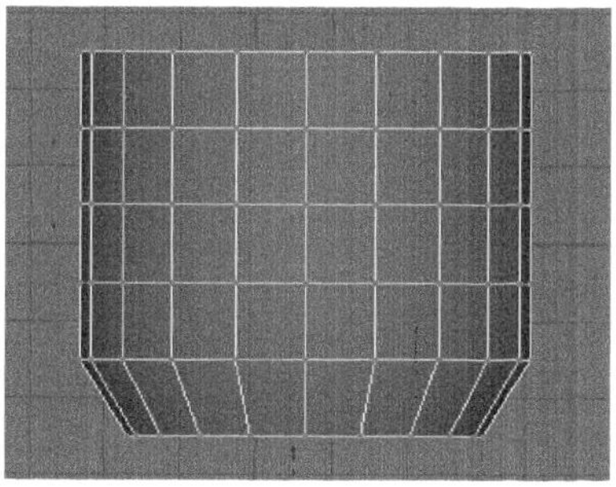

Figure 2-61 *Bottom vertices of the cylinder scaled*

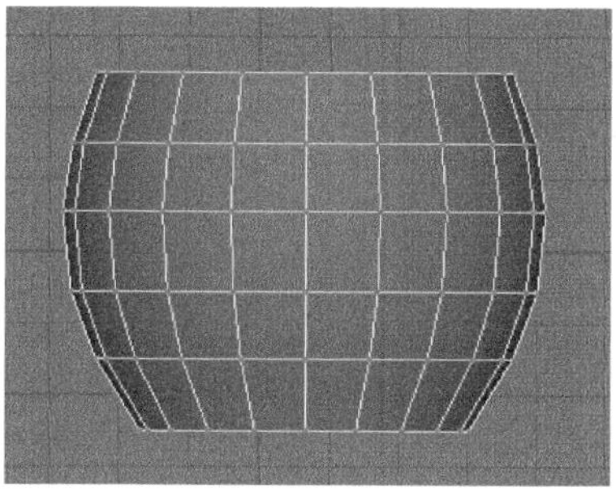

Figure 2-62 *Basic shape of the mug created*

Next, you need to add segments at the top and bottom.

8. Make sure the **Modeling** menuset is selected in the **Menuset** drop-down list. Choose **Mesh Tools > Tools > Insert Edge Loop** from the menubar. Next, click at the top and bottom region of *mug*; two edges are inserted, refer to Figure 2-63. Deactivate the **Insert Edge Loop** tool by pressing the W key and then press 3 to view *mug* in the smooth mode.
9. Maximize the persp viewport. Press 1 to switch back to the original mode. Make sure *mug* is selected and then press and hold the right mouse button; a marking menu is displayed. Choose **Face** from the marking menu; the face selection mode is activated. Now, select the top faces of *mug* using the SHIFT key, refer to Figure 2-64. Next, choose **Edit Mesh > Components > Extrude** from the menubar.
10. Invoke the **Scale Tool** and scale down the selected faces uniformly, refer to Figure 2-65.
11. Again, choose **Edit Mesh > Components > Extrude** from the menubar; the **polyExtrudeFace2** In-View Editor is displayed in the viewport, refer to Figure 2-66. Enter **-0.3** in the **Thickness** edit box of the **polyExtrudeFace2** In-View Editor, refer to Figure 2-66; the shaded faces are extruded.

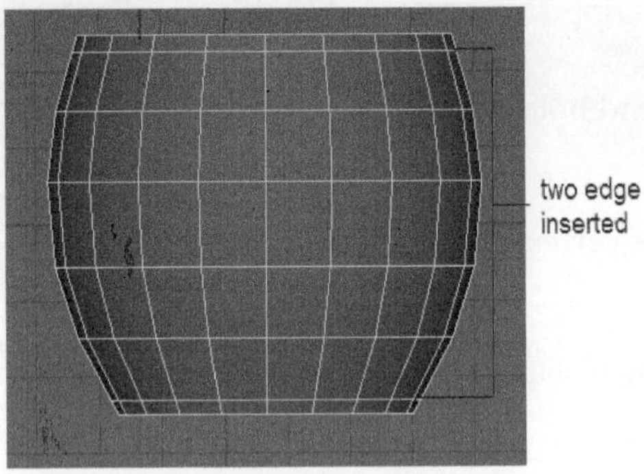

Figure 2-63 Two edges inserted at the top and bottom of the cylinder

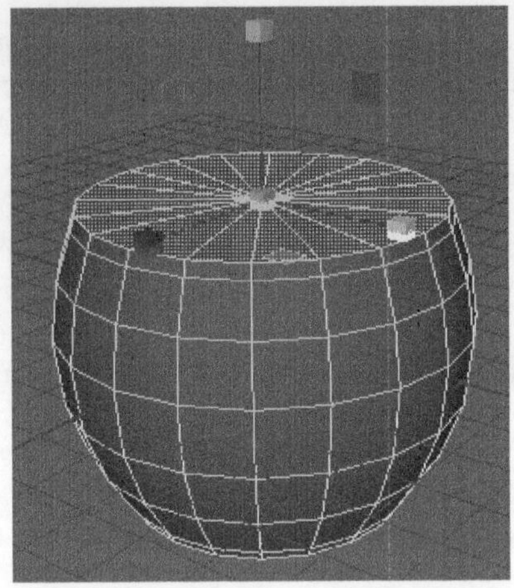

Figure 2-64 Top faces of the cylinder selected

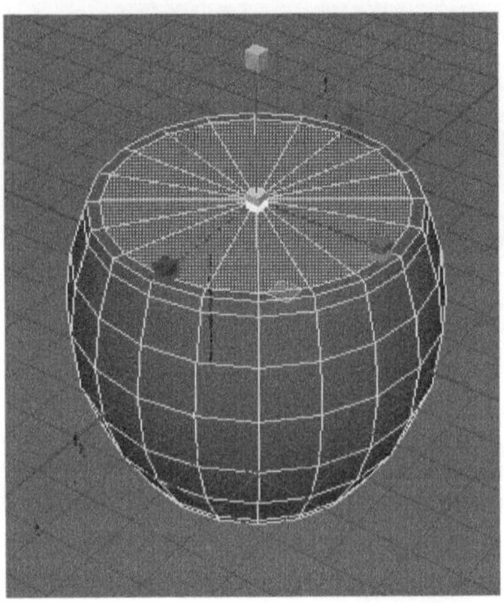

*Figure 2-65 Selected top faces of the mug scaled down using **Scale Tool***

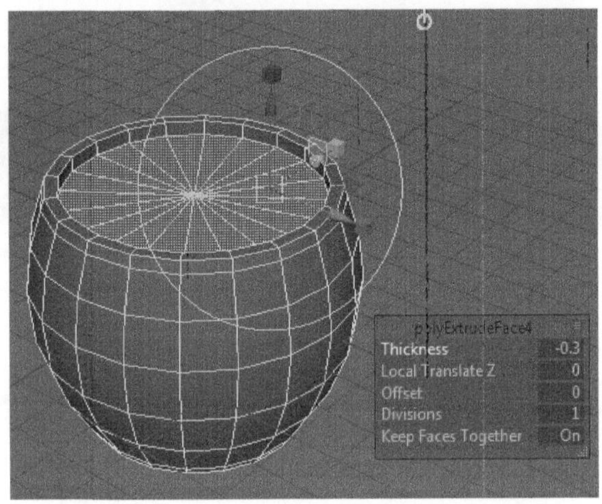

*Figure 2-66 The **polyExtrudeFace2** In-View Editor displayed*

12. Press the G key to invoke the **Extrude** tool again and enter the value **-1.6** in the **Thickness** edit box; the top faces of *mug* are extruded downward.

Note
The G key is used to repeat the last performed action in Maya.

13. Press G again to invoke the **Extrude** tool, and enter the value **-2** in the **Thickness** edit box. Next, enter **0.8** in the **Offset** edit box; the selected polygon is extruded inward.

14. Maximize the top-Y viewport such that you can view the inner area of *mug*. Press 3 to view the object in the smooth mode. To rectify the distortion in the geometry, you need to add edges. Press 1 and choose **Mesh Tools > Tools > Insert Edge Loop** tool; the shape of the cursor changes and then insert two edges inside the mug, refer to Figure 2-67. Deactivate the **Insert Edge Loop** tool by pressing W.

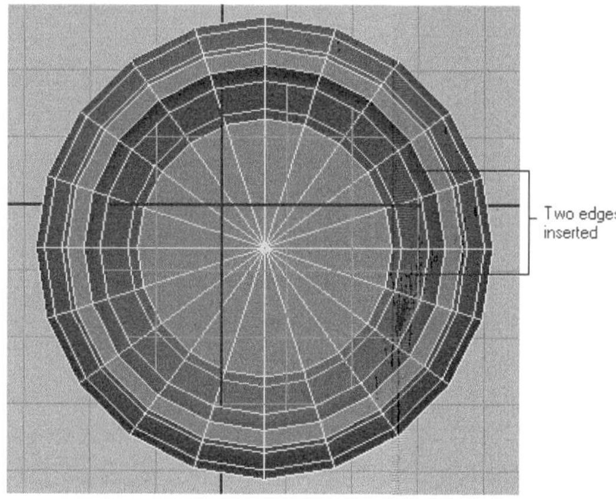

Figure 2-67 Two edge loops added inside the mug

Creating the Handle of the Mug

In this section, you need to create the handle of the mug.

1. Maximize the side-X viewport. Move the cursor over *mug* and then press and hold the right mouse button; a marking menu is displayed. Choose **Edge** from the marking menu; the edge selection mode is activated.

2. Select two edges of *mug*, refer to Figure 2-68. Next, choose **Edit Mesh > Components > Bevel > Option Box**; the **Bevel Options** dialog box is displayed. Now, enter the value **1** in the **Width** edit box and choose the **Bevel** button; the selected edges will be beveled, as shown in Figure 2-69.

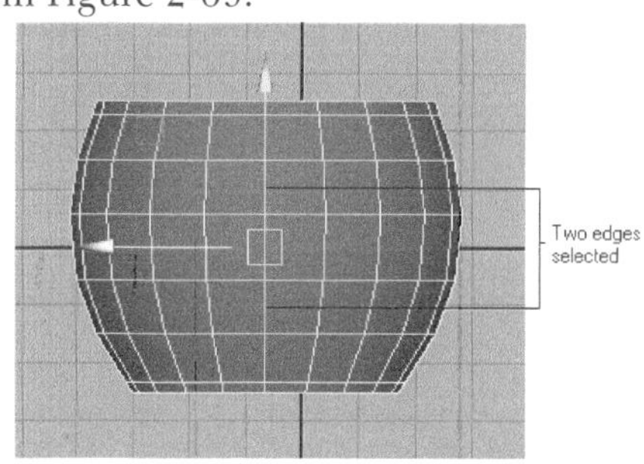

Figure 2-68 Two edges of mug selected

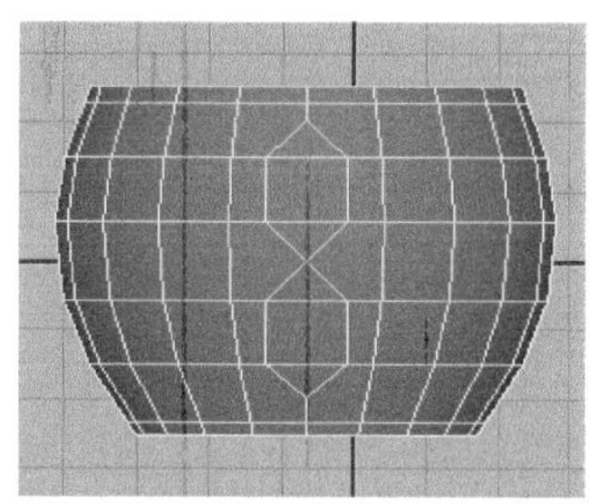

Figure 2-69 Selected edges beveled

3. Move the cursor over *mug* and then press and hold the right mouse button; a marking menu is displayed. Choose **Face** from the marking menu; the face selection mode is activated. Next, select a face of *mug*, as shown in Figure 2-70.

4. Choose **Edit Mesh > Components > Extrude** from the menubar. Next, invoke **Scale Tool** by pressing the R key and scale down the selected face of *mug* uniformly upto 70%. You can check the scale size in the status line, as shown in Figure 2-71.

5. Select the face of *mug*, as shown in Figure 2-72. Repeat the procedure as done in Step 4 to scale down the face, refer to Figure 2-73.

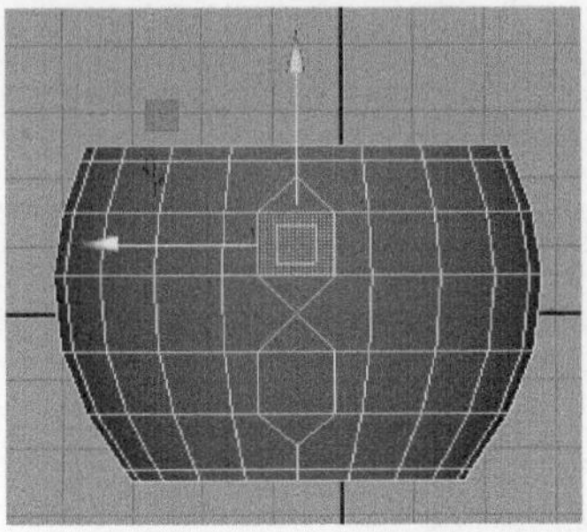

Figure 2-70 A face of mug selected

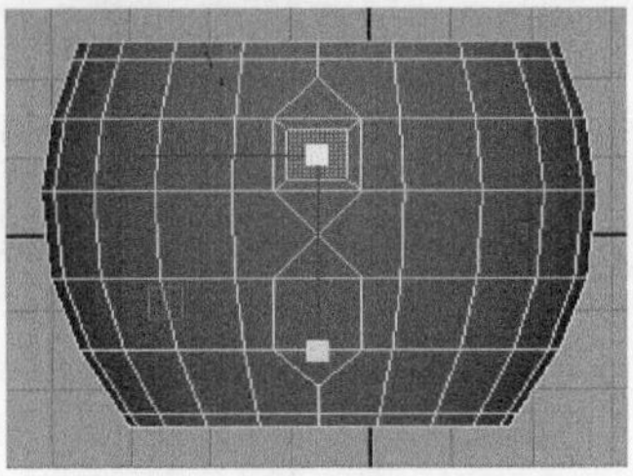

Figure 2-71 Face of the mug scaled down

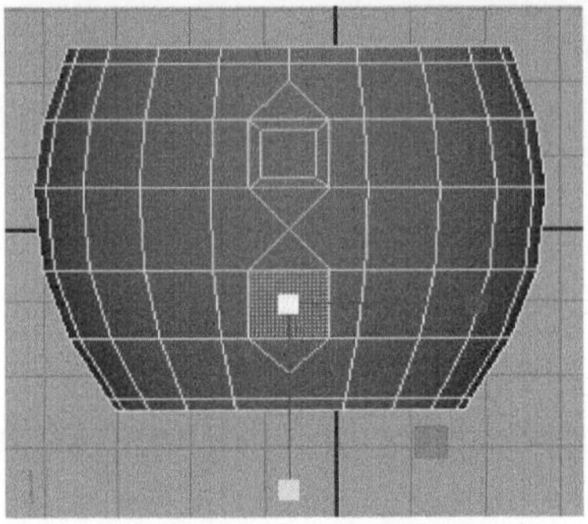

Figure 2-72 A face of the mug selected

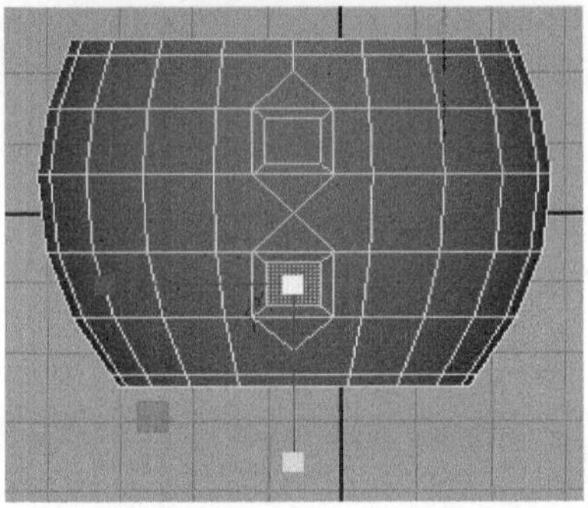

Figure 2-73 A face of the mug scaled down

6. Maximize the persp viewport. Make sure that both the scaled faces are selected, and then invoke the **Extrude** tool by pressing the G key. Next, enter the value **0.8** in the **Thickness** edit box of the **polyExtrudeFace4 In-View Editor.**

7. Deactivate the **Extrude** tool by pressing the W key. Make sure the two extruded faces are selected. Next, choose **Edit Mesh > Components > Bridge > Option Box** from the menubar; the **Bridge Options** dialog box is displayed. Enter the values in the **Bridge Options** dialog box, as shown in Figure 2-74. Next, choose the **Apply** button and close the dialog box; the extruded faces are connected to each other.

8. Make sure *mug* is selected and then press and hold the right mouse button on it; a marking menu is displayed. Next, choose **Object Mode** from the marking menu; the object selection mode is activated.

9. Select *mug* and then choose **Mesh > Remesh > Smooth** from the menubar; the mesh of *mug* is smoothened. Press SPACEBAR; the four viewports display the *mug* after applying **Smooth Tool**, as shown in Figure 2-75.

Changing the Background Color of the Scene

In this section, you will change the background color of the scene.

1. Choose **Windows > Editors > Outliner** from the menubar; the **Outliner** window is displayed. Select the **persp** camera in the **Outliner** window; the **perspShape** tab is displayed in **Attribute Editor**.

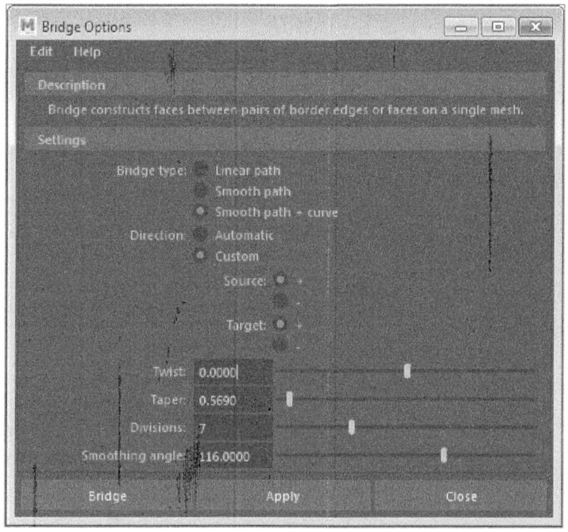

*Figure 2-74 The **Bridge Options** dialog box*

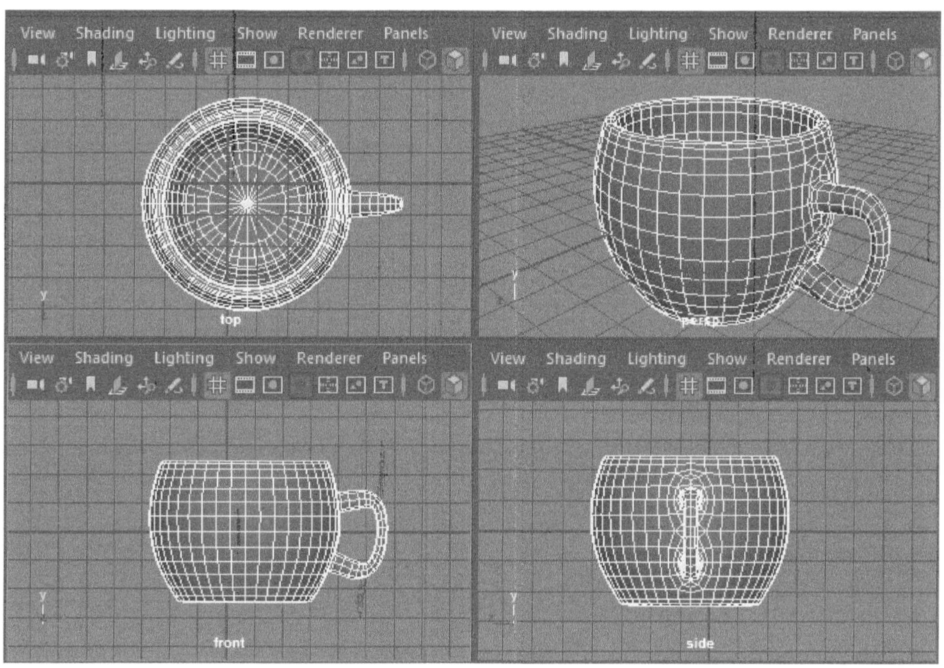

Figure 2-75 The mug displayed in all viewports

2. In the **perspShape** tab, expand the **Environment** node and drag the **Background Color** slider bar toward right to change the background color to white.

Saving and Rendering the Scene

In this section, you will save the scene that you have created and then render it. You can view the final rendered image of the scene by downloading the *c02_maya_2017_rndr.zip* file from *www.cadcim.com*. The path of the file is as follows: *Textbooks > Animation and Visual Effects > Maya > Autodesk Maya 2017: A Comprehensive Guide*

1. Choose **File > Save Scene** from the menubar.

2. Maximize the persp viewport. Choose the **Render the current frame** button from the Status Line; the **Render View** window is displayed. This window shows the final output of the scene, refer to Figure 2-57.

Tutorial 2

In this tutorial, you will create the model of a skateboard, as shown in Figure 2-76, using the polygon modeling techniques. (**Expected time: 30 min**)

Figure 2-76 *The model of a skateboard*

The following steps are required to complete this tutorial:

a. Create a project folder.
b. Create the deck.
c. Create the base.
d. Create the wheels.
e. Change the background color of the scene.
f. Save and render the scene.

Creating a Project Folder

Create a new project folder with the name *c02_tut2* at *\Documents\maya2017* and then save the file with the name *c02tut2*, as discussed in Tutorial 1.

Creating the Deck

In this section, you need to create the deck of the skateboard using the **Cube** tool.

1. Maximize the top-Y viewport. Choose **Create > Objects > Polygon Primitives > Cube > Option Box** from the menubar; the **Tool Settings (Polygon Cube Tool)** window is displayed on the left of the viewport. Enter the required values in the **Tool Settings (Polygon Cube Tool)** window, as shown in Figure 2-77. Next, click in the top-Y viewport; a cube is created in the top-Y viewport, as shown in Figure 2-78.

2. In the **Channel Box / Layer Editor**, click on **pCube1**. Next, enter **deck** in the text box and press ENTER; the **pCube1** is renamed as *deck*.

3. In the top-Y viewport, press and hold the right mouse button on *deck*; a marking menu is displayed. Choose **Vertex** from the marking menu; the vertex selection mode is activated.

Next, select the vertices, as shown in Figure 2-79. Next, choose **Scale Tool** by pressing the R key and scale the vertices uniformly, refer to Figure 2-80.

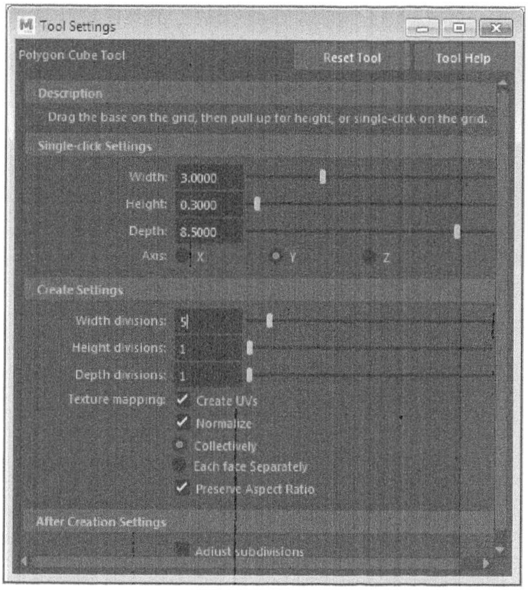

Figure 2-77 The ***Tool Settings (Polygon Cube Tool)*** *window*

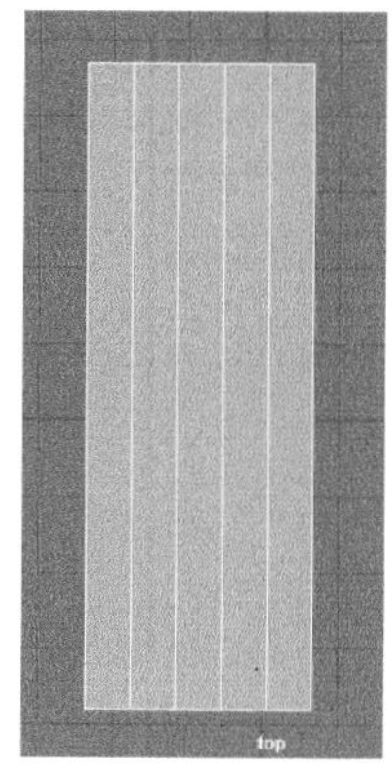

Figure 2-78 A cube created

4. Similarly, scale the other vertices to create the basic shape of *deck*, as shown in Figure 2-81.

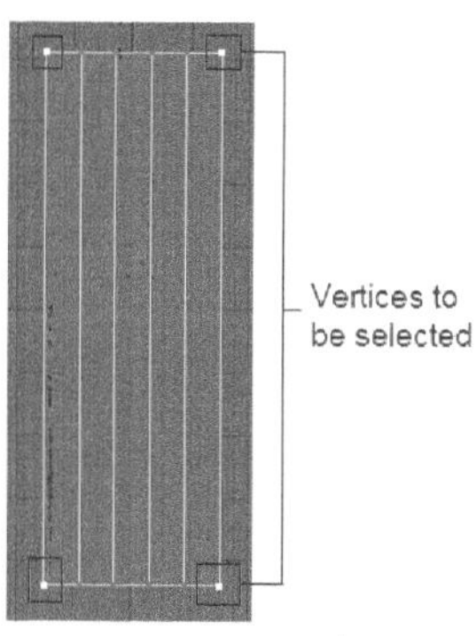

Figure 2-79 The vertices selected

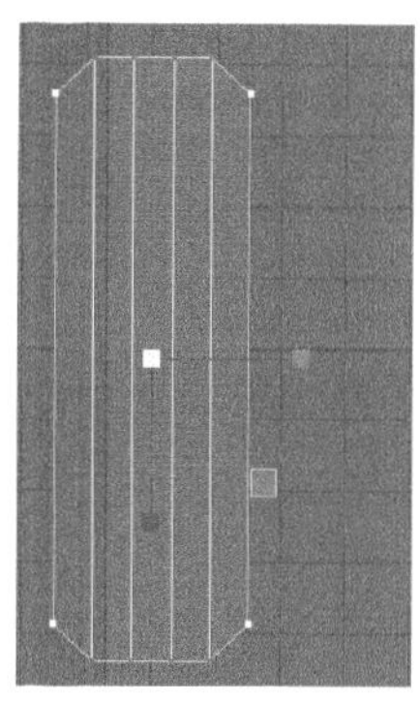

Figure 2-80 The selected vertices scaled

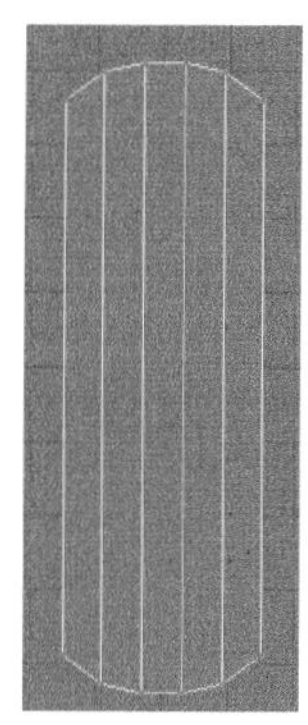

Figure 2-81 The basic shape of the deck

5. Press and hold the right mouse button on *deck*; a marking menu is displayed. Next, choose **Object Mode** from the marking menu; the object selection mode is activated. Select *deck* and maximize the front-Z viewport.

6. Make sure the **Modeling** menuset is selected from the **Menuset** drop-down list in the Status Line. Next, choose **Mesh Tools > Tools > Insert Edge Loop** tool from the menubar; the shape of the cursor changes. Click on the top and bottom vertical edge and create two new segments on *deck*, as shown in Figure 2-82.

7. Maximize the top-Y viewport and repeat the previous step to create two segments on *deck*, as shown in Figure 2-83. Choose the **Select Tool** to deactivate the **Insert Edge Loop** tool.

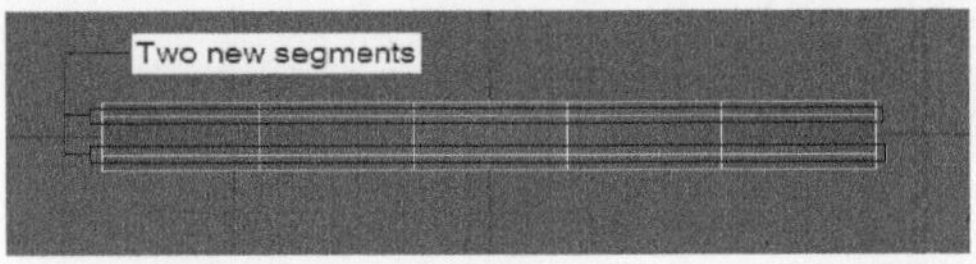

Figure 2-82 Two new segments created in the front-Z viewport

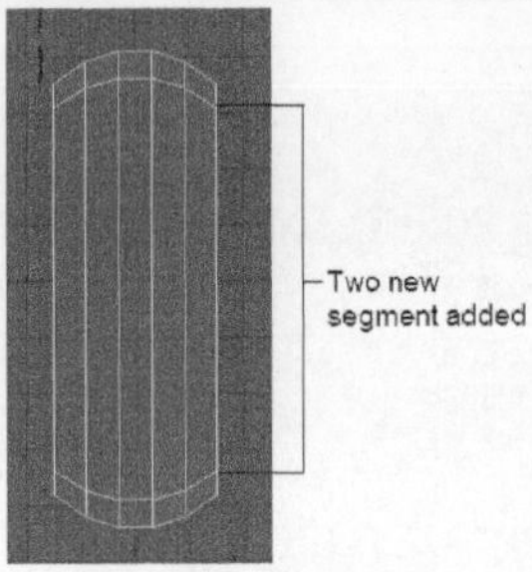

Figure 2-83 Two segments created in the top-Y viewport

8. Press and hold the right mouse button on *deck*; a marking menu is displayed. Choose **Object Mode** from the marking menu; the object selection mode is activated.

9. Make sure *deck* is selected and choose **Mesh > Remesh > Smooth > Option Box** from the menubar; the **Smooth Options** dialog box is displayed. In the **Smooth Options** dialog box, make sure the **Division levels** value is set to **1**. Now, choose the **Smooth** button; the geometry of *deck* is smoothened.

Creating the Base

In this section, you need to create the base of the skateboard using the **Cube** polygon primitive.

1. Maximize the front-Z viewport. Choose **Create > Objects > Polygon Primitives > Cube > Option Box** from the menubar; the **Tool Settings (Polygon Cube Tool)** window is displayed in the viewport. Enter the required values in the **Tool Settings (Polygon Cube Tool)** window, as shown in Figure 2-84. Next, click in the front-Z viewport; a cube is created in the front-Z viewport, as shown in Figure 2-85.

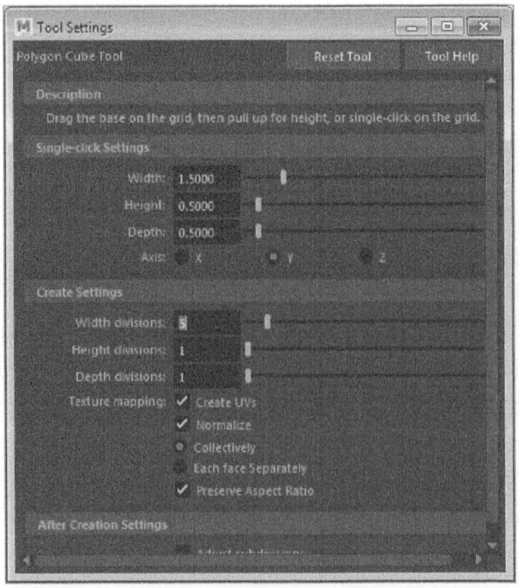

*Figure 2-84 The **Tool Settings (Polygon Cube Tool)** window*

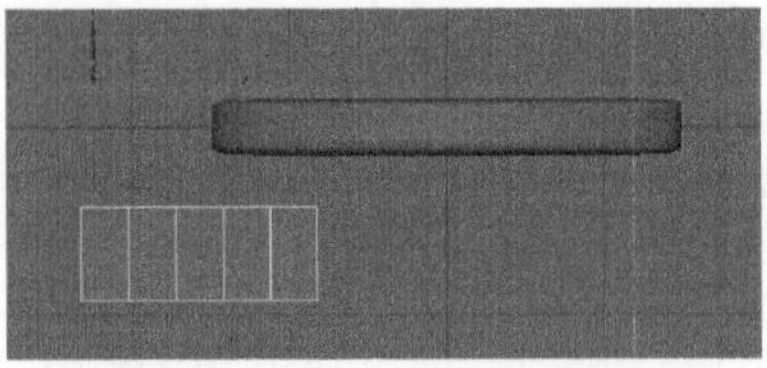

Figure 2-85 The cube created

2. In the **Channel Box / Layer Editor**, click on **pCube1** tab. Next, enter **base** in the text box and press ENTER; **pCube1** tab is renamed as *base*.

3. In the front-Z viewport, press and hold the right mouse button on *base*; a marking menu is displayed. Choose **Vertex** from the marking menu; the vertex selection mode is activated. Next, select the two bottom center vertices and then choose **Move Tool** from the Tool Box. Now, adjust the vertices on *base* to get the result shown in Figure 2-86.

4. Maximize the side-X viewport. Select the left most vertices in the side-X viewport and then drag them along the -Z axis to reduce the size of *base*, as shown in Figure 2-87.

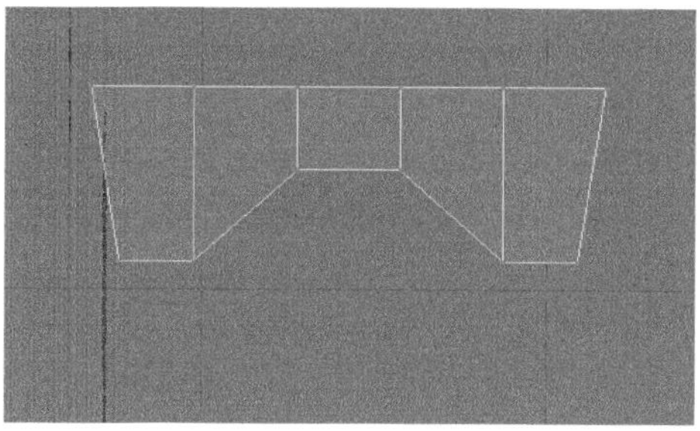

Figure 2-86 *The adjusted vertices of the base*

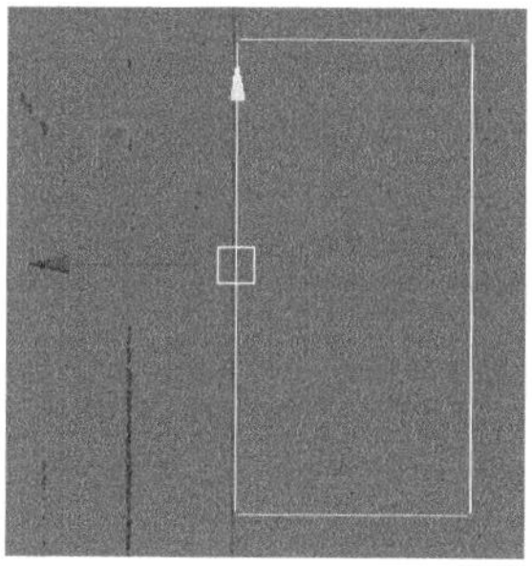

Figure 2-87 *Dragging the selected vertices along the -Z axis*

5. Press and hold the right mouse button on *base*; a marking menu is displayed. Next, choose **Object Mode** from the marking menu; the object selection mode is activated.

6. Select *base* and maximize the front-Z viewport. Next, choose **Mesh Tools > Tools > Insert Edge Loop** tool from the menubar. Using this tool, insert four new segments, as shown in Figure 2-88. Choose the **Select Tool** to deactivate the **Insert Edge Loop** tool.

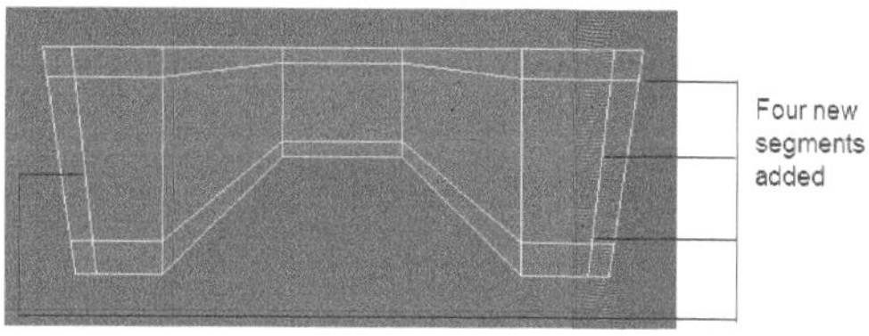

Figure 2-88 *Four new segments inserted in the front-Z viewport*

7. Press and hold the right mouse button on *base*; a marking menu is displayed. Choose **Object Mode** from the marking menu; the object selection mode is activated.

8. Select *base* and choose **Mesh > Remesh > Smooth** from the menubar; the geometry of *base* is smoothened.

   Next, you need to create the bolts.

9. Choose **Create > Objects > Polygon Primitives > Cylinder > Option box** from the menubar; the **Tool Settings (Polygon Cylinder Tool)** window is displayed. Enter the required

values in the **Tool Settings (Polygon Cylinder Tool)** window, as shown in Figure 2-89. Click in the front-Z viewport; a cylinder is created.

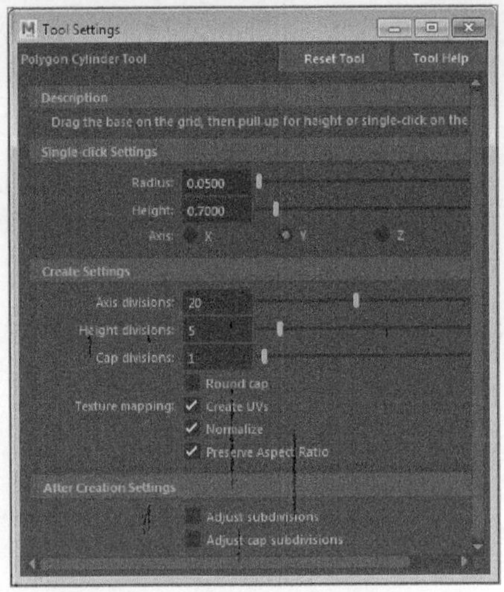

***Figure 2-89** The **Tool Settings (Polygon Cylinder Tool)** window*

10. In the **Channel Box / Layer Editor**, click on **pCylinder1**. Next, enter **bolt** in the text box and press ENTER; **pCylinder** is renamed as *bolt*.

11. Choose **Move Tool** from the Tool Box and align *bolt* with base in all viewports. Next, choose the **Rotate Tool** from the Tool Box to rotate and align it with both front and side-X viewports, as shown in Figures 2-90 and 2-91.

12. Activate the side-X viewport. Make sure *bolt* is selected and press CTRL+D; a duplicate copy of *bolt* is created with the name *bolt1*. Set the following parameters in the **Channel Box / Layer Editor** of *bolt1*:

    Rotate X: **90** Rotate Z: **0**

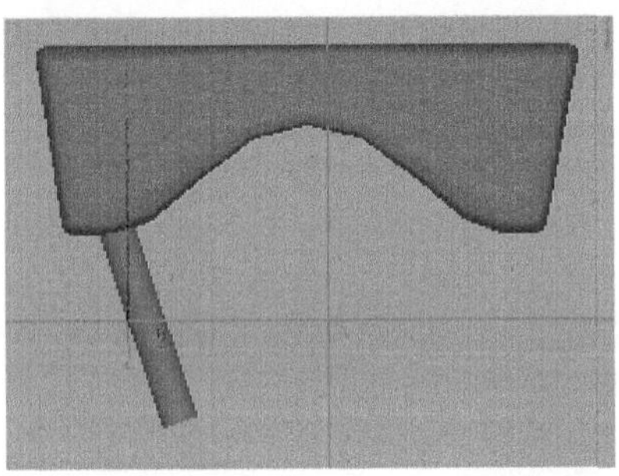

***Figure 2-90** The cylinder rotated and aligned in the front-Z viewport*

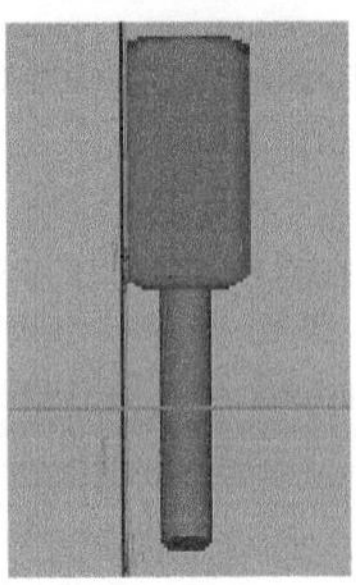

***Figure 2-91** The cylinder rotated and aligned in the side-X viewport*

13. Choose **Scale Tool** from the Tool Box and scale *bolt1* uniformly. Next, choose **Move Tool** from the Tool Box and align it in all viewports, as shown in Figure 2-92.

    Next, you need to create *truck*.

14. Maximize the front-Z viewport. Choose **Create > Objects > Polygon Primitives > Cylinder > Option box** from the menubar; the **Tool Settings (Polygon Cylinder Tool)** window is displayed in the viewport. In the **Tool Settings (Polygon Cylinder Tool)** window, set the parameters as follows:

    Radius: **0.25** Height: **1** Axis: **Z**
    Axis divisions: **10** Height divisions: **3** Cap Divisions: **10**

    Next, click in the viewport; the cylinder is created, as shown in Figure 2-93.

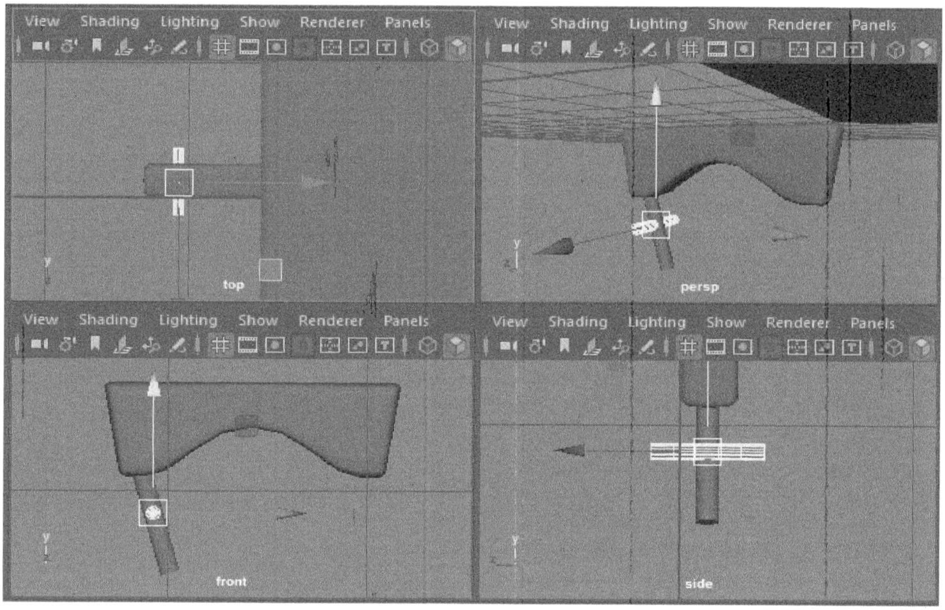

Figure 2-92 Aligning bolt1 in all viewports

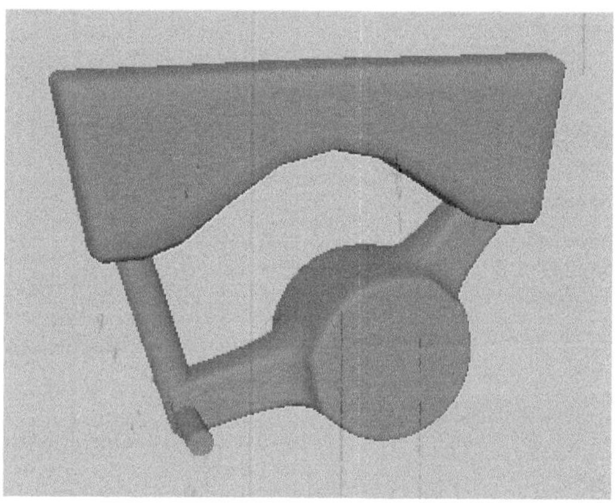

Figure 2-93 The wheel aligned with bolt1 in all viewports

15. In the **Channel Box / Layer Editor**, click on **pCylinder1**. Next, enter **truck** in the text box and press ENTER; the **pCylinder1** is renamed as *truck*.

16. Maximize the persp viewport. Press and hold the right mouse button over *truck* and choose **Face** from the marking menu displayed; the face selection mode is activated. Select the faces 1 and 5 of *truck*, refer to Figure 2-94. Next, choose **Edit Mesh > Components > Extrude** from the menubar; the **polyExtrudeFace2** In-View Editor is displayed. Enter **1** in the **Thickness** edit box; the faces of *truck* are extruded, as shown in Figure 2-95.

17. Maximize the front-Z viewport. Choose the **Mesh Tools > Tools > Insert Edge Loop** tool from the menubar and add new segments to *truck*, as shown in Figure 2-96. Choose **Select Tool** to deactivate **Insert Edge Loop** tool.

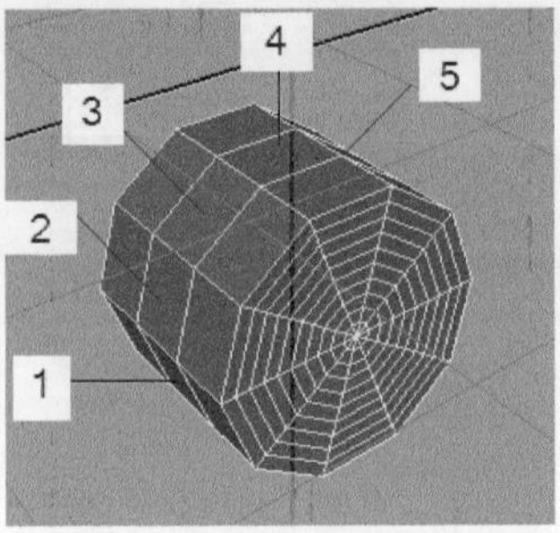

Figure 2-94 The cylinder after extrusion in the persp viewport

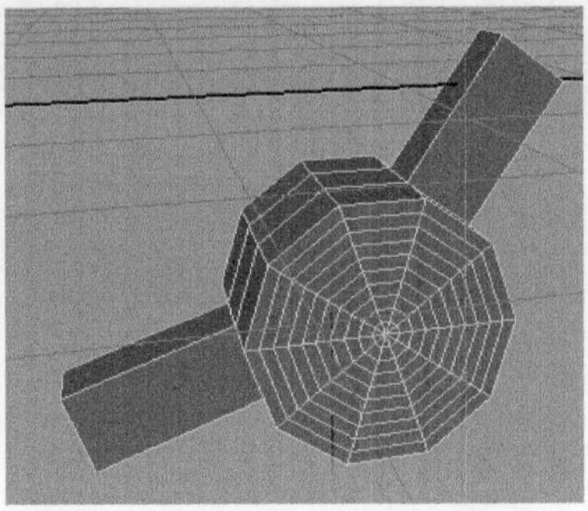

Figure 2-95 The cylinder after extrusion in the persp viewport

18. Press and hold the right mouse button on *truck*; a marking menu is displayed. Choose **Object Mode** from it; the object selection mode is activated. Next, select *truck* and choose **Mesh > Remesh > Smooth > Option Box** from the menubar; the **Smooth Options** dialog box is displayed.

19. In the dialog box, enter **2** in the **Division levels** edit box and then choose the **Smooth** button; the geometry of *truck* is smoothened. Next, align *truck, base, bolt* and *bolt1* in all viewports using **Move Tool, Rotate Tool**, and **Scale Tool** uniformly, refer to Figure 2-97.

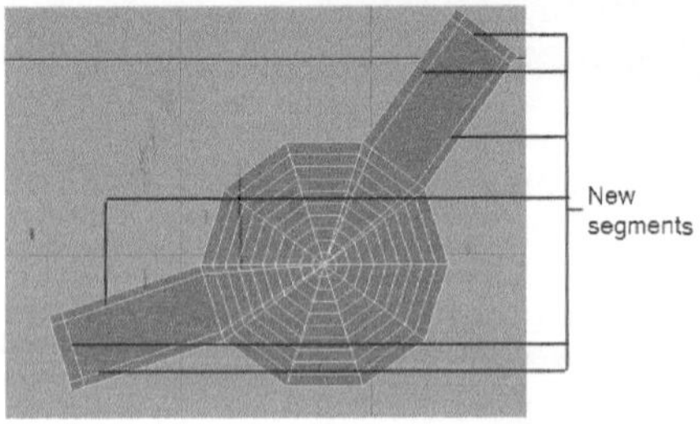

Figure 2-96 New segments added to truck

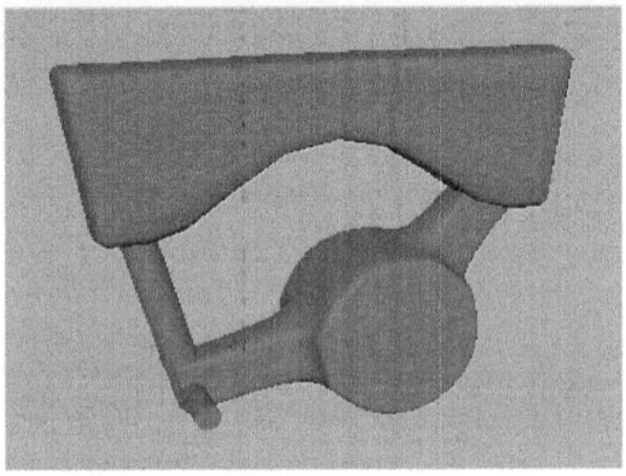

Figure 2-97 The parts aligned with base in the front-Z viewport

20. Press and hold the SHIFT key and select *base, truck, bolt,* and *bolt1* in the persp viewport. Next, choose **Mesh > Combine > Combine** from the menubar; the selected parts are combined and a group with the name **base1** is created.

21. In the **base1** area of the **Channel Box / Layer Editor**, enter **90** in the **Rotate Y** edit box and then press the ENTER key.

22. Align **base1** in all viewports using **Move Tool** and **Scale Tool** from the Tool Box to make it proportional with the deck, as shown in Figure 2-98.

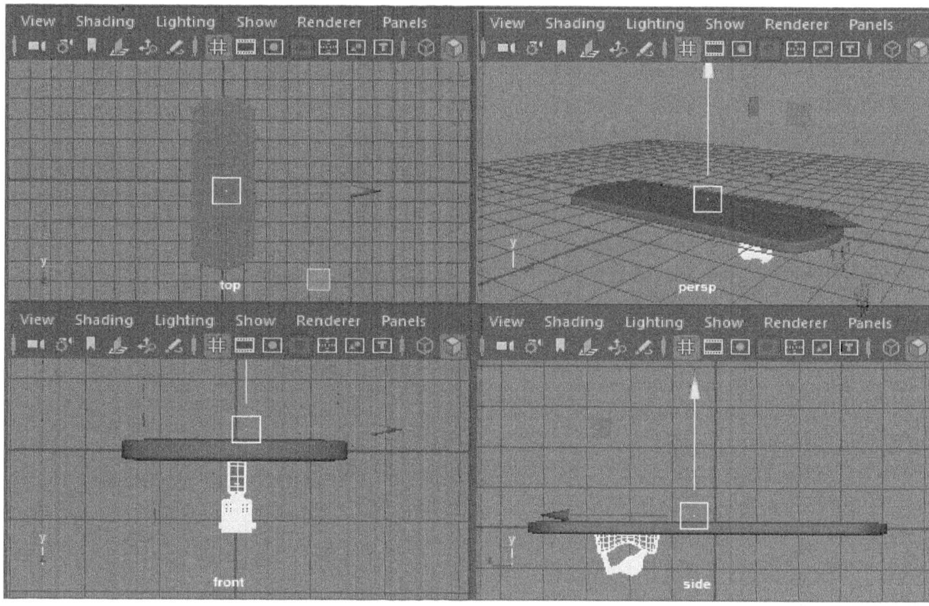

*Figure 2-98 The **base1** aligned in all viewports*

Creating Wheels

In this section, you need to create wheels for the skateboard using the **Torus** polygon primitive.

1. Choose **Create > Objects > Polygon Primitives > Torus** from the menubar. Next, click in the top-Y viewport to create a torus.

2. In the **INPUTS** area of the **Channel Box / Layer Editor**, expand the **polyTorus1** node and set the following parameters:

   Radius: **0.1** Section radius: **0.1**

3. In the **pTorus1** area of the **Channel Box/Layer Editor**, enter **90** in the **Rotate Z** edit box.

4. In the **Channel Box / Layer Editor**, rename **pTorus1** as *wheel*, as done earlier.

5. Scale and align *wheel* with *bolt1* in all viewports using **Move Tool** from the Tool Box, as shown in Figure 2-99.

6. Maximize the front-Z viewport. Make sure the *wheel* is selected and then press CTRL+D; a duplicate copy of *wheel* is created with the name *wheel1*. Next, move *wheel1* in the opposite direction to *wheel*, as shown in Figure 2-101.

7. Maximize the persp viewport. Select *base1, wheel,* and *wheel1* by using the SHIFT key and then choose **Mesh > Combine > Combine** from the menubar; the selected parts are combined to form a single polygon object with the name **base2**.

8. Choose **Modify > Pivot > Center Pivot** from the menubar; the pivot point of the combined **base2** is set to center. Next, press CTRL+D; a duplicate copy of the selected mesh is created in the viewport.

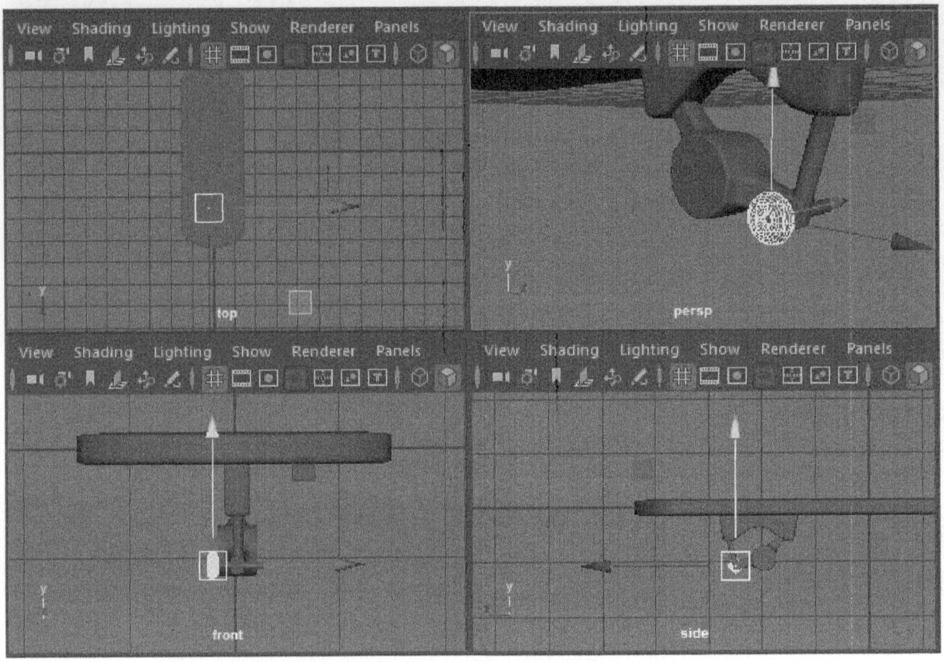

Figure 2-99 The wheel aligned with bolt1 in all viewports

9. Maximize the side-X viewport. Next, move *base3* along the Z axis to align with *deck* and also enter **180** in the **Rotate Y** edit box to rotate *base3*, refer to Figure 2-101.

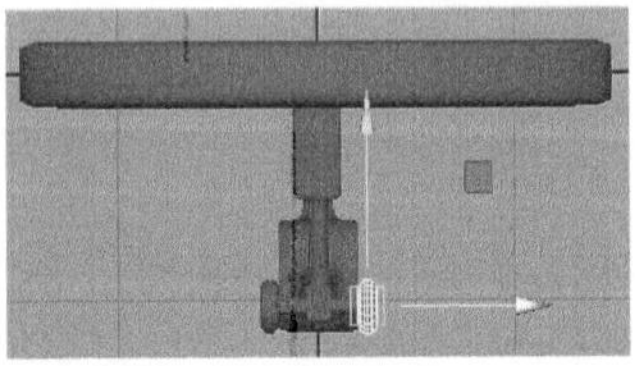

Figure 2-100 *The wheel1 moved to opposite direction to wheel*

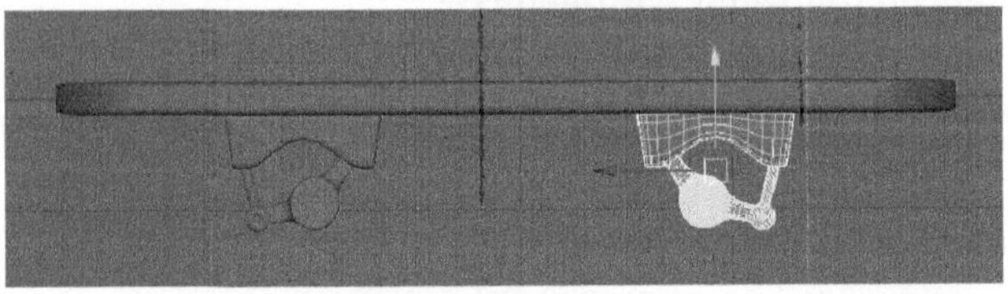

Figure 2-101 *The base3 moved and rotated*

10. Select *deck*. Press and hold the right mouse button on *deck*; a marking menu is displayed. Choose **Vertex** from the marking menu; the vertex selection mode is activated. Next, select the vertices and move up along the Y axis using **Move Tool**, as shown in Figure 2-102.

11. Press and hold the right mouse button on *deck*; a marking menu is displayed. Choose **Object Mode** from the marking menu; the object selection mode is activated.

12. Maximize the persp viewport and select all parts of the skateboard in the persp viewport. Next, choose **Mesh > Combine > Combine** from the menubar; the selected parts are combined.

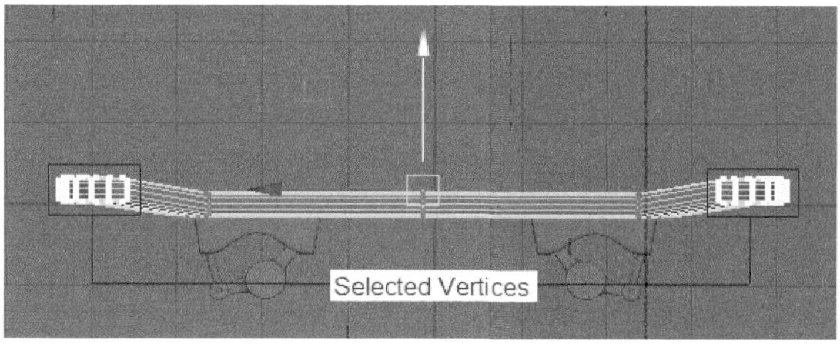

Figure 2-102 *Moving the selected vertices up along the Y axis*

Changing the Background Color of the Scene

In this section, you will change the background color of the scene.

1. Choose **Windows > Editors > Outliner** from the menubar; the **Outliner** window is displayed. Select the **persp** camera in the **Outliner** window; the **perspShape** tab is displayed in the **Attribute Editor**.

Note

If the **Attribute Editor** *is not visible in the interface, press CTRL + A to make it visible.*

2. In the **perspShape** tab, expand the **Environment** area and drag the **Background Color** slider bar toward right to change the background color to white.

Saving and Rendering the Scene

In this section, you will save the scene that you have created and then render it. You can view the final rendered image of the model by downloading the *c02_maya_2017_rndr.zip* file from *www.cadcim.com*. The path of the file is as follows: *Textbooks > Animation and Visual Effects > Maya > Autodesk Maya 2017: A Comprehensive Guide.*

1. Choose **File > Save Scene** from the menubar.

2. Maximize the persp viewport, if it is not already maximized. Choose the **Render the current frame** button from the Status Line; the **Render View** window is displayed. This window shows the final output of the scene, refer to Figure 2-76.

Self-Evaluation Test

Answer the following questions and then compare them to those given at the end of this chapter:

1. Which of the following geometric shapes is formed by connecting a polygonal base and an apex?

   (a) **Prism** (b) **Pyramid**
   (c) **Sphere** (d) **Cube**

2. Which of the following shortcuts can be used to display an object in the object selection mode?

   (a) **F8** (b) **F9**
   (c) **F10** (d) **F11**

3. The __________ is used to merge two vertices together by dragging the source vertex toward the target vertex.

4. The __________ option is used to subtract the last selected geometry from the geometry that was selected first.

5. A__________ is a curve in three dimensional space such that its angle to a plane perpendicular to the axis is constant.

6. The __________ solids are those primitives in which all sides and angles are equal and all faces are identical.

7. The __________ tool is used to reduce the number of polygons in the selected region of an object.

8. The **Insert Edge Loop Tool** is used to create beveled transition surfaces on a profile curve. (T/F)

9. The **Chamfer** tool is used to merge the selected edges and vertices that are within a numerically specified threshold distance from each other. (T/F)

10. The **Bridge** tool is used to connect two edges or two faces of a polygon object. (T/F)

Review Questions

Answer the following questions:

1. Which of the following tools is used to add smoothness to a sharp edge?

   (a) **Extrude** (b) **Duplicate face**
   (c) **Bevel** (d) **Merge to Center**

2. Which of the following primitives is formed by an alternate arrangement of hexagons and pentagons?

   (a) **Prism** (b) **Helix**
   (c) **Soccer ball** (d) **Sphere**

3. The __________ option is used to create a duplicate copy of a selected face.

4. The __________ tool is used to add segments on both the sides of a selected edge.

5. The __________ tool is used to ungroup the combined polygon objects into separate polygon objects.

6. The __________ tool is used to make a polygon object smooth by adding divisions to it.

7. The __________ operation is used to merge two intersecting objects by deleting the intersecting geometry between them.

8. The **Combine** tool is used to group two or more polygon meshes into a single polygon object. (T/F)

9. The **Multi-Cut** tool is used to manually add segments between two edges of an object. (T/F)

10. The **Detach** tool is used to split a vertex into multiple vertices. (T/F)

EXERCISES

The rendered output of the models used in the following exercises can be accessed by downloading the file *c02_maya_2017_exr.zip* from *www.cadcim.com*. The path of the file is as follows: *Textbooks > Animation and Visual Effects > Maya > Autodesk Maya 2017: A Comprehensive Guide.*

Exercise 1

Using various polygon modeling techniques, create the model of a USB cable, as shown in Figure 2-103. **(Expected time: 30 min)**

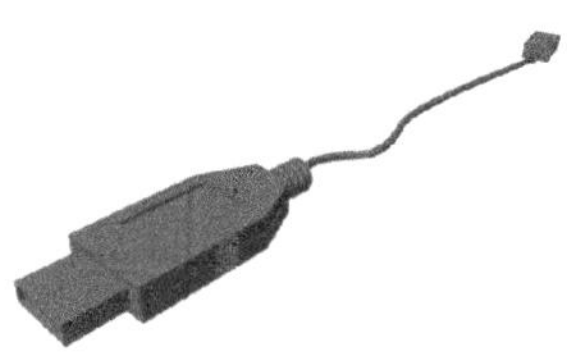

Figure 2-103 *Model to be created in Exercise 1*

Exercise 2

Using various polygon modeling techniques, create a scene, as shown in Figure 2-104.
(Expected time: 30 min)

Figure 2-104 *Scene to be created in Exercise 2*

Exercise 3

Using polygon primitive modeling techniques, create a scene, as shown in Figure 2-105.
(Expected time: 30 min)

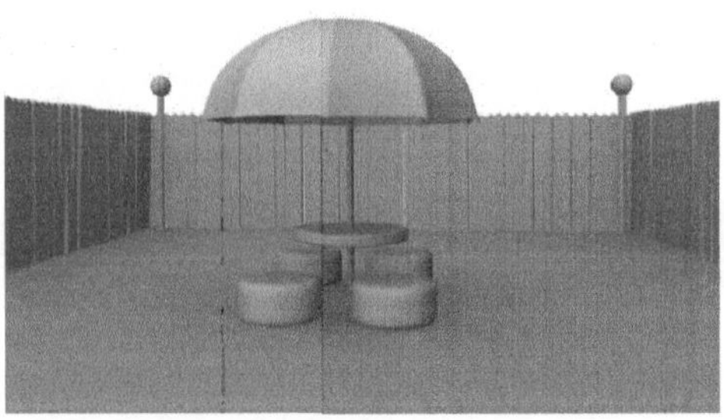

Figure 2-105 *Scene to be created in Exercise 3*

Answers to Self-Evaluation Test

1. b, **2.** a, **3. Merge Vertex Tool**, **4. Difference**, **5.** helix, **6.** platonic, **7. Reduce**, **8.** F, **9.** F, **10.** T

Chapter 3

NURBS Curves and Surfaces

Learning Objectives

After completing this chapter, you will be able to:

- *Create NURBS Primitives*
- *Create NURBS curves*
- *Create surfaces*

INTRODUCTION

In Maya, there are three different types of modeling: NURBS, polygon, and subdivision surface. NURBS, which stands for Non-Uniform Rational B-Splines, is an industry standard for designing and modeling surfaces. NURBS modeling is suitable for modeling surfaces with complex curves. NURBS surfaces can be manipulated interactively with ease. Before modeling an object, you need to visualize it in 3D terms. Visualization of an object in 3D terms helps you in determining the type of modeling that you need to use for creating the object. In this chapter, you will learn about various NURBS modeling tools and techniques.

NURBS PRIMITIVES

In this chapter, you will learn about NURBS curves and surfaces. NURBS (Non-Uniform Rational B-Spline) is a mathematical representation of 3D geometry that can describe any shape accurately. NURBS modeling is basically used for creating curved shapes and lines.

In Maya, there are default NURBS objects that resemble various geometrical objects. These NURBS objects are grouped together under the NURBS Primitives group in the menubar. To access the NURBS primitives, choose **Create > Objects > NURBS Primitives** from the menubar; a cascading menu will be displayed with all the default NURBS primitives. Some of the NURBS primitives can also be accessed from the Shelf, refer to Figure 3-1. In order to access the NURBS modeling tools for the NURBS primitives, make sure that the **Curves/Surfaces** Shelf tab is chosen from the Shelf. You need to turn on the **Interactive Creation** menu before creating the NURBS Primitives by click-drag method. To do so, choose **Create > Objects > NURBS Primitives > Interactive Creation** from the menubar. The types of NURBS Primitives are discussed next.

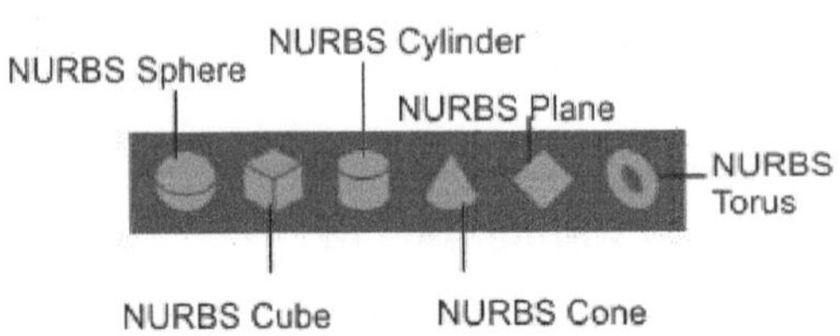

Figure 3-1 *Accessing NURBS primitives from the Shelf*

Creating a Sphere

Menubar:	Create > Objects > NURBS Primitives > Sphere
Shelf:	Curves/Surfaces > NURBS Sphere

A sphere is a solid object and every point on its surface is equidistant from its center, as shown in Figure 3-2. To create a sphere, choose **Create > Objects > NURBS Primitives > Sphere** from the menubar; the instructions to create a sphere will be displayed on the grid. Alternatively, choose the **NURBS Sphere** tool from the **Curves/Surfaces** Shelf tab. You can create a sphere either dynamically or by entering values using the keyboard. Both the methods are discussed next.

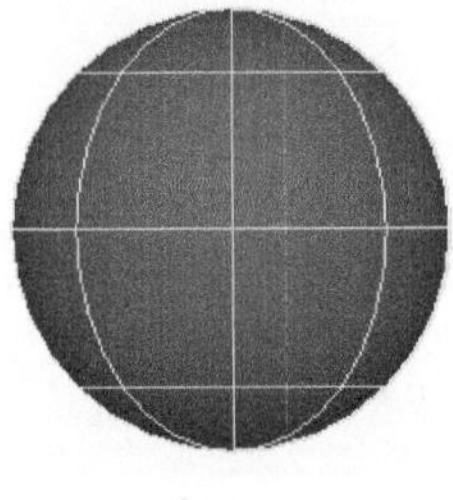

Figure 3-2 *The NURBS sphere*

Creating a Sphere Dynamically

To create a sphere dynamically, choose **Create > Objects > NURBS Primitives > Sphere** from the menubar; you will be prompted to drag the cursor on the grid to draw the sphere in the viewport. Press and hold the left mouse button, and drag the cursor up or down to define the radius of the sphere as required. Now, release the left mouse button; the sphere will be created in all viewports and will be visible in the **Smooth Shade all** mode. Press the numeric key 4 to change the display to the **Wireframe** mode. Alternatively, you can choose **Shading > Wireframe** from the **Panel** menu to change the display to the **Wireframe** mode. Press the numeric key 5 or choose **Shading > Smooth Shade All** from the **Panel** menu to revert to the **Smooth Shade all** mode.

Creating a Sphere by Using the Keyboard

To create a sphere by using the keyboard, double-click on the **NURBS Sphere** tool in the **Curves/ Surfaces** Shelf tab; the **Tool Settings (NURBS Sphere Tool)** window will be displayed, as shown in Figure 3-3. In this window, set the properties of the sphere by using the keyboard and then click in the viewport; the sphere will be created in all viewports. Alternatively, choose **Create > Objects > NURBS Primitives > Sphere > Option Box** from the menubar; to invoke **Tool Settings (NURBS Sphere Tool)** window. Choose **Reset Tool** at the top of the **Tool Settings (NURBS Sphere Tool)** window to reset the settings of the **NURBS Sphere** tool. The most commonly used options in this window are discussed next.

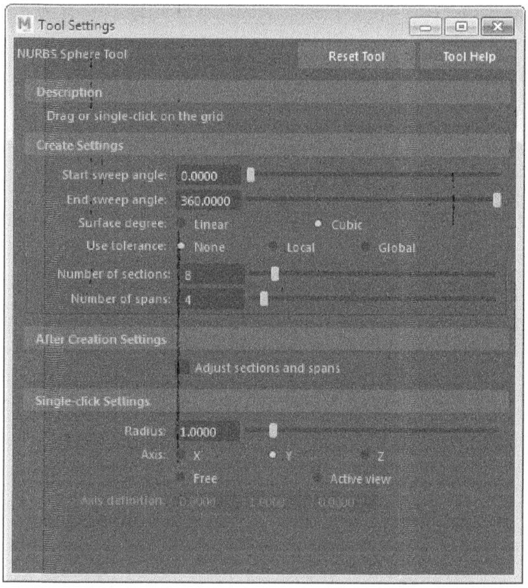

***Figure 3-3** The **Tool Settings (NURBS Sphere Tool)** window*

Description Area

The text in the **Description** area gives you information about the method of creating sphere in the viewport.

Create Settings Area

The options in the **Create Settings** area of the **Tool Settings (NURBS Sphere Tool)** window are used to adjust the parameters of the NURBS sphere. The options in this area are discussed next.

Start sweep angle and End sweep angle: The **Start sweep angle** and **End sweep angle** options are used to specify the start and end angles for a sphere. Move the sliders on the right of these parameters to change the values or enter the values in their respective text boxes. The values in these sliders range from 0 to 360 degrees. You can create partial sphere, as shown in Figure 3-4 by changing the values in the **Start sweep angle** and **End sweep angle** edit boxes.

Start sweep angle = 270
End sweep angle = 90

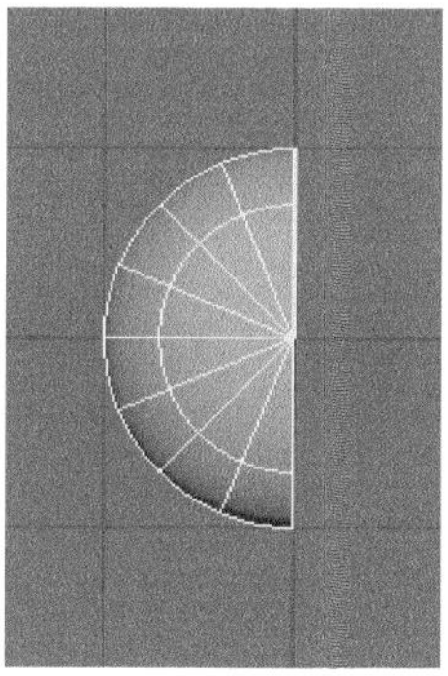

***Figure 3-4** Partial sphere created*

Surface degree: The **Surface degree** attribute is used to create a sphere with a faceted or smooth appearance. This attribute consists of two radio buttons: **Linear** and **Cubic**. The **Linear** radio button is used to give a faceted appearance to the sphere. The **Cubic** radio button is selected by default and gives a smooth appearance to the sphere, refer to Figure 3-5. Note that the number of segments remains the same on the sphere while using any of these two radio buttons.

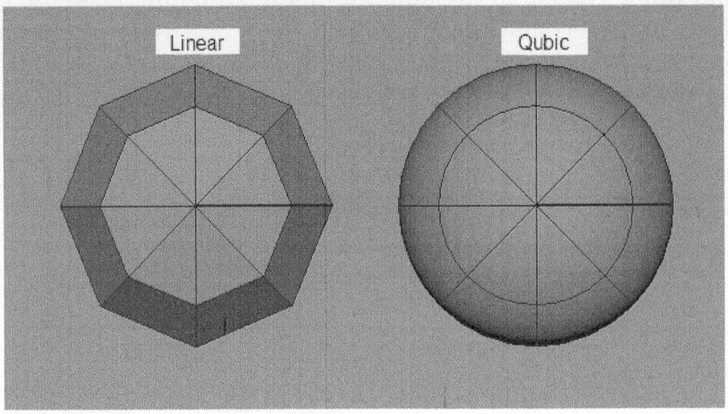

***Figure 3-5** The faceted and smooth appearances of spheres*

Use Tolerance: The **Use Tolerance** attribute is used to improve the accuracy of the primitive's by increasing or decreasing the number of sections and spans. If the **Use Tolerance** attribute is set to **None**, you can make the number of sections and spans on a sphere separately. If the **Use Tolerance** attribute is set to **Local**, you can change the number of sections and spans uniformly by moving the slider on the right of the attribute. If the **Use Tolerance** attribute is set to **Global**, you can change the number of sections and spans by moving the slider on the right of the **Positional** attribute in **Windows > Editors > Settings/Preferences > Preferences**.

Number of sections and Number of spans: The **Number of sections** and **Number of spans** edit boxes are used to adjust the surface curves on a sphere, refer to Figure 3-6. The more the number of sections or spans on a NURBS object, the more will be its smoothness. Surface curves are also known as Isoparms. You can enter the values directly in these edit boxes to set the number of sections/spans on a NURBS object. Alternatively, you can move the sliders on the right of these edit boxes.

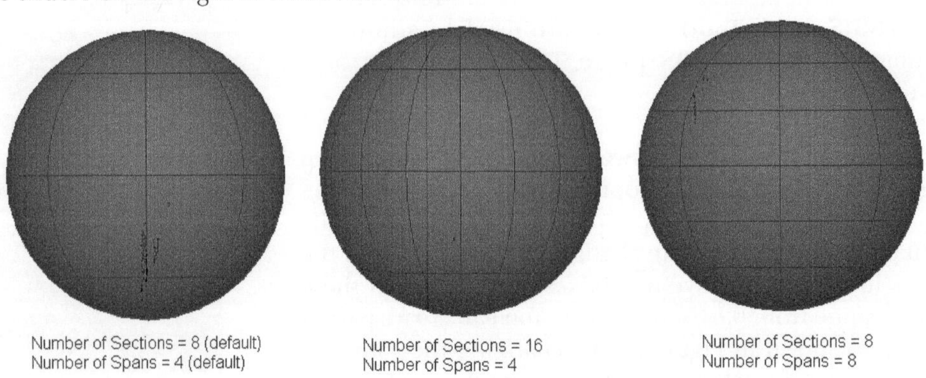

***Figure 3-6** The number of sections and spans on spheres*

After Creation Settings Area

The options in this area are used to adjust the number of sections and spans on a sphere after it is created in the viewport. To do so, select the **Adjust sections and spans** check box from this area and drag the cursor to create a sphere in the viewport. Next, you can drag the cursor to add or reduce sections in the sphere.

Single-click Settings Area

The options in this area are used to set the radius and axis of formation of the NURBS sphere. The settings of this area will be applicable only if the sphere is created using the single-click method. The options in this area are discussed next.

Radius: The **Radius** attribute is used to set the radius of the sphere by entering required value in the **Radius** edit box. Alternatively, you can drag the slider on the right of the attribute.

Axis: The **Axis** attribute is used to set the axis for creating a NURBS sphere. It has three radio buttons: **X**, **Y**, and **Z**. By default, the **Y** radio button is selected. You can use these radio buttons to set the axis for creating a NURBS sphere. Figure 3-7 shows the NURBS spheres created on the X, Y, and Z axes.

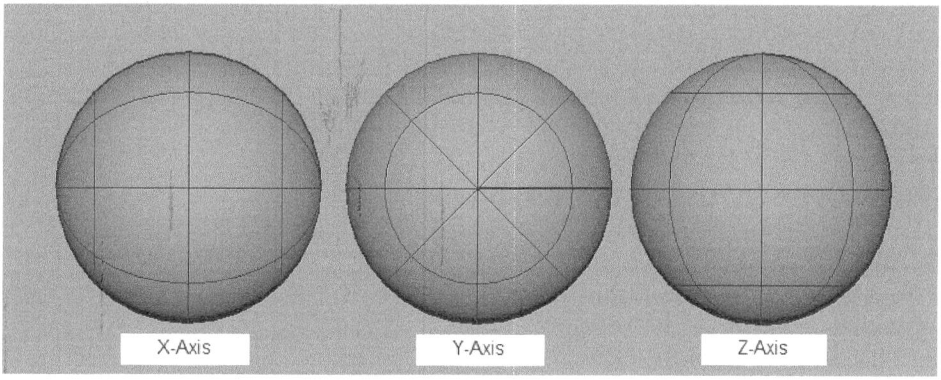

***Figure 3-7** Spheres created on X, Y, and Z axes*

Modifying the Names and other Parameters of a Sphere

You can change the name and parameters of a sphere in the viewport. To do so, select a sphere in the viewport; the **Channel Box / Layer Editor** will be displayed, refer to Figure 3-8. Now, to change the name of the selected sphere, click on **nurbsSphere#** in the **Channel Box / Layer Editor**; an edit box will appear. Specify a new name for the sphere and then press ENTER. You can also modify the sphere by using the parameters in the **INPUTS** area of the **Channel Box / Layer Editor**; the change will be reflected on the sphere in the viewport. To dynamically modify the parameters in the **INPUTS** area, select the attribute label in the **Channel Box / Layer Editor**. Next, place the cursor in the viewport, press and hold the middle mouse button, and then drag it horizontally in the viewport to make the changes.

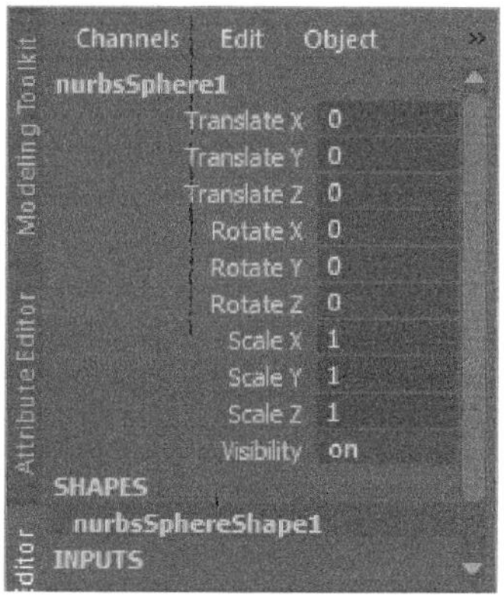

Figure 3-8** The **Channel Box / Layer Editor

Creating a Cube

Menubar:	Create > Objects > NURBS Primitives > Cube
Shelf:	Curves/Surfaces > NURBS Cube

A cube is a three-dimensional shape with six sides, as shown in Figure 3-9. To create a **NURBS** cube, choose **Create > Objects > NURBS Primitives > Cube** from the menubar; the instructions to create the cube will be displayed on the grid. Alternatively, to create a cube, you can choose the **NURBS Cube** tool from the **Curves/Surfaces** Shelf tab. You can also create a cube dynamically or by entering values using the keyboard. Both the methods are discussed next.

Figure 3-9 The NURBS cube

Creating a Cube Dynamically

To create a cube dynamically, choose **Create > Objects > NURBS Primitives > Cube** from the menubar; you will be prompted to drag the cursor on the grid to draw a cube in the viewport. Press and hold the left mouse button and drag the cursor on the grid to define the base of the cube, as required. Now, release the left mouse button to get the desired base. Next, press and hold the left mouse button again and drag the cursor up to set the height of the cube and then release the left mouse button; the cube will be created in all viewports.

Creating a Cube by Using the Keyboard

To create a cube by using the keyboard, double-click on the **NURBS Cube** tool in the **Curves/Surfaces** Shelf tab; the **Tool Settings (NURBS Cube Tool)** window will be displayed on the left of the viewport, as shown in Figure 3-10. In this window, set the properties of the cube by using the keyboard and then click in the viewport; a cube will be created in all viewports. Alternatively, choose **Create > Objects > NURBS Primitives > Cube > Option Box** from the menubar; to invoke the **Tool Settings** **(NURBS Cube Tool)** window. Choose **Reset Tool** at the top of the **Tool Settings (NURBS Cube Tool)** window to reset the settings of the **NURBS Cube** tool. The most commonly used options in this window are discussed next.

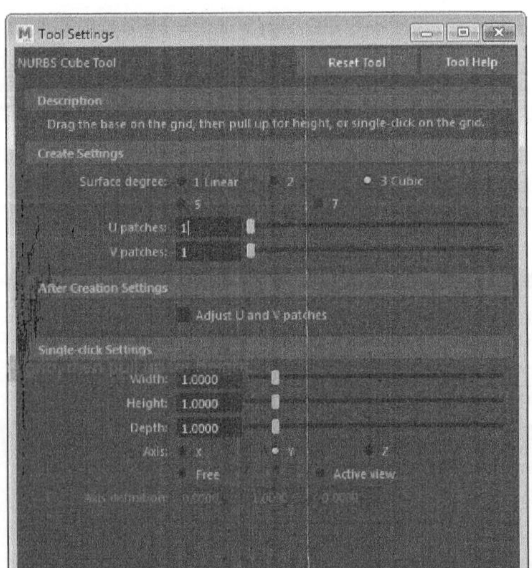

*Figure 3-10 The **Tool Settings (NURBS Cube Tool)** window*

Description Area

The **Description** area displays the information about the method of creating the cube in the viewport.

Create Settings Area

The options in the **Create Settings** area of the **Tool Settings (NURBS Cube Tool)** window are used to set the parameters of the NURBS cube. Various options in this area are discussed next.

Surface degree: The radio buttons in the **Surface degree** attribute are used to create a cube with a faceted or smooth appearance. This attribute consists of five radio buttons: **1 Linear**, **2**, **3 Cubic**, **5**, and **7**.

U patches and V patches: The **U patches** and **V patches** edit boxes are similar to the **Number of sections** and **Number of spans** edit boxes in the **Tool Settings (NURBS Sphere Tool)** window and are used to create surface patches on the cube.

Single-click Settings: The options in this area are used to set the width, height, and depth for creating the NURBS cube. The settings will be applicable only if the cube is created using the single-click method.

Width, **Height**, and **Depth**: You can adjust the width, height, and depth of the NURBS cube by entering values in the **Width**, **Height**, and **Depth** edit boxes, respectively. Alternatively, you can set these values by moving the slider on the right of these edit boxes.

Modifying the Names and Other Properties of the Cube

You can modify the name and other properties of the cube using the **Channel Box / Layer Editor**, as discussed in the NURBS sphere section.

Creating a Cylinder

Menubar:	Create > Objects > NURBS Primitives > Cylinder
Shelf:	Curves/Surfaces > NURBS Cylinder

A cylinder is a solid geometry with straight parallel sides and circular sections, as shown in Figure 3-11. To create a cylinder in the viewport, choose **Create > Objects > NURBS Primitives > Cylinder** from the menubar; the instructions to create the cylinder will be displayed on the grid in the viewport. Alternatively, you can choose the **NURBS Cylinder** tool from the **Curves/Surfaces** Shelf tab. You can create a cylinder either dynamically or by entering values using the keyboard. Both the methods of creating the cylinder are discussed next.

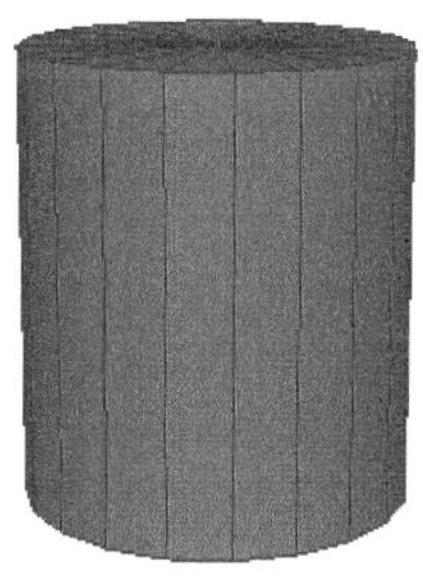

Figure 3-11 *The NURBS cylinder*

Creating a Cylinder Dynamically

To create a cylinder dynamically, choose **Create > Objects > NURBS Primitives > Cylinder** from the menubar; you will be prompted to drag the cursor on the grid. Press and hold the left mouse button and drag the cursor on the grid to define the base of the cylinder. Next, release the left mouse button to get the desired base. Now, press and hold the left mouse button again, drag the cursor up to set the height of the cylinder and then release the left mouse button; the cylinder will be created in all viewports.

Creating a Cylinder by Using the Keyboard

To create a cylinder by using the keyboard, double-click on the **NURBS Cylinder** tool in the **Curves / Surfaces**Shelf tab; the **Tool Settings (NURBS Cylinder Tool)** window will be displayed, as shown in Figure 3-12. Set the properties of the cylinder to be created in the viewport using various options available in the **Tool Settings (NURBS Cylinder Tool)** window and click in the viewport; a cylinder will be created in all viewports. Alternatively, choose **Create > Objects > NURBS Primitives > Cylinder > Option Box** from the menubar to invoke the **Tool Settings** (**NURBS Cylinder Tool**) window. Choose **Reset Tool** at the top of the **Tool Settings (NURBS Cylinder Tool)** window to reset the settings of the **NURBS Cylinder** tool. The options in the **Tool Settings** (**NURBS Cylinder Tool**) window are similar to those of the **NURBS Sphere** tool.

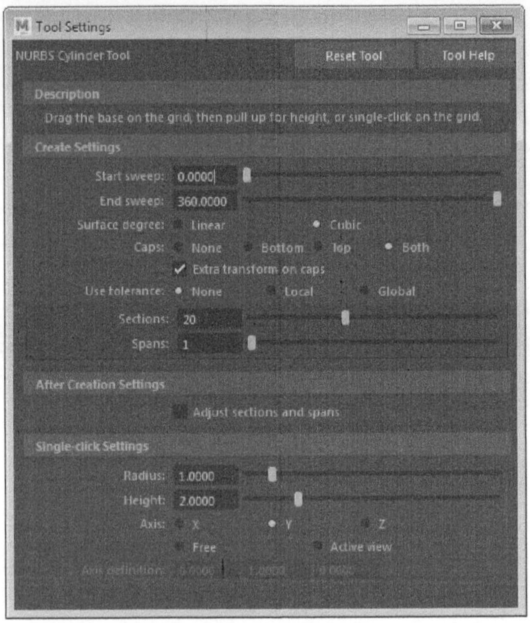

*Figure 3-12 The **Tool Settings (NURBS Cylinder Tool)** window*

Modifying the Names and other Properties of Cylinder

You can modify the name and properties of the cylinder by using the **Channel Box / Layer Editor**, as discussed in the NURBS sphere section.

Creating a Cone

Menubar:	Create > Objects >NURBS Primitives > Cone
Shelf:	Curves/Surfaces > NURBS Cone

A cone is an object with a circular base and its sides tapered up to a point, as shown in Figure 3-13. To create a cone, choose **Create > Objects > NURBS Primitives > Cone** from the menubar. Alternatively, you can create a cone by invoking the **NURBS Cone** tool from the **Curves/Surfaces** Shelf tab. You can create a cone either dynamically or by entering values using the keyboard. Both the methods of creating a cone are discussed next.

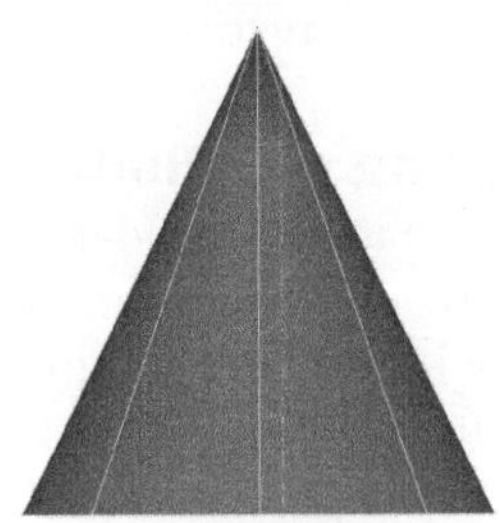

Figure 3-13 The NURBS cone

Creating a Cone Dynamically

To create a cone dynamically, choose **Create > Objects > NURBS Primitives > Cone** from the menubar; you will be prompted to drag the cursor on the grid. Press and hold the left mouse button and drag the cursor on the grid to define the base of the cone. Next, release the left mouse button to get the desired base. Now, press and hold the left mouse button again and drag the cursor up to set the height of the cone. Next, release the left mouse button; the cone will be created in all viewports.

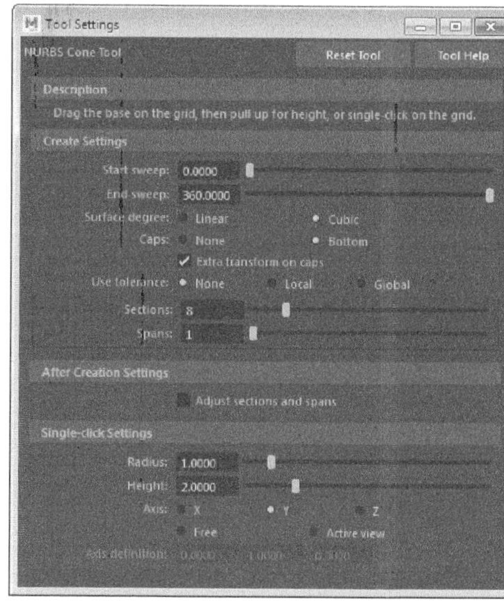

Figure 3-14 The Tool Settings (NURBS Cone Tool) window

Creating a Cone by Using the Keyboard

To create a cone by using the keyboard, double-click on the **NURBS Cone** tool in the **Curves/Surfaces** Shelf tab; the **Tool Settings (NURBS Cone Tool)** window will be displayed on the left of the viewport, as shown in Figure 3-14. In this window, set the properties of the cone by using the keyboard and then choose the **Create** Button click in the viewport; the cone will be created in all viewports. Alternatively, choose **Create > Objects > NURBS Primitives > Cone > Option Box** from the menubar to invoke the **Tool Settings (NURBS Cone Tool)** window. Choose **Reset Tool** at the top of the **Tool Settings (NURBS Cone Tool)** window to reset the settings of the **NURBS Cone** tool. The options in the **Tool Settings (NURBS Cone Tool)** window are similar to those of the **NURBS Sphere** tool.

Creating a Plane

Menubar:	Create > Objects > NURBS Primitives > Plane
Shelf:	Curves/Surfaces > NURBS Plane

A plane is a two-dimensional flat surface, as shown in Figure 3-15. To create a NURBS plane, choose **Create > Objects > NURBS Primitives > Plane** from the menubar. Alternatively, you can create a plane by invoking the **NURBS Plane** tool from the **Curves/Surfaces** Shelf tab. You can create a plane either dynamically or by entering values using the keyboard. Both the methods of creating a plane are discussed next.

Figure 3-15 The NURBS plane

Creating a Plane Dynamically

To create a plane dynamically, choose **Create > Objects > NURBS Primitives > Plane** from the menubar; you will be prompted to drag the cursor on the grid. Next, press and hold the left mouse button and drag the cursor on the grid; a plane will be created in all viewports.

Creating a Plane by Using the Keyboard

To create a plane by using the keyboard, double-click on the **NURBS Plane** tool in the **Curves/Surfaces** Shelf tab; the **Tool Settings (NURBS Plane Tool)** window will be displayed on the left of the viewport, as shown in Figure 3-16. Next, in this window, set the properties of the plane by using the keyboard and then click in the viewport; the plane will be created in all viewports. Alternatively, choose **Create > Objects > NURBS Primitives > Plane > Option Box** from the menubar to invoke the **Tool Settings (NURBS Plane Tool)** window. Choose **Reset Tool** at the top of the **Tool Settings (NURBS Plane Tool)** window to reset the settings of the **NURBS Plane** tool. The options in the **Tool Settings (NURBS Plane Tool)** window are similar to those of the **NURBS Cube** tool.

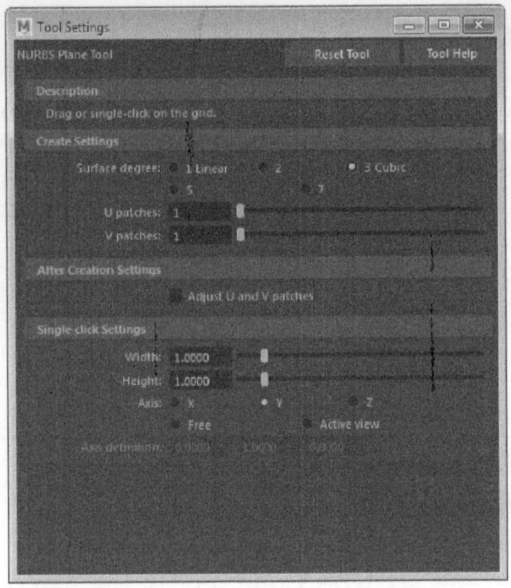

*Figure 3-16 The **Tool Settings (NURBS Plane Tool)** window*

Creating a Torus

Menubar:	Create > Objects > NURBS Primitives > Torus
Shelf:	Curves/Surfaces > NURBS Torus

A torus is created by revolving a circular profile around a circular or an elliptical path, as shown in Figure 3-17. To create a NURBS torus, choose **Create > Objects > NURBS Primitives > Torus** from the menubar. Alternatively, you can create a torus by choosing the **NURBS Torus** tool from the **Curves/Surfaces** Shelf tab. You can create a torus either dynamically or by entering values using the keyboard. Both the methods of creating a torus are discussed next.

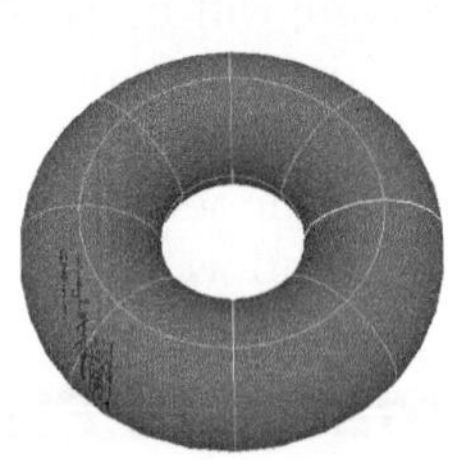

Figure 3-17 The NURBS torus

Creating a Torus Dynamically

To create a torus dynamically, choose **Create > Objects > NURBS Primitives > Torus** from the menubar; you will be prompted to drag the cursor on the grid to create a torus in the viewport. Press and hold the left mouse button, drag the cursor on the grid to define the radius of the torus, and then release the left mouse button. Now, press and hold the left mouse button again and drag the cursor to edit the section radius. Next, release the left mouse button; the torus will be created in all viewports.

Creating a Torus by Using the Keyboard

To create a torus by using the keyboard, double-click on the **NURBS Torus** tool in the **Curves / Surfaces** Shelf tab; the **Tool Settings (NURBS Torus Tool)** window will be displayed, as shown in Figure 3-18. In this window, set the properties of the torus by using the keyboard and then click in the viewport to create a torus. Alternatively, choose **Create > Objects > NURBS Primitives > Torus > Option Box** from the menubar to invoke the **Tool Settings (NURBS Torus Tool)** window. Choose the **Reset Tool** button at the top of the **Tool Settings (NURBS Torus Tool)** window to reset the settings of the **NURBS Torus** tool. The options in the **Tool Settings (NURBS Torus Tool)** window are similar to those of the **NURBS Sphere** tool.

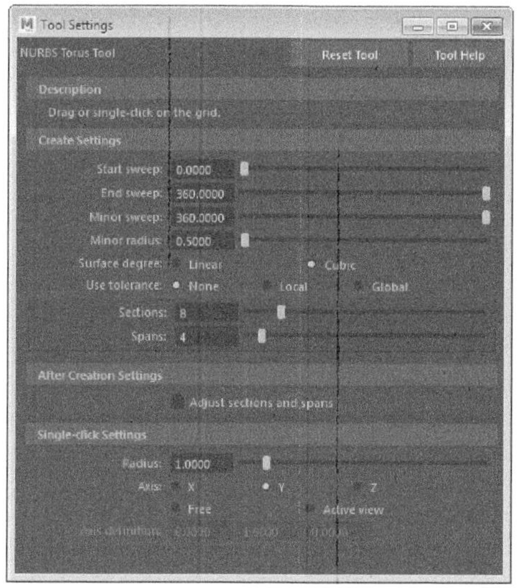

Figure 3-18 *The* **Tool Settings (NURBS Torus Tool)** *window*

Creating a Circle

Menubar:	Create > Objects > NURBS Primitives > Circle
Shelf:	Curves/Surfaces > NURBS Circle

A circle is a closed plane curve in which every point on the curve is equidistant from the center, as shown in Figure 3-19. To create a circle, choose **Create > Objects > NURBS Primitives > Circle** from the menubar. Alternatively, you can create a circle by choosing the **NURBS Circle** tool from the **Curves/Surfaces** Shelf tab. You can create a circle either dynamically or by entering values using the keyboard. Both the methods of creating circle are discussed next.

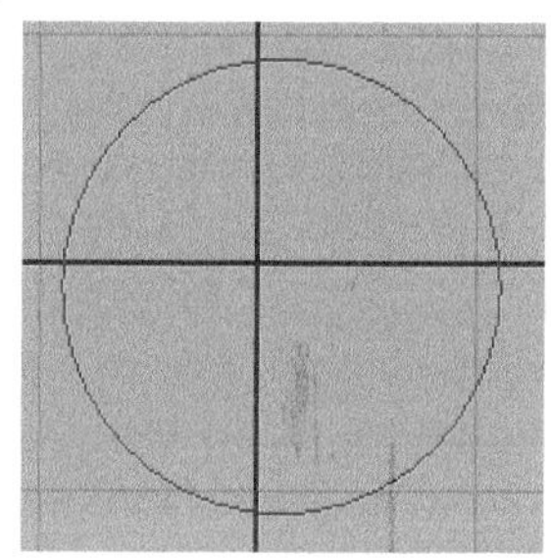

Figure 3-19 *The NURBS circle*

Creating a Circle Dynamically

To create a circle dynamically, choose **Create > Objects > NURBS Primitives > Circle** from the menubar; you will be prompted to drag the cursor on the grid. Press and hold the left mouse button and drag the cursor on the grid and then release the left mouse button; the circle will be created in all viewports.

Creating a Circle by Using the Keyboard

To create a circle by using the keyboard, double-click on the **NURBS Circle** tool in the **Curves** Shelf tab; the **Tool Settings (NURBS Circle Tool)** window will be displayed, as shown in Figure 3-20. In this window, set the properties of the circle by using the keyboard and then click in the viewport to create a circle in all viewports. Alternatively, choose **Create > Objects > NURBS Primitives > Circle > Option Box** from the menubar to invoke the **Tool Settings (NURBS Circle Tool)** window. Choose the **Reset Tool** button at the top of the **Tool Settings (NURBS Circle Tool)** window to reset the settings of the **NURBS Circle** tool. The options in this window are similar to those of the **NURBS Sphere** tool.

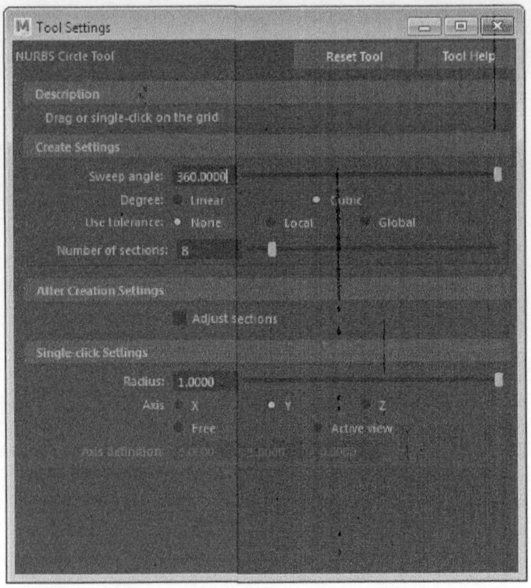

*Figure 3-20 The **Tool Settings (NURBS Circle Tool)** window*

Creating a Square

Menubar:	Create > Objects > NURBS Primitives > Square
Shelf:	Curves/Surfaces > NURBS Square

A square is a four-sided regular polygon with equal sides, as shown in Figure 3-21. To create a square, choose **Create > Objects > NURBS Primitives > Square** from the menubar. Alternatively, you can create a square by invoking the **NURBS Square** tool from the **Curves** Shelf tab. You can create a square either dynamically or by entering values by using the keyboard. Both the methods of creating a square are discussed next.

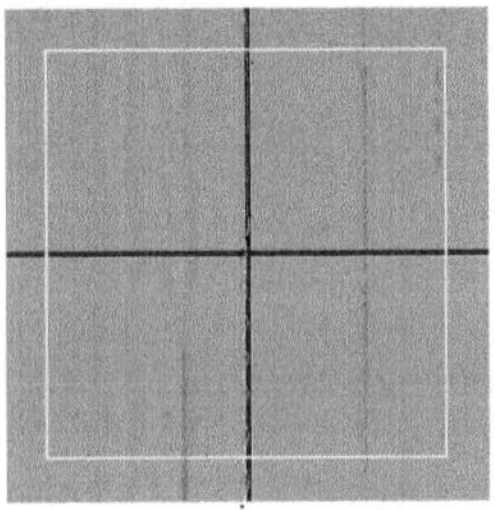

Figure 3-21 The NURBS square

Creating a Square Dynamically

To create a square dynamically, choose **Create > Objects > NURBS Primitives > Square** from the menubar; you will be prompted to drag the cursor on the grid. Press and hold the left mouse button and drag the cursor on the grid. Next, release the left mouse button; the square will be created in all viewports.

Creating a Square by Using the Keyboard

To create a square by using the keyboard, double-click on the **NURBS Square** tool in the **Curves** Shelf tab; the **Tool Settings (NURBS Square Tool)** window will be displayed on the left of the viewport, as shown in Figure 3-22. Set the properties of the square using various options available in the **Tool Settings (NURBS Square Tool)** window and click in the viewport to create a square in all viewports. Alternatively, choose **Create > NURBS Primitives > Square > Option Box** from the menubar to invoke the **Tool Settings (NURBS Square Tool)** window. Choose the **Reset Tool** button at the top of the **Tool Settings (NURBS Square Tool)** window to reset the settings of the **NURBS Square** tool. The options in this window are similar to those discussed in the **NURBS Cube** tool.

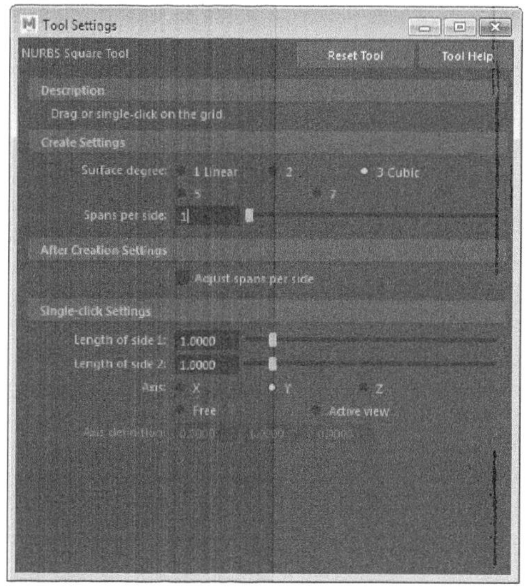

*Figure 3-22 The **Tool Settings (NURBS Square Tool)** window*

Interactive Creation

Menubar: Create > Objects > NURBS Primitives > Interactive Creation

The **Interactive Creation** option is used to create objects dynamically. It is a toggle option in the **NURBS Primitives** cascading menu. The **Interactive Creation** option is not selected by default. To select this option, choose **Create > Objects > NURBS Primitives > Interactive Creation** from the menubar. It allows you to edit an object as required. If you clear this option, you need to modify the object using the **Channel Box**.

Exit on Completion

Menubar: Create > Objects > NURBS Primitives > Exit on Completion

The **Exit on Completion** option is used to exit the Nurbs Primitive command after the creation of a primitive in the viewport. To do so, choose **Create > NURBS Primitives > Exit on Completion** from the menubar. Deselect this option to interactively create multiple primitives of the same type until another tool is chosen. This option is activated only when the **Interactive Creation** option is selected.

WORKING WITH NURBS COMPONENTS

Each NURBS object has certain components such as **Isoparm**, **Hull**, **Surface Patch**, **Surface UV**, **Control Vertex**, and **Surface Point**, refer to Figures 3-23 to 3-28. To view the components of a NURBS object, select the NURBS object in the viewport and choose **Display > NURBS** from the menubar; a cascading menu will be displayed. Choose the component that you want to modify from the cascading menu; the selected component will be displayed in the viewport. Alternatively, press and hold the right mouse button over the object and choose the required component from the marking menu.

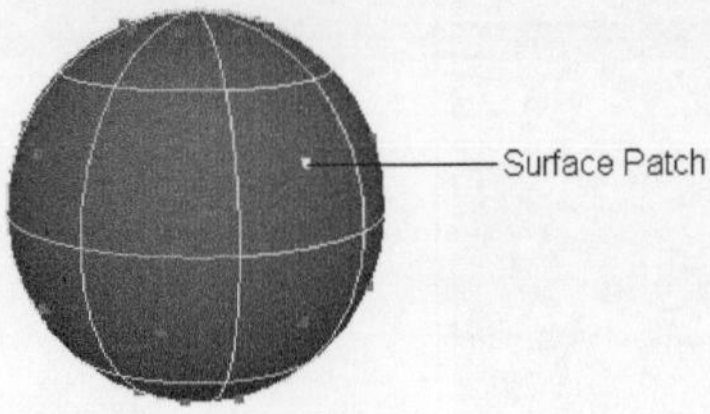

Figure 3-23 ***Surface Patch*** *of the NURBS*

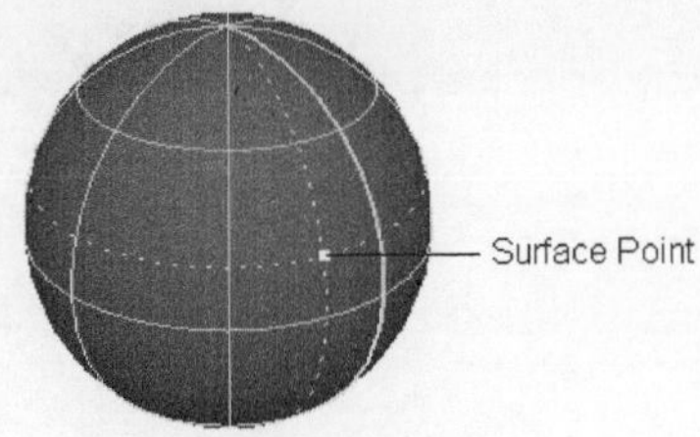

Figure 3-24 ***Surface Point*** *of the NURBS*

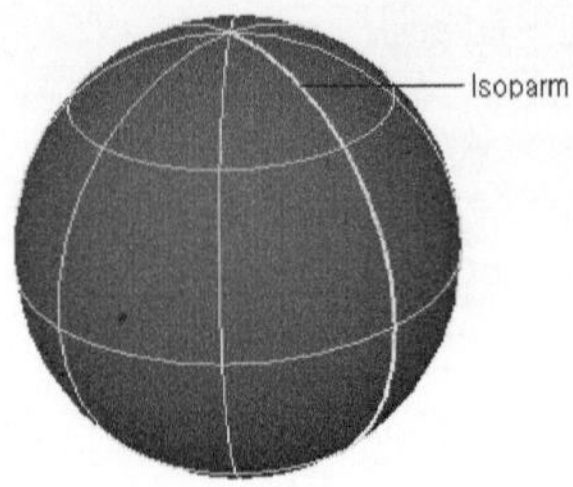

Figure 3-25 ***Isoparm*** *of the NURBS*

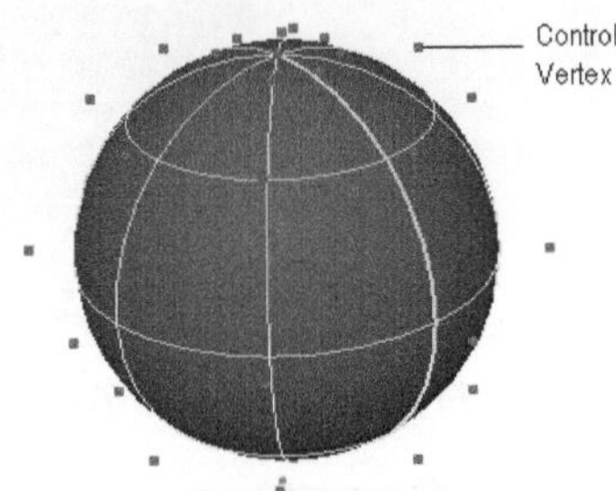

Figure 3-26 ***Control Vertex*** *of the NURBS*

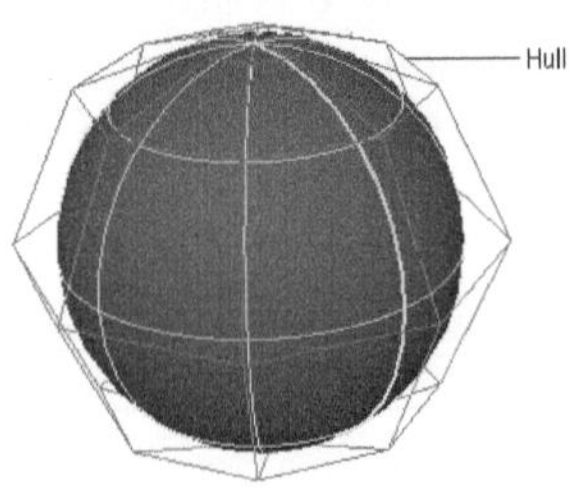

Figure 3-27 ***Hull*** *of the NURBS*

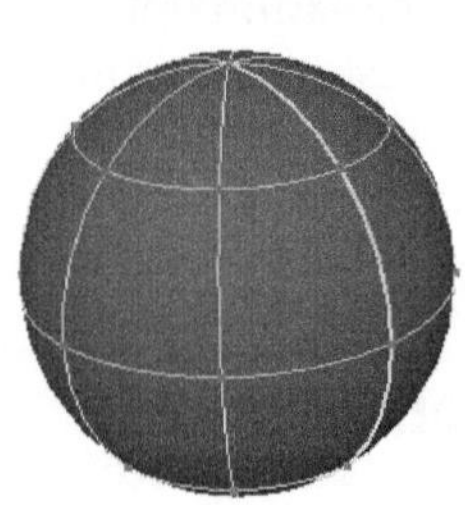

Figure 3-28 ***Surface UV*** *of the NURBS*

TOOLS FOR CREATING NURBS CURVES

In Maya, you can create NURBS curves using various tools. The tools used to create NURBS curves are discussed next.

CV Curve Tool

Menubar: Create > Objects > Curve Tool > CV Curve Tool

The **CV Curve Tool** is used to create curves in the viewport. A CV curve comprises of control vertices or CVs. To create a CV curve, choose **Create > Objects > Curve Tools > CV Curve Tool** from the menubar; the cursor will change into a plus sign. Next, click on different places in the viewport to create a curve. The first CV of the curve will be displayed as a box, and the second CV will be displayed as letter U. The box defines the starting point of the curve, and the letter U defines the direction of the curve. Press ENTER to finish the curve creation process. To edit the properties of a curve, choose **Create > Objects > Curve Tools >**

CV Curve Tool Option Box from the menubar; the **Tool Settings (CV Curve Tool)** window will be displayed, as shown in Figure 3-29. The options in the window are discussed next.

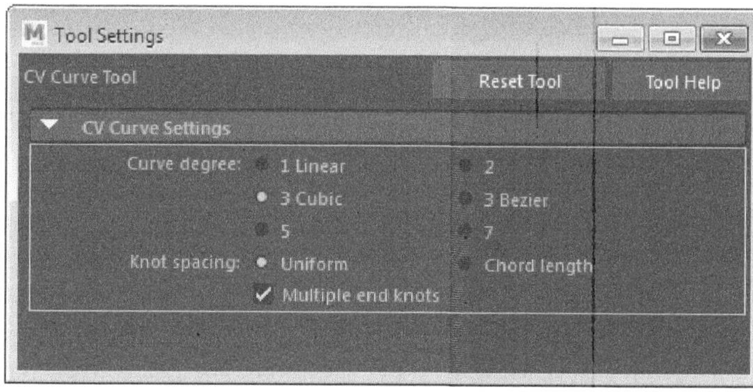

*Figure 3-29 The **Tool Settings (CV Curve Tool)** window*

Curve degree

The radio buttons corresponding to the **Curve degree** attribute are used to define the smoothness of a curve. By default, the **3 Cubic** radio button is selected in the **Curve degree** area. The higher the degree of curve, the smoother it will be.

Knot spacing

The radio buttons corresponding to the **Knot spacing** attribute are used to define the distribution of the knots on the curve. Knots are the parametric locations(u) along the curve. The **Knot spacing** attribute has two radio buttons: **Uniform** and **Chord length**. The **Uniform** radio button is selected by default and is used to create the U parametric location values that are easier to predict. The **Chord length** radio button is used to distribute the curvature in such a way that the surface displays a symmetrical texture applied over it.

Tip

*By default, **CV Curve Tool** is not present in the **Curves** Shelf tab. To add **CV Curve Tool** to the Shelf, press and hold CTRL+SHIFT and choose **Create > CV Curve Tool** from the menubar; **CV Curve Tool** icon will be displayed in the Shelf.*

EP Curve Tool

Menubar: Create > Objects > Curve Tools > EP Curve Tool
Shelf: Curves/Surfaces > EP Curve Tool

The **EP Curve Tool** is also used to create an outline of a curve by placing edit points on it. To create an outline, choose **Create > Objects > Curve Tools > EP Curve Tool** from the menubar; the cursor sign will change into a plus sign. Now, click on different places in the viewport to create a curve. Next, press ENTER to finish the curve creation process. To modify the properties of the EP curve, choose **Create > Objects > Curve Tools > EP Curve Tool > Option Box** from the menubar; the **Tool Settings (EP Curve Tool)** window will be displayed. Alternatively you can invoke this window form the **Curve / Surfaces** Shelf tab by double-click on the icon in the Shelf tab; the **Tool Settings (EP Curve Tool)** window will be displayed. The options in the **Tool Settings (EP Curve Tool)** window are similar to those discussed in the **Tool Settings (CV Curve Tool)** window.

Note

*The process of creating a curve using **EP Curve Tool** is different from that of **CV Curve Tool**. In both the cases, if **3 cubic** is selected from the **Curve degree** attribute, then the curve created using **CV Curve Tool** will create a smooth curve in the fourth segment, whereas in case of **EP curve Tool**, a smooth curve will be created in the third segment.*

Pencil Curve Tool

Menubar:	Create > Objects > Curve Tools > Pencil Curve Tool
Shelf:	Curves/Surfaces > Pencil Curve Tool

The **Pencil Curve Tool** works similar to the brush tool available in other softwares. This tool is used to draw a freehand NURBS curve. To do so, choose **Create > Objects > Curve Tools > Pencil Curve Tool** from the menubar; the cursor will change into a pencil sign. Next, press and hold the left mouse button and drag the cursor in the viewport to create a curve. To set the properties of the curve, choose **Create > Objects > Curve Tools > Pencil Curve Tool > Option Box** from the menubar; the **Tool Settings (Pencil Curve Tool)** window will be displayed. Alternatively you can invoke this window form the **Curves/Surfaces** Shelf tab by double-click on the icon in the **Curves/Surfaces** Shelf tab; the **Tool Settings (Pencil Curve Tool)** window will be displayed. The options in the **Tool Settings (Pencil Curve Tool)** window are similar to those discussed in the **Tool Settings (EP Curve Tool)** window.

Arc Tools

Menubar:	Create > Objects > Curve Tools
Shelf:	Curves/Surfaces > Three Point Circular Arc

The **Arc Tools** are used to create arc curves by specifying points in the viewport. In Maya, there are two types of arc tools: **Three Point Circular Arc** and **Two Point Circular Arc**. To create an arc, choose **Create > Objects > Curve Tools** from the menubar; a cascading menu will be displayed. Choose **Two Point Circular Arc** from the cascading menu to create an arc by defining the start and end points of the arc. Similarly, choose the **Three Point Circular Arc** from the cascading menu to create an arc by defining the start point, the curve point, and the end point.

TOOLS FOR CREATING SURFACES

Maya provides a number of tools to create complex three dimensional surface models. To view the tools that are used to create various surfaces, select the **Modeling** option from the **Menuset** drop-down list in the Status Line. Next, choose the **Surfaces** menu to display all the surfacing tools in Maya, refer to Figure 3-30.

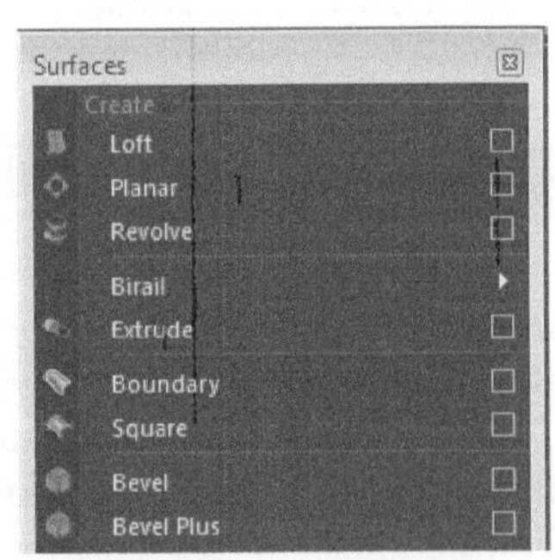

***Figure 3-30** The **Surface** floating menu*

Loft Tool

Menubar:	Surfaces > Create > Loft

The **Loft** tool is used to skin a surface along the profile curves. While using this tool, at least two profile curves are required to create a NURBS surface. To create a NURBS surface by using this tool, create three curves, as shown in Figure 3-31. Next, press and hold the SHIFT key and select the curves in the viewport. Now, choose **Surfaces > Create > Loft** from the menubar; the NURBS curves are lofted with a surface in the viewport, as shown in Figure 3-32. To set the properties of the lofted surface created, choose **Surfaces > Create > Loft > Option Box** from the menubar; the **Loft Options** dialog box will be displayed, as shown in Figure 3-33. The options in the **Loft Options** dialog box are discussed next.

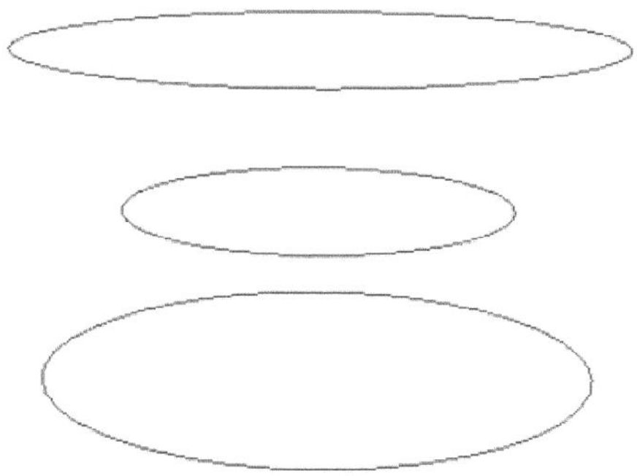

*Figure 3-31 The NURBS curves before applying the **Loft** tool*

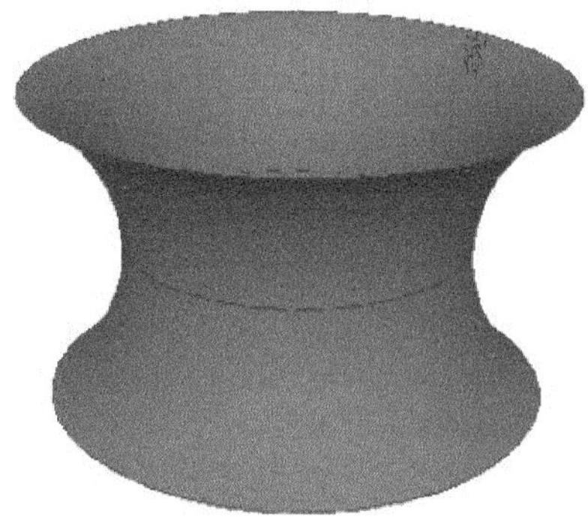

*Figure 3-32 The lofted surface created after applying the **Loft** tool*

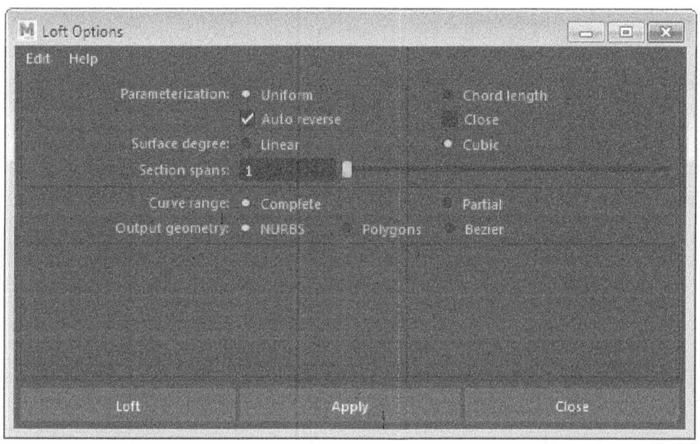

*Figure 3-33 The **Loft Options** dialog box*

Parameterization

The radio buttons corresponding to the **Parameterization** attribute are used to modify the parameters of the lofted surface. The **Uniform** radio button is used to set the number of control points uniformly along the curve. The **Chord length** radio button is used to parameterize the curve such that its value is proportional to the chord length. The **Auto reverse** check box is selected by default and is used to create a NURBS surface in the reverse order of selection of NURBS curves. Figure 3-34 shows the surface created with the **Close** check box cleared. Figure 3-35 shows the surface created with the **Close** check box selected.

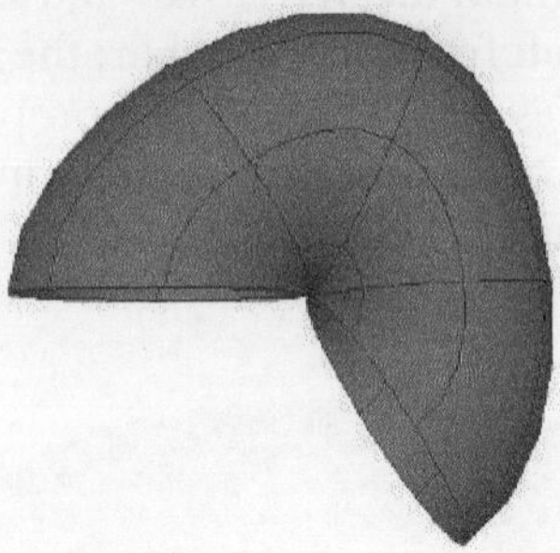

Figure 3-34 *Surface created with the* ***Close*** *check box cleared*

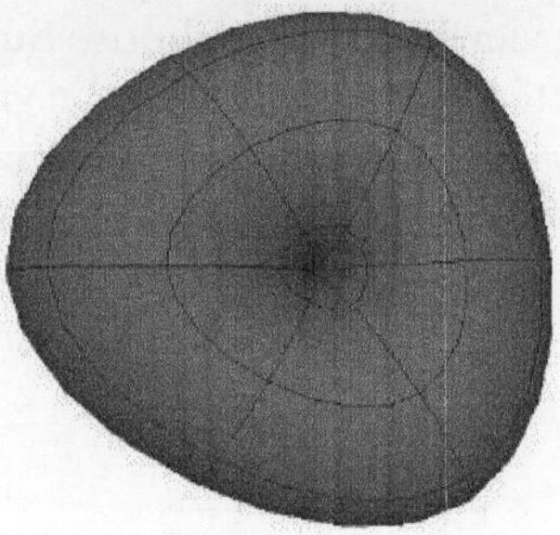

Figure 3-35 *Surface created with the* ***Close*** *check box selected*

Surface degree

The **Surface degree** attribute is used to specify the smoothness of a NURBS surface. The **Cubic** radio button corresponding to this attribute is selected by default. The **Linear** radio button is used to create the surface with edgy facets. To create a NURBS surface, choose **Create > Objects > Curve Tools > CV Curve Tool** from the menubar and then create NURBS curves in the viewport, as shown in Figure 3-36. Next, select the **Linear** or **Cubic** radio button corresponding to the **Surface degree** attribute in the **Loft Options** dialog box; the NURBS surfaces will be displayed, as shown in Figures 3-37 and 3-38.

Figure 3-36 *NURBS curves for creating a surface*

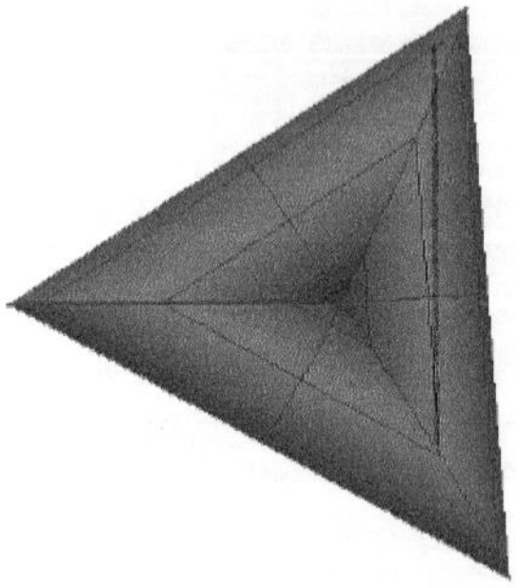

Figure 3-37 *Surface created on selecting the* ***Linear*** *radio button*

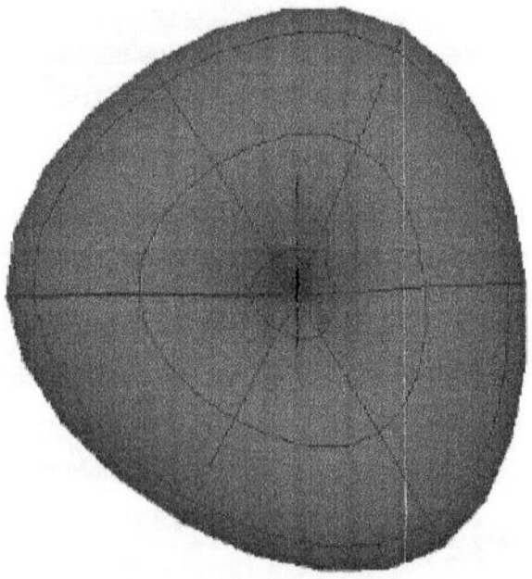

Figure 3-38 *Surface created on selecting the* ***Cubic*** *radio button*

Section spans

The **Section spans** edit box is used to specify the number of spans on the NURBS surface. To do so, enter a value in the edit box to specify the number of sections in the NURBS surface. Alternatively, adjust the slider on the right of the **Section spans** edit box. More the number of spans, more will be the smoothness of the NURBS surface.

Output geometry

The options in the **Output geometry** are used to specify the type of outputs of the NURBS surface. Select the required radio button to get the output surface as **NURBS**, **Polygons**, or **Bezier**. After setting the options in the **Loft Options** dialog box, choose the **Loft** button to create a NURBS surface.

Alternatively, choose the **Apply** button to create a NURBS surface. The function of the **Loft** and the **Apply** buttons is quite similar. On choosing the **Loft** button, the loft command will be applied to the NURBS curves and the **Loft Options** dialog box will be closed. On the other hand, on choosing the **Apply** button, the loft command will be applied to the NURBS curves without closing the **Loft Options** dialog box.

Planar Tool

Menubar: Surfaces > Create > Planar

The **Planar** tool is used to create a NURBS surface with all the vertices lying on the same plane. To create a NURBS surface using this tool, create a close curve using a curve tool. The curve should form a close loop and should at least have three sides. Next, choose **Surfaces > Create > Planar** from the menubar; a NURBS surface will be created. To set the properties of the NURBS surface, choose **Surfaces > Create > Planar > Option Box** from the menubar; the **Planar Trim Surface Options** dialog box will be displayed, as shown in Figure 3-39. The options in this dialog box are discussed next.

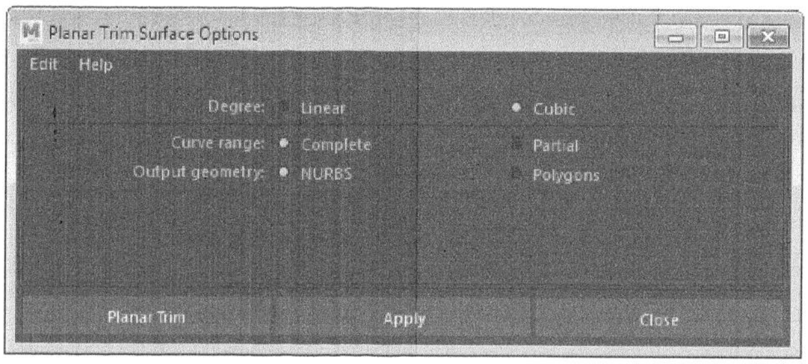

*Figure 3-39 The **Planar Trim Surface Options** dialog box*

Degree

The radio buttons corresponding to the **Degree** attribute are used to add smoothness to the edges of the surface created. By default, the **Cubic** radio button is selected. As a result, a planar surface with smooth edges is created. You can select the **Linear** radio button to create a planar surface with rough edges.

Curve range

The radio buttons corresponding to the **Curve range** attribute are used to set curves for creating a planar surface. The **Complete** radio button is selected by default and is used to create a planar surface along the selected curve. The **Partial** radio button is used to display manipulators on the planar surface using **Show Manipulator** tool and edit the plane along the input curve.

Output geometry

The **Output geometry** attribute specifies the type of geometry to be created. Select the **NURBS** radio button to set the output geometry as NURBS. Select the **Polygons** radio button to set the output geometry as polygon.

Revolve Tool

Menubar: Surfaces > Create > Revolve

The **Revolve** tool is used to create a surface around a profile curve along a selected axis. The axis of revolution depends on the location of the pivot point of an object. To create a revolved surface, choose **Create > Objects > Curve Tools > EP Curve Tool** from the menubar and then create a profile curve in the front-Z viewport, refer to Figure 3-40. Select the profile curve and choose **Surfaces > Create > Revolve** from the menubar; the profile curve will rotate around its pivot point, thus creating a revolved surface, as shown in Figure 3-41. Alternatively, you can choose **Surfaces > Create > Revolve > Option Box** from the menubar; the **Revolve Options** dialog box will be displayed, as shown in Figure 3-42. The options in this dialog box are discussed next.

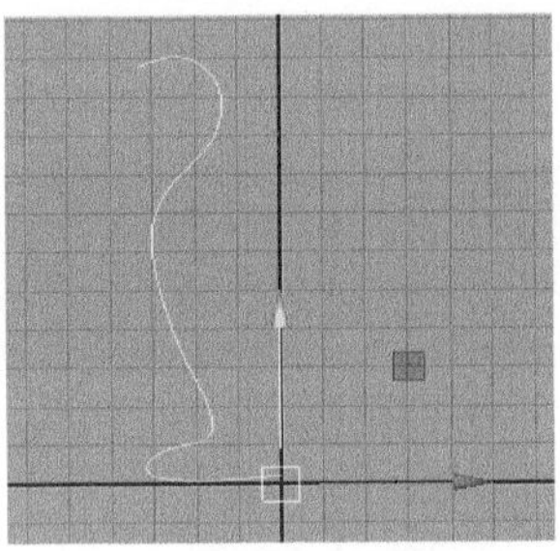

Figure 3-40 The profile curve created

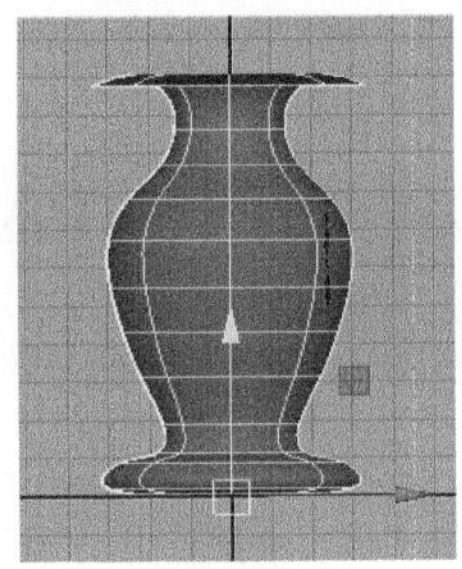

*Figure 3-41 The NURBS surface created after using the **Revolve** tool*

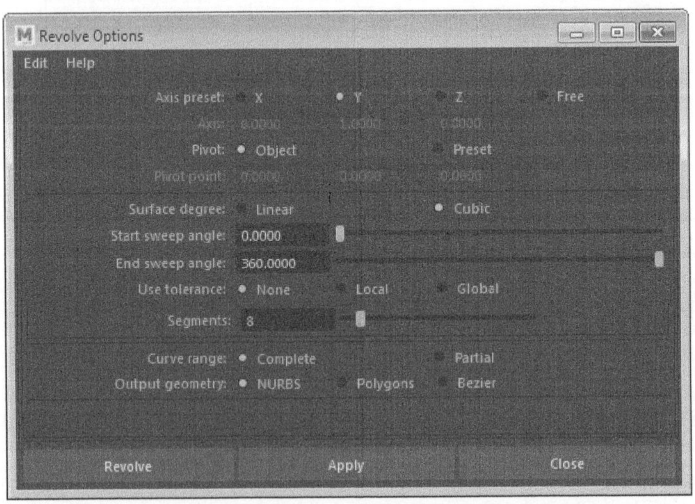

*Figure 3-42 The **Revolve Options** dialog box*

Axis preset

The options corresponding to the **Axis preset** parameter are used to set the axis about which the curve will revolve. You can select the required radio button to set the axis of revolution of the curve. By default, the revolution axis is Y. You can also select the **Free** radio button to enter the value of the axis manually.

Axis

The edit boxes corresponding to the **Axis** attribute are inactive by default. On selecting the **Free** radio button in the **Axis preset** attribute, the **Axis** edit boxes will be enabled. Now, you can specify the axis about which you want to revolve the NURBS curve in the viewport.

Pivot

The options corresponding to the **Pivot** attribute are used to define the rotation of the object from the default pivot location. It has two radio buttons: **Object** and **Preset**. The **Object** radio button is selected by default and is used to rotate an object at the default pivot location (0, 0, 0). Select the **Preset** radio button to change the X, Y, and Z location of the pivot point.

Surface degree

The **Surface degree** attribute is used to determine whether the direction of the surface created will be linear or cubic. It has two radio buttons: **Linear** and **Cubic**. If you select the **Linear** radio button, the surface will be formed with edgy facets. If you select the **Cubic** radio button, the edgy facets of the surface will become smooth.

Start sweep angle and End sweep angle

The **Start sweep angle** and **End sweep angle** edit boxes are used to define the degree of revolution of a curve. By default, the values in these edit boxes are set to 0 and 360, respectively. You can drag the slider next to these edit boxes to change the values as required.

Use tolerance

The radio buttons corresponding to the **Use tolerance** attribute are used to define the accuracy of the revolved NURBS surface. There are three radio buttons in this area: **None**, **Local**, and **Global**. By selecting the **None** radio button, you can make changes in the number of segments of the NURBS surface. The more the number of segments, the more will be the smoothness of the NURBS surface.

Segments

The **Segments** attribute is used to set the number of segments that are used to create the revolved surface. More the number of segments, more will be the smoothness of the surface. Either enter the required value in the attribute or drag the slider next to it. The default value in this attribute is 8.

Curve range

The **Curve range** attribute is used to determine whether the entire profile will be revolved or only a part of profile curve will be revolved about its pivot point. There are two radio buttons corresponding to the **Curve range** attribute: **Complete** and **Partial**. The **Complete** radio button is selected by default and is used to revolve the entire profile curve about the pivot point. The **Partial** radio button is used to create a revolved surface by revolving a part of profile curve about its pivot point. You can also edit the curve range for rotation. To do so, select the revolved surface in the viewport; the **Channel Box / Layer Editor** will be displayed. Next, choose **subCurve1** from the **INPUTS area**; the **subCurve1** options will be displayed in the **Channel Box / Layer Editor**. Set the **Min Value** and the **Max Value** of **subCurve1** in the **Channel Box / Layer Editor**. Alternatively, you can edit *subCurve1* by using the **Show Manipulator Tool**. Choose **Modify > Transform > Transformation Tools > Show Manipulator Tool** from the menubar. Next, drag the Curve Segment Manipulator to set the partial curve range, refer to Figure 3-43, and then choose the **Revolve** tool to create the NURBS surface.

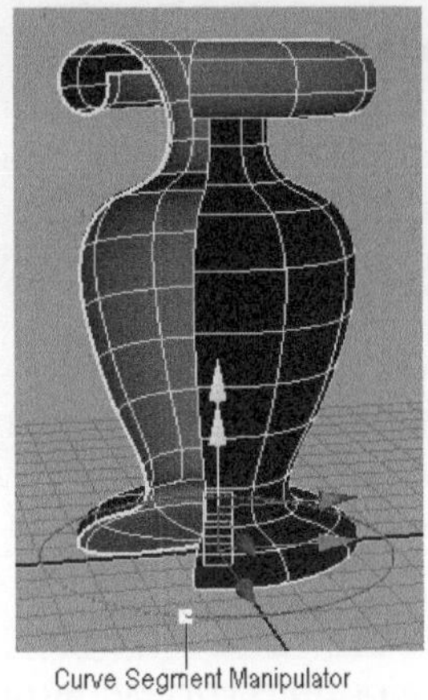

Figure 3-43 *Dragging the Curve Segment Manipulator*

Output geometry

The **Output geometry** parameter is used to define the type of geometry to be created using the NURBS curve. The radio buttons in this area are used to convert the NURBS curve into four different types of geometries: NURBS, Polygons, Subdiv, and Bezier (Subdiv refers to subdivision surfaces). Select the required geometry to set the type of output geometry.

Birail Tool

Menubar:	Surfaces > Create > Birail

The **Birail** tool works similar to the **Extrude** tool. This tool is used to create surfaces using one curve or two profile curves along two path curves. You can create complex NURBS surfaces using this tool. Maya has three different types of **Birail** tools: **Birail 1 Tool**, **Birail 2 Tool**, and **Birail 3+ Tool**. Before creating a NURBS surface using different **Birail** tools, the following points should be kept in mind:

1. The profile curves and the path curves must touch each other and have continuity.
2. All profile curves should have the same number of CVs.
3. All path curves should also have the same number of CVs.
4. Press C to snap the curve of the profile curve and the path curve together.
5. If the profile curve and the path curve do not have the same number of CVs, you will have to draw the curves again.

Extrude Tool

Menubar:	Surfaces > Create > Extrude

The **Extrude** tool is used to extrude a particular object by sweeping its profile curve along the path curve. To extrude a surface, two curves are required: a profile curve and a path curve. The profile curve gives shape to a surface, whereas the path curve defines the path on which the shape will sweep to create a surface. To create an extruded surface, select the two curves in the viewport. The first curve selected will act as the profile curve, whereas the second curve will act as the path curve. Now, choose **Surfaces > Create > Extrude** from the menubar to extrude the surface. You can use this method to create objects such as curtains, parts of a vehicle, and so on. To adjust the properties of the **Extrude** tool, choose **Surfaces > Create > Extrude > Option Box** from the menubar; the **Extrude Options** dialog box will be displayed, as shown in Figure 3-44. The options in this dialog box are discussed next.

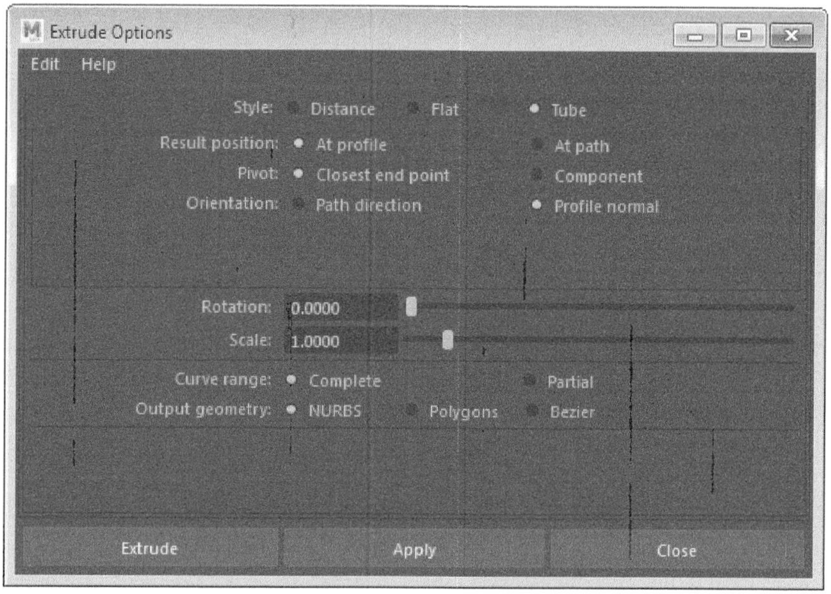

***Figure 3-44** The **Extrude Options** dialog box*

Style

The **Style** attribute consists of three radio buttons: **Distance**, **Flat**, and **Tube**. The **Tube** radio button is selected by default and is used to maintain a cross-section along the path, with the reference vector remaining tangent to the path. The **Distance** radio button is used to extrude the profile in a straight line. The **Flat** radio button is used to maintain the orientation path of the profile curve.

Result position

The radio buttons corresponding to the **Result position** attribute are used to set the position at which the extruded surface will be created. By default, the **At profile** radio button is selected. It is used to position the extruded surface along the profile curve. The **At path** radio button is used to set the position of the extruded surface along the path curve. This attribute is available only if you set the **Style** to **Tube** or **Flat**.

Pivot

The **Pivot** attribute is used to set the pivot point of an extruded surface and will be activated only when the **Tube** radio button is selected in the **Style** attribute. The two radio buttons corresponding to the **Pivot** attribute are: **Closest end point** and **Component**. By default, the **Closest end point** radio button is selected. As a result, an extruded surface is created close to the center of the bounding box of the profile curves. The **Component** radio button is used to create an extruded surface along the components of the profile curve. Figure 3-45 shows a profile curve and a path curve to create an extruded surface. Figures 3-46 and 3-47 show extruded surfaces created on selecting the **Closest end point** and **Component** radio buttons, respectively.

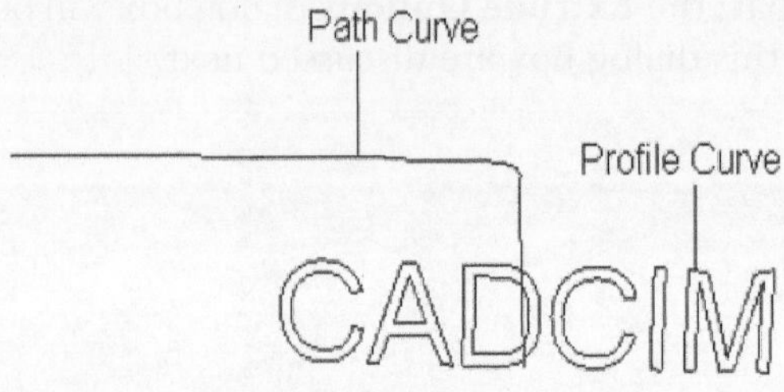

***Figure 3-45** The profile curve and the path curve for creating an extruded surface*

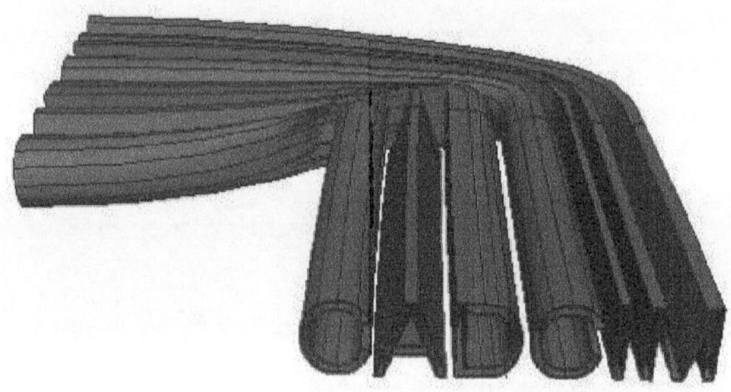

***Figure 3-46** Extruded surface created on selecting the **Closest end point** radio button*

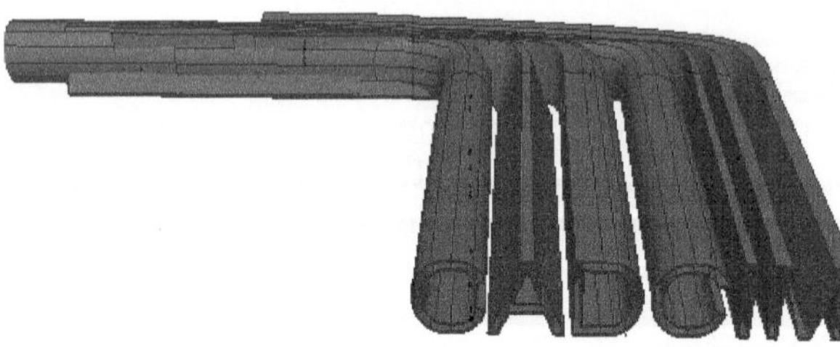

***Figure 3-47** Extruded surface created on selecting the **Component** radio button*

Orientation

The radio buttons corresponding to the **Orientation** attribute are used to set the orientation of an extruded surface. The **Orientation** attribute is available only when the **Tube** radio button is selected in the **Extrude Options** dialog box. The **Path direction** radio button is used to extrude the profile curve along the direction of path curve. By default, the **Profile normal** radio button is selected. The **Profile normal** radio button is used to extrude the surface such that the path curve is created normal to the profile curve.

Rotation

The **Rotation** attribute is used to rotate the profile curve along path. To do so, specify the angle of rotation in this attribute.

Scale

The **Scale** attribute is used to scale the profile while extruding it along the path curve. To do so, specify the scale factor in this attribute.

Curve range and Output geometry

The radio buttons corresponding to the **Curve range** and **Output geometry** attributes are the same as discussed in the revolved surface section. On selecting the **Distance** radio button from the **Style** attribute, some other options are displayed, as shown in Figure 3-48. These options are discussed next.

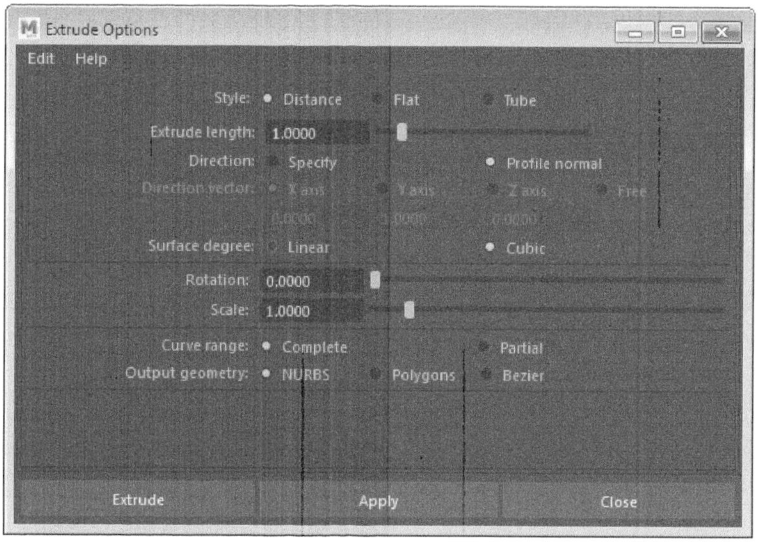

*Figure 3-48 The **Extrude Options** dialog box with the **Distance** radio button selected*

Extrude length

The **Extrude length** attribute is used to define the length of extrusion.

Direction

The radio buttons corresponding to the **Direction** attribute is used to define the direction of extrusion. It consists of two radio buttons: **Specify** and **Profile normal**. The **Profile normal** radio button is used to set the direction of the path to normal. The **Specify** radio button is used to manually set the direction for creating the surface in a particular axis. For example, if you select the X-axis, the extrusion will take place only in the X-direction.

Surface degree

The **Surface degree** attribute is used to give smoothness or sharpness to the surface created. This attribute consists of two radio buttons: **Linear** and **Cubic**. The **Linear** radio button is used to create sharp edges near the isoparms. The **Cubic** radio button is used to create smooth surfaces.

Boundary Tool

Menubar:	Surfaces > Create > Boundary

The **Boundary** tool is used to create a surface by filling the boundary curves. This tool creates a NURBS surface by filling the space between the curves. It is not necessary for the curves to have a closed loop, but they should intersect with each other at some point. To apply the **Boundary** tool, create four curves in the viewport, as shown in Figure 3-49. Press and hold the SHIFT key and select all the curves in opposite pairs to maintain continuity. Now, choose **Surfaces > Create > Boundary** from the menubar to create the NURBS surface. To adjust the properties of the **Boundary** tool, choose **Surfaces > Create > Boundary > Option Box** from the menubar; the **Boundary Options** dialog box will be displayed, as shown in Figure 3-50. The options in this dialog box are similar to those discussed in other surfacing tools.

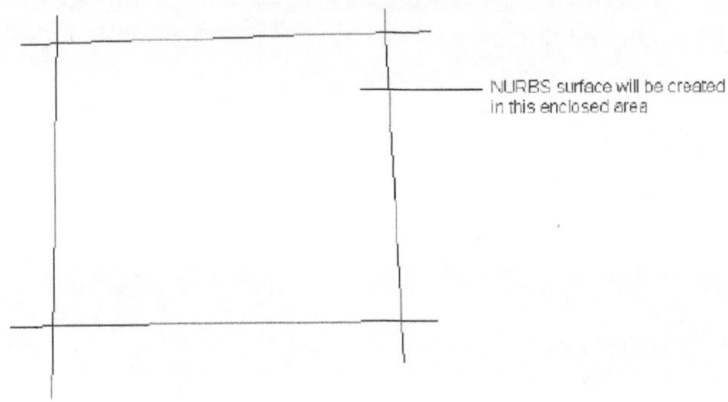

Figure 3-49 *Four NURBS curves created*

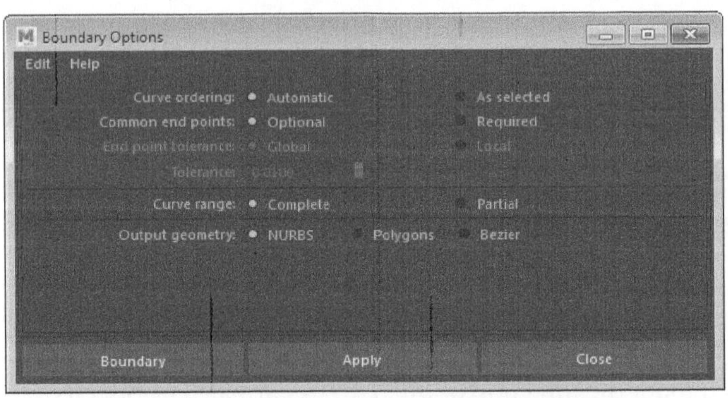

Figure 3-50 *The **Boundary Options** dialog box*

Square Tool

Menubar:	Surfaces > Create > Square

The **Square** tool is used to create a four-sided NURBS surface from the intersecting curves. On choosing this tool, a NURBS surface is created by filling the region defined by four intersecting curves. This tool is similar to the **Boundary** tool with the only difference that in the **Boundary** tool, you can select curves in any order, whereas in the **Square** tool, you need to select them in clockwise or counterclockwise direction. To use this tool, create four intersecting curves in the viewport. Next, press and hold the SHIFT key and select the curves either in clockwise or counterclockwise direction. Now, choose **Surfaces > Create > Square** from the menubar; the NURBS surface will be created.

Bevel Tool

Menubar:	Surfaces > Create > Bevel

The **Bevel** tool is used to create a NURBS surface by using the three-dimensional edge effect applied on the selected curves. The surface created by the **Bevel** tool has an open area that can be filled by using the **Planar** tool. To create a surface by using the **Bevel** tool, create a NURBS circle in the top-Y viewport, as shown in Figure 3-51. Next, choose **Surfaces > Create > Bevel** from the menubar; a beveled surface will be created, as shown in Figure 3-52. You can adjust the properties of the beveled surface in the **Channel Box / Layer Editor** by changing the values in the **bevel1** node of the **INPUTS** area as required, refer to Figure 3-53.

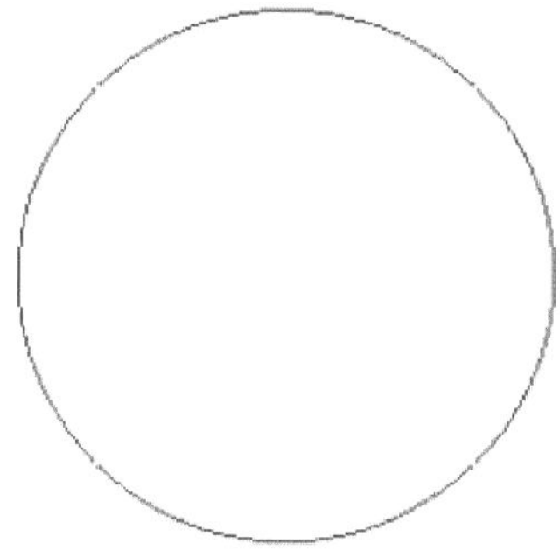

Figure 3-51 *A NURBS circle*

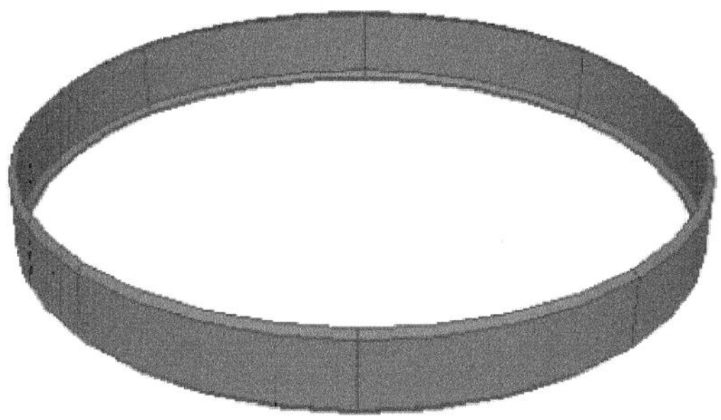

Figure 3-52 *The bevel surface created*

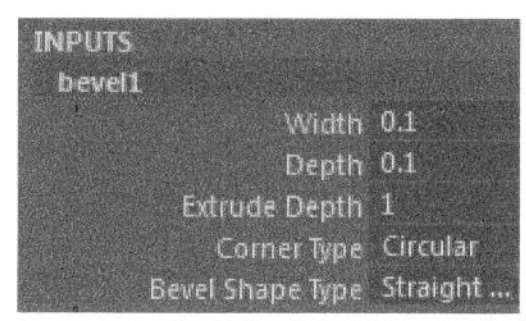

Figure 3-53 *The **bevel1** node in the **INPUTS** area*

Bevel Plus Tool

Menubar:	Surfaces > Create > Bevel Plus

The **Bevel Plus** tool is used to extrude the closed curves and add beveled transition to the extruded surface. To create a surface by using this tool, create a NURBS circle in the top-Y viewport, as shown in Figure 3-54 and then choose **Surfaces > Create > Bevel Plus** from the menubar; a beveled surface will be created, as shown in Figure 3-55. You can adjust the properties of the beveled surface in the **Channel Box / Layer Editor** by changing the values in the **bevelPlus1** node of the **INPUTS** area as required, refer to Figure 3-56.

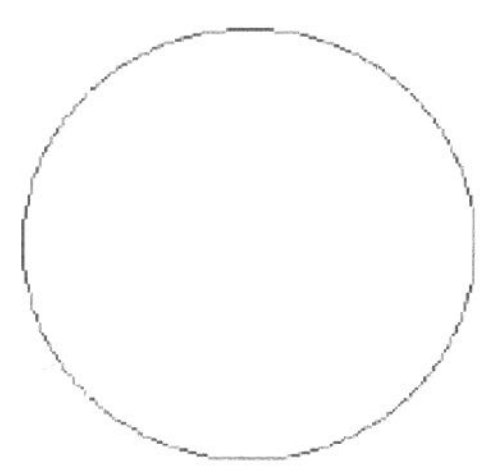

Figure 3-54 *A NURBS circle created in the top-Y viewport*

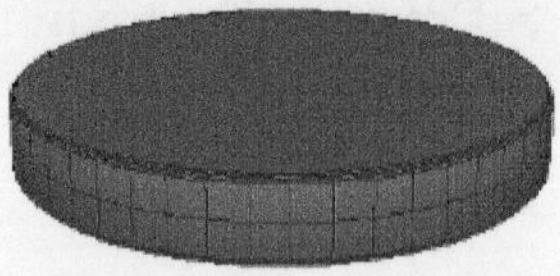

*Figure 3-55 The beveled surface created using the **Bevel Plus** tool*

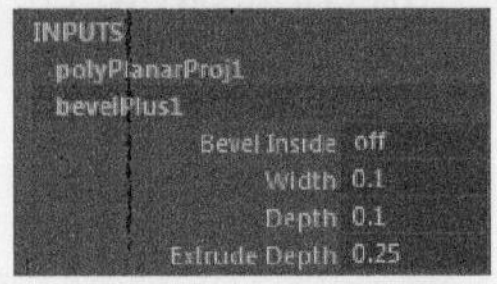

*Figure 3-56 The **bevelPlus1** node displayed in the **INPUTS** area*

TUTORIALS

Tutorial 1

In this tutorial, you will create 3D model of a teapot, as shown in Figure 3-57, using the curve tools and the surface tools. (Expected time: 15 min)

The following steps are required to complete this tutorial:

a. Create a project folder.
b. Create the body of the teapot.
c. Create the handle of the teapot.
d. Create the spout of the teapot
e. Create the lid of the teapot.
f. Change the background color of the scene.
g. Save and render the scene.

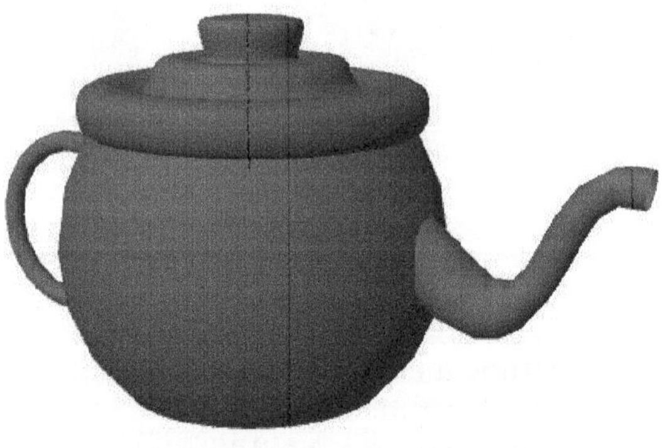

Figure 3-57 The teapot model

Creating a Project Folder

Create a new project folder with the name *c03_tut1* at *\Documents\maya2017* and then save the file with the name *c03tut1*, as discussed in Tutorial 1 of Chapter 2.

Creating the Body of the Teapot

In this section, you will create the body of the teapot using the **NURBS Circle** and **Loft** tools.

1. Select the **Modeling** menuset from the **Menuset** drop-down list in the Status Line. Choose the **Four View** button from the Tool Box to switch to four views. Move the cursor to the top-Y viewport and then press the SPACEBAR key to maximize the top-Y viewport.

2. Choose **Create > Objects > NURBS Primitives > Circle** from the menubar and click in the top-Y viewport; a NURBS Circle is created in the viewport.

3. In the **Channel Box / Layer Editor**, expand the **makeNurb Circle1** area in the **INPUTS** area and enter **3** in the **Radius** edit box, refer to Figure 3-58.

4. Choose the **Four View** button from the Tool Box to switch to four views. Move the cursor to the front-Z viewport and then press the SPACEBAR key to maximize the front-Z viewport. In the front-Z viewport, make sure the NURBS Circle is selected and choose **Edit > Duplicate > Duplicate** from the menubar; another copy of the circle is created. Next, choose **Move Tool** from the Tool Box and move the duplicate circle up along the Y-axis, refer to Figure 3-59.

5. Make sure the duplicate circle is selected and then press CTRL+D; a copy of the circle is created. Next, choose **Move Tool** from the Tool Box and move the third circle and place it in the middle of the first and second circles, as shown in Figure 3-60.

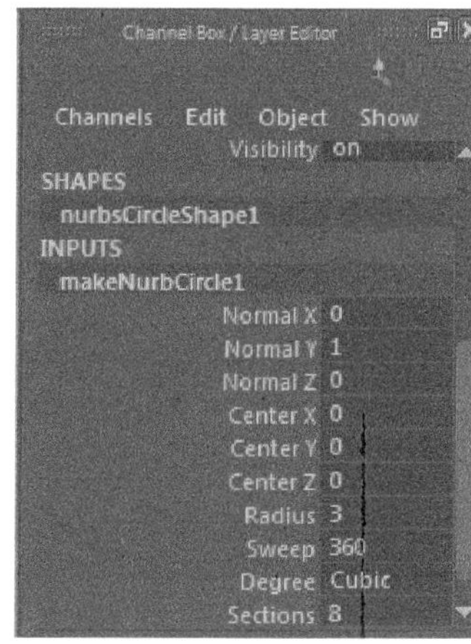

***Figure 3-58** The **Channel Box / Layer Editor** for the circle*

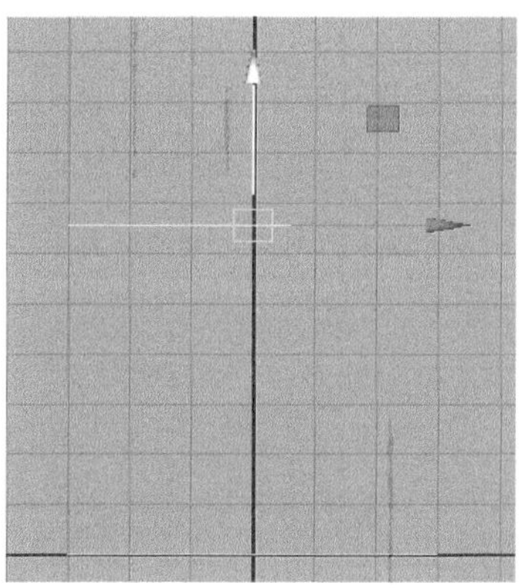

***Figure 3-59** Duplicate copy of the circle created in the front-Z viewport*

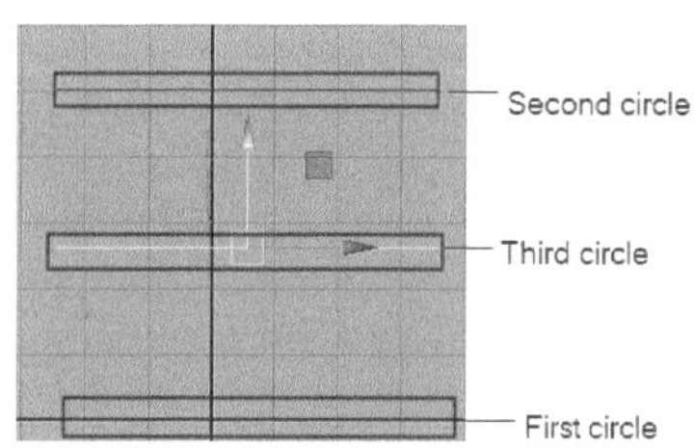

***Figure 3-60** Third copy of the circle placed between the first and second circles*

6. Invoke **Scale Tool** and scale the third circle uniformly, refer to Figure 3-61.

   Next, you will create a NURBS surface.

7. Press and hold the SHIFT key and select the first, third and second circles. Choose **Surfaces > Create > Loft** from the menubar; the lofted surface is created in the viewport, refer to Figure 3-62.

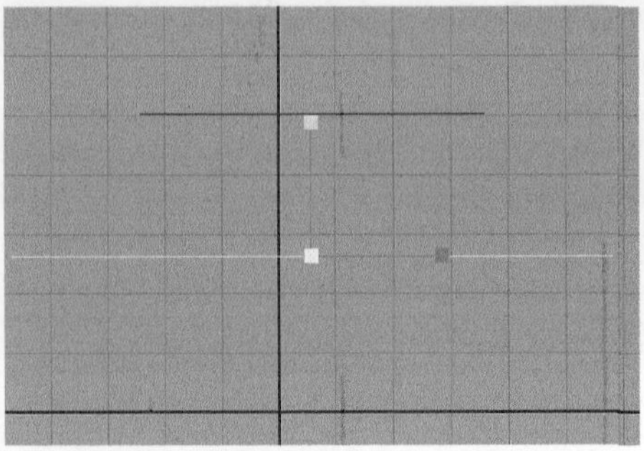

Figure 3-61 *The third circle scaled using* ***Scale Tool*** *in the front-Z viewport*

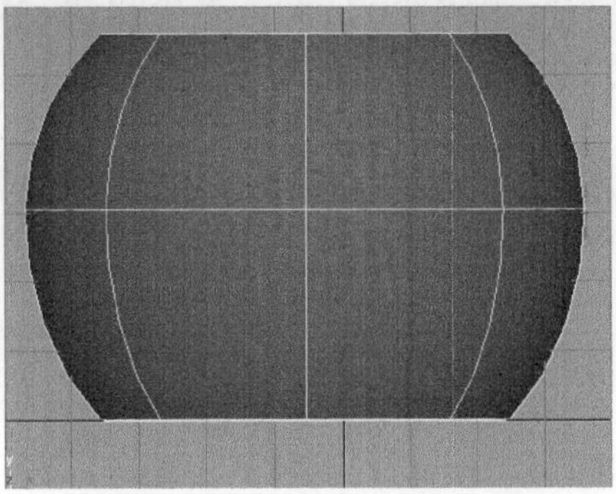

Figure 3-62 *The three circles lofted using the* ***Loft*** *tool*

8. Choose **Windows > Editors > Outliner** from the menubar; the **Outliner** window is displayed. Now select the **NURBS Circle.** Select the first circle and choose **Surfaces > Create > Planar** from the menubar; a flat surface is created at the bottom.

Creating the Handle of the Teapot

In this section, you will create the handle of the teapot by using the **Three Point Circular Arc** and **Extrude** tools.

1. Choose **Create > Objects > Curve Tools > Three Point Circular Arc** from the menubar and create an arc in the front-Z viewport by defining the start point, the curve point, and the endpoint, refer to Figure 3-63. Choose **Create > Objects > NURBS Primitives > Circle** from the menubar and click in the front-Z viewport; a circle is created in the viewport. In the **Channel Box / Layer Editor,** expand the **makeNurbCircle2** node in the **INPUTS** area. Next, enter **0.25** in the **Radius** edit box.

2. Make sure the circle is selected. Enter **90** in the **Rotate X** edit box in the **Channel Box / Layer Editor**. Figure 3-64 displays the circle created in the front-Z viewport.

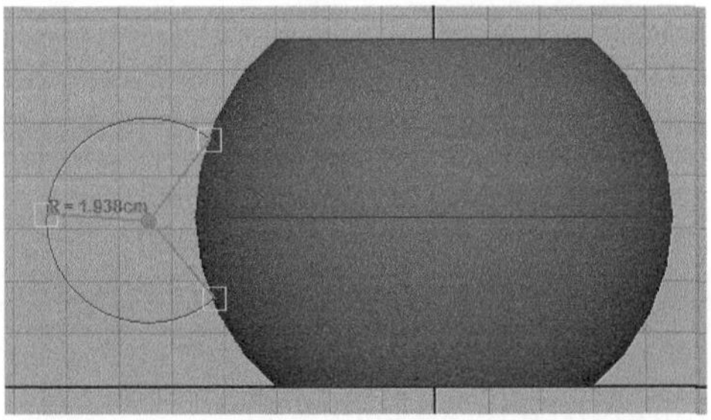

Figure 3-63 *An Arc created using the* ***Three Point Circular Arc*** *tool*

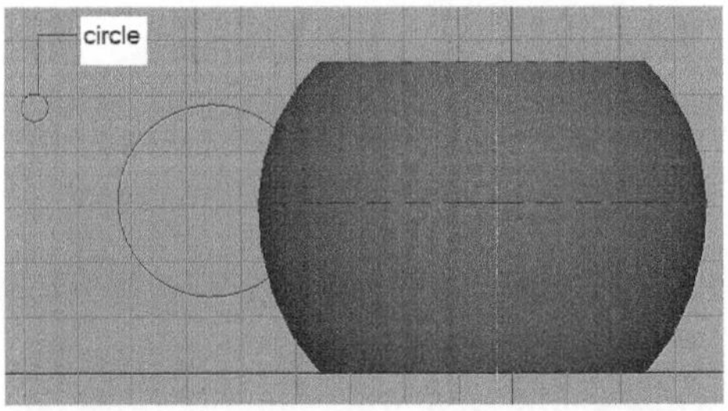

Figure 3-64 *A Circle created in the front-Z viewport*

3. Make sure the circle is selected and then select the arc by using the SHIFT key. Next, choose **Surfaces > Create > Extrude > Option Box** from the menubar; the **Extrude Options** dialog box is displayed. In this dialog box, set the parameters, as shown in Figure 3-65. Next, choose the **Apply** button and then the **Close** button; the circle is extruded along the arc.

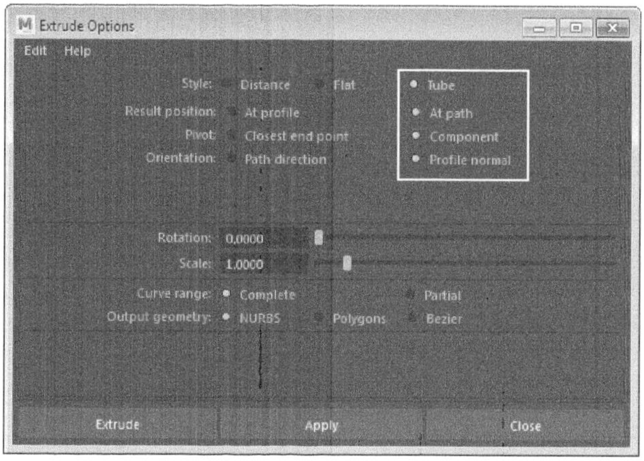

Figure 3-65 The ***Extrude Options*** *dialog box*

4. Choose the **Four View** button from the Tool Box to switch to four views. Move the cursor to the persp viewport and then press the SPACEBAR key to maximize the persp viewport. Press 5 to view the surface in the shaded mode, if not in the shaded mode. Choose **Move Tool** and **Rotate Tool**, if required. Next, align the handle on the body of the teapot, as shown in Figure 3-66.

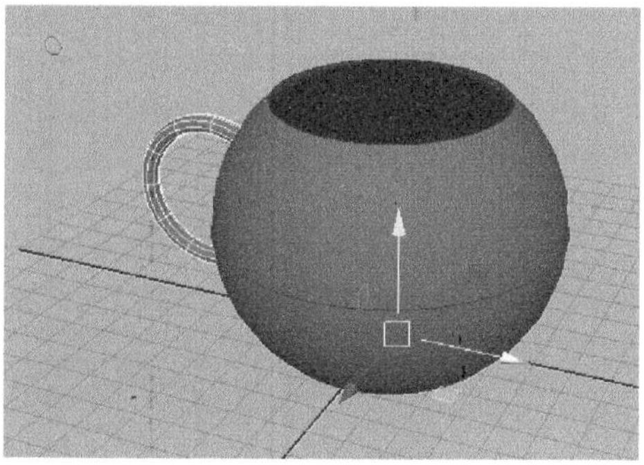

Figure 3-66 Handle aligned with the teapot

Creating the Spout of the Teapot

In this section, you will create the spout of the teapot by using the **EP Curve Tool** and the **Extrude** tool.

1. Choose the **Four View** button from the Tool Box to switch to four views. Move the cursor to the front-Z viewport and then press the SPACEBAR key to maximize the front-Z viewport. Choose **Create > Objects > Curve Tools > EP Curve Tool > Option Box** from the menubar; the **Tool Settings (EP Curve Tool)** window is displayed. Select the **5** radio button corresponding to the **Curve degree** attribute.

2. Create a profile curve in the front-Z viewport from bottom to top, as shown in Figure 3-67 and then press ENTER.

3. Choose **Create > Objects > NURBS Primitives > Circle** from the menubar and click in the front-Z viewport; a circle is created in the viewport. Make sure the circle is selected in the viewport. In the **Channel Box / Layer Editor**, expand the **makeNurbCircle3** node in the **INPUTS** area and enter **0.4** in the **Radius** edit box and **90** in the **Rotate X** edit box; the circle is rotated in the front-Z viewport, as shown in Figure 3-68.

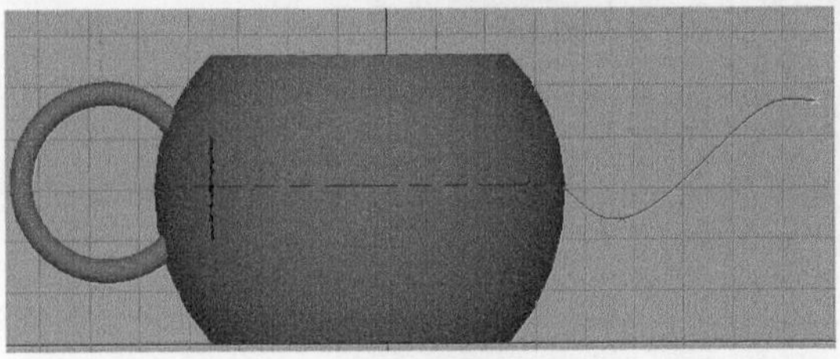

Figure 3-67 Profile curve created for the spout

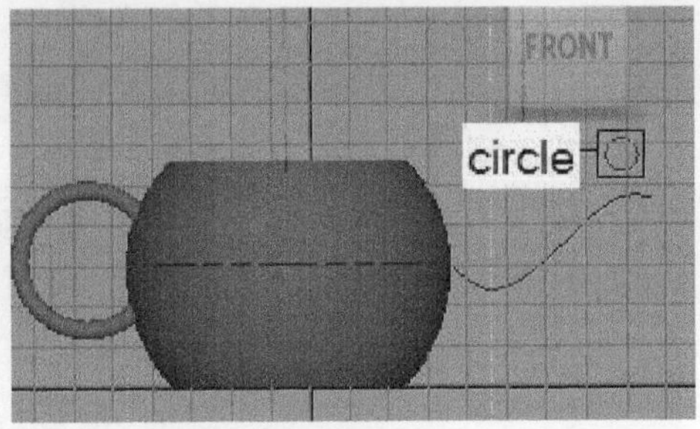

Figure 3-68 A Circle created in the front-Z viewport

Tip
To get the exact shape of the curve, you need to modify it. To do so, select the curve and then right click on it. Next, choose ***Control Vertex*** *from the marking menu displayed. Now, you can select a vertex and modify the shape of the curve using* ***Move Tool****.*

4. In the front-Z viewport, make sure the circle is selected and then select the profile curve of the spout by using the SHIFT key. Next, choose **Surfaces > Create > Extrude > Option Box** from the menubar; the **Extrude Options** dialog box is displayed. In this dialog box, set the parameters, refer to Figure 3-69. Choose the **Apply** button and then the **Close** button; the profile curve of the spout is extruded.

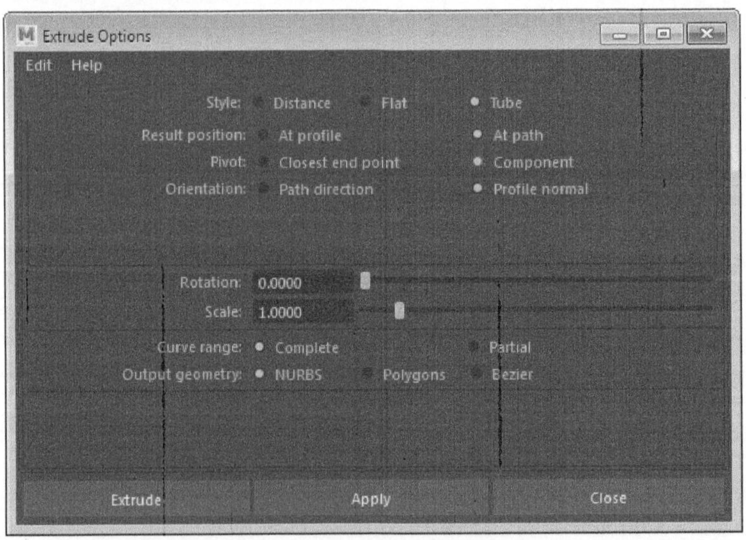

Figure 3-69 The ***Extrude Options*** *dialog box*

5. Choose the **Four View** button from the Tool Box to switch to four views. Move the cursor to the persp viewport and then press the SPACEBAR key to maximize the persp viewport. Place the spout on the body of the teapot using **Move Tool** if required, as shown in Figure 3-70.

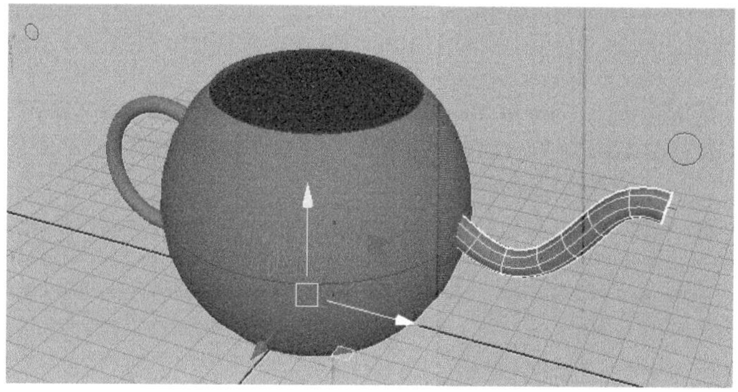

Figure 3-70 The spout placed on the teapot

6. Make sure the spout is selected. Press and hold the right mouse button over the spout; a marking menu is displayed. Choose **Control Vertex** from the marking menu; vertex selection mode is activated.

7. Choose the **Four View** button from the Tool Box to switch to four views. Move the cursor to the front-Z viewport and then press the SPACEBAR key to maximize the front-Z viewport. Select the vertices of the spout, as shown in Figure 3-71. Next, invoke **Scale Tool** and scale the selected vertices uniformly, as shown in Figure 3-72.

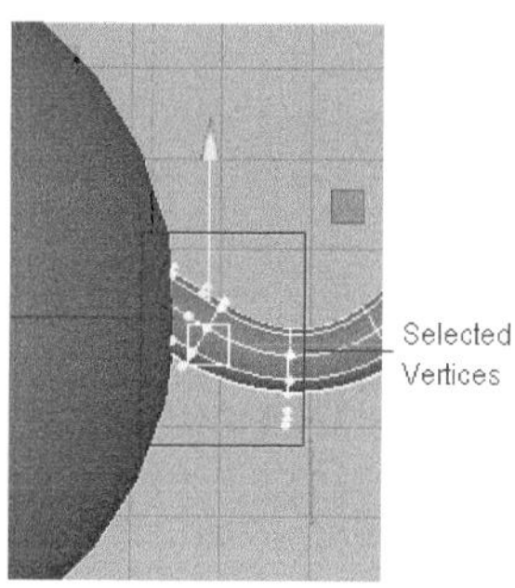

Figure 3-71 Vertices of the spout selected

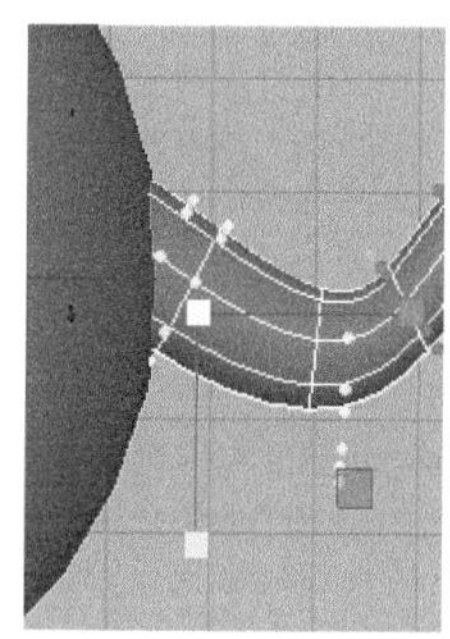

Figure 3-72 Selected vertices scaled

8. Modify the shape of the spout to refine it using **Scale Tool** and **Move Tool**, as shown in Figure 3-73.

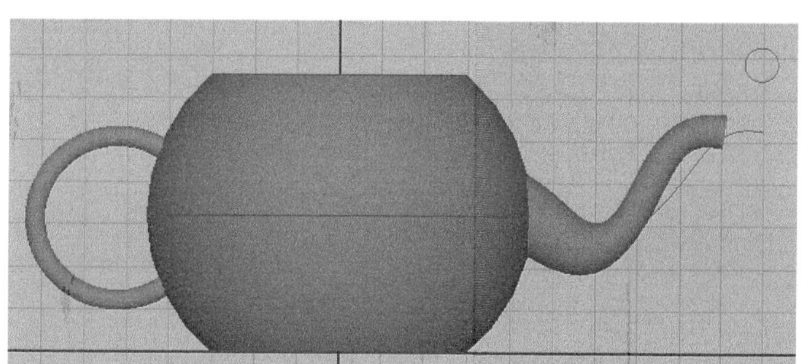

Figure 3-73 The refined shape of the spout

Creating the Lid of the Teapot

In this section, you will create the lid of the teapot using **EP Curve Tool** and the **Revolve** tool.

1. Choose **Create > Objects > Curve Tools > EP Curve Tool > Option Box** from the menubar; the **Tool Settings (EP Curve Tool)** window is displayed. Select the **3 Cubic** radio button corresponding to the **Curve Degree** attribute.

2. In the front-Z viewport, create a profile curve from bottom to top for the lid of the teapot using **EP Curve Tool**, as shown in Figure 3-74 and press ENTER. Next, press and hold the **D** key and set the pivot point of the curve, as shown in Figure 3-75.

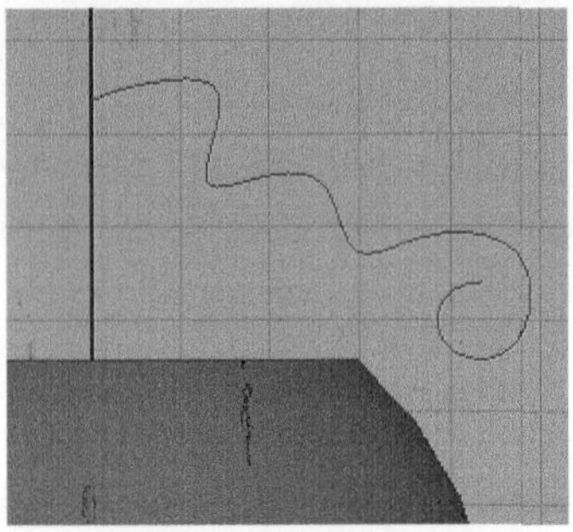

Figure 3-74 *Profile curve created for the lid*

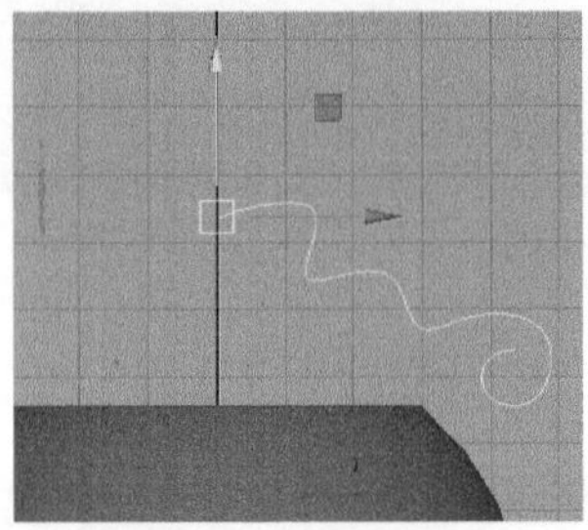

Figure 3-75 *Pivot point of the curve aligned*

3. Make sure the profile curve is selected. Next, choose **Surfaces >Create > Revolve** from the menubar; the profile curve rotates at 360 degrees and the lid is created.

4. Choose the **Four View** button from the Tool Box to switch to four views. Move the cursor to the persp viewport and then press the SPACEBAR key to maximize the persp viewport. Scale and align the lid on the body of the teapot using **Move Tool** and **Scale Tool**, as shown in Figure 3-76.

Figure 3-76 *The lid placed on the teapot*

Note

*To set the pivot point of any surface, press the INSERT key; the shape of the gizmo will change. Before applying the **Revolve** tool on the selected curve, adjust the pivot point at the center of the curve from where the new surface will be created. If you delete the profile curve after applying the **Revolve** tool, you cannot modify the shape.*

Changing the Background Color of the Scene

In this section, you will change the background color of the scene.

1. Choose **Windows > Editors > Outliner** from the menubar; the **Outliner** window is displayed. Select the **persp** camera in the **Outliner** window; the **perspShape** tab is displayed in the **Attribute Editor**.

2. In the **perspShape** tab, expand the **Environment** area and drag the **Background Color** slider bar toward right to change the background color to white.

Saving and Rendering the Scene

In this section, you will save the scene that you have created and then render it. You can view the final rendered image of the scene by downloading the *c03_maya_2017_rndr.zip* file from *www.cadcim.com*. The path of the file is as follows: *Textbooks > Animation and Visual Effects > Maya > Autodesk Maya 2017: A Comprehensive Guide.*

1. Choose **File > Save Scene** from the menubar.

2. Maximize the persp viewport, if it is not already maximized. Choose the **Render the current frame** button from the Status Line; the **Render View** window is displayed. This window shows the final output of the scene, refer to Figure 3-57.

Tutorial 2

In this tutorial, you will create the 3D model of a tea cup, as shown in Figure 3-77, using curve tools and surface methods. **(Expected time: 30 min)**

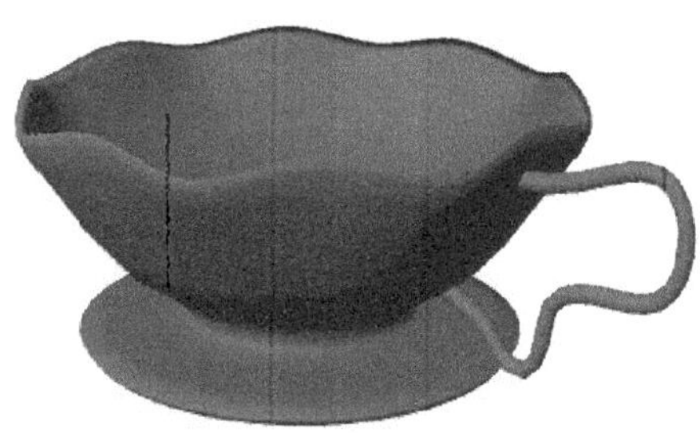

Figure 3-77 *The tea cup*

The following steps are required to complete this tutorial:

a. Create a project folder.
b. Create a profile curve.
c. Create the tea cup using the **Revolve** tool.
d. Create creases in the tea cup.
e. Create the handle of the tea cup.
f. Change the background color of the scene.
g. Save and render the scene.

Creating a Project Folder

Create a new project folder with the name *c03_tut2* at *\Documents\maya2017* and then save the file with the name *c03tut2*, as discussed in Tutorial 1 of Chapter 2.

Creating a Profile Curve

In this section, you will create a profile curve for the tea cup using **CV Curve Tool**.

1. Choose the **Four View** button from the Tool Box to switch to four views. Move the cursor to the front-Z viewport and then press the SPACEBAR key to maximize the front-Z viewport. Choose **Create > Objects > Curve Tools > EP Curve Tool** from the menubar.

2. In the front-Z viewport, create a profile curve starting from the origin, as shown in Figure 3-78. Next, press the ENTER key.

Creating the Tea Cup Using the Revolve Tool

In this section, you will create the tea cup using the **Revolve** tool.

1. Choose the **Four View** button from the Tool Box to switch to four views. Move the cursor to the persp viewport and then press the SPACEBAR key to maximize the persp viewport. Select the profile curve in the viewport. Next, choose **Surfaces > Create > Revolve** from the menubar; the tea cup is created, as shown in Figure 3-79.

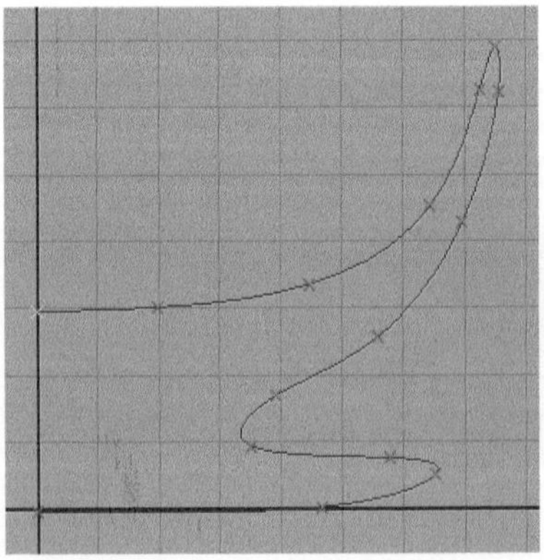

Figure 3-78 The profile curve for the tea cup

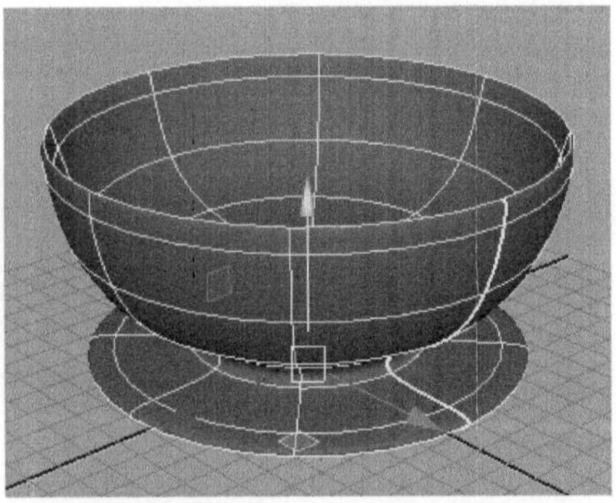

Figure 3-79 The tea cup created

Creating Creases in the Tea Cup

In this section, you will add creases to the tea cup to give it the required shape.

1. In the persp viewport, make sure the tea cup is selected. Next, press and hold the right mouse button over the tea cup; a marking menu is displayed. Choose **Isoparm** from the marking menu.

2. Choose a vertical isoparm of the tea cup and then drag the cursor; a dotted impression of the isoparm is created on the cup, refer to Figure 3-80.

3. Press and hold the SHIFT key and similarly create dotted impression of other vertical isoparms, as shown in Figure 3-80. You may need to rotate the viewport to select the vertical isoparms.

4. Make sure that **Surfaces** menuset is selected from the **Menuset** drop-down list in the Status Line. **Curves > Insert Knot** from the menubar; the new isoparms are created on the tea cup, as shown in Figure 3-81.

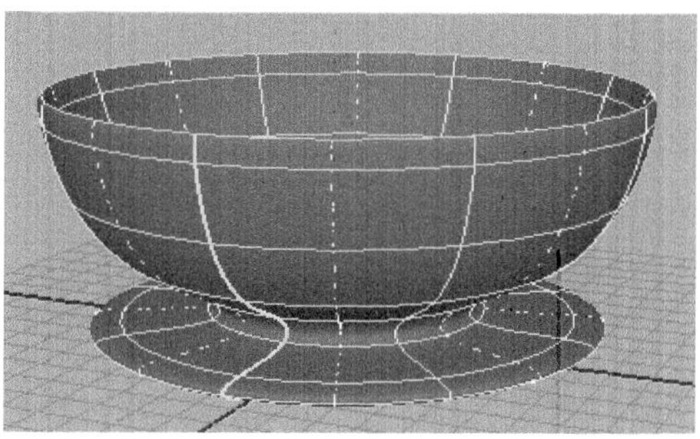

Figure 3-80 *Dotted impression of the isoparms*

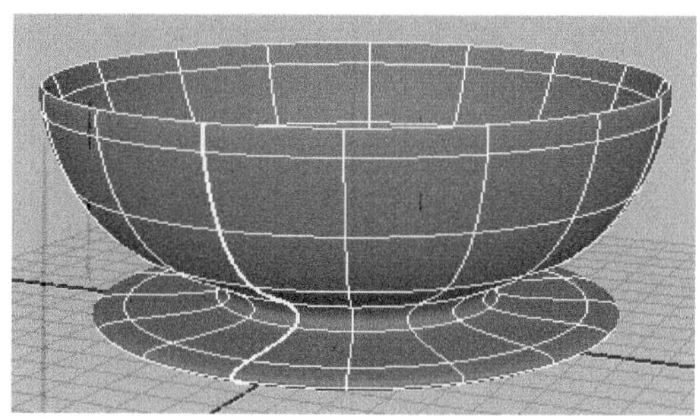

Figure 3-81 *New isoparms created*

5. Choose the **Four View** button from the Tool Box to switch to four views. Move the cursor to the front-Z viewport and then press the SPACEBAR key to maximize the front-Z viewport.

6. Press and hold the right mouse button over the tea cup; a marking menu is displayed. Choose **Control Vertex** from the marking menu; the vertex selection mode is activated. Next, press and hold the SHIFT key to select the vertices, as shown in Figure 3-82.

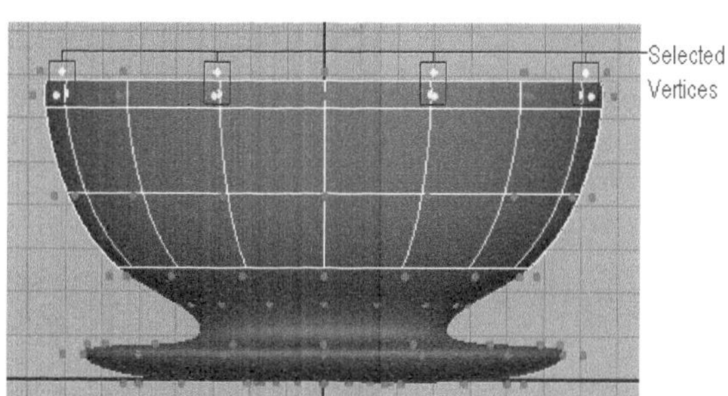

Figure 3-82 *Vertices selected*

7. Choose **Move Tool** from the Tool Box and move the selected vertices downward along the Y-axis; creases are created in the tea cup, as shown in Figure 3-83.

8. Choose the **Four View** button from the Tool Box to switch to four views. Move the cursor to the top-Y viewport and then press the SPACEBAR key to maximize the top-Y viewport.

9. Make sure that the vertices are selected in the top-Y viewport. Next, choose the **Scale Tool** from the Tool Box and scale the selected vertices outward uniformly, as shown in Figure 3-84.

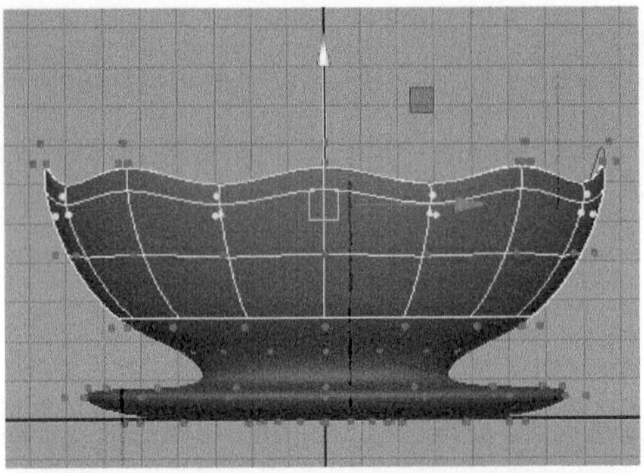

Figure 3-83 *Crease created in the tea cup*

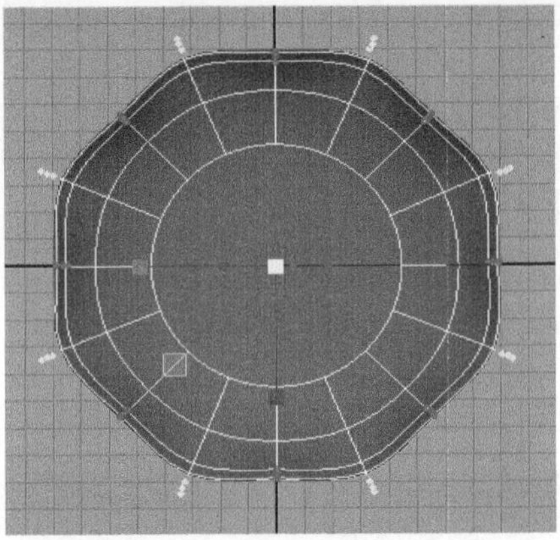

Figure 3-84 *Selected vertices scaled outward*

Creating the Handle of the Tea Cup

In this section, you will create the handle of the cup by using **CV Curve Tool**.

1. Choose the **Four View** button from the Tool Box to switch to four views. Move the cursor to the front-Z viewport and then press the SPACEBAR key to maximize the front-Z viewport. Choose **Create > Objects > Curve Tools > CV Curve Tool** from the menubar and draw a profile curve, as shown in Figure 3-85 and then press the ENTER key.

2. Choose the **Four View** button from the Tool Box to switch to four views. Move the cursor to the top-Y viewport and then press the SPACEBAR key to maximize the top-Y viewport. Choose **Create > Objects > NURBS Primitives > Circle** from the menubar and create a circle in the top-Y viewport.

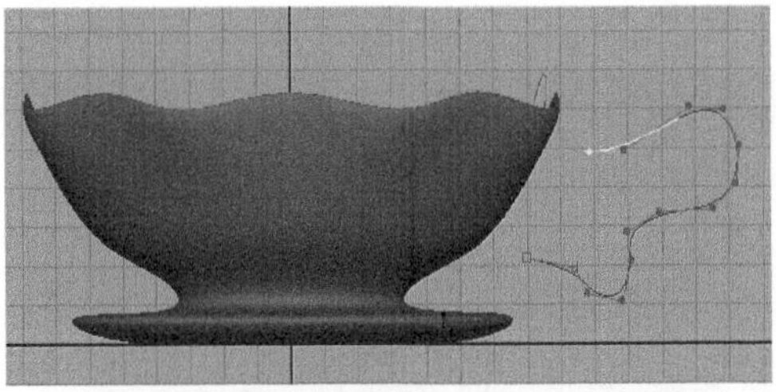

Figure 3-85 *The profile curve drawn*

3. Make sure the NURBS Circle is selected in the viewport. Set the parameters in the **nurbsCircle1** area of the **Channel Box / Layer Editor**, as shown in Figure 3-86.

4. In the **Channel Box / Layer Editor**, expand the **makeNurbCircle1** node in the **INPUTS** area and enter **0.2** in the **Radius** edit box.

5. Choose the **Four View** button from the Tool Box to switch to four views. Move the cursor to the persp viewport and then press the SPACEBAR key to maximize the persp viewport.

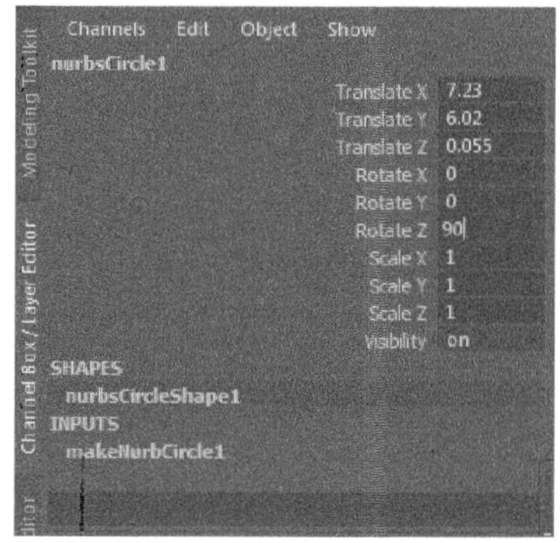

Figure 3-86** The **nurbsCircle1** area in the **Channel Box / Layer Editor

6. Make sure the NURBS circle is selected and then select the profile curve using the SHIFT key. Next, choose **Surfaces > Create > Extrude** from the menubar; the extruded surface is created, refer to Figure 3-87. Next, select the extruded surface. In the **extrude1** tab of the **Attribute Editor**, make sure the **Component Pivot** is selected from the **Use Component Pivot** drop-down list.

7. Choose **Move Tool** and **Rotate Tool** to adjust the handle with the tea cup to get the final output, as shown in Figure 3-88.

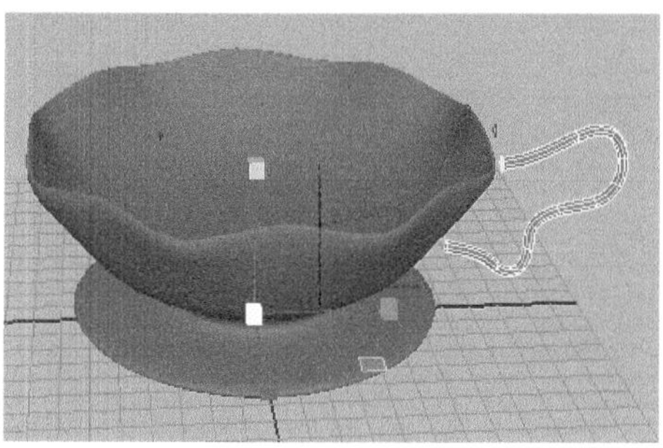

***Figure 3-87** The extruded surface displayed*

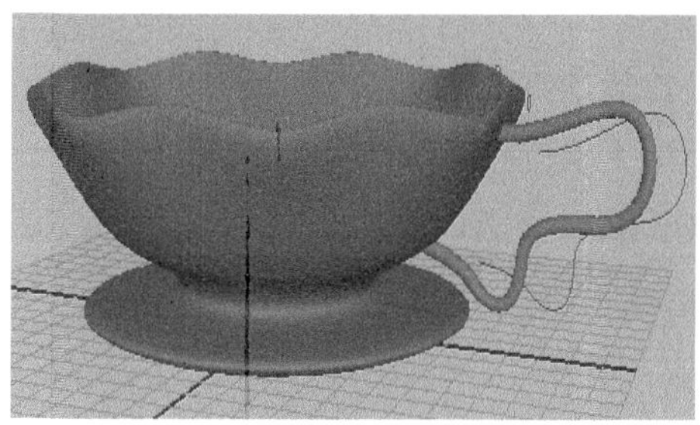

***Figure 3-88** Final output of the cup*

Changing the Background Color of the Scene

In this section, you will change the background color of the scene.

1. Choose **Windows > Editors > Outliner** from the menubar; the **Outliner** window is displayed. Select the **persp** camera in the **Outliner** window; the **perspShape** tab is displayed in the **Attribute Editor**.

2. In the **perspShape** tab, expand the **Environment** area and drag the **Background Color** slider bar toward right to change the background color to white.

Saving and Rendering the Scene

In this section, you will save the scene that you have created and then render it. You can view the final rendered image of the scene by downloading the *c03_maya_2017_rndr.zip* file from *www.cadcim.com*. The path of the file is mentioned in Tutorial 1.

1. Choose **File > Save Scene** from the menubar.

2. Maximize the persp viewport, if it is not already maximized. Choose the **Render the current frame** button from the Status Line; the **Render View** window is displayed. This window shows the final output of the scene, refer to Figure 3-77.

Self-Evaluation Test

Answer the following questions and then compare them to those given at the end of this chapter:

1. Which of the following objects has a circular base and sides tapered to a point?

    (a) **Cone** (b) **Cylinder**
    (c) **Torus** (d) **Square**

2. Which of the following objects has every point equidistant from its center?

    (a) **Plane** (b) **Circle**
    (c) **Torus** (d) **Sphere**

3. The options in the _________ area are used to define the distribution of the knots on the curve.

4. NURBS stands for _________.

5. The default NURBS objects in Maya are grouped together under _________.

6. The _________ tool is used to create a surface around a profile curve along a selected axis.

7. You can switch from the wireframe mode to the object mode by pressing 4 on the keyboard. (T/F)

8. A cube is a two-dimensional shape with six square or rectangular sides. (T/F)

9. A square is a six-sided regular polygon with six equal sides and six right angles. (T/F)

10. The **Boundary** tool is used to create a surface by filling a surface between the boundary curves. (T/F)

Review Questions

Answer the following questions:

1. Which of the following is not a component of NURBS surface?

   (a) **Isoparm** (b) **Vertex**
   (c) **Hull** (d) **Surface patch**

2. Which of the following tools works similar to the brush tool in other software?

   (a) **EP Curve Tool** (b) **CV Curve Tool**
   (c) **Pencil Curve Tool** (d) **Arc Tool**

3. Which of the following keys is required to adjust the center pivot of an object?

   (a) SPACEBAR (b) HOME
   (c) CTRL (d) INSERT

4. __________ is a four-sided regular polygon with equal sides.

5. The __________ option is used to determine whether the direction of the surface created will be linear or cubic.

6. __________ is the addition of surface between two or more specified curves.

7. The __________ option is used to create a sphere with a faceted or a smooth appearance.

8. The __________ is a solid object in which the surface is at an equal distance from the center.

9. The **Square** tool is used to create a surface from the intersecting NURBS curves. (T/F)

10. The NURBS curves which are used to create the NURBS surfaces by using the **Loft** tool, should have curves with equal number of vertices. (T/F)

EXERCISES

The rendered output of the models used in the following exercises can be accessed by downloading the *c03_maya_2017_exr.zip* file from *www.cadcim.com*. The path of the file is as follows: *Textbooks > Animation and Visual Effects > Maya > Autodesk Maya 2017: A Comprehensive Guide.*

Exercise 1

Create the model of an apple, as shown in Figure 3-89. **(Expected time: 15 min)**

Figure 3-89 *Model of an apple*

Exercise 2

Create the model of a lantern, as shown in Figure 3-90. **(Expected time: 15 min)**

Figure 3-90 *Model of a lantern*

Exercise 3

Create the model of a castle, as shown in Figure 3-91. **(Expected time: 30 min)**

Figure 3-91 Model of a castle

Exercise 4

Create the model of a candle stand, as shown in Figure 3-92. **(Expected time: 15 min)**

Exercise 5

Create the model of a table, as shown in Figure 3-93. **(Expected time: 15 min)**

Figure 3-92 Model of a candle stand

Figure 3-93 Model of a Table

Answers to Self-Evaluation Test

1. a, **2.** d, **3. Knot Spacing**, **4.** Non uniform rational B-Spline, **5.** NURBS Primitives, **6. Revolve**, **7.** F, **8.** F, **9.** F, **10.** T

Chapter 4

NURBS Modeling

Learning Objectives

After completing this chapter, you will be able to:

- *Understand NURBS editing techniques*
- *Convert NURBS objects to polygons*

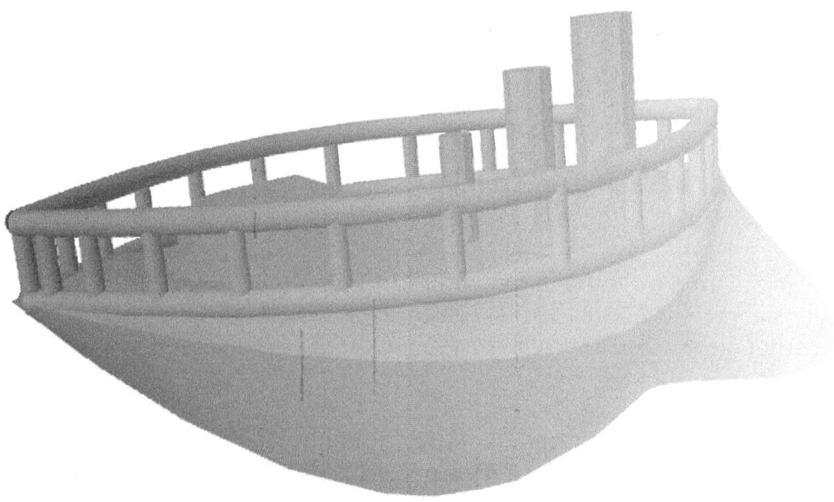

INTRODUCTION

NURBS stands for Non Uniform Rational B-Spline. NURBS are used for creating 3D curves and surfaces, and complex 3D organic models having smooth surfaces and curves. In the previous chapter, you have learned about different methods of creating NURBS surfaces. In this chapter, you will learn about various editing techniques used for modifying NURBS surfaces.

WORKING WITH NURBS TOOLS

The NURBS tools are used to edit NURBS surfaces. The most commonly used tools in NURBS modeling are discussed next.

Duplicate NURBS Patch

Menubar: Surfaces > Edit NURBS Surfaces > Duplicate NURBS Patch

The **Duplicate NURBS Patch** tool is used to create new surface from an existing NURBS patch. To understand the working of this tool, choose **Create > Objects > NURBS Primitives > Sphere** from the menubar and create a NURBS sphere in the viewport. Press and hold the right mouse button over the sphere and then choose **Surface Patch** from the marking menu displayed, as shown in Figure 4-1; the surface patch component of the NURBS sphere will be activated. Now, select the surface patch that you want to duplicate. Choose **Surface > Edit NURBS Surfaces > Duplicate NURBS Patch** from the menubar; a duplicate surface patch will be created. Invoke **Move Tool** from the Tool Box and move the duplicate surface patch away from the NURBS sphere. Note that the pivot point of the duplicate surface patch will remain at the same position as that of the NURBS sphere. To reset the pivot point to the center of the duplicate patch, choose **Modify > Pivot > Center Pivot** from the menubar; the pivot point will be reset.

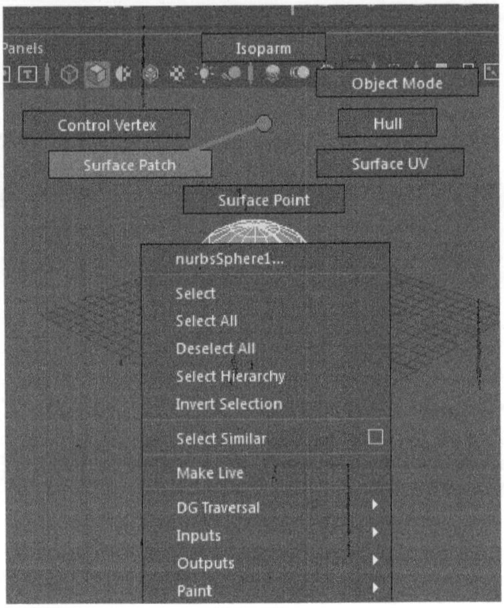

*Figure 4-1 Choosing **Surface Patch** from the marking menu*

Project Curve on Surface

Menubar: Surfaces > Edit NURBS Surfaces > Project Curve on Surface

The **Project Curve on Surface** tool is used to project a NURBS curve on a NURBS surface. To understand the working of this tool, choose **Create > Objects > NURBS Primitives > Square** from the menubar and create a square in the front-Z viewport. Now, choose **Surfaces > Create > Planar** from the menubar to create a NURBS surface. Next, choose **Create > Curve Tools > EP Curve Tool** from the menubar to create a curve, as shown in Figure 4-2 and make sure the NURBS curve is selected. Press and hold the SHIFT key and select the NURBS surface. Now, choose **Surface > Edit NURBS Surfaces > Project Curve on Surface** from the menubar to project the curve on the surface and activate the persp viewport; the NURBS curve will be projected over the NURBS surface, as shown in Figure 4-3.

Note

The curve will be projected at the exact position as visible through the camera of that particular viewport.

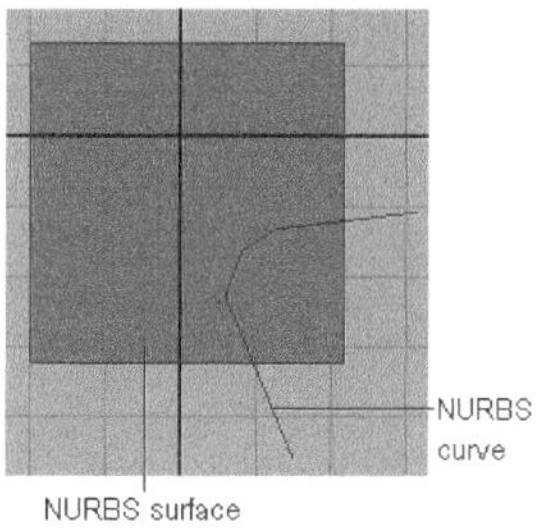

Figure 4-2 *The NURBS curve created*

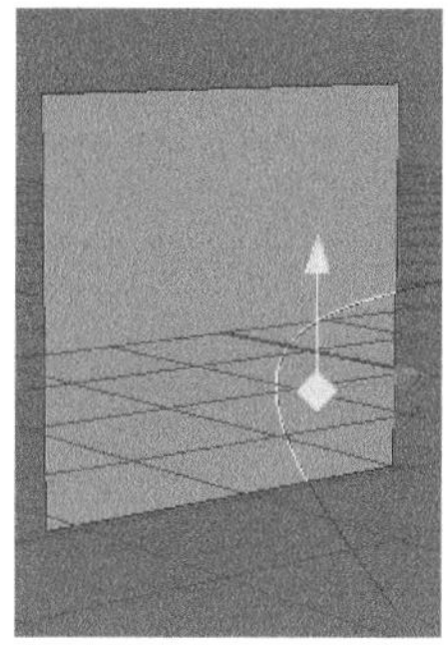

Figure 4-3 *The NURBS curve projected on the NURBS surface*

Intersect

Menubar: Surfaces > Edit NURBS Surfaces > Intersect

The **Intersect** tool is used to create a new segment at the intersection of two NURBS surfaces. To understand the working of this tool, create two surfaces, as discussed earlier, and align them such that they intersect each other, refer to Figure 4-4. Select both the surfaces and choose **Surfaces > Edit NURBS Surfaces > Intersect** from the menubar to create a new segment at the location where the two plane intersect. Choose the **Move Tool** from the Tool Box; the selection handles will be displayed at the intersection point, refer to Figure 4-4. You can now move these handles to align the intersection point anywhere on the NURBS surface.

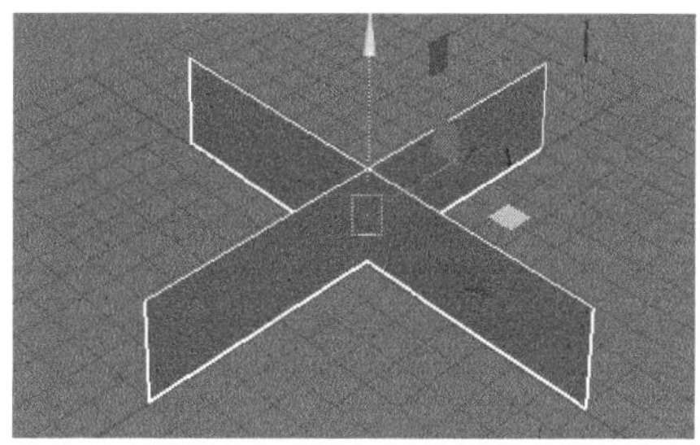

Figure 4-4 *The aligned surfaces and selection handles*

Trim Tool

Menubar: Surfaces > Edit NURBS Surfaces > Trim Tool

The **Trim Tool** is used to hide a particular area from the NURBS surface defined by curves. To understand the working of this tool, project a curve on a surface, as discussed in the **Project Curve on Surface** section. Next, select the NURBS surface in the viewport and choose **Surfaces > Edit NURBS Surfaces > Trim Tool** from the menubar; the NURBS surface will be displayed in the wireframe mode with a dotted outline. Select the part that you want to retain from the surface and press ENTER; the surface will be trimmed. You can also change the settings of **Trim Tool** as required. To retain the selected part from the NURBS surface and trim the unselected part from the NURBS surface, choose **Surfaces > Edit NURBS Surfaces > Trim Tool > Option Box** from the menubar; the **Tool Settings (Trim Tool)** window will be displayed on the viewport, as shown in Figure 4-5. The **Keep** radio button is used. The **Discard** radio button is used to trim the selected part from the NURBS surface and keep the unselected part intact.

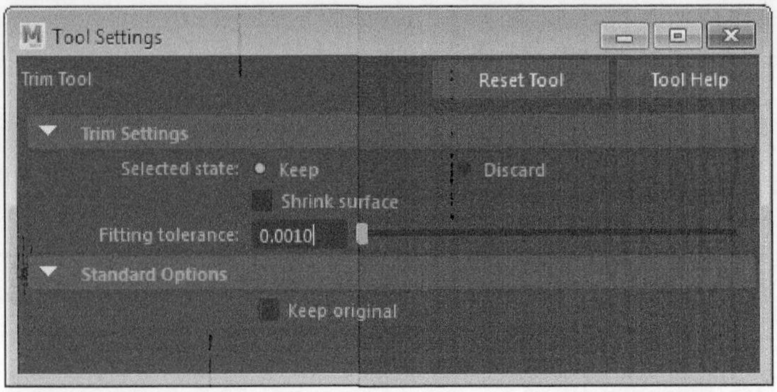

*Figure 4-5 The **Tool Settings (Trim Tool)** window*

Untrim

Menubar:	Surfaces > Edit NURBS Surfaces > Untrim

The **Untrim** tool is used to untrim the last trimmed surface. To understand the working of this tool, select the trimmed surface and choose **Surfaces > Edit NURBS Surfaces > Untrim** from the menubar; the surface sets back to its original untrimmed state.

Attach

Menubar:	Surfaces > Edit NURBS Surfaces > Attach

The **Attach** tool is used to attach two selected NURBS surfaces. To understand the working of this tool, create two NURBS surfaces in the viewport, as shown in Figure 4-6. Next, select the two surfaces and choose **Surface > Edit NURBS Surfaces > Attach > Option Box** from the menubar; the **Attach Surfaces Options** dialog box will be displayed, as shown in Figure 4-7. By default, the **Blend** radio button is selected in the **Attach method** area. Choose the **Apply** button; the selected surfaces will be connected, as shown in Figure 4-8. You can also select the **Connect** radio button from the **Attach** method area to connect the end of a surface to the end of another surface, as shown in Figure 4-9.

Figure 4-6 The two NURBS surfaces

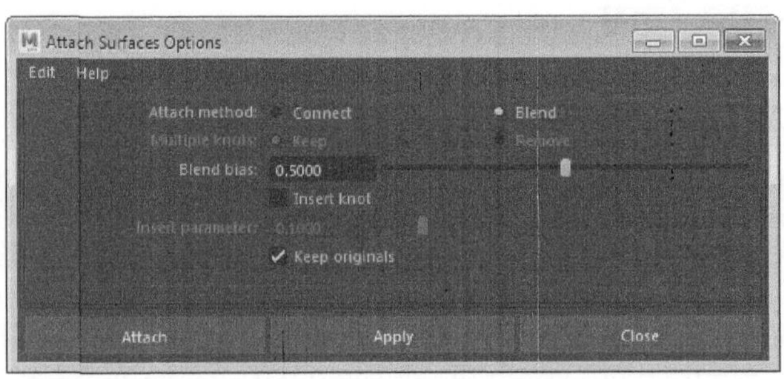

*Figure 4-7 The **Attach Surfaces Options** dialog box*

Note

*The **Attach Surfaces** tool does not attach trimmed surfaces. In such cases, surfaces need to be untrimmed before attaching them using this tool.*

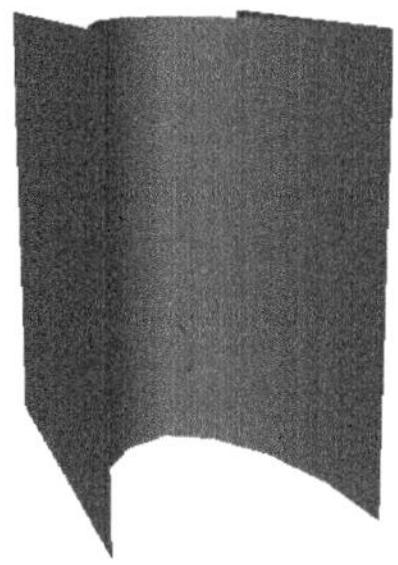

Figure 4-8 *Surfaces connected on selecting the **Blend** radio button*

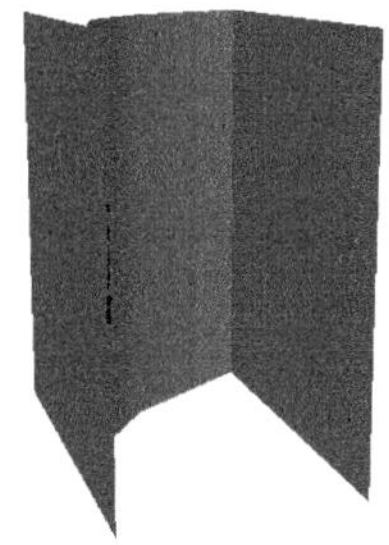

Figure 4-9 *The surfaces connected on selecting the **Connect** radio button*

Tip

*You can make changes in the attached surfaces by using the **attachSurface1** tab in the **Attribute Editor**. To do so, choose **Window > Editors > General Editors > Attribute Editor** from the menubar; the **Attribute Editor** will be displayed. Choose the **attachSurface#** tab from the **Attribute Editor**; the attributes of the attached surface will be displayed, as shown in Figure 4-10. You can apply different styles on the surface by using the parameters in the **Attribute Editor**.*

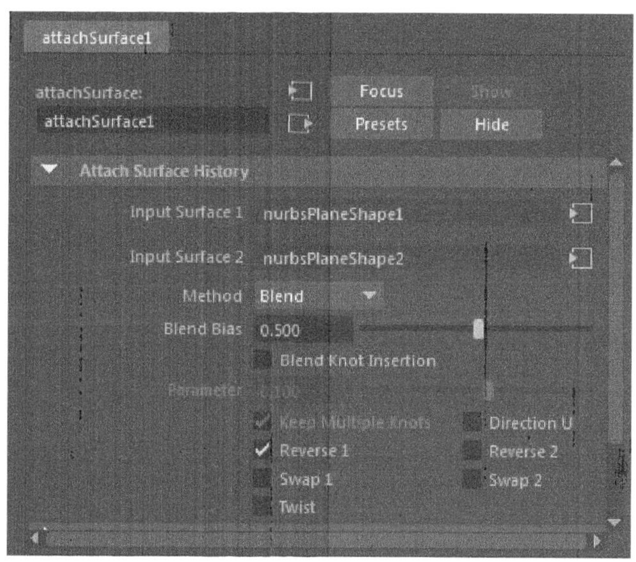

Figure 4-10 *The **attachSurface1** tab in the **Attribute Editor***

Attach Without Moving

Menubar: Surfaces > Edit NURBS Surfaces > Attach Without Moving

The **Attach Without Moving** tool is used to attach two NURBS surfaces or curves by selecting their respective isoparms. To understand the working of this tool, create two NURBS surfaces and select two isoparms, one each from the two surfaces. Now, choose **Surfaces > Edit NURBS**

Surfaces > Attach Without Moving from the menubar; the two surfaces will be attached along with the two isoparms.

Align

Menubar: Surfaces > Edit NURBS Surfaces > Align

The **Align** tool is used to align the selected NURBS surfaces tangentially. To understand the working of this tool, select the NURBS surfaces that you want to align. Choose **Surfaces > Edit NURBS Surfaces > Align > Option Box** from the menubar; the **Align Surfaces Options** dialog box will be displayed, as shown in Figure 4-11. Now, you can use different options in this dialog box to align the selected NURBS surfaces as required.

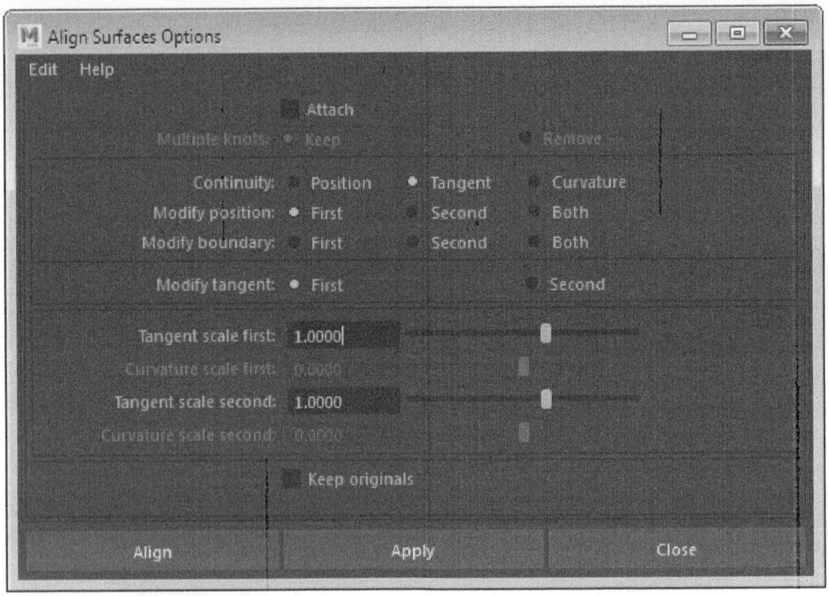

Figure 4-11 *The* ***Align Surfaces Options*** *dialog box*

Detach

Menubar: Surfaces > Edit NURBS Surfaces > Detach

The **Detach** tool is used to break NURBS surfaces into parts. To understand the working of this tool, select the isoparm of a surface and then choose **Surfaces > Edit NURBS Surfaces > Detach** from the menubar; the surface will get detached from the selected isoparm.

Open/Close

Menubar: Surfaces > Edit NURBS Surfaces > Open/Close

The **Open/Close** tool is used to open or close the NURBS surfaces. To open a closed surface, select the closed surface and choose **Surfaces > Edit NURBS Surfaces > Open/Close** from the menubar; the closed surface will be opened, as shown in Figure 4-12. Similarly, to close an open surface, select the opened surface in the viewport and choose **Surfaces > Edit NURBS**

Surfaces > Open/Close from the menubar; the opened surface will change into a closed surface, as shown in Figure 4-13.

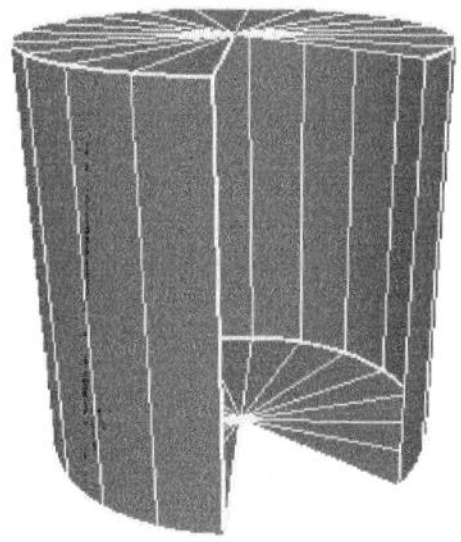

Figure 4-12 *The opened NURBS surface*

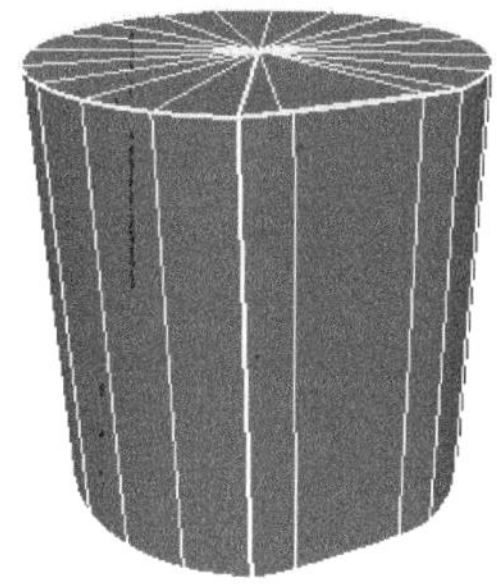

Figure 4-13 *The closed NURBS surface*

Extend

Menubar: Surfaces > Edit NURBS Surfaces > Extend

The **Extend** tool is used to extend a NURBS surface. To extend a NURBS surface, select a NURBS surface in the viewport. Then, press and hold the right mouse button on the NURBS surface and choose **Isoparm** from the marking menu displayed. Now, select the isoparm that you want to extend from the NURBS surface and choose **Surfaces > Edit NURBS Surfaces > Extend** from the menubar; the selected surface will be extended. To set the attributes of the extended surface, choose **Surfaces > Edit NURBS Surfaces > Extend > Option Box** from the menubar; the **Extend Surface Options** dialog box will be displayed, as shown in Figure 4-14. Modify the values in the dialog box to make changes in the working of the **Extend** tool. Figures 4-15 and 4-16 display a hut roof before and after using the **Extend** tool, respectively. Any change made in the original surface will also be displayed in the offset surface created.

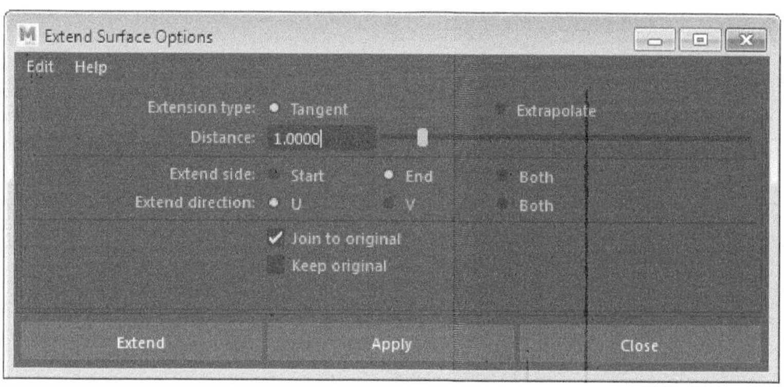

Figure 4-14 *The* ***Extend Surface Options*** *dialog box*

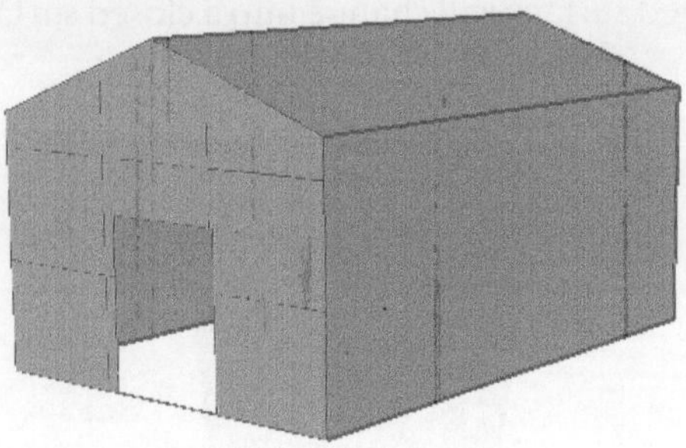

*Figure 4-15 The hut roof before using the **Extend Surfaces** tool*

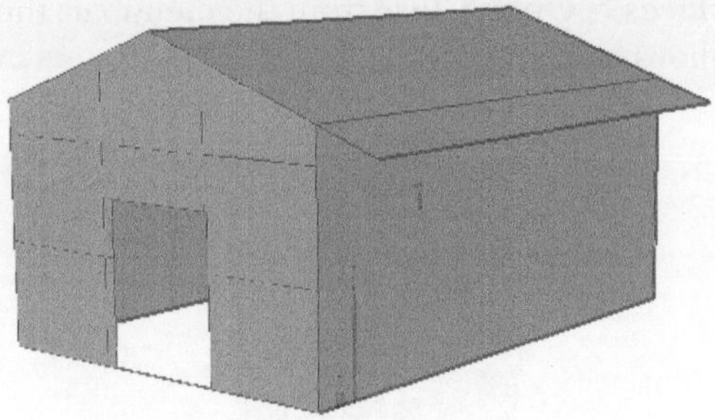

*Figure 4-16 The hut roof after using the **Extend Surfaces** tool*

Insert Isoparms

Menubar: Surfaces > Edit NURBS Surfaces > Insert Isoparms

The **Insert Isoparms** tool is used to insert an isoparm on a NURBS surface. To understand the working of this tool, select a NURBS surface. Next, press and hold the right mouse button on the NURBS surface and choose **Isoparm** from the marking menu; the isoparms will be highlighted on the selected NURBS object. Now, press and hold the left mouse button on any NURBS isoparm and drag the mouse to specify the position for the new isoparm; a yellow dotted line will appear over the NURBS surface, as shown in Figure 4-17. Next, choose **Surfaces > Edit NURBS Surfaces > Insert Isoparms** from the menubar; a new isoparm will be inserted in place of the yellow dotted line.

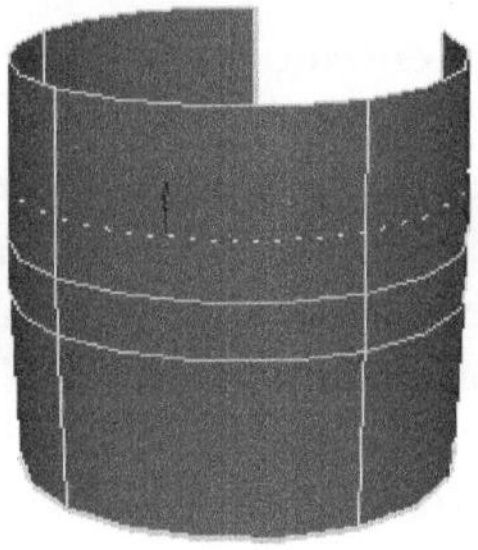

Figure 4-17 The yellow dotted line displayed on the NURBS surface

Tip

*To create multiple isoparms, press and hold the SHIFT key over a NURBS isoparm and then drag the mouse; multiple yellow dotted lines will appear on the NURBS surface. Now, choose **Surfaces > Edit NURBS Surfaces > Insert Isoparms** from the menubar; multiple isoparms will be created.*

Offset

Menubar: Surfaces > Edit NURBS Surfaces > Offset

The **Offset** tool is used to create a copy of the selected surface by creating an offset at a specified distance. To understand the working of this tool, select a NURBS surface in the viewport and then choose **Surfaces > Edit NURBS Surfaces > Offset** from the menubar; a copy of the selected NURBS surface will be created. To set the properties of the **Offset** tool, choose **Surfaces > Edit NURBS Surfaces > Offset > Option Box** from the menubar; the **Offset Surface Options** dialog box will be displayed, as shown in Figure 4-18. The **Offset distance** attribute in the dialog box is used to specify the distance of the copied surface from the original surface.

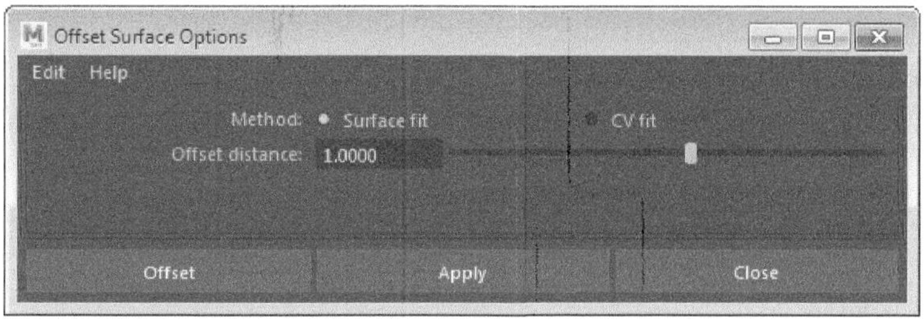

*Figure 4-18 The **Offset Surface Options** dialog box*

Rebuild

Menubar: Surfaces > Edit NURBS Surfaces > Rebuild

The **Rebuild** tool is used to rebuild the NURBS surface by changing the parameters of the surface, or by increasing or decreasing the number of U and V spans on a selected NURBS surface. To understand the working of this tool, select the NURBS surface that you want to rebuild and choose **Surfaces > Edit NURBS Surfaces > Rebuild > Option Box** from the menubar; the **Rebuild Surface Options** dialog box will be displayed, as shown in Figure 4-19. The options in this dialog box are discussed next.

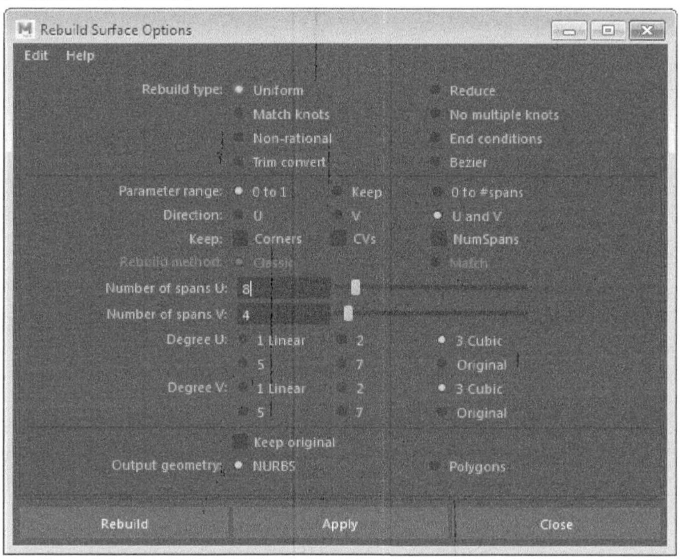

*Figure 4-19 The **Rebuild Surface Options** dialog box*

Rebuild type

The radio buttons corresponding to the **Rebuild type** attribute are used to select the rebuild type. On selecting a rebuild type, various options related to it are displayed in the dialog box. The various rebuild types are discussed next. You need to specify the **Rebuild type** attribute by choosing any of the following radio buttons:

Uniform

The **Uniform** radio button is used to rebuild the surface with uniform parameterization. On selecting this radio button, you can modify the number of U and V spans and their degree as required.

Reduce
The **Reduce** radio button is used to remove the knots from the selected NURBS surface.

Match knots
The **Match knots** radio button is used to match the curve degree, knot values, number of spans, and sections of other surfaces.

No multiple knots
The **No multiple knots** radio button is used to remove the extra knots formed while rebuilding a surface.

Non-rational
The **Non-rational** radio button is used to convert a rational surface into a non-rational surface.

End conditions
The **End conditions** radio button is used to rebuild the positioning of the CVs and knots of the selected NURBS surface.

Trim convert
The **Trim convert** radio button is used to convert a trimmed NURBS surface into a non-trim NURBS surface.

Bezier
The **Bezier** radio button is used to rebuild a NURBS surface as a bezier surface.

Parameter range
The radio buttons in the **Parameter range** attribute are used to specify how the U and V parameters will be affected while rebuilding a surface. These three radio buttons are discussed next.

0 to 1
The **0 to 1** radio button is used to specify the U and V parameters from 0 to 1 of the rebuild surface.

Keep
The **Keep** radio button is used to match the U and V parameters with that of the original surface.

0 to #spans
The **0 to #spans** radio button is used to get the rebuild surface spans to have integers knot values.

Direction
The radio buttons in this area are used to determine the parametric direction of the surface for removing the knots in the **U**, **V**, or both **U** and **V** directions.

Keep

The **Keep** attribute is used to ensure that some particular characteristics of the original object or surface are retained while creating a new surface. Select the **Corners**, **CVs** or **NumSpans** radio button to retain the corresponding characteristics.

Rebuild Method

The **Rebuild Method** radio buttons are activated only when the **Match Knots** radio button is selected from the **Rebuild type** parameter. The radio buttons in this area are used to rebuild the surface by specifying the quality of the new surface. Select the **Classic** radio button to get the surface quality similar to that obtained with the version 5.0 and earlier versions of Maya. Select the **Match** radio button to get a better quality for surfaces having multiple knots at the end.

Number of spans U and Number of spans V

The **Number of spans U** and **Number of spans V** options are used to set the number of spans in the U and V directions of the rebuilt surface respectively.

Degree U and Degree V

The **Degree U** and **Degree V** attributes are used to set the degree of the rebuilt surface.

Keep original

The **Keep original** check box is used to keep the original surface and rebuild a new surface.

Use tolerance

The **Use tolerance** area will be available only on selecting the **Non-Rational** or **Reduce** radio button in the **Rebuild type** area. The radio buttons in this area are used to set the distance between a point on the original and rebuilt surfaces. The **Global** radio button is used to set the positional value as the original value. The **Local** radio button is used to enter the tolerance value manually. The smaller the tolerance value, the more the rebuild surface will resemble the original surface.

Output geometry

The **Output geometry** attribute is used to specify the geometry type for the rebuilt surface. You can select the **NURBS** or **Polygons** radio button to specify the output geometry.

Reverse Direction

Menubar: Surfaces > Edit NURBS Surfaces > Reverse Direction

The **Reverse Direction** tool is used to reverse or swap the U and V directions of a selected surface. To understand the working of this tool, select a NURBS surface in the viewport and then choose **Surfaces > Edit NURBS Surfaces > Reverse Direction > Option Box** from the menubar; the **Reverse Surface Direction Options** dialog box will be displayed, as shown in Figure 4-20. Select the required radio button from the **Surface direction** area of this dialog box and then choose the **Reverse** button to reverse or swap the surface direction.

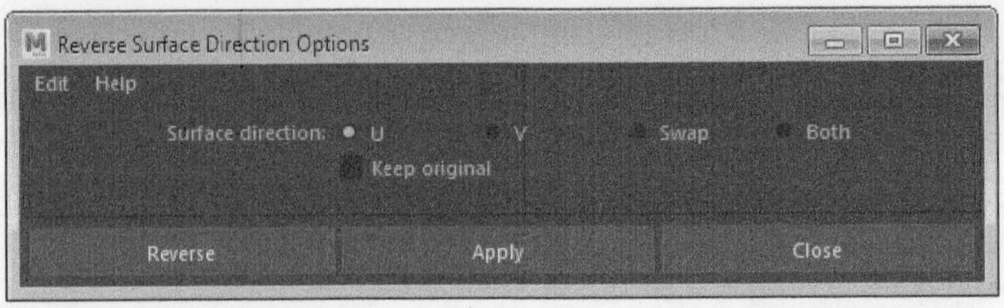

Figure 4-20 The ***Reverse Surface Direction Options*** *dialog box*

Sculpt Geometry Tool

Menubar:	Surfaces > Edit NURBS Surfaces > Sculpt Geometry Tool

The **Sculpt Geometry Tool** is used to sculpt a NURBS or polygon object manually in the viewport. On invoking this tool, the cursor will change into a brush icon. To sculpt an object, select the NURBS surface in the viewport and choose **Surfaces > Edit NURBS Surfaces > Sculpt Geometry Tool > Option Box** from the menubar; the **Tool Settings (Sculpt Geometry Tool)** window will be displayed on the viewport, as shown in Figure 4-21.

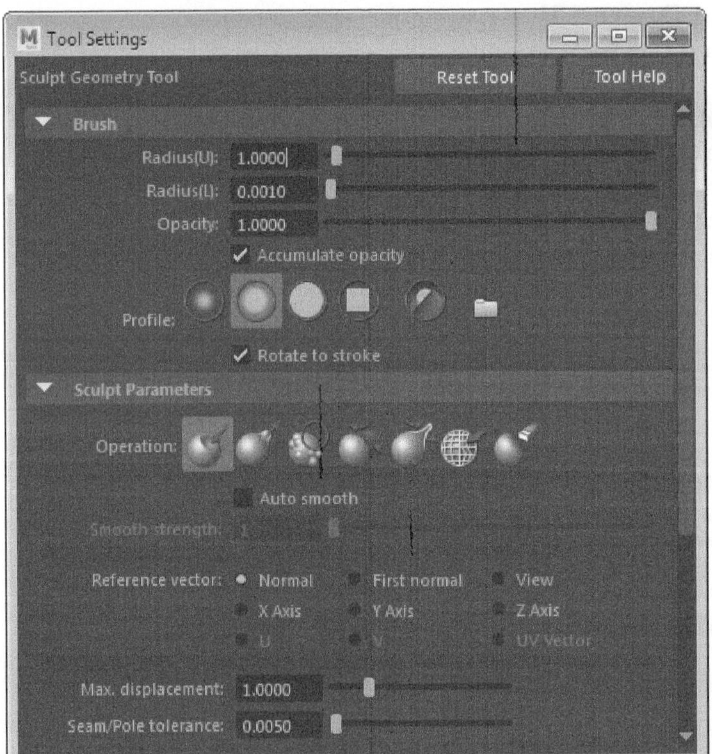

Figure 4-21 Partial view of the ***Tool Settings (Sculpt Geometry Tool)*** *window*

The more the number of segments on an object, the better sculpting can be done on it using the **Sculpt Geometry Tool**. You can sculpt an object using seven different options: **Push**, **Pull**, **Smooth**, **Relax**, **Pinch**, **Slide** and **Erase**. All these methods are discussed next.

Push

The **Push** option is used to push down the selected NURBS mesh. To do so, create a NURBS plane in the viewport. Next, choose **Surfaces > Edit NURBS Surfaces > Sculpt Geometry Tool > Option Box** from the menubar; the **Tool Settings (Sculpt Geometry Tool)** window will be displayed on the viewport, refer to Figure 4-21. Choose the **Push** button in the **Sculpt Parameters** area; the cursor will be displayed, as shown in Figure 4-22. Press and hold the left mouse button and move the cursor over the NURBS plane to sculpt the NURBS plane. Figure 4-23 shows a NURBS plane before sculpting and Figure 4-24 shows the NURBS plane sculpted using the **Push** tool.

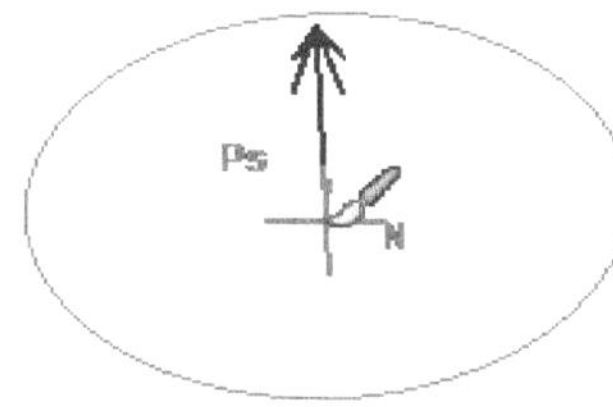

Figure 4-22 *The **Sculpt Geometry Tool** cursor*

Figure 4-23 *The NURBS plane before sculpting*

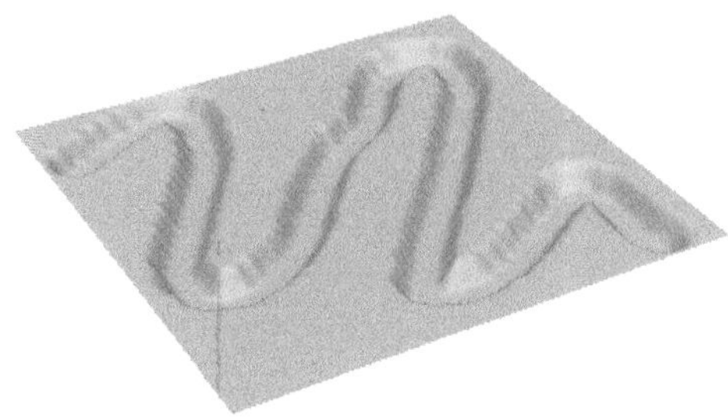

Figure 4-24 *The NURBS plane sculpted using the **Push** tool*

Pull

The **Pull** tool is used to pull the NURBS mesh from the surface. This tool works similar to the **Push** tool and the method to apply it on a NURBS plane is same as that of the **Push** tool. Figure 4-25 shows a NURBS plane sculpted using the **Pull** tool.

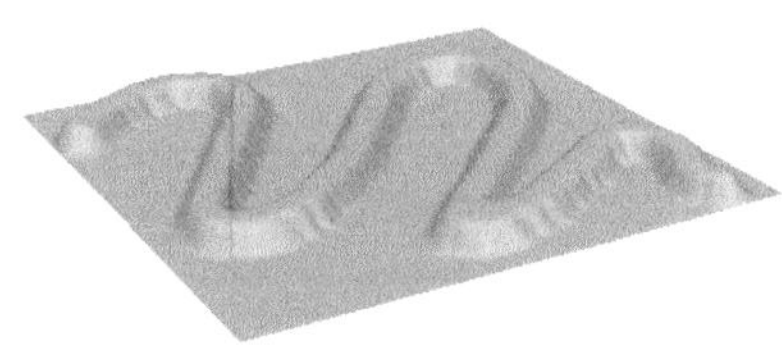

Figure 4-25 *The NURBS plane sculpted using the **Pull** tool*

Smooth

The **Smooth** tool is used to paint on a mesh to give it a smoother look. To use this tool, follow the same procedure as discussed in the **Push** tool and choose the **Smooth** button from the **Sculpt Parameters** area of the **Tool Settings (Sculpt Geometry Tool)** window. Figure 4-26 shows a surface before smoothening and Figure 4-27 shows the surface after smoothening.

Relax

The **Relax** tool works similar to the **Smooth** tool. It is used to relax the bumps over the surface, thus maintaining the overall shape of the mesh.

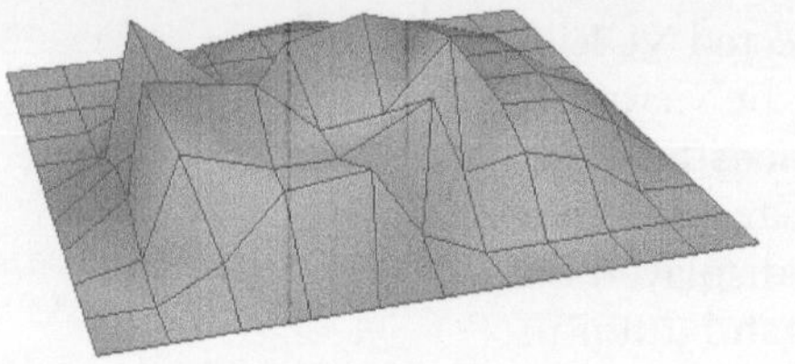

Figure 4-26 Surface before smoothening

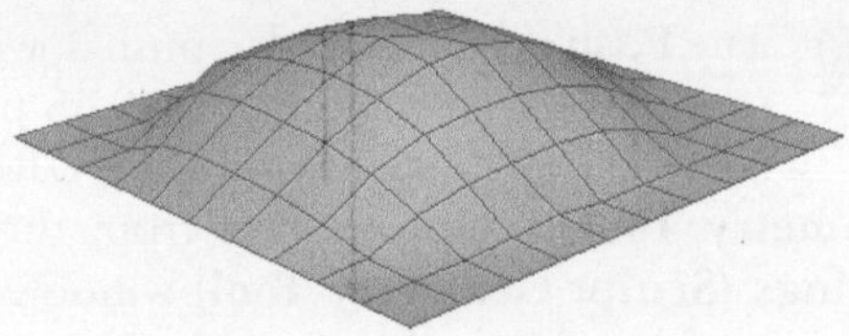

Figure 4-27 Surface after smoothening

Pinch

The **Pinch** tool is used to pull selected vertices toward each other. It helps in bringing the vertices closer in order to make sharp or well defined creases.

Slide

The **Slide** tool is used to slide the vertices of the surface in the direction of the stroke Figure 4-28 shows a surface before sliding the vertices and Figure 4-29 shows the surface after sliding the vertices.

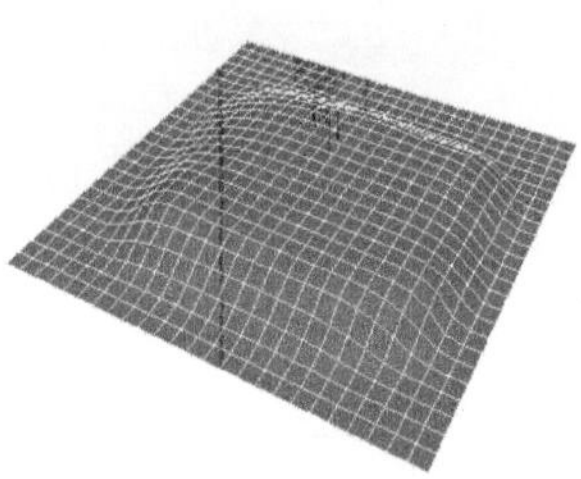

Figure 4-28 Surface before sliding

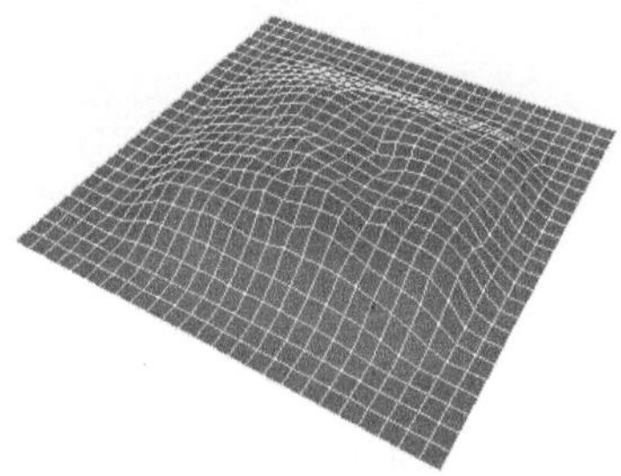

Figure 4-29 Surface after sliding

Erase

The **Erase** tool is used to erase the changes made on the surface by using the other **Sculpt Geometry** tools like **Push** or **Pull**. Figure 4-30 shows a surface before erasing changes on it and Figure 4-31 shows the surface after erasing changes on it.

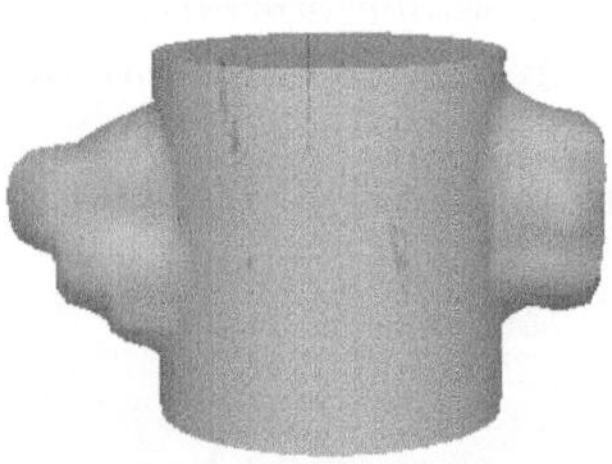

Figure 4-30 Surface before erasing

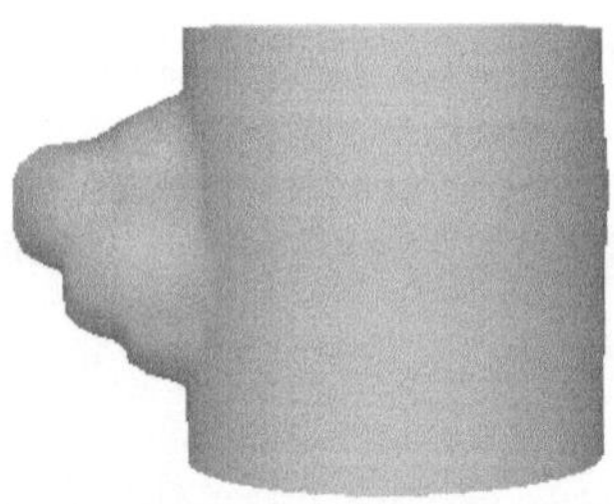

Figure 4-31 Surface after erasing

CONVERTING OBJECTS

In Maya, you can convert an object from one form to another. To do so, select an object in the viewport and choose **Modify > Objects > Convert** from the menubar; a cascading menu will be displayed. Choose the conversion type from the cascading menu to specify the output geometry for the selected object. The most commonly used options in this cascading menu are discussed next.

Converting NURBS to Polygons

Menubar:	Modify > Objects > Convert > NURBS to Polygons

The **NURBS to Polygons** conversion tool is used to convert a NURBS mesh into a polygonal object. To do so, select a NURBS mesh to be converted and then choose **Modify > Objects Convert > NURBS to Polygons > Option Box** from the menubar; the **Convert NURBS to Polygons Options** dialog box will be displayed in the viewport, as shown in Figure 4-32. You can use this dialog box to set the options for the conversion of the object from NURBS to polygons. Some of the options in this dialog box are discussed next.

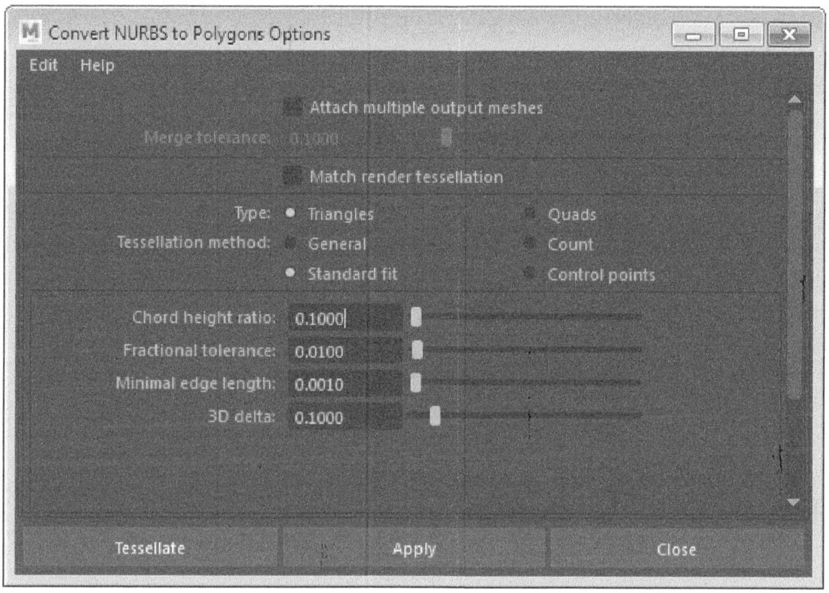

Figure 4-32 The ***Convert NURBS to Polygons Options*** *dialog box*

Type

The **Type** attribute is used to set the output of the geometry after the conversion has taken place. If you select the **Triangles** radio button, then three-sided polygons will be created on the surface, as shown in Figure 4-33. If you select the **Quads** radio button, then four-sided polygons will be created on the surface, as shown in Figure 4-34.

Tessellation method

The **Tessellation method** attribute is used to convert a NURBS mesh into a set of polygons. In Maya, there are four tessellation methods that are discussed next. You can select a radio button corresponding to this parameter to specify the tessellation method to be used.

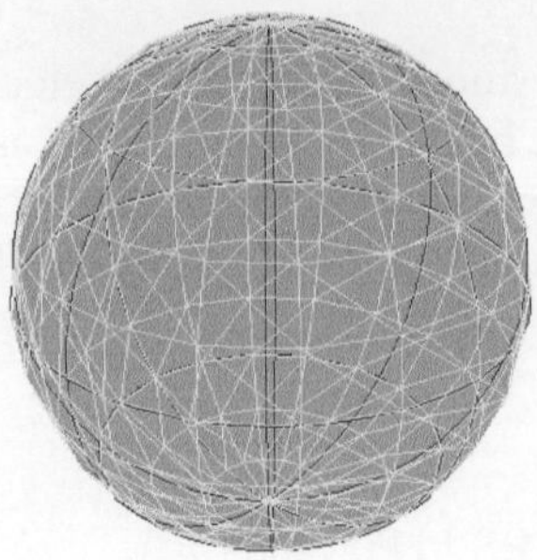

Figure 4-33 Surface created on selecting the ***Triangles*** *polygon type radio button*

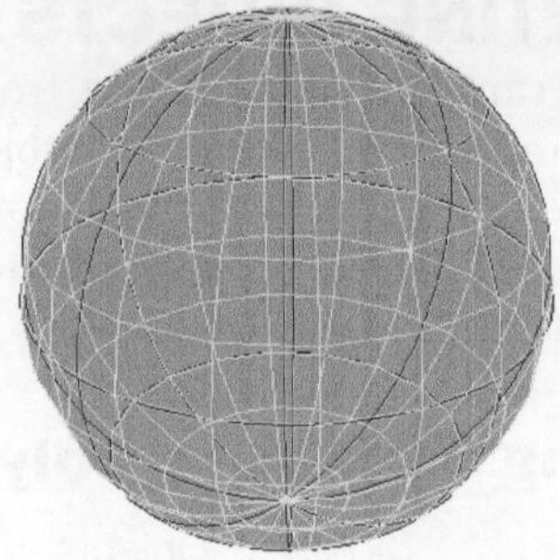

Figure 4-34 Surface created on selecting the ***Quads*** *polygon type radio button*

General

The **General** radio button is used to define the number of polygons in the U or in the V direction. On selecting this radio button, various options for setting the tessellation are displayed.

Standard fit

The **Standard fit** radio button is selected by default. This method is used to determine when to stop the tessellation by setting the fractional tolerance value. On selecting this radio button, the options related to it are displayed.

Count

The **Count** radio button is used to specify the polygon count in the mesh after the mesh has been converted into polygons. The more the count value, the smoother will be the object.

Control points

The **Control points** radio button is used to create a new mesh while matching its CVs to the original NURBS surface. The resulting polygons will be quads by default.

Converting NURBS to Subdiv

Menubar: Modify > Objects > Convert > NURBS to Subdiv

The **NURBS to Subdiv** conversion tool is used to convert a NURBS mesh into a subdiv mesh. To do so, select the NURBS object in the viewport and choose **Modify > Objects > Convert > NURBS to Subdiv > Option Box** from the menubar; the **Convert NURBS/Polygons to Subdiv Options** dialog box will be displayed, as shown in Figure 4-35. Some of the options in the **Convert NURBS/Polygons to Subdiv Options** dialog box are discussed next.

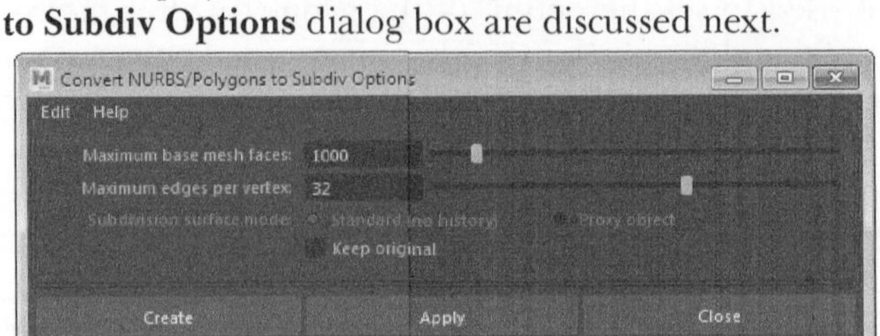

Figure 4-35 The ***Convert NURBS/Polygons to Subdiv Options*** *dialog box*

Maximum base mesh faces

The **Maximum base mesh faces** attribute is used to set the maximum number of faces that the original surface can have, such that it can be successfully converted into a subdivision surface.

Maximum edges per vertex

The **Maximum edges per vertex** attribute is used to set the maximum number of edges that each vertex can have in the original surface, such that it can be successfully converted into a subdivision surface.

Keep original

The **Keep original** check box is used to keep the original NURBS object mesh after creating the new subdivision surface.

TUTORIALS

Tutorial 1

In this tutorial, you will create the model of a cowboy hat, as shown in Figure 4-36, using NURBS. **(Expected time: 15 min)**

Figure 4-36 *The model of a cowboy hat*

The following steps are required to complete this tutorial:

a. Create a project folder.
b. Create a NURBS cylinder.
c. Add details to the hat.
d. Change background color of the scene.
e. Save and render the scene.

Creating a Project Folder

Create a new project folder with the name *c04_tut1* at *\Documents\maya2017* and then save the file with the name *c04tut1*, as discussed in Tutorial 1 of Chapter 2.

Creating a NURBS Cylinder

In this section, you will create a NURBS cylinder to form the base structure of the cowboy hat.

1. Maximize the top-Y viewport and then choose **Create > Objects > NURBS Primitives > Cylinder** from the menubar and create a cylinder in the viewport.

2. Rename **nurbsCylinder1** to *hat*. Next, in the **Channel Box / Layer Editor**, expand the **makeNurbCylinder1** node and set parameters, as shown in Figure 4-37.

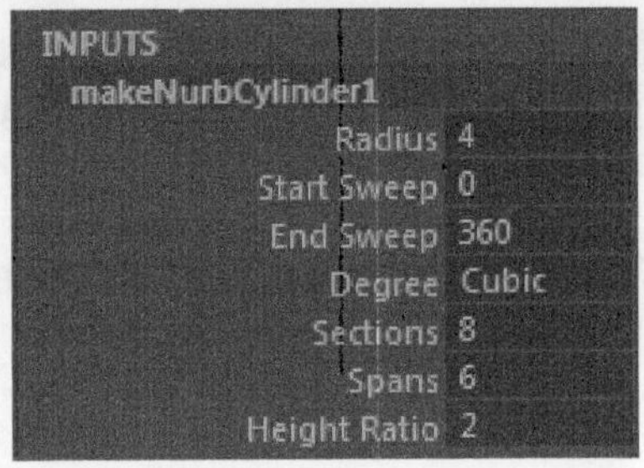

Figure 4-37 The INPUTS node

3. In the front-Z viewport, press and hold the right mouse button on the *hat*; a marking menu is displayed. Choose **Control Vertex** from the marking menu; the vertex selection mode is activated. Now, select the vertices, as shown in Figure 4-38. Next, invoke **Scale Tool** from the Tool Box and scale up the vertices uniformly in the front-Z viewport, as shown in Figure 4-39.

4. Make sure the vertices of *hat* are selected. Select the green handle of **Scale Tool** and scale the selected vertices downward along the Y-axis; the mesh gets modified, as shown in Figure 4-40.

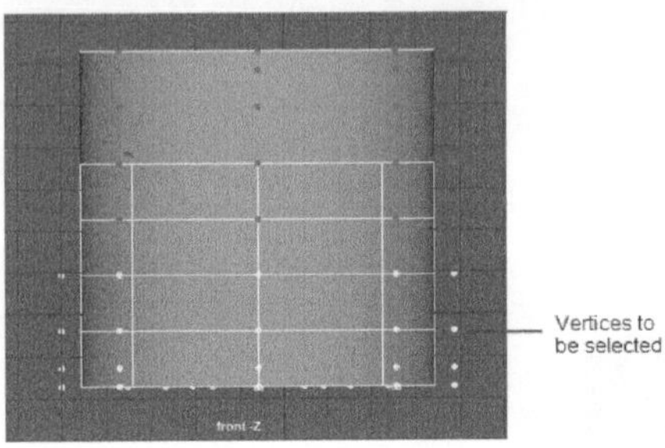

Figure 4-38 *Vertices to be selected*

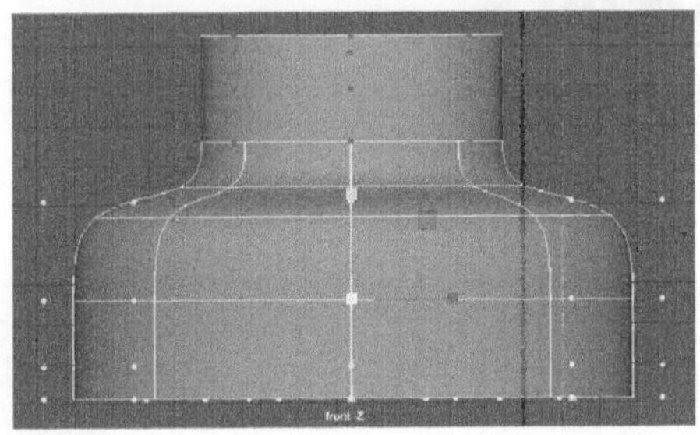

Figure 4-39 *Scaling the selected vertices uniformly*

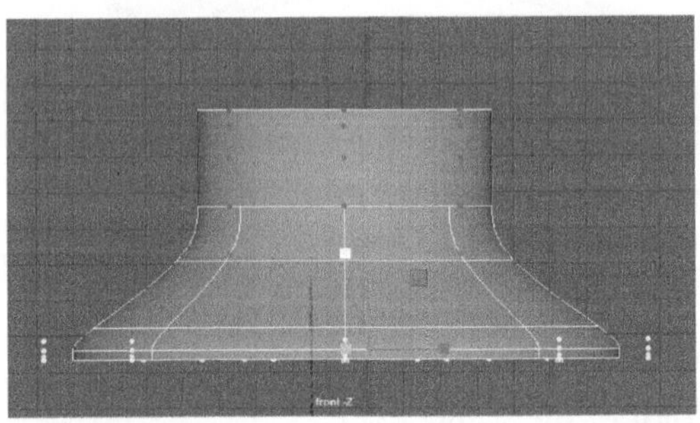

Figure 4-40 *Scaling the selected vertices along the Y axis*

Adding Details to the Hat

In this section, you will add details to the hat to give it the look of a cowboy hat.

1. Maximize the top-Y viewport. Next, press and hold the SHIFT key and marquee-select the vertices, refer to Figure 4-41. Choose **Scale Tool** from the Tool Box, and scale the selected vertices inward along the Z-axis using the yellow handle; the mesh gets scaled, as shown in Figure 4-42.

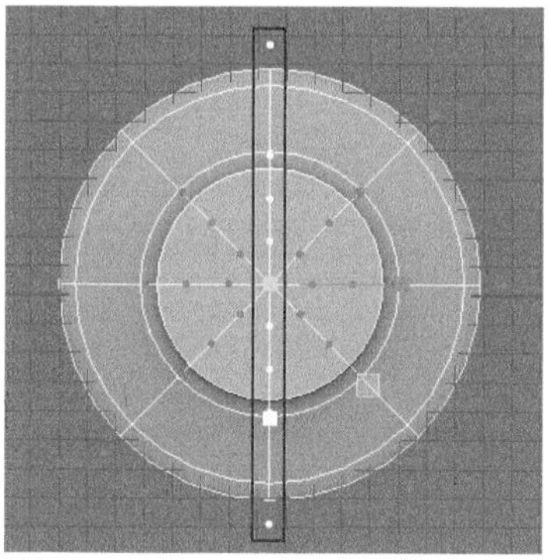

Figure 4-41 The vertices selected

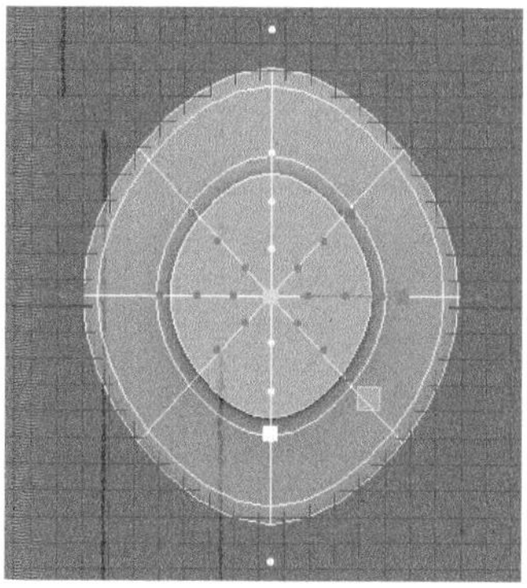

Figure 4-42 Scaled mesh

2. Maximize the side-X viewport. Next, marquee-select the vertices using the SHIFT key, as shown in Figure 4-43. Next, choose **Move Tool** and move the vertices downward along the Y-axis, as shown in Figure 4-44.

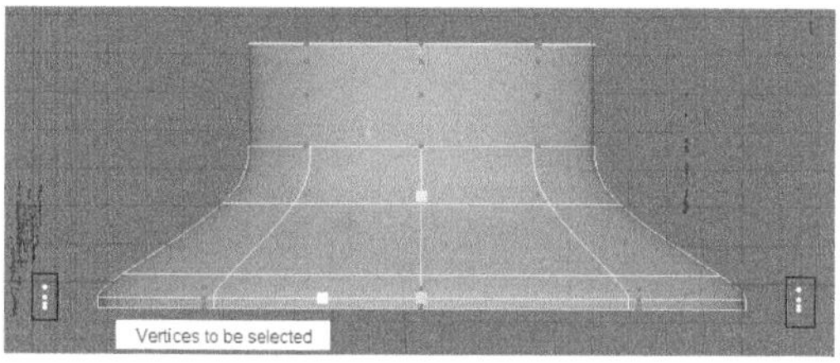

Figure 4-43 Vertices to be selected

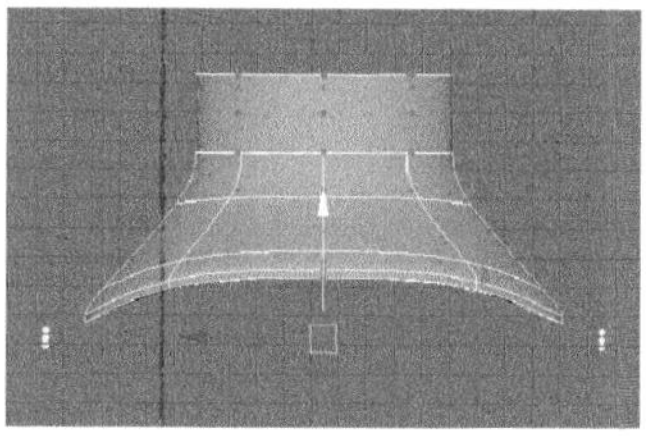

Figure 4-44 The modified mesh after moving the vertices

3. Maximize the persp viewport. Press and hold the right mouse button over the lower part of *hat*; a marking menu is displayed. Next, choose **Object Mode** from the marking menu; the object selection mode is activated.

4. Select the model in the persp viewport. Next, press and hold the right mouse button over the lower part of *hat* and choose **Isoparm** from the marking menu; the color of the edges of *hat* changes to blue.

5. In the persp viewport, select the isoparm, as shown in Figure 4-45. Drag the isoparm outward; a dotted isoparm is displayed on *hat*. Next, choose the **Modeling** menuset from the **Menuset** drop-down list in the Status Line and then choose **Surfaces > Insert Isoparms** from the menubar; a new isoparm is added, as shown in Figure 4-46.

6. Make sure *hat* is selected. Next, choose **Edit > Delete > Delete All by Type > History** from the menubar; the history of all actions performed on the model is deleted.

7. Maximize the side-X viewport. Next, press and hold the right mouse button on *hat*; a marking menu is displayed. Choose **Control Vertex** from the marking menu; the vertex selection mode is activated. Next, marquee-select the vertices of *hat* by using the SHIFT key, as shown in Figure 4-47. Next, invoke **Move Tool** from the Tool Box, and move the vertices upward along the Y axis, as shown in Figure 4-48.

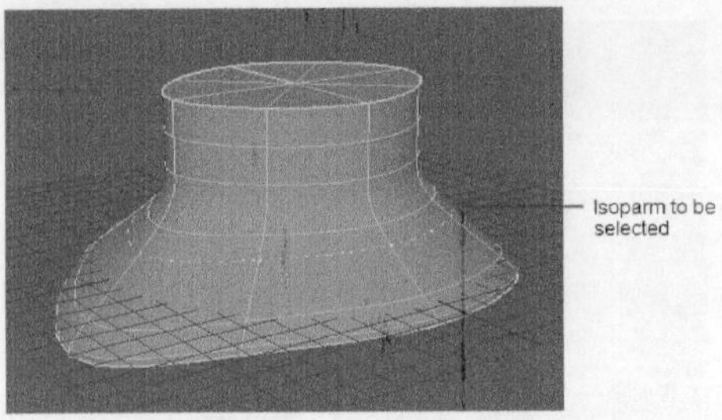

Figure 4-45 *Selecting an isoparm*

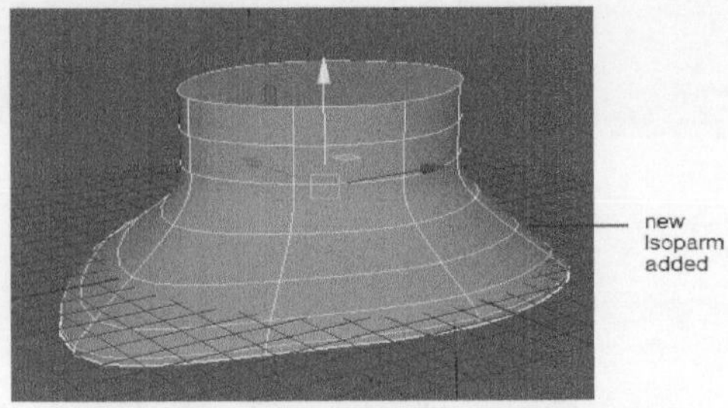

Figure 4-46 *A new isoparm added*

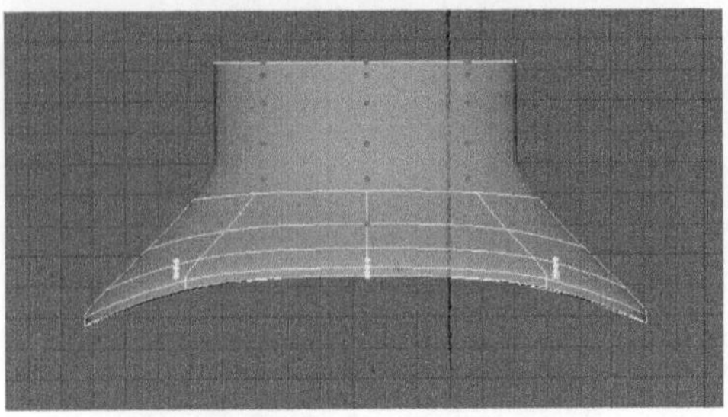

Figure 4-47 *Vertices to be selected*

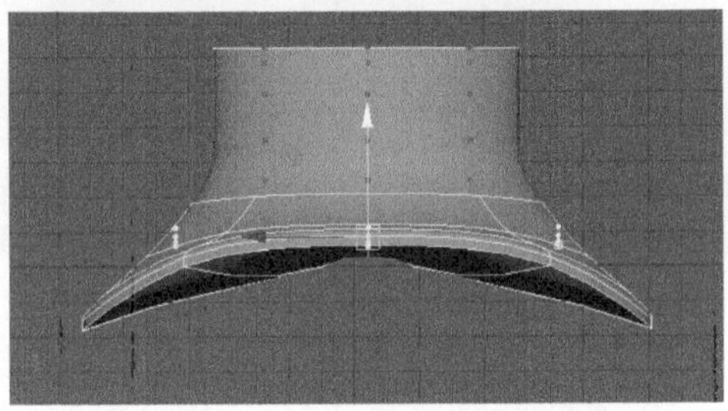

Figure 4-48 *The modified mesh*

8. Press and hold the right mouse button over *hat* and choose **Object Mode** from the marking menu displayed; the object selection mode is activated. Maximize the top-Y viewport. Choose **View > Predefined Bookmarks > Bottom** from the **Panel** menu; the bottom viewport is activated.

9. Insert two new isoparms on *hat*, as discussed in steps 4 and 5. Figure 4-49 displays two isoparms added to *hat* in bottom viewport.

10. Press and hold the right mouse button over the cylinder and choose **Control Vertex** from the marking menu displayed; the vertex selection mode is activated. Next, select the vertices using the SHIFT key, as shown in Figure 4-50.

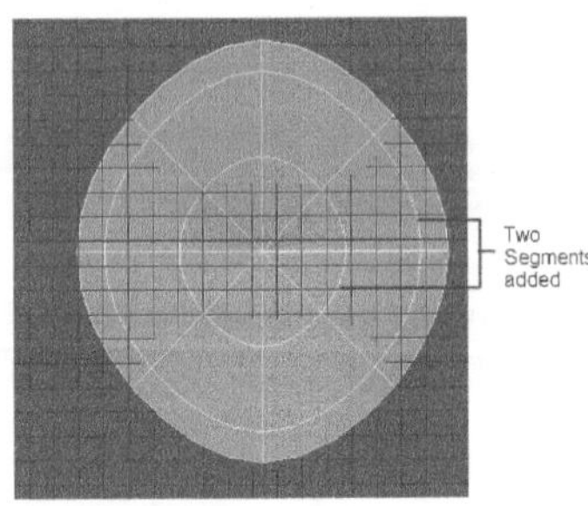

Figure 4-49 *The two new isoparms added*

11. Choose **View > Predefined Bookmarks > Right Side** from the **Panel** menu; the right side-X viewport is activated. Choose **Move Tool** from the Tool Box and move the selected vertices upward along the Y axis to get the final output, refer to Figure 4-51.

Changing the Background Color of the Scene

In this section, you will change the background color of the scene.

1. Choose **Windows > Editors > Outliner** from the menubar; the **Outliner** window is displayed. Select the **persp** camera in the **Outliner** window; the **perspShape** tab is displayed in the **Attribute Editor**.

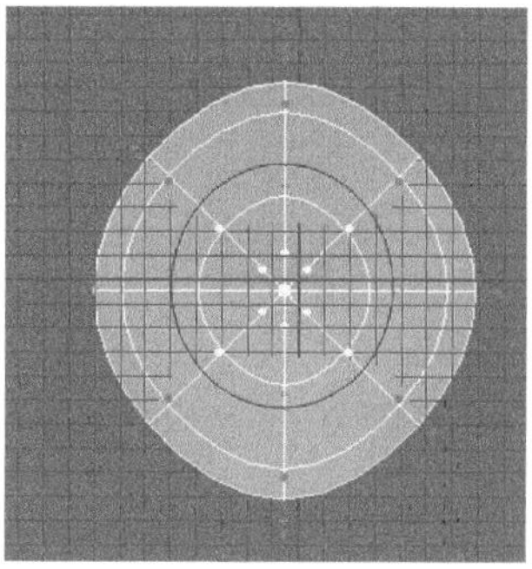

Figure 4-50 Selecting vertices

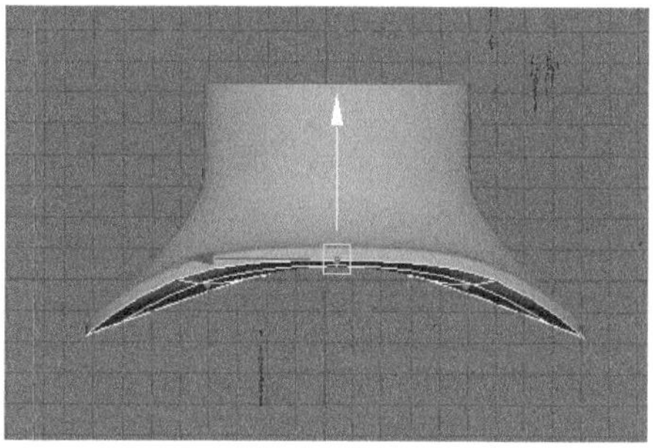

Figure 4-51 The final output

2. In the **perspShape** tab, expand the **Environment** area and drag the **Background Color** slider bar toward right to change the background color to white.

Saving and Rendering the Scene

In this section, you will save the scene that you have created and then render it. You can view the final rendered image of this scene by downloading the *c04_maya_2017_rndr.zip* file from *www.cadcim.com*. The path of the file is as follows: *Textbooks > Animation and Visual Effects > Maya > Autodesk Maya 2017: A Comprehensive Guide*

1. Choose **File > Save Scene** from the menubar.

2. Maximize the persp viewport, if it is not already maximized. Choose the **Render the current frame** button from the Status Line; the **Render View** window is displayed. This window shows the final output of the scene, refer to Figure 4-36.

Tutorial 2

In this tutorial, you will create the model of a ship, as shown in Figure 4-52 using the NURBS and polygon tools. **(Expected time: 30 min)**

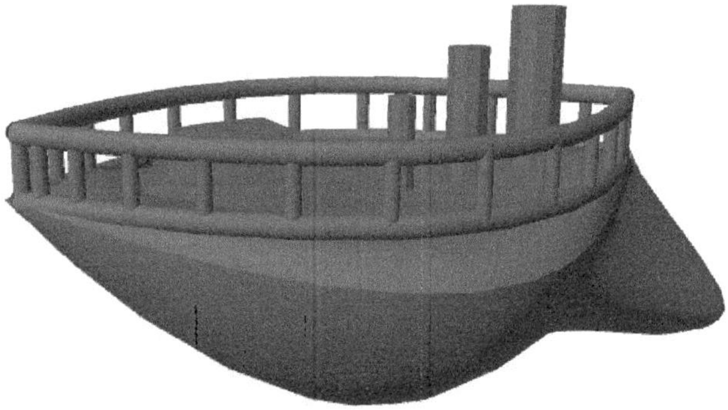

Figure 4-52 Model of a ship

The following steps are required to complete this tutorial:

a. Create a project folder.
b. Create the hull of the ship.
c. Create railings.
d. Create the deck.
e. Create the chimney.
f. Change the background color of the scene.
g. Save and render the scene.

Creating a Project Folder

Create a new project folder with the name *c04_tut2* at *\Documents\maya2017* and then save the file with the name *c04tut2,* as discussed in Tutorial 1 of Chapter 2.

Creating the Hull of the Ship

In this section, you will create the hull of the ship using the NURBS curves and the loft method.

1. Maximize the side-X viewport and choose **Create > Objects > Curve Tools > EP Curve Tool > Option Box** from the menubar; the **Tool Settings (EP Curve Tool)** window is displayed on the left of the viewport. In this window, select the **5** radio button from the **Curve Degree** attribute. Next, create a curve for the base of the ship in the side-X viewport, as shown in Figure 4-53.

   To get the exact shape, select the curve and right-click on it to display a marking menu. Next, choose **Control Vertex** from the marking menu; the vertex mode is activated.

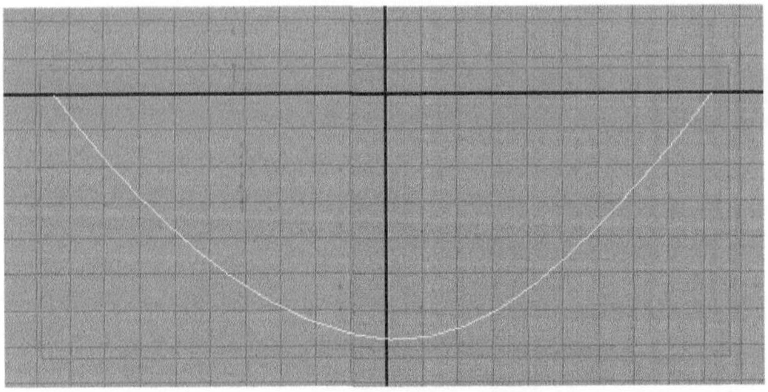

Figure 4-53 *Curve created for the base of the ship*

   Now, you can select a vertex and modify the shape by using **Move Tool**.

2. Choose **Move Tool** from the Tool Box. Next, press and hold the d key and set the pivot point to the right end of the curve by moving the manipulators.

3. Make sure the curve is selected. Choose **Edit > Duplicate > Duplicate Special > Option Box** from the menubar; the **Duplicate Special Options** dialog box is displayed, refer to Figure 4-54. Enter the values in the dialog box, as shown in Figure 4-54, and then choose the **Duplicate Special** button; duplicate curves are created in the viewport.

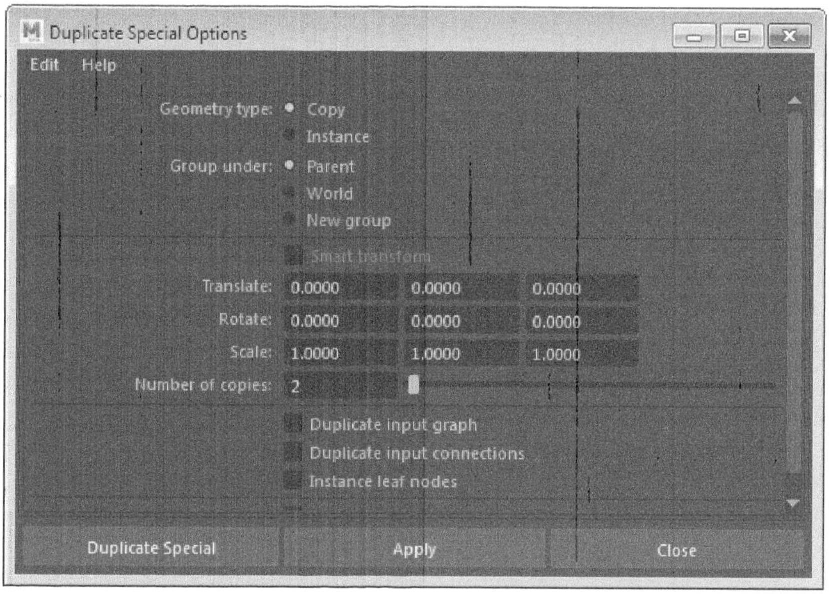

Figure 4-54 *The **Duplicate Special Options** dialog box*

4. Select the duplicate curves one by one and rotate them along the Z axis using **Rotate Tool**, as shown in Figure 4-55.

5. Press and hold the SHIFT key and then select all the curves in the viewport one by one from bottom to top.

6. Choose **Surfaces > Create > Loft** from the menubar; a surface is created defining half of the ship base, as shown in Figure 4-56.

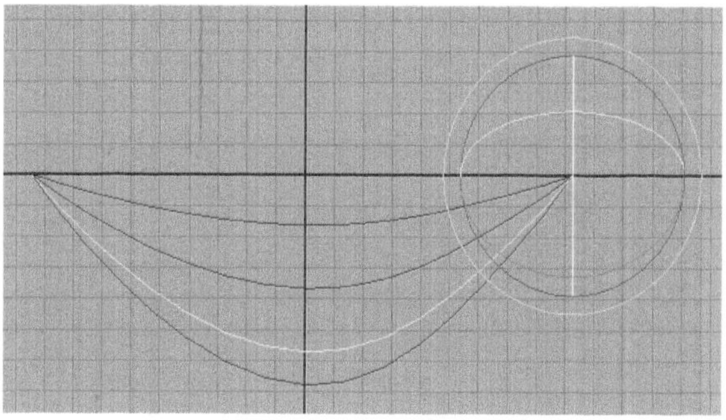

Figure 4-55 *The duplicate curve rotated*

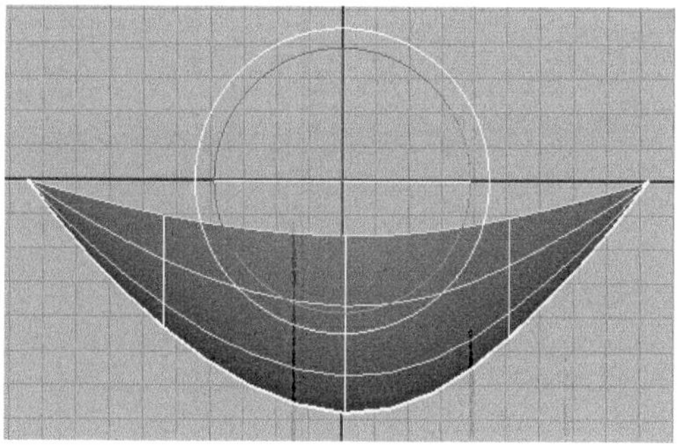

Figure 4-56 *Surface created*

7. Make sure the lofted surface is selected and then choose **Move Tool**. Next, press and hold the D key and set the pivot point to the right end of the surface by moving the manipulators.

8. Choose **Window > Editors > Outliner** from the menubar; the **Outliner** window is displayed. In the **Outliner** window, select all the curves by using the SHIFT key. Next, choose **Display > Object > Hide > Hide Selection** from the menubar; the selected curves are hidden. Close the **Outliner** window.

9. In the side-X viewport, select the NURBS surface. Now, choose **Surfaces > Edit NURBS Surfaces > Rebuild > Option Box** from the menubar; the **Rebuild Surface Options** dialog box is displayed. Set the parameters in this dialog box, as shown in Figure 4-57, and then choose the **Rebuild** button; the selected surface is rebuilt.

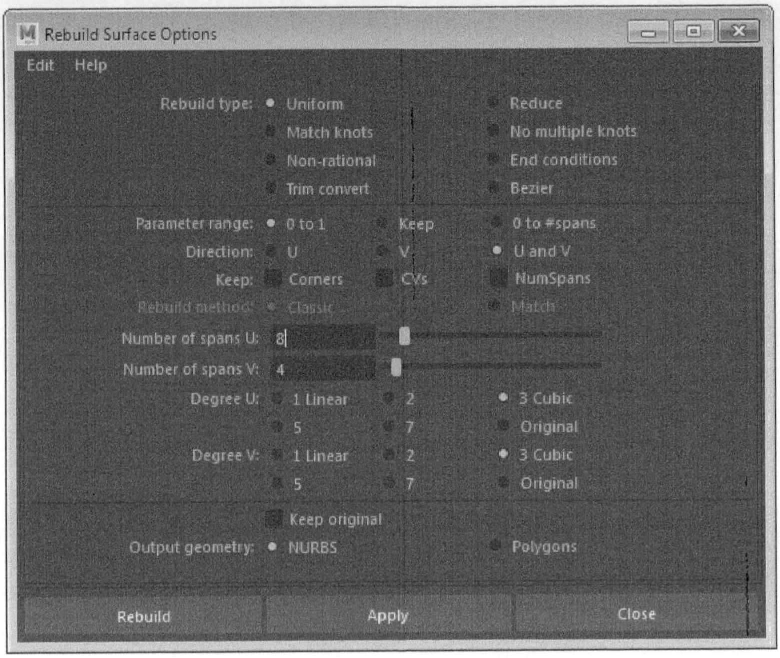

*Figure 4-57 The **Rebuild Surface Options** dialog box*

10. Make sure the rebuilt surface is selected. Next, press and hold the right mouse button over it and choose **Control Vertex** from the marking menu displayed; the vertex selection mode is activated. Next, marquee-select the vertices using the SHIFT key, as shown in Figure 4-58. Move the vertices downward to create the tail of the ship, as shown in Figure 4-59.

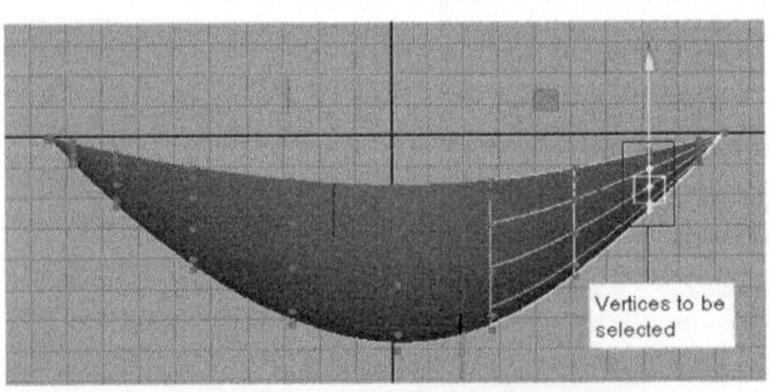

***Figure 4-58** Selecting vertices*

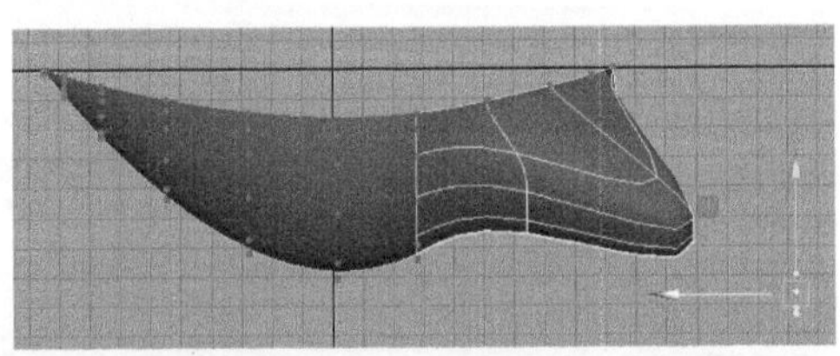

***Figure 4-59** Vertices moved downward to create the tail of the ship*

11. Maximize the persp viewport. Press and hold the right mouse button; a marking menu is displayed. Choose **Object Mode** from the marking menu; the object selection mode is activated. Select the surface of the ship and choose **Edit > Duplicate > Duplicate Special > Option Box** from the menubar to create a copy of the half part of the ship; the **Duplicate Special Options** dialog box is displayed. In this dialog box, select the **Copy** radio button and make sure **-1** is entered in the first **Scale** edit box and enter **1** in the **Number of copies** edit box.

Next, choose the **Duplicate Special** button; a copy of the selected surface is created in the persp viewport, refer to Figure 4-60.

12. Make sure the copy of the surface is selected. Next, choose **Curves > Reverse Direction** from the menubar; the curve direction of the selected surface is reversed, as shown in Figure 4-60.

13. Make sure that one of the surfaces is selected. Press and hold the right mouse button over the surface; a marking menu is displayed. Choose **Isoparm** from the marking menu; the isoparm selection mode is activated.

14. Press and hold the right mouse button over another surface; a marking menu is displayed. Choose **Isoparm** from the marking menu; the isoparm selection mode is activated. Next, press SHIFT and select the topmost isoparm of both the surfaces, as shown in Figure 4-61. Next, choose **Surfaces > Create > Loft** from the menubar; a surface is created between the selected isoparms.

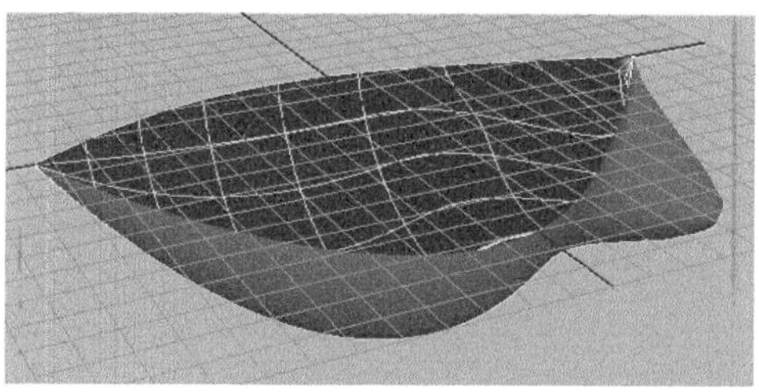

Figure 4-60 *The duplicate surface created*

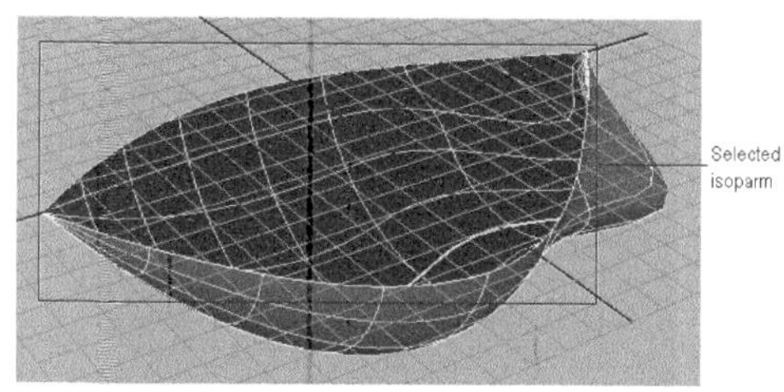

Figure 4-61 *The two selected isoparms*

15. Make sure the newly created surface is selected and choose **Surfaces > Edit NURBS Surfaces > Rebuild > Option Box** from the menubar; the **Rebuild Surfaces Options** dialog box is displayed. In this dialog box, make sure **8** is entered in the **Number of spans U** edit box. Next, choose the **Rebuild** button; the newly created surface is rebuilt.

16. Maximize the top-Y viewport and press and hold the right mouse button on the selected surface; a marking menu is displayed. Choose **Isoparm** from the marking menu displayed and insert the two isoparms using the SHIFT key, as shown in Figure 4-62. Now, choose **Surfaces > Edit NURBS Surfaces > Insert Isoparms** from the menubar; two new isoparms are added to the surface.

17. Maximize the side-X viewport. Invoke **Move Tool** and move the newly created surface up along the Y axis.

18. In the side-X viewport, press and hold the right mouse button over the newly created surface; a marking menu is displayed. Choose **Control Vertex** from the marking menu; the vertex selection mode is activated. Select all the vertices of the newly created surface. Next, maximize the top-Y viewport and deselect the center vertices by pressing the SHIFT key and select all the corner vertices, as shown in Figure 4-63.

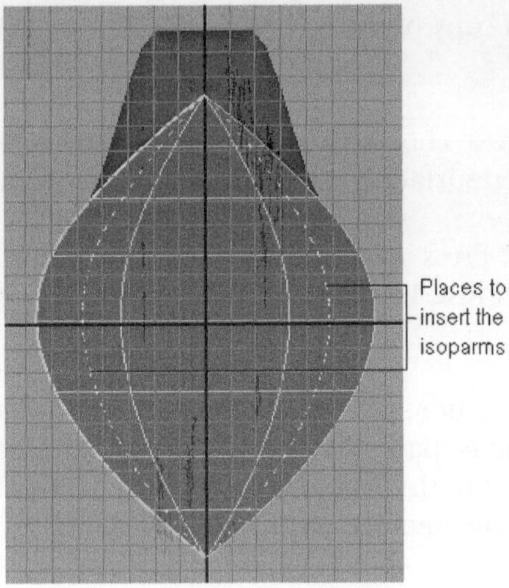

Figure 4-62 Inserting isoparms

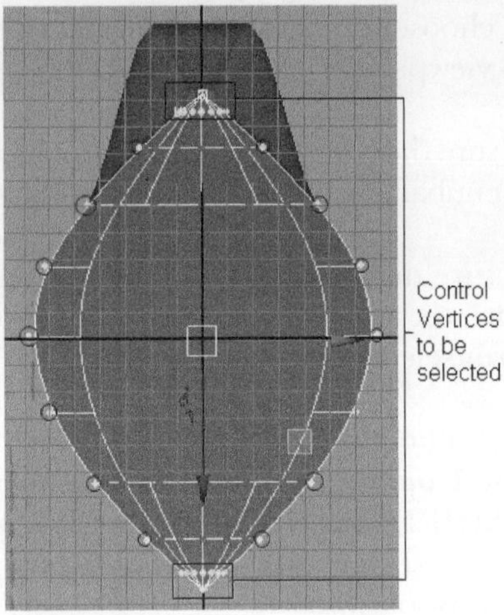

Figure 4-63 The vertices selected

19. Maximize the persp viewport and then choose **Move Tool** from the Tool Box and move the selected vertices downward along the Y axis, as shown in Figure 4-64.

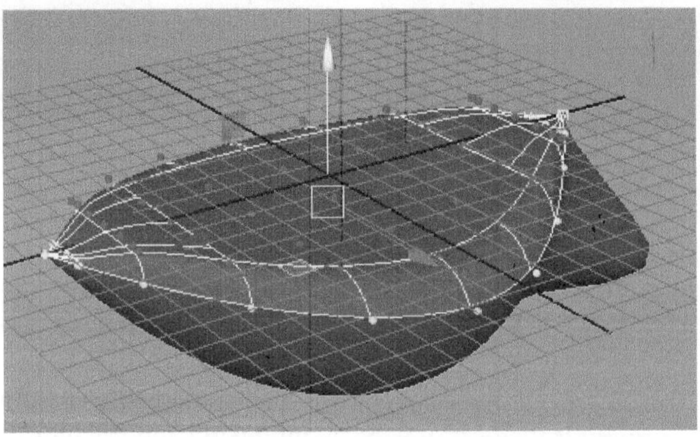

Figure 4-64 Moving the vertices along the Y axis

Creating Railings

In this section, you will create railings for the ship by using the NURBS cylinder and then align the cylinders on a curve.

1. Maximize the top-Y viewport. Choose **Create > Objects > Curve Tools > EP Curve Tool** from the menubar and create a curve, refer to Figure 4-65. Now, move the curve using **Move Tool**. Figure 4-65 displays the position of the NURBS curve in all viewports.

2. Maximize the persp viewport and choose **Create > Objects > NURBS Primitives > Cylinder** from the menubar and create a cylinder in the viewport. Next, select the upper cap of the cylinder and delete it. Similarly, delete the lower cap of the cylinder.

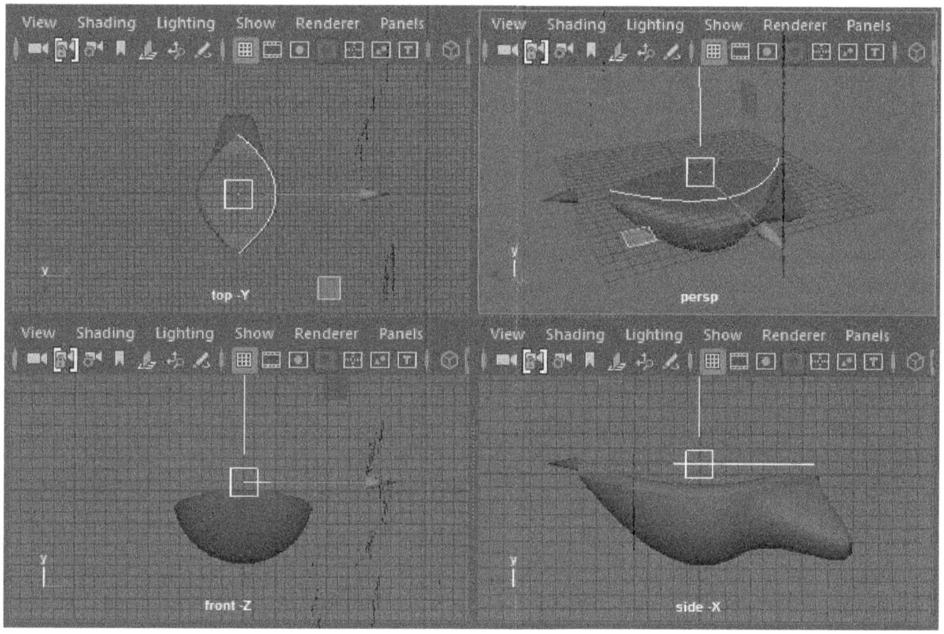

***Figure 4-65** The NURBS curve aligned in all viewports*

3. Select the cylinder. In **Channel Box / Layer Editor**, expand **makeNurbCylinder1** node in the **INPUTS** area and set the following parameters of the cylinder:

   Radius: **0.2** Sections: **10** Height Ratio: **10**

4. Select the **Animation** menuset from the **Menuset** drop-down list in the Status Line. Next, select the curve and then press and hold the SHIFT key and select the cylinder. Choose **Constrain > Motion Paths > Attach to Motion Path > Option Box** from the menubar; the **Attach to Motion Path Options** dialog box is displayed in the viewport.

5. In this dialog box, choose **Start/End** radio button in the **Time range** attribute and make sure **30** is entered in the **End Time** edit box. Next, choose the **Attach** button; cylinder gets attached to the curve.

6. Choose **Visualize > Snapshot > Create Animation Snapshot > Option Box** from the menubar; the **Animation Snapshot Options** dialog box is displayed in the viewport. Enter **30** in the **End Time** edit box, **2** in the **Increment** edit box, and then choose the **Snapshot** button; the cylinders are aligned on the curve surface, as shown in Figure 4-66.

Note
*The value in the **End Time** edit box may vary depending on the size of the NURBS surface created.*

7. Maximize the front-Z viewport and choose **Create > Objects > NURBS Primitives > Circle** from the menubar and create a circle on the curve in the viewport, refer to Figure 4-67. Make sure the circle is selected in the front-Z viewport. In the **Channel Box / Layer Editor**, enter **90** in the **Rotate X** and **-38** in the **Rotate Y** edit boxes. Next, expand **makeNurbCircle1**

node in the **INPUTS** area of the **Channel Box / Layer Editor** and set the radius of the circle to **0.3**.

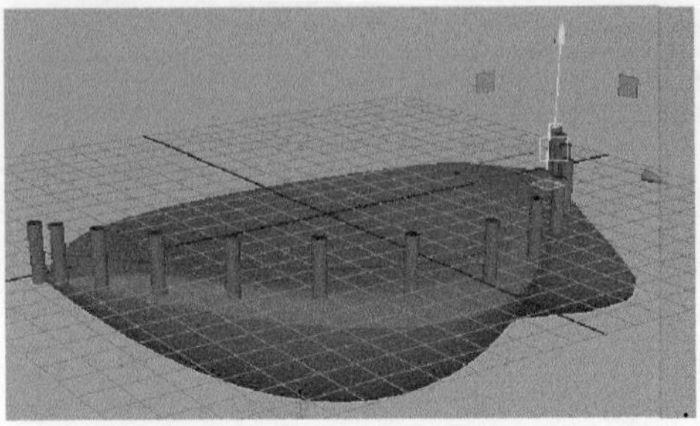

Figure 4-66 *The cylinders aligned on the curve surface*

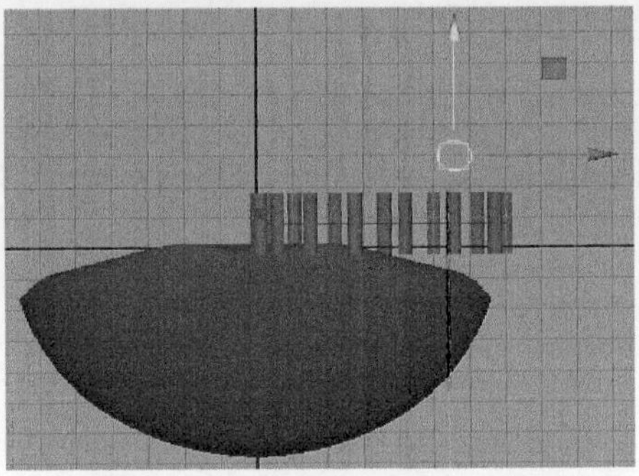

Figure 4-67 *The handrail created*

8. Select the **Modeling** menuset from the **Menuset** drop-down list in the Status Line. Now, select the circle and then the curve from the viewport. Choose **Surfaces > Extrude > Option Box** from the menubar; the **Extrude Options** dialog box is displayed. In this dialog box, make sure the **Tube** radio button is selected corresponding to the **Style** attribute. Also, select the **At path** radio button corresponding to the **Result position** attribute and **Component** radio button corresponding to the **Pivot** attribute. Next, choose the **Extrude** button; the circle is extruded and the handrail is created, refer to Figure 4-68.

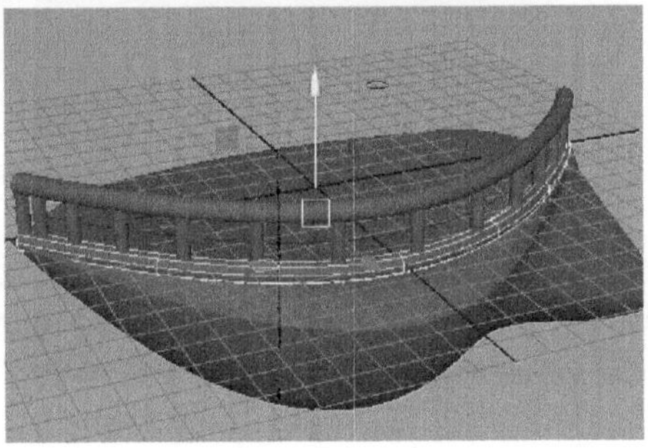

Figure 4-68 *The handrail aligned*

9. Maximize the persp viewport. Next, invoke the **Move Tool** and move the handrail up along the Y axis to align it, refer to Figure 4-68. Now, press CTRL+D; a copy of handrail is created and then align it using **Move Tool**, as shown in Figure 4-68

10. Choose **Windows > Editors > Outliner** from the menubar; the **Outliner** window is displayed. In the **Outliner** window, select the **curve5** and the **nurbsCircle1** curve; the nurb circle and the handrail curve is selected in the viewport. Next, choose **Display > Object > Hide > Hide Selection** from the menubar to hide the selected curves.

11. Select the complete railing and press CTRL+G; the selected railing is grouped. Choose **Edit > Delete > Delete by Type > History** from the menubar; the history of the surfaces created earlier is deleted. Next, choose **Modify > Transform > Freeze Transformations** from the menubar and then press d to set the pivot in the center of the ship, if it is not in the center.

12. Make sure the complete railing is selected andchoose **Edit > Duplicate > Duplicate Special** from the menubar; the copy of railings is created and placed on the other half of the ship. Next, choose **Curves > Edit >Reverse Direction** from the menubar; the curve direction of the copied railing surface is reversed, as shown in Figure 4-69.

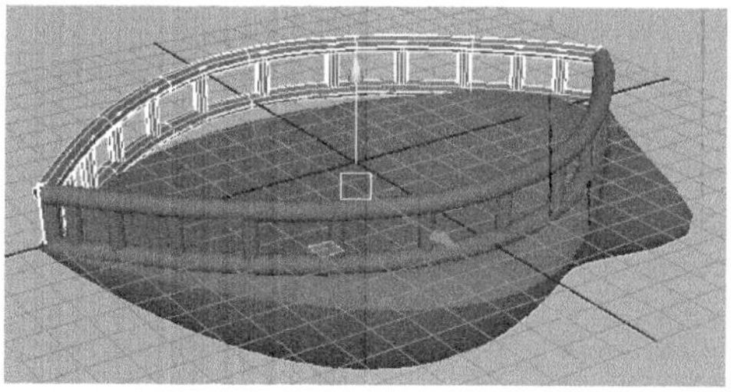

Figure 4-69 Copied railing surface is reversed

Creating the Deck

In this section, you will create the deck of the ship using the polygon modeling method.

1. Maximize the top-Y viewport. Choose **Create > Objects > Polygon Primitives > Cube** from the menubar. Next, create a cube in the viewport. In the **Channel Box / Layer Editor**, expand the **polyCube1** node of the **INPUTS** area and set the parameters as follows:

   Width: **5** | Subdivisions Width: **2**
   Height: **1** | Subdivision Depth: **4**
   Depth: **5**

2. Press and hold the right mouse button on the cube; a marking menu is displayed. Choose **Vertex** from the marking menu displayed. Next, choose **Scale Tool** from the Tool Box and adjust the vertex of the cube to form the shape, as shown in Figure 4-70.

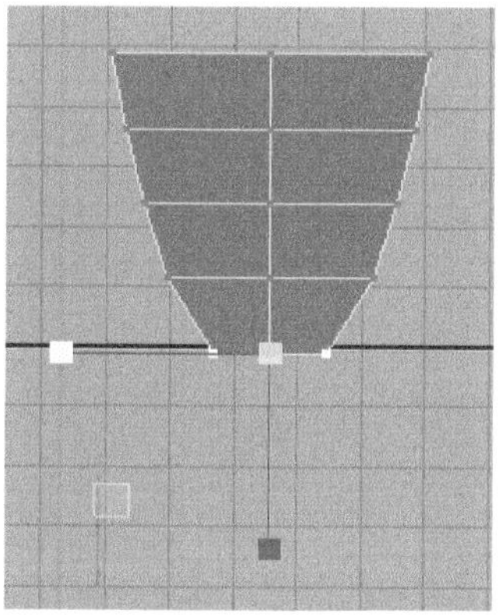

Figure 4-70 The shape of the deck created

3. Maximize the persp viewport. Press and hold the right mouse button on the cube; a marking menu is displayed. Choose **Object Mode** from the marking menu displayed. Next, select the cube and choose **Edit > Duplicate > Duplicate** from the menubar; a copy of cube is created. Similarly, create one more duplicate of the deck. Choose **Move Tool** and then **Scale Tool** to align the duplicated decks on the ship, as shown in Figure 4-71.

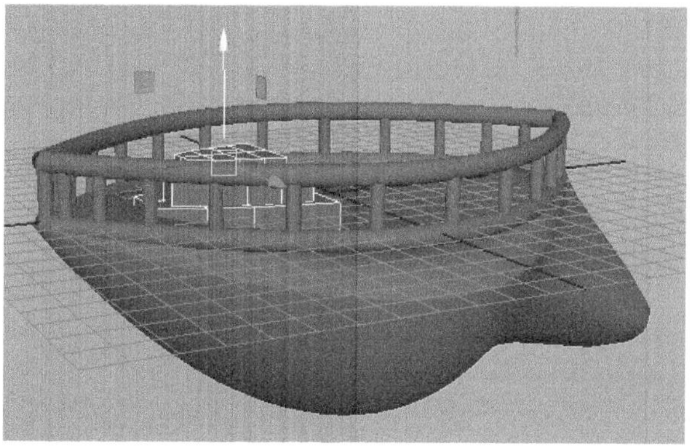

Figure 4-71 The duplicate decks aligned together

Creating the Chimney

In this section, you will create the chimney for the ship using the **Polygon Cylinder** tool.

1. Maximize the top-Y viewport. Choose **Create > Objects > Polygon Primitives > Cylinder** from the menubar and create three cylinders in the viewport. The cylinders will act as chimneys for the ship. In the **Channel Box / Layer Editor**, set the parameters as given next.

Note

The radius and height of the cylinders may vary depending on the size of the ship. Therefore, you need to set the respective values accordingly.

Cylinder	Radius	Height
Cylinder1	0.8	8
Cylinder2	0.6	6
Cylinder3	0.4	4

2. Maximize the persp viewport and align the cylinders to create the chimneys, as shown in Figure 4-72.

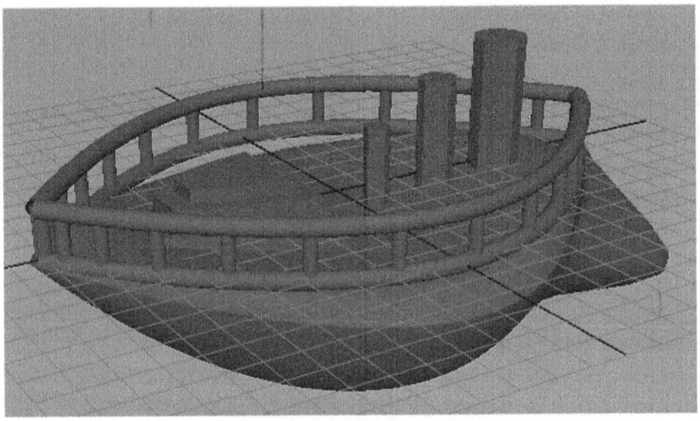

Figure 4-72 *The chimneys created*

Changing the Background Color of the Scene

In this section, you will change the background color of the scene.

1. Choose **Windows > Editors > Outliner** from the menubar; the **Outliner** window is displayed. Select the **persp** camera in the **Outliner** window; the **perspShape** tab is displayed in the **Attribute Editor**.

2. In the **perspShape** tab, expand the **Environment** area and drag the **Background Color** slider bar toward right to change the background color to white.

Saving and Rendering the Scene

In this section, you will save the scene that you have created and then render it. You can view the final rendered image of this scene by downloading the *c04_maya_2017_rndr.zip* file from *www.cadcim.com.* The path of the file is as follows: *Textbooks > Animation and Visual Effects > Maya > Autodesk Maya 2017: A Comprehensive Guide.*

1. Choose **File > Save Scene** from the menubar.

2. Maximize the persp viewport, if not already maximized. Choose the **Render the current frame** button from the Status Line; the **Render View** window is displayed. This window shows the final output of the scene, refer to Figure 4-52.

Self-Evaluation Test

Answer the following questions and then compare them to those given at the end of this chapter:

1. Which of the following tools is used to create a new segment at the intersection of two surfaces?

   (a) **Intersect Surfaces** (b) **Untrim Surfaces**
   (c) **Attach Surfaces** (d) None of these

2. Which of the following tools is used to paint a mesh to give it a smoother look?

   (a) **Pull** (b) **Push**
   (c) **Smooth** (d) **Relax**

3. The __________ tool is used to rebuild the U and V spans.

4. The __________ tool is used to undo the last trim operation.

5. The __________ tool is used to reverse the U and V directions of selected surface.

6. The __________ **Geometry Tool** is used to sculpt a NURBS or polygon object manually in the viewport.

7. The **NURBS to Subdiv** conversion tool is used to convert a NURBS mesh into a subdiv mesh. (T/F)

8. The **Sculpt Geometry Tool** is used to sculpt a NURBS or polygon object manually in the viewport. (T/F)

9. The **Offset Surfaces** tool is used to create the copy of a selected surface at a particular distance. (T/F)

10. The **Insert Isoparms** tool is used to insert an isoparm into an existing NURBS surface. (T/F)

Review Questions

Answer the following questions:

1. Which of the following operations is used to relax bumps over a surface?

    (a) **Push** (b) **Pull**
    (c) **Relax** (d) **Erase**

2. Which of the following tools is used to create a copy of the selected surface by creating an offset at a specified distance?

    (a) **Offset Surface** (b) **Attach Surface**
    (c) **Align Surface** (d) **Detach Surface**

3. The __________ tool is used to extend an edge of the NURBS surface.

4. The __________ **knots** radio button is used to remove the extra knots formed while rebuilding a surface.

5. The **Pinch** operation is used to pull the selected vertices toward each other while using the **Sculpt Geometry Tool**. (T/F)

6. The **Extend Surfaces** tool is used to extend the edge of a NURBS surface. (T/F)

7. The **Reverse Surface Direction** tool is used to reverse or swap the U and V directions of a selected surface. (T/F)

8. The **Erase** operation is used to push the NURBS mesh inside a surface. (T/F)

9. The **Extend Surfaces** tool is used to rebuild a NURBS surface. (T/F)

10. The **Detach** tool is used to detach a surface by selecting isoparm. (T/F)

EXERCISES

The rendered output of the models used in the following exercises can be accessed by downloading the *c04_maya_2017_exr.zip* from *www.cadcim.com*. The path of the file is as follows: *Textbooks > Animation and Visual Effects > Maya > Autodesk Maya 2017: A Comprehensive Guide.*

Exercise 1

Use various NURBS modeling techniques to create the model of a handbag, as shown in Figure 4-73. **(Expected time: 45 min)**

Figure 4-73 *The model of a handbag*

Exercise 2

Use various NURBS modeling techniques to create the model of a chair, as shown in Figure 4-74. **(Expected time: 30 min)**

Figure 4-74 *The model of a chair*

Answers to Self-Evaluation Test

1. a, **2.** c, **3. Rebuild Surfaces**, **4. Untrim Surfaces**, **5. Reverse Surface Direction**, **6. Sculpt**, **7.** T, **8.** T, **9.** T, **10.** T

Chapter 5

UV Mapping

Learning Objectives

After completing this chapter, you will be able to:

- *Use different UV mapping techniques*
- *Use the UV Editor*
- *Use various tools and options in the UV Editor*

INTRODUCTION

UV mapping is a process of creating or editing UVs for an object. The U and V denote the axes of the 2D texture and they determine how the texture will be applied to the surface of an object. Therefore, it is important to use the mapping space efficiently to minimize seams and distortions in a model. The look of your model depends on the way you project the texture on the surface of the model by arranging the UVs. In this chapter, you will learn to use the tools and techniques needed to create good UV maps.

UV MAPPING

UV mapping is a technique in which a 3D object is unfolded and split into 2D patches. It is used to place texture directly on the surface mesh. The UV coordinates are used to position textures on the surfaces. To access various UV mapping techniques, select **Modeling** from the **Menuset** drop-down list in the Status Line. Next, choose the required mapping technique which is required. There are six types of UV mapping used in Maya. These types are discussed next.

Cylindrical

Menubar: UV > Create > Cylindrical

The cylindrical mapping technique is used for cylindrical projection of UVs on a polygonal object. This technique works best for objects that can be completely enclosed in the cylindrical projection area. Before applying cylindrical mapping, you need to assign texture to the object. To understand the cylindrical mapping, create a polygon cylinder in the viewport and press and hold the right mouse button over it; a marking menu will be displayed. Choose **Assign Favorite Material > Lambert** from the marking menu; the **Attribute Editor** will be displayed on the right side of the viewport. In the **Attribute Editor**, choose the checker button on the right of the **Color** attribute in **lambert#** tab; the **Create Render Node** window will be displayed. Choose the **Checker** button from this window; the checker texture will be assigned to the object. Press 6 to display the checker texture on the object. You will observe that the checker pattern created on the object is in distorted form.

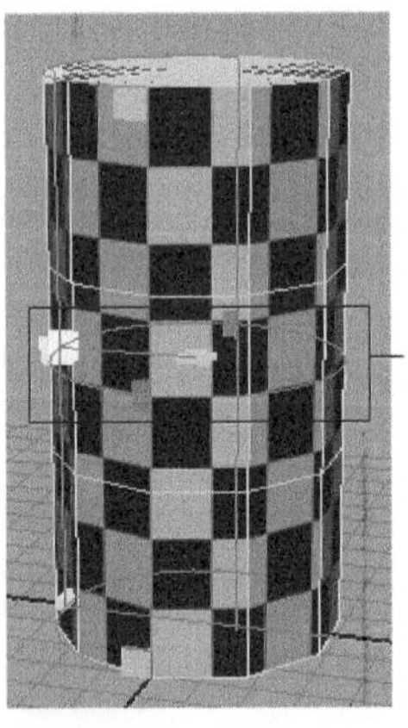

Figure 5-1 *The cylindrical mapping projection manipulators*

The checker texture helps you to judge how the texture will appear. If the checkers in the checker map stretch, the texture will also stretch. To avoid the texture from stretching, select the cylinder from the viewport and choose **UV > Create > Cylindrical** from the menubar; the cylindrical mapping projection manipulators will be displayed on the object, as shown in Figure 5-1.

You can now use these manipulators to adjust the cylindrical mapping as required. You can also change the default settings of the cylindrical mapping. To do so, choose **UV > Create > Cylindrical > Option Box** from the menubar; the **Cylindrical Mapping Options** dialog box will be displayed, as shown in Figure 5-2. In this dialog box, set the values of the attribute as required and then choose the **Project** button.

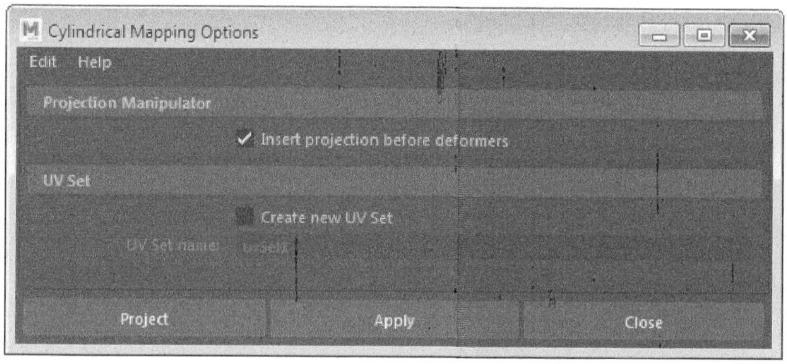

*Figure 5-2 The **Cylindrical Mapping Options** dialog box*

Planar

Menubar: UV > Create > Planar

The planar mapping technique is used to map UV texture coordinates on the mesh through an imaginary plane. This is the best suited technique for objects with a flat surface. On applying this projection to an object, the projection manipulator handles will be displayed on that object, as shown in Figure 5-3. Using these manipulator handles, you can set the planar mapping. You can also apply the planar mapping on specific faces of an object. To do so, select a polygonal object from the viewport. Next, press and hold the right mouse button over the object; a marking menu will be displayed. Choose **Face** from the marking menu displayed; the face selection mode will be activated. Now, you can select the faces on which you want to apply the planar mapping. After selecting the faces, choose **UV > Create > Planar** from the menubar; the planar mapping will be applied on the selected faces.

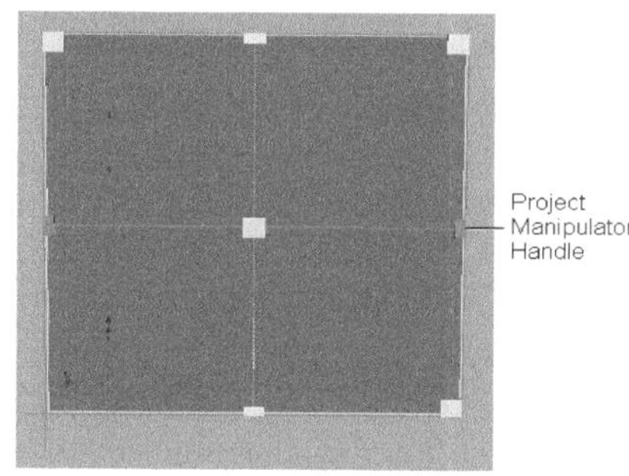

Figure 5-3 The planar mapping projection manipulator handle

You can also modify the default settings of the planar mapping. To do so, choose **UV > Create > Planar > Option Box** from the menubar; the **Planar Mapping Options** dialog box will be displayed, as shown in Figure 5-4. The options in this dialog box are discussed next.

Projection Manipulator Area

The options in this area are used to modify the settings of the projection of planar mapping on the selected object or the face of an object in the viewport. Various attributes in this area are discussed next.

Fit projection to

The radio buttons corresponding to the **Fit projection to** attribute are used to position the projection manipulator on to the selected object. On selecting the **Best plane** radio button, the planar mapping manipulator will be positioned on the selected faces of the polygonal object. On selecting the **Bounding box** radio button, the planar mapping manipulator will be positioned within the bounding box of the selected polygonal object.

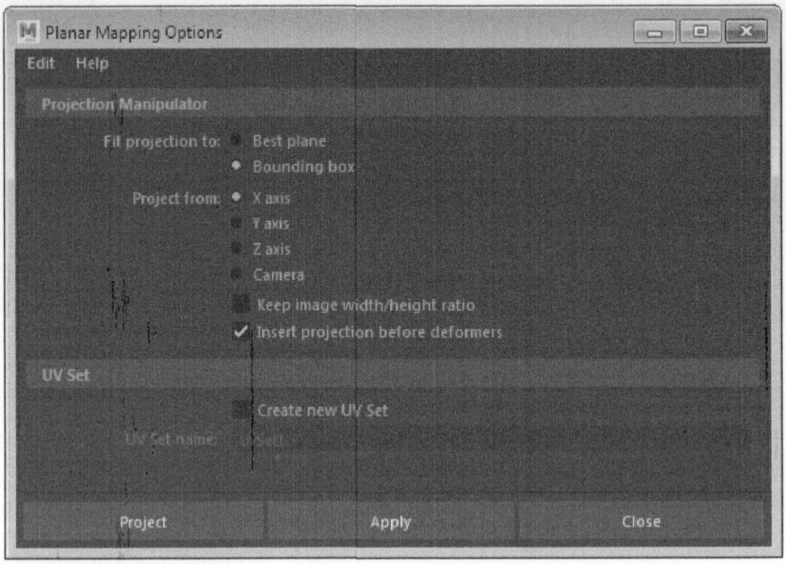

*Figure 5-4 The **Planar Mapping Options** dialog box*

Project from

The radio buttons available for the **Project from** attribute are used to project the planar mapping manipulator on a particular axis. You can select the **X axis**, **Y axis**, **Z axis**, or **Camera** radio button to aim the projection of planar mapping on the majority of object's faces. On selecting the **Keep image width/height ratio** check box, the width to height ratio will remain same as that of the image and the projected image will not distort. By default, the **Insert projection before deformers** check box is selected to ensure that the texture will adhere to the object even after deformation is applied to it.

UV Set Area

The options in this area are used to manually create a new UV set and place UVs created by the projection in that set. To create a new UV set, select the **Create new UV Set** check box from the **UV Set** area; the **UV Set name** text box will be activated. In this text box, enter the desired name for the UV set and choose the **Project** button from the dialog box; a new UV set with the specified name will be created.

Tip

*You can also apply planar mapping on an object by using the marking menu. To do so, select the object from the viewport, press and hold the SHIFT key, and then right-click on the object; a marking menu will be displayed. Choose **Mapping > Planar Map** from the marking menu displayed; the planar mapping will be applied on the selected object.*

Spherical

Menubar: UV > Create > Spherical

The spherical mapping technique is used to map UVs onto the selected object by projecting them on a sphere. This technique works best for spherical objects that can be completely enclosed in a spherical projection area. Before applying spherical mapping to an object, you need to assign a texture to the object. To do so, create the object in the viewport and press and hold the right mouse button over it; a marking menu will be displayed. Choose **Assign Favorite Material > Lambert** from the marking menu; the **Attribute Editor** will be displayed on the right side of the viewport. In the **Attribute Editor**, choose the checker button on the right of the **Color** attribute; the **Create Render Node** window will be displayed. Choose the **Checker** button from this window; the checker texture will be assigned to the object. Press 6 to display the checker texture on the object. You will observe that the created checker pattern is in a distorted form. Next, select the object in the viewport, press and hold the SHIFT key, and then press the right mouse button; a marking menu will be displayed. Choose **Mapping > Spherical Map** from the marking menu; the spherical mapping manipulators will be displayed on the selected object, refer to Figure 5-5. You can adjust these mapping manipulators to set the mapping coordinates. You can also change the default settings of the spherical mapping. To do so, choose **UV > Create > Spherical > Option Box** from the menubar; the **Spherical Mapping Options** dialog box will be displayed, as shown in Figure 5-6. Set the required parameters in the dialog box and then choose the **Project** button.

Figure 5-5 The spherical mapping projection manipulators

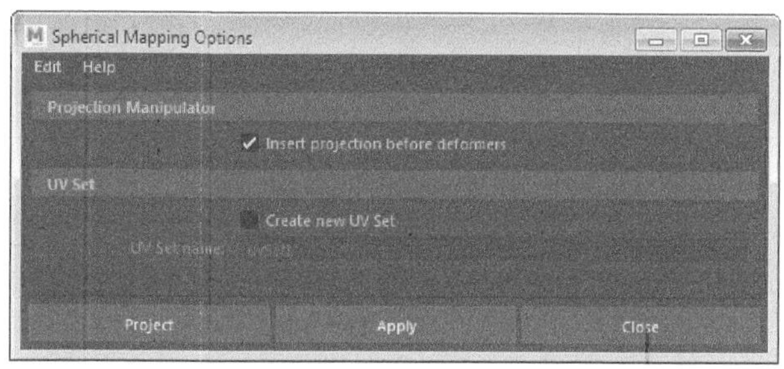

*Figure 5-6 The **Spherical Mapping Options** dialog box*

Contour Stretch

Menubar: UV > Create > Contour Stretch

The contour stretch technique is used to project a texture image onto the selected polygons of an object. Contour stretch mapping analyzes a four-cornered selection to determine how to stretch the UV coordinates of the polygons over the image. It does not have the same alignment and positioning options as are available in other mapping methods.

Automatic

Menubar: UV > Create > Automatic

The automatic mapping technique is used to project UV texture coordinates on the selected objects from multiple angles at the same time. This type of mapping is mainly used to create UVs for complex objects on which other mapping techniques cannot be applied. The automatic mapping technique is best suitable for the objects that are hollow and are projected outward. On applying this technique, a number of projection planes of different colors are created around the polygonal object, as shown in Figure 5-7.

The color of a projection plane indicates the projection orientation of the object. For example, the light blue color of the projection plane indicates that the projection face is oriented away from the polygonal object, whereas the lavender color of the projection plane indicates that this plane is facing toward the polygonal object. You can also change the default settings of the automatic UV mapping. To do so, choose **UV > Create > Automatic > Option Box** from the menubar; the **Polygon Automatic Mapping Options** dialog box will be displayed, as shown in Figure 5-8. The options available in the **Mapping Settings** area are discussed next.

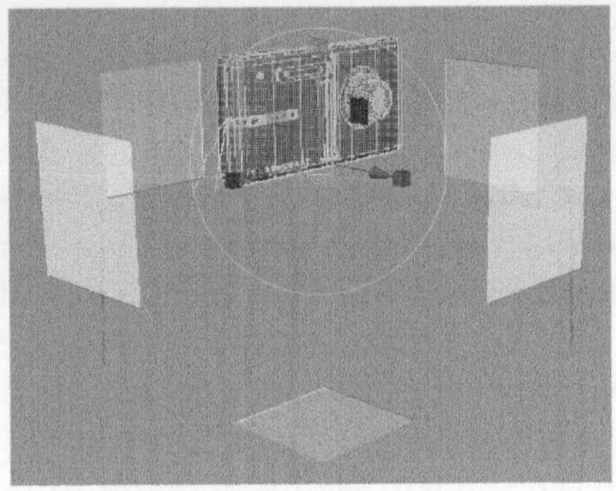

Figure 5-7 *The projection planes created on applying automatic mapping*

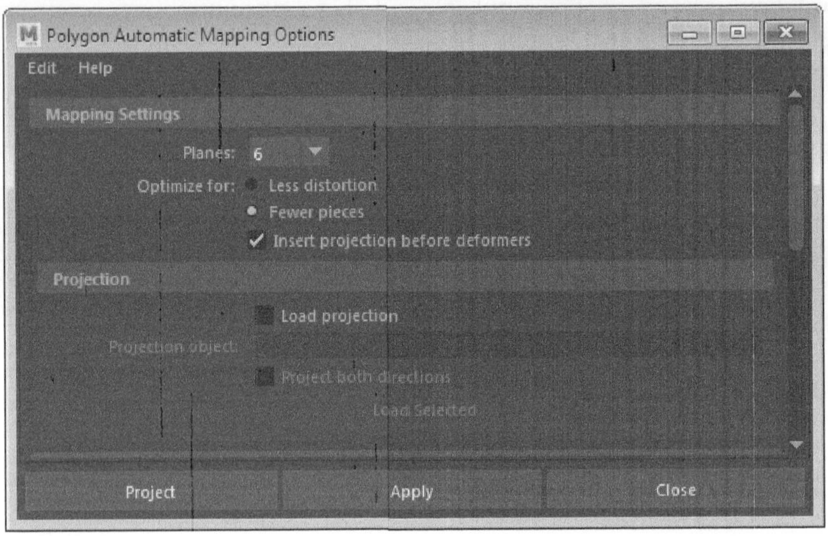

Figure 5-8 *The* ***Polygon Automatic Mapping Options*** *dialog box*

Mapping Settings Area

The **Mapping Settings** area consists of different attributes that are used to modify the settings of projections of automatic mapping on the selected object. The options in this area are discussed next.

Planes

The **Planes** drop-down list is used to specify the number of projection planes for automatic mapping. Higher the value specified for the number of projection planes, more will be the number of shells created in the **UV Editor**, which in turn, will reduce distortion. Shells are different parts of the 2D texture coordinates created from a 3D model in the **UV Editor**. To apply automatic mapping, select the object in the viewport, and choose **UV > Create > Automatic > Option Box** from the menubar; the **Polygon Automatic Mapping Options** dialog box will be displayed. In this dialog box, select **4** from the **Planes** drop-down list and then choose the **Project** button; the selected object will be unwrapped and four projection planes will be created automatically. Now, choose **UV > Editors > UV Editor** from the menubar; the **UV Editor** window will be displayed with UV shells created in the UV Editor window, as shown in Figure 5-9. Similarly, select **8** from the **Planes** drop-down list and then choose the **Project** button; the selected object will be unwrapped and eight projection planes will be created automatically. Now, choose **UV > Editors > UV Editor** from the menubar; the UV shells will be displayed in the **UV Editor** window, as shown in Figure 5-10.

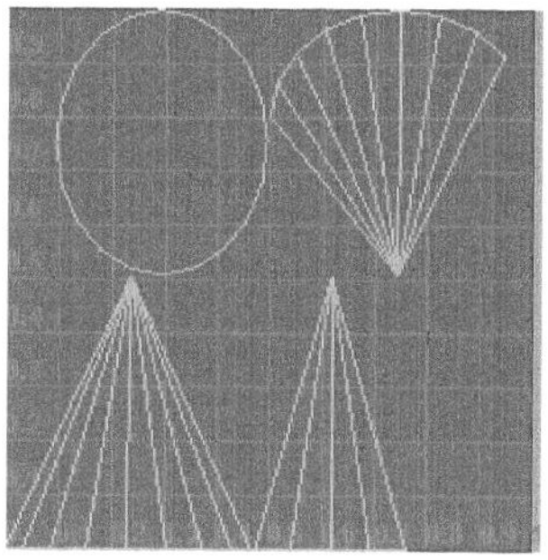

Figure 5-9 *UV shells created on selecting the* ***4*** *option in the* ***Planes*** *drop-down list*

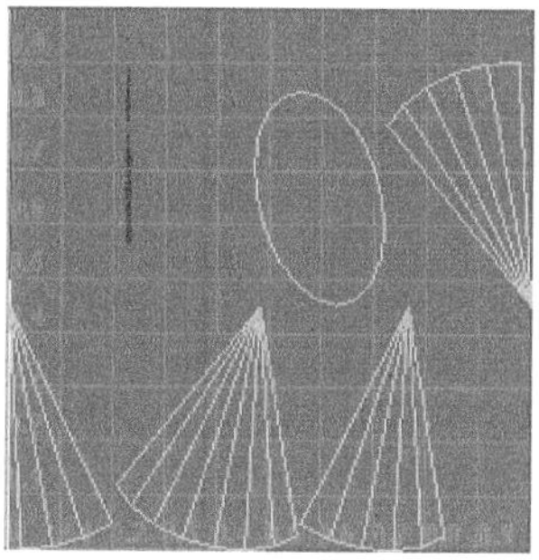

Figure 5-10 *UV shells created on selecting the* ***8*** *option in the* ***Planes*** *drop-down list*

Optimize for

The radio buttons available for the **Optimize for** attribute are used to set the optimization type for the automatic projection. By default, the **Fewer pieces** radio button is selected for the **Optimize for** attribute. As a result, the projection planes that are not ideal for texture mapping are created which leads to the formation of larger shells, as shown in Figure 5-11. Select the **Less distortion** radio button to project all planes in the **UV Editor** at equal distance, as shown in Figure 5-12. Select the **Insert projection before deformers** check box, if not already selected, before applying any texture to the object. It prevents the texture from deforming while the object is being animated in the viewport.

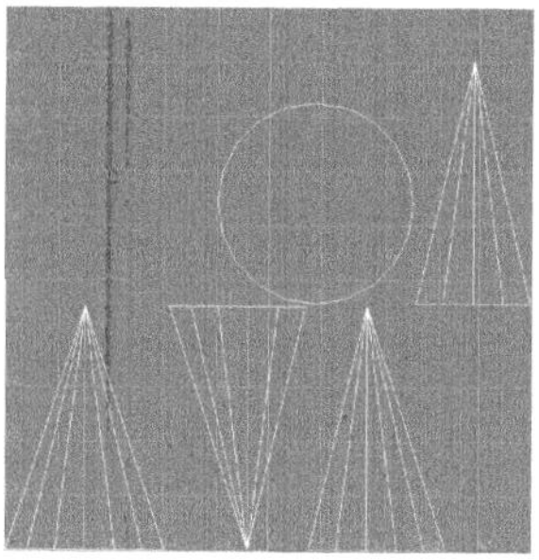

Figure 5-11 *Planes projected using the* ***Fewer pieces*** *radio button*

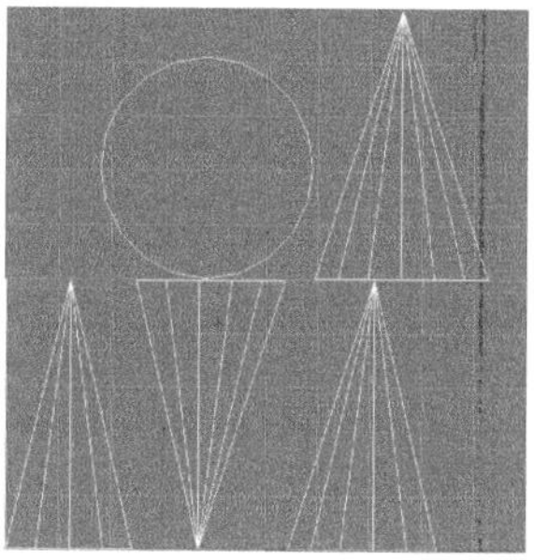

Figure 5-12 *Planes projected using the* ***Less distortion*** *radio button*

Camera-Based

Menubar: UV > Create > Camera-Based

The **Camera-Based** tool is used to create UV texture for the coordinates on a polygonal object, based on the current camera view. In this type of projection, UVs are created on the object based on faces visible in the view plane. To create UVs using this tool, select a polygonal object from the viewport, press and hold the right-mouse button over it, and then choose **Face** from the marking menu displayed; the face mode will be activated. Now, select the faces for which you want to create the UVs. After selecting the faces, choose **UV > Create > Camera-Based** from the menubar; the projection will be applied to the selected faces.

UV EDITOR

Menubar: UV > Editors > UV Editor

The **UV Editor**, as shown in Figure 5-13, is used to edit UV texture coordinates. The options in this window are used to view and edit the UV texture coordinates within a 2D view.

Tip
*To pan in the **UV Editor**, press and hold the middle mouse button along with the ALT key.*

For example, to view the UV coordinates of a cube, create a cube in the viewport. Make sure the cube is selected in the viewport and then choose **UV > Editors > UV Editor** from the menubar; the **UV Editor** will be displayed with the UV texture coordinates for the cube primitive, refer to Figure 5-13. In this window, the tools are grouped together in the toolbar and are discussed next.

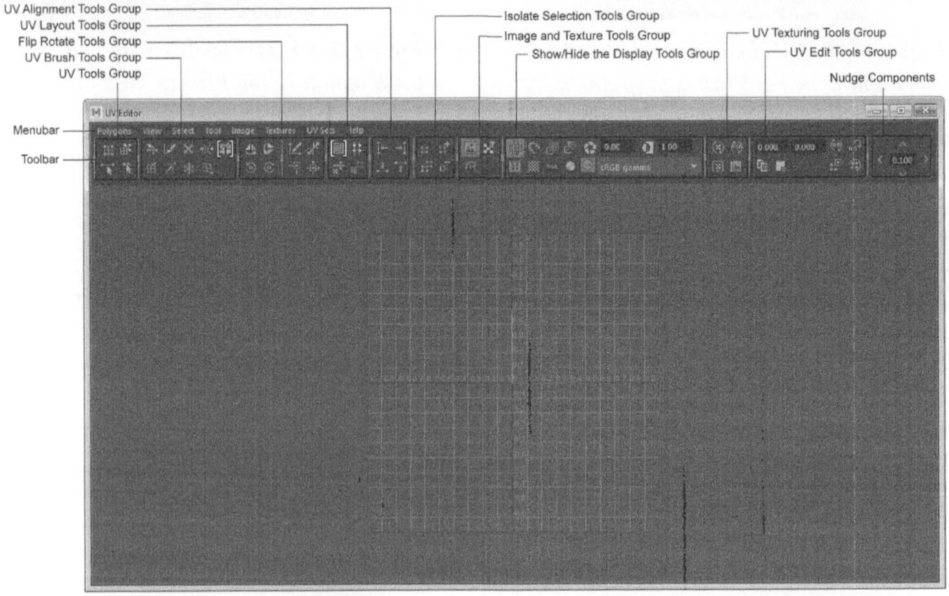

Figure 5-13 The UV Editor

UV Tools Group

The tools in the **UV Tools** group of the **UV Editor** are used to select and move the UVs of the selected object. These tools are discussed next.

UV Lattice Tool

UV Editor menubar: Tool > UV Lattice Tool

The **UV Lattice Tool** is used to create a lattice around the UVs to deform the 2D texture coordinates. To do so, choose the **UV Lattice Tool** button from the **UV Editor** toolbar. Now, press and hold the right mouse button in the **UV Editor** area; a marking menu will be displayed. Choose **UV** from the marking menu and marquee select the UVs of the object; a UV lattice will be displayed on the selected UVs, as shown in Figure 5-14. Now, you can deform the 2D coordinates by moving the selected UVs as required.

Move UV Shell Tool

UV Editor menubar: Tool > Move UV Shell Tool

The **Move UV Shell Tool** is used to select and move a particular shell. To do so, click on the shell using the **Move UV Shell Tool**; its UVs are selected, refer to Figure 5-15. Now, you can move the selected shell, as required.

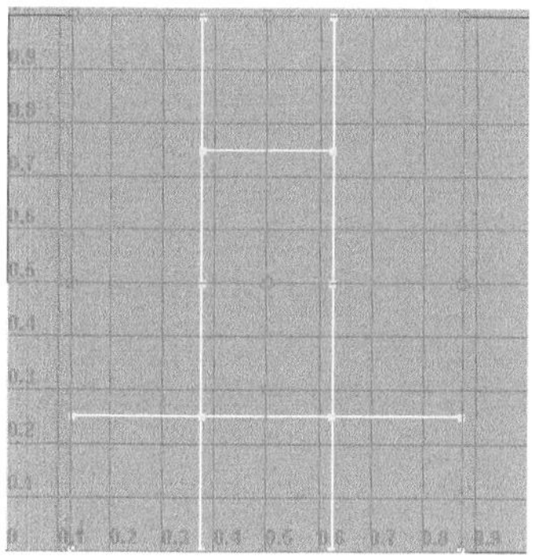

*Figure 5-14 Lattice created using the **UV Lattice Tool***

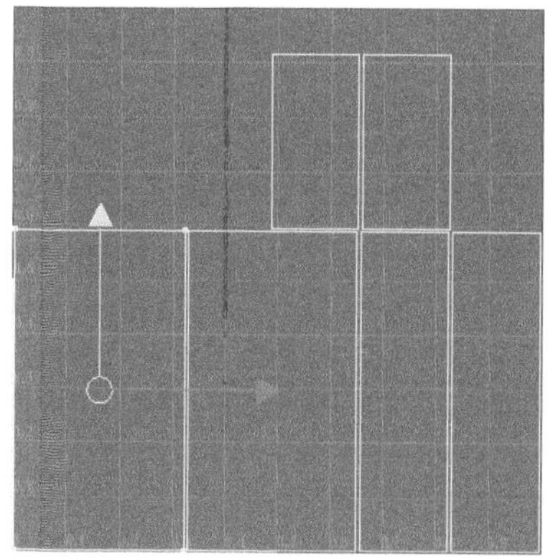

Figure 5-15 The UVs of the shell selected

Select Shortest Edge Path Tool

UV Editor menubar: Select > Select Shortest Edge Path Tool

The **Select Shortest Edge Path Tool** is used to select the direct path between two selected vertices. To do so, invoke this tool from the **UV Editor** toolbar in the **UV Editor**. Now, press and hold the right mouse button anywhere in the **UV Editor** area; a marking menu will be displayed. Choose **Vertex** from the marking menu displayed. Now, select any two vertices from the UV shell using the SHIFT key; the shortest edge between the two selected vertices will be highlighted in orange color.

Tweak UV Tool

UV Editor menubar: Tool > Tweak UV Tool

The **Tweak UV Tool** is used to reposition the selected UVs in the **UV Editor**. To do so, invoke the **Tweak UV Tool**. Now, press and hold the right mouse button anywhere in the **UV Editor** area; a marking menu will be displayed. Choose **UV** from the marking menu displayed. Now, select the UVs that you want to move.

UV Brush Tools Group

Enhanced

The tools in the UV brush tools group of the **UV Editor** are used to unfold, relax, and smooth UVs. To do so, choose the required tool and paint on the UVs of the selected object. These tools are discussed next.

Unfold UV Tool

UV Editor menubar: Tool > Unfold UV Tool

The **Unfold UV Tool** is used to unfold the overlapped UVs. To do so, choose the **Unfold UV Tool** from the **UV Editor** toolbar in the **UV Editor**. Next, paint on the UVs of the selected object. To change the brush size, press and hold the B key and drag the mouse cursor on the viewport.

Cut UV Tool

UV Editor menubar: Tool > Cut UV Tool

The **Cut UV Tool** is used to split UVs by dragging the cursor along edges. To do so, choose the **Cut UV Tool** from the **UV Editor** toolbar in the **UV Editor**. Now, click and drag the cursor along the edge; the edge will split into two edges. Press CTRL to temporarily activate the **Sew UV Tool** and weld the UVs together.

Grab UV Tool

UV Editor menubar: Tool > Grab UV Tool

The **Grab UV Tool** moves UVs along the direction of dragging the cursor. This tool is useful for making subtle adjustments to the texture of the model. To use this tool, place the cursor on the UVs that you want move and then drag the cursor to change the polygons of the UVs.

Pinch UV Tool

UV Editor menubar: Tool > Pinch UV Tool

The **Pinch UV Tool** pulls UVs toward the center of the tool cursor, so that the texture occupies less space on the model. Press CTRL to push UVs away from the center of the cursor, creating the inverse effect.

Symmetrize UV Tool

UV Editor menubar: Tool > Symmetrize UV Tool

The **Symmetrize UV Tool** is used to mirror UVs across the U and V axes. The symmetry line is displayed as bold line.

Optimize UV Tool

UV Editor menubar: Tool > Optimize UV Tool

The **Optimize UV Tool** is used to make the spacing between the UVs on a mesh uniform. This fixes the distortion or overlapping in UVs.

Sew UV Tool

UV Editor menubar: Tool > Sew UV Tool

The **Sew UV Tool** is used for welding UVs by dragging the brush along edges. Press CTRL to temporarily activate the **Cut UV Tool**.

Pin UV Tool

UV Editor menubar: Tool > Pin UV Tool

The **Pin UV Tool** locks the position of UVs. Locked UVs turn into blue color. Press CTRL and click to unlock the locked UVs.

Smear UV Tool

UV Editor menubar: Tool > Smear UV Tool

The **Smear UV Tool** is used to move the UVs in the direction tangent to their original position on the surface.

UV Smudge Tool

UV Editor menubar: Tool > UV Smudge Tool

The **UV Smudge Tool** moves the selected UVs and also affects the position of the adjacent UVs to some extent. To move the UVs, select one of the UVs from the UV shell in the **UV Editor**. Next, choose the **Tool > UV Smudge Tool** from the **UV Editor** menubar; a circle will be displayed around the cursor, refer to Figure 5-16. Press and hold the left mouse button and drag the cursor in the **UV Editor** to reposition the UVs.

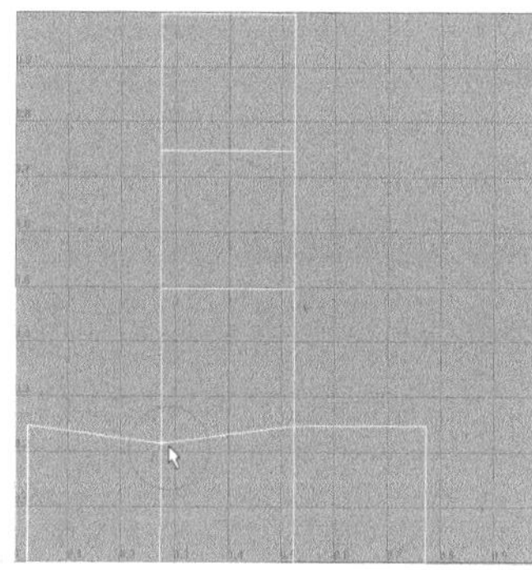

Figure 5-16** Moving a UV using the **UV Smudge Tool

Smooth UV Tool

UV Editor menubar: Tool > Smooth UV Tool

The **Smooth UV Tool** is used to relax or unfold the selected UV shell in the **UV Editor**. To do so, select the UVs that you want to unfold or relax and choose the **Tool > Smooth UV Tool** from the **UV Editor** menubar; the **Unfold** and **Relax** sliders will be displayed in the **UV Editor**, as shown in Figure 5-17. Hover the cursor on the **Unfold** or **Relax** button and drag the cursor toward right; the selected UVs will be relaxed or unfolded.

Note

1. *To exit the **Smooth UV Tool**, press W.*
2. *While selecting UVs, the manipulator automatically snaps to the nearest UV.*

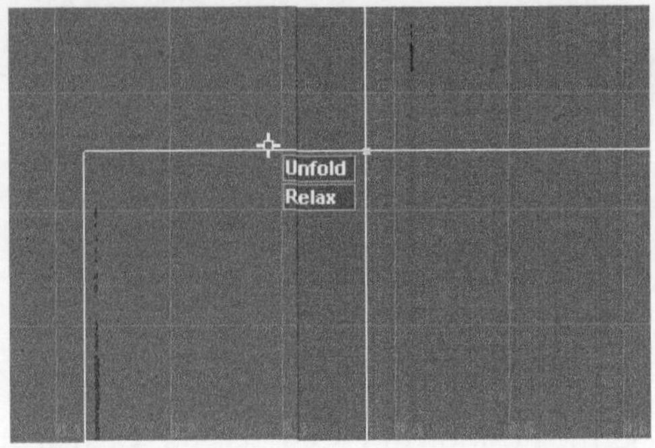

*Figure 5-17 The **Unfold** and **Relax** sliders*

Flip/Rotate Tools Group

The tools in the **Flip/Rotate tools group** are used to modify the orientation of the selected UVs. These tools are discussed next.

Flip selected UVs in U direction

The **Flip selected UVs in U direction** tool is used to flip the selected UVs in the U direction. To do so, select the UVs that you want to flip and then choose the **Flip selected UVs in U direction** tool from the **UV Editor** toolbar; the selected UVs will be flipped.

Flip selected UVs in V direction

The **Flip selected UVs in V direction** tool is used to flip the selected UVs in the V direction. To do so, select the UVs that you want to flip and then choose the **Flip selected UVs in V direction** tool from the **UV Editor** toolbar; the selected UVs will be flipped.

Rotate selected UVs counterclockwise

The **Rotate selected UVs counterclockwise** tool is used to rotate the selected UVs by 45 degrees in counterclockwise direction. To do so, select the UVs to be rotated and then choose the **Rotate selected UVs counterclockwise** tool from the **UV Editor** toolbar; the UVs will be rotated by 45 degrees, which is the default angle of rotation. You can also change the default rotation angle for the UVs. To do so, right-click on the **Rotate selected UVs counterclockwise** tool in the **UV Editor**; the **Rotate UVs Counterclockwise Options** dialog box will be displayed, as shown in Figure 5-18. In this dialog box, enter the desired angle value for the **Counterclockwise** attribute or move the slider on the right to change the rotation angle. Next, choose the **Apply** button.

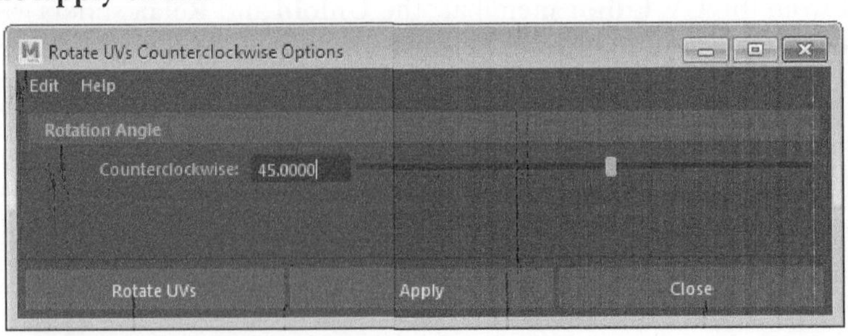

*Figure 5-18 The **Rotate UVs Counterclockwise Options** dialog box*

Rotate selected UVs clockwise

The **Rotate selected UVs clockwise** tool is used to rotate the selected UVs in clockwise direction. To do so, select the UVs to be rotated and then choose the **Rotate selected UVs clockwise** tool from the **UV Editor** toolbar; the UVs will be rotated by 45 degrees. You can also change the default rotation angle of the UVs. To do so, right-click on the **Rotate selected UVs clockwise** tool in the **UV Editor** toolbar; the **Rotate UVs Clockwise Options** dialog box will be displayed. In this dialog box, enter the desired angle value for the **Clockwise angle** attribute or move the slider on the right to change the rotation angle. Next, choose the **Apply** and then the **Close** button.

UV Layout Tools Group

The tools in this group are used to arrange the selected UVs in the layout. These tools are discussed next.

Layout UVs

UV Editor menubar: Polygons > Layout

The **Layout UVs** tool is used to reposition the UV shells in such a way that they do not overlap in the UV texture space. It fits the selected UVs in the 0 to 1 space.

Snap selected UVs to user specified grid

The **Snap selected UVs to user specified grid** tool is used to move the selected UVs to their nearest grid intersection point. To understand the working of this tool, select the UVs in the UV shell from the **UV Editor** and right-click on the **Snap selected UVs to user specified grid** tool from the **UV Editor** toolbar; the **Grid UVs Options** dialog box will be displayed, as shown in Figure 5-19. The options in this dialog box are used to set the grid size for the **UV Editor**. Set the options as required and choose the **Apply** and then the **Close** button; the selected UVs will move to their nearest grid intersection in the **UV Editor**.

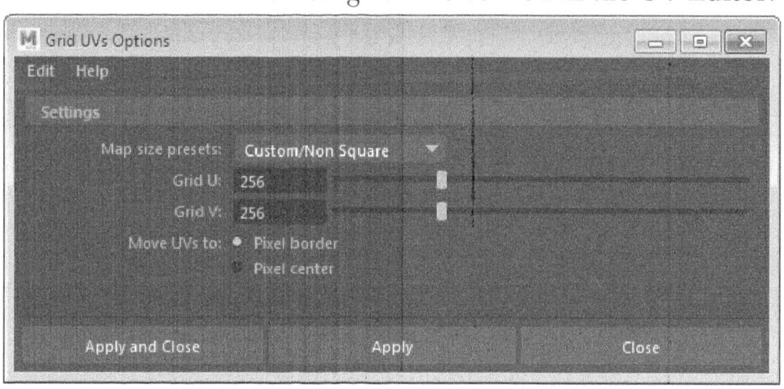

*Figure 5-19 The **Grid UVs Options** dialog box*

Unfold selected UVs

UV Editor menubar: Polygons > Unfold

The **Unfold selected UVs** tool is used to unwrap the selected UVs in the **UV Editor**. To do so, select the UVs in the UV shell from the **UV Editor** and choose the **Unfold selected**

UVs tool from the **UV Editor** toolbar; the selected UVs will be unfolded without overlapping each other.

Automatically move UVs for better texture space distribution

The **Automatically move UVs for better texture space distribution** tool is used to arrange UVs of the selected mesh to create a better layout. This tool works similar to the **Unfold selected UVs** tool and spreads the UV mesh uniformly in the **UV Editor**.

UV Alignment Tools Group

The tools in the UV alignment group are used to align the selected UVs in the U and V directions. These tools are discussed next.

Align selected UVs to minimum U value

UV Editor menubar:	Polygons > Align > Option Box

The **Align selected UVs to minimum U value** tool is used to align the selected UVs vertically to the minimum U value. To align the UVs, select the UVs that you want to align and choose the **Align selected UVs to minimum U value** tool from the **UV Editor** toolbar.

Align selected UVs to maximum U value

UV Editor menubar:	Polygons > Align > Option Box

The **Align selected UVs to maximum U value** tool is used to align the selected UVs vertically to the maximum U value. To align the UVs, select the UVs that you want to align and choose the **Align selected UVs to maximum U value** tool from the **UV Editor** toolbar.

Align selected UVs to minimum V value

UV Editor menubar:	Polygons > Align > Option Box

The **Align selected UVs to minimum V value** tool is used to align the selected UVs horizontally to the minimum V value. To align the UVs, select the UVs to align and choose the **Align selected UVs to minimum V value** tool from the **UV Editor** toolbar.

Align selected UVs to maximum V value

UV Editor menubar:	Polygons > Align > Option Box

The **Align selected UVs to maximum V value** tool is used to align the selected UVs horizontally to the maximum V value. To do so, select the UVs that you want to align and choose the **Align selected UVs to maximum V value** tool from the **UV Editor** toolbar.

Isolate Selection Tools Group

The tools in this group are used to work on the selected UVs independently by hiding the rest of the UVs. The tools in this group are discussed next.

Toggle isolate select mode

UV Editor menubar: View > Isolate Select > View Set

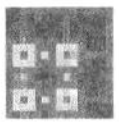

The **Toggle isolate select mode** tool is used to toggle between the display of the selected UVs and the isolated UVs in the **UV Editor**. To do so, select the UVs of the object to be displayed from the **UV Editor** and then choose the **Toggle isolate select mode** tool from the **UV Editor** toolbar to toggle the display of the selected UVs and the isolated UVs.

Add selected UVs to the isolate select set

UV Editor menubar: View > Isolate Select > Add Selected

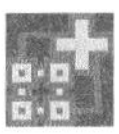

The **Add selected UVs to the isolate select set** tool is used to add the selected UVs to the isolated UVs group. To do so, select the isolated UVs group from the **UV Editor**, if it is not selected. Next, in the **UV Editor**, select the UVs that you want to add to the isolated UVs and then choose the **Add selected UVs to the isolate select set** tool from the **UV Editor** toolbar; the selected UVs will be added to the isolate select set.

Remove all UVs of the selected object from the isolate select set

UV Editor menubar: View > Isolate Select > Remove All

The **Remove all UVs of the selected object from the Isolate select set** tool is used to remove the set in the **UV Editor**.

Remove selected UVs to the isolate select set

UV Editor menubar: View > Isolate Select > Remove Selected

The **Remove selected UVs to the isolate select set** tool is used to remove the selected UVs from the isolated UVs group. To do so, make sure the isolate select set UVs group is selected in the **UV Editor**. Now, select the UVs that you want to remove from the isolated select set group in the **UV Editor**. Now, choose the **Remove selected UVs to the isolate select set** tool from the **UV Editor** toolbar; the selected UVs will be removed from the isolated select set.

Image and Texture Tools Group

The tools in the image and texture group are used to toggle the display of texture images and to adjust their appearances. The tools in this group are discussed next.

Display image on/off

UV Editor menubar: Image > Display Image

The **Display image on/off** tool is used to toggle the display of the texture images in the **UV Editor**.

Toggle filtered image on/off

UV Editor menubar: Image > Display Unfiltered

The **Toggle filtered image on/off** tool is used to toggle between the display of low resolution texture image and high resolution texture image.

Dim image on/off

UV Editor menubar: Image > Dim Image

The **Dim image on/off** tool is used to toggle between the bright and dim texture image. Choose the **Dim image on/off** tool from the **UV Editor** tool; the brightness of the texture image in the **UV Editor** will be reduced.

Show/Hide the Display Tools Group

Enhanced

The tools in the Show/Hide the Display Tools group are used to adjust alpha channels other texture properties. These tools are discussed next.

View grid on/off

UV Editor menubar: View > Grid

The **View grid on/off** tool is used to display or hide the grid in the **UV Editor**.

Pixel snap on/off

UV Editor menubar: Image > Pixel Snap

The **Pixel snap on/off** tool is used to automatically snap the selected UVs to pixel boundaries.

Toggle shaded UV display

The **Toggle shaded UV display** tool is used to toggle the display of semi-transparent UV shells such that you can view the overlapping UVs in the **UV Editor**.

Display UV distortion

The **Display UV distortion** tool is used to point out the UVs by coloring the squashed or stretched faces in the **UV Editor**. The errors are indicated by different colors as a red face indicates stretching, a blue face indicates compression, and a white face indicates optimal UVs.

Toggle the display of texture borders for the active mesh

The **Toggle the display of texture borders for the active mesh** tool is used to toggle the display of texture borders on the UV shells. To do so, choose this tool from the **UV Editor** toolbar; the border of UV texture coordinates will be displayed as a thick line.

Display checkered tiles

The **Display checkered tiles** tool is used to find out problems like stretched and overlapping UVs, by applying checker texture to UV mesh.

Display RGB channels

UV Editor menubar: Image > Display RGB Channels

The **Display RGB channels** tool is used to display the color channels of the selected texture image.

Display alpha channel

UV Editor menubar: Image > Display Alpha Channel

The **Display alpha channel** tool is used to display the transparency channel. To do so, choose the **Display alpha channel** tool from the **UV Editor** toolbar. As a result, the alpha channels of the selected texture image will be displayed.

Adjust the brightness for display

This tool is used to adjust the brightness for display between the default and modified values. You can also specify a custom value in the edit box available next to this tool.

Adjust the contrast, or brightness of the midtones in the image for display

This tool is used to adjust the brightness of the midtones between default and modified values. To enter a custom value, enter it in the edit box available next to this tool.

View Transform

This tool is used to toggle view transform on and off. By default, the sRGB gamma transform is applied. You can select a different transform from the drop-down list available next to this tool. This is useful when you want to see raw color values

UV Texturing Tools Group

The tools in this group are used to perform functions such as baking textures, updating texture group, and so on. Texture baking is a method to render multiple materials and shaders including scene lighting, shadows, and complicated materials into a single texture. The tools in this group are discussed next.

UV Texture Editor baking on/off

UV Editor menubar: Image > UV Texture Editor Baking

The **UV Texture Editor baking** on/off tool is used to bake textures and store them in the memory of the system.

Update PSD networks

UV Editor menubar:	Image > Update PSD Networks

The **Update PSD Networks** tool is used to update the current PSD texture used in the scene. To understand the working of this tool, modify the PSD texture connected to Maya PSD node in Photoshop and choose the **Update PSD Networks** tool from the **UV Editor** toolbar; the PSD texture used in the scene will be updated.

Force editor texture rebake

The **Force editor texture rebake** tool is used to rebake the texture. If the **UV Texture Editor Baking** option is selected in the Image menu, you must rebake the texture using this tool after making changes to the texture.

Use image ratio on/off

UV Editor menubar:	Image > Use Image Ratio

The **Use image ratio on/off** tool is used to toggle the display of square texture space, with the texture space having the same ratio of width to height as the image itself in the **UV Editor**. Figure 5-20 displays the square texture space. Figure 5-21 displays the texture space having the same width to height ratio as the image itself.

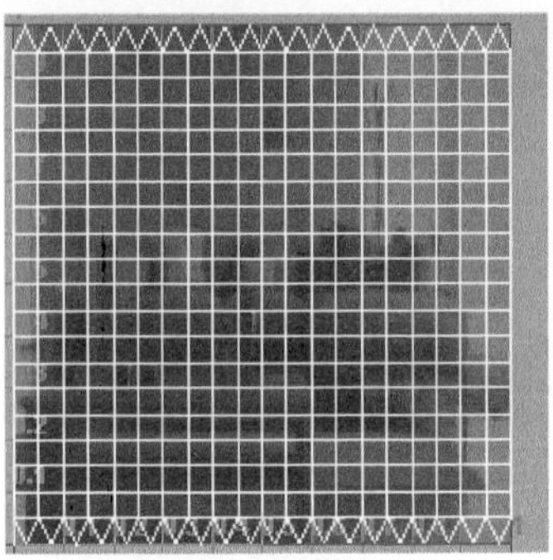

Figure 5-20 *The square texture space displayed*

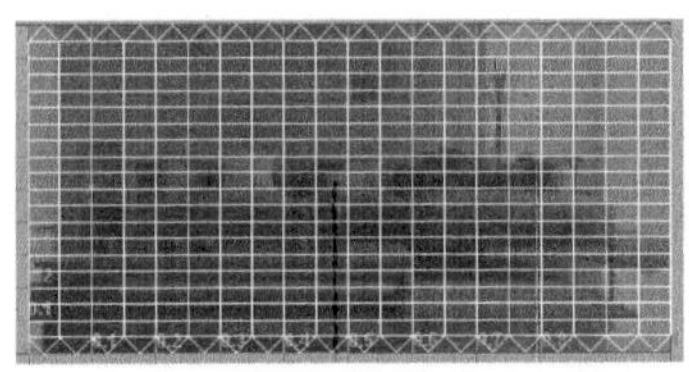

Figure 5-21 *The texture space displayed having the same ratio*

UV Edit Tools Group

The options in this group are used to edit the UVs of the selected object. These options are discussed next.

Enter value to set/transform in U and Enter value to set/transform in V

The **Enter value to set/transform in U** and **Enter value to set/transform in V** edit boxes show the coordinates of the selected UVs. You can set the U and V coordinates of the selected UV shell in the **UV Editor**. To do so, select the UV shell and enter the UV coordinate values in the corresponding edit boxes of the toolbar. Next, press ENTER; the selected UVs are transformed to the values specified.

Refresh the current UV values

The **Refresh the current UV values** tool is used to update the UV values of the selected UVs. On selecting a particular UV, the U and V coordinate values are displayed in the **Enter value to set/transform in U** and **Enter value to set/transform in V** edit boxes. However, on moving the UVs, the values do not change dynamically in the input area. Choose the **Refresh the current UV values** tool from the **UV Editor** to update the UV coordinates.

Toggles the mode of the UV entry fields between absolute UV position and relative transformation tool values

The **Toggles the mode of the UV entry fields between absolute UV position and relative transformation tool values** tool is used to toggle the entry mode of the UV coordinates between absolute and relative values.

Copy colors, UVs, and or shader from a face to the clipboard

The **Copy colors, UVs, and or shader from a face to the clipboard** tool is used to copy the selected UV points and the faces of an object to the clipboard.

Paste colors, UVs, and or shaders to face(s) from clipboard

The **Paste colors, UVs, and or shaders to face(s) from clipboard** tool is used to paste the selected UV points and the faces from the clipboard.

Toggle copy/paste for faces/UVs

The **Toggle copy/paste for faces/UVs** tool is used to activate the **Copy/Paste** buttons in the **UV Editor** toolbar. Choose the **Toggle copy/paste for faces/UVs** tool from the **UV Editor** toolbar; the **Paste U value to selected UVs** and **Paste V value to selected UVs** tools will be activated.

Cycles the UVs of the selected face counter clockwise

The **Cycle UVs of the selected face counter clockwise** tool is used to cycle the U and V values of the selected faces counterclockwise.

Nudge components

The **Nudge components** tool is used to reposition the selected components in the **UV Editor**.

TUTORIALS

Tutorial 1

In this tutorial, you will model and then texture a wooden box. The final rendered output of the model is displayed in Figure 5-22. **(Expected time: 15 min)**

Figure 5-22 The final rendered output of the model

The following steps are required to complete this tutorial:

a. Create a project folder.
b. Download the texture file.
c. Create a polygon cube.
d. Fit the texture using the 2D UV coordinates.
e. Change the background color of the scene.
f. Save and render the scene.

Creating a Project Folder

Create a new project folder with the name *c05_tut1* at *\Documents\maya2017* and then save the file with the name *c05tut1,* as discussed in Tutorial 1 of Chapter 2.

Downloading the Texture File

In this section, you need to download the texture file.

1. Download the *c05_maya_2017_tut.zip* file from *www.cadcim.com*. The path of the file is as follows: *Textbooks > Animation and Visual Effects > Maya > Autodesk Maya 2017: A Comprehensive Guide.*

2. Extract the contents of the zip file to the *Documents* folder. Next, copy the *woodbox-texture.jpg* file from *\Documents\maya2017\c05_maya_2017_tut* to *\Documents\maya2017\c05_tut1\sourceimages.*

Creating a Polygon Cube

In this section, you need to create a polygon cube.

1. Choose **Create > Objects > Polygon Primitives > Cube** from the menubar and click in the viewport; a cube is created in the persp viewport.

2. In the **Channel Box / Layer Editor**, expand the **polyCube1** node in the **INPUTS** area and then set **8** as the value for the **Width, Height**, and **Depth** attributes.

Fitting Texture Using the 2D UV Coordinates

In this section, you need to apply the texture to the polygon cube using the 2D UV coordinates.

1. Choose **Windows > Editors > Rendering Editors > Hypershade** from the menubar; the **Hypershade** window is displayed.

2. Choose the **Lambert** shader from the **Create** panel; a lambert shader node is created in the **Browser** panel with the name **lambert#**. Press and hold the CTRL key and double-click on the **lambert#** shader in the **Browser** panel; the **Rename node** dialog box is displayed, as shown in Figure 5-23. Enter **Wood box** in the **Enter new name** text box and then choose the **OK** button; the **Lambert** shader is renamed to *Wood box*. Also, the **Wood box** tab is displayed in **Property Editor**.

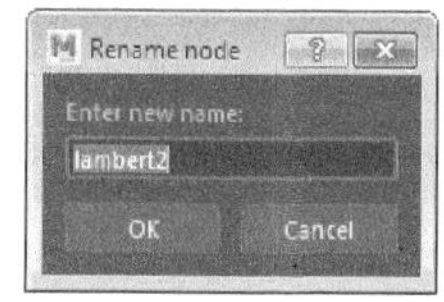

Figure 5-23 *The* ***Rename node*** *dialog box*

3. In the **Property Editor** panel of the **Wood box** tab, click on the checker button next to the **Color** attribute, as shown in Figure 5-24; the **Create Render Node** window is displayed. In this window, choose the **File** button; the **File Attributes** area is displayed in the **file1** tab of the **Property Editor**. Choose the folder icon located on the right of the **Image Name** attribute; the **Open** dialog box is displayed. In this dialog box, select the **woodbox-texture.jpg** file and then choose the **Open** button.

4. Select the polygon cube in the viewport. In the **Hypershade** window, press and hold the right mouse button over the **Wood box** shader; a marking menu is displayed. Choose the **Assign Material To Selection** option from this marking menu; the texture is applied to the cube. Now, click anywhere in the viewport and press 6 to view the texture in the viewport. Figure 5-25 shows the polygon cube with the texture applied.

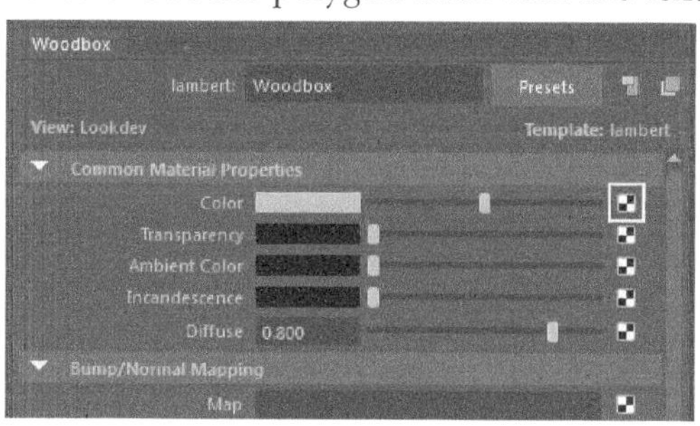

Figure 5-24 *Clicking on the checker button next to the* ***Color*** *attribute in the* ***Common Material Properties*** *panel*

Figure 5-25 *The wood texture applied to the cube*

5. Make sure the cube is selected and then choose **Windows > Editor > Modeling Editors > UV Editor** from the menubar; the **UV Editor** is displayed. Next, choose **View > Grid** from the **UV Editor** menubar; the grid becomes invisible and the UV shell for the cube is displayed, as shown in Figure 5-26.

6. Press and hold the right mouse button in the empty space of the **UV Editor**; a marking menu is displayed. Choose **UV** from this marking menu and select all the UVs. Invoke **Scale Tool** from the Tool Box; various handles are displayed. Scale the selected UVs using

the marque selection along the X axis by dragging the red handle, align the edges with the vertical lines of the *woodbox-texture.jpg*.

The entire texture is mapped on to the cube, except the two areas that are not covered in the V area. Figure 5-27 shows the selected 2D UV texture coordinates after scaling them.

Note

*In the **UV Editor**, the area of the texture within the UV coordinates will only be visible on the object in the viewport.*

7. Press and hold the right mouse button in the empty space of the **UV Editor**; a marking menu is displayed. Next, choose **Edge** from the marking menu. Select edge 12 from the **UV Editor**, refer to Figure 5-28. Now, choose **Polygons > Cut UV Edges** from the **UV Editor** menubar; the UVs of selected edges are separated from the edge. Next, select edge 4, refer to Figure 5-27 and choose **Polygons > Move and Sew UV Edges** from the **UV Editor** menubar; the edge corresponding to the selected edge of the 2D texture coordinate is moved and sewed. Figure 5-29 displays the 2D UV coordinate partially mapped over the texture.

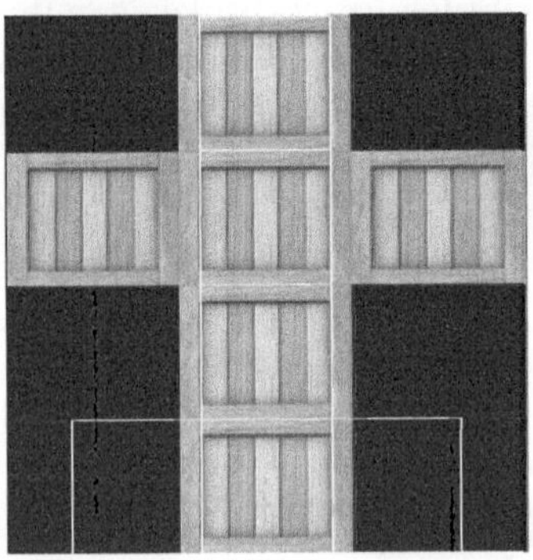

Figure 5-26 The UV shell for cube

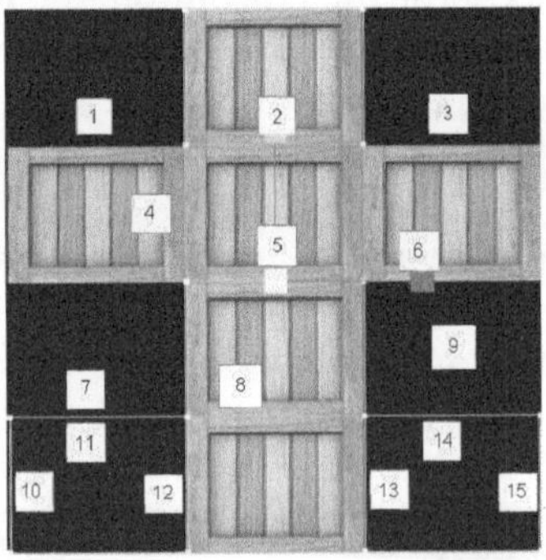

Figure 5-27 The 2D UV texture coordinates after scaling

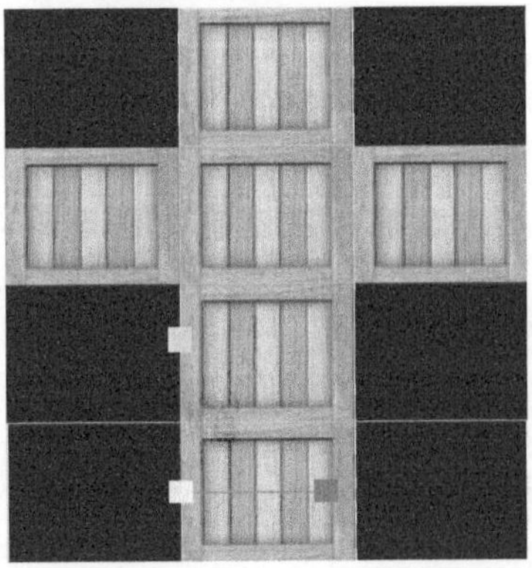

*Figure 5-28 Edge 12 to be selected from the **UV Editor***

Figure 5-29 The 2D UV coordinate partially mapped over the texture

8. In the **UV Editor**, select edge 13, refer to Figure 5-27. Choose **Polygons > Cut UV Edges** from the **UV Editor** menubar; the UVs of selected edges are separated from the edge. Now, select edge 6, refer to Figure 5-27. Choose **Polygons > Move and Sew UV Edges** from the menubar; the edge corresponding to the selected edge of the 2D texture coordinate is moved and sewed to match the 2D UV coordinate completely with the texture. Figure 5-30 displays the UV coordinate completely mapped over the texture.

9. Close the **UV Editor** and the **Hypershade** window. Now, you can rotate the view in the persp viewport to check that the texture is properly applied on the polygon cube, or not. You can also scale the UVs, if the texture is stretched.

***Figure 5-30** The 2D UV coordinate completely mapped over the texture*

Changing the Background Color of the Scene

In this section, you need to change the background color of the scene.

1. Choose **Windows > Editors > Outliner** from the menubar; the **Outliner** window is displayed. Click on the **persp** camera in the **Outliner** window; the **perspShape** tab is displayed in the **Attribute Editor**.

2. In the **perspShape** tab, expand the **Environment** area and drag the **Background Color** slider bar toward right to change the background color to white. Close the **Outliner** window.

Saving and Rendering the Scene

In this section, you will save the scene that you have created and then render it. You can view the final rendered image of the model by downloading the *c05_maya_2017_rndr.zip* file from *www.cadcim.com.* The path of the file is as follows: *Textbooks > Animation and Visual Effects > Maya > Autodesk Maya 2017: A Comprehensive Guide.*

1. Choose **File > Save Scene** from the menubar.

2. Maximize the persp viewport, if it is not already maximized. Choose the **Render the current frame** button from the Status Line; the **Render View** window is displayed. The final output of the model is shown in Figure 5-31.

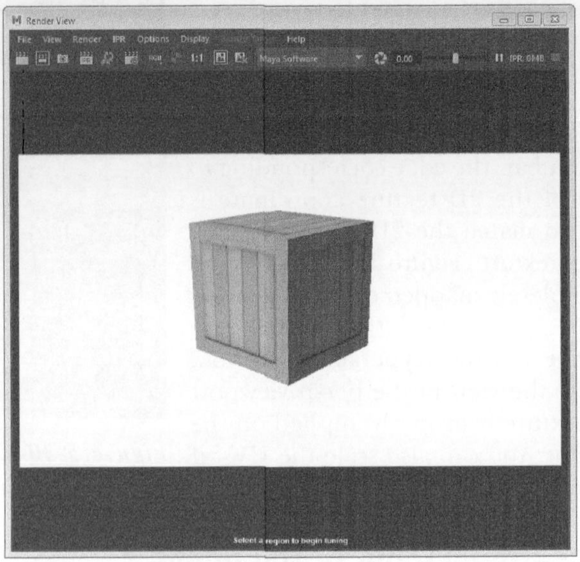

*Figure 5-31 The **Render View** window displaying the final rendered image*

Tutorial 2

In this tutorial, you will create the model of a hut and then unwrap it, refer to Figures 5-32 and 5-33. **(Expected time: 30 min)**

Figure 5-32 Front view of the unwrapped model of the hut

Figure 5-33 Back view of the unwrapped model of the hut

The following steps are required to complete this tutorial:

a. Create a project folder.
b. Create the hut.
c. Assign a texture to the hut.

d. Unwrap the hut.
e. Change the background color of the scene.
f. Save and render the scene.

Creating a Project Folder

Create a new project folder with the name *c05_tut2* at *\Documents\maya2017* and then save the file with the name *c05tut2*, as discussed in Tutorial 1 of Chapter 2.

Creating the Hut

In this section, you need to create the model of the hut.

1. Maximize the front-Z viewport. Choose **Create > Objects > Polygon Primitives > Cube** from the menubar and click on the viewport; a cube is created in the viewport.

2. Make sure that the cube is selected in the viewport. In the **Channel Box / Layer Editor**, expand the **polyCube1** node of the **INPUTS** area and set the parameters as follows:

   Width: **8** Height: **7**
   Depth: **8** Subdivisions Width: **2**

3. Next, rename the cube to **hut**, as discussed earlier.

4. Make sure *hut* is selected. Press and hold the right mouse button over it; a marking menu is displayed. Choose **Vertex** from the marking menu; the vertex selection mode is activated. Next, marquee-select the top-center vertices of *hut*, refer to Figure 5-34. Choose **Move Tool** from the Tool Box and move the selected vertices upward along the Y-axis, refer to Figure 5-34.

5. Make sure the **Modeling** menuset from the **Menuset** drop-down list is selected. Next, press and hold the right mouse button over *hut*; a marking menu is displayed. Choose **Object Mode** from the marking menu; the object selection mode is activated. Select *hut* and then choose **Mesh Tools > Tools > Insert Edge Loop** from the menubar and insert four edges, refer to Figure 5-35. Now, choose **Scale Tool** from the Tool Box and scale the inserted horizontal edges along the Y axis to make them straight, refer to Figure 5-35. Choose **Move Tool** from the Tool Box and align the horizontal lines, as shown in figure 5-35.

6. Press and hold the right mouse button over *hut*; a marking menu is displayed. Choose **Face** from the marking menu; the face selection mode is activated. Next, select the faces of *hut*, as shown in Figure 5-36, and press DELETE; the selected faces are deleted.

7. Press and hold the right mouse button over *hut*; a marking menu is displayed. Choose **Edge** from the marking menu; the edge selection mode is activated. Now, select the edges of *hut*, refer to Figure 5-37.

8. Choose **Edit Mesh > Components > Extrude** from the menubar; the **polyExtrudeEdge1** In-View Editor is displayed in the viewport. Next, invoke **Scale Tool** by pressing the R key and uniformly scale the selected edges inward, refer to Figure 5-38.

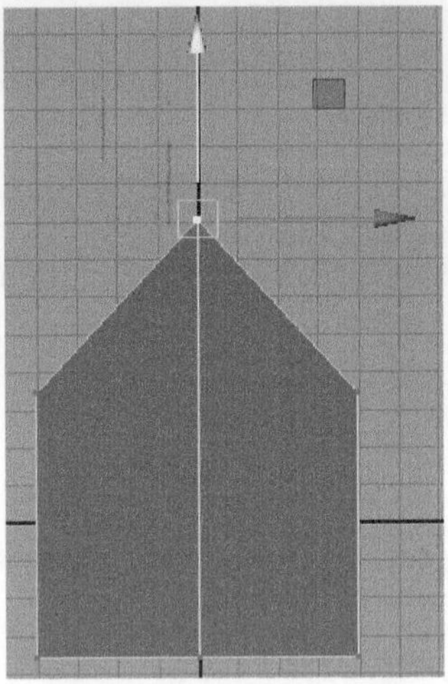

Figure 5-34 Vertices moved upward

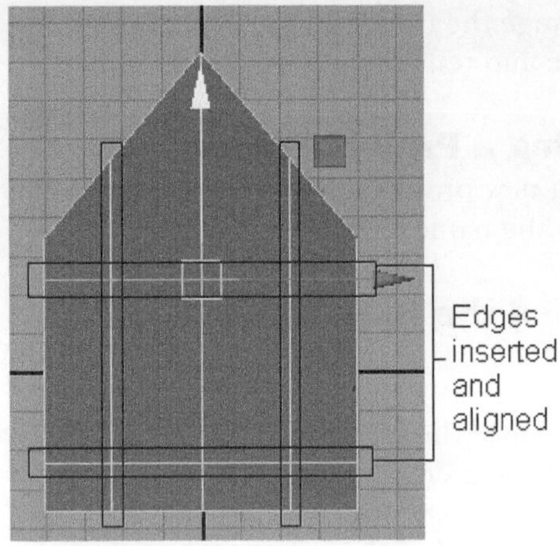

Figure 5-35 Four edges inserted in the hut

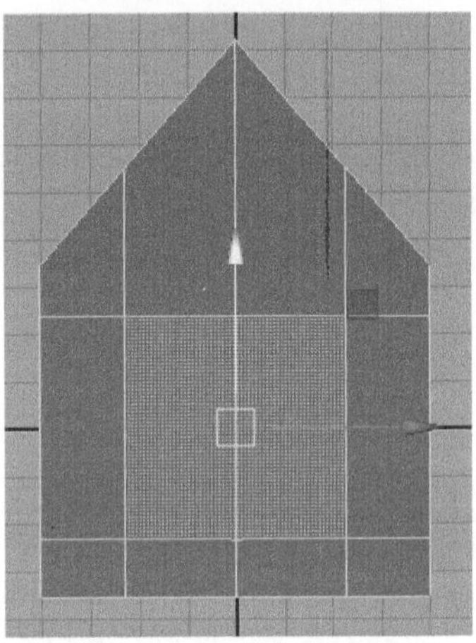

Figure 5-36 The faces to be selected

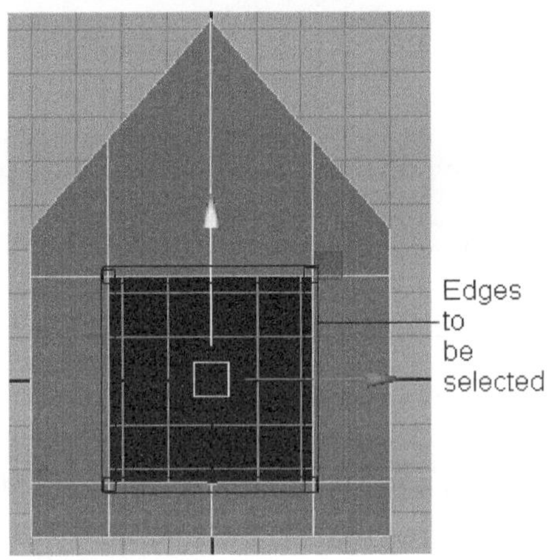

Figure 5-37 The edges to be selected

9. Maximize the persp viewport. Next, press and hold the right mouse button over *hut*; a marking menu is displayed. Choose **Face** from the marking menu; the face selection mode is activated. Select the faces using the SHIFT key, refer to Figure 5-39 and choose **Edit Mesh > Components > Extrude** from the menubar; the **polyExtrudeFace1** In-View Editor is displayed in the viewport. Enter **0.2** in the **Thickness** edit box of the **polyExtrudeFace1** In-View Editor, refer to Figure 5-39.

10. Select the top faces of the hut using the SHIFT key, as shown in Figure 5-40. Next, choose **Edit Mesh > Components > Extrude** from the menubar, the **polyExtrudeFace2** In-View Editor is displayed in the viewport. Enter **0.25** in the **Thickness** edit box of the **polyExtrudeFace2** In-View Editor, refer to Figure 5-41.

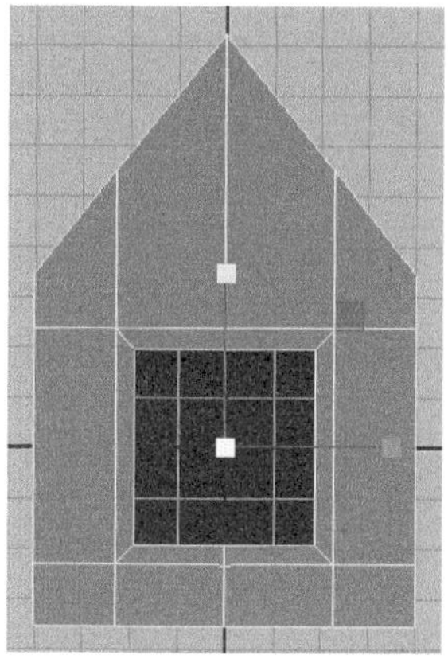

Figure 5-38 Scaling the edges of the hut inward

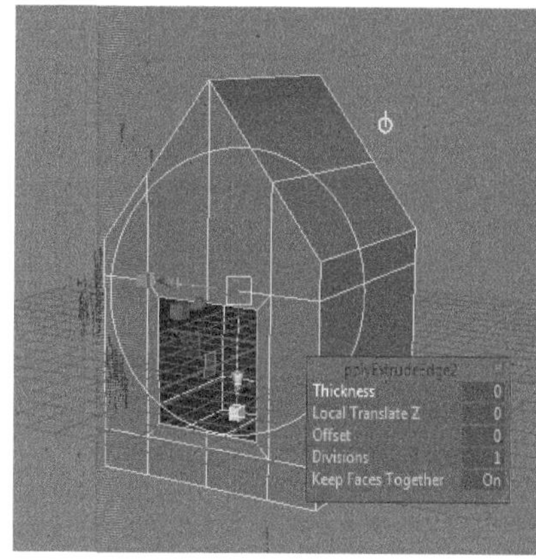

Figure 5-39 The faces of hut extruded

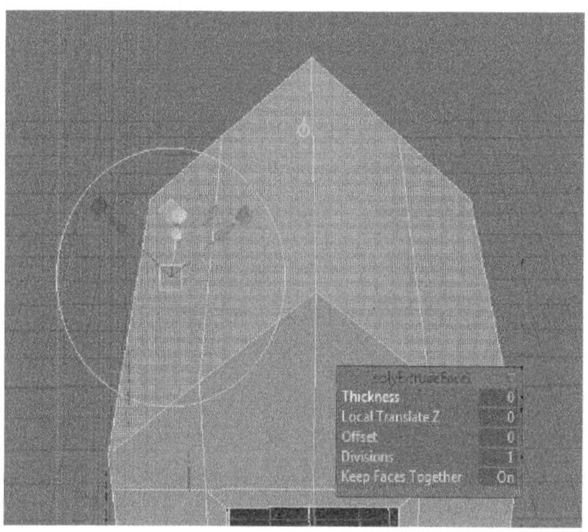

Figure 5-40 The selected faces of the hut

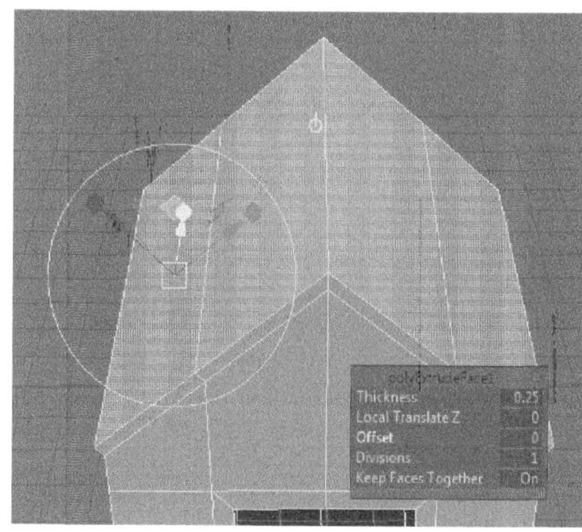

Figure 5-41 Selected faces of the hut extruded

Assigning Texture to the Hut

In this section, you need to assign texture to the hut.

1. Choose **Select Tool** from the Tool Box; the **Extrude** tool is deactivated. Press and hold the right mouse button over *hut*; a marking menu is displayed. Choose **Object Mode** from the marking menu; the object selection mode is activated. Select the *hut*. Next, press and hold the right mouse button over it; a marking menu is displayed. Choose **Assign Favorite Material > Lambert** from this marking menu, as shown in Figure 5-42; the **lambert2** tab is displayed in the **Attribute Editor**.

2. In the **Common Material Attributes** area of the **lambert2** tab, click on the checker button beside the **Color** attribute; the **Create Render Node** window is displayed. Choose the **Checker** button from this window, as shown in Figure 5-43.

3. Press 6; the checker texture is displayed on *hut*. You will notice that the checker pattern appears distorted.

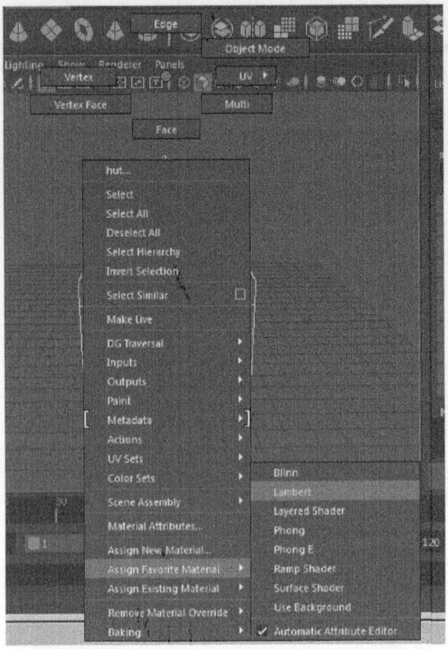

Figure 5-42 Choosing the ***Lambert*** *material from the marking menu*

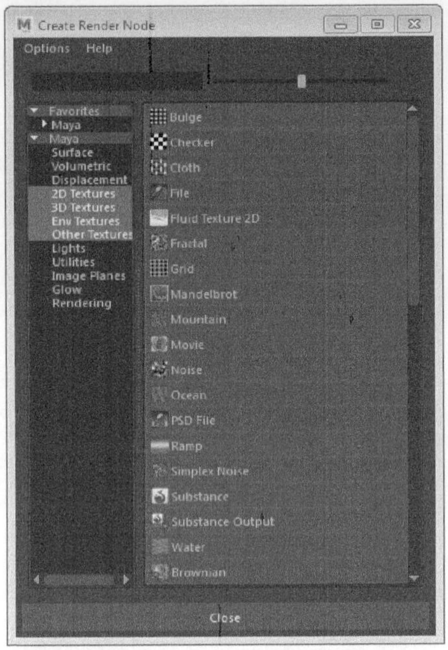

Figure 5-43 Choosing the ***Checker*** *button from the* ***Create Render Node*** *window*

Unwrapping the Hut

In this section, you need to unwrap the hut for proper distribution of UVs.

1. In the persp viewport, press and hold the right mouse button over *hut*; a marking menu is displayed. Choose **Face** from the marking menu; the face selection mode is activated. Select the front faces of *hut*, as shown in Figure 5-44. Next, choose **UV > Create > Planar > Option Box** from the menubar; the **Planar Mapping Options** dialog box is displayed. In the **Projection Manipulator** area of the dialog box, select the **Z axis** radio button in the **Project from** attribute. Next, choose the **Apply** button; the checker pattern is distributed uniformly. Choose the **Close** button to close the dialog box.

2. Choose **Windows > Editors > Modeling Editors > UV Editor** from the menubar; the **UV Editor** is displayed with unwrapped hut, as shown in Figure 5-45.

3. In the **UV Editor**, move the selected part out of the UV texture area, as shown in Figure 5-46.

   Next, you will project a uniform texture on the left side of the *hut*.

4. In the persp viewport, press and hold the right mouse button over *hut*; a marking menu is displayed. Choose **Face** from this marking menu; the face selection mode is activated. Next, select the faces of the left part of *hut*, as shown in Figure 5-47.

5. Choose **UV > Create > Planar > Option Box** from the menubar; the **Planar Mapping Options** dialog box is displayed. In the **Projection Manipulator** area of the dialog box, select the **X axis** radio button in the **Project from** parameter. Next, choose the **Apply** button; the

checker pattern is distributed uniformly. Now, choose the close button to close the dialog box.

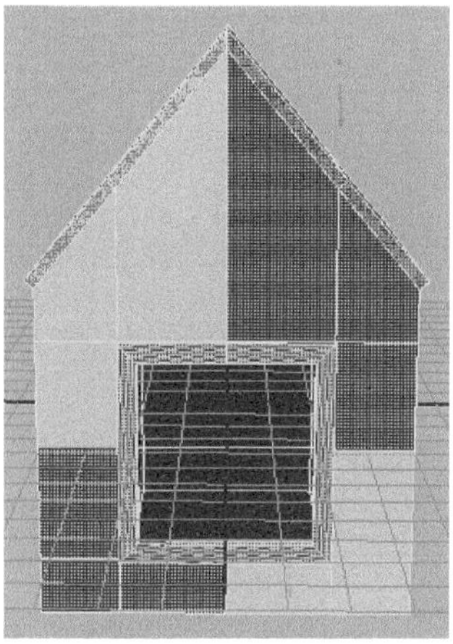

Figure 5-44 *Front faces of the hut selected*

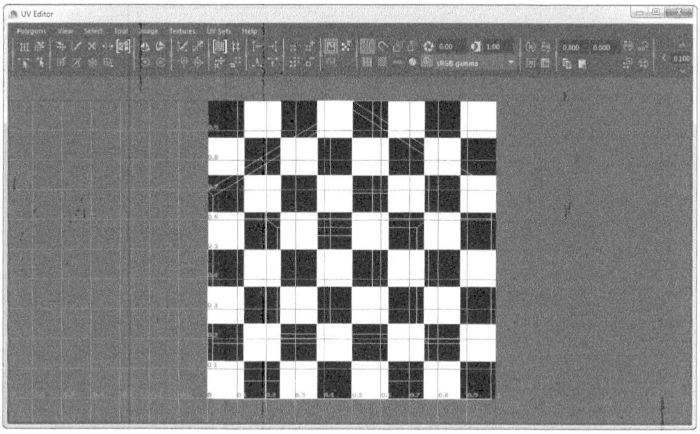

Figure 5-45 *The **UV Editor** displaying the unwrapped hut*

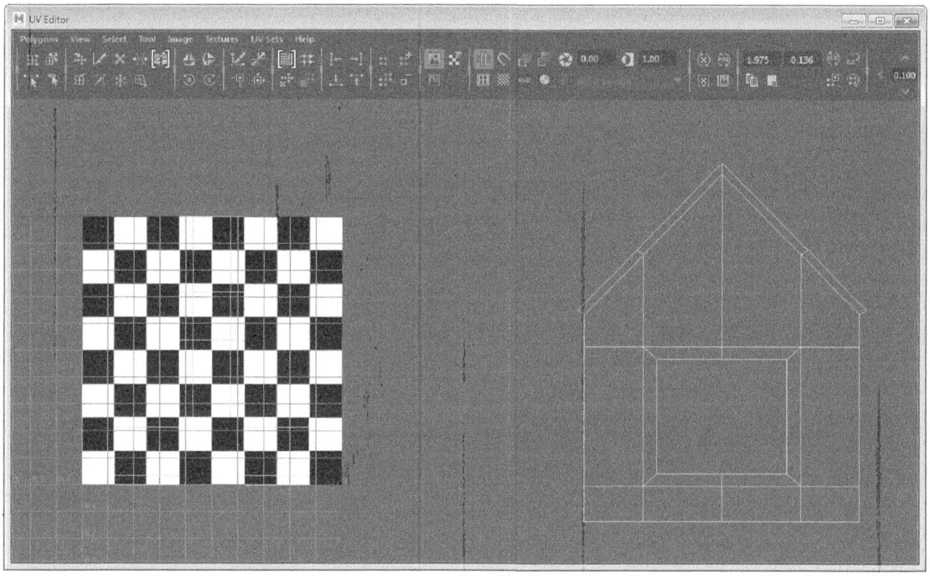

Figure 5-46 *Scaling the front part of the hut*

6. In the **UV Editor**, move the selected part of *hut* in such a way that it lies at the left side to the front part of *hut*. Next, invoke the **Scale Tool** and scale the hut uniformly, as shown in Figure 5-48.

7. Repeat the same procedure to unwrap the right part of the *hut*, and then move it to the right of the front part in the **UV Editor**, refer to Figure 5-49. Next, press and hold the right mouse button over the front part of *hut* in the **UV Editor**; a marking menu is displayed. Choose **Edge** from the marking menu. Next, select the right edges of the front part, as

shown in Figure 5-49. You will notice that the left edges of the right side of *hut* get selected automatically.

Figure 5-47 *Faces of the left part of hut selected*

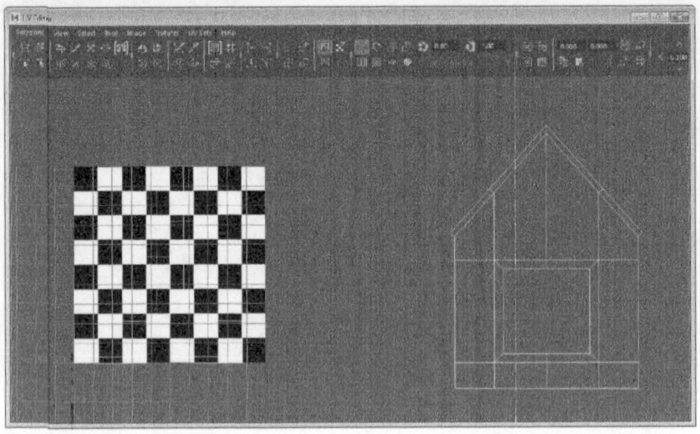

Figure 5-48 *Scaling the UVs of side and front parts of the hut*

8. In the **UV Editor**, choose the **Polygons > Move and sew UV edges** tool from the menubar; the selected edges get attached, as shown in Figure 5-50.

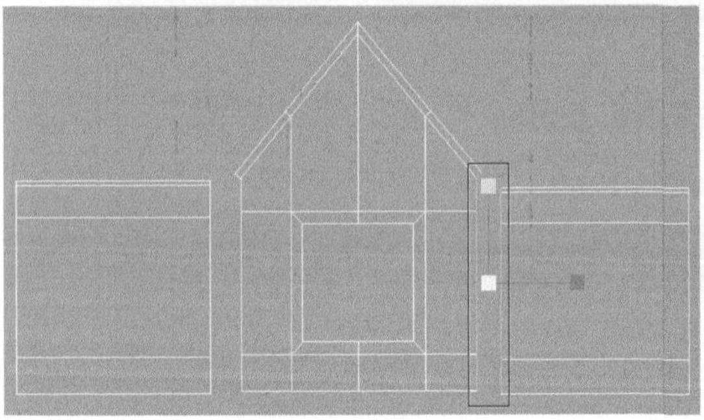

Figure 5-49 *Right edge of the front part selected*

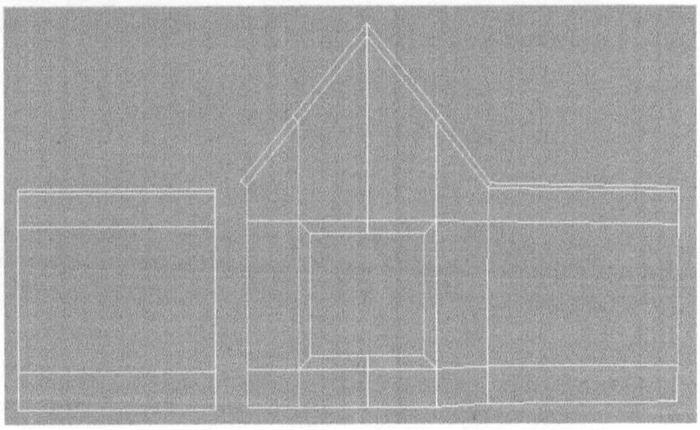

Figure 5-50 *The right side edges of the front attached to left side edges of the right part*

9. Similarly, choose the left edges of the front part of *hut*. You will notice that the left edges of the left part of *hut* get selected. On choosing the **Move and sew the selected edges** tool from the menubar, the faces get distorted.

10. Press and hold the right mouse button over the left side of *hut*; a marking menu is displayed. Choose **UV** from the marking menu and then marquee select all the UVs of the left part of *hut*, as shown in Figure 5-51.

11. Choose the **Flip selected UVs in U direction** tool from the **UV Editor** toolbar; the selected UVs flip in the U direction.

12. Press and hold the right mouse button over the left part of *hut*; a marking menu is displayed. Choose **Edge** from the marking menu. Next, choose the right edges of the left part of *hut*

and then choose the **Move and sew the selected edges** tool from the **UV Editor** toolbar; the selected edges of the front and side parts of *hut* are attached, as shown in Figure 5-52.

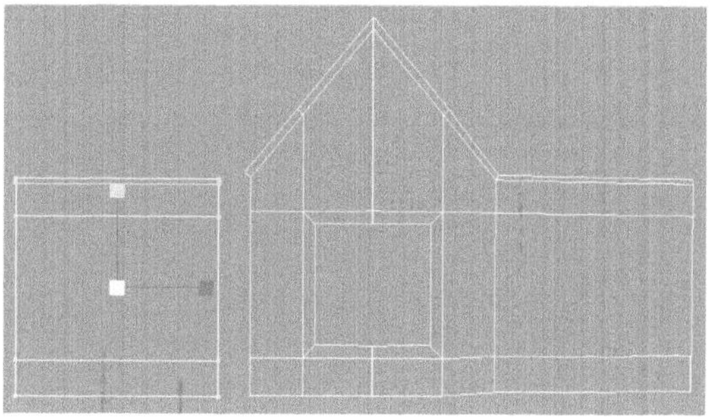

Figure 5-51 *UVs of the left part selected*

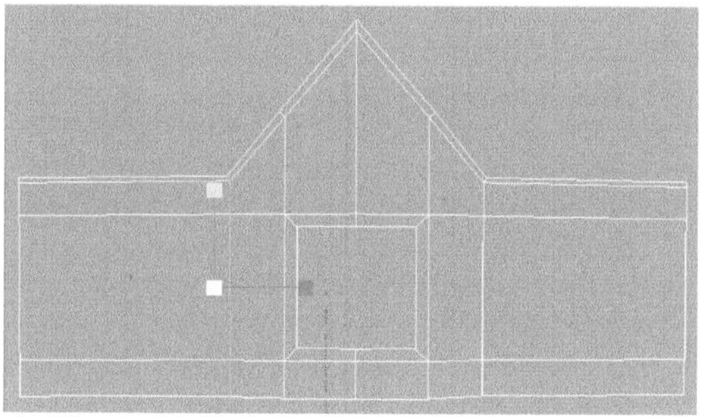

Figure 5-52 *Front and left parts of the hut*

13. In the persp viewport, press and hold the right mouse button over the *hut*; a marking menu is displayed. Choose **Face** from the marking menu and select the faces of the roof of *hut*, and choose **UV > Create > Automatic** from the menubar; the checkers are distributed uniformly, as shown in Figure 5-53.

14. In the **UV Editor**, the UVs of the roof are split into two parts. Press and hold the CTRL and then right mouse button over the roof part; a marking menu is displayed. Choose **To UV > To UV** from the marking menu. Now, press W to invoke the **Move Tool** in the **UV Editor** and move the UVs of roof parts outside the UV texture area, as shown in Figure 5-54.

Figure 5-53 *Uniformly distributed checkers on the roof of hut*

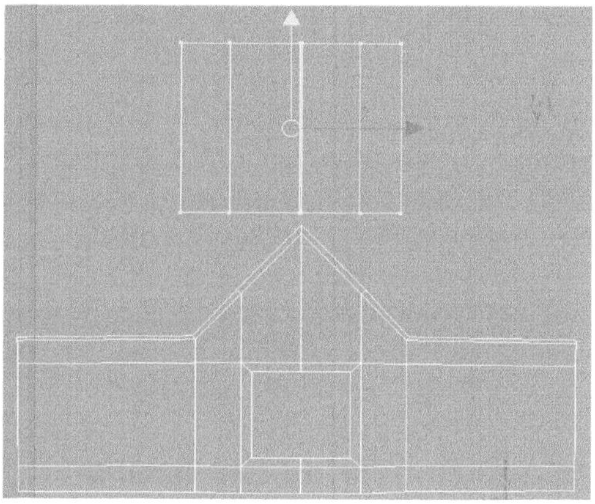

Figure 5-54 *Moving the roof part of the hut out of the UV texture area*

Next, you need to merge the edges.

15. Press and hold the right mouse button over the roof part of the *hut*; a marking menu is displayed. Choose **Edge** from the marking menu and select the edges, as shown in Figure 5-55.

16. Choose the **Move and sew the selected edges** tool from the **UV Editor** toolbar; the selected edges of the roof are automatically attached. If the checkers are stretched, scale the UVs of

the roof accordingly in the **UV Editor**, as shown in Figure 5-56. The checkers in the viewport should form a square shape.

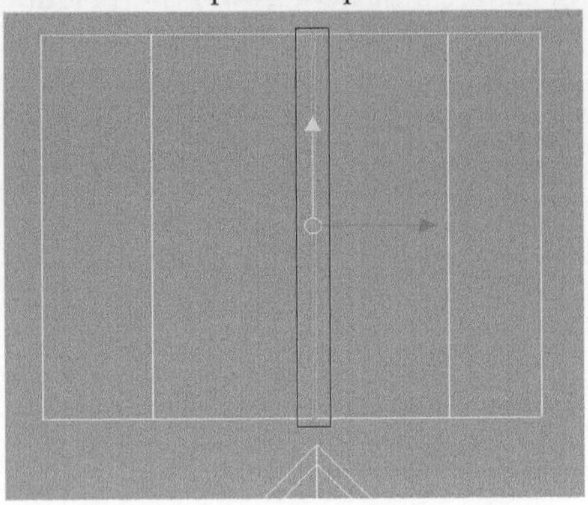

Figure 5-55 *Edges selected*

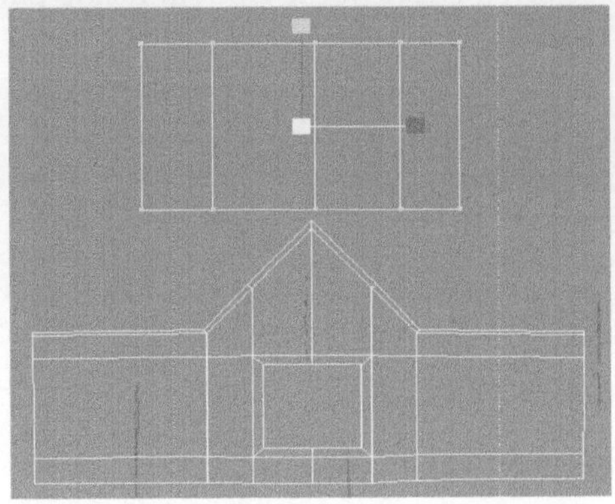

Figure 5-56 *UVs of the roof scaled*

17. Similarly, unwrap the back side and bottom sides of *hut* using the **Planar** tool. The final model will have uniform distribution of checkers on all the sides, as shown in Figure 5-57.

Note
The checkers in the viewport should form a square shape.

Changing the Background Color of the Scene

In this section, you will change the background color of the scene.

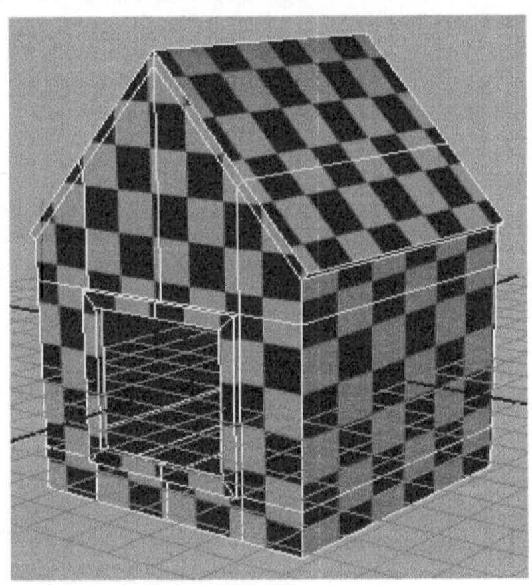

Figure 5-57 *Final model of hut with uniform distribution of checkers*

1. Choose **Windows > Editors > Outliner** from the menubar; the **Outliner** window is displayed. Select the **persp** camera in the **Outliner** window; the **perspShape** tab is displayed in the **Attribute Editor**.

2. In the **perspShape** tab, expand the **Environment** area and drag the **Background Color** slider bar toward right to change the background color to white.

Saving and Rendering the Scene

In this section, you will save the scene that you have created and then render it. You can view the final rendered image of the model by downloading the *c05_maya_2017_rndr.zip* file from *www.cadcim.com*. The path of the file is as follows: *Textbooks > Animation and Visual Effects > Maya > Autodesk Maya 2017: A Comprehensive Guide.*

1. Choose **File > Save Scene** from the menubar.

2. Maximize the persp viewport, if it is not already maximized. Choose the **Render the current frame** button from the Status Line; the **Render View** window is displayed. The final output of the scene is shown in Figures 5-32 and 5-33.

Self-Evaluation Test

Answer the following questions and then compare them to those given at the end of this chapter:

1. Which of the following tools is used to change the position of the selected UVs and their neighboring UVs?

   (a) **Move UV Shell Tool** (b) **UV Smudge Tool**
   (c) **UV Lattice Tool** (d) **Flip Selected UVs in V Direction**

2. Which of the following mapping techniques is used to map complex objects?

   (a) Planar (b) Spherical
   (c) Cylindrical (d) Automatic

3. The **Rotate Selected UVs counterclockwise** tool is used to rotate the selected UVs by __________ degrees.

4. The __________ creates UVs by creating a spherical projection around a polygonal object.

5. You can view and edit the 2D texture coordinates of an object by using the __________.

6. Press __________ to show or hide the texture image in the viewport.

7. The **Cycle UVs** tool is used to rotate the U and V values of a selected polygon. (T/F)

8. Spherical mapping is mainly used for planar objects. (T/F)

9. The navigation options in the **UV Editor** are different from those that are displayed in the normal viewport area. (T/F)

10. The Counter Stretch mapping technique is used to apply texture in triangulated surface. (T/F)

Review Questions

Answer the following questions:

1. Which of the following is a UV mapping technique used in Maya?

   (a) Planar (b) Cylindrical
   (c) Spherical (d) All of these

2. Which of the following tools is used to create a lattice around the UVs for deformation?

   (a) **UV Lattice Tool** (b) **UV Smudge Tool**
   (c) **Move UV Shell Tool** (d) **Smooth UV Tool**

3. You can change the number of projection planes in the __________ UV mapping technique.

4. The __________ tool is used to unwrap a selected mesh without overlapping the UVs.

5. __________ is used to create UVs on a polygonal object by creating a bounding box around it.

6. The __________ tool is used to arrange the UVs in a cleaner layout based on the settings in the **Layout UVs Options** dialog box.

7. You can project the Planar mapping manipulators in the camera axis. (T/F)

8. Automatic mapping is mainly used for the objects that are hollow or projected outward. (T/F)

9. You can map a texture on to the 2D UV coordinates by scaling UVs in the **UV Editor**. (T/F)

10. The **Sew the selected object or UVs together** tool is used to attach the UVs along the selected borders, but it cannot be used to move them together in the **UV Editor**. (T/F)

EXERCISES

The rendered output of the models used in the following exercises can be accessed by downloading the *c05_maya_2017_exr.zip* file from *www.cadcim.com*. The path of the file is as follows: *Textbooks > Animation and Visual Effects > Maya > Autodesk Maya 2017: A Comprehensive Guide.*

Exercise 1

Create a model of the interior of a house, as shown in Figure 5-58, and unwrap it.

(Expected time: 20 min)

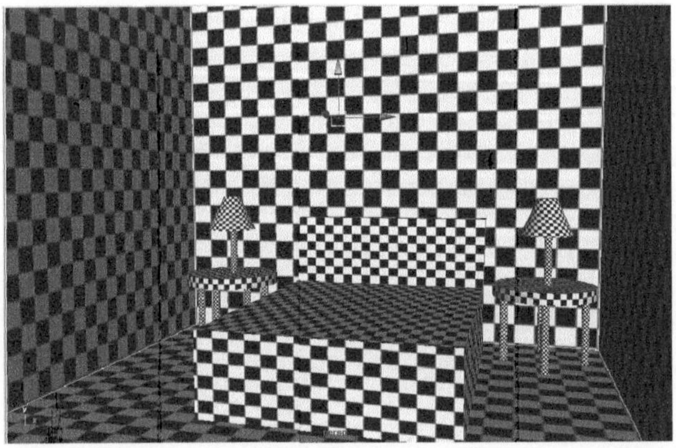

Figure 5-58 *The unwrapped model of the interior of a house*

Exercise 2

Create a model of the exterior of a house, as shown in Figure 5-59, and unwrap it.

(Expected time: 20 min)

Figure 5-59 *The unwrapped model of the exterior of a house*

Answers to Self-Evaluation Test

1. b, **2.** d, **3.** 45, **4. Spherical mapping**, **5. UV Editor**, **6.** 6, **7.** T, **8.** F, **9.** F, **10.** F

Chapter 6

Shading and Texturing

Learning Objectives

After completing this chapter, you will be able to:

- *Navigate in the Hypershade window*
- *Use shaders*
- *Apply textures and colors to objects*

INTRODUCTION

In this chapter, you will learn to give a realistic look to the objects by applying textures to them. For example, while creating a brick wall, you first need to apply a brick texture and then apply the bump on the wall. On doing so, the darker area of the texture will display bumps on the surface on rendering.

WORKING IN THE Hypershade WINDOW

Main menubar: Windows > Editors > Rendering Editors > Hypershade

The options in the **Hypershade** window can be used to create, edit, and connect the rendering nodes such as textures, materials, and lights. To open this window, choose **Windows > Editors > Rendering Editors > Hypershade** from the menubar; the **Hypershade** window will be displayed, as shown in Figure 6-1. The components of the **Hypershade** window are discussed next.

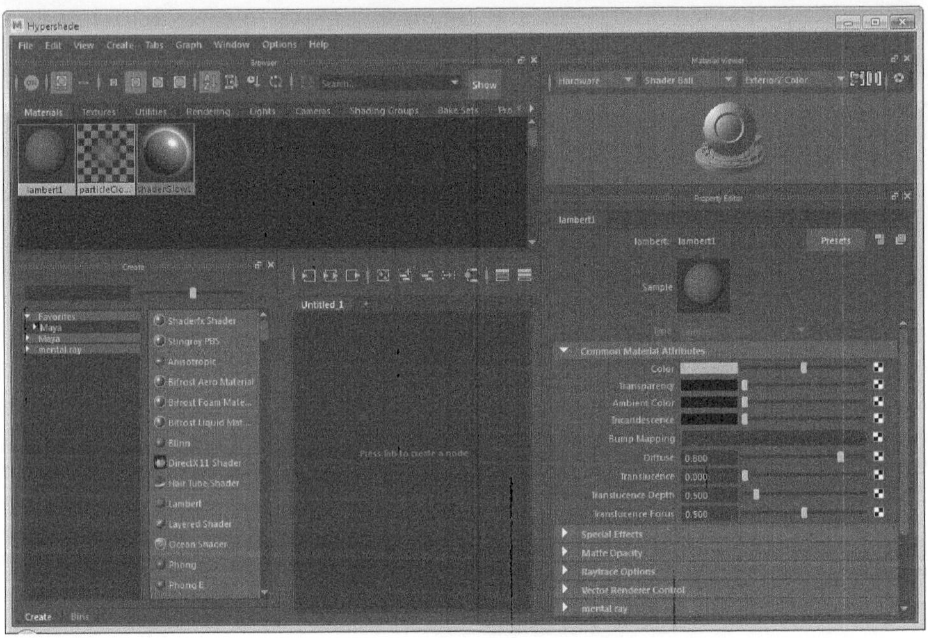

*Figure 6-1 The **Hypershade** window*

Create Panel

The **Create** panel is located on the left of the **Untitled_1** tab in the **Hypershade** window, refer to Figure 6-1. This panel consists of different types of nodes that are used to create different shading effects. These nodes are divided into three categories: **Favorites**, **Maya**, and **mental ray**. These categories are further divided into sections. You can also search the nodes by their respective names in the **Hypershade** window. To do so, enter the name of the required node in the search text box located at the top of the **Create Panel**; the render node with that particular name will be displayed in the node list. To increase or decrease the size of node icons, drag the slider bar located on the right of the search text box. On moving the slider bar to right, the size of the icons will increase, and on moving it to left, the size of the icons will decrease. The **Create** panel is discussed in detail later in this chapter.

Browser Panel

The top panel of the **Hypershade** window contains ten tabs that are used to access rendering components, refer to Figure 6-2. These tabs also correspond to various objects present in the viewport. For example, the **Materials** tab contains all materials that have been used in the scene and the **Lights** tab contains lights that are added to the scene, and so on.

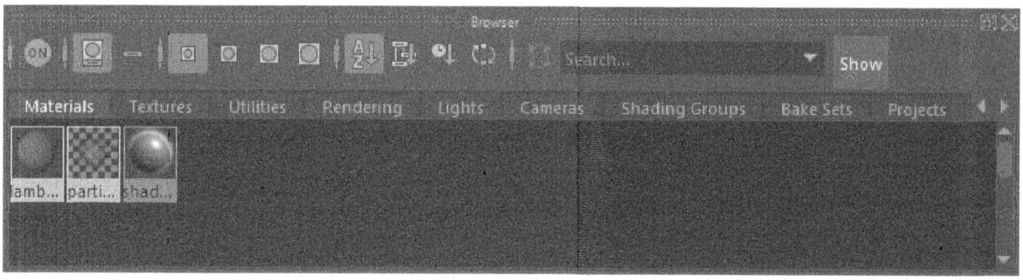

*Figure 6-2 The **Browser** tab in the **Hypershade** window*

Browser Panel Toolbar

The Browser panel toolbar is located on the top of the **Browser** panel, as shown in Figure 6-3. The buttons in this toolbar are used to control viewing, listing, and ordering of the options in the different tabs of the **Browser** panel.

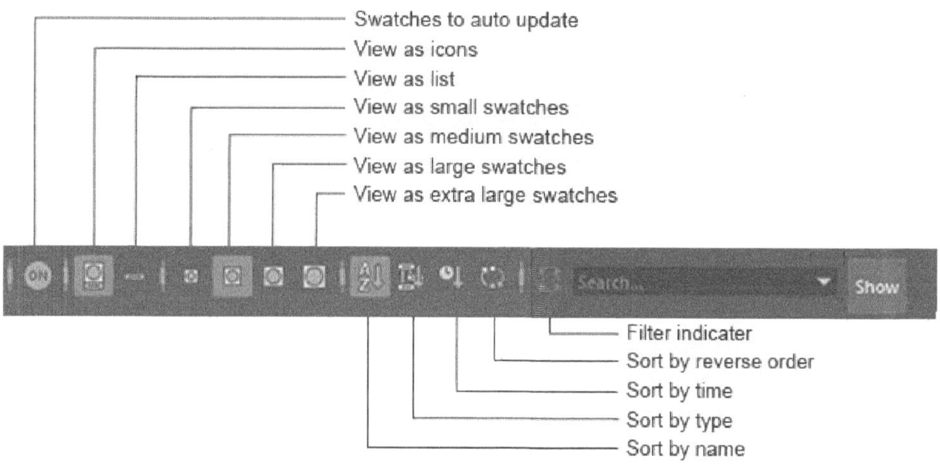

*Figure 6-3 The Browser panel toolbar in the **Hypershade** window*

Swatches to auto update

This button is used to toggle on and off the swatch generation functionality for all nodes.

View as icons

This button is used to display node swatches as icons.

View as list

 This button is used to display names of various node swatches in the form of a list in the **Browser** panel.

View as small/medium/large/extra large swatches

 These buttons are used to change the size of the swatches.

Sort by name

 This button is used to arrange node swatches alphabetically (A-Z) in the **Hypershade** window.

Sort by type

 This button is used to arrange nodes according to their shader types. For example, on choosing this button, all the **Blinn** shaders will be grouped together in a single group and all the **Anisotropic** shaders will be grouped together under another group. Apart from grouping and arranging similar types of shaders, you can also use this button to arrange the types of shaders alphabetically.

Sort by time

 This button is used to arrange nodes according to the time of their creation (oldest to newest). It means that the nodes created first will be displayed first, then the next, and so on.

Sort by reverse order

 This button is used to reverse the arrangement of nodes in the **Hypershade** window, irrespective to their sequence of placement in the **Untitled_1** tab of the **Hypershade** window.

Work Area

This area is located on the right of the **Create** panel. By default, the **Untitled_1** tab is displayed in this panel, refer to Figure 6-1. The Work Area displays the shading network for the selected node. A shading network is an arrangement of nodes that affect the final look of the surface on which the material is applied.

A toolbar, referred to as the Work Area toolbar, is located on the top of the Work Area. It consists of various buttons that are used to control shading and texturing, refer to Figure 6-4. Some of the commonly used buttons in this toolbar are discussed next.

Input connections

 The **Input connections** button is used to display the input connections of the selected material node in the Work Area.

Input and output connections

 This button is used to display the input and output connections of the selected material node in the Work Area.

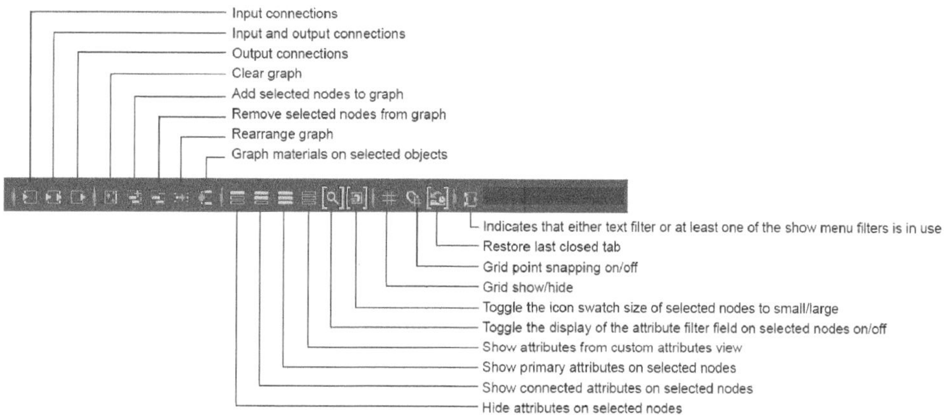

Figure 6-4 *The main toolbar of the* ***Hypershade*** *window*

Output connections

This button is used to display only the output connections of the selected material node in the Work Area.

Clear graph

This button is used to clear the nodes and shading networks in the Work Area. Alternatively, you can choose **Graph > Clear Graph** from the menubar in the **Hypershade** window.

Add selected nodes to graph

This button is used to add the selected material node in the work area. Alternatively, you can choose **Graph > Add Selected to Graph** from the menubar in the **Hypershade** window.

Remove selected nodes from graph

This button is used to remove selected nodes from the Work Area. Alternatively, you can choose **Graph > Remove Selected from Graph** from the menubar in the **Hypershade** window.

Rearrange graph

This button is used to rearrange nodes in the Work Area such that all nodes and networks are displayed properly in a defined manner. Alternatively, you can choose **Graph > Rearrange Graph** from the menubar in the **Hypershade** window.

Graph materials on selected objects

This button is used to display the shading group networks of the selected object. Alternatively, you can choose **Graph > Graph Materials on Selected Objects** from the menubar in the **Hypershade** window.

Hide attributes on selected nodes

This button is used to hide the attributes of selected nodes. In this mode, only the input and output master ports are shown.

Show connected attributes on selected nodes

This button changes the view mode to the connected mode. In this mode, the input and the output master ports as well as the connected node attributes are shown.

Show primary attributes on selected nodes

This button changes the view mode of the selected nodes to full. In this mode, the input and the output master ports as well as the primary node attributes are displayed.

Show attributes from custom attribute view

This button is used to view all the nodes created in the **Hypershade** window.

Toggle the display of the attribute filter field on selected nodes on/off

This button is used to display and hide the attribute filter field on the material nodes.

Toggle the icon swatch size of selected nodes to small/large

This button is used to toggle swatch icon size larger or smaller.

Grid show/hide

This button is used to show or hide the background grid.

Grid point snapping on/off

This button is used to snap the nodes to the grid.

Restore last closed tab

This button is used to restore last closed or deleted tab. This icon becomes active when you have deleted a tab.

Indicates that either text filter or at least one of the show menu filters is in use

By default, the cameras, shading groups, and shading nodes are displayed in the **Untitled_1** tab. You can filter nodes by name using the text box on the right of this button. When no filter is applied, this icon appears gray.

PROPERTY EDITOR

In Maya, the shaders are controlled by attributes. To view these attributes, click on a shader in the **Browser** panel of the **Hypershade** window; all attributes of the corresponding shader will be displayed in the **Property Editor**, refer to Figure 6-5. You can tear off the **Property Editor** panel from the **Hypershade** window. By choosing top right button you can toggle between **Lookdev view** and **Attribute Editor view**.

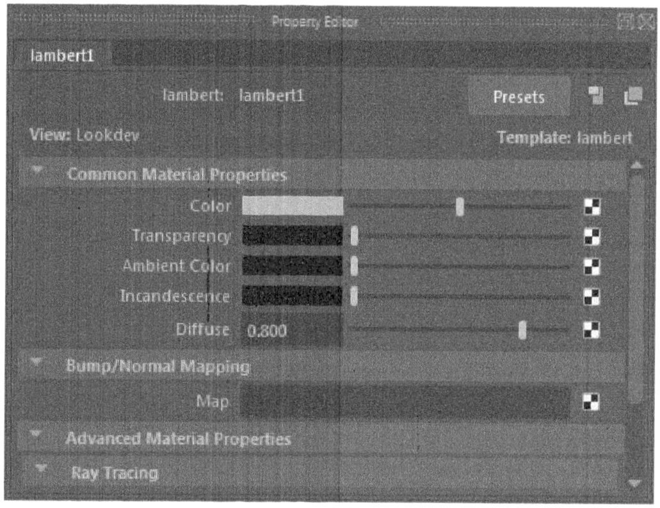

*Figure 6-5 The **Property Editor** displaying the Lambert shader attributes*

Common Material Attributes

The **Common Material Attributes** area consists of general attributes of an object. These attributes are discussed next.

Color

The **Color** attribute is used to assign a basic color to the surface. To do so, click on the color swatch on the right of the **Color** attribute; the **Color History** palette will be displayed, as shown in Figure 6-6. Choose a color from the **Color History** palette and then click anywhere outside the palette; the shader will display the color selected from this window. Next, adjust the brightness of the color by dragging the slider available on the right of the **Color** attribute.

You can also apply a map instead of a particular color on a shader. To do so, click on the checker box corresponding to the **Color** attribute; the **Create Render Node** window will be displayed, as shown in Figure 6-7. Now, you can choose either the **File** or **PSD File** button from the **Create Render Node** window to apply maps or textures.

The **File** button allows you to add images as maps and textures, whereas the **PSD File** button allows you to add the Photoshop file as maps and textures. If you choose the **File** button from the **Create Render Node** window, the **File Attributes** area will be displayed in the **Property Editor**. Choose the folder button on the right of the **Image Name** attribute; the **Open** window will be displayed. Choose the image file from the location on the disk and then choose the **Open** button. Similarly, add the PSD texture by choosing the **PSD File** button from the **Create Render Node** window.

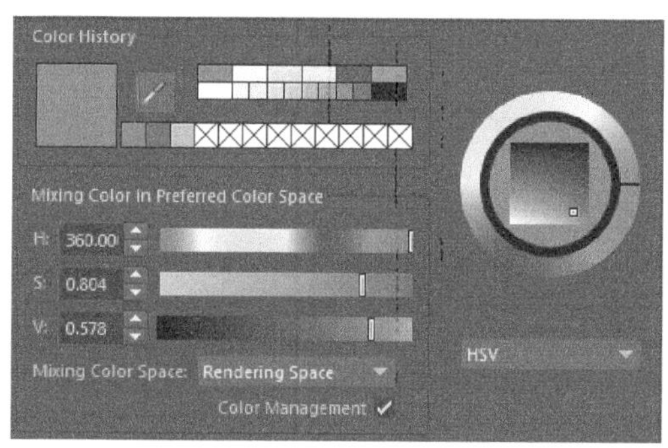

*Figure 6-6 The **Color History** palette*

Transparency

The **Transparency** attribute is used to make an object transparent. To set the transparency of an object, adjust the slider on the right of the **Transparency** attribute in the **Property Editor**. You can also apply a transparency map to an object. To do so, choose the checker button on the right of the **Transparency** attribute; the **Create Render Node** window will be displayed, refer to Figure 6-7. Choose the required map from the default maps and textures in the **Create Render Node** window and then choose the **Close** button. The lighter area in the material map will become transparent and the darker area will become opaque.

Ambient Color

The **Ambient Color** attribute is black by default; therefore it does not affect the default color of the material. When you make the ambient color brighter, it affects the material color by adding more light to it. To vary the effect of ambient color, drag the slider on the right of the **Ambient Color** attribute. Figure 6-8 shows the uppermost sphere with **Ambient Color** set to black, the middle sphere with **Ambient Color** set to medium gray, and the bottommost sphere with **Ambient Color** set to white.

*Figure 6-7 The **Create Render Node** window*

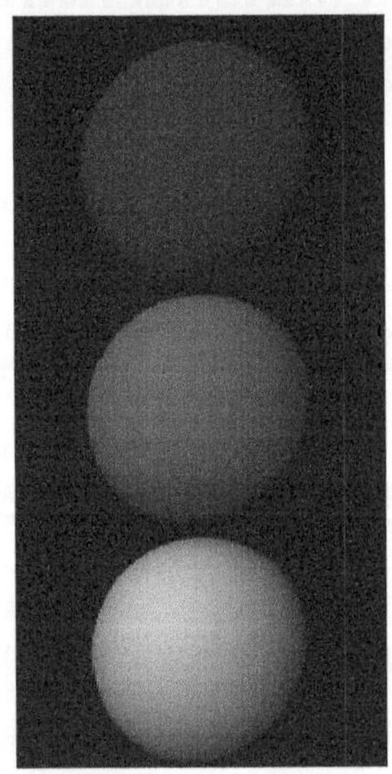

***Figure 6-8** The spheres showing the effect of the **Ambient Color** attribute*

Incandescence

The **Incandescence** attribute is used to self-illuminate an object such that the object creates a self-illuminating effect around it. For example, you can illuminate a bulb or tube light. Figure 6-9 shows the difference between a normal sphere (left) and a sphere with the **Incandescence** attribute (right) applied to it.

Diffuse

The **Diffuse** attribute is used to control the distribution of light on the surface of an object. The higher the **Diffuse** value, the more is the illumination on the surface when light falls on it. On the contrary, the lower the **Diffuse** value, the more is the light absorbed by that particular surface, resulting into a darker area, especially while making a metallic surface.

Bump/Normal Mapping

The **Bump Mapping** attribute is used to add bump effect to an object on rendering. This attribute does not modify the surface of the object, but it shows roughness on the surface on rendering. To apply bump map to an object, choose the checker button on the right of the **Bump Mapping** attribute; the **Create Render Node** window will be displayed, refer to Figure 6-7. Select the map or texture to which you want to apply the bump and then choose the **Close** button. Render the object to see the bump effect. Figure 6-10 shows the object after applying different textures to the **Bump Mapping** attribute.

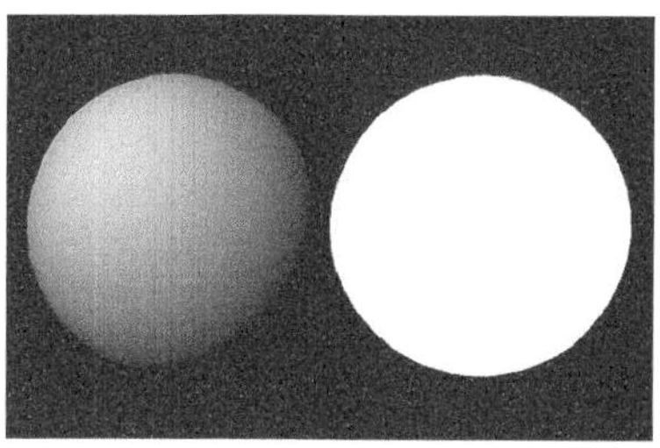

Figure 6-9 *Spheres showing the effect of the* ***Incandescence*** *attribute*

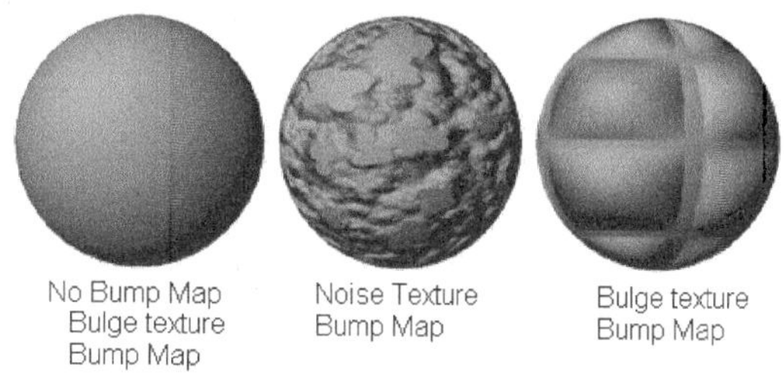

Figure 6-10 *Object after applying different textures to the* ***Bump Mapping*** *attribute*

Special Effects

The options in this area are used to set the parameters of special effects applied to an object. These special effects are visible only when the object is rendered. This area consists of only the **Glow Intensity** attribute to add glow effect on the edges of objects. To display the **Glow Intensity** attribute, choose the **Toggle between Lookdev view and Attribute Editor view** button available on the top-right corner of the **Property Editor**. The glow effect is discussed next.

Glow Intensity

The **Glow Intensity** attribute is used to add glow to the edges of an object, as shown in Figure 6-11. To add glow intensity to an object, enter the required value in the **Glow Intensity** edit box located in the **Special Effects** area, or drag the slider on the right of the **Glow Intensity** attribute. Next, choose the **Render the current frame** button from the Status Line to render and adjust the glow as required. You can also hide the source of the glow object. To do so, select the **Hide Source** check box from the **Special Effects** area. You can also add a light glow source to an object. To do so, choose the checker button on the right of the **Glow Intensity** attribute; the **Create Render Node** window will be displayed. Select the **Glow** option on the left pane of the window and then select the **Optical FX** option from the right pane of the window, as shown in Figure 6-12. The **Optical FX** option will be added to the object. Now, render the scene to see the final effect.

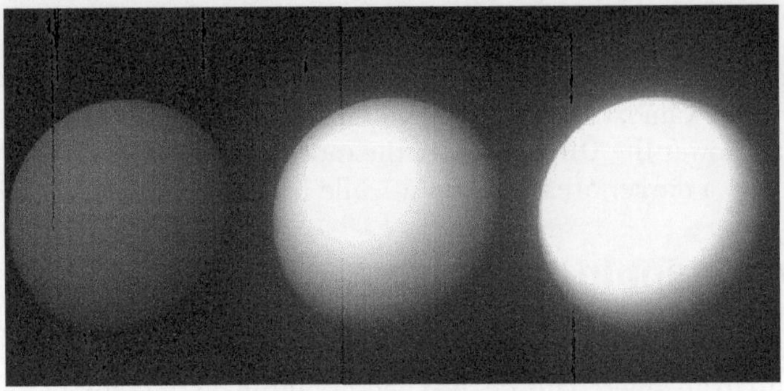

Figure 6-11 Spheres with different glow intensities

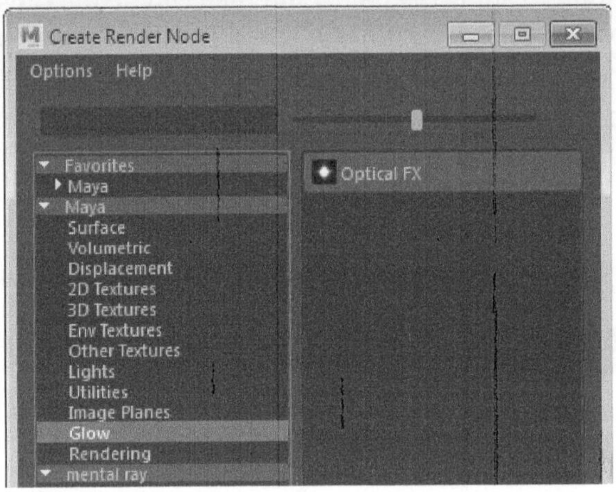

*Figure 6-12 The **Optical FX** option displayed*

Matte Opacity

The options in this area are used to calculate the matte (alpha channel or mask) for the material. The **Matte Opacity Mode** drop-down list in the **Matte Opacity** area has three options: **Black Hole**, **Solid Matte**, and **Opacity Gain**.

EXPLORING THE SHADERS

As you know, that the **Create** panel is located on the bottom-left in the **Hypershade** window. This panel has different types of nodes, which are used to create different shading networks. These nodes are divided into three categories: **Favorites**, **Maya**, and **mental ray**. These categories are further divided into sections. Among these sections, the **Surface** section which comes under the **Maya** category consists of all shaders/nodes that are required to apply texture to an object. The **Surface** section is discussed next.

Note

*The **mental ray** categories are displayed only when the **mental ray** renderer is installed and activated from the **Plug-in Manager** dialog box.*

Surface

By default, all shaders/nodes of this section are displayed in this section. The **Surface** section is mainly used to define the physical appearances of objects. The most commonly used shaders in the **Surface** section are discussed next.

Shaderfx Shader

The **Shaderfx Shader** helps you in creating your own advanced viewport shaders by connecting various shading nodes. The resulting materials can be visualized real time in Viewport 2.0 while connecting various shaders.

Stingray PBS

The **Stingray PBS** shader is used to assign a physically based shader. This shader uses roughness and normal and metallic maps to create a balance between diffusion/reflection and microsurface detail/reflectivity.

Anisotropic

The **Anisotropic** shader is used to create deformed surfaces such as foil wrapper, wrapped plastic, hair, or brushed metal. The directions of the highlights change according to direction of the object in the viewport. Due to this property, the elliptical or anisotropic highlights are created, as shown in Figure 6-13. Some of the examples of the objects created by applying the **Anisotropic** shader are CDs, feather, and utensils.

***Figure 6-13** The **Anisotropic** shader applied to an object*

Bifrost Aero Material

The **Bifrost Aero Material** shader is a mental ray material that creates atmospheric effects such as smoke and mist. This shader gets automatically applied to the aero and bifrost Aero Mesh objects while creating a Bifrost simulation. It is a volume ray marcher that accumulates the shading contributions from emission, absorption, and scattering at each step based on the density.

Bifrost Foam Material

The **Bifrost Foam Material** shader is used to create bubbles, foam, and spray effects. By using this shader, you can also generate foam if you emit liquid into an existing liquid with a different density, such as in the case of a hot-tub liquid effect.

Bifrost Liquid Material

The **Bifrost Liquid Material** shader is used to render the Bifrost voxels or the mesh. This shader is automatically applied to the bifrost and bifrostMesh objects while creating a Bifrost simulation. It uses many of the standard mental ray attributes. You can change the velocity and vorticity in the Bifrost channels area to remap the diffuse, reflection, and refraction colors.

Blinn

The **Blinn** shader is mainly used to create shiny metallic surfaces such as brass and aluminium. Figure 6-14 shows the **Blinn** shader applied to a sphere.

Hair Tube Shader

The **Hair Tube Shader** is mainly used for hair. The **HairTubeShader** node is automatically created while converting nHair into polygons. To apply a new **Hair Tube Shader** on a newly created nHair, the nHair must be converted into a polygon.

Lambert

The **Lambert** shader is mainly used to create unpolished surfaces. This shader diffuses and scatters light evenly on the object created in the viewport, thus giving it an unpolished appearance. It has no specular highlighting properties. Figure 6-15 shows a sphere with the **Lambert** shader applied to it.

*Figure 6-14 The **Blinn** shader applied to a sphere*

*Figure 6-15 The **Lambert** shader applied to a sphere*

Layered Shader

The **Layered Shader** is used when multiple materials are needed to be applied to the surface of an object. Figure 6-16 shows an object with the **Layered Shader** applied to it. It helps in creating a surface with distinct look and style. In this shader, different textures and shades are blended together to give a realistic look to the surface of an object. The **Layered Shader** takes more time in rendering.

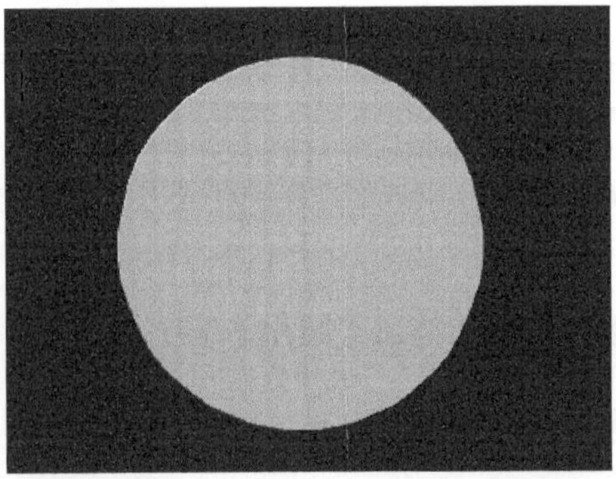

*Figure 6-16 The **Layered Shader** applied to an object*

To apply the **Layered Shader**, choose **Windows > Editors > Rendering Editors > Hypershade** from the menubar; the **Hypershade** window will be displayed. In the **Hypershade** window, choose the **Layered Shader** from the left of the **Create** panel; **layeredShader1** will be created in the **Untitled_1** tab. Next, choose the **Lambert** and **Anisotropic** shaders from the **Create** area; the **lambert2** and **anisotropic1** shaders will be created in the **Untitled_1** tab. Click on the **layeredShader1** shader in the **Untitled_1** tab; the **layeredShader1** tab will be displayed in the **Property Editor**, as shown in Figure 6-17. Next, press and hold the middle mouse button over the **lambert2** shader in the **Hypershade** window and drag it to the green swatch in the **Layered Shader Attributes** area of the **Attribute Editor**; the **lambert2** swatch is created in the **Layered Shader Attributes** area.

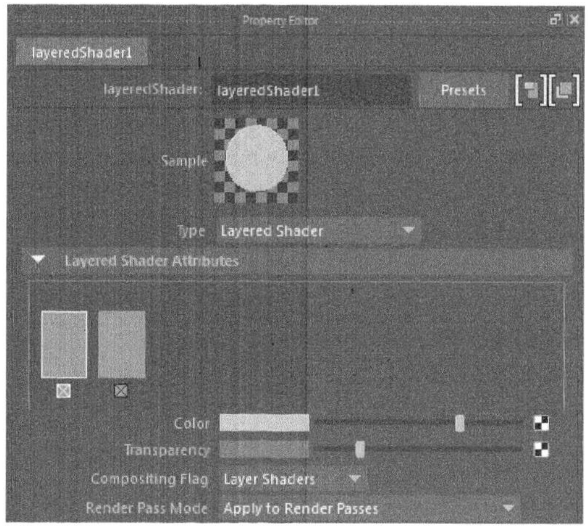

Figure 6-17** The **layeredShader1** tab in the **Property Editor

Similarly, add the **anisotropic1** shader to the green swatch in the **Layered Shader Attributes** area of the **Property Editor**; the **anisotropic1** swatch is created in the **Layered Shader Attributes** area. Choose the cross box under the green swatch to delete swatch from the **Layered Shader Attributes** area. Now, double-click on the **lambert2** shader and adjust the transparency of this shader from the **Common Material Attributes** area of the **lambert2** shader in the **Attribute Editor**. Next, choose the gray color swatch of the **Color** attribute; the **Color History** palette will be displayed. Select the required color for the shader from this palette and then click anywhere outside the palette to close the **Color History** palette. Finally, select the object in the viewport and then press and hold the right mouse button over the **layeredShader1** shader in the **Hypershade** window. Next, choose **Assign Material To Viewport Selection** from the marking menu displayed; the **layeredShader1** shader will be applied to the object.

Ocean Shader

The **Ocean Shader** is used to create realistic ocean. It can also be used to stimulate waves in the viewport. To use this shader, create a plane in the viewport with the **Width Subdivisions** and **Height Subdivisions** set to **20** each. Next, choose **Windows > Editors > Rendering Editors > Hypershade** from the menubar; the **Hypershade** window will be displayed. Choose **Ocean Shader** from the **Hypershade** window; the **oceanShader1** will be created in the **Browser** area. Select the plane in the viewport, and press and hold the right mouse button over the **OceanShader1** in the **Hypershade** window; a marking menu will be displayed. Choose **Assign Material To Viewport Selection** from the marking menu; the material will be applied to the plane in the viewport. Choose the **Render the current frame** button from the Status Line to render the scene; the plane rendered using **Ocean Shader** is shown in Figure 6-18.

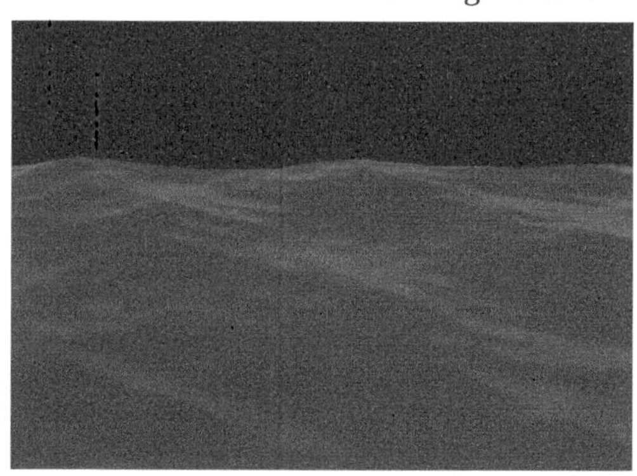

Figure 6-18** The plane rendered using **Ocean Shader

You can also set the properties of the **Ocean Shader** to modify the wavelengths and other attributes related to waves. To do so, select the plane in the viewport and then press and hold the right mouse button over it; a marking menu will be displayed. Choose **Material Attributes** from the marking menu. Expand the **Common Material Attributes** area in the **Property Editor**. This area shows the general attributes of an ocean, mainly the colors that can be applied to the ocean, as shown in Figure 6-19. You can also set the attributes of ocean in this area as required. To do so, expand the **Ocean Attributes** area. On expanding this area, three more areas will be displayed, namely **Wave Height**, **Wave Turbulence**, and **Wave Peaking**. The attributes in the **Wave Height** area are used to specify the height of the waves relative to their wavelengths. The attributes in the **Wave Turbulence** area are used to give variation in the movement of the waves while animating at different frequencies. The attributes in the **Wave Peaking** area are used to set the depth of the crests in the wavelengths.

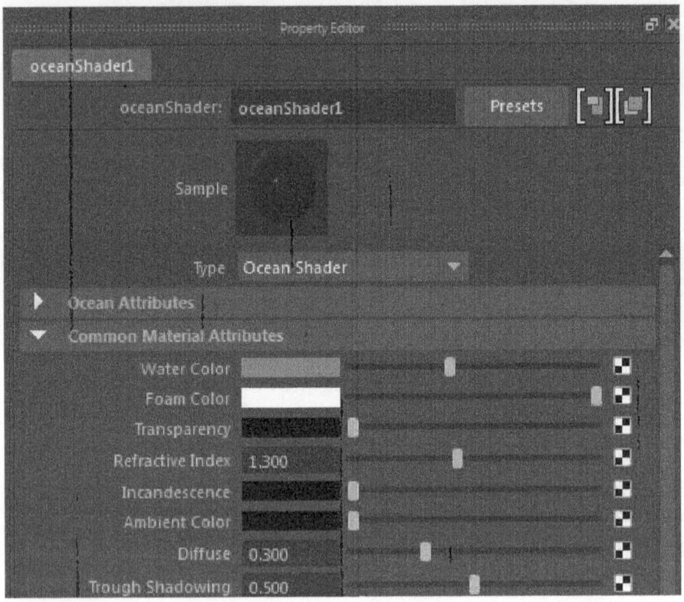

Figure 6-19** The **Common Material Attributes** area of the **Ocean Shader

Note

*If you apply the **Ocean Shader** to an object and then choose the **Play forwards** button, you will notice that the in-built animation is being played in the viewport. Also, while using the **Ocean Shader**, you always need to apply general lighting to brighten the scene.*

Phong

The **Phong** shader is used to add shine to an object, as shown in Figure 6-20. A phong surface reflects light, thus creating a specular highlight on the object. The **Phong** shader has certain characteristics such as diffusion and specularity that can be used to create smooth light reflecting surfaces. For example, you can create plastics, glass, ceramics, and most of the metals by using the **Phong** shader.

Phong E

The **Phong E** shader is used to produce glossy surfaces. This shader is perfect for creating plastics, bathroom accessories, and car modeling. Figure 6-21 shows the **Phong E** shader applied to a sphere.

*Figure 6-20 The **Phong** shader applied to a sphere*

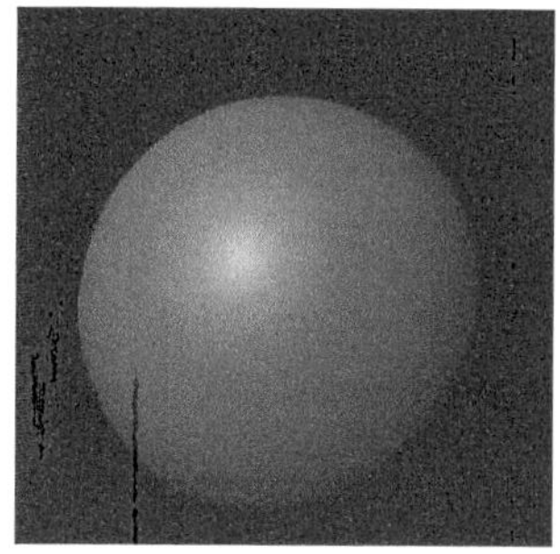

*Figure 6-21 The **Phong E** shader applied to a sphere*

Ramp Shader

The **Ramp Shader** is used to apply additional control over the colors of shader with respect to change in light and direction of the object in the viewport. All attributes related to colors in this shader are controlled by ramps. Ramps are known as gradients and are used to create smooth transitions among different colors. You can apply the **Ramp Shader** to an object in the viewport. To do so, invoke the **Hypershade** window and choose the **Ramp Shader** from the **Create** panel. Next, click on the **rampShader1** shader in the **Untitled_1** tab; the attributes of the **rampShader1** will be displayed in the **rampShader1** tab in the **Property Editor**, as shown in Figure 6-22 and then click on the color ramp on the right of the **Selected Color** attribute; a new color entry will be created. Drag the circular handle on top of the new color node to adjust it, as shown in Figure 6-23.

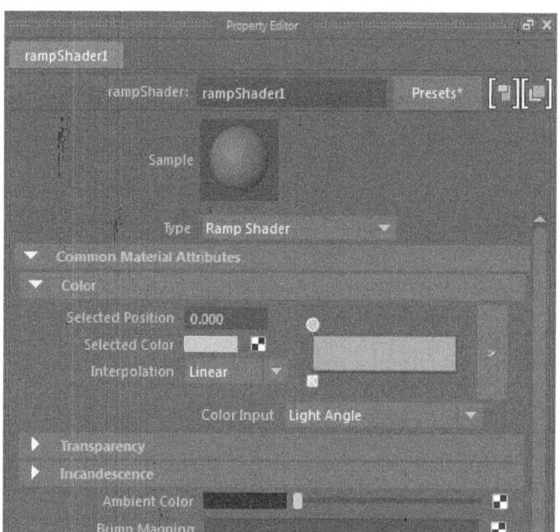

*Figure 6-22 The **rampShader1** tab in the **Property Editor***

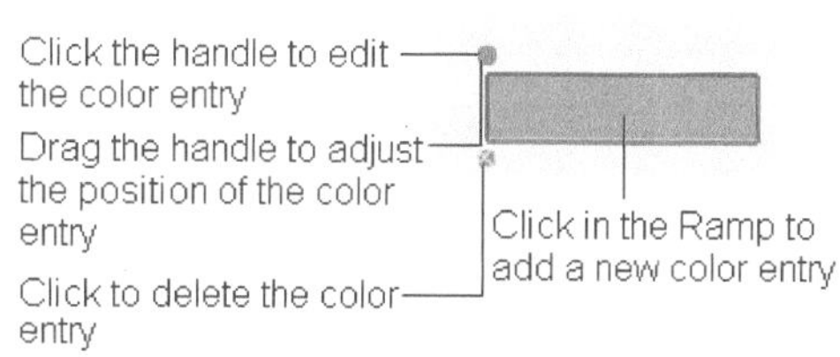

*Figure 6-23 The color ramp in the **Color** area of the **rampShader1***

Select the circular handle and choose the color swatch on the right of the **Selected Color** attribute. To add a map to a particular color entry, select the handle and choose the checker box on the right of the **Selected Color** attribute; the **Create Render Node** window will be displayed. In the **Create Render Node** window, choose the **Mountain** texture and then select the object in the viewport. Next, press and hold the right mouse button on the **rampShader1** in the **Hypershade** window and choose the **Assign Material To Viewport Selection** option from the marking menu; the object after applying the **rampShader1** will appear, refer to Figure 6-24.

Note

*You can also assign different color effects to an object by changing the values of the **Interpolation** and **Color Input** attributes in the **rampShader1** tab of the **Property Editor**.*

Shading Map

The **Shading Map** shader is used to apply a non-photorealistic effect on an object in the viewport, as shown in Figure 6-25. This shader works in accordance with the basic shaders, **Phong** and **Blinn**. When you apply this shader to an object, first the color of the basic shader is applied to the object and then this color is replaced by the **Shading Map** shader, thus creating a non-photorealistic effect on it. The hue and brightness of the original color affects the mapping on the object. To apply the **Shading Map** shader to an object, choose **Shading Map** from the **Create** panel in the **Hypershade** window. Next, select the object in the viewport, press and hold the right mouse button over the **Shading Map** shader, and choose **Assign Material To Viewport Selection** from the marking menu; the **Shading Map** shader will be applied to the object in the viewport.

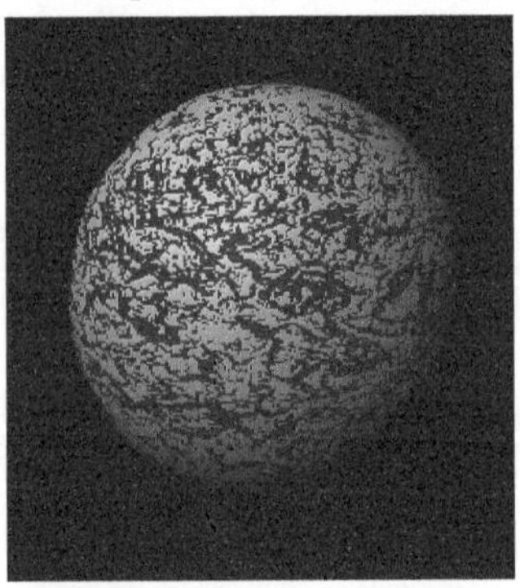

*Figure 6-24 The **Ramp Shader** applied to sphere*

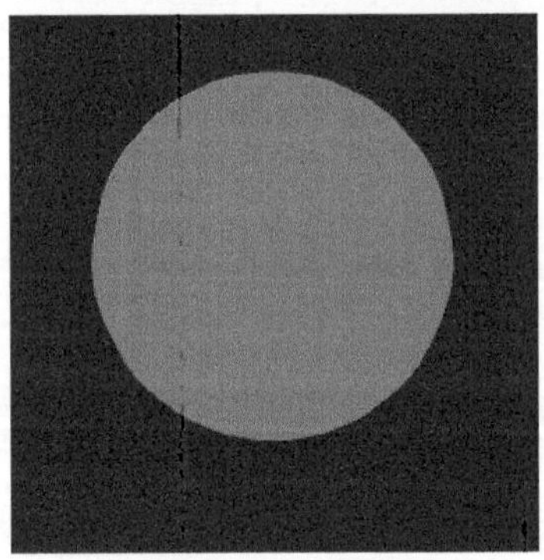

*Figure 6-25 The **Shading Map** shader applied to sphere*

Surface Shader

The **Surface Shader** is used to connect a keyable attribute to a shading group, and then to connect the shading group to an object. For example, you can connect the rotation of an object to the **Out Color** attribute of a **Surface Shader**, so that the color of the object changes according to its rotation.

Use Background

The **Use Background** shader is used to merge the object created in the viewport to the image applied in the background such that the object seems to be a part of the background.

TUTORIALS

Tutorial 1

In this tutorial, you will create a polygon cube and apply the texture of an old house to it, refer to Figure 6-26. **(Expected time: 30 min)**

Figure 6-26 *The textured model of the cube*

The following steps are required to complete this tutorial:

a. Create a project folder.
b. Download texture files.
c. Create a polygon cube.
d. Apply the checker pattern to the cube.
e. Create a texture in Adobe Photoshop.
f. Apply the texture to the cube.
g. Change the background color of the scene.
h. Save and render the scene.

Creating a Project Folder

Create a new project folder with the name *c06_tut1* at *\Documents\maya2017* and then save the file with the name *c06tut1* as discussed in Tutorial 1 of Chapter 2.

Downloading Texture Files

In this section, you will download the texture files.

1. Download the *c06_maya_2017_tut.zip* file from *www.cadcim.com*. The path of the file is as follows: *Textbooks > Animation and Visual Effects > Maya > Autodesk Maya 2017: A Comprehensive Guide*

2. Extract the contents of the zip file to the Documents folder. Navigate to *\Documents\c06_maya_2017\tut* and then copy the entire texture to the *\Documents\maya2017\c06_tut1\sourceimages*.

Creating a Polygon Cube

In this section, you will create a cube using cube polygon primitive.

1. Choose **Create > Objects > Polygon Primitives > Cube > Option Box** from the menubar; the **Tool Settings (Polygon Cube Tool)** window is displayed. Alternatively, double-click on the **Polygon Cube** icon in the **Polygons** tab of the Shelf to display the **Tool Settings (Polygon Cube Tool)** window.

Note

*Before creating a polygon cube by this method, make sure the **Interactive Creation** menu is selected from **Create > Objects > Polygon Primitives** cascading menu.*

2. Enter values in this window, as shown in Figure 6-27. Next, click in the persp viewport; a cube is displayed in the persp viewport.

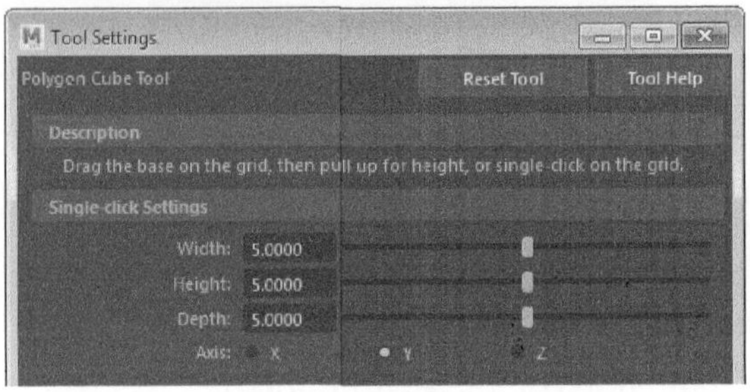

*Figure 6-27 Partial view of the **Tool Settings (Polygon Cube Tool)** window*

Applying the Checker Pattern to the Cube

In this section, you will apply the checker pattern to the cube.

1. Choose **Windows > Editors > Rendering Editors > Hypershade** from the menubar; the **Hypershade** window is displayed.

2. Choose the **Lambert** shader from the **Create** panel in the **Hypershade** window; the **Lambert** shader with the name **lambert2** is created in the **Browser** panel. Next, press the CTRL key and double-click on the **lambert2** shader in the **Browser** panel; the **Rename node** dialog box is displayed. Enter **initial_texture** in the **Enter new name** edit box, and then choose the **OK** button; the **lambert2** shader is renamed as *initial_texture*.

3. Click on the **initial_texture** shader in the **Browser** panel; the **initial_texture** tab is displayed in the **Property Editor**.

4. In the **Common Material Attributes** area of the **initial_texture** tab, click on the checker button corresponding to the **Color** attribute, refer to Figure 6-28; the **Create Render Node** window is displayed.

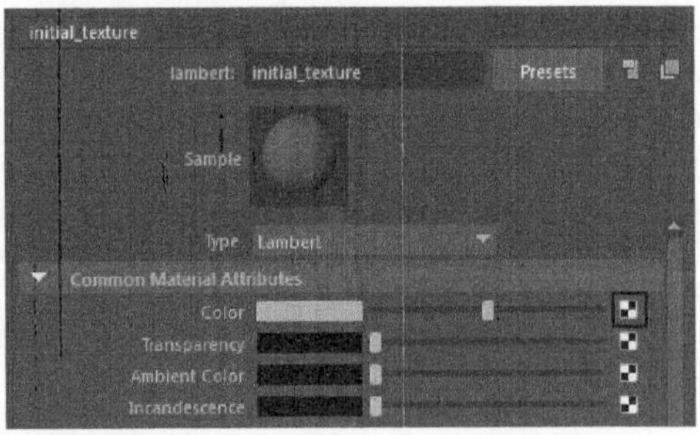

***Figure 6-28** Choosing the checker button corresponding to the **Color** attribute*

5. Choose the **Checker** button from the **Create Render Node** window, refer to Figure 6-29.

6. Select the polygon cube in the viewport. Now, in the **Untitled_1** tab of the **Hypershade** window, press and hold the right mouse button on the **initial_texture** shader; a marking menu is displayed. Choose the **Assign Material To Viewport Selection** option from the marking menu, as shown in Figure 6-30; the *initial_texture* shader is applied to the polygon cube. Press 6; the texture is displayed on the cube in the viewport.

Figure 6-29 *Choosing the **Checker** button from the **Create Render Node** window*

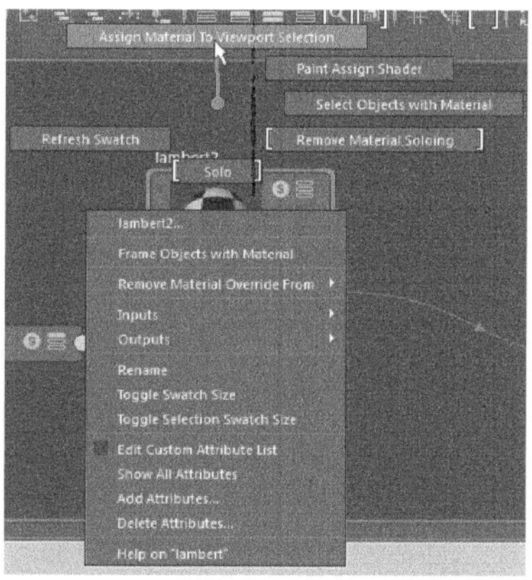

Figure 6-30 *Choosing **Assign Material To Viewport Selection** from the marking menu*

7. Make sure the cube is selected in the viewport. Select the **Modeling** menuset from the **Menuset** drop-down list, if it is not already selected. Choose **UV > Editors > UV Editor**; the **UV Editor** is displayed, as shown in Figure 6-31.

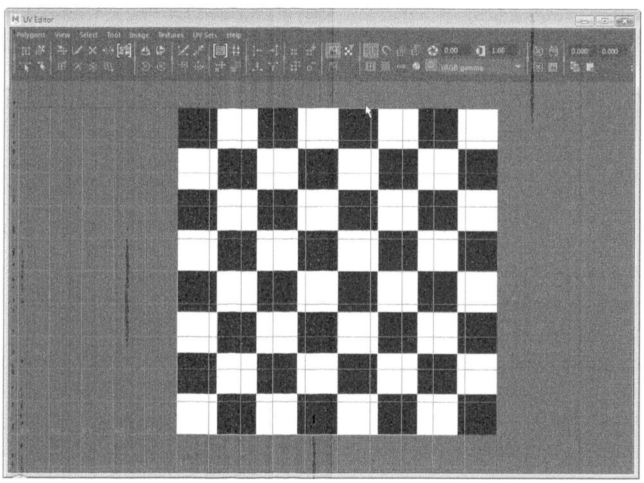

Figure 6-31 *The UV Editor*

8. In the **UV Editor**, choose the **Toggle the display of texture borders for the active mesh** button ; the uvs of the cube are highlighted. Now, choose **Polygons > UV Snapshot** from the **UV Editor** menubar; the **UV Snapshot** dialog box is displayed, as shown in Figure 6-32. Choose the **Browse** button; the **Save Snapshot** dialog box is displayed. In this dialog box, browse to the location *\Documents\maya2017\c06_tut1\images*. Next, save the UV snapshot with the name **UV snapshot** and choose the **Save** button; the **Save Snapshot** dialog box closes. Next, enter **1024** in the **Size X** edit box in the **UV snapshot** dialog box; you will notice that **1024** in the **Size Y** edit box is automatically entered. Choose the **OK** button from the **UV Snapshot** dialog box. Close the **Hypershade** and the **UV Texture Editor** windows.

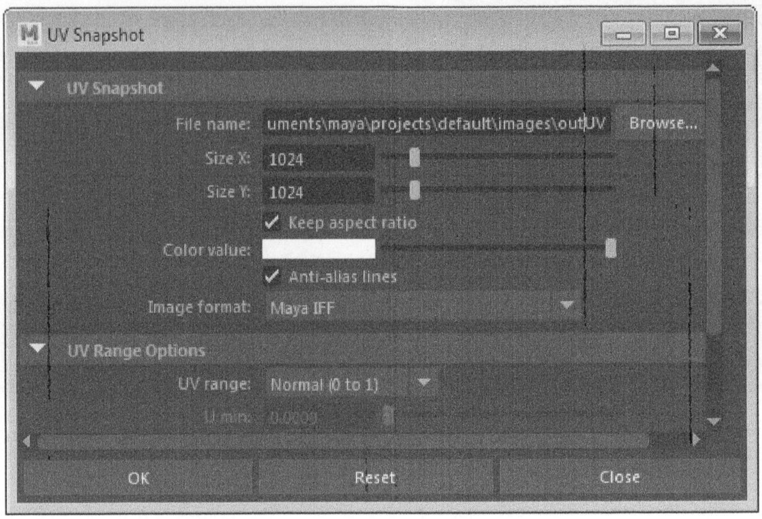

***Figure 6-32** The **UV Snapshot** dialog box*

Now, you will open the *UV snapshot.iff* file in Adobe Photoshop.

Creating a Texture in Adobe Photoshop

In this section, you will create a texture for the cube using Adobe Photoshop.

1. Open the *UV snapshot.iff* file in Adobe Photoshop. The file opens in the canvas area and a layer with the name **Layer 0** is created in the **Layers** panel.

2. Choose the **Create a new layer** button in the **Layers** panel; a new layer with the name **Layer 1** is created.

3. Make sure the newly created layer is selected and set **Set foreground color** to black color in the **Tool Box**. Next, press ALT+BACKSPACE; the **Layer 1** is filled with black color.

4. Move this layer below the **Layer 0**; the faces are now visible in the canvas area, as shown in Figure 6-33.

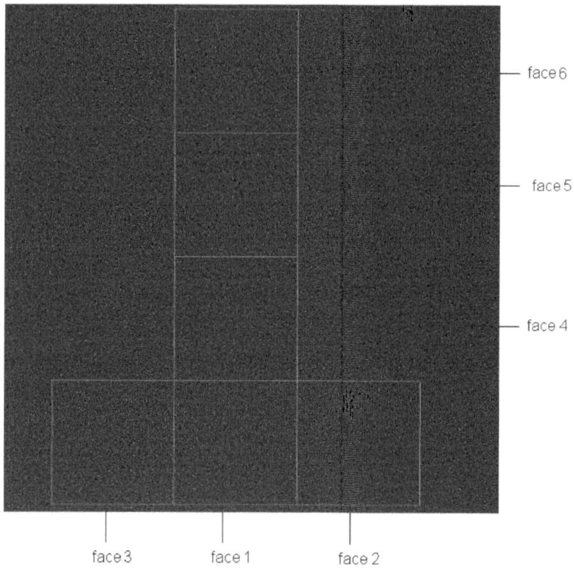

Figure 6-33 UVs in the canvas area of Photoshop

5. Choose **File > Open** from the menubar; the **Open** dialog box is displayed. In this dialog box, browse to *\Documents\maya2017\c06_tut1\sourceimages\frontwalltexture.jpg* and choose the **Open** button; the *frontwalltexture.jpg* is loaded. Choose **Move Tool**, and drag the image and place it on face 1, refer to Figure 6-34. Press CTRL+T; **Transform Tool** is activated. Next, scale the image such that it fits into face 1, as shown in Figure 6-34. Next, press ENTER; the transformation is applied.

6. Choose **Burn Tool** and darken **Layer 2**.

7. Create a new layer, and using **Brush Tool**, create different patterns to make the image dirty with opacity equal to 15 and brush size equal to 5, as shown in Figure 6-35.

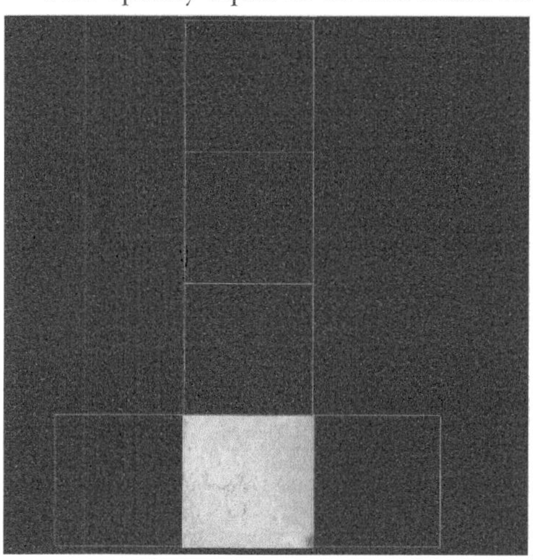

Figure 6-34 Fitting the image into the face 1

Figure 6-35 Different patterns created on the image

8. Open the files *doortexture.jpg* and *windowtexture.jpg* from the *sourceimages* folder, as discussed earlier. Next, choose **Move Tool** and place the images on face 1. Invoke **Transform Tool** by pressing CTRL+T, and scale the textures to fit them on face 1, as shown in Figure 6-36.

Figure 6-36 The textures placed on the face 1

9. Select the layer having door, and then choose the **Add a layer style** button from the **Layers** panel; a flyout is displayed. Choose the **Bevel & Emboss** option from the flyout; the **Layer Style** dialog box is displayed. In this dialog box, enter the values, as shown in Figure 6-37. Now, choose the **OK** button, a depth is created in the door. Repeat the same procedure to create depth in the window.

10. Select the layer having window in the canvas and press and hold ALT, and then drag the layer; a duplicate copy of the window is created. Next, place the window on face 1, as shown in Figure 6-38.

11. Open the *sidewallstexture.jpeg* file from the *sourceimages* folder, as discussed earlier, and place it on face 2 and face 3. Create different patterns on the faces using **Burn Tool** and **Brush Tool**, as shown in Figure 6-39.

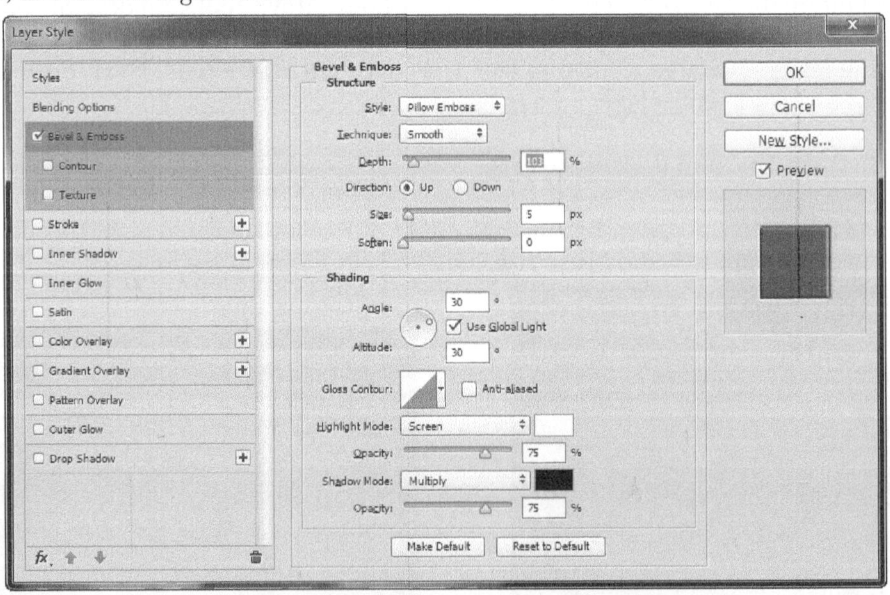

*Figure 6-37 The **Layer Style** dialog box*

Figure 6-38 A copy of window created on face 1

Figure 6-39 Patterns created on face 2 and face 3

12. Similarly, apply the *roof.jpeg, backside.jpeg,* and *ground.jpeg* texture files at the top, back, and base of the cube, respectively, as shown in Figure 6-40. Next, create different patterns on the textures to make the textures worn out, as shown in Figure 6-40. Make the area below the windows darker to show seepage in the walls. Next, turn off **Layer 0** so that the seams are not visible in the texture.

13. Choose **File > Save As** from the menubar; the **Save As** dialog box is displayed. In this dialog box, enter **Cube_UVs** in the **File Name** text box. Next, make sure the **Photoshop (*.PSD;*.PDD)** option is selected in the **Format** drop-down list. Next, browse to *\Documents\maya2017\c06_tut1\sourceimages* and choose the **Save** button; the file is saved at the specified location.

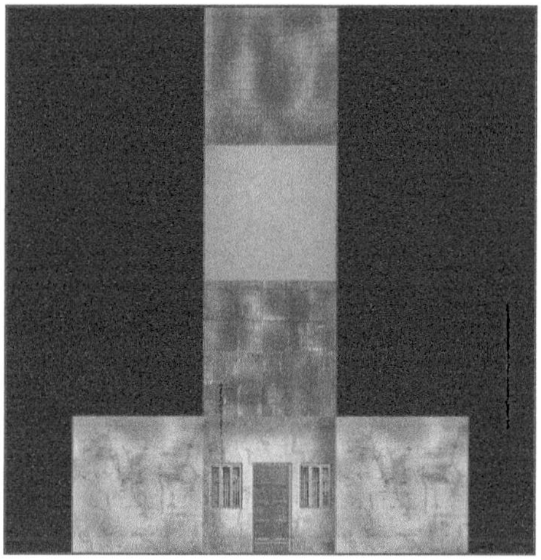

Figure 6-40 Patterns created on all faces

Next, you will switch back to Autodesk Maya and apply the texture created in Photoshop to the cube.

Applying the Texture to the Cube

In this section, you will apply the texture created in Photoshop to the cube.

1. Make sure the cube is selected in the viewport, choose **Windows > Editors > Rendering Editors > Hypershade** from the menubar; the **Hypershade** window is displayed.

2. Choose the **Lambert** shader from the **Create** panel; the **Lambert** shader with the name **lambert3** is created in the **Untitled_1** tab. Press CTRL and then double-click on the **lambert3** shader in the **Create** panel; the **Rename node** dialog box is displayed. Enter **oldhouse** in the text box and press ENTER; the **lambert3** shader is renamed as *oldhouse*. Click on the **oldhouse** shader; the **oldhouse** tab is displayed in the **Property Editor**.

3. In the **oldhouse** tab, click on the checker button corresponding to the **Color** attribute in the **Common Material Attributes** area; the **Create Render Node** window is displayed. Choose the **PSD File** button from the **Create Render Node** window; the **psdFileTex1** tab is displayed in the **Property Editor**, as shown in Figure 6-41.

4. Click on the folder icon on the right of the **Image Name** text box in the **File Attributes** area; the **Open** dialog box is displayed. Next, browse and select the **Cube_UVs.psd** and then choose the **Open** button.

5. Select the cube in the persp viewport. In the **Browser** panel of the **Hypershade** window, press and hold the right mouse button over the **oldhouse** shader; a marking menu is displayed. Choose the **Assign Material To Selection** option from the marking menu; the texture is applied to all sides of the cube, as shown in Figure 6-42. Close the **Hypershade** window.

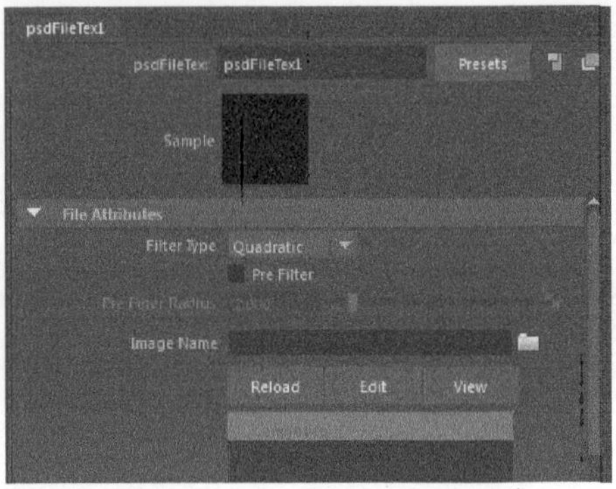

Figure 6-41 The psdFileTex1 tab

Figure 6-42 The texture applied to all sides of the cube

Changing the Background Color of the Scene

In this section, you will change the background color of the scene.

1. Choose **Windows > Editors > Outliner** from the menubar; the **Outliner** window is displayed. Click on the **persp** camera in the **Outliner** window; the **perspShape** tab is displayed in the **Attribute Editor**.

2. Expand the **Environment** area in the **perspShape** tab and drag the **Background Color** slider bar toward right to change the background color to white.

Saving and Rendering the Scene

In this section, you will save the scene that you have created and then render it. You can view the final rendered image of the scene by downloading the *c06_maya_2017_rndr.zip* file from *www.cadcim.com*. The path of the file is as follows: *Textbooks > Animation and Visual Effects > Maya > Autodesk Maya 2017: A Comprehensive Guide*.

1. Choose **File > Save Scene** from the menubar.

2. Maximize the persp viewport, if it is not already maximized. Choose the **Render the current frame** button from the Status Line; the **Render View** window is displayed. This window shows the final output of the scene, refer to Figure 6-26.

Tutorial 2

In this tutorial, you will create the model of an eyeball and then apply texture to it, as shown in Figure 6-43. **(Expected time: 15 min)**

The following steps are required to complete this tutorial:

a. Create a project folder.
b. Create the NURBS sphere.
c. Assign material to the sphere.
d. Change the background color of the scene.
e. Save and render the scene.

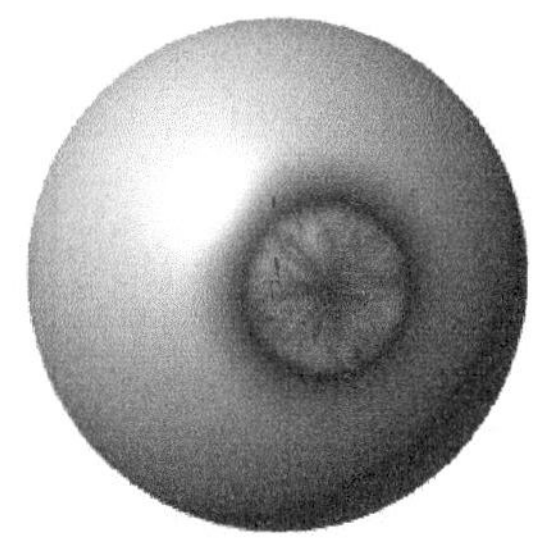

Figure 6-43 *Model of an eyeball*

Creating a Project Folder

Create a new project folder with the name *c06_tut2* at *\Documents\maya2017* and then save the file with the name *c06tut2*, as discussed in Tutorial 1 of Chapter 2.

Creating the NURBS Sphere

In this section, you will create the NURBS sphere for the eyeball.

1. Maximize the front-Z viewport and then choose **Create > Objects > NURBS Primitives > Sphere** from the menubar. Next, create a NURBS sphere in the viewport.

   Radius : **2** Rotate X : **90** Rotate Z : **-90**

2. Maximize the persp viewport.

Assigning Material to the Sphere

In this section, you will create a material for the eyeball and then assign it to the NURBS sphere.

1. Choose **Windows > Editors > Rendering Editors > Hypershade** from the menubar; the **Hypershade** window is displayed. Select the **Blinn** shader from the **Create** area in this window; the **blinn1** shader is created in the **Browser** panel of the **Hypershade** window.

2. Press and hold the CTRL key and double-click on the **blinn1** shader in the **Browser** panel; the **Rename node** dialog box is displayed. Enter **eye** in the **Enter new name** text box and then choose the **OK** button; the **blinn1** shader is renamed as **eye**.

3. Select the sphere in the viewport. Press and hold the right mouse button on the **eye** shader in the **Browser** panel of the **Hypershade** window and choose **Assign Material to Selection** from the marking menu; the *eye* shader is applied to the sphere.

4. Click on the *eye* shader in the **Hypershade** window; the **eye** tab is displayed in the **Property Editor**.

5. In the **Common Material Attributes** area of the **eye** tab, choose the checker button on the right of the **Color** attribute; the **Create Render Node** window is displayed. Choose the **Ramp** button from the **Create Render Node** window; the **ramp1** shader tab is created in the **Property Editor**.

6. In the **ramp1** shader tab, select the **U Ramp** option from the **Type** drop-down list and **Bump** from the **Interpolation** drop-down list in the **Ramp Attributes** area. Next, press 6 to view the texture in the viewport.

   By default, two color nodes are available in the ramp color area. You will create two more nodes. To do so, follow the steps given next.

7. Click on the ramp color area twice in the **Ramp Attributes** area; two more nodes are created. Next, arrange the nodes, as shown in Figure 6-44.

8. Select the color node 1, refer to Figure 6-45, from the **Ramp Attributes** area in the **ramp1** tab and then click on the color swatch of the **Selected Color** attribute; the **Color History** palette is displayed. Make sure that the **HSV** option is selected in the drop-down list below the color wheel in the **Ramp Attributes** area. Next, make sure the **HSV** values in the **Color History** palette are as follows:

   H: **0** S: **0** **V: 0**

9. Select the color node 2 from the **Ramp Attributes** area in the **ramp1** tab and then click on the color swatch in the **Selected Color** attribute; the **Color History** palette is displayed. Next, enter the following **HSV** values in the **Color History** palette:

   H: **0** S: **0** **V: 1**

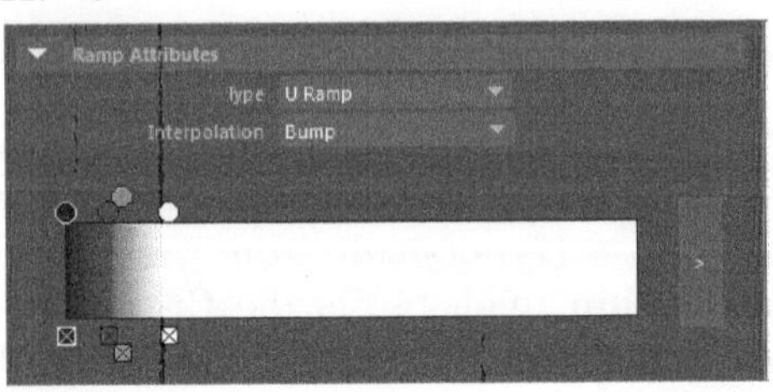

Figure 6-44 *The nodes in the color area of the* ***ramp1*** *shader*

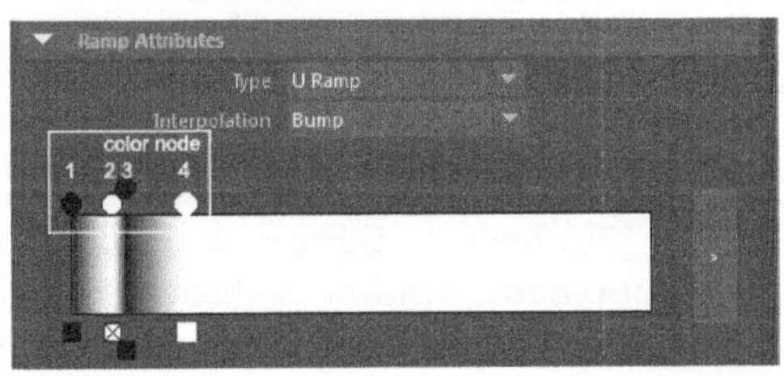

Figure 6-45 *The color nodes arranged in the color area*

10. Select the color node 3 from the **Ramp Attributes** area in the **ramp1** tab and then click on the color swatch in the **Selected Color** attribute; the **Color History** palette is displayed. Next, enter the following **HSV** values in the **Color History** palette:

    H: **0** S: **0** **V: 0**

11. Select the color node 4 from the **Ramp Attributes** area in the **ramp1** tab and then click on the color swatch in the **Selected Color** attribute; the **Color History** palette is displayed. Next, make sure the **HSV** values in the **Color History** palette are as follows:

H: **0** S: **0** **V: 1**

Figure 6-45 shows the nodes after the colors are assigned and are arranged in the color area. Figure 6-46 displays the eyeball after material is applied to it.

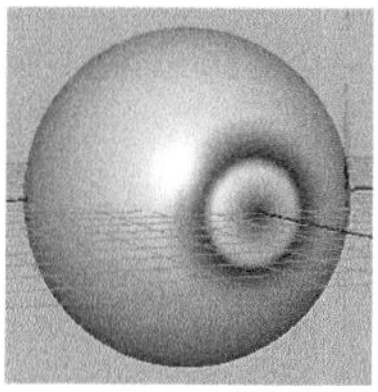

Figure 6-46 *Initial eyeball material applied to the NURBS sphere*

12. Select the color node 2 from the **Ramp Attributes** area in the **Property Editor**, refer to Figure 6-45. Next, click on the checker button on the right of the **Selected Color** attribute; the **Create Render Node** window is displayed. Choose **Fractal** from the **Create Render Node** window, as shown in Figure 6-47; the fractal is applied to the eyeball, as shown in Figure 6-48. Also, the **fractal1** tab is displayed in the **Property Editor**.

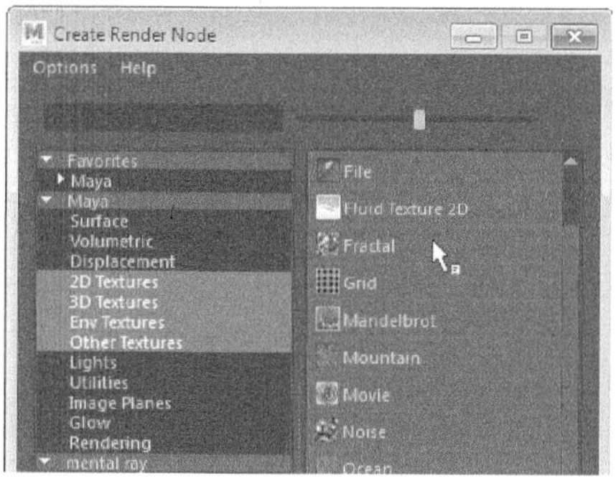

Figure 6-47 *Choosing* ***Fractal*** *from the* ***Create Render Node*** *window*

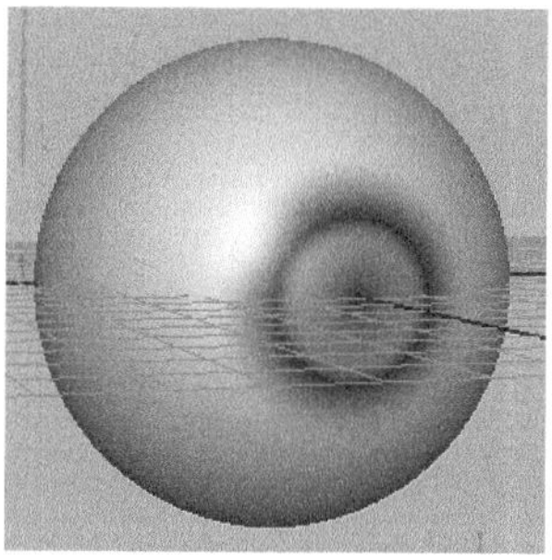

Figure 6-48 *Eyeball after applying the fractal texture*

13. Make sure the **fractal1** tab is selected in the **Property Editor**. Expand the **Color Balance** area and choose the gray color swatch on the right of the **Default Color** attribute; the **Color History** palette is displayed. In the **Color History** palette, set the following values for **H**, **S**, and **V**:

H: **199** S: **0.967** **V: 0.779**

14. In the **Color Balance** area, choose the color swatch corresponding to the **Color Gain** attribute; the **Color History** palette is displayed. In the **Color History** palette, set the following values of **H**, **S**, and **V**:

H: **199** S: **0.8** **V: 1**

15. In the **Color Balance** area, choose the color swatch corresponding to the **Color Offset** attribute; the **Color History** palette is displayed. In the **Color History** palette, set the following values of **H**, **S**, and **V**:

H: **191** S: **0.967** **V: 0.3**

Changing the Background Color of the Scene

In this section, you will change the background color of the scene.

1. Choose **Windows > Editors > Outliner** from the menubar; the **Outliner** window is displayed. Select the **persp** camera in the **Outliner** window; the **perspShape** tab is displayed in the **Attribute Editor**.

2. Expand the **Environment** area in the **perspShape** tab and drag the **Background Color** slider bar toward right to change the background color to white.

Saving and Rendering the Scene

In this section, you will save and then render the scene that you have created. You can view the final rendered image of the scene by downloading the *c06_maya_2017_rndr.zip* file from *www.cadcim.com*. The path of the file is as follows: *Textbooks > Animation and Visual Effects > Maya > Autodesk Maya 2017: A Comprehensive Guide.*

1. Choose **File > Save Scene** from the menubar.

2. Maximize the persp viewport, if it is not already maximized. Choose the **Render the current frame** button from the Status Line; the **Render View** window is displayed. This window shows the final output of the scene, refer to Figure 6-43.

Tutorial 3

In this tutorial, you will create the model of a bulb and then apply multiple textures to it. The final rendered output is shown in Figure 6-49. **(Expected time: 20 min)**

The following steps are required to complete this tutorial:

a. Create a project folder.
b. Create the model of a bulb.
c. Apply chrome texture to the bottom of the bulb.
d. Apply texture to the glass portion of the bulb.
e. Add lights.
f. Save and render the scene.

***Figure 6-49** The final rendered output*

Creating a Project Folder

Create a new project folder with the name *c06_tut3* at *\Documents\maya2017* and then save the file with the name *c06tut3*, as discussed in Tutorial 1 of Chapter 2.

Creating the Model of the Bulb

In this section, you will create two profile curves using **EP Curve Tool** to create a bulb.

1. Choose **Create > Objects > Curve Tools > EP Curve Tool** from the menubar.

2. Maximize the front-Z viewport and draw two profile curves, as shown in Figure 6-50. Make sure **Move Tool** is active. Next, press and hold the D key and set the pivot point for both the curves at the center of the grid by moving the pivot point manipulators if the pivot points are not at the center.

3. Select both the profile curves in the front-Z viewport and then choose the **Modeling** menuset from the **Menuset** drop-down list in the Status Line.

4. Choose **Surfaces > Create > Revolve** from the menubar; the profile curves rotate at 360 degrees. As a result, the bulb is created in the viewport, as shown in Figure 6-51.

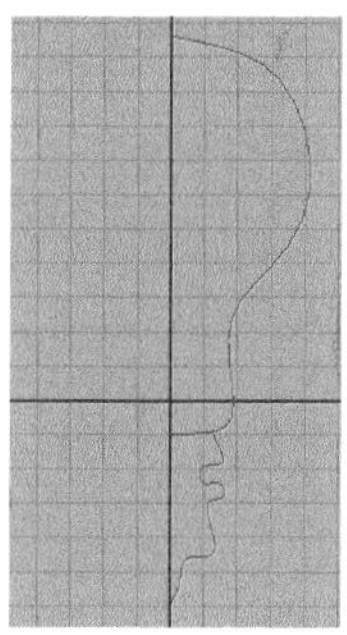

Figure 6-50 *The profile curves for the bulb*

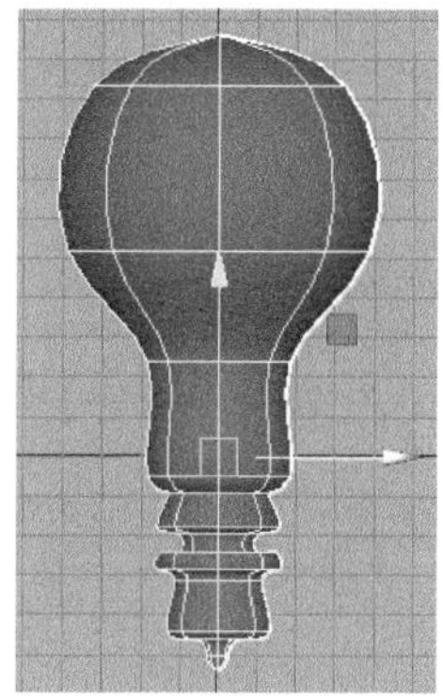

Figure 6-51 *The bulb created using the **Revolve** tool*

Note

*After applying the **Revolve** tool, if the surface of the profile curve is black then select the surface and choose **Surfaces > Edit NURBS Surfaces > Reverse Direction** from the menubar; the profile curve is reversed.*

Applying the Chrome Texture to the Bottom of the Bulb

In this section, you will create the chrome texture and apply it to the bottom of the bulb.

1. Choose **Windows > Editors > Rendering Editors > Hypershade** from the menubar; the **Hypershade** window is displayed.

2. Choose the **Blinn** shader from the **Create** panel in the **Hypershade** window; the **Blinn** shader named **blinn1** is displayed in the **Browser** panel.

3. Press the CTRL key and double-click on the **blinn1** shader in the **Browser** panel; the **Rename node** dialog box is displayed. Enter **Chrome** as the new name of the shader in this dialog box and choose the **OK** button; the shader is renamed to **Chrome**.

4. Select the bottom part of the bulb in the viewport. In the **Hypershade** window, press and hold the right mouse button on the *Chrome* shader and choose **Assign Material to Selection** from the marking menu displayed; the *Chrome* shader is applied at the bottom part of the bulb.

5. In the **Hypershade** window, click on the **Chrome** shader; the **Chrome** tab is displayed in the **Property Editor**.

6. In the **Chrome** tab, expand the **Specular Shading** area. If this area is not available in the **Property Editor panel**, choose **Toggle between Lookdev view and Attribute Editor view** from the top right area of the **Property Editor** panel. Make sure the values for the attributes are set, as shown in Figure 6-52

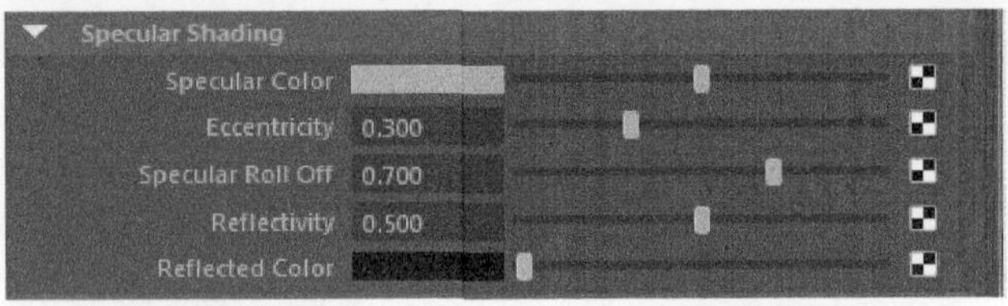

*Figure 6-52 The **Specular Shading** area*

7. Click on the checker button corresponding to the **Reflected Color** attribute in the **Specular Shading** area; the **Create Render Node** window is displayed.

8. Choose the **Env Ball** button from the **Create Render Node** window, as shown in Figure 6-53; the **envBall1** tab is displayed in the **Property Editor**.

9. In the **Environment Ball Attributes** area of the **envBall1** tab, choose the checker button on the right of the **Image** option; the **Create Render Node** window is displayed. Choose the **Stucco** button from the **Create Render Node** window, as shown in the Figure 6-54; the **Stucco1** tab is displayed in the **Property Editor**.

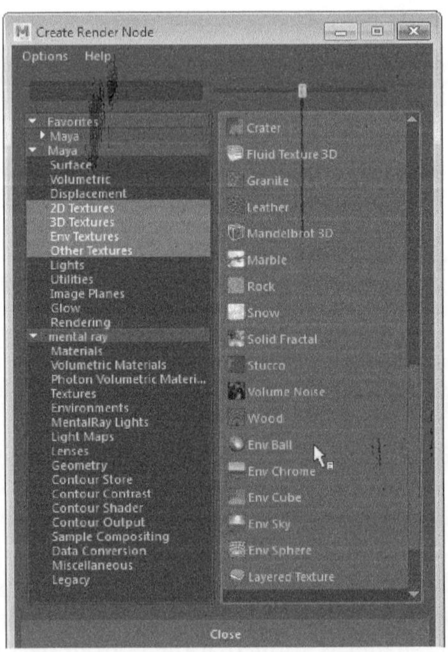

*Figure 6-53 Choosing **Env Ball** from the **Create Render Node** window*

*Figure 6-54 Choosing **Stucco** from the **Create Render Node** window*

10. In the **Stucco Attributes** area of the **Stucco1** tab, enter **40** as the value of the **Shaker**. Next, choose the color swatch corresponding to the **Channel 1** attribute; the **Color History** palette is displayed. In the **Color History** palette, set the following values of **H**, **S**, and **V**:

    H: **0** S: **0** **V: 0.4**

11. In the **Stucco Attributes** area of the **Stucco1** tab, choose the color swatch corresponding to the **Channel 2** attribute; the **Color History** palette is displayed. In the **Color History** palette, set the following values for **H**, **S**, and **V**:

    H: **0** S: **0** **V: 1**

Note

*The **Stucco** texture is a color map. It randomly mixes any two colors as channel 1 and 2 to create a final combination of colors as cloud or stain.*

Applying Texture to the Glass Portion

In this section, you will apply texture to the glass portion of the bulb and add glow to it.

1. Choose the **Lambert** shader from the **Create** panel of the **Hypershade** window; the **lambert2** shader is created in the **Untitled_1** tab of the **Hypershade** window. Press CTRL and then double-click on it in the **Browser** panel; the **Rename node** dialog box is displayed. Type **Bulb** in the **Enter new name** text box and choose the **OK** button to close the dialog box. Next, assign the *Bulb* shader to the glass portion of the bulb, as discussed earlier.

2. In the **Hypershade** window, select the ***Bulb*** shader; the **Bulb** tab is displayed in the **Property Editor**.

3. In the **Common Material Attributes** area of the **Bulb** tab, choose the color swatch corresponding to the **Color** attribute; the **Color History** palette is displayed. In the **Color History** palette, set the following values for **H**, **S**, and **V**:

   H: **46** S: **1** **V: 1**

4. In the **Common Material Attributes** area of the **Bulb** tab, choose the color swatch corresponding to the **Incandescence** attribute; the **Color History** palette is displayed. In the **Color History** palette, set the following values for **H**, **S**, and **V**:

   H: **60** S: **0.451** **V: 0.902**

5. Expand the **Special Effects** area and then enter **0.147** as the value of **Glow Intensity**.

6. Close the **Hypershade** window.

Adding Light

In this section, you will add lights to the scene.

1. Choose **Create > Object > Lights > Directional Light** from the menubar; a directional light is created in the viewport. Set the translation and rotation parameters of the directional light in **Channel Box / Layer Box Editor** as follows:

   Translate Y: **2.49** Translate Z: **-2.94** Rotate X: **-123.2**

2. Press CTRL+A; the **Attribute Editor** is displayed. In the **directionalLightShape1** tab of the **Attribute Editor**, enter **1.2** as the value of the **Intensity**. Next, choose the color swatch corresponding to the **Color** attribute; the **Color History** palette is displayed. In the **Color History** palette, set the following values for **H**, **S**, and **V**:

   H: **65** S: **0.658** V: **0.975**

Saving and Rendering the Scene

In this section, you will save the scene that you have created and render it by using the **mental ray** renderer. You can view the final rendered image of the model by downloading the *c06_maya_2017_rndr.zip* file from *www.cadcim.com*. The path of the file is as follows: *Textbooks > Animation and Visual Effects > Maya > Autodesk Maya 2017: A Comprehensive Guide.*

1. Choose the **Display Render Settings** button on the Status Line; the **Render Settings** window is displayed. Select **mental ray** from the **Render Using** drop-down list.

2. Choose the **Render the current frame** button from the Status Line; the **Render View** window is displayed. This window shows the final output of the scene, refer to Figure 6-49.

3. Choose **File > Save Scene** from the menubar to save the scene.

Self-Evaluation Test

Answer the following questions and then compare them to those given at the end of this chapter:

1. Which of the following numeric keys is used to view the object in the shaded mode?

   (a) 1 (b) 5
   (c) 4 (d) 3

2. In the **Ocean Shader**, the __________ attribute is used to specify the height of the waves relative to its length.

3. The __________ shader is used to apply multiple materials to the surface of an object.

4. The __________ shader is used to apply a non-photorealistic effect on an object.

5. In the **Hypershade** window, the main toolbar is located below the _________.

6. The _________ attribute is used to illuminate an object such that the object creates a self-illuminating effect around it.

7. The **Transparency** attribute is used to make an object opaque. (T/F)

8. The **Lambert** shader is mainly used to create polished surfaces. (T/F)

Review Questions

Answer the following questions:

1. Which of the following attributes is used to add glow to the edges of an object?

   (a) **Incandescence** (b) **Ambient Color**
   (c) **Glow Intensity** (d) None of these

2. When you double-click on any of the shader swatches, then related attributes appear in the _________.

3. The _________ parameter is used to adjust the density of mask channels.

4. The _________ button is used to arrange the shader icons alphabetically (A-Z).

5. The _________ connections are created automatically by Maya based on the type of node selected.

6. The properties of the **Anisotropic** shader change according to the direction of the object it is applied on. (T/F)

7. The **Clear graph** tool is used to rearrange the nodes in the current layout such that all nodes and networks are displayed properly in the **Hypershade** window. (T/F)

8. The **View as icons** button is used to display the default name of the shader icons. (T/F)

EXERCISES

The rendered output of the models used in the following exercises can be accessed by downloading the *c06_maya_2017_exr.zip* file from *www.cadcim.com*. The path of the file is as follows: *Textbooks > Animation and Visual Effects > Maya > Autodesk Maya 2017: A Comprehensive Guide.*

Exercise 1

Create the model of a house, shown in Figure 6-55. Unwrap it and then apply textures to it to get the final output, as shown in Figure 6-56. **(Expected time: 30 min)**

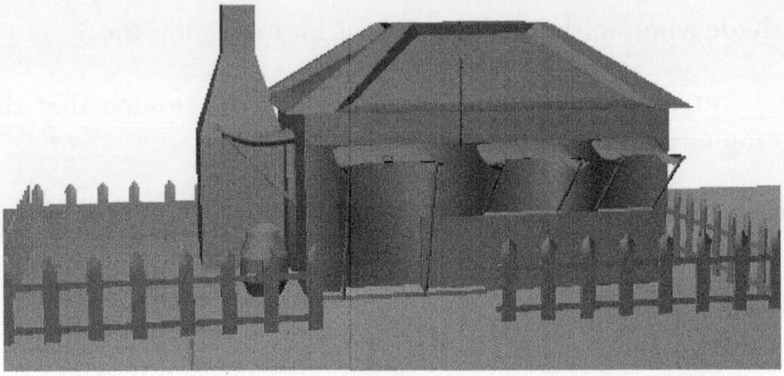

Figure 6-55 *The house model before applying the textures*

Figure 6-56 *The house model after applying the textures*

Exercise 2

Create the model of a house, shown in Figure 6-57, and then apply textures to it to get the final output, as shown in Figure 6-58. **(Expected time: 30 min)**

Figure 6-57 *The house model before applying the textures*

Figure 6-58 *The house model after applying the textures*

Exercise 3

Create a scene showing a model of the study table with objects, as shown in Figure 6-59, and apply textures to the objects in the scene, as shown in the same figure.

(Expected time: 30 min)

Figure 6-59 *Model of a study table after applying textures*

Answers to Self-Evaluation Test

1. b, **2. Weight Height**, **3. Layered Shader**, **4. Shading Map**, **5.** menubar, **6. Incandescence**, **7.** T, **8.** F

Chapter 7

Lighting

Learning Objectives

After completing this chapter, you will be able to:

- *Work with standard Maya lights*
- *Add glow and halo effects to lights*
- *Apply the Physical Sun and Sky effect to a scene*
- *Work with the camera*

INTRODUCTION

Lights are objects that produce real lighting effects like street lights, flash lights, house-hold lights or office lamp, and so on. When there is no light in a scene, the scene is rendered with default lighting. Moreover, light objects can be used to project the images. In this chapter, you will learn about various lights that you can use in your scene to give it realistic lighting effects.

TYPES OF LIGHTS

There are six types of lights in Maya. To create a light, choose **Create > Objects > Lights** from the menubar; a cascading menu will be displayed. Choose the required light from the cascading menu and click in the viewport; the light will be created in your scene. Different types of lights in Maya are discussed next.

Ambient Light

Menubar:	Create > Objects > Lights > Ambient Light

The ambient light is a single point light that projects the rays uniformly in all directions and lights up the scene. To create an ambient light, choose **Create > Objects > Lights > Ambient Light** from the menubar; ambient light will be created at the center of the viewport. You can modify the attributes of this light. To do so, select the ambient light in the viewport. Next, choose **Windows > Editors > General Editor > Attribute Editor** from the menubar; the **Attribute Editor** displaying the properties of the ambient light will be displayed on the right of the viewport. Some of the attributes in Maya are common for all lights. These attributes are discussed next.

Ambient Light Attributes Area

The options in this area control the general attributes of the ambient light. To set these attributes, select the light in the viewport and choose **Windows > Editors > General Editors > Attribute Editor** from the menubar; the **Attribute Editor** will be displayed. Expand the **Ambient Light Attributes** area, if not already expanded; various options will be displayed, refer to Figure 7-1. These options are discussed next.

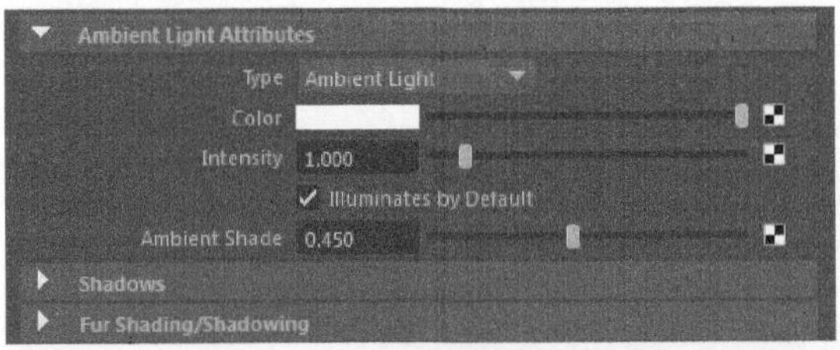

*Figure 7-1 The **Ambient Light Attributes** area*

Type

The options in the **Type** drop-down list are used to display the type of light to be displayed in the viewport. To change a light, select the required option from the **Type** drop-down list; the current light will be replaced by the light selected from this drop-down list.

Color

The **Color** attribute is used to set the color of the light. To do so, choose the color swatch on the right of the **Color** attribute; the **Color History** palette will be displayed, as shown in Figure 7-2. Set the desired color for the light in this palette and click anywhere outside this palette; the selected color will be applied to the light. You can also assign a texture to the light. To do so, choose the checker box on the right of the **Color** attribute, refer to Figure 7-1; the **Create Render Node** window will be displayed. Choose the desired texture map from the **Create Render Node** window and then choose the **Close** button; the texture will be assigned to the light. To see the effect of the light you need to render the scene. To do so, invoke the **Render the current frame** button from the Status Line. Figure 7-3 shows an ambient light without applying the checker map to the **Color** attribute and Figure 7-4 shows the ambient light with the checker map assigned to the **Color** attribute.

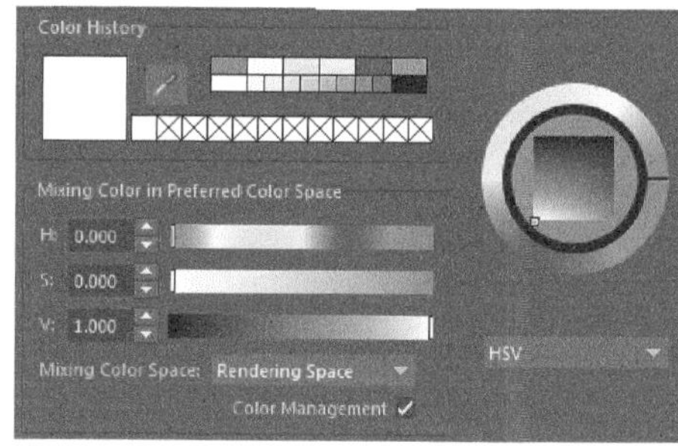

*Figure 7-2 The **Color History** palette*

*Figure 7-3 Ambient light without applying the checker map to the **Color** attribute*

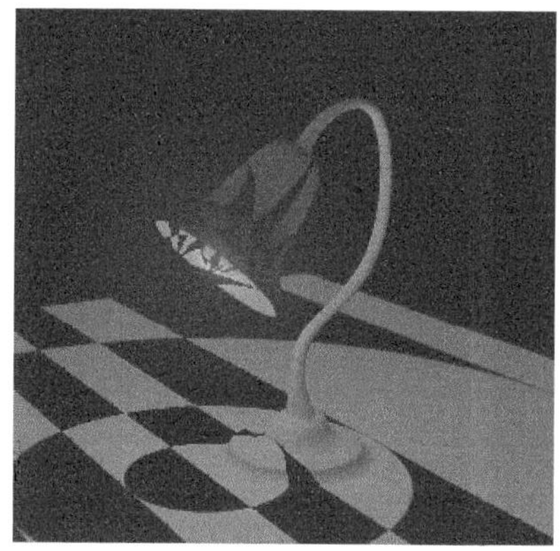

*Figure 7-4 Ambient light with the checker map assigned to the **Color** attribute*

Intensity

The **Intensity** attribute is used to set the brightness of the light. To do so, enter the desired value in the **Intensity** edit box or move the slider at its right to adjust the intensity. If the value specified in this edit box is 0, there will be no illumination in the scene at all and it will appear completely black on rendering. The **Illuminates by Default** check box is selected by default and is used to illuminate all objects in the viewport. When this check box is cleared, the light would only illuminate the objects to which it is linked. You will learn about light linking later in the chapter.

Ambient Shade

The **Ambient Shade** attribute is used to control the proportion of directional light to the ambient light. To apply ambient shade, enter a value in the **Ambient Shade** edit box or adjust the slider at the right of this edit box. The ambient shade value ranges from 0 to 1. If the value in this attribute is set to 0, the light will come from all the directions, and if the value in this attribute is set to 1, the light will come from the point where the light is placed. In other words, the ambient light will act like a point light, when the value of the **Ambient Shade** attribute is 1. The default value of the **Ambient Shade** attribute is 0.45. Figure 7-5 shows the ambient light when the **Ambient Shade** value is set to **0.25** and Figure 7-6 shows the ambient light when the ambient shade value is set to **1**.

Figure 7-5 Ambient light with the ***Ambient Shade*** *value set to* ***0.25***

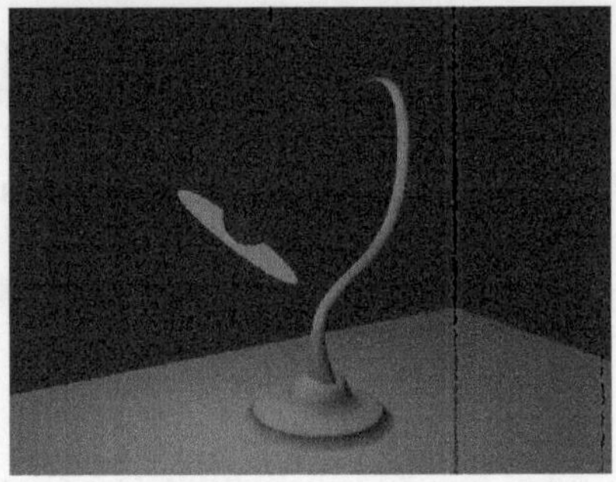

Figure 7-6 Ambient light with the ***Ambient Shade*** *value set to* ***1***

Shadows Area

The options in this area are used to define the color of the shadow produced by the light. By default, the shadow color is black. You can also map textures to the shadows.

Raytrace Shadow Attributes

The attributes in this area are used to control the appearance of raytrace shadows produced by the light. Raytrace shadows are soft and transparent shadows. These shadows will be visible in the render only when raytracing is enabled in the **Render Settings** window. To do so, choose **Windows > Editors > Rendering Editors > Render Settings** from the menubar; the **Render Settings** window will be displayed. Choose the **Maya Software** tab and expand the **Raytracing Quality** area. In this area, select the **Raytracing** check box to enable raytracing.

Use Raytrace Shadows

The **Use RayTrace Shadows** check box is used to ensure that the raytrace shadows are displayed in the scene.

Shadow Radius

This attribute is used to control the softness of the shadow edges by increasing or decreasing the size or angle of light.

Shadow Rays

This attribute is used to control the grain of the soft shadow edges. The higher the number of shadow rays, the softer will be the grain of the shadow edges, but it will also increase the render time.

Ray Depth Limit

This attribute is used to specify the maximum number of times a light ray can be reflected or refracted.

Directional Light

Menubar: Create > Objects > Lights > Directional Light

The directional light is used to create a distant point light. The light rays coming from the directional light are parallel to each other. To create a directional light, choose **Create > Objects >**

Lights > Directional Light from the menubar; a directional light will be created on the grid in the viewport, as shown in Figure 7-7. You can also modify the attributes of this light. To do so, select the light in the viewport; the **Attribute Editor** showing the attributes of the directional light will be displayed on the right of the viewport. Some of the attributes of the directional light are same as those of the ambient light as discussed earlier. The remaining attributes are discussed next.

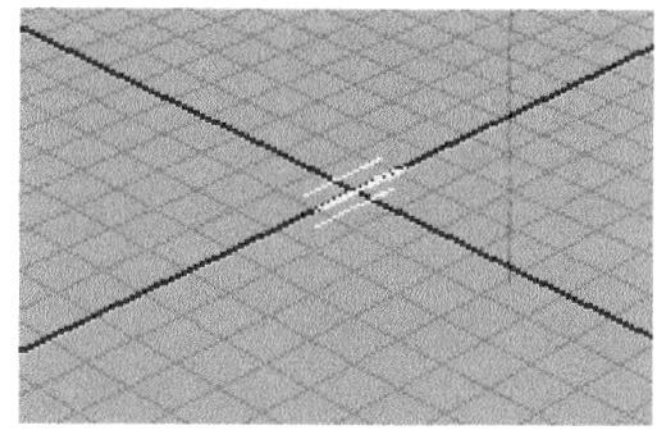

Figure 7-7 *A directional light created*

Depth Map Shadow Attributes

The attributes in this area are used to control the depth map shadows produced by the light. A depth map shadow gives good result and does not take more render time. A depth map contains the depth data rendered from a light's position in the scene. Some of the attributes in this area are discussed next.

Use Depth Map Shadows

This attribute is used to enable depth map shadow calculations.

Resolution

This attribute is used to set the resolution of the depth map shadows. On increasing the resolution, the render time of the depth map shadows also increases.

Filter Size

This attribute is used to control the softness of the shadow edges. The higher the value of the filter size, the softer will be the shadow edges but it will also increase the render time.

Bias

This attribute is used to offset the depth map toward or away from the light.

Note

*1. Directional light can be used to view the area illuminated by it. To do so, makes sure the light is selected and then choose **Panels > Look Through Selected** from the **Panel** menu; you can now look through the selected light. Use ALT+MMB to pan the view, ALT+ RMB to zoom in and out the view, and the ALT+ LMB to rotate in the viewport. To go back to the view, choose **Panels > Perspective > persp** from the **Panel** menu.*

*2. You can set the focus point of the selected light by using the light manipulators from the menubar. To do so, choose **Display > Object > Show > Light Manipulators** from the menubar; the light manipulators will be displayed on the selected light. To hide them, choose **Display > Object > Hide > Light Manipulators** from the menubar. Similarly, you can display the light manipulators for all the lights in Maya.*

Point Light

Menubar: Create > Objects > Lights > Point Light

The point light is a single source of light which projects light evenly in all directions. To create a point light, choose **Create > Objects > Lights > Point Light** from the menubar; a point light will be created at the center of the viewport, as shown in Figure 7-8. Most of the attributes of the point light are similar to the attributes of the ambient light. Some of its other attributes are discussed next.

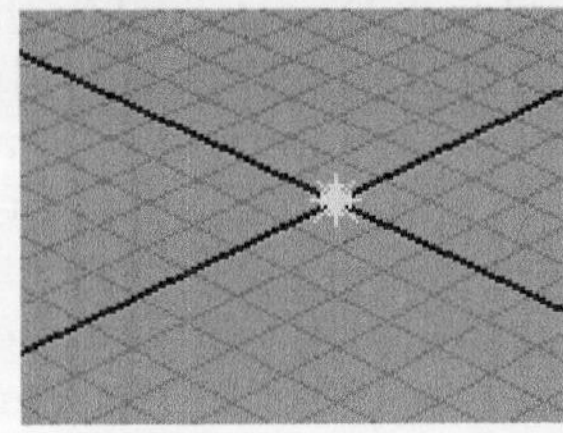

Figure 7-8 A point light created

Light Effects

The attributes in this area are used to modify the visual aspects of a selected light. To do so, select point light in the viewport and choose **Windows > Editors > General Editors > Attribute Editor** from the menubar; the **Attribute Editor** will be displayed. Expand the **Light Effects** area in the **Attribute Editor**, if it is not already expanded, refer to Figure 7-9. The attributes in this area are discussed next.

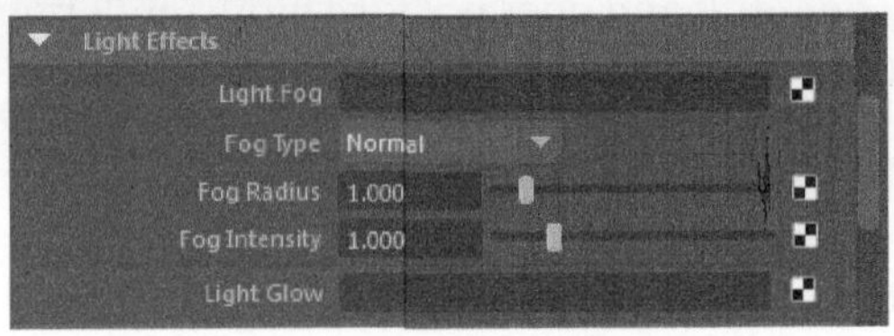

*Figure 7-9 The **Light Effects** area*

Light Fog

The **Light Fog** attribute is used to add the fog effect to the scene. To do so, choose the checker box corresponding to the **Light Fog** attribute in the **Attribute Editor**, refer to Figure 7-10; the **Light Fog Attributes** area will be displayed, as shown in Figure 7-10. Adjust the attributes in the **Light Fog Attributes** area as required. The density of the fog will be higher near the light and it decreases gradually as you move away from it.

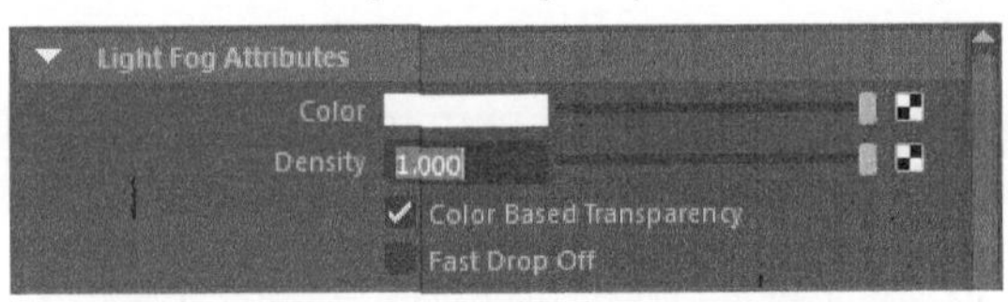

*Figure 7-10 The **Light Fog Attributes** area*

Fog Type

The options in the **Fog Type** drop-down list are used to select the type of fog to be used. By default, the **Normal** option is selected in the **Fog Type** drop-down list. Select the **Linear** option if you want the fog to diminish slowly from the center of the light. By selecting the **Exponential** option, the fog will diminish quickly from the center of the light.

Fog Radius

The **Fog Radius** attribute is used to set the radius of the fog for the selected light.

Fog Intensity

The **Fog Intensity** attribute is used to increase or decrease the intensity of the fog.

Light Glow

The **Light Glow** attribute is used to add glow to the selected light. On choosing the checker box on the right of this attribute, the **opticalFX1** node will be added to the selected light and it will be displayed in the **Attribute Editor**, refer to Figure 7-11.

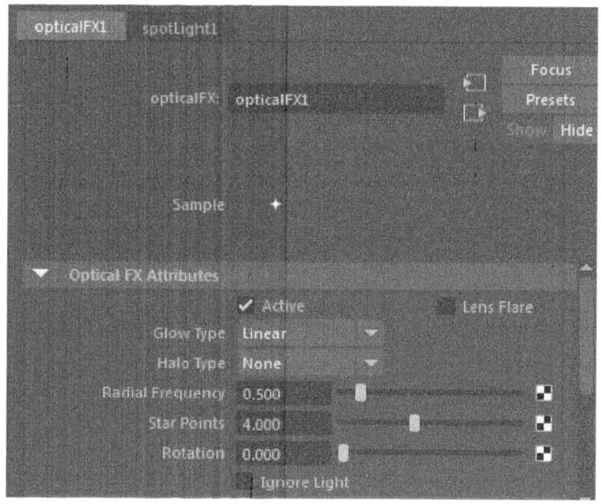

Figure 7-11 *The* ***opticalFX1*** *node added to the light*

Spot Light

Menubar: Create > Objects > Lights > Spot Light

The spot light evenly throws a beam of light within a narrow range in a conical shape, refer to Figure 7-12. Figure 7-13 shows a flower pot illuminated by a spot light. To create a spot light, choose **Create > Objects > Lights > Spot Light** from the menubar; the spot light will be created at the center of the viewport. Most of the attributes of the spot light are similar to those of the ambient light. Some of its other attributes are discussed next.

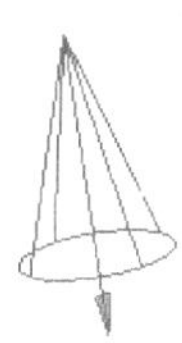

Figure 7-12 *The spot light*

Figure 7-13 *A flower pot illuminated by a spot light*

Spot Light Attributes Area

The attributes in this area are used to adjust the angles of the spot light. These attributes are discussed next.

Decay Rate

This drop-down list is available only in the **Spot**, **Area**, and **Point lights**. It is used to determine the rate at which the light decreases or fades away with distance. The options in this drop-down list are discussed next.

No Decay

The **No Decay** option is used to illuminate all the objects in the scene when there is no decay in the light.

Linear

The **Linear** option is used to linearly decrease the intensity of light linearly with distance. This rate is slower than the real world light.

Quadratic

The **Quadratic** option is used to decrease the intensity of light proportionally to the square of distance. This rate imitates the real world decay rate.

Cubic

The **Cubic** option is used to decrease the intensity of the light proportionally to the cube of distance.

Cone Angle

The **Cone Angle** attribute is used to increase or decrease the illumination of the spot light. By default, the angle value in this attribute is set to 40.00.

Penumbra Angle

The **Penumbra Angle** attribute controls the angle from the edge of the beam of the spot light where the intensity of the spot light falls to zero. The higher the value of the **Penumbra Angle** attribute, the lower will be the intensity of the edges, as shown in Figures 7-14 and 7-15.

Figure 7-14 *Spot Light with* ***Penumbra Angle = 0***

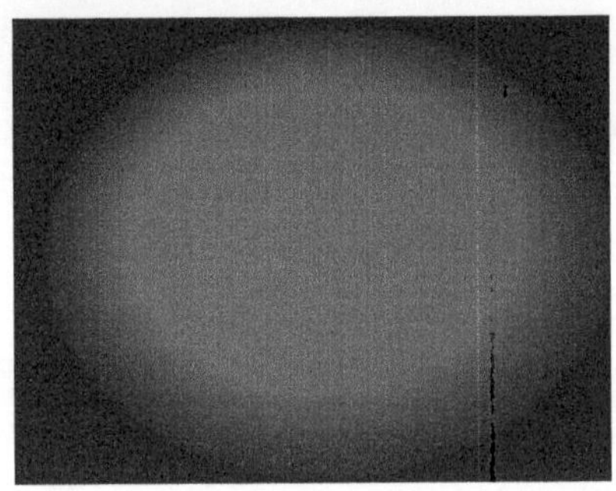

Figure 7-15 *Spot Light with* ***Penumbra Angle = 10***

Dropoff

The **Dropoff** attribute is used to control the intensity of the light from the center to the edge of the spot light beam area. The higher the value of this attribute, the lower will be the intensity of the spot light beam.

Light Effects Area

The attributes in the **Light Effects** area are used to assign fog effects to the light. These attributes are discussed next.

Light Fog

The **Light Fog** attribute is used to add fog effect to the selected light. Choose the checker box on the right of the **Light Fog** attribute; the light fog attributes will be added to the selected light in the **Attribute Editor**.

Fog Spread

The **Fog Spread** attribute is used to spread the fog coming from a spot light. The more the **Fog Spread** value, the thicker will be the fog at the edges of the spot light, as shown in Figures 7-16 and 7-17.

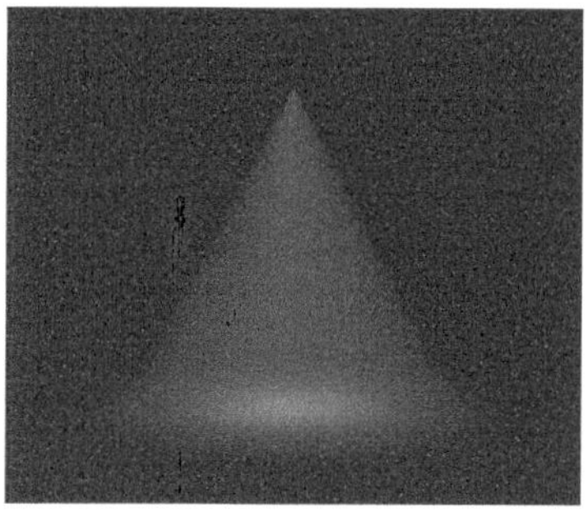

Figure 7-16 Spot Light with ***Fog Spread*** *= 1*

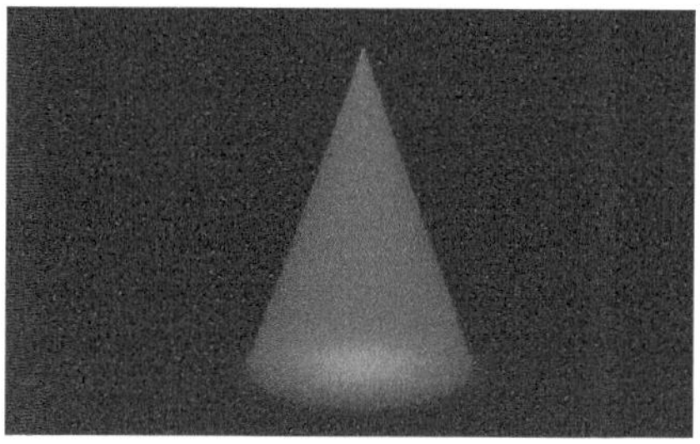

Figure 7-17 Spot Light with ***Fog Spread*** *= 5*

Fog Intensity

The **Fog Intensity** attribute is used to adjust the fog intensity of the selected light. If you want the light to be displayed in a certain shape, or as if it is coming from a half opened door, you can do so by adjusting its parameters. To do so, select the **Barn Doors** check box in the **Light Effects** area of the **Attribute Editor**; the attributes related to the barn doors will be activated. Set the required values in the **Barn Doors** edit boxes and render the scene to display the effect. The default values in all the edit boxes are shown in Figure 7-18.

You can also create shadows of an object in the viewport. To do so, expand the **Shadows** area in the **Attribute Editor**. Next, select the **Use Depth Map Shadows** check box from the **Depth Map Shadow Attributes** area to activate shadows in the viewport, as shown in Figure 7-19.

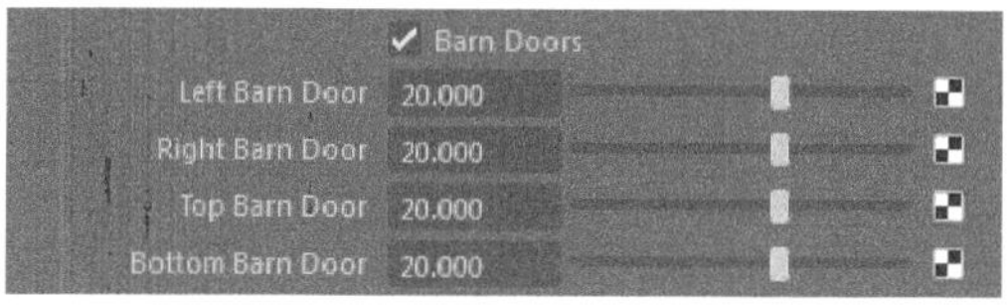

Figure 7-18 The ***Barn Doors*** *attributes*

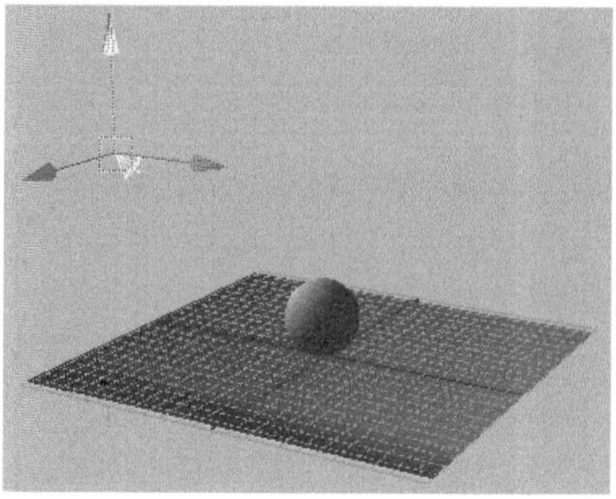

Figure 7-19 The shadow effect displayed

Area Light

Menubar: Create > Objects > Lights > Area Light

The area light is a type of light that has a two-dimensional rectangular light source. It emits light from a rectangular area. The larger the size of the light, the more illuminated the scene will be. To create an area light, choose **Create > Objects > Lights > Area Light** from the menubar; an area light will be created at the center of the viewport, as shown in Figure 7-20. It is used to create high quality still images. Therefore, the scene with an area light will take more time for rendering as compared to the other lights. The attributes of this light are similar to those of the **ambient light** except the **Decay Rate** which is discussed next.

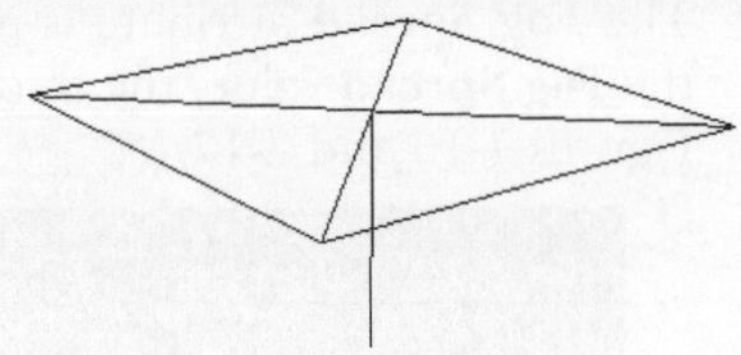

Figure 7-20 *The area light*

Decay Rate

This drop-down list is available only in the **Spot**, **Area**, and **Point** lights. It is used to determine the rate at which the light decreases or fades away with distance. The options in this drop-down list are discussed next.

No Decay

The **No Decay** option is used to illuminate all objects in the scene when there is no decay in the light.

Linear

The **Linear** option is used to linearly decrease the intensity of light with distance. This rate is slower than the real world light.

Quadratic

The **Quadratic** option is used to decrease the intensity of light proportionally to the square of distance. This rate imitates the real world decay rate.

Cubic

The **Cubic** option is used to decrease the intensity of the light proportionally to the cube of distance.

Volume Light

Menubar:	Create > Objects > Lights > Volume Light

The volume light is used to add a volume light to the scene. This light is represented by the icon shown in Figure 7-21. The innermost area of the volume light icon represents the visual extent of the light. You can also use this light as a negative light. For example, you can use it to remove illumination from a particular area or to lighten up the dark shadows in the scene. To create a volume light, choose **Create > Objects > Lights > Volume Light** from the menubar; a volume light will be created at the center of the viewport, as shown in Figure 7-21. Figure 7-22 shows the effect of the volume light. The attributes of the volume light are similar to those discussed in other lights.

Object Light

Menubar:	Create > Objects > Lights > mental ray > Object Light

The object light is used to change a mesh object into a mental ray object light in a scene. To understand the function of this tool, create a sphere in the viewport, as shown in Figure 7-23. Next, select the sphere and then choose **Create > Objects > Lights > mental ray > Object Light** from the menubar; the mesh object changes into a light object, as shown in Figure 7-24. To see the effect of the light, render the scene.

Figure 7-21 The volume light

Figure 7-22 The volume light effect

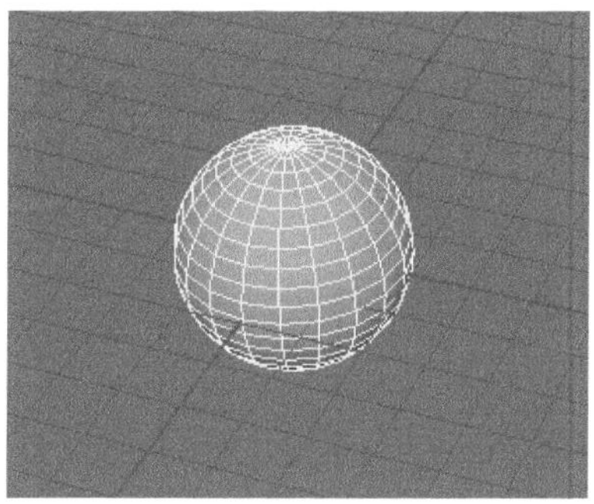

Figure 7-23 The Sphere

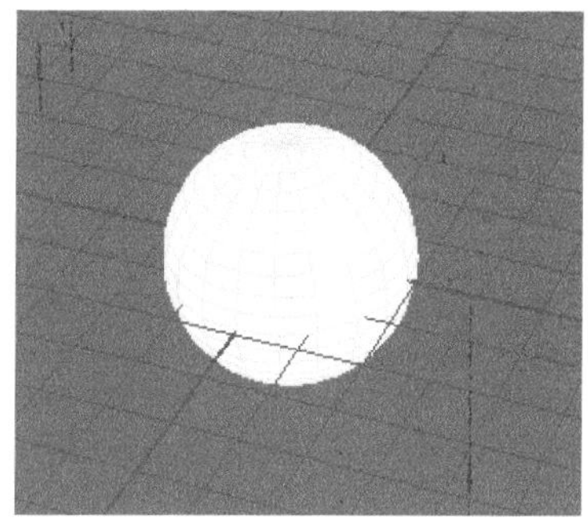

Figure 7-24 The mesh object changed into a light object

Physical Area Light

Menubar: Create > Objects > Lights > mental ray > Physical Area Light

In Maya, area lights are two-dimensional rectangular light sources, refer to Figure 7-25. You can use the standard transform tools to resize them. Compared to other light sources, area lights take longer to render but they produce better quality lighting and shadows. These lights are physically based therefore they don't have the decay option. This physical area light casts rays from the sample points on the objects to create smooth shadows.

Physical Sun

Menubar: Create > Objects > Lights > mental ray > Physical Sun

The physical Sun and environment sky lights are used to produce accurate renderings of daylight scenes. When you create a physical sun light in a scene, the **mia_physicalsun** shader will be created and is automatically connected to all the existing renderable cameras. Similarly, when you create an environment sky light, the **mia_phsicalsky** shader will be created and will get connected to all the renderable cameras.

The physical sun and sky effect is discussed later in the chapter.

Environment Sky

Menubar:	Create > Objects > Lights > mental ray > Environment Sky

Refer to physical sun section for the description of this light.

Environment Image (IBL)

Menubar:	Create > Objects > Lights > mental ray > Environment Image (IBL)

The environment image (IBL) light is used to simulate light emitted from an indefinitely distant sphere to create image-based lighting, refer to Figure 7-26. Image based lighting is a technique to render photorealistic images. With image-based lighting, you will use a photograph of a real environment to illuminate the scene.

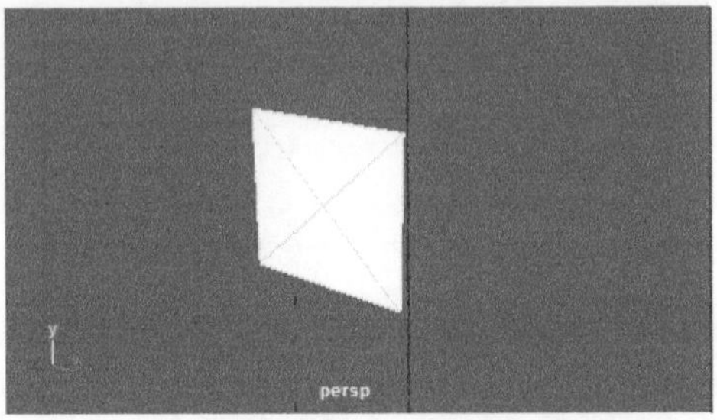

Figure 7-25 *The Physical area light*

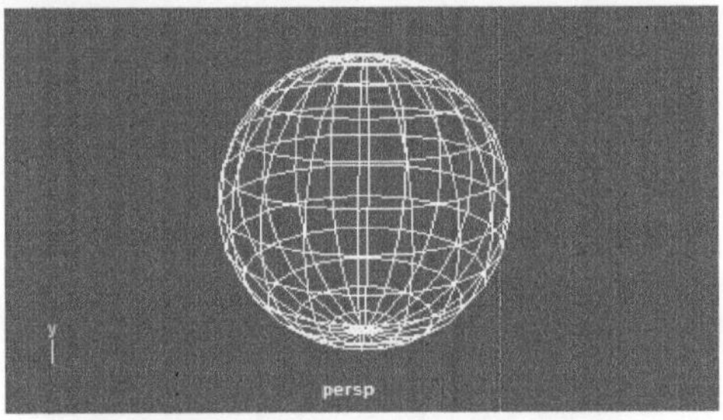

Figure 7-26 *The Environment Image (IBL) light*

GLOW AND HALO EFFECTS

The glow and halo effects are used to add a realistic effect to the scene. These effects can be added to any light by using the **Attribute Editor**. To add these effects to a light, select the light in the viewport and choose **Windows > Editors > General Editors > Attribute Editor** from the menubar; the **Attribute Editor** displaying the attributes of the selected light will be displayed. Choose the checker box on the right of the **Color** attribute, as shown in Figure 7-27; the **Create Render Node** window will be displayed in the viewport. Select the **Glow** option from the left pane of the **Create Render Node** window.

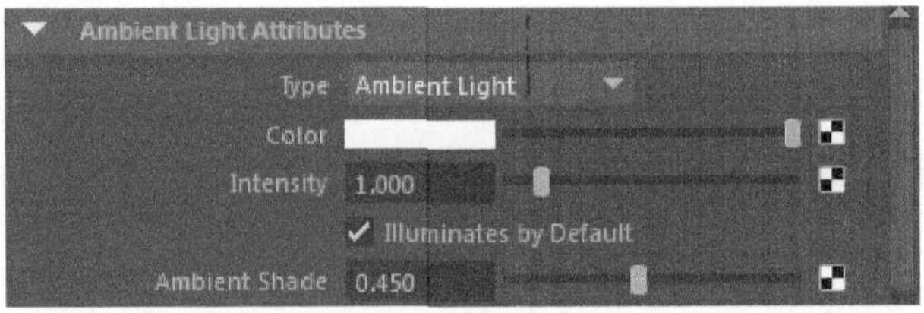

Figure 7-27 *Choosing the checker box next to the* ***Color*** *attribute*

Next, choose **Optical FX** from the right pane of the window; the **Optical FX Attributes** area will be displayed in the **Attribute Editor**, as shown in Figure 7-28.

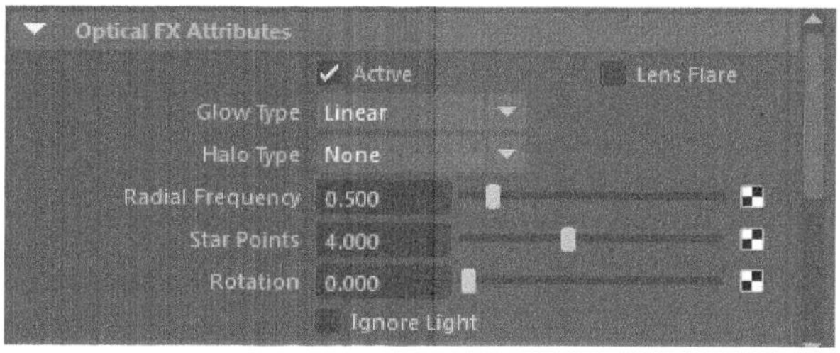

Figure 7-28 *The **Optical FX Attributes** area*

Optical FX Attributes Area

The attributes in this area are used to control the visual aspect of glow, halo, and lens effects. Various attributes in this area are discussed next.

Active

The **Active** check box is used to toggle the display of optical effects on rendering. This check box is selected by default.

Lens Flare

The **Lens Flare** check box is used to create a bright light source illuminating the surfaces of a lens of a camera. This is called the lens effect. It reduces the contrast and creates bright streak patterns on an image.

To apply this effect to a scene, select the **Lens Flare** check box from the **Optical FX Attributes** area; the lens effect will be created on the selected light. Figure 7-29 shows the light without lens flare and Figure 7-30 shows the light with lens flare.

Figure 7-29 *Light without lens flare*

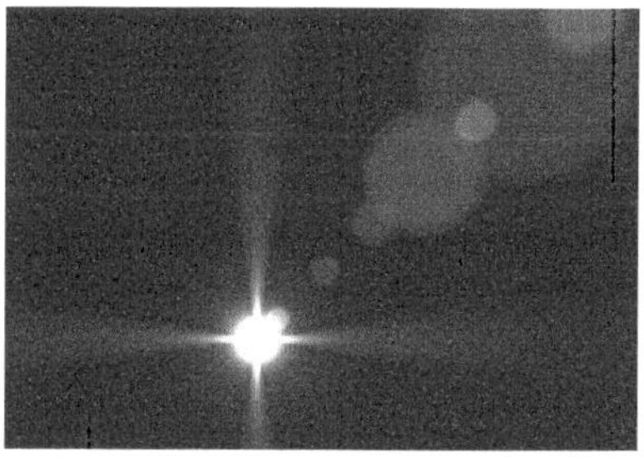

Figure 7-30 *Light with lens flare*

Glow Type

The options in the **Glow Type** drop-down list are used to apply various glow effects to the selected light. The options available in this drop-down list are: **None**, **Linear**, **Exponential**, **Ball**, **Lens Flare**, and **Rim Halo**.

Figures 7-31 through 7-35 show all the glow effects on selecting different options from this drop-down list.

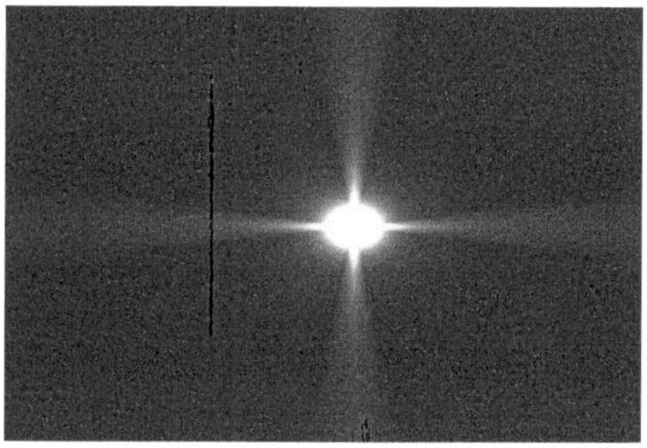

Figure 7-31 *The **Linear** glow effect*

*Figure 7-32 The **Exponential** glow effect*

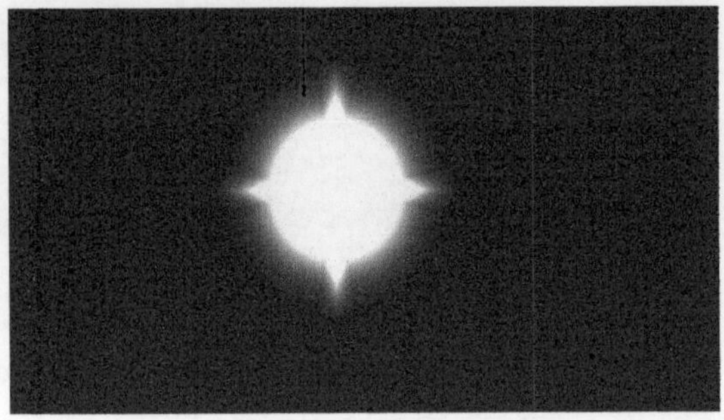

*Figure 7-33 The **Ball** glow effect*

*Figure 7-34 The **Lens Flare** glow effect*

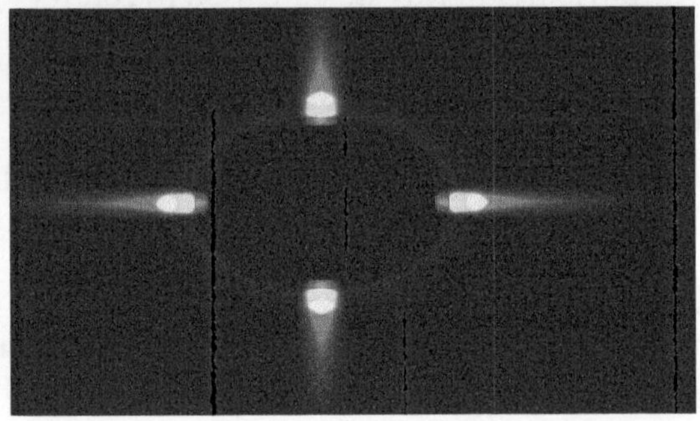

*Figure 7-35 The **Rim Halo** glow effect*

Halo Type

The options in the **Halo Type** drop-down list are used to apply different halo effects to the selected light. The options available are **None**, **Linear**, **Exponential**, **Ball**, **Lens Flare**, and **Rim Halo**. Figures 7-36 through 7-40 show various halo effects applied to the light.

Radial Frequency

The **Radial Frequency** attribute is used to control the smoothness of the glow radial noise. The default value of this attribute is set to 0.5.

Star Points

The **Star Points** attribute is used to change the number of star points emitting from a light. Figures 7-41 and 7-42 show lights on entering different values in the **Star Points** edit box. The default value of this attribute is set to 4.

*Figure 7-36 The **Linear** halo effect*

*Figure 7-37 The **Exponential** halo effect*

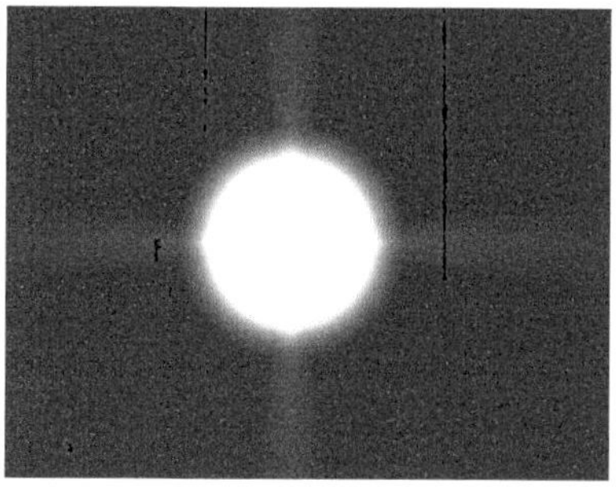

*Figure 7-38 The **Ball** halo effect*

*Figure 7-39 The **Lens Flare** halo effect*

Rotation

The **Rotation** attribute is used to rotate the star effects and the glow noise from the center of the light.

The value of slider next to this attribute ranges from 0 to 360, but you can also enter any other value as per your requirement in this edit box.

The default value of this attribute is 0.

*Figure 7-40 The **Rim** halo effect*

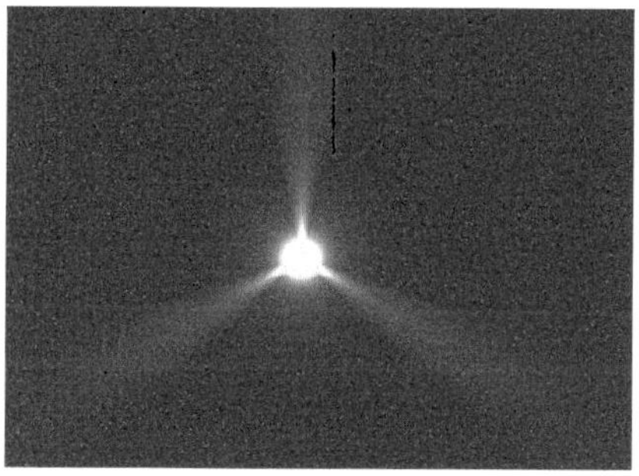

*Figure 7-41 Light with **Star Points = 3***

*Figure 7-42 Light with **Star Points = 15***

PHYSICAL SUN AND SKY EFFECT

The **Physical Sun and Sky** option is used to add a natural daylight effect to a scene by using the **mental ray** renderer.

Note

*This feature will only be available when the **mental ray** renderer is installed and active. If the **mental ray** renderer is not active, choose **Windows > Editors > Settings/Preferences > Plug-in Manager** from the menubar; the **Plug-in Manager** dialog box will be displayed, as shown in Figure 7-43. In this dialog box, select the **Loaded** and **Auto Load** check boxes on the right of the **Mayatomr.mll** plug-in type and then choose the **Refresh** button. Next, choose the **Close** button.*

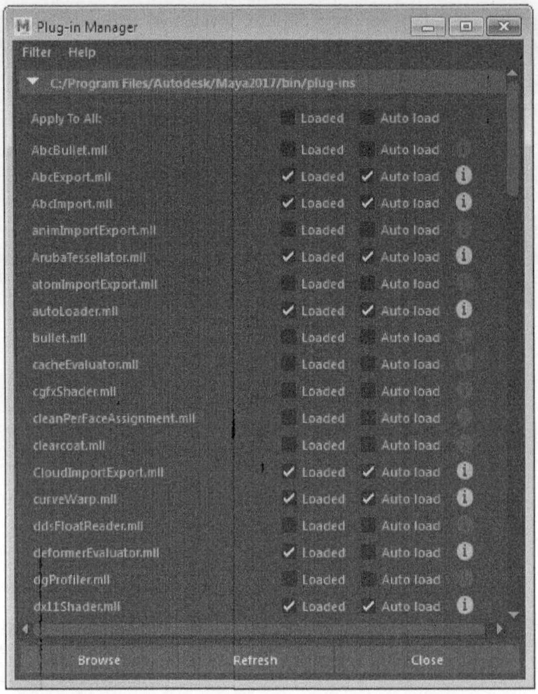

*Figure 7-43 The **Plug-in Manager** dialog box*

Now, choose the **Display render settings** button from the Status Line; the **Render Settings** window will be displayed in the viewport. Select **mental ray** from the **Render Using** drop-down list, if not already selected. Choose the **Quality** tab from the **Render Setting** window and then choose the **Show advanced Setting** check box.

All the attributes of advanced lighting will be displayed. Next, choose the **Scene** tab and expand **Camera > Environment** area, if not already expanded, refer to Figure 7-44.

Next, choose the **Create** button on the right of the **Physical Sun and Sky** attribute; a directional light will be created in the viewport. Figure 7-45 shows the Physical Sun and Sky effect applied to a scene in rendering.

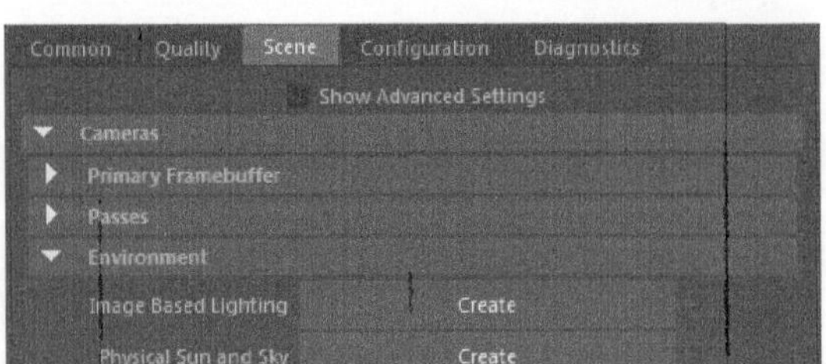

*Figure 7-44 The **Environment** area*

Figure 7-45 The Physical Sun and Sky effect applied to a scene

LIGHT LINKING

Light linking is a process of linking light to specific objects in a scene. To link lights, the light affects only the object to which it is linked in the scene. To link an object to the light, select the light and then select the **Rendering** menu from the **Menuset** drop-down list in the Status Line. Next, choose **Lighting/Shading > Light Linking > Light Linking Editor > Light-Centric** from the menubar; the **Relationship Editor** will be displayed in the viewport, refer to Figure 7-46. Select the light that you want to link from the **Light Sources** area and then select the objects from the **Illuminated Objects** area of the **Relationship Editor**; now the light source will illuminate only the linked objects. Next, close the **Relationship Editor**.

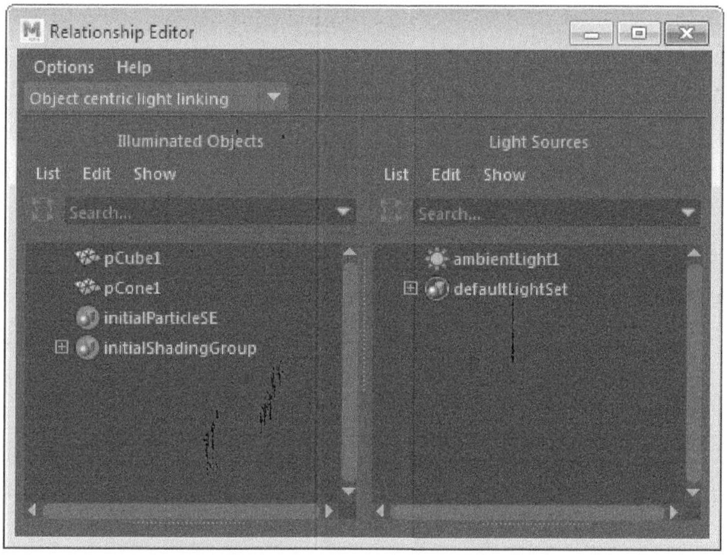

Figure 7-46** The **Relationship Editor

CAMERAS

In Maya, cameras are used to view a scene from different angles. These cameras work in a similar way as the still and video cameras in the real world. There are five types of cameras in Maya: Camera, Camera and Aim, Camera Aim and Up, Stereo Camera, and Multi-Stereo Rig. These camera types are created with the help of the **Camera**, **Camera and Aim**, **Camera Aim and Up**, **Stereo Camera**, and **Multi-Stereo Rig** tools, respectively. These tools are discussed next.

Camera

Menubar: Create > Objects > Cameras > Camera

The **Camera** tool is used to create a basic camera in the scene. The camera created using this tool is ideal for static scenes and simple animations. To create a camera using this tool, choose **Create > Objects > Cameras > Camera** from the menubar; a camera will be created in the viewport, as shown in Figure 7-47. You can adjust the camera to focus on any object, as shown in Figure 7-48. You can also set the properties of the camera in the **Attribute Editor**. To do so, select the camera; the **Attribute Editor** will be displayed with the **Camera Attributes** area expanded, as shown in Figure 7-49. The attributes in this area are discussed next.

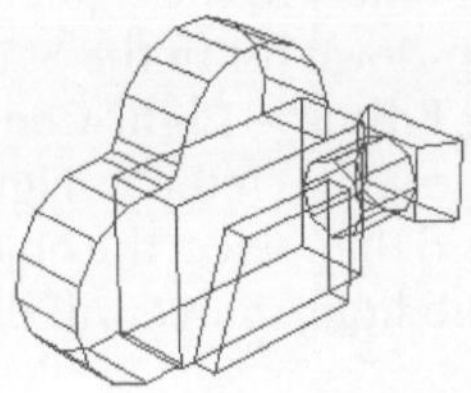

Figure 7-47 A camera created

Figure 7-48 The camera focusing on an object

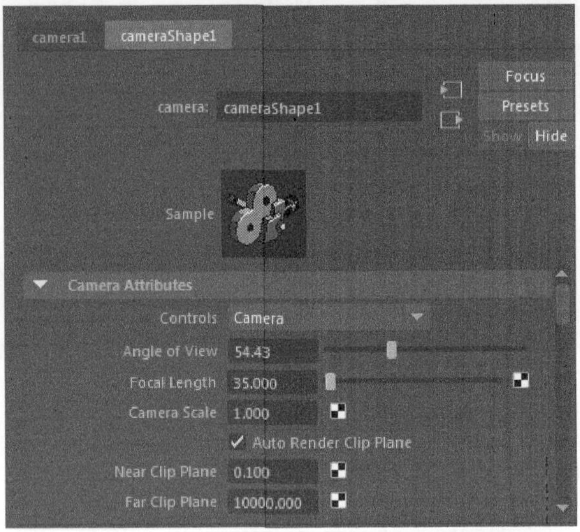

Figure 7-49** Partial view of the **Camera Attributes** area in the **Attribute Editor

Controls

The options in the **Controls** drop-down list are used to display the type of camera which will currently display in the viewport.

Angle of View

The **Angle of View** attribute is used to specify the angle of view of the camera. This attribute is affected by the value specified in the **Focal Length** edit box.

Focal Length

The **Focal Length** attribute is used to specify the focal length of the camera in millimeters. On increasing the value of the **Focal Length** attribute, the camera will zoom in and size of the objects in the camera view will be increased and vice versa.

Camera Scale

The **Camera Scale** attribute is used to scale the size of the camera that is indirectly proportional to the scene.

Auto Render Clip Plane

The **Auto Render Clip Plane** check box affects only the **Maya Software** renderer. When this check box is selected, the near and far clipping planes are automatically set to enclose all the objects within the view of the camera. You must set the values for the planes manually for **Hardware**, **Maya Software**, and **mental ray** renderers.

Near Clip Plane and Far Clip Plane

The near and far clipping planes are two imaginary planes located at two specific distances. You can specify the value of these planes in the **Near Clip Plane** and **Far Clip Plane** edit boxes. The objects between these two planes will be rendered in the camera view.

Note

1. The clipping planes are not visible in the scene.

*2. Clear the **Auto Render Clip Plane** check box, if you want to render the images to be used in a depth based compositing.*

3. If a part of a project is in front of the near clipping plane, only the part of the object beyond the near clipping plane will be rendered.

*4. For the **Maya Software** renderer, if a part of the object is beyond the far clipping plane, the entire object is rendered.*

*5. For the **mental ray** renderer, if any object is opaque and a part of it is beyond the far clipping plane, then it will not be clipped. If the object is semi-transparent, the part of the object behind the far clipping plane will be clipped.*

Camera and Aim

Menubar: Create > Objects > Cameras > Camera and Aim

The **Camera and Aim** tool is used to create a basic camera and an aim vector control. To do so, choose **Create > Objects > Cameras > Camera and Aim** from the menubar; a camera will be created in the viewport, refer to Figure 7-50. This control is used to aim the camera at a specified point in the scene, refer to Figure 7-51.

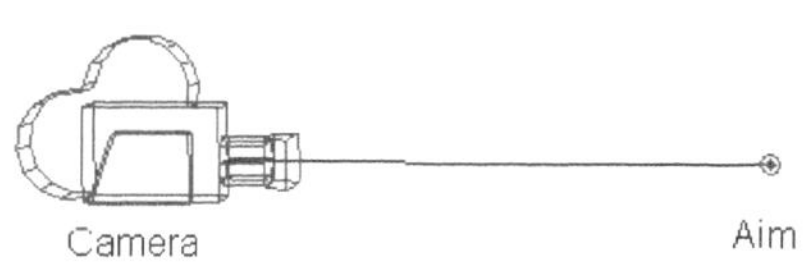

Figure 7-50 *A camera with an aim created*

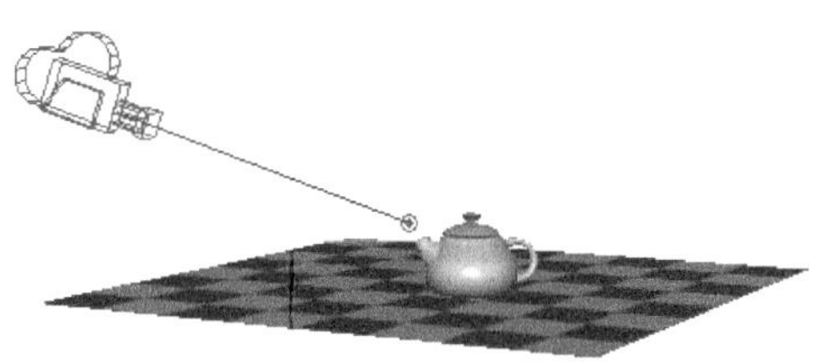

Figure 7-51 *The camera aiming at a point in the scene*

Camera, Aim and Up

Menubar:	Create > Objects > Cameras > Camera, Aim and Up

The **Camera, Aim and Up** tool is used to create a basic camera with an aim vector and an up vector controls. To do so, choose **Create > Objects > Cameras > Camera, Aim and Up** from the menubar; a camera will be created in the viewport, as shown in Figure 7-52.

This aim vector control is used to aim the camera at a specified point in the scene. The up vector control is used to rotate the camera, refer to Figure 7-53.

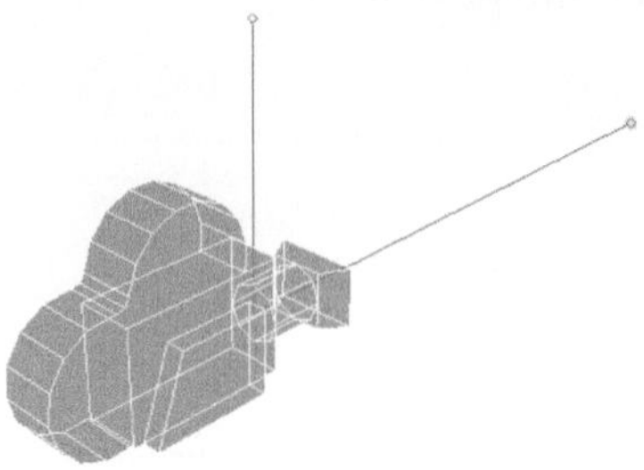

Figure 7-52 *A camera with the aim vector and up vector controls*

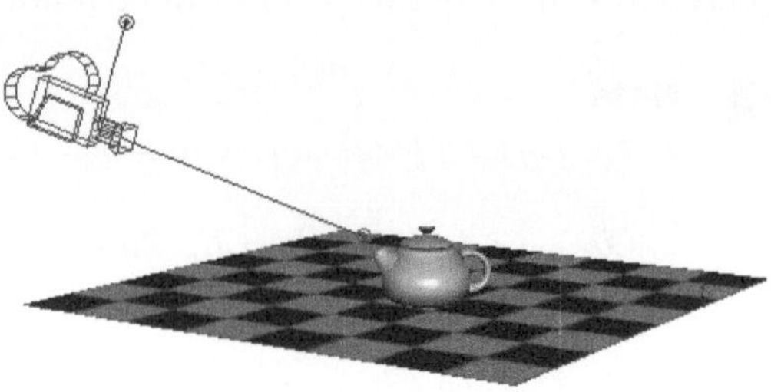

Figure 7-53 *A camera with the aim vector and up vector controls focusing on a point in the scene*

Stereo Camera

Menubar:	Create > > Objects > Cameras > Stereo Camera

The **Stereo Camera** tool is used to create stereoscopic cameras to produce an anaglyph or parallel image. This image when composited in a compositor produces renders with a depth illusion. To create a stereo camera, choose **Create > Objects > Cameras > Stereo Cameras** from the menubar; a stereo camera will be created in the viewport.

MultiStereo Rig

Menubar:	Create > Objects > Cameras > Multi Stereo Rig

The **Multi Stereo Rig** tool is used to create multi-camera rig for stereo cameras. By default, it is done by three layered camera rig.

TUTORIALS

Tutorial 1

In this tutorial, you will create a scene in which the light is scattering through a cylindrical object, as shown in Figure 7-54. **(Expected time: 15 min)**

The following steps are required to complete this tutorial:

a. Create a project folder.
b. Create a cylinder.
c. Adding a point light in the scene.
d. Save and render the scene.

Figure 7-54 The light scattering through a cylinder

Creating a Project Folder

Create a new project folder with the name *c07_tut1* at *\Documents\maya2017* and then save the file with the name *c07tut1* as discussed in Tutorial 1 of Chapter 2.

Creating a Cylinder

In this section, you will create a cylindrical object through which the light will scatter in all directions.

1. Maximize the top viewport. Next, choose **Create > Objects > Polygon Primitives > Cylinder** from the menubar and then create a cylinder.

2. In the **Channel Box / Layer Editor**, expand the **polyCylinder1** node in the **INPUTS** area and set the parameters as follows:

   Radius: **2** Height: **10**
   Subdivisions Axis: **50** Subdivisions Height: **25**

3. In the **Channel Box / Layer Editor**, enter **2** in the **Scale X**, **Scale Y**, and **Scale Z** edit boxes and enter **0** in the **Translate X** and **Z** edit boxes, and **10** in the **Translate Y** edit box.

4. Maximize the persp viewport. Next, press and hold the right mouse button on the cylinder; a marking menu is displayed. Choose **Face** from the marking menu; the face selection mode is activated. Next, delete the top and bottom faces of the cylinder.

5. Delete some more faces of the cylinder randomly, as shown in Figure 7-55.

6. Choose **Create > Objects > Polygon Primitives > Plane** from the menubar. Next, create a plane in the persp viewport. Now, choose **Move Tool** from the Tool Box and place the plane below the cylinder.

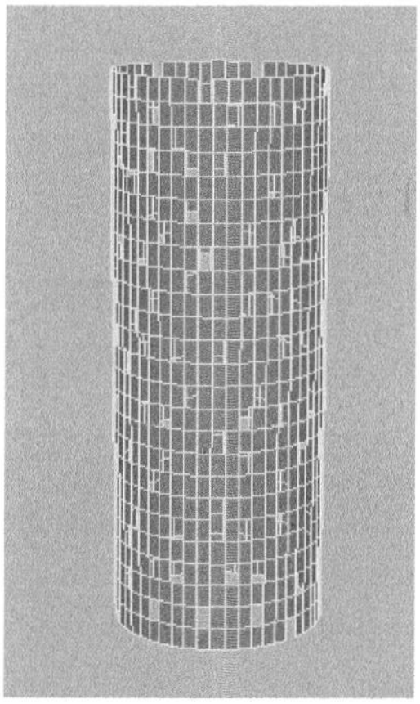

***Figure 7-55** Randomly deleted faces*

7. In the **Channel Box / Layer Editor**, expand the **polyPlane1** node in the **INPUTS** area and set the parameters as follows:

   Width: **80** Height: **80**

8. Make sure the **Modeling** menuset is selected from the **Menuset** drop-down list in the Status Line. Next, press and hold the right mouse button on the cylinder; a marking menu is displayed. Choose **Face** from the marking menu; the face selection mode is activated. Select all the faces of the cylinder. Next, choose **Edit Mesh > Components > Extrude** from the menubar; the **polyExtrudeFace1** In-View Editor is displayed in the viewport. Now, enter **0.6** in the **Thickness** edit box of the **polyExtrudeFace1** In-View Editor. Press W to exit the tool.

9. Press and hold the right mouse button on the cylinder; a marking menu is displayed. Choose **Object Mode** from the marking menu; the object selection mode is activated.

Adding a Point Light to the Scene

In this section, you will add a point light to the scene. It will act as the source of light.

1. Choose **Create > Objects > Lights > Point Light** from the menubar; a point light is created in the viewport.

2. In the **Channel Box / Layer Editor**, enter **10** in the **Translate Y** edit box.

3. Make sure the point light is selected in the viewport. Next, press CTRL+A; the **pointLightShape1** tab is displayed in the **Attribute Editor** with the attributes of the point light.

4. In the **Point Light Attributes** area, click on the color swatch on the right of the **Color** attribute; the **Color History** palette is displayed. Set the color of the light to orange. Alternatively, select **RGB, 0 to 1.0** option from the drop-down list located in the bottom right of the **Color History** palette and then set the values as given below:

   R: **0.667** G: **0.35** B: **0.078**

   Next, click anywhere outside the palette to close it and then enter **30** in the **Intensity** edit box.

5. In the **Light Effects** area of the **pointLightShape1** tab, choose the checker button on the right side of the **Light Fog** attribute; the **lightFog1** tab is displayed in the **Attribute Editor**.

6. Select the point light in the viewport. Make sure that the **pointLightShape1** tab is chosen, in the **Attribute Editor** and then set the parameters in the **Light Effects** area as follows:

   Fog Radius: **40** Fog Intensity: **4**

7. Choose the checker button on the right side of the **Light Glow** attribute; the **opticalFX1** tab is displayed in the **Attribute Editor**.

8. Select the point light in the viewport. In the **pointLightShape1** tab in the **Attribute Editor**, expand the **Shadows** area and select the **Use Depth Map Shadows** check box in the **Depth Map Shadow Attributes** area.

9. In the **Depth Map Shadow Attributes** area, set the parameters as follows:

   Resolution: **1024** Fog Shadow Samples: **50**

10. In the **sphereShape#** tab of the **Attribute Editor**, expand the **Render Stats** area. Next, select the **Volume Samples Override** check box and enter **2** in the **Volume Samples** edit box.

Saving and Rendering the Scene

In this section, you will save the scene that you have created and then render it. You can view the final rendered image of the scene by downloading the *c07_maya_2017_rndr.zip* file from *www.cadcim.com*. The path of the file is as follows: *Textbooks > Animation and Visual Effects > Maya > Autodesk Maya 2017: A Comprehensive Guide.*

1. Choose **File > Save Scene** from the menubar.

2. Maximize the persp viewport, if it is not already maximized. Choose the **Render the current frame** button from the Status Line; the **Render View** window is displayed. This window shows the final output of the scene, refer to Figure 7-54.

Tutorial 2

In this tutorial, you will add lights to an underwater scene to get the final output, as shown in Figure 7-56. **(Expected time: 30 min)**

Figure 7-56 *The final output*

The following steps are required to complete this tutorial:

a. Create a project folder.
b. Download and open the file.

c. Add lights to the scene.
d. Save and render the scene.

Creating a Project Folder

Create a new project folder with the name *c07_tut2* at *\Documents\maya2017*, as discussed in Tutorial 1 of Chapter 2.

Downloading and Opening the File

In this section, you will download and open the file.

1. Download the *c07_maya_2017_tut.zip* file from *www.cadcim.com*. The path of the file is as follows: *Textbooks > Animation and Visual Effects > Maya > Autodesk Maya 2017: A Comprehensive Guide*.

2. Extract the contents of the zip file to the *Documents* folder. Next, navigate to *\Documents\c07_maya_2017\tut* and then copy all the texture files to *\Documents\maya2017\c07_tut2\sourceimages*.

3. Choose **File > Open Scene** from the menubar; the **Open** dialog box is displayed. In this dialog box, browse to *\Documents\c07_maya_2017_tut* and select **c07_tut2_start** file from it. Choose the **Open** button; the file opens.

4. Now, choose **File > Save Scene As** from the menubar; the **Save As** dialog box is displayed. As the project folder is already set, the path *\Documents\maya2017\c07_tut2\scenes* is displayed in the **Look In** drop-down list. Save the file with the name *c07tut2.mb* in this folder.

Adding Lights to the Scene

In this section, you will add spot light to the scene.

1. Choose **Create > Objects > Lights > Spot Light** from the menubar; the spot light is created in the viewport. In the **Channel Box / Layer Editor**, set the parameters as follows:

Translate X: **1.034**	Translate Y: **51.527**	Translate Z: **1.499**
Rotate X: **121.306**	Rotate Y: **73.369**	Rotate Z: **-180**

   Figure 7-57 displays the light after entering the values in the **Channel Box / Layer Editor**.

2. Make sure the spot light is selected in the viewport. Choose **Display > Object > Show > Light Manipulators** from the menubar; the light manipulators are displayed, refer to Figure 7-58. Select the manipulator ring 10, press and hold the left mouse button on it, and then move it downward till the number on the ring changes to about 100; the fog area of the light is increased.

3. In the perps viewport, make sure the spot light is selected. Choose **Display > Object > Hide > Light Manipulators** from the menubar to hide the manipulators.

4. Choose **Windows > Editors > General Editors > Attribute Editor** from the menubar; the **spotLightShape1** tab is displayed in the **Attribute Editor**. In this tab, choose the checker button on the right of the **Color** attribute; the **Create Render Node** window is displayed. Choose the **File** button from this window; the **File Attributes** area is displayed in the **Attribute Editor**.

Figure 7-57 *The spot light in the front viewport*

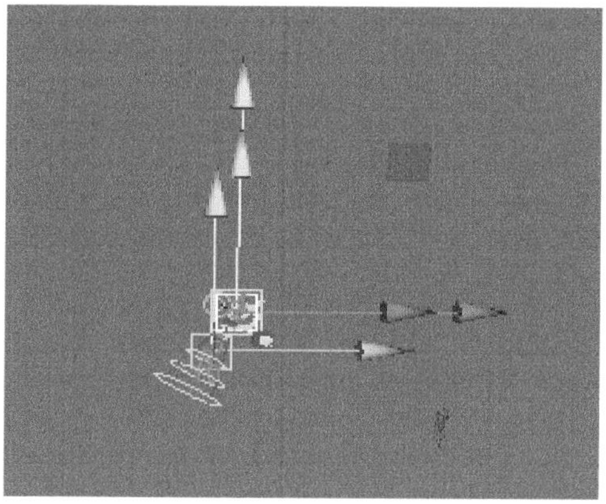

Figure 7-58 *The light manipulators*

5. Choose the folder icon corresponding to the **Image Name** attribute in the **Attribute Editor**; the **Open** dialog box is displayed. In this dialog box, select **texture_light.jpg** and then choose the **Open** button to open the selected file.

6. Select the spot light and enter **60** in the **Cone Angle** attribute in the **Spot Light Attributes** area of the **spotLightShape1** tab. Expand the **Light Effects** area and then choose the checker button on the right of the **Light Fog** attribute; the fog effect is applied to the spot light.

7. Select the spot light. In the **Attribute Editor**, enter **1.5** in the **Fog Spread** edit box and **2** in the **Fog Intensity** edit box. Make sure the persp viewport is active and choose the **Render the current frame** button from the Status Line; the fog effect is displayed, as shown in Figure 7-59.

Figure 7-59 *The Fog effect displayed*

8. Choose **Create > Objects > Lights > Ambient Light** from the menubar; the ambient light is created in the viewport. In the **Channel Box / Layer Editor**, set the parameters as follows:

   Translate X: **65** Translate Y: **26** Translate Z: **152**

9. Choose **Panels > Perspective > camera1** from the **Panel** menu to switch from the persp view to the camera view. Adjust the view of the camera in the viewport, if required.

Saving and Rendering the Scene

In this section, you will save the scene that you have created and then render it. You can view the final rendered image of the scene by downloading the *c07_maya_2017_rndr.zip* file from *www.cadcim.com*. The path of the file is as follows: *Textbooks > Animation and Visual Effects > Maya > Autodesk Maya 2017: A Comprehensive Guide.*

1. Choose **File > Save Scene** from the menubar.

2. Maximize the persp viewport, if it is not already maximized. Choose the **Render the current frame** button from the Status Line; the **Render View** window is displayed. This window shows the final output of the scene, refer to Figure 7-56.

Self-Evaluation Test

Answer the following questions and then compare them to those given at the end of this chapter:

1. Which of the following lights is used to focus on an object?

   (a) spot light (b) ambient light
   (c) area light (d) none of these

2. A __________ emits light from a specific point and radiates in a conical shape.

3. An __________ behaves more like a point light as its **Ambient Shade** parameter approaches to 1.

4. The __________ is a phenomenon of linking light with some specific objects in a scene.

5. The __________ attribute is used to control the brightness of the spot light near edges.

6. The __________ attribute helps you control the smoothness of the glow radial noise.

7. The physical sun and sky feature works only with the **mental ray** renderer. (T/F)

8. The **Focal Length** attribute is used to zoom in and out the camera. (T/F)

9. The working of the spot light is similar to that of the directional light. (T/F)

10. The **Camera and Aim** tool is used to create a basic camera and an aim vector control. (T/F)

Review Questions

Answer the following questions:

1. Which of the following attributes is used to control the smoothness of the glow radial noise?

   (a) **Halo Type** (b) **Radial frequency**
   (c) **Star Points** (d) **Rotation**

2. The __________ attribute is used to spread fog coming from the spot light.

3. The __________ attribute is used to control the intensity of the light flowing from the center to the edge of the spot light beam area.

4. The __________ attribute is used to increase or decrease the illumination of the spot light.

5. The __________ check box is used to add the lens flare effect to the selected light.

6. The **Focal Length** attribute is used to specify the focal length of the camera measured in centimeters. (T/F)

EXERCISE

The rendered output of the models used in the following exercise can be accessed by downloading the *c07_maya_2017_exr.zip* file from *www.cadcim.com*. The path of the file is as follows: *Textbooks > Animation and Visual Effects > Maya > Autodesk Maya 2017: A Comprehensive Guide.*

Exercise 1

Apply the physical sun and sky effect to the textured scene shown in Figure 7-60 to get the output shown in Figure 7-61. **(Expected time: 15 min)**

Figure 7-60 *The textured scene*

Figure 7-61 *The physical sun and sky effect applied to the scene*

Answers to Self-Evaluation Test

1. a, **2. Spot Light**, **3.** Ambient Light, **4.** Light linking, **5. Dropoff**, **6. Radial**, **7.** T, **8.** T, **9.** T, **10.** F

Chapter 8

Animation

Learning Objectives

After completing this chapter, you will be able to:

- *Understand the basic concepts of animation*
- *Understand different types of animation*
- *Use the Graph Editor for editing animation*
- *Use Animation layers*

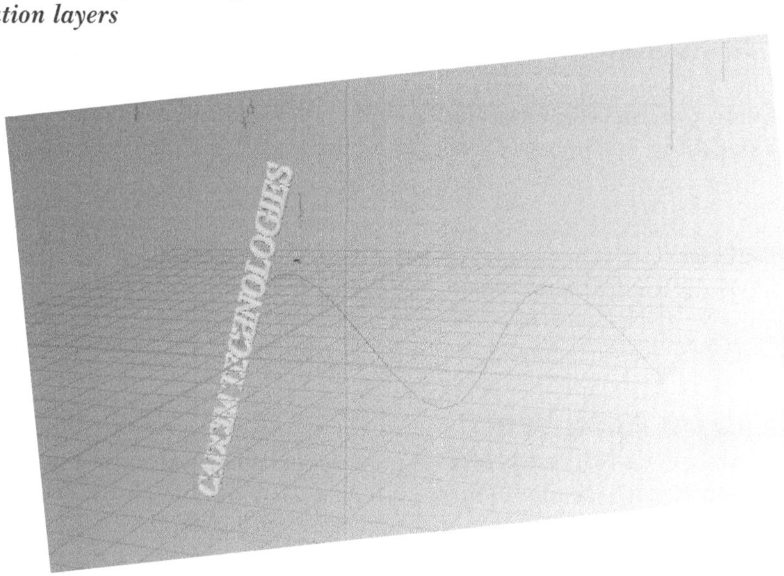

INTRODUCTION

Animation is a process of displaying a sequence of images in order to create an illusion of movement. In this chapter, you will animate models using various animation techniques such as keyframe animation, path animation, nonlinear animation, and technical animation.

To animate a 3D object, you need to record its position, rotation, and scale on different frames. These frames are known as keyframes. The keys between the keyframes contain information about the actions performed in the animation. When an animation is played, the frames are displayed one after the other in quick succession which creates an optical illusion of motion. In this chapter, you will also learn about the playback control buttons available at the bottom of the interface and various additional tools used for creating an animation.

ANIMATION TYPES

In Maya, you can create animation using different techniques such as Keyframe Animation, Effects Animation, Nonlinear Animation, Path Animation, Motion Capture Animation, and Technical Animation. Some of these techniques are discussed below.

Keyframe Animation

The Keyframe animation is used to animate objects by manually setting the keyframes over time. It is the most commonly used animation type as it is highly flexible and helps to create complex animations easily.

Effects Animation

The Effects animation is also known as the dynamic animation. It is used to create and simulate physical phenomena such as fire and smoke. Animation of fluids, particles, and hair/fur are some examples of effects animation.

Nonlinear Animation

The Nonlinear animation is an advanced method of animation. It is used to blend, duplicate, and split animation clips to achieve different motion effects. The nonlinear animation is controlled by using the **Trax Editor**. For example, you can loop the walk cycle of your character by using Graph Editor.

Path Animation

The Path animation is used to animate an object's translation and rotation attributes on the basis of a NURBS curve. This type of animation is used to animate an object along a path such as a moving car on the road or a moving train on the railtrack.

Motion Capture Animation

The Motion Capture animation is the process of recording human body movement for immediate or delayed analysis and playback. It is used to animate a character by using the motion capturing devices. A motion capture device helps in real time monitoring and recording of data.

Technical Animation

The Technical Animation is used to animate an object by linking the translation and rotation attributes of one object with another object. The linking is done by setting driven keys in such a way that the attributes of one object are governed by the attributes of another object. For example, if you want to animate a locomotive engine, you need to link various parts of the engine by using the technical animation.

ANIMATION CONTROLS

In Maya, you can edit and view an animation. It can be done using various buttons such as Playback Controls, Animation Preferences, and so on. Some of these buttons are discussed below.

Playback Controls

The Playback Controls, shown in Figure 8-1, are used to control the animation in a scene. These buttons are located on the Time Slider at the bottom of the interface. The animation playback control buttons in Maya are discussed next.

Figure 8-1 *The playback controls*

Play forwards

The **Play forwards** button is used to play the animation in the forward direction. When you choose this button, it turns into the **Stop playback** button.

Play backwards

The **Play backwards** button is used to play the animation in backward direction. When you choose the **Play backwards** button, it turns into the **Stop playback** button.

Stop playback

The **Stop playback** button is used to stop the animation. You can stop an animation at any frame. Alternatively, you can press the ESC key to stop the animation.

Step forward one key

The **Step forward one key** button is used to jump from the current key to the next key in forward direction in the active time segment.

Step back one key

The **Step back one key** button is used to jump from the current key to the next key in backward direction in the active time segment.

Step back one frame

The **Step back one frame** button is used to step backward by one frame at a time in backward direction. You can view the current frame on the Time Slider when it moves from one frame to another. The keyboard shortcut for this button is ALT+,(comma).

Step forward one frame

The **Step forward one frame** button is used to step one frame at a time in forward by one frame in the active time segment. The keyboard shortcut for this button is ALT+.(dot).

Go to end of playback range

The **Go to end of playback range** button is used to go to the last frame of the active time segment.

Go to start of playback range

The **Go to start of playback range** button is used to go to the first frame of the active time segment.

Animation preferences

The **Animation preferences** button is used to display the **Preferences** dialog box with the **Time Slider** option selected by default in the **Categories** list. The options in this dialog box are used to edit the animation settings in Maya. To do so, choose the **Animation preferences** button located below the **Go to end of playback range** button in the playback control area; the **Preferences** dialog box will be displayed in the viewport, as shown in Figure 8-2.

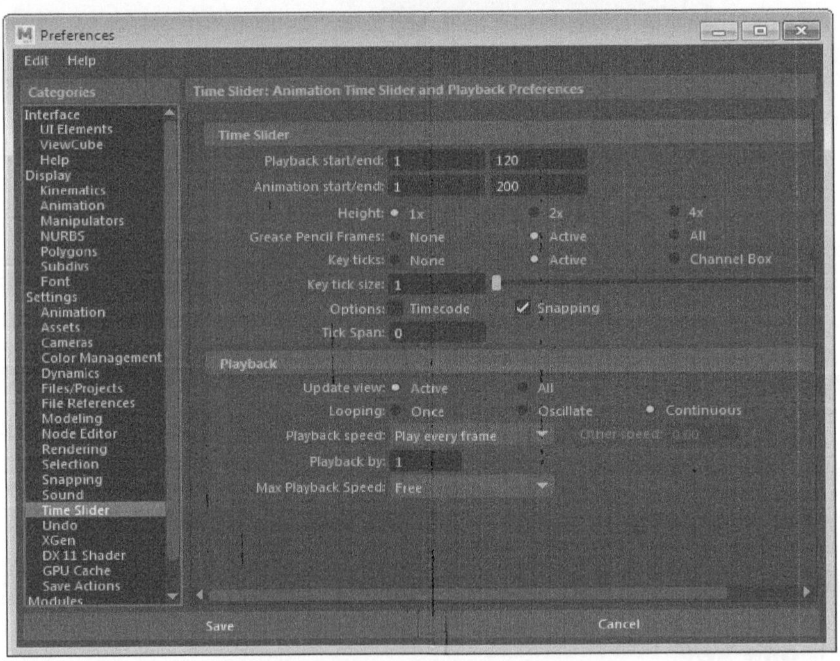

*Figure 8-2 The **Preferences** dialog box*

Alternatively, you can choose **Windows > Editors > Settings/Preferences > Preferences** from the menubar; the **Preferences** dialog box will be displayed. Next, choose **Time Slider** from the **Categories** list in this dialog box; the **Time Slider: Animation Time Slider and Playback Preferences** area will be displayed on the right of this dialog box. Adjust the required parameters in the **Playback** area of this dialog box. The options in this dialog box are discussed next.

Time Slider

The options in the **Time Slider** area are used to specify the time range, play back start/end, and so on. Various options in the **Time Slider** area are discussed below.

Playback start/end

The **Playback start/end** edit boxes are used to determine the start and end time of the playback range. The default playback values of the start time and end time are 1.00 and 120.00, respectively.

Animation start/end

The **Animation start/end** edit boxes are used to determine the start and end time of animation range. The default values of animation start time and end time are 1.00 and 200.00, respectively.

Height

The radio buttons corresponding to the **Height** attribute are used to specify the height of the Time Slider.

Grease Pencil Frames

The radio buttons corresponding to the **Grease Pencil Frames** attribute are used to display the **Grease Pencil** frames. By default, the **Active** radio button is selected.

Key ticks

The radio buttons corresponding to the **Key ticks** attribute are used to specify the appearance of the line markers on the Time Slider. By default, the **Active** radio button is selected.

Key tick size

The **Key tick size** attribute is used to specify the thickness of the line markers on the Time Slider.

Options

The check boxes corresponding to the **Options** attribute are used to choose between current time in video standard timecode or animation is snapped to nearest integer value. By default, the **Snapping** check box is selected.

Tick Span

The **Tick Span** attribute is used to specify the interval between the ticks displayed in the Time Slider. The default value for this attribute is 0.

Playback

The options in this area are used to change the playback settings of the scene.

Update view

The radio buttons corresponding to the **Update view** attribute are used to play the animation clip in the current active view only. By default, the **Active** radio button is selected. On selecting the **All** radio button, the animation clip will be played in all the views.

Looping
The radio buttons corresponding to the **Looping** attribute are used to specify the way the playback will start/end. By default, the **Continuous** radio button is selected.

Playback speed
The options in the **Playback speed** drop-down list are used to specify the speed of the playback. By default, the **Play every frame** option is selected.

Playback by
The **Playback by** attribute is used to play the animation clip at every frame. For example, if it is set to **10.00**, the animation will be played on every 10th frame.

Max Playback Speed
The options in the **Max Playback Speed** drop-down list are used to clamp the playback speed of the current animation. By default, the **Free** option is selected.

COMMONLY USED TERMS IN ANIMATION
In Maya, some terms are used very commonly.. These terms are discussed next.

Frame Rate
The frame rate is termed as the number of frames or images displayed per second in a sequence. It is abbreviated as fps (frames per second). It is the total number of frames played per second in an animation.

Range
The term range is used to define the total length of an animation. The range of an animation is calculated in frames. For calculating the range of an animation, multiply the frame rate with the total time of animation. For example, if you have a frame rate of 24 fps and the total time of the animation is 5 secs, then the range of the animation will be: 24 X 5 = 120 frames.

Setting Keys
Setting keys is defined as the process of specifying the translational, rotational, and scale values of an object on a particular frame. For example, to set a key for translation of an object, select the object that you need to animate and choose a frame in the timeline on which you want to set the key. Then, select the **Animation** menuset from the **Menuset** drop-down list in the Status Line. Next, choose **Key > Set > Set Key** from the menubar; the key will be set at the selected frame in the timeline. In the **Channel Box / Layer Editor**, press and hold the right mouse button on any translate axis; a flyout will be displayed. Choose **Key Selected** from the flyout; the key for the selected translate axis will set. On setting the keys, the default background color of the attributes in the **Channel Box / Layer Editor** will change to peach color, indicating that the keys are set for the selected attributes.

> **Tip**
> *You can set the keys for animation by pressing the 'S' key.*

UNDERSTANDING DIFFERENT TYPES OF ANIMATIONS

In the beginning of this chapter, you learned in brief about different types of animations. Now, you will learn to animate objects using some of these animation types.

Path Animation

The path animation method is used to animate an object along a path. To do so, activate the top-Y viewport, choose **Create > Objects > Curve Tools > EP Curve Tool** from the menubar, and then create a curve, refer to Figure 8-3. Next, choose **Create > Objects > NURBS Primitives > Sphere** from the menubar and create a sphere in the viewport, as shown in Figure 8-3. Now, press and hold the SHIFT key and select the sphere first and then the curve. Next, select the **Animation** menuset from the **Menuset** drop-down list in the Status Line. Next, choose **Constrain > Motion Paths > Attach to Motion Path** from the menubar; the sphere will be attached to the curve. Choose the **Play forwards** button from the playback controls; the sphere will start moving along the path. You can also use a closed path to animate an object.

Sometimes, when you choose the **Play forwards** button from the animation playback controls, the sphere may not sail smoothly on the curve. To overcome this problem, select the sphere from the viewport and choose **Constrain > Motion Paths > Flow Path Object** from the menubar; a lattice will be created for the object throughout the curve. The lattice provides smoothness to the motion of the sphere. To detach the sphere from the curve, select it. In the **Channel Box / Layer Editor**, press and hold the SHIFT key and select the **Translate X**, **Translate Y**, **Translate Z**, **Rotate X**, **Rotate Y**, and **Rotate Z** options. Now, press and hold the right mouse button over the selected attributes; a flyout will be displayed. Choose **Break Connections** from the flyout; the sphere will be detached from the curve. Similarly, you can detach the curve from the sphere.

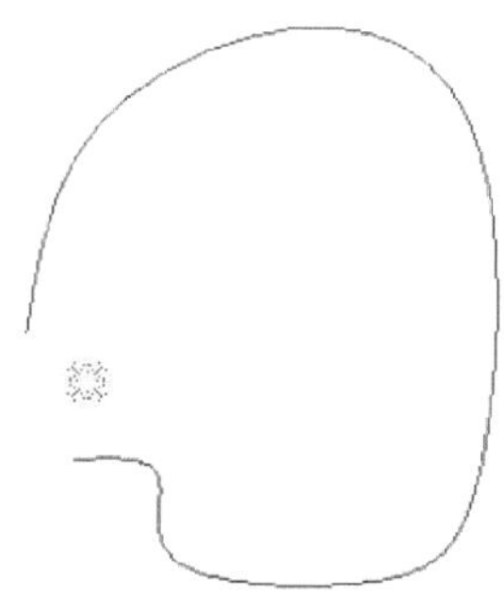

Figure 8-3 *The NURBS curve and the sphere*

Tip

To animate multiple objects on a single path curve, select the objects that you want to animate and then choose the path curve; all the objects will get attached to the path through their pivot points.

Note

*If object gets distorted on applying the **Flow Path Object** option, choose **Windows > Editors > Outliner** from the menubar and select the **FFD1 lattice** and **FFD1Base** options from the **Outliner** window. Then, scale the two selected lattices such that the object fits well into the lattice structure.*

Keyframe Animation

The keyframe animation method is the standard method used for animating an object. It is used to animate an object by creating smooth transitions between different keyframes. This is done by setting the keys for the object at two extreme positions. Maya interpolates the value for the keyed attributes with the change in the timeline between the two set keys.

You can set the key for animating an object by pressing 'S' on the keyboard. Alternatively, select the frame at which you want to set the key and choose **Key > Set > Set Key** from the menubar; a keyframe will be set at the selected frame. You can also use the auto keyframe method to set the keys for creating an animation. To do so, activate the persp viewport and choose **Create > Objects > Polygon Primitives > Cube** from the menubar; you will be prompted to create a polygon cube in the viewport. Create a polygon cube in the viewport. Next, choose the **Animation preferences** button located below the animation playback controls; the **Preferences** dialog box will be displayed with the **Time Slider: Animation Time Slider and Playback Preferences** area on the right of the **Preferences** dialog box, as shown in Figure 8-4. Set the required parameters in this dialog box and choose the **Save** button.

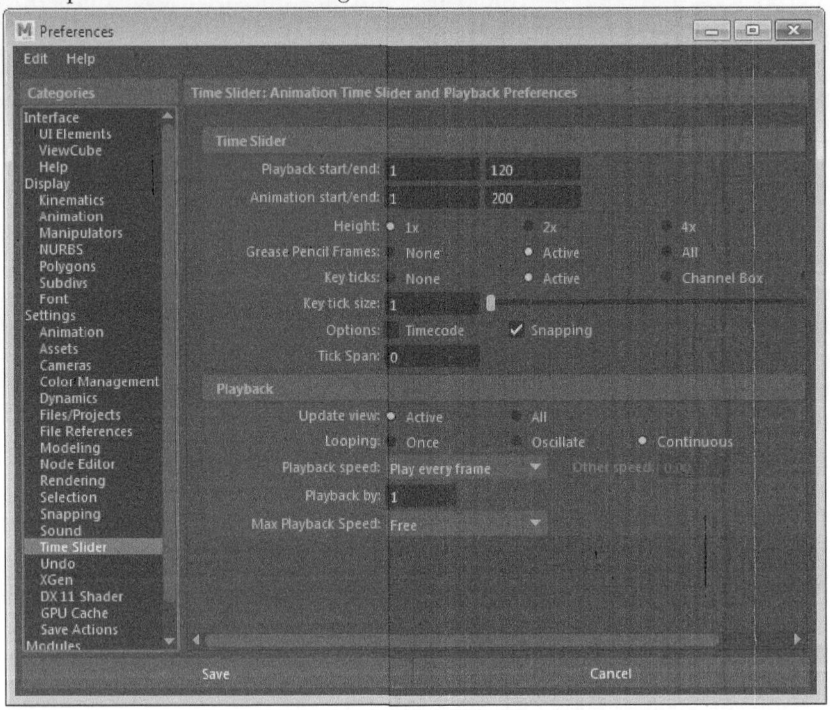

***Figure 8-4** The **Time Slider: Animation Time Slider and Playback Preferences** area*

Select the polygon cube from the viewport and choose **Modify > Transform > Freeze Transformations** from the menubar; the move, rotate and scale attributes of the cube will be set to **0**. Set the Time Slider to frame **1**. Next, choose **Key > Set > Set Key** from the menubar; the key will be set on frame **1** and then set the value in the Time Slider to frame **300**. Next, set the **Translate X** value in the **Channel Box / Layer Editor** to **15** and choose **Key > Set > Set Key** from the menubar; the key will be set for the selected frame. Now, choose the **Play forwards** button from the playback controls to preview the animation. Move the Time Slider to frame **150**. Next, set the **Translate Z** value to **5**. Now, choose **Key > Set > Set Key** from the menubar to set the key. Then, choose the **Play forwards** button from the playback controls to preview the animation; the cube will move along the curve path.

If you want the cube to rotate while animating, select the cube and set the current time indicator to frame **0** on the timeline. Now, press SHIFT+E to set the keys for rotation. In the **Channel Box / Layer Editor**, set the Time Slider to frame **24** and set the **Rotate Y** attribute to **300** in the

Channel Box / Layer Editor. Then, press SHIFT+E again; the keys for rotation will be set. Finally, choose the **Play forwards** button from the animation playback controls to preview the animation; the cube will rotate on its own axis. To translate the position of the cube in the viewport, move the current time indicator to frame **1** in the timeline. Now, press SHIFT+W to set the keys for translation. Next, move the current time indicator to frame **24** and set the **Translate X** attribute to **20** in the **Channel Box / Layer Editor**. Press SHIFT+W to set the translate key and choose the **Play forwards** button from the playback controls to preview the animation; the cube will translate and rotate simultaneously. You can also set the keys for animation by enabling the **Auto keyframe toggle** button in the timeline. It is a toggle button which turns blue when active and sets the keys automatically, refer to Figure 8-5.

***Figure 8-5** The **Auto keyframe toggle** button*

Nonlinear Animation

The nonlinear animation is used to animate an object that is independent of time. These clips can be used repeatedly to add motion to your scene which saves a lot of time for creating the animation. To apply nonlinear animation to an object, you need to use the **Trax Editor**. To display the **Trax Editor**, choose **Windows > Editors > Animation Editors > Trax Editor** from the menubar; the **Trax Editor** will be displayed, as shown in Figure 8-6.

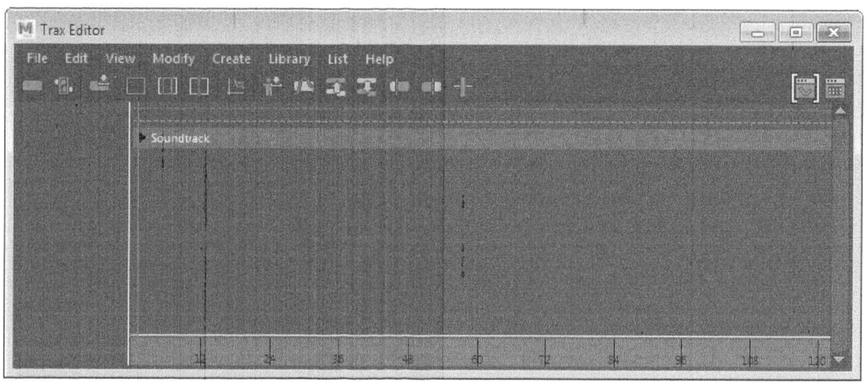

Figure 8-6** The **Trax Editor

KEY MENUS

The **Key** menus contain tools that are used to edit and control animations in Maya. These menus are discussed next.

Working with Keys

The options to manipulate the keys are discuss next.

Set Key

The **Set Key** option is used to set a key for an object in the viewport. To set a key on the timeline, select the object and choose **Key > Set > Set Key** from the menubar; a red-colored key will be created indicating that a keyframe is set on the selected frame in the timeline for the selected object, refer to Figure 8-7.

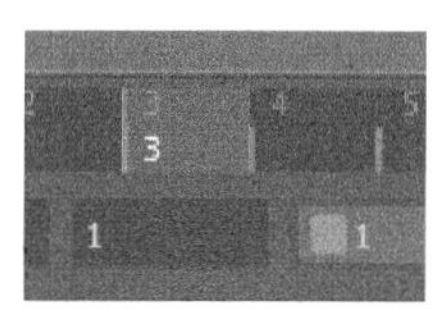

***Figure 8-7** The keyframe created*

Set Key on Translate/Rotate/Scale

The **Set Key on Translate/Rotate/Scale** option is used to set the transform keys for rotating, translating, or scaling an object. To do so, choose **Key > Set** from the menubar; a cascading menu will be displayed. Select the required option from the cascading menu; the transform key will be set for the selected option. For example, if you want to set the keys for rotation, choose **Key > Set > Set Key on Rotate** from the menubar; the keys will be set only for rotation.

Set Breakdown Key

The **Set Breakdown Key** option is used to create a key that will maintain proportional time relationship between the adjacent keys. On doing so, the color of the selected key will change to green in the timeline.

Set Driven Key

The **Set Driven Key** option is used to link different objects together such that the attributes of one object control the attributes of another object. In this case, one object acts as a driver and the other object acts as a driven, and all attributes of the driven object are controlled by the driver. To set the driver and the driven objects, choose **Key > Set > Set Driven Key > Set** from the menubar; the **Set Driven Key** dialog box will be displayed, as shown in Figure 8-8. Now, select the object that you want to set as the driver key from the viewport and choose the **Load Driver** button from the **Set Driven Key** dialog box; the selected object will act as the driver key and its attributes will be displayed on the right in the **Set Driven Key** dialog box. Next, select the required object from the viewport and choose the **Load Driven** button from the **Set Driven Key** dialog box; the selected object will be the driven key. The **Set Driven Key** dialog box is discussed in detail in the next chapter.

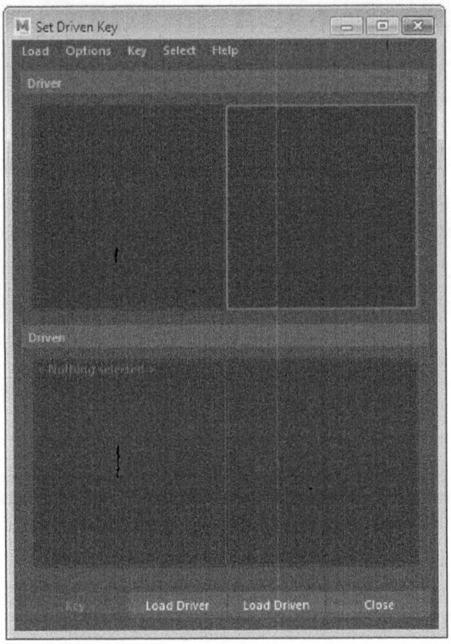

*Figure 8-8 The **Set Driven Key** dialog box*

Cut Key

The **Cut** key option is used to cut keys from the timeline.

Copy Key

The **Copy** key option is used to copy keys from the timeline.

Paste Key

The **Paste** key option is used to paste keys from the clipboard to the place where the current time indicator is located.

Delete Key

The **Delete** key option is used to delete the selected keys from the timeline.

Bake Animation

The **Bake Animation** option is used to bake the current simulation. To bake an animation, choose **Key > Edit > Bake Animation** from the menubar.

Hold Current Keys

The **Hold Current Keys** option is used to set all keys for animated attributes of the selected object in the viewport at the current time.

Ghost Selected

Ghosting is a technique in which an animator rapidly flips through drawings to evaluate the timing of the action he is working on. To activate it, choose **Visualize > Ghost > Ghost Selected > Option Box** from the menubar; the **Ghost Options** dialog box will be displayed, as shown in Figure 8-9. Now, when you animate an object, the object will be trailed by the shadow of the corresponding ghost object. This will help you to calculate the time taken for animation. You can set the required parameters for ghosting in the **Ghost Options** dialog box.

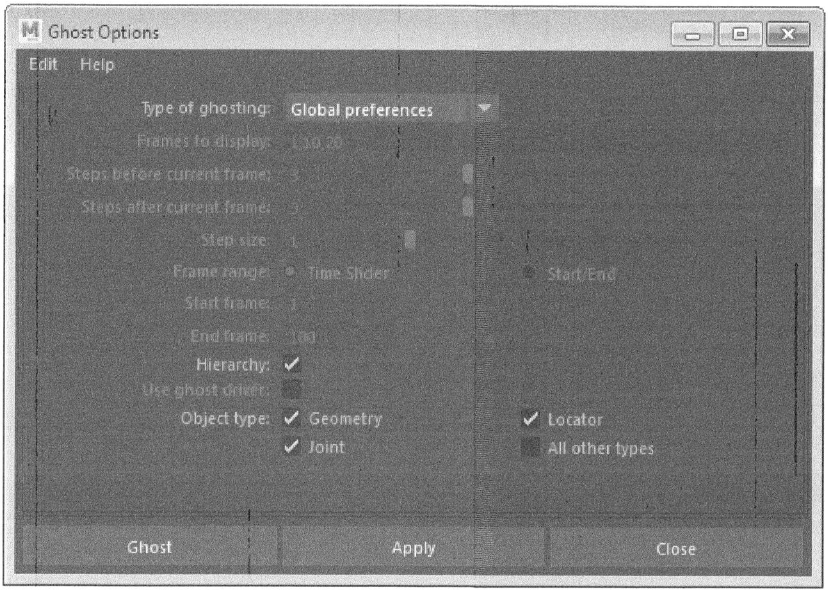

Figure 8-9 The ***Ghost Options*** *dialog box*

Unghost Selected

The **Unghost Selected** option is used to undo the changes made by the **Ghost Selected** option. To do so, choose **Visualize > Ghost > Unghost Selected** from the menubar; the selected object will be unghosted.

Unghost All

The **Unghost All** option is used to unghost the objects in the viewport that were ghosted previously. To do so, choose **Visualize > Ghost > Unghost All** from the menubar; all objects that were ghosted previously will be unghosted.

The Playback Menu

The **Playback** menu consists of various options that are used to modify the animations as required. The **Playback** options is discussed next.

Playblast

The **Playblast** option is used to create a low resolution preview of the animation that you can use to review the animation and rectify errors. You can also change the format and quality of the playblast by using this option. To do so, choose **Playback > Playblast > Option Box** from the menubar; the **Playblast Options** dialog box will be displayed, refer to Figure 8-10. You can set the options in the dialog box as required.

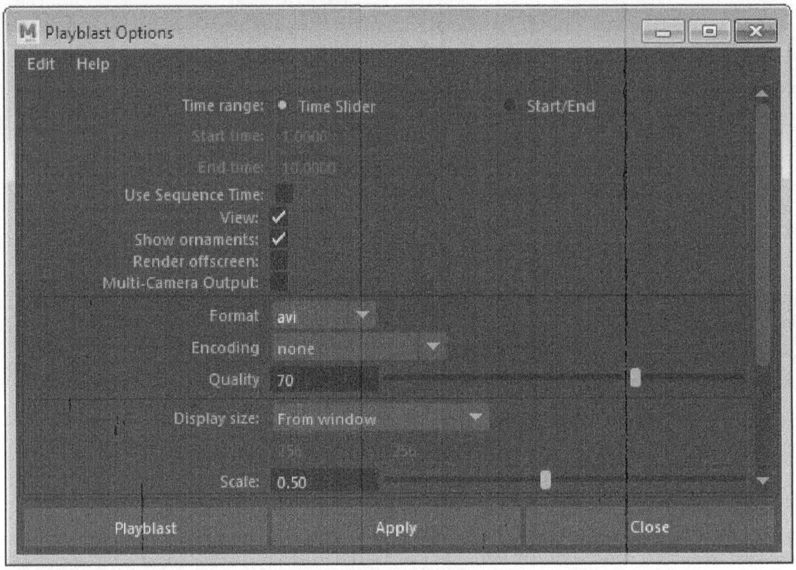

*Figure 8-10 The **Playblast Options** dialog box*

Graph Editor

Menu:	Windows > Editors > Animation Editors > Graph Editor

The **Graph Editor** is used to edit the animation curves, refer to Figure 8-11. This window displays graphical representation of the animated object in the viewport. The graph helps you to change or set the values of keys in this window as required. The **Graph Editor** is used to store all the information about animation and provides you a direct access to fine-tune the animation. Each animation in Maya generates a value vs time graph. In this graph, the horizontal axis represents the time and the vertical axis represents the value. In the **Graph Editor**, the keyframes are represented by points on curves. You can move these points freely to fine-tune the animation. To move a point on the curve, select a key, press and hold the middle mouse button, and then drag the point in the timeline to adjust the animation as required. You can also snap the keys to the grids in the editor using the snap icons from the **Graph Editor** toolbar.

Note

*To navigate in the **Graph Editor**, you can use the same shortcuts that are used to navigate in the viewport.*

All the tools of the **Graph Editor** are displayed in the **Graph Editor** toolbar, as shown in Figures 8-12 and 8-13. The tools and options in the **Graph Editor** toolbar are discussed next.

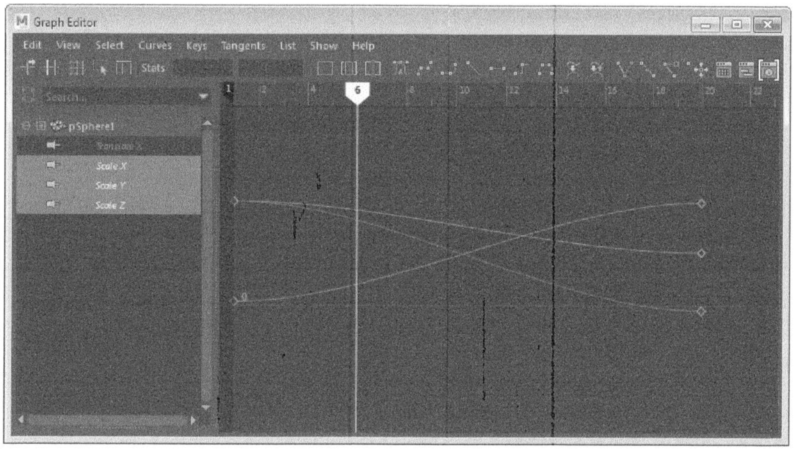

*Figure 8-11 The **Graph Editor***

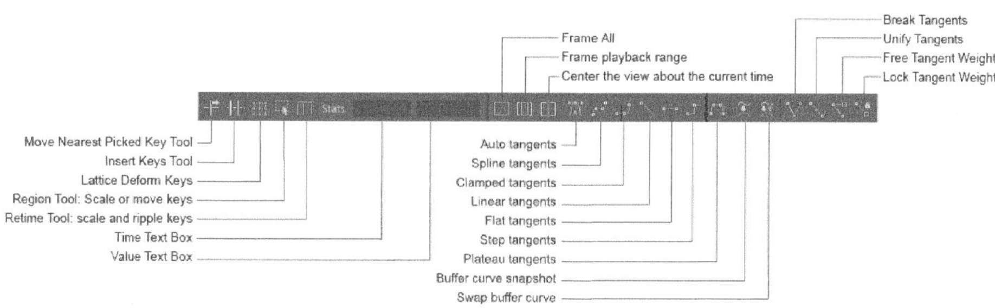

*Figure 8-12 The **Graph Editor** toolbar (part-I)*

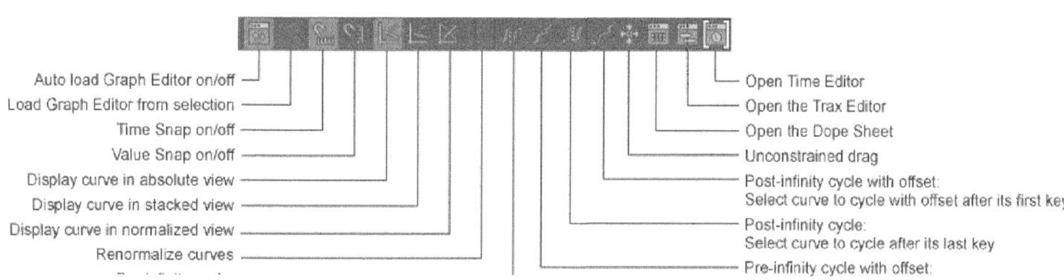

*Figure 8-13 The **Graph Editor** toolbar (part-II)*

Move Nearest Picked Key Tool

The **Move Nearest Picked Key Tool** works on a single key at a time. It is different from the **Move Tool** as it moves keys individually. Select a key from the timeline and then choose the **Move Nearest Picked Key Tool** button from the toolbar. Now, press the middle mouse button in the **Graph Editor** to move the selected key for making changes in the animation.

Insert Keys Tool

The **Insert Keys Tool** is used to add a new key to an animation curve. To do so, select the curve on which you want to add a new key and then choose the **Insert Keys Tool** button from the **Graph Editor** toolbar. Now, click the middle mouse button on the selected curve; a new key will be created without changing the shape of the original animation curve.

Lattice Deform Keys

The **Lattice Deform Keys** tool is used to draw a lattice around a group of keys in the **Graph Editor** so that the selected keys can be transformed uniformly. To transform the keys using this tool, choose the **Lattice Deform Keys Tool** button from the **Graph Editor** toolbar. Next, press and hold the left mouse button and then select the keys in the **Graph Editor**; a lattice will be formed around the selected keys. Now, you can deform the lattice to transform the selected keys. This tool provides a high level of control over animation.

Region Tool: Scale or move keys

The **Region Tool: Scale or move keys** tool is used to move or scale the selected keys in the **Graph Editor**. To do so, choose the **Region Tool: Scale or move keys** button from the **Graph Editor** toolbar. Next, select the key on the curve and then move the key in any direction by using the middle mouse button.

Retime Tool: scale and ripple keys

The **Retime Tool: Scale and ripple keys** tool is used to directly adjust the timing of key movements in an animation sequence. To adjust the timing, choose the **Retime Tool: Scale and ripple keys** tool from the **Graph Editor** toolbar. Next, double-click in the graph to create retime markers around segments of the animation curves you want to adjust.

Frame all

The **Frame all** tool is used to frame all the keys of the curve in the **Graph Editor**. To do so, choose the **Frame all** tool from the **Graph Editor** toolbar; all the keys in the **Graph Editor** will zoom in to fit in the **Graph Editor**.

Frame playback range

The **Frame playback range** tool is used to frame all the keys present in the current playback range in the **Graph Editor**. To do so, choose the **Frame playback range** button from the **Graph Editor** toolbar; the keys present in the current playback range are displayed in the **Graph Editor**. Alternatively, press f to frame keys in the **Graph Editor**.

Center the view about the current time

The **Center the view about the current time** tool is used to adjust the view of the **Graph Editor** with the current Time Slider in the timeline. The red line in the **Graph Editor** indicates the current time of animation in the timeline. If you play the animation, the red line will also move simultaneously.

Auto tangents

The **Auto tangents** tool is used to make the selected curve smooth by automatically adjusting the keys on the curve. By default, this tangent type is turned off.

Spline tangents

The **Spline tangents** tool is used to adjust the tangents on a curve so that curve becomes smoother. To adjust the tangents, select an animation key on the animation curve in the **Graph Editor** and then choose the **Spline tangents** tool from the **Graph Editor** toolbar. Alternatively, choose **Tangents > Spline** from the **Graph Editor** menubar, as shown in Figure 8-14.

Clamped tangents

The **Clamped tangents** tool has the characteristics of both the **Spline tangents** and the **Linear tangents** tools and it works similar to these tools.

Linear tangents

The **Linear tangents** tool is used to create a straight animation curve by joining two keys on the selected curve. Figures 8-15 and 8-16 show the animation curve before and after using the **Linear tangents** tool.

Note

*The process of using or accessing the remaining tangent tools is similar as discussed for the **Spline tangents** tool.*

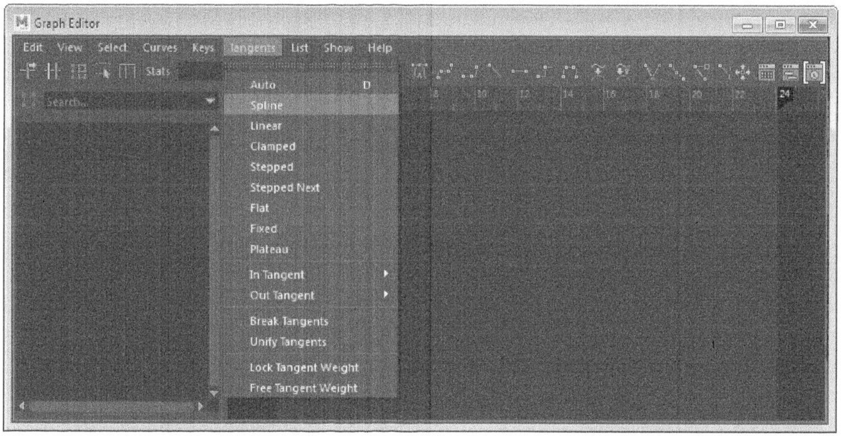

*Figure 8-14 The **Tangents** menu in the **Graph Editor***

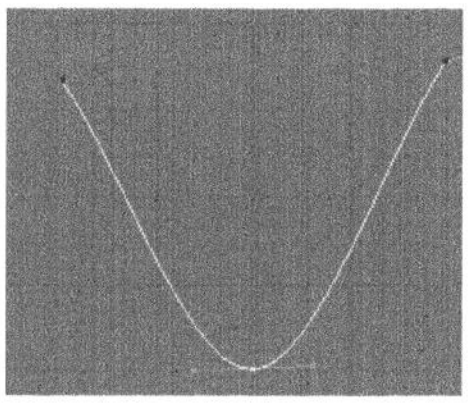

*Figure 8-15 The animation curve before using the **Linear tangents** tool*

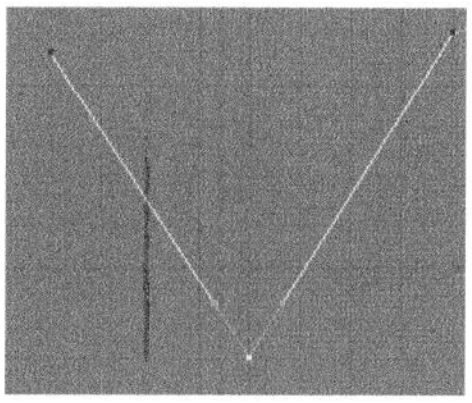

*Figure 8-16 The animation curve after using the **Linear tangents** tool*

Flat tangents

The **Flat tangents** tool is used to set the tangent of the selected curves horizontally. When you throw a ball up in the air, the ball stays at the topmost point for a moment before it comes down. To represent such an animation, you can use the **Flat tangents** tool. Figures 8-17 and 8-18 show the animation curve before and after using the **Flat tangents** tool.

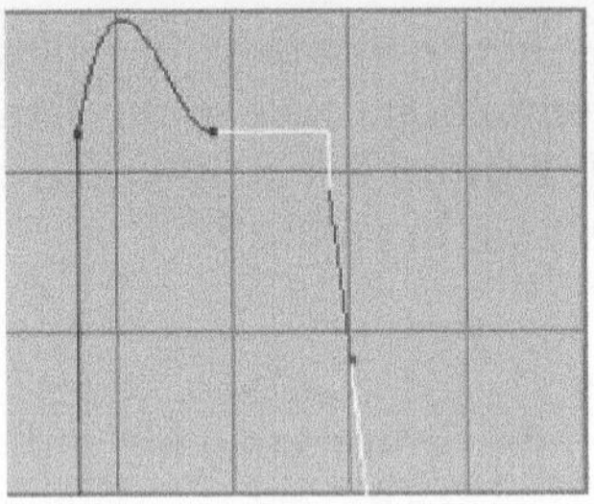

***Figure 8-17** The animation curve before using the **Flat tangents** tool*

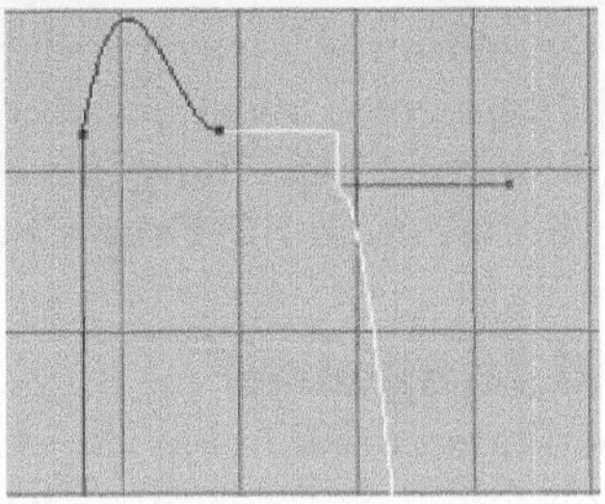

***Figure 8-18** The animation curve after using the **Flat tangents** tool*

Step tangents

The **Step tangents** tool is used to change a flat curve in the shape of steps, refer to Figures 8-19 and 8-20. You can also create the effect of the blinking light using this tool.

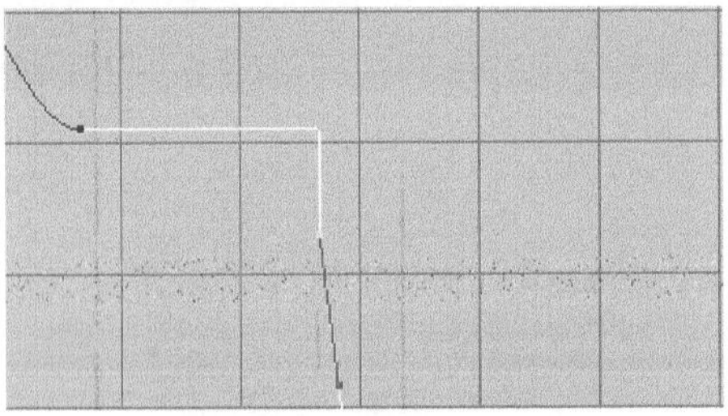

***Figure 8-19** The animation curve before using the **Stepped tangents** tool*

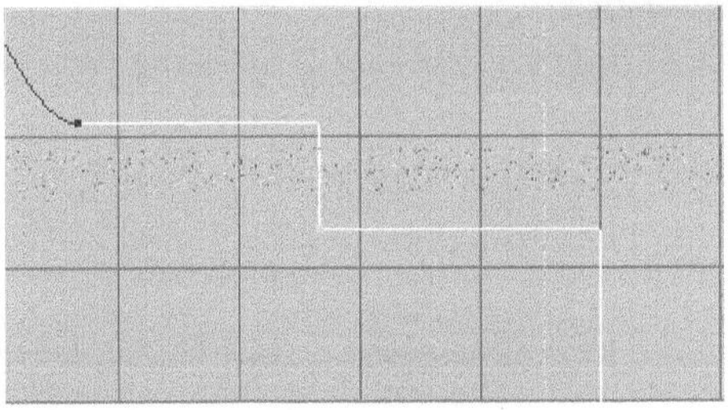

***Figure 8-20** The animation curve after using the **Stepped tangents** tool*

Plateau tangents

The **Plateau tangents** tool works similar to the **Spline tangents** and **Clamped tangents** tools. It is used to set the animation curves in such a way that they do not go beyond the position of their respective keyframes, refer to Figures 8-21 and 8-22.

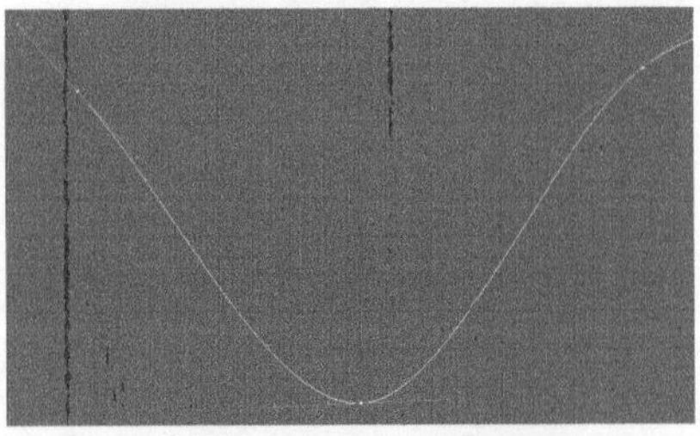

***Figure 8-21** The animation curve before using the **Plateau tangents** tool*

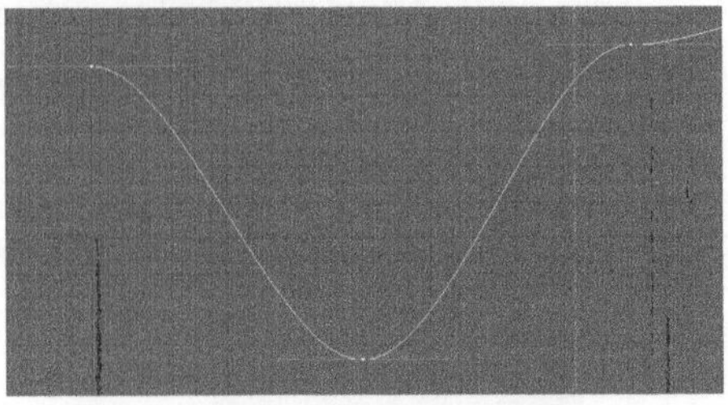

***Figure 8-22** The animation curve after using the **Plateau tangents** tool*

Buffer curve snapshot

The **Buffer curve snapshot** tool is used to take a snapshot of the selected curve. To take a snapshot, select the curve. Next, invoke the **Buffer Curve Snapshot** tool from the **Graph Editor** toolbar; the buffer curve snapshot will be taken for the selected curve. To view the buffer curve snapshot, choose **View > Show Buffer Curves** from the **Graph Editor** menubar, as shown in Figure 8-23.

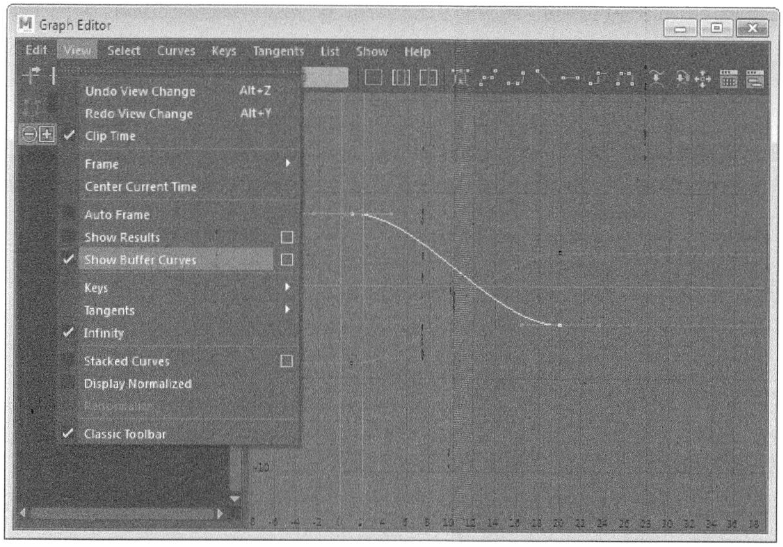

*Figure 8-23 Choosing the **Show Buffer Curves** option from the **View** menu in the **Graph Editor** menubar*

Tip

Tangents can be edited using the marking menus displayed by pressing CTRL +SHIFT and the middle mouse button.

Swap buffer curve

The **Swap buffer curve** tool is used to swap between the original curve and the edited curve. You can use the **Buffer curve snapshot** tool and the **Swap buffer curves** tool to compare the changes made in the animation curve. The changes in the animation curve will be indicated by a grey line.

Break tangents

The **Break tangents** tool is used to break the tangents joined to a key such that both handles of the broken tangent work separately to fine-tune the animation. Note that the broken tangent will be displayed in blue color.

Unify tangents

The **Unify tangents** tool is used to retain tangents at their original location. This tool works in such a way that if you manipulate changes in one tangent, the other tangent of the key will be equally affected. If you break two tangents, which are joined to a key using the **Break tangents** tool and then apply the **Unify tangents** tool on them, the two tangents will start acting as a single tangent.

Free tangent weight

The **Free tangent weight** tool is used to change the angle and weight of the selected key. You can apply this tool only to a weighted curve.

Lock tangent weight

The **Lock tangent weight** tool is used to lock the tangent weight. You can visually identify the weight of locked and unlocked tangents. By default, an unlocked tangent is displayed in green color in the **Graph Editor**. On invoking the **Lock tangent weight** tool, both the tangents will be displayed in same color. You can apply this tool only for a weighted curve.

Auto load Graph Editor on/off

The **Auto load Graph Editor on/off** tool is activated by default. It is used to automatically make changes in the curves of the objects selected in the **Outliner** window.

Load Graph Editor from selection

The **Load Graph Editor from selection** tool can be chosen only if the **Auto load Graph Editor on/off** tool is deactivated. On choosing this tool, the objects selected in the **Outliner** window will not be linked with the curves selected in **Graph Editor**.

Time snap on/off

The **Time snap on/off** tool is used to move the keys in the graph view to their nearest integer time unit value by applying force on them. By default, this tool is active.

Value snap on/off

The **Value snap on/off** tool is used to move the keys in the graph view to their nearest integer value by applying force on them.

Display curve in absolute view

Enhanced

The **Display curve in absolute view** tool allows you to display a graph view in the absolute mode. In this mode, the graph view shows all key values relative to zero. You can press the 1 key to activate the absolute view.

Display curve in stacked view

Enhanced

The **Display curve in stacked view** tool is used to display individual curves in stack. In this stacked view mode, no overlapping of curves is displayed. Each curve displays its own value axis which is normalized between 1 and -1, by default. You can press the 2 key to activate the absolute view.

Display curve in normalized view

Enhanced

The **Display curve in normalized view** tool is used to activate the normalized view. In this mode, the large key values are scaled down or small key values are scaled up to fit within -1 to 1 range. You can press the 3 key to activate the absolute view.

Renormalize curves

The **Renormalize curves** tool in the **Graph Editor** toolbar is used to quickly normalize the selected curve to fit the key values of the selected animation curves within the range of normalization. The normalization range is between -1 and 1.

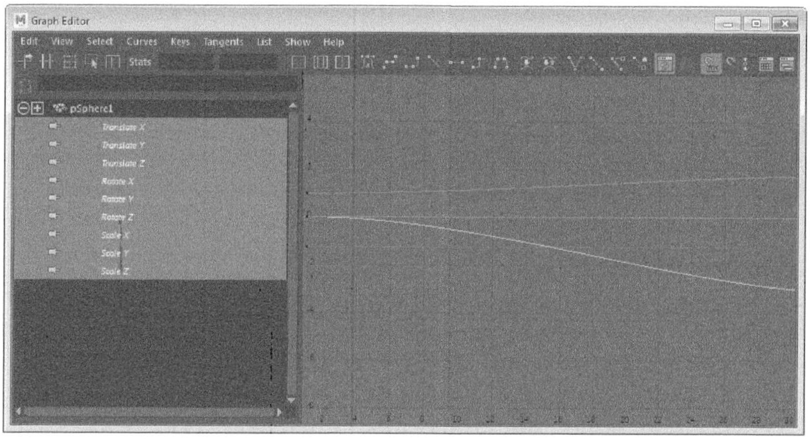

*Figure 8-24 The stacked curve displayed in the **Graph Editor***

Pre-infinity cycle

The **Pre-infinity cycle** tool is used to copy a selected animation curve and then repeat the animation infinitely in the graph view before the selected curve. The copied animation curve will be displayed as a dotted line, as shown in Figure 8-25.

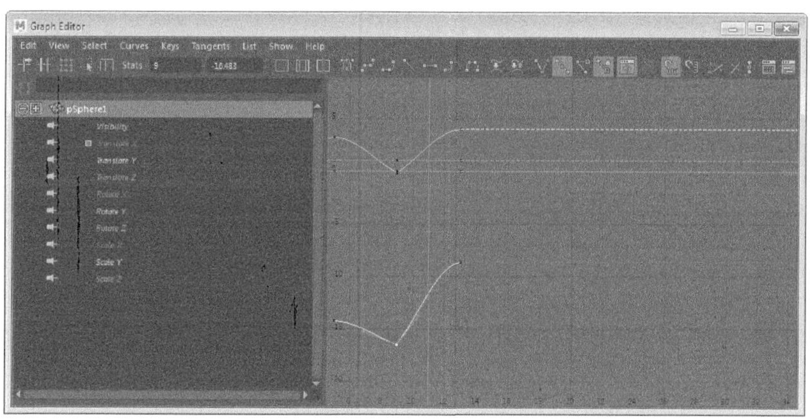

*Figure 8-25 The pre-infinity cycle graph in the **Graph Editor***

Pre-infinity cycle with offset

The **Pre-infinity cycle with offset** tool is also used to repeat the selected animation curve infinitely through the graph view. This tool differs from the **Pre-infinity cycle** tool as it adds the first key value of the original curve to the last key value of the cycled curve.

Post-infinity cycle

The **Post-infinity cycle** tool is used to copy an animation curve and then join it after the same curve infinite number of times. Therefore, unlike the **Pre-infinity cycle** tool, this tool copies the animation curve and repeats it after the curve. The copied animation curve will be displayed as a dotted line.

Post-infinity cycle with offset

The **Post-infinity cycle with offset** tool is used to cycle curve with offset after its first key. It works similar to the **Pre-Infinity cycle with offset** tool, except that on using this tool the last key value of the original curve is added to the first key value of the cycled curve.

Unconstrained drag

The **Unconstrained drag** tool is used to constrain the movement of drag of the selected curve in the X and Y directions. To do so, press the left mouse button on the **Unconstrained drag** tool; the tool icon will change to **Constrained x-axis drag**. Now, select the tool and then press the middle mouse button in the **Graph Editor** to move the selected curve in the x-axis only. Again, press the left mouse button on the **Unconstrained drag** tool; the tool icon will change to **Constrained y-axis drag**. Press the middle mouse button in the **Graph Editor** to move the selected curve in the y-axis only.

Open the Dope Sheet

The **Open the Dope Sheet** tool is used to switch between the **Graph Editor** and **Dope Sheet** to set the animation keys of the current object into the **Dope Sheet** area, refer to Figure 8-26. The **Dope Sheet** window is used to display the time horizontally in blocks. To invoke the **Dope Sheet**, choose **Windows > Editors > Animation Editors > Dope Sheet** from the menubar.

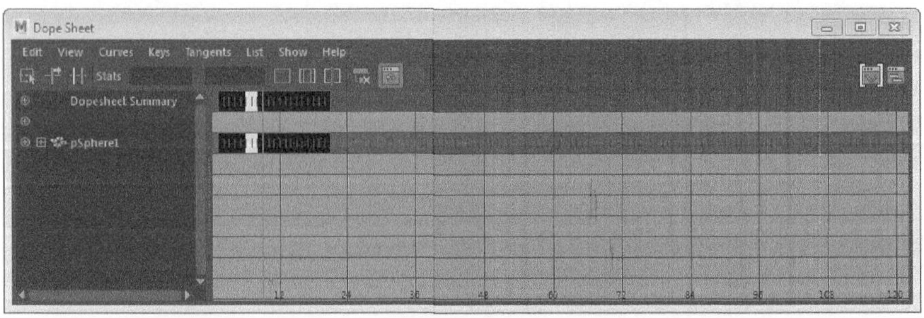

*Figure 8-26 The **Dope Sheet***

Open the Trax Editor

The **Open the Trax Editor** tool is used to load the **Trax Editor** along with the animation clips of the current object. To load it, choose **Windows > Editors > Animation Editors > Trax Editor** from the menubar; the **Trax Editor** window will be displayed. In this editor, you can position, scale, cycle, and blend the animation sequences as required.

ANIMATION LAYERS

Animation layers are used to add or blend two animations together. In other words, these layers help you to organize a keyframe animation without overlapping the original animation. You can control these animations using the **Animation Layer Editor**. To open the animation layer, select the object; the **Channel Box / Layer Editor** will be displayed on the right of the viewport. To activate the **Animation Layer Editor**, choose the **Anim** tab from the **Channel Box / Layer Editor**; the attributes for the animation will be displayed in the **Channel Box / Layer Editor**, as shown in Figure 8-27. To set the **Animation Layer Editor** as a floating window, choose **Show > Floating Window** from the **Channel Box / Layer Editor**; the **Animation Layer Editor** floating window will be displayed. You can create a number of animation layers using this editor.

Creating an Animation Layer

To create an animation layer in the **Channel Box / Layer Editor**, choose the **Anim** tab; the **Animation Layer Editor** floating window will be activated. Now, choose the **Layers** menu from the **Animation Layer Editor** menubar; a flyout will be displayed, as shown in Figure 8-28. Choose **Create Empty Layer** from the flyout; a new layer will be created. Alternatively, choose the **Create Empty Layer** button available on the right of the **Channel Box / Layer Editor** to create a new layer, refer to Figure 8-29. The **Animation Layer Editor** contains various buttons that help you to control animations. These buttons are discussed next.

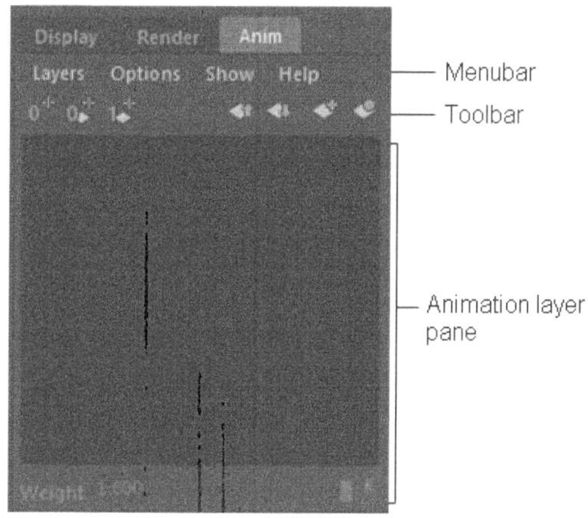

Figure 8-27 The Animation Layer Editor

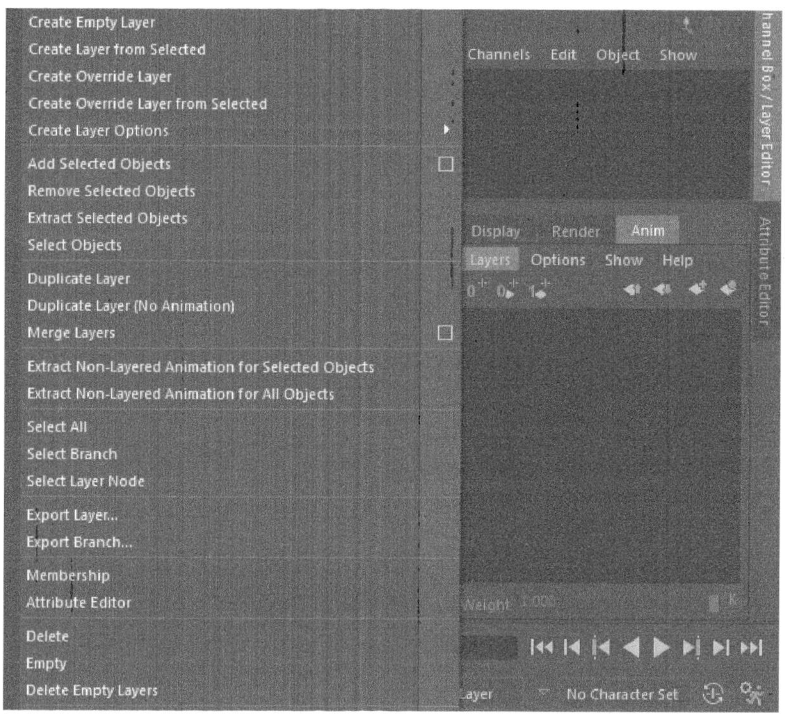

*Figure 8-28 Flyout displayed on choosing the **Layers** menu from the **Animation Layer Editor** menubar*

Zero Key Layer

The **Zero Key Layer** button is used to set the start and end time for the animation in a particular layer. It defines a point of time at which the layer's animation has no offset from the original animation. For example, if you keyframe an animation of 100 frames and want to modify the animation between the frames 40 and 60, then you can choose this button to set the zero key at frames 40 and 60 to define the range of animation for editing. Now, any change made between these frames will not affect the original animation.

Zero Weight and Key Layer

The **Zero Weight and Key Layer** button is used to set the key with zero weight in the **Animation Layer Editor**. Setting the weight of a layer means determining the amount of animation that will be played at the final stage.

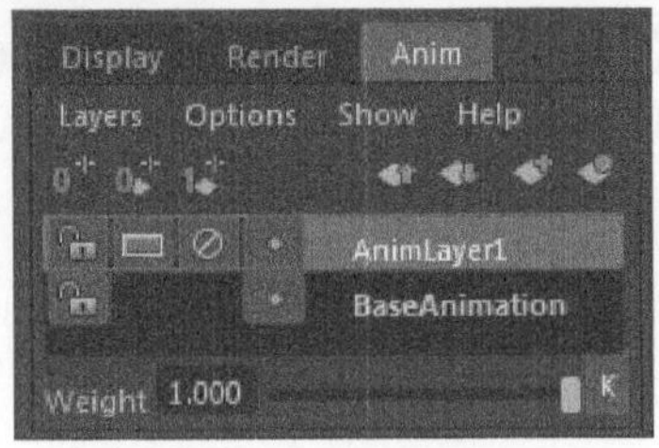

Figure 8-29 A new layer created in the ***Animation Layer Editor***

Set Weight to 1.0 and Key Layer

The **Set Weight to 1.0 and Key Layer** button is used to set the key with the layer weight **1** in the **Animation Layer Editor**.

Move selection up in list

The **Move Selection up in list** button is used to move the selected layer one step up from the original position in the **Animation Layer Editor**.

Move selection down in list

The **Move Selection down in list** button is used to move the selected layer one step down from the original position in the **Animation Layer Editor**.

Create Empty Layer

The **Create Empty Layer** button is used to create an empty layer in the layer pane of the **Animation Layer Editor**.

Create Layer from Selected

The **Create Layer from Selected** button is used to create a layer in the layer pane of the **Animation Layer Editor** such that the new layer contains all attributes of the selected object.

The **Animation Layer Pane** in the **Animation Layer Editor** is discussed next.

Animation Layer Pane

The animation layer pane displays the hierarchy of animation layers that have been created. By default, the animation layers in this pane are arranged from bottom to top, as shown in Figure 8-30. Whenever you create a new layer, it gets added at the top of the **Animation Layer Pane**. You can change the arrangement of these layers by choosing **Options > Reverse Layer Stack** from the **Animation Layer Editor** menubar. On doing so, the layers will be arranged from top to bottom, as shown in Figure 8-31. Also, all newly created layers will be added at the bottom of the layer stack.

Apart from the layers created, there is one more layer in the animation layer pane called **BaseAnimation** layer. This layer is created by default, refer to Figure 8-31. It is not an animation layer, but it represents the animation that is not assigned to other layers in the **Animation Layer Editor**. The animation layer pane has three major components, which affect animation layers in the hierarchy. These components are discussed next.

Figure 8-30 *Layer arrangement from bottom to top*

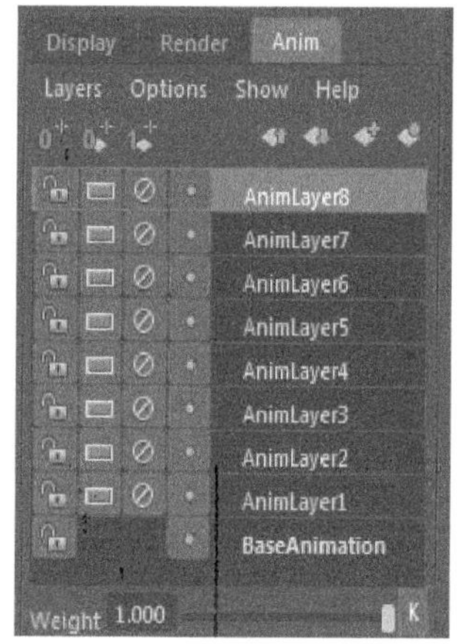

Figure 8-31 *Layer arrangement from top to bottom*

Animation Layer Buttons

The animation layer buttons are displayed in front of each animation layer in the **Animation Layer Editor.** These buttons are discussed next.

Lock Layer

The **Lock Layer** button is used to lock an animation layer. A locked animation layer cannot be keyframed further, unless it is unlocked. Also, only the frames that were keyframed before locking the animation layer will be played in the final animation. When you choose the **Lock Layer** button the color of the set keys changes from red to grey in the timeslider.

Solo Layer

The **Solo Layer** button is used to make the selected layer solo. On doing so, the solo layer will be the only layer that will be played in the final animation.

Mute Layer

The **Mute Layer** button is used to make the selected layer mute. On doing so, the animation of the mute layer will not be evaluated in the final output.

Ghost/Color Layer

The **Ghost/Color Layer** button is used to preview the position of an object on each added layer while it is being animated. You can turn the ghosting on or off by choosing this button. Note that the ghost option cannot be applied to objects in the top most layer of the hierarchy. To display ghosts for the selected objects, choose **Options > Auto ghost selected objects** from the **Animation Layer Editor** menubar. Select the objects that you want to ghost from the viewport and then choose the **Ghost/Color Layer** button; the effect of ghosting will be displayed on the selected objects. To display the effect of ghosting on all objects in the **Animation Layer Editor**, choose **Options > Auto ghosts objects in layer** from the **Animation Layer Editor** menubar.

By default, the color of this button is dark red. To change the color of the **Ghost/Color Layer** button, right-click on this button; the **Color Index Settings** dialog box will be displayed, as shown in Figure 8-32. Change the color of the ghost button by dragging the slider on the right of the **Select Color** option in the **Color Index Settings** dialog box.

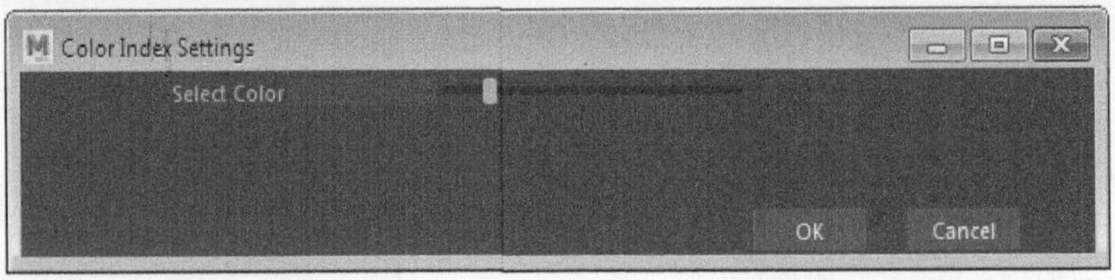

*Figure 8-32 The **Color Index Settings** dialog box*

Active Keying Feedback

The **Active Keying Feedback** is the visual feedback of layers in the **Animation Layer Pane**. The visual feedback is indicated by the colored indicators located on the right of each keyed layer in the **Animation Layer Pane**. Depending upon the active keying feedback, a layer can further be classified into three animation layer states: **Active**, **Affected**, and **Selected**. The **Active** animation layer represents the layer that receives keys. The **Affected** animation layer represents the layer that receives the attributes of the object selected in the viewport, but it will not be selected. The **Selected** animation layer represents the layer that is highlighted in the **Channel Box / Layer Editor**. The active keying feedback indicators are discussed next.

Green

A layer with the green indicator represents that the selected layer is in active animation state and it can receive keys.

Red

A layer with red indicator indicates that the layer containing attributes of the selected object in the viewport is not active. You cannot set the key to the objects in a layer with the red indicator.

Weight Slider

The **Weight** slider is located at the bottom of the **Animation Layer Editor**. This slider is used to control the amount of animation to be played on the selected layer. It is similar to setting transparency between two layers.

By default, the value of the **Weight** slider is set to **1**, which indicates that the animation of the selected layer will be played completely. Set the **Weight** slider value to **0** to mute the animation of the selected layer.

Adding Attributes in Animation Layers

When you create a new layer in the **Animation Layer Editor**, by default some general attributes are added to that layer. You can also add specific attributes to a layer as required. To do so, choose

Layers > Add Selected Objects > Option Box from the **Animation Layer Editor** menubar; the **Add Objects To Animation Layers Options** dialog box will be displayed, as shown in Figure 8-33. Before setting the options in this dialog box, first select the object from the viewport and then set its parameters as required.

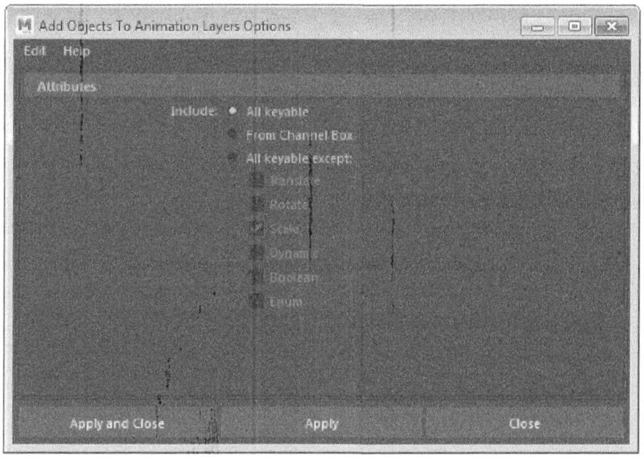

Figure 8-33 The ***Add Objects To Animation Layers Options*** *dialog box*

You can also add attributes to a layer using the **Channel Box / Layer Editor**. To do so, first select the layer to which you want to add attributes and then select the object from the viewport whose attributes you want to add to that layer. Now, from the **Channel Box / Layer Editor**, select the attributes you want to add to the layer in the **Animation Layer Editor**. Now, press and hold the right mouse button over the selected attribute in the **Channel Box / Layer Editor**; a flyout will be displayed. Choose **Add To Selected Layers** from the flyout; the selected attribute will be added to the animation layer. Also, the color of the selected attribute will be changed in the **Channel Box / Layer Editor**, indicating that it is now linked with the layer.

Removing Attributes from Animation Layers

You can also remove the attributes of an objects from the **Animation Layer Editor**. To do so, select the object whose attributes you want to remove. Next, select the layer from which you want to remove the attributes of the selected object and also, select the attribute that you want to remove from the **Channel Box / Layer Editor**. Next, press and hold the right mouse button over the attribute in the **Channel Box / Layer Editor** that you want to remove; a flyout will be displayed. Choose **Remove Selected Objects** from the flyout to remove the selected attribute. The color of the selected attribute will be changed, indicating that it is no longer linked with the layer.

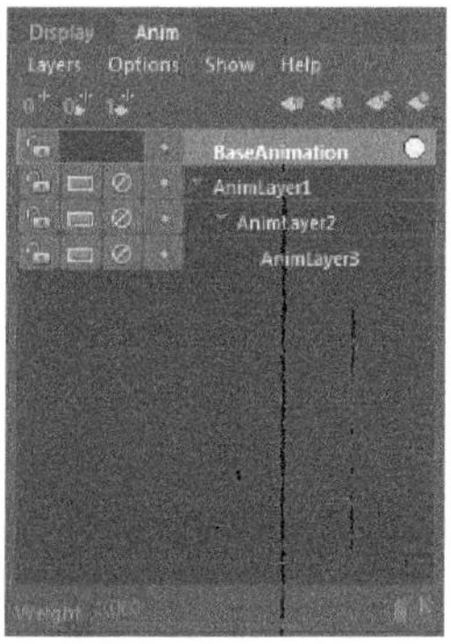

Figure 8-34 *Layers showing the parent-child relationship*

Creating the Parent-Child Relationship in the Animation Layer Editor

The Animation Layer **hierarchy** is used to parent and unparent an animation layer. To create a parent-child relationship between layers, select a layer from the **Animation Layer Editor**, drag it using the middle mouse button and drop it over another layer. The layer on which another layer is dropped will now act as the parent layer of the dropped layer. Also, a down arrow will be displayed in the parent layer, as shown in Figure 8-34. Similarly, you can create any number of parent-child relationships in the **Animation Layer Editor**. You can also unparent a layer in the **Animation Layer Editor**.

TUTORIALS

Tutorial 1

In this tutorial, you will animate text along a path, as shown in Figures 8-35 and 8-36, using profile curves. **(Expected time: 30 min)**

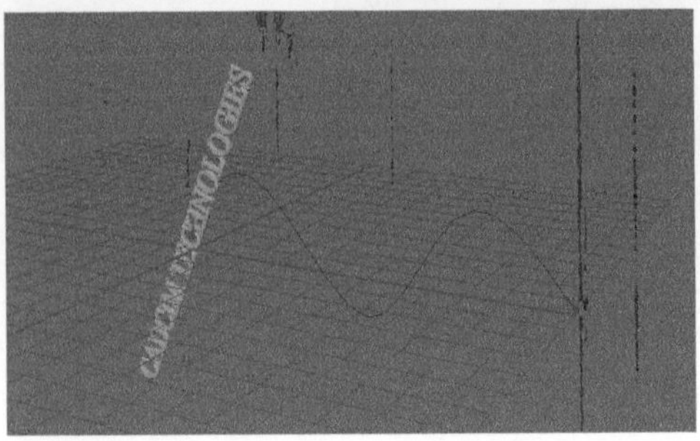

Figure 8-35 The text animation at frame 42

Figure 8-36 The text animation at frame 54

The following steps are required to complete this tutorial:

a. Create a project folder.
b. Create text for the logo.
c. Create path for animating the text.
d. Fine-tune the animation.
e. Save and render the scene.

Creating a Project Folder

Create a new project folder with the name *c08_tut1* at *\Documents\maya2017* and then save the file with the name *c08tut1*, as discussed in Tutorial 1 of Chapter 2.

Creating Text for the Logo

In this section, you will create text for the logo.

1. In the persp viewport, choose **Create > Objects > Type** from the menubar; **3D Type** text is displayed in the viewport, as shown in Figure 8-37.

2. Change the type attributes of the text in **Attribute Editor**, as shown in Figure 8-38.

Creating Path for Animating the Text

In this section, you will create a path to animate the text on it.

1. Activate the front-Z viewport and choose **Create > Objects > Curve Tools > EP Curve Tool > Option Box** from the menubar; the **Tool Settings (EP Curve Tool)** window is displayed on the left side of the viewport. Select the **3 Cubic** radio button corresponding to the **Curve**

degree attribute in this window and then close the window. Next, create a profile curve in the front-Z viewport, as shown in Figure 8-39.

Figure 8-37 3D Type text Displayed in Persp viewport

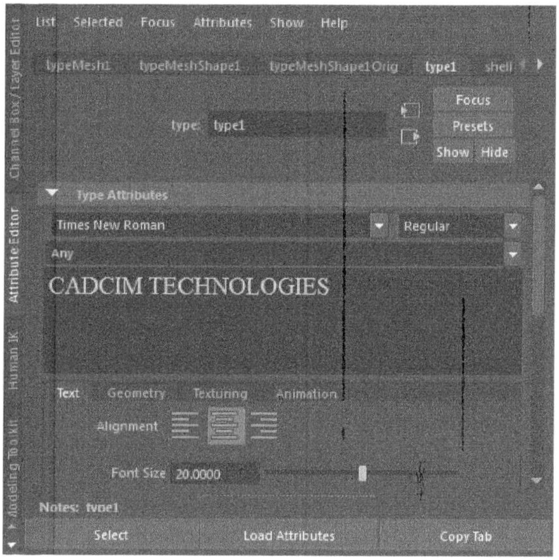

Figure 8-38 The 3D text displayed in the persp viewport

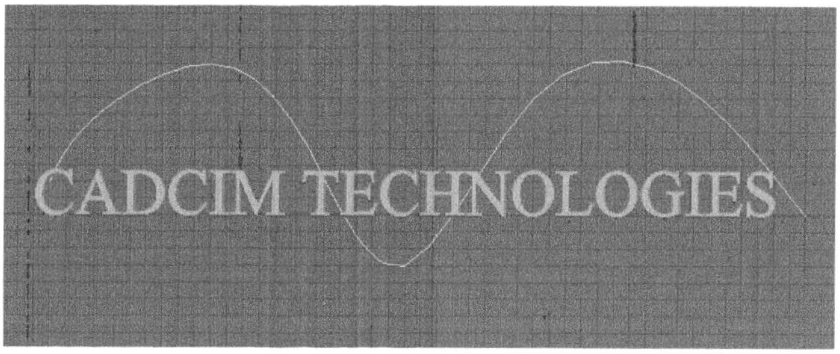

Figure 8-39 The profile curve displayed in the front-Z viewport

2. Set the start frame to **1** and the end frame to **100** in the timeline, as shown in Figure 8-40.

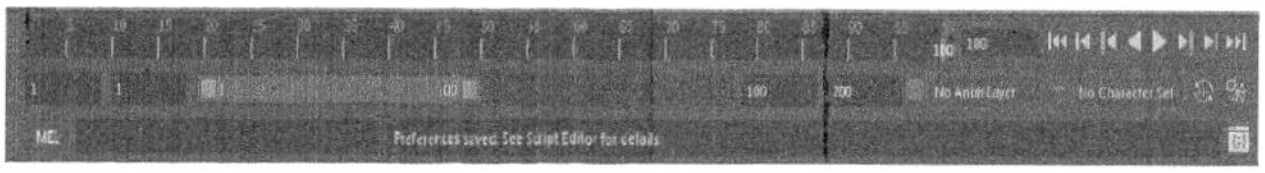

Figure 8-40 The start and end frames set in the timeline

3. Maximize the persp viewport. Select the text and then select the path with the SHIFT key. Select the **Animation** menuset from the **Menuset** drop-down list in the Status Line. Next, choose **Constrain > Motion Paths > Attach to Motion Path > Option Box** from the menubar; the **Attach to Motion Path Options** dialog box is displayed. Set the attributes in this dialog box, as shown in Figure 8-41.

4. After setting all the attributes, choose the **Attach** button from the **Attach to Motion Path Options** dialog box; the 3D text is attached to the path at path's pivot point. Next, choose the **Play forwards** button from playback controls to preview the animation. Figure 8-42 shows a 3D text attached to the profile curve.

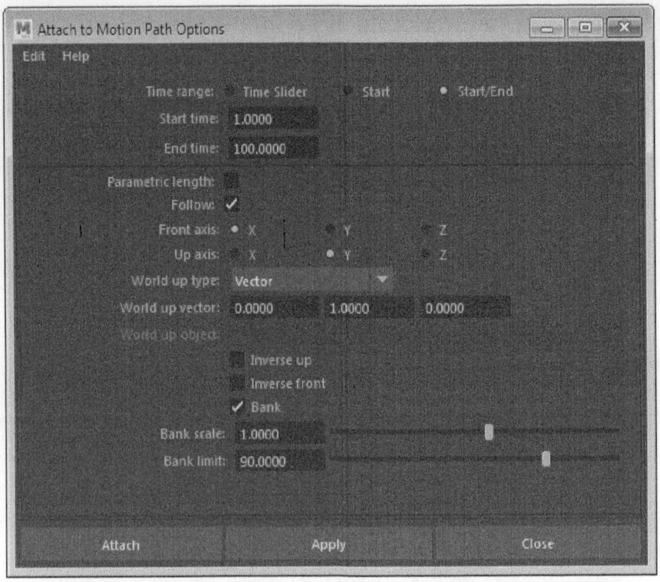

*Figure 8-41 The **Attach to Motion Path Options** dialog box*

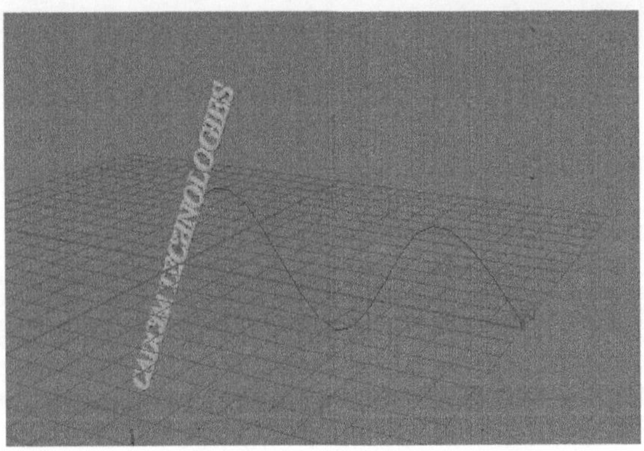

Figure 8-42 The 3D text attached to the profile curve

5. Make sure the text is selected in the persp viewport and choose the **Scale Tool** from the Tool Box. Next, scale down the text uniformly so that it becomes very small, as shown in Figure 8-43.

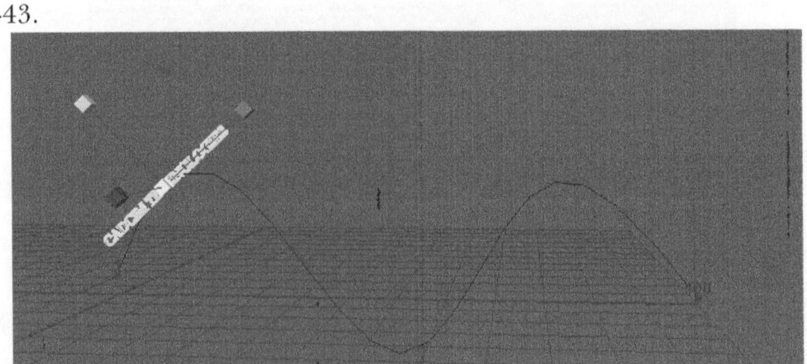

Figure 8-43 The 3D text scaled

Fine-tuning the Animation

In this section, you will fine-tune the animation so that the 3D text flows smoothly on the path.

1. Make sure the 3D text is selected in the viewport and then choose **Constrain > Create > Motion Paths > Flow Path Object > Option Box** from the menubar; the **Flow Path Object Options** dialog box is displayed.

2. Set the attributes in the **Flow Path Object Options** dialog box, as shown in Figure 8-44, and then choose the **Flow** button; the 3D text surface gets distorted and a lattice is displayed, as shown in Figure 8-45.

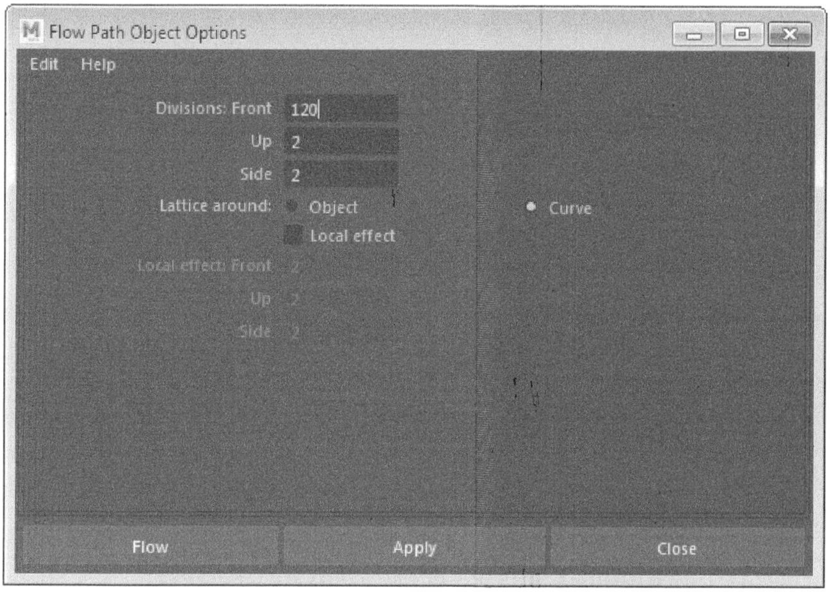

***Figure 8-44** The **Flow Path Object Options** dialog box*

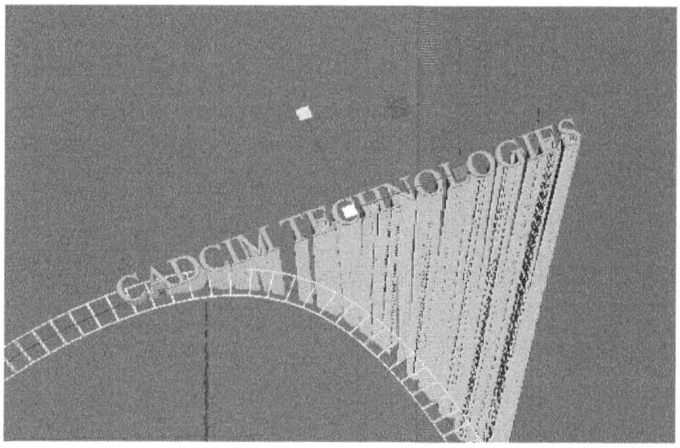

***Figure 8-45** The lattice around the curve*

3. Choose **Windows > Editors > Outliner** from the menubar; the **Outliner** window is displayed. In the **Outliner** window, select the **ffd1Lattice** and **ffd1Base** using the SHIFT key; the respective lattices are selected in the viewport. Next, close the **Outliner** window.

4. In the persp viewport, uniformly scale the two selected lattices outward such that the 3D text surface is enclosed entirely inside the lattice structure, as shown in Figure 8-46.

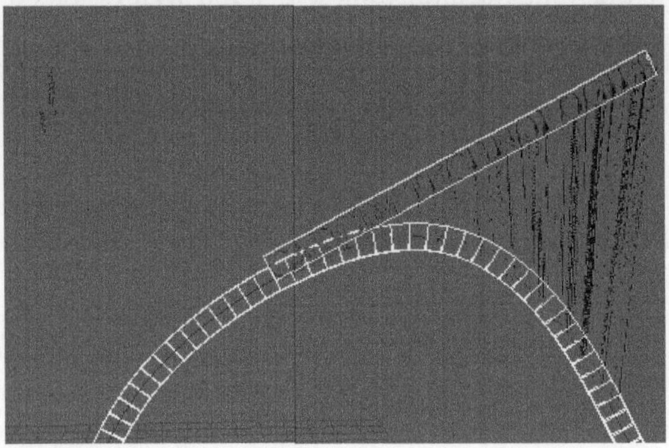

Figure 8-46 *The enlarged lattice area around the path*

5. Choose the **Play forwards** button from the playback controls area to preview the animation. If the 3D text surface gets distorted again, scale the lattices once again.

Saving and Rendering the Scene

In this section, you will save the scene that you have created and then render it. You can view the final rendered image sequence of the scene by downloading the *c08_maya_2017_rndr.zip* file from *www.cadcim.com*. The path of the file is as follows: *Textbooks > Animation and Visual Effects > Maya > Autodesk Maya 2017: A Comprehensive Guide.*

1. Choose **File > Save Scene** from the menubar to save the scene.

2. Maximize the persp viewport, if it is not already maximized.

3. Change the background color of the scene to white.

4. Choose the **Display render settings** tool from the Status Line; the **Render Settings** window is displayed. Enter **animation_logo** in the **File name prefix** text box in the **File Output** area. Next, select **AVI (avi)** from the **Image format** drop-down list.

5. In the **Frame Range** area of the **Render Settings** window, enter **70** in the **End Frame** edit box.

Note

The AVI image format is not available for the ***mental ray*** *renderer. However, you can render a tif, targa, exr, or jpeg sequence using the* ***mental ray*** *renderer. When you render an image sequence, you need to select the extension style from the* ***Frame/Animation ext*** *drop-down list in the* ***Render Settings*** *window. Once the sequence is rendered, you can play it using the Fcheck utility. The default path of this utility is as follows: C:\Program Files\Autodesk\maya2017\bin.*

6. Choose the **Maya Software** tab from the **Render Settings** window. Next, select **Production quality** from the **Quality** drop-down list in the **Edge Anti-aliasing Quality** area. Next, choose the **Close** button to close the **Render Settings** window.

7. Select the **Rendering** menuset from the **Menuset** drop-down list in the Status Line. Next, choose **Render > Batch Render > Batch Render > Option Box** from the menubar; the **Batch Render Animation** dialog box is displayed.

8. Make sure the **Use all available processors** check box is selected in the **Batch Render Animation** dialog box. Next, choose the **Batch render and close** button from the dialog box; the rendering process is started.

   You can view the rendering progress by choosing the **Script Editor** button from the Command Line.

Tip
You can also add color and glow to the 3D text surface by using the ***Attribute Editor****. To do so, select the 3D text in the viewport, press and hold the right mouse button over it, and then choose* ***Assign Favorite Material > Lambert*** *from the marking menu; the* ***lambert2*** *tab is displayed in the* ***Attribute Editor****. In this tab, expand the* ***Special Effects*** *area and move the slider placed on the right of the* ***Glow Intensity*** *option to set the intensity for the 3D text. Choose* ***Render the current frame*** *from the Status Line to render the scene.*

Tutorial 2

In this tutorial, you will create a bouncing ball animation. **(Expected time: 30 min)**

The following steps are required to complete this tutorial:

a. Create the project folder.
b. Create a ball.
c. Create and refine the animation.
d. Save and render the scene.

Creating the Project Folder

Create a new project folder with the name *c08_tut2* at *\Documents\maya2017* and then save the file with the name *c08tut2*, as discussed in Tutorial 1 of Chapter 2.

Creating the Model of a Ball

In this section, you will create a ball using the polygon sphere.

1. Activate the top-Y viewport. Choose **Create > Objects > Polygon Primitives > Sphere** from the menubar and create a sphere in the viewport.

2. In the **Channel Box / Layer Editor**, expand the **polySphere1** node in the **INPUTS** area and make sure **1** is entered in the **Radius** edit box.

3. In the **Channel Box / Layer Editor**, click on **pSphere1**; a text box is activated. Next, enter **ball** in the text box and press ENTER; the **pSphere1** is renamed as *ball*.

4. Choose **Create > Objects > Polygon Primitives > Plane** from the menubar and create a plane below the *ball*. Next, activate the persp viewport. Choose **Move Tool** from the Tool Box and place *ball* on the plane, as shown in Figure 8-47.

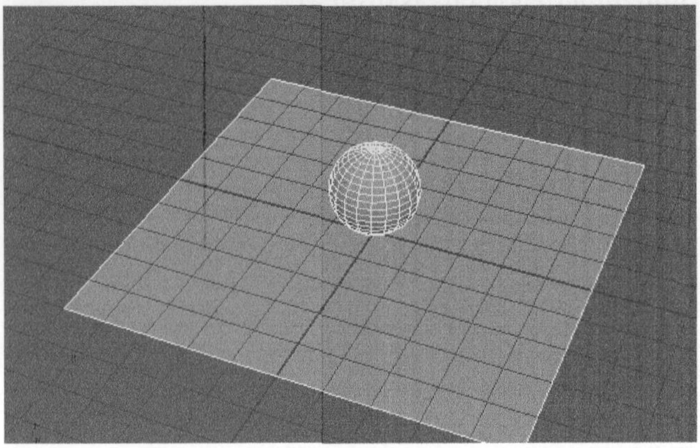

Figure 8-47 Ball placed on the plane

5. Select the plane in the persp viewport. Expand the **polyPlane1** area in the **INPUTS** node of **Channel Box / Layer Editor** and set the parameters as follows:

Width: **30** Height: **30**

Create and Refine the Animation

In this section, you will set the animation keys to create the bouncing ball animation.

1. Select the **Animation** menuset from the **Menuset** drop-down list.

2. Select *ball* in the viewport and then choose **Modify > Transform > Freeze Transformations** from the menubar; the transformation values of *ball* are set to 0.

3. Choose **Windows > Editors > Settings/Preferences > Preferences** from the menubar; the **Preferences** dialog box is displayed. Choose **Time Slider** from the **Categories** list of the dialog box; the **Time Slider: Animation Time Slider and Playback Preferences** area is displayed in the **Preferences** dialog box.

4. Enter **50** in the second edit box corresponding to the **Playback start/end** attribute. Next, make sure the **Real-time [24 fps]** option is selected from the **Playback speed** drop-down list, refer to Figure 8-48. Next, choose the **Save** button; the **Preferences** dialog box closes.

5. Make sure *ball* is selected and the frame 1 is selected in the timeline. In the **Channel Box / Layer Editor**, enter **9** in the **Translate Y** edit box; *ball* moves upward along the Y axis, refer to Figure 8-49. Next, choose **Key > Set > Set Key**; the key is set at frame 1. Alternatively, press the S key to set the key.

6. Select frame 25 and enter **-0.002** in the **Translate Y** edit box of the **Channel Box / Layer Editor**; *ball* touches the plane. Next, press the S key; the key is set at frame 25.

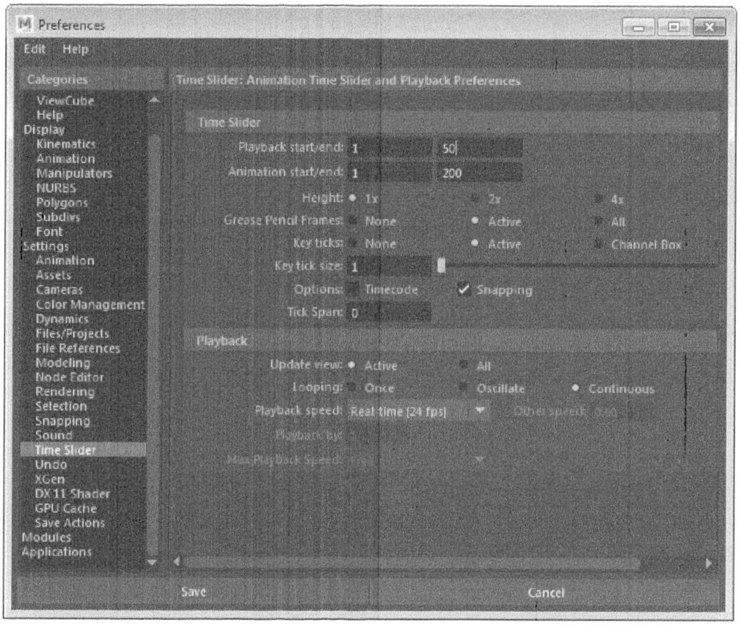

Figure 8-48 *Setting the options in the* ***Preferences*** *dialog box*

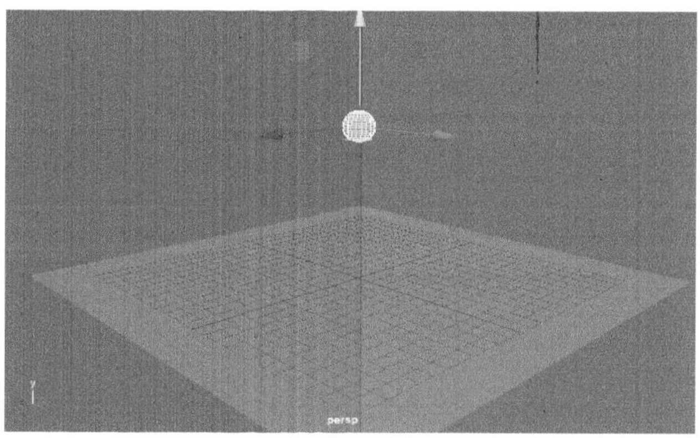

Figure 8-49 *Position of the ball changed*

7. Select frame 50 and then enter **9** in the **Translate Y** edit box of the **Channel Box / Layer Editor**; *ball* moves upward along the Y axis. Next, press the S key; the key is set at frame 50.

   Next, you will scale down *ball* at frame 25.

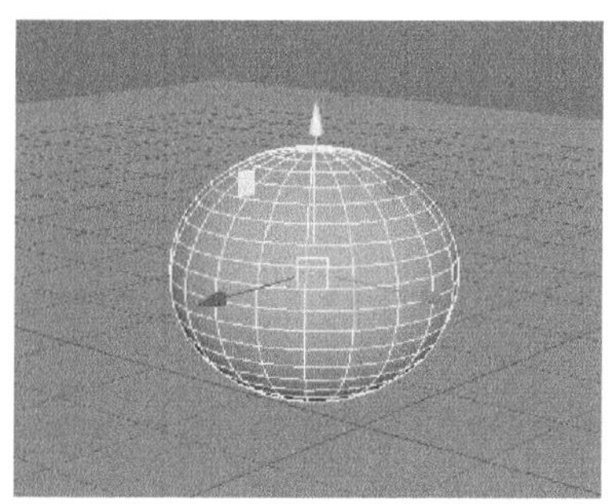

Figure 8-50 *The ball squashes*

8. Select frame 25 and enter **0.85** in the **Scale Y** edit box of the **Channel Box / Layer Editor**; *ball* gets squashed, as shown in Figure 8-50. Also, move the *ball* downward

along the Y axis such that it touches the plane. Next, press the S key; the key is set at frame 25.

9. Select frame 24 and enter **1** in the **Scale Y** edit box of the **Channel Box / Layer Editor**; *ball* gets stretched. Now, enter **0** in the **Translate Y** edit box of the **Channel Box / Layer Editor**; *ball* moves upward. Next, press the S key; the key is set at frame 24.

10. Select frame 26 and enter **1** in the **Scale Y** edit box of the **Channel Box / Layer Editor**; *ball* gets stretched. Now, enter **0** in the **Translate Y** edit box of the **Channel Box / Layer Editor**; *ball* moves upward. Next, press the S key; the key is set at frame 26.

11. Choose the **Play forwards** button from the playback control area to preview the animation; *ball* starts bouncing like a rubber ball.

Note

*If the ball penetrates into the plane, you need to adjust the **Translate Y** value at frames 25 and 26.*

Saving and Rendering the Scene

In this section, you will save the scene that you have created and then render it. You can view the final rendered image sequence of the scene by downloading the *c08_maya_2017_rndr.zip* file from *www.cadcim.com*. The path of the file is as follows: *Textbooks > Animation and Visual Effects > Maya > Autodesk Maya 2017: A Comprehensive Guide*.

1. Choose **File > Save Scene** from the menubar to save the scene.

2. For rendering the scene, refer to Tutorial 1 of this chapter.

Tutorial 3

In this tutorial, you will create the model of a wall clock and then animate its second hand using the **Graph Editor**. **(Expected time: 30 min)**

The following steps are required to complete this tutorial:

a. Create the project folder.
b. Create the model of a wall clock.
c. Set the animation keys and refine them.
d. Save and render the scene.

Creating the Project Folder

Create a new project folder with the name *c08_tut3* at *\Documents\maya2017* and then save the file with the name *c08tut3*, as discussed in Tutorial 1 of Chapter 2.

Creating the Model of a Wall Clock

In this section, you will create the basic model of a wall clock using the NURBS and polygon modeling methods.

1. Maximize the top-Y viewport. Choose **Create > Objects > NURBS Primitives > Circle** from the menubar and create a circle in the viewport. In the **Channel Box / Layer Editor**,

enter **5** in the **Radius** edit box in the **makeNurbCircle1** node of the **INPUTS** area and press ENTER.

2. In the front-Z viewport, create another circle. In the **Channel Box / Layer Editor**, enter **0.5** in the **Radius** edit box in the **makeNurbCircle2** node of the **INPUTS** area and press ENTER.

3. Select the **Modeling** menuset from the **Menuset** drop-down list. Make sure the smaller circle is selected and then select the bigger circle by using the SHIFT key. Next, choose **Surfaces > Extrude > Options Box** from the menubar; the **Extrude Options** dialog box is displayed. In this dialog box, select the **At Path** radio button corresponding to the **Result Position** attribute. Also, select the **Component** radio button corresponding to the **Pivot** attribute. Now, choose the **Extrude** button; the circle is extruded.

4. Maximize the persp viewport. Choose **Windows > Editors > Outliner** from the menubar; the **Outliner** window is displayed. Select **nurbsCircle1** from the **Outliner** window. Close the **Outliner** window. Next, choose **Surfaces > Create > Planar** from the menubar; a circular NURBS surface is created. Figure 8-51 shows the base of wall clock in the persp viewport. Make sure the surface is selected. Next, choose **Curves > Reverse Direction** from the menubar; the curve direction of the selected surface is reversed.

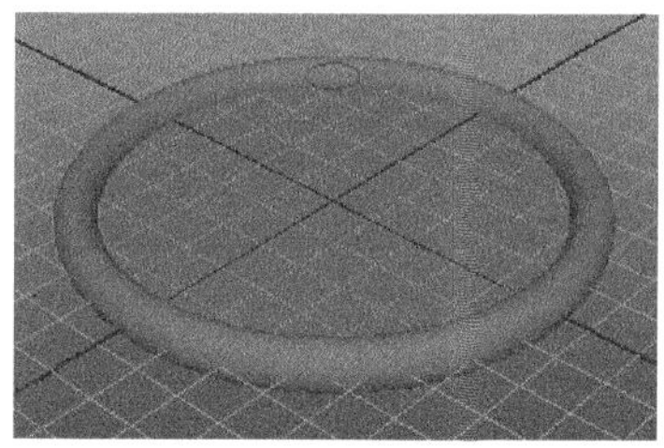

Figure 8-51 *The base of wall clock*

Next, you will create the text for the wall clock.

5. Choose **Create > Objects > Type** from the menubar; the settings for the text are displayed in the **Type Attributes** area of the **Attribute Editor**. In the **Type Attributes** area, select the 3D Type text and enter **3**, the **3D Type** text is replaced with 3 in the viewports.

6. Make sure **3** is selected in the viewport. In the **Channel Box / Layer Editor**, set the parameters as follows:

Scale X : **0.14**	Scale Y : **0.14**	Scale Z : **0.14**
Translate X: **3**	Translate Z: **0.7**	Rotate X: **-90**

7. Similarly, create numbers 9, 6, and 12. Next, arrange the text at the top-Y and persp viewports at appropriate places on the dial of the wall clock, as shown in Figure 8-52.

8. Maximize the top-Y viewport. Choose **Create > Objects > Polygon Primitives > Cylinder** from the menubar and create a cylinder at the center of the grid in the top-Y viewport. Next, set the following parameters in the **polyCylinder1** node in the **INPUTS** area of the **Channel Box / Layer Editor**:

Radius: **0.3**	Height: **0.2**	Subdivisions Caps: **0**

Next, align the cylinder at the center of the wall clock.

9. In the top-Y viewport, choose **Create > Objects > Polygon Primitives > Cube** from the menubar and create a cube in the top-Y viewport. Next, set the following parameters in the **polyCube1** area of the **INPUTS** node of the **Channel Box / Layer Editor**:

   Width: **0.3** Height: **0.1** Depth: **3.5**

   Next, rename **pCube1** to *second hand* and align it with the cylinder on the wall clock, as shown in Figure 8-53.

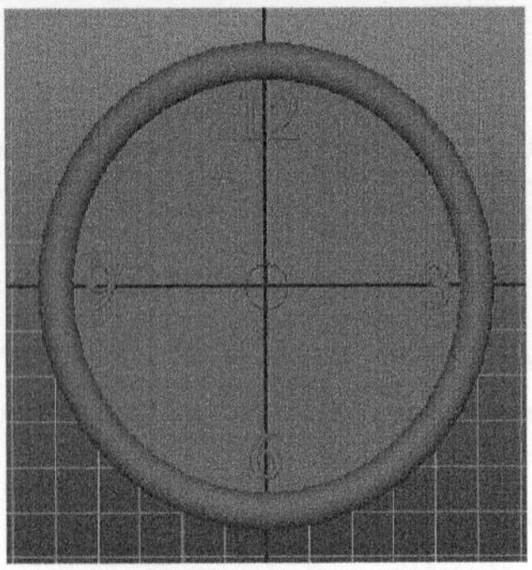

Figure 8-52 *The text arranged on the clock model*

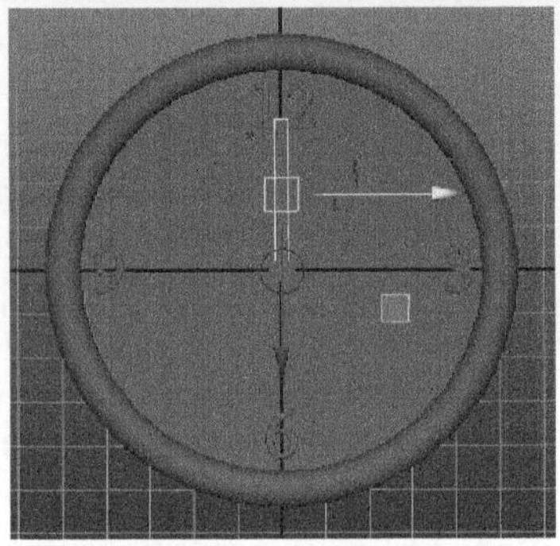

Figure 8-53 *The second hand of the clock*

10. Make sure that the **Move Tool** is active and then press the INSERT key to display the pivot point manipulators. Next, move the pivot point of the second hand to the center of the wall clock dial. Press the INSERT key again to deactivate the manipulators.

Setting and Refining Animation Keys Using the Graph Editor

In this section, you will animate the second hand of the clock using the **Graph Editor**.

1. Select the second hand from the viewport. Next, choose **Modify > Freeze Transformations** from the menubar; the transformation values of the second hand are set to 0.

2. Set the timeslider from **1** to **5400**. Make sure that the second hand is selected at frame 1 and press S to set the key on frame 1. Now, move the timeslider to frame 30 by pressing ALT+. (dot). Next, in the **Channel Box / Layer Editor**, enter **-6** in the **Rotate Y** edit box and press s to set the animation key at frame 30.

3. Choose **Windows > Editors > Animation Editors > Graph Editor** from the menubar; the **Graph Editor** is displayed. Select **Rotate Y** from the left panel in the **Graph Editor**; the **Rotate Y** animation curve is displayed. Now, select the **Rotate Y** animation curve from the right panel in the **Graph Editor** by clicking on it.

4. Choose **View > Infinity** from the **Graph Editor** menubar; the graph in the **Graph Editor** continues till the end. Choose **Curves > Post Infinity > Cycle with Offset** from the **Graph Editor** menubar. Next, play the animation.

5. To make the movement of the *second hand* smooth, select the **Rotate Y** animation curve from the **Graph Editor**. Next, choose **Tangents > Stepped** from the **Graph Editor** menubar to set the tangency to **Stepped** in the **Graph Editor**. Close the **Graph Editor**.

6. Preview the animation; the movement of the *second hand* becomes smoother.

7. Choose the **Animation Preferences** button from the right of the **Auto keyframe toggle** button; the **Preferences** dialog box is displayed. In this dialog box, choose the **Settings** option from the **Categories** area. Next, select **NTSC (30 fps)** from the **Time** drop-down list. Choose the **Time Slider** option from the **Categories** area and make sure the **Real-time [30 fps]** option is selected in the **Playback speed** drop-down list. Next, choose the **Save** button to save the preferences.

8. Preview the animation to view the animation of the second hand in the clock.

Note
Using the steps given in this tutorial, you can create a complete clock with the minute and hour hands also.

Saving and Rendering the Scene

In this section, you will save the scene that you have created and then render it. You can view the final rendered image sequence of the scene by downloading the *c08_maya_2017_rndr.zip* file from *www.cadcim.com*. The path of the file is as follows: *Textbooks > Animation and Visual Effects > Maya > Autodesk Maya 2017: A Comprehensive Guide.*

1. Choose **File > Save Scene** from the menubar to save the scene.

2. For rendering the scene, refer to Tutorial 1 of this chapter.

Self-Evaluation Test

Answer the following questions and then compare them to those given at the end of this chapter:

1. In which of the following animation types, you can transform objects by setting keyframes?

   (a) Keyframe (b) Nonlinear
   (c) Technical (d) Effects

2. Which of the following editors is used to edit animation curves?

   (a) **Graph Editor** (b) **Expression Editor**
   (c) **Trax Editor** (d) None of these

3. The __________ option is used to paste keys from the virtual memory to the place where the current time indicator is located.

4. The __________ option is used to import the motion-captured data to apply a realistic animation to the character.

5. The __________ button is used to make the selected layer a solo layer in the **Animation Layer Editor**.

6. The **Spline tangents** tool is used to adjust the tangent on a curve so that it becomes smooth between the keys. (T/F)

7. The technical animation type is used to animate an object by linking the translation and rotation attributes of one object with another object. (T/F)

8. The **Buffer Curve Snapshot** tool is used to take a snapshot of the selected curve. (T/F)

9. The **Unify Tangent** tool is used to uniformly adjust the handles at the bottom side of the key. (T/F)

10. The **Post-Infinity Cycle** tool is used to copy an animation curve and repeat it infinitely through the graph view. (T/F)

Review Questions

Answer the following questions:

1. Which of the following options is used to define the total length of an animation?

   (a) **Range** (b) **Frame Rate**
   (c) Keyframe Animation (d) None of these

2. The __________ method is used to animate an object on a particular path.

3. The __________ tool is used to copy an animation curve and then join it after the same curve infinite number of times.

4. The __________ tool is used to lock the tangent weight.

5. The __________ animation is used to blend, duplicate, and split animation clips to achieve different motion effects.

6. The __________ of the **Playback range** button is used to move the frame to the last frame of the active time segment.

7. The function of the **Plateau tangents** tool is similar to the **Spline tangents** and **Clamped tangents** tools. (T/F)

8. The playback control buttons are used to control the animation in the viewport. (T/F)

EXERCISE

The rendered image sequence of the scene used in the following exercise can be accessed by downloading the *c08_maya_2017_exr.zip* from *www.cadcim.com*. The path of the file is as follows: *Textbooks > Animation and Visual Effects > Maya > Autodesk Maya 2017: A Comprehensive Guide.*

Exercise 1

Download the file *c08_maya_2017_exr.zip* from *www.cadcim.com*. Extract the contents from the zipped file and open the scene shown in Figure 8-54. Then use the **Graph Editor**, animate the intensity of the bulb. **(Expected time: 15 min)**

Figure 8-54 *The animated intensity of the bulb*

Answers to Self-Evaluation Test

1. a, **2.** a, **3. Paste Keys**, **4. Motion Capture**, **5. Solo Layer**, **6.** T, **7.** T, **8.** T, **9.** T, **10.** T

Chapter 9

Rigging, Constraints, and Deformers

Learning Objectives

After completing this chapter, you will be able to:

- *Understand different types of joints*
- *Understand the parent and child relationship*
- *Use different deformers for animating an object*
- *Use different types of constraints*
- *Use the set driven keys to link objects*

INTRODUCTION

Rigging is the process of preparing an object or a character for animation. To rig an object, you need to add bones and joints to it. Bones and joints are grouped together to form a complete skeleton. Skeleton provides support to an object in the same way as the human skeleton does to the human body. In this process, the skeleton is joined to the corresponding object by the skinning method. This method is discussed in detail later in this chapter. In this chapter, you will learn about bones and joints.

BONES AND JOINTS

Bones and joints act as the building blocks for creating a skeleton. They are visible in the viewport but cannot be rendered. Each joint may have one or more bones attached to it, as shown in Figure 9-1. Make sure the **Rigging** menuset is selected from the **Menuset** drop-down list. To create a bone, choose **Skeleton > Joints > Create Joints** from the menubar.

By default, the size of bones and joints is set to 1. To change the size of bones and joints, choose **Display > Object > Animation > Joint Size** from the menubar; the **Joint Display Scale** dialog box will be displayed, as shown in Figure 9-2.

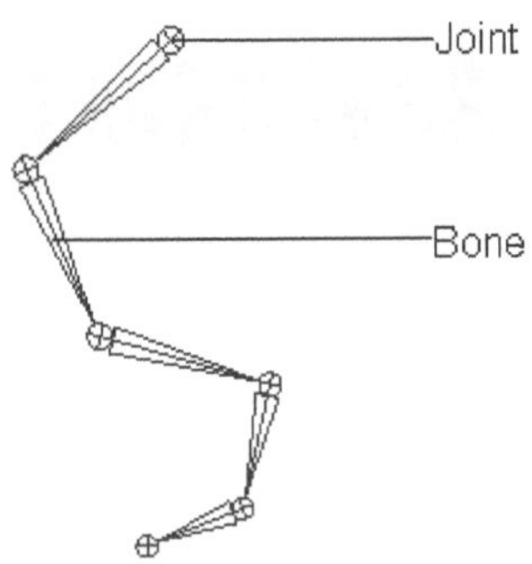

Figure 9-1 The bones and joints

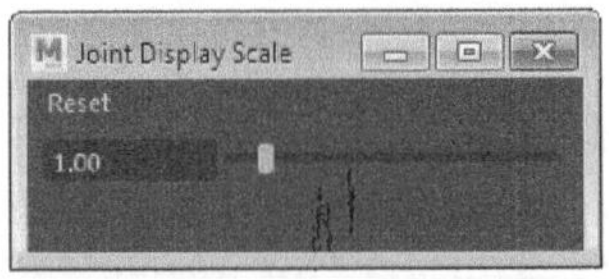

*Figure 9-2 The **Joint Display Scale** dialog box*

In this dialog box, enter the required value for the joint size in the edit box and press ENTER. Alternatively, move the slider on the right of the edit box to adjust the size of joints and bones. The **Reset** button is used to reset the value of joint size. You can also set the joint size by using the **Preferences** dialog box. To do so, choose **Windows > Editors > Setting/Preferences > Preferences** from the menubar; the **Preferences** dialog box will be displayed. In this dialog box, select **Kinematics** from the **Categories** list; the **Kinematics: Kinematic Display Preferences** area will be displayed on the right of the **Preferences** dialog box, refer to Figure 9-3. Now, enter a value in the **Joint size** edit box or move the slider on the right of the edit box to adjust the joint size in the **Inverse Kinematics** area of the **Preferences** dialog box.

CREATING A BONE STRUCTURE

To create a bone structure in a scene, select the **Rigging** menuset from the **Menuset** drop-down list in the Status Line and activate the front-Z, side-X, or top-Y viewport. Next, choose **Skeleton > Joints > Create Joints** from the menubar and then click in the viewport; the bone will be created in the viewport. Press ENTER to exit **Joint Tool**.

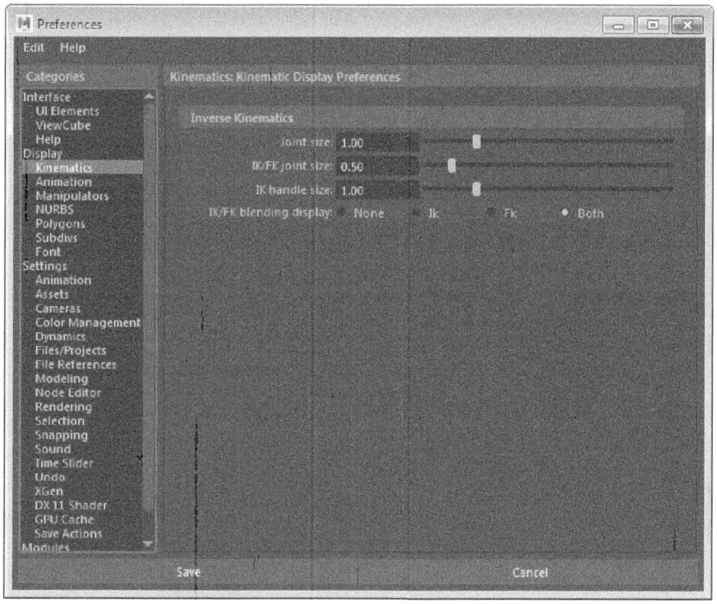

*Figure 9-3 The **Preferences** dialog box*

To animate a joint system, you need to first set the local axes of all joints. To display the local axis of a joint, select the joint from the joint system created in the viewport and choose **Display > Objects > Transform Display > Local Rotation Axes** from the menubar; the local axes will be displayed on a single joint, as shown in Figure 9-4. Similarly, to display the local axes of all joints in a skeleton, select the topmost joint in the skeleton hierarchy and choose **Select > Hierarchy** from the menubar. Next, choose **Display > Object > Transform Display > Local Rotation Axes** from the menubar; the local axes will be displayed on all joints, as shown in Figure 9-5.

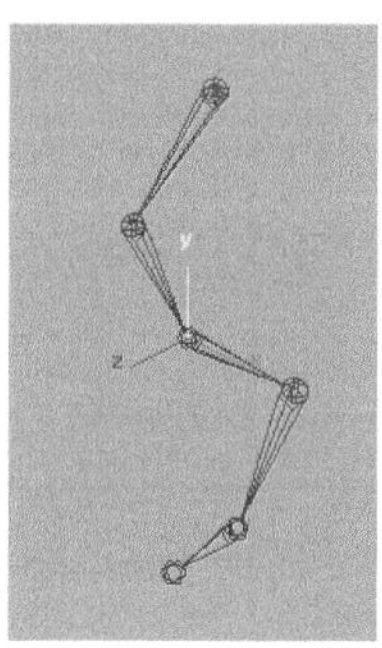

Figure 9-4 The local axes displayed on a single joint

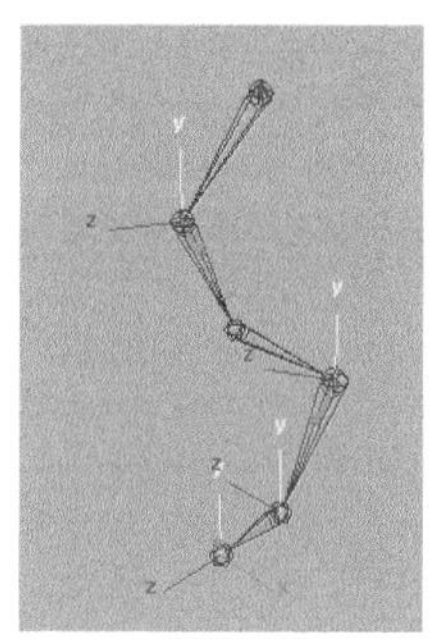

Figure 9-5 The local axes displayed on the entire hierarchy

Types of Joints

In Maya, there are three types of joints that determine the movement of the bones attached to them. These joints are discussed next.

Ball Joint

The ball joint provides free movement to a joint in the skeleton. This type of joint can rotate about all three of its local axes freely. The human shoulder is an example of the ball joint.

Universal Joint

The universal joint provides motion to bones only in two directions. This means the joint can move freely along two axes only. The human wrist is an example of the universal joint.

Hinge Joint

The hinge joint provides rotation to bones in one direction only. The human knee is an example of the hinge joint.

PARENT-CHILD RELATIONSHIP

The parent-child relationship is the most important relationship. The parent object passes its transformations down the hierarchy chain to its children, and each child object inherits all properties of its parent. Note that a parent object can have more than one child object but not vice versa.

To understand the parent-child relationship, create two NURBS spheres in the viewport such that one sphere is larger than the other, as shown in Figure 9-6. Select the smaller sphere, press and hold the SHIFT key, and then select the larger sphere. Now, choose **Edit > Hierarchy > Parent** from the menubar; the larger sphere will become the parent of the smaller sphere. Note that the object that you select later will act as parent of the object that you selected earlier. Invoke **Move Tool** from the Tool Box and move the parent object; the child object will move along with the parent object.

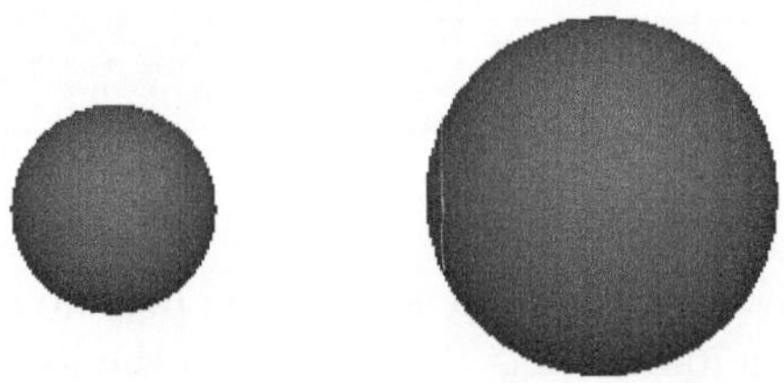

Figure 9-6 *The spheres created*

KINEMATICS

Kinematics is the science of motion. In the case of skeletons used in Maya, kinematics specifies the motion of bones. Kinematics is of two types: Forward and Inverse.

In Forward Kinematics (FK), the child objects are animated based on the transformations of the parent object. It is a one-way process, in which, if a parent object moves, the child objects will also move. However, if a child object moves, the parent object will not move. In other words, you can use the topmost object in the hierarchy to animate the entire chain. Note that when you create a hierarchy, the Forward Kinematics is set by default.

The Inverse Kinematics (IK) is just the opposite of the Forward Kinematics. In Inverse Kinematics, you can use the object at the bottom of hierarchy to animate the entire chain. In this kinematics, if you move a child object, the objects that are higher in the hierarchy will also move accordingly.

DEFORMERS

The deformers are the tools that are used to modify the geometry of an object. You can deform any object in Maya. Various deformers in Maya are discussed next.

Blend Shape Deformer

Main menubar: Deform > Create > Blend Shape

The **Blend Shape** deformer is used to change the shape of an object into another object. The original object that is used in this process is known as the base object, and the object into which the base object gets blended is known as the target object.

To deform the shape of the polygonal base object, create a copy of the base object and modify its shape to create a target object, as shown in Figure 9-7. Now, select the target object, press and hold the SHIFT key, and then select the base object. Next, select the **Rigging** menuset from the **Menuset** drop-down list in the Status Line and choose **Deform > Create > Blend Shape** from the menubar; the blending will be done on the base object.

Now, to view the blending of the object in the viewport, you need to set the parameters in the **Attribute Editor**. To do so, select the base object and choose **Windows > Editors > General Editors > Attribute Editor** from the menubar; the **Attribute Editor** will be displayed. Choose the **blendShape1** tab from the **Attribute Editor**. In the **Blend Shape Attributes** area of this tab, select **World** from the **Origin** drop-down list. Next, in the **Weight** area of this tab, move the slider of **pSphere2** to the right to view the blending of the object in the viewport.

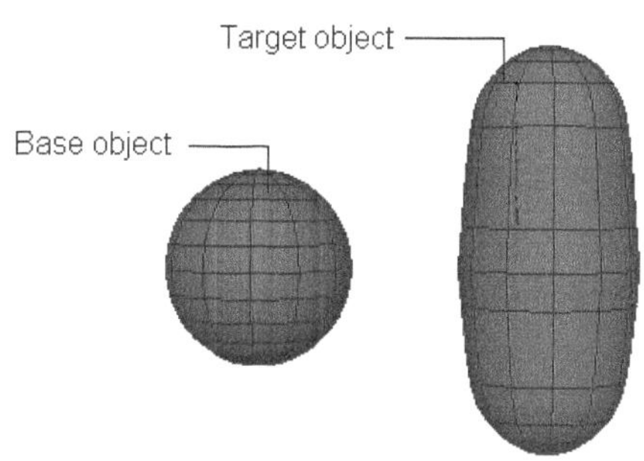

Figure 9-7 *The base and target objects*

Note

*You can apply the **Blend Shape** deformer on mesh objects only if they have equal number of vertices. The **Blend Shape** deformer is mainly used for creating facial expressions.*

Curve Warp Deformer

New

Menubar: Deform > Create > Curve Warp Deformer

The **Curve Warp Deformer** is used to stretch or animate an object along a curve. To do so, create a polygon cube (base object) and a curve. Select the base object and the curve using the SHIFT key. Now, choose **Deform > Create > Curve Warp Deformer** from the menu bar; the polygon cube will be wrapped along the curve, refer to Figure 9-8.

To view the deformation of the object in the viewport, choose the **polyCube1** tab from the **Attribute Editor**. In the **Poly Cube History** area of this tab, move the **Height** slider to the right to view the deformation of the object in the viewport.

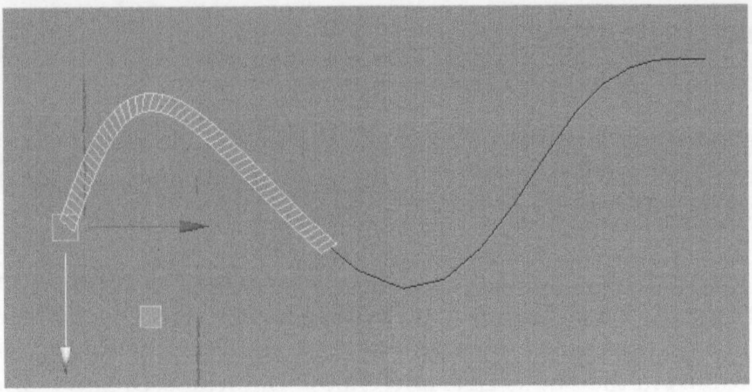

Figure 9-8 The object after applying the ***Curve Warp Deformer***

Cluster Deformer

Menubar:	Deform > Create > Cluster

The **Cluster** deformer is used to modify a particular area of the polygon mesh. To do so, select a group of vertices from the object that you want to deform. Next, choose **Deform > Create > Cluster** from the menubar; a C symbol will be displayed in the viewport. Select the C symbol and move it using **Move Tool**; the group of vertices that you selected earlier will move along with it. Figures 9-9 and 9-10 show an object before and after applying the **Cluster** deformer, respectively.

Figure 9-9 The object before applying the ***Cluster*** *deformer*

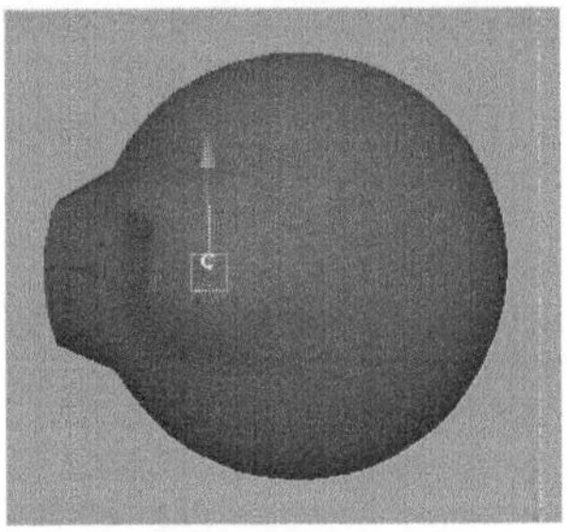

Figure 9-10 The object after applying the ***Cluster*** *deformer*

Delta Mush Deformer

Menubar:	Deform > Create > Delta Mush

The **Delta Mush** deformer is used to filter the deformation artifacts on a skinned object. It removes the artifacts by making the final result closer to the original geometry in the rest position. It produces smooth result when the mesh is deformed.

Lattice Deformer

Menubar:	Deform > Create > Lattice

The **Lattice** deformer is used to modify an object using lattices. To modify an object using lattices, create the object in the viewport. Next, select the object and choose **Deform > Create > Lattice** from the menubar; lattice will be created around the selected object, as shown in Figure 9-11.

To control the influence of lattice on the mesh, select the lattice in the viewport and enter the required value in the **ffd1** area of the **OUTPUTS** node in the **Channel Box / Layer Editor**, as shown in Figure 9-12. To set the number of lattice segments, set the required values in the **S Divisions**, **T Divisions**, and **U Divisions** edit boxes of the **SHAPES** node in the **Channel Box / Layer Editor**.

Figure 9-11 *Lattice created around the selected object*

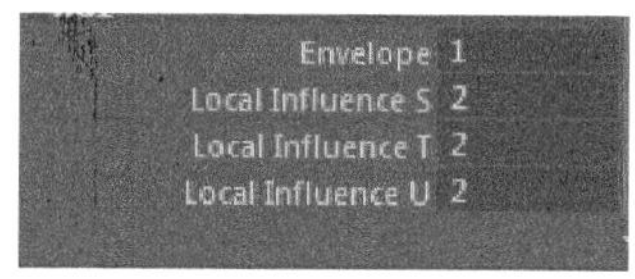

Figure 9-12 *The **ffd1** area in the **OUTPUTS** node*

After setting the required parameters of the lattice, you can deform the object. To do so, select the lattice, press and hold the right mouse button in the viewport, and choose **Lattice Point** from the marking menu displayed; the lattice points will be displayed around the selected object. Now, select these lattice points to deform the object as required. A very good example of lattice deformer is sack animation. To create a sack animation, first create a sack model and then select it. Next, choose **Deform > Create > Lattice** from the menubar; a lattice will be created around the sack model. Select the lattice and press and hold the right mouse button in the viewport and choose **Lattice Point** from the marking menu displayed. Now, you can modify the sack model using the lattice points. Next, set the keys as discussed in Chapter 9.

Wrap Deformer

Menubar: Deform > Create > Wrap

The **Wrap** deformer is used to deform an object using NURBS surfaces, NURBS curves, or polygonal surfaces (meshes). To apply the **Wrap** deformer to an object, create a polygonal plane and add segments to it. Next, create polygonal sphere in the viewport. The polygonal sphere should be placed such that it intersects with the polygonal plane at some point. Next, invoke **Move Tool** from the Tool Box and select the polygonal sphere. Next, press and hold the SHIFT key and select the polygonal plane. Now, choose **Deform > Create > Wrap** from the menubar to apply the **Wrap** deformer. To view the deformation on sphere, select the vertices of plane and move them. You will notice changes on sphere.

ShrinkWrap Deformer

Menubar: Deform > Create > ShrinkWrap

The **ShrinkWrap** deformer is used to shrink the shape of a wrapper object according to the target object. To apply the **ShrinkWrap** deformer to an object, select it and then select a target object using the SHIFT key. Now, choose **Deform > Create > ShrinkWrap** from the menubar to apply the **ShrinkWrap** deformer.

Pose Space Deformation

New

Menubar: Deform > Create > Post Space Deformation

The **Pose Space Deformation** deformer is used to fix the skin deformation problem in a pose. These problems occur at the articulation points of the character such as shoulder, underarm, knee, and groin areas.

Soft Modification Deformer

Menubar: Deform > Create > Soft Modification

The **Soft Modification** deformer is used to deform high density surface meshes without adjusting the vertices manually. The falloff attributes of this deformer are adjustable. To use this deformer, create a polygonal plane in the viewport and add segments to it. Next, choose **Deform > Soft Modification** from the menubar; a colored falloff area will be created at the center of the plane, as shown in Figure 9-13.

The colored area defines the deformer on the surface. The darker the color is, the greater will be the influence of deformation. By default, the amount of deformation is greatest at the center and it gradually decreases toward the end. Move the manipulators in this area to deform the plane as required.

Nonlinear Deformers

In Maya, there are different types of nonlinear deformers. These are discussed next.

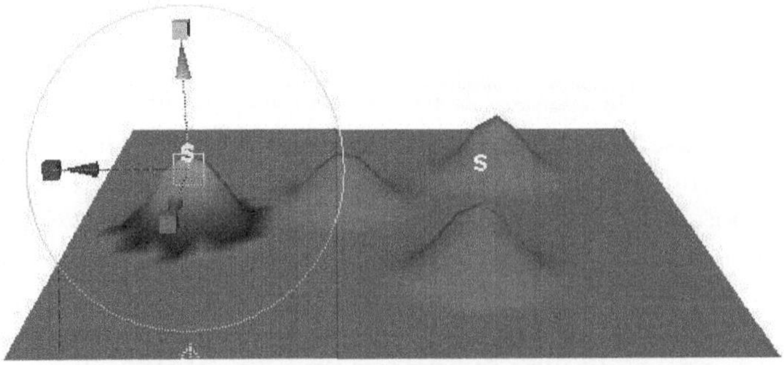

***Figure 9-13** A colorful falloff area created*

Bend Deformer

Menubar:	Deform > Create > Nonlinear > Bend

The **Bend** deformer is used to bend an object along a circular arc. Figures 9-14 and 9-15 show a cylinder before and after applying the **Bend** deformer, respectively. To bend an object, select the object in the viewport. Next, choose **Deform > Create > Nonlinear > Bend** from the menubar; the **Bend** deformer will be applied to the selected object. Again, select the object in the viewport and choose **Windows > Editors > General Editors > Attribute Editor** from the menubar; the **Attribute Editor** will be displayed, as shown in Figure 9-16. Choose the **bend1** tab from the **Attribute Editor** and adjust the attributes in the **Nonlinear Deformer Attributes** area to bend the object, refer to Figure 9-15.

Note

You should avoid changing the number of CVs, vertices, or other lattice points after applying a deformer on an object. Any change in the object will lead to a change in the functioning of that particular deformer.

Figure 9-14 *The object before applying the **Bend** deformer*

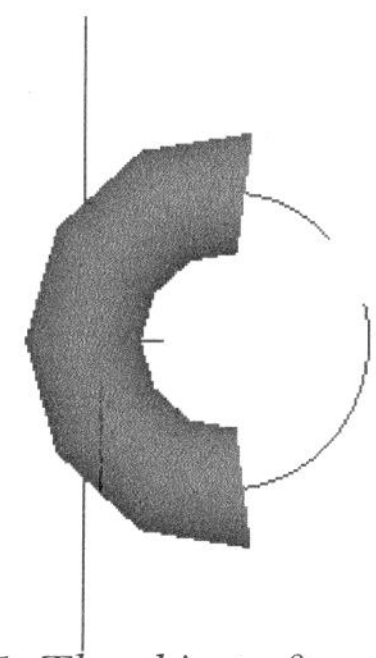

Figure 9-15 *The object after applying the **Bend** deformer*

Flare Deformer

Menubar:	Deform > Create > Nonlinear > Flare

The **Flare** deformer is used to taper an object along two axes. Figures 9-17 and 9-18 shows a cylinder before and after applying the **Flare** deformer, respectively. To taper an object using this deformer, select a NURBS cylinder in the viewport. Next, choose **Deform > Create > Nonlinear > Flare** from the menubar; the **Flare** deformer will be applied to the object, refer to Figure 9-18. Again, select the cylinder in the viewport and choose **Windows > Editors > General Editors > Attribute Editor** from the menubar; the **Attribute Editor** will be displayed, as shown in Figure 9-19. Choose the **flare1** tab from the **Attribute Editor** and set the values for various attributes in the **Nonlinear Deformer Attributes** area to deform the object, refer to Figure 9-19.

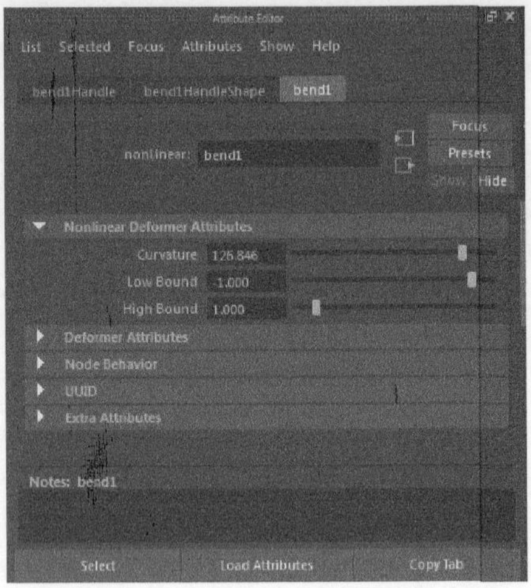

*Figure 9-16 The **Nonlinear Deformer Attributes** area in the **bend1** tab*

*Figure 9-17 The cylinder before applying the **Flare** deformer*

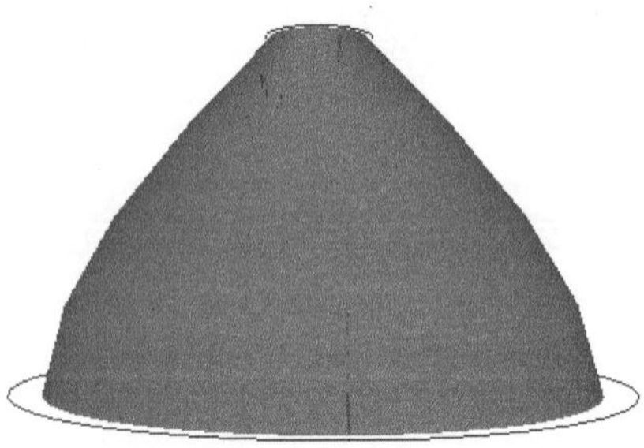

*Figure 9-18 The cylinder modified using the **Flare** deformer*

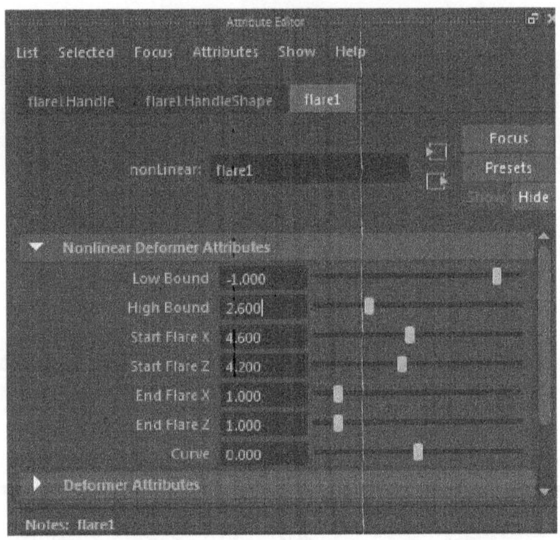

*Figure 9-19 Partial view of the **Flare** deformer attributes in the **Attribute Editor***

Sine Deformer

Menubar: Deform > Create > Nonlinear > Sine

The **Sine** deformer is used to deform an object in the shape of a sine wave. Figures 9-20 and 9-21 show a cylinder before and after applying the **Sine** deformer, respectively. To apply this deformer, select an object in the viewport and then choose **Deform > Create > Nonlinear > Sine** from the menubar; the **Sine** deformer will be applied to the object and the **Attribute Editor** will be displayed, refer to Figure 9-22. Next, choose the **sine1** tab from the **Attribute Editor** and set the values of various attributes in the **Nonlinear Deformer Attributes** area to deform the object.

*Figure 9-20 The cylinder before applying the **Sine** deformer*

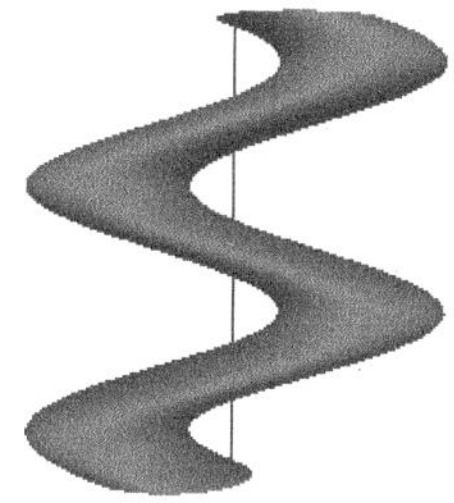

*Figure 9-21 The cylinder after applying the **Sine** deformer*

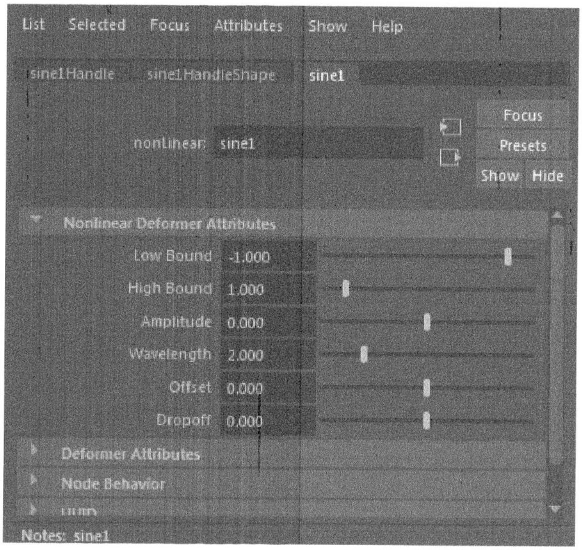

*Figure 9-22 Partial view of the **Sine** deformer attributes in the **Attribute Editor***

Squash Deformer

Menubar:	Deform > Create > Nonlinear > Squash

The **Squash** deformer is used to squash and stretch an object along a specific axis. Figures 9-23 and 9-24 show a cylinder before and after applying the **Squash** deformer, respectively. To squash or stretch an object, select the object in the viewport and choose **Deform > Create > Nonlinear > Squash** from the menubar; the **Squash** deformer will be applied to the selected object. Again, select the deformer in the viewport and choose **Windows > Editors > General Editors > Attribute Editor** from the menubar; the **Attribute Editor** will be displayed, refer to Figure 9-25. Choose the **squash1** tab from the **Attribute Editor** and set the values of attributes in the **Nonlinear Deformer Attributes** area to deform the object.

*Figure 9-23 An object before applying the **Squash** deformer*

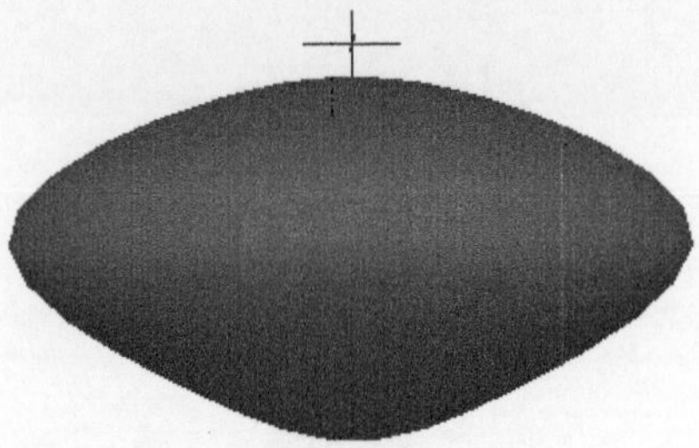

*Figure 9-24 An object after applying the **Squash** deformer*

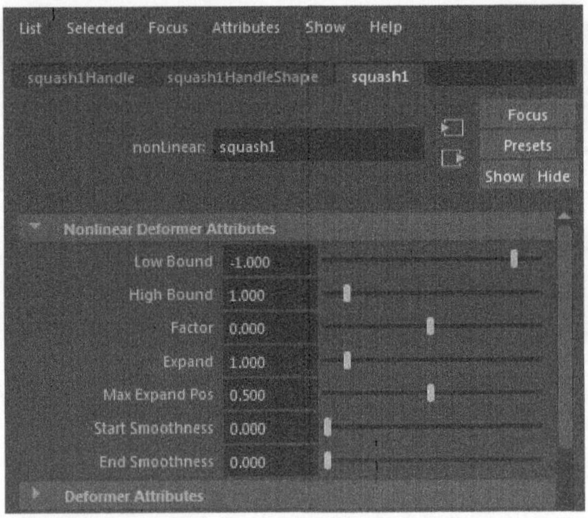

*Figure 9-25 Partial view of the **Squash** deformer attributes in the **Attribute Editor***

Twist Deformer

Menubar:	Deform > Create > Nonlinear > Twist

The **Twist** deformer is used to twist an object about an axis. Figures 9-26 and 9-27 show a cylinder before and after applying the **Twist** deformer, respectively. To apply this deformer, select an object in the viewport and choose **Deform > Create > Nonlinear > Twist** from the menubar; the **Twist** deformer will be applied to the object. Now, select the object again from the viewport and choose **Windows > Editors > General Editors > Attribute Editor** from the menubar; the **Attribute Editor** will be displayed. Choose the **twist1** tab from the **Attribute Editor** and set the values of various attributes in the **Nonlinear Deformer Attributes** area to deform the object, as shown in Figure 9-28.

Wave Deformer

Menubar:	Deform > Create > Nonlinear > Wave

The **Wave** deformer is used to propagate waves on an object in the X and Z directions. Figures 9-29 and 9-30 show a plane before and after applying the **Wave** deformer, respectively.

To apply the **Wave** deformer, select an object in the viewport and then increase the number of segments on it from the **Channel Box / Layer Editor**. Next, choose **Deform > Create > Nonlinear > Wave** from the menubar; the **Wave** deformer will be applied to the selected object. Select the object again and choose **Windows > Editors > General Editors > Attribute Editor** from the menubar; the **Attribute Editor** will be displayed. Next, choose the **wave1** tab from the **Attribute Editor** to deform the selected object as desired. The attributes of the **Wave** deformer are similar to those of the **Sine** deformer and are shown in Figure 9-31.

Figure 9-26 *The cylinder before applying the **Twist** deformer*

Figure 9-27 *The cylinder after applying the **Twist** deformer*

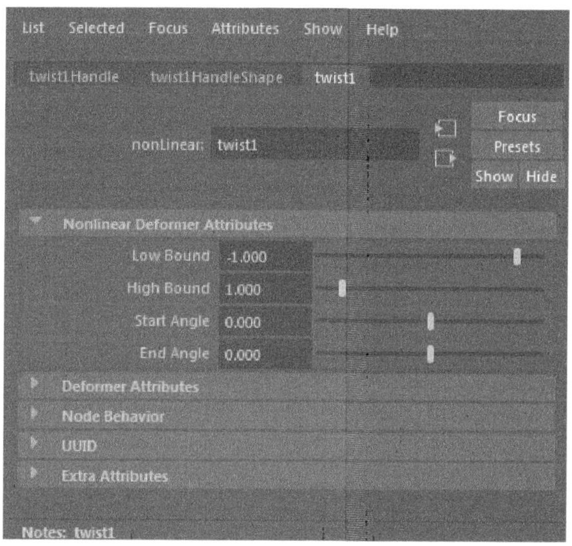

Figure 9-28 *The **Nonlinear Deformer Attributes** area in the **twist1** tab*

Figure 9-29 *The plane before applying the **Wave** deformer*

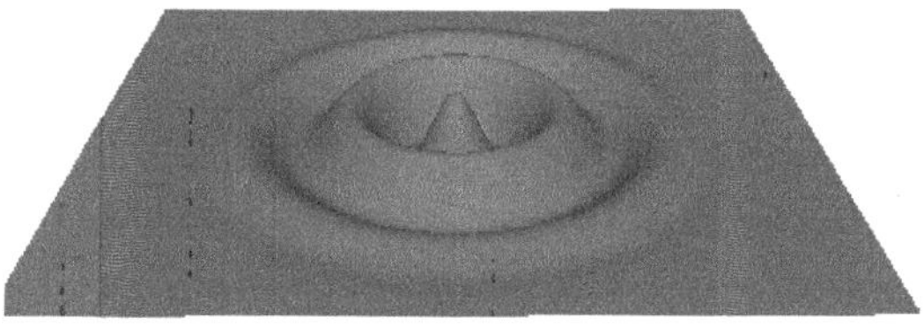

Figure 9-30 *The plane after applying the **Wave** deformer*

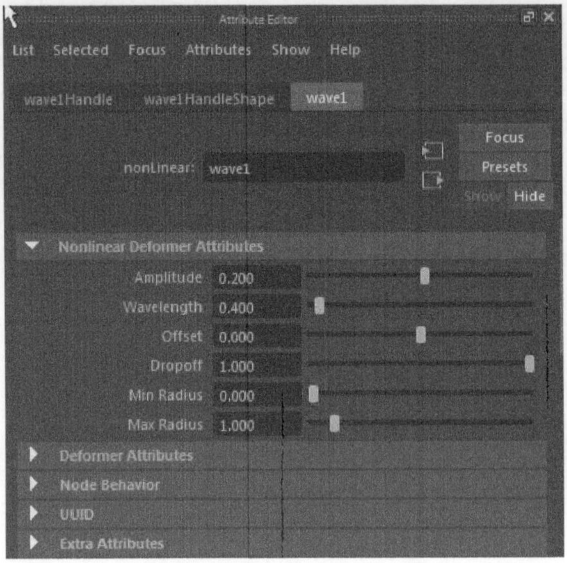

*Figure 9-31 Partial view of the **Wave** deformer attributes in the **Attribute Editor***

Sculpt Deformer

Menubar:	Deform > Create > Sculpt

The **Sculpt** deformer is used to create a rounded deformation on an object. To apply the **Sculpt**, select an object or the vertices of an object where you need deformation. Now, choose **Deform > Create > Sculpt** from the menubar; a spherical influence object called sculpt sphere will be created around the selected object or vertices. Now, move this sculpt sphere to deform the object. Note that the object will be sculpted better if there are more number of segments on the object.

Texture Deformer

Menubar:	Deform > Create > Texture

The **Texture** deformer is used to deform objects using a texture pattern. You can use the procedural noise or a displacement map for the texture. To apply the **Texture** deformer, select an object and choose **Deformers > Create > Texture** from the menubar, the **Texture** deformer will be applied to the object. In the **Attribute Editor**, choose the **textureDeformer1** tab. Next, choose the checker button corresponding to the **Texture** attributes; the **Create Render Node** window will be displayed. Choose the **Noise** button from the **Create Render Node** window; the shape of the object will change.

Jiggle Deformer

Menubar:	Deform > Create > Jiggle > Jiggle Deformer

The **Jiggle** deformer is used to shake an object or its parts while animating. This deformer is applied to a complete object or to its CVs, lattice points, and vertices. For example, you can use this deformer to show the affect of shaking the stomach of a fat man or a wrestler while he is walking.

Wire Deformer

Menubar: Deform > Create > Wire

The **Wire** deformer is used to change the shape of an object by setting one or more of its NURBS curves. This deformer is mainly used for setting lips or eyebrow deformations. To understand the working of **Wire** deformer, create a plane in the viewport and enter **10** in the **Subdivisions Width** and **Subdivisions Height** edit boxes, respectively. Next, choose **Create > Objects > Curve Tools > EP Curve Tool** from the menubar and create a curve on the plane in the viewport. Next, invoke **Move Tool** from the Tool Box, and click anywhere in the viewport to deselect the selection, if any. Now, select the **Rigging** menuset from the **Menuset** in the Status Line and choose **Deform > Create > Wire** from the menubar. Then, select the objects from the viewport that are required to be deformed and press ENTER. Now, select the curve and press ENTER; the curve will change the shape of the object.

Wrinkle Deformer

Menubar: Deform > Create > Wrinkle

The **Wrinkle** deformer is used to create a detailed wrinkle effect on an object. The **Wrinkle** deformer works in collaboration with **Wire** deformer and **Cluster** deformer. The **Wrinkle** deformer is preferably used on NURBS surfaces. To understand the working of this tool, create a NURBS sphere in the viewport. Next, select the **Rigging** menuset from the **Menuset** drop-down list in the Status Line. Next, choose **Deform > Create > Wrinkle** deformer from the menubar; a UV region will be highlighted on the selected surface. The UV surface allows you set the wire cluster to deform the object. Use the middle mouse button to shape the UV region and press ENTER; a 'C' icon is created on the object. The 'C' icon is the cluster deformer handle that is used to deform the object. Invoke **Move Tool** to move vertices and deform the object as required.

Point On Curve Deformer

Menubar: Deform > Create > Point On Curve

The **Point On Curve** deformer is used to deform points on the NURBS curve. To understand the working of this deformer, create a curve using the **EP Curve Tool** in the viewport. Next, right-click on a point on the curve and then choose **Curve Point** from the marking menu displayed. Next, click on the curve; a point will be created. Next, select the **Rigging** menuset from the **Menuset** in the Status Line and then choose **Deform > Create > Point On Curve** from the menubar; a star-shaped point will be created on the curve. Next, invoke **Move Tool** from the Tool Box, and move the point in any direction in the viewport. As a result, the curve will also move along with it.

APPLYING CONSTRAINTS

Constraints are used to restrict the motion of an object to a particular mode by specifying their limits. Different types of constraints in Maya are discussed next.

Parent Constraint

Menubar: Constrain > Create > Parent

The **Parent** constraint is used to relate the orientation of one object with the other object such that both of them follow the parent-child relationship. To apply this constraint, create two objects in the viewport. Select one object, press and hold the SHIFT key, and then select the other object. Next, choose **Constrain > Create > Parent** from the menubar to apply the **Parent** constraint to the selected objects. Change the position of the parent object; the objects follow the parent-child relationship. The **Parent** constraint is different from the **Point** and **Orient** constraints. When an object is rotated using the **Point** or **Orient** constraint, the constrained object rotates about its local axis. Whereas in case of the **Parent** constraint, the constrained object rotates with respect to the world axis.

Point Constraint

Menubar: Constrain > Create > Point

The **Point** constraint is used to restrict the movement of an object such that the constrained object follows the movement of another object. To apply this constraint, create two cubes of different sizes in the viewport. Next, select the **Rigging** menuset from the Status Line. Now, select one cube, and press and hold the SHIFT key to select another cube. Next, choose **Constrain > Create > Point** from the menubar to coordinate the motion of one cube with another cube. The object selected first controls the movement of the object selected later. On applying the **Point** constraint, the objects may overlap when they are moved. To avoid this situation, choose **Constrain > Create > Point > Option Box** from the menubar; the **Point Constraint Options** dialog box will be displayed, as shown in Figure 9-32. The **Offset** attribute in this dialog box is used to set the distance between the two selected objects. Enter the required values in the **Offset** edit boxes and choose the **Add** button from the dialog box; the **Point** constrain will be applied to the selected object.

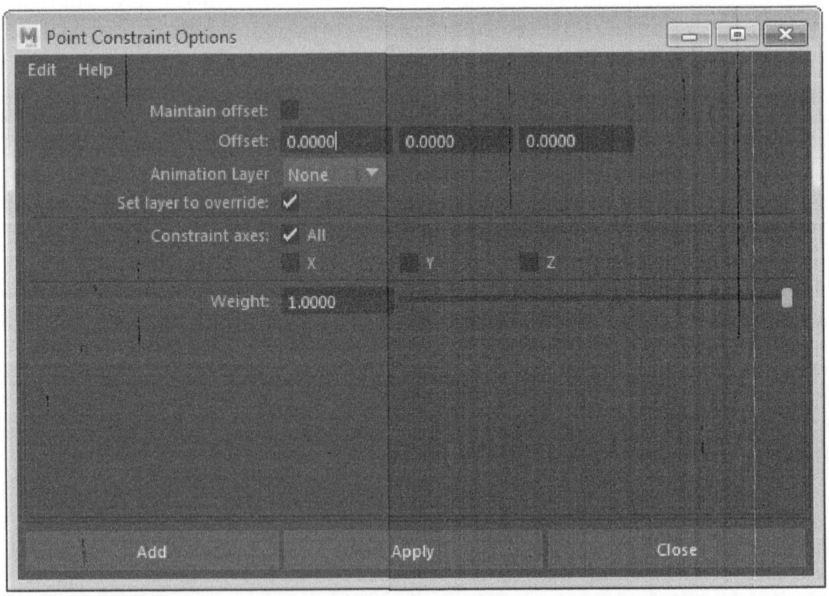

*Figure 9-32 The **Point Constraint Options** dialog box*

Note

The working of a constraint is opposite to that of the parent-child relationship. In a parent-child relationship, the object selected later acts as the parent, but in case of constraints, the object selected first acts as the parent of the object selected later.

Aim Constraint

Menubar: Constrain > Create > Aim

The **Aim** constraint is used to aim one object at another object. To create one object aiming at another object, create two objects in the viewport. Next, select one object, press and hold the SHIFT key and then select another object. Choose **Constrain > Create > Aim** from the menubar; the constraint will be applied to the objects. Now, the object selected first will act as the aim for the object selected later. You can also set the object to aim in a particular direction. To do so, choose **Constrain > Create > Aim > Option Box** from the menubar; the **Aim Constraint Options** dialog box will be displayed, as shown in Figure 9-33. Set the required axis in the **Constraint axes** area and choose the **Add** button; the object will be set to aim in a particular direction.

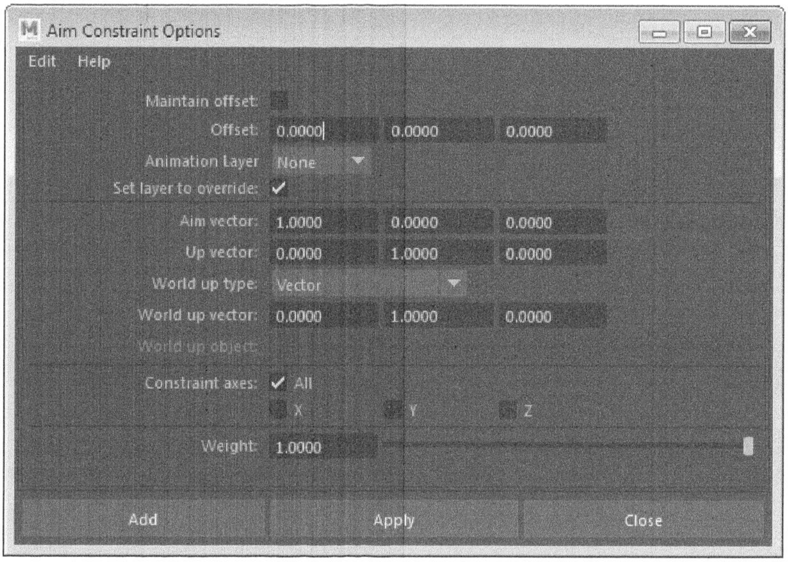

*Figure 9-33 The **Aim Constraint Options** dialog box*

Orient Constraint

Menubar: Constrain > Create > Orient

The **Orient** constraint is used to match the orientation of one object to the other such that the objects are aligned together. To do so, create two objects in the viewport. Select one object, press and hold the SHIFT key and then select another object. Choose **Constrain > Create > Orient** from the menubar; the constraint will be applied to the objects. Now, invoke **Rotate Tool** from the Tool Box, select the object created first, and then rotate it; the other object will also rotate with it. To set the constrain axes, choose **Constrain > Create > Orient > Option Box** from the menubar; the **Orient Constraint Options** dialog box will be displayed, as shown in Figure 9-34. In this dialog box, set the required constraint axis in the **Constraint axes** area and choose the **Add** button.

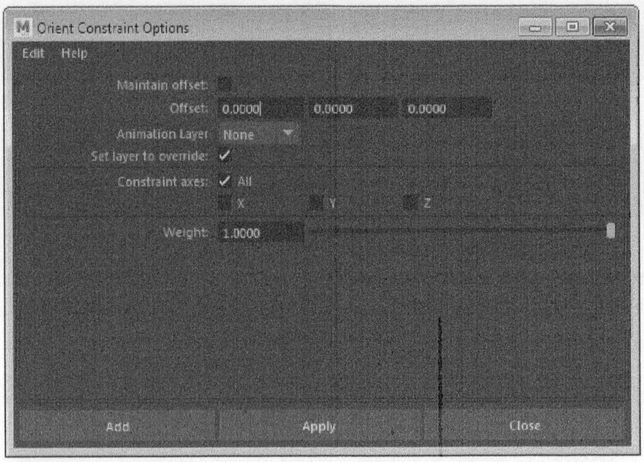

*Figure 9-34 The **Orient Constraint Options** dialog box*

Scale Constraint

Menubar: Constrain > Create > Scale

The **Scale** constraint is used to match the orientation of one object with the other object such that the scaling of one object matches with the other object. To apply this constraint, create two objects in the viewport. Select one object, press and hold the SHIFT key, and then select the other object. Next, choose **Constrain > Create > Scale** from the menubar; the **Scale** constraint will be applied to the objects. Now, invoke **Scale Tool** from the Tool Box and select the object that you created first and scale it; the other object will also be scaled with it.

Geometry Constraint

Menubar: Constrain > Create > Geometry

The **Geometry** constraint is used to restrict one object to the geometry of another object. To apply this constraint, create a plane and a sphere in the viewport. Select the plane from the viewport, press and hold the SHIFT key, and then select the sphere. Now, choose **Constrain > Create > Geometry** from the menubar; the movement of the sphere will be restricted to the geometry of the plane. Invoke **Move Tool** from the Tool Box and move the sphere; the sphere will not move beyond the geometry of the plane.

Normal Constraint

Menubar: Constrain > Create > Normal

The **Normal** constraint is used to orient the selected objects together in such a way that they align with the normal vectors of the mesh object. To apply this constraint, create two objects in the viewport. Next, select the objects created, and choose **Constrain > Create > Normal** from the menubar to align one object to the normal vector of another object. On applying the **Normal** constraint, the constrained object will move along the normal vector of another object. For example, if you want to show a person sweating, instead of animating the sweat drops manually, apply the **Normal** constraint to it; the sweat drops will move while the drop is still attached to the skin.

Tangent Constraint

Menubar: Constrain > Create > Tangent

The **Tangent** constraint is used to keep an object aligned and oriented toward a curve. To apply this constraint, create an object and a curve in the viewport. Next, select both entities and choose **Constrain > Create > Tangent** from the menubar; the object will be constrained on the curve in such a way that the object moves along the curve. For example, you can use the **Tangent** constraint to animate a locomotive such that it moves on the track.

Pole Vector Constraint

Menubar: Constrain > Create > Pole Vector

The **Pole Vector** constraint is used to constrain one object with the other object such that the end of one pole vector moves with the movement of another object. Select two entities from the viewport and choose **Constrain > Create > Pole Vector** from the menubar; the constrained object will move with the movement of another object with which it is constrained. The **Pole Vector** constraint is mainly used for setting up joints in a character setup.

Point On Poly Constraint

Menubar: Constrain > Create > Point On Poly

The **Point On Poly** constraint is used to constrain an object with the mesh or another object such that the object remains stuck to the mesh or another object even if the mesh is deformed or moved from one place to another. To apply this constraint, create two objects in the viewport. Next, select the objects created and choose **Constrain > Crate > Point On Poly** from the menubar. This constraint can be used to create objects such as a handle on the door which remains stuck to the door even if the door is deformed.

Closest Point Constraint

Menubar: Constrain > Create > Closest Point

The **Closest Point** constraint is used to calculate the closest point on a mesh, NURBS surface or curve relative to an input position. To apply the **Closest Point** constraint, select the object created in the viewport and choose **Constrain > Create > Closest Point** from the menubar.

ADDING CONSTRAINT TO ANIMATION LAYERS

In Maya, you can add various constraints to animation layers. To do so, activate the **Animation Layer Editor** by choosing the **Anim** tab. Now, create a new animation layer in the **Animation Layer Editor** and rename it as **constrain** in the **Channel Box / Layer Editor**. Next, select the target objects followed by the object on which you want to apply constraint from the viewport and choose **Constrain > Create > Orient > Option Box** from the menubar; the **Orient Constraint Options** dialog box is displayed. In the **Orient Constraint Options** dialog box, choose the layer to which you want to add constraint from the **Animation Layer** drop-down list. Next, choose the **Add** button; the constraint will be added to the selected layer.

HumanIK CHARACTER CONTROLS

The **HumanIK** tool is used to set a complete character with full body parts. To invoke the **HumanIK** tool, choose **Windows > Editors > Animation Editors > HumanIK** from the menubar; the **Character Controls** window will be displayed on the right of the viewport, as shown in Figure 9-35. The options of this window are discussed next.

Character Drop-down List

The **Character** drop-down list displays the list of characters present in the scene. If there are no characters in the scene, the **None** option is selected, refer to Figure 9-35.

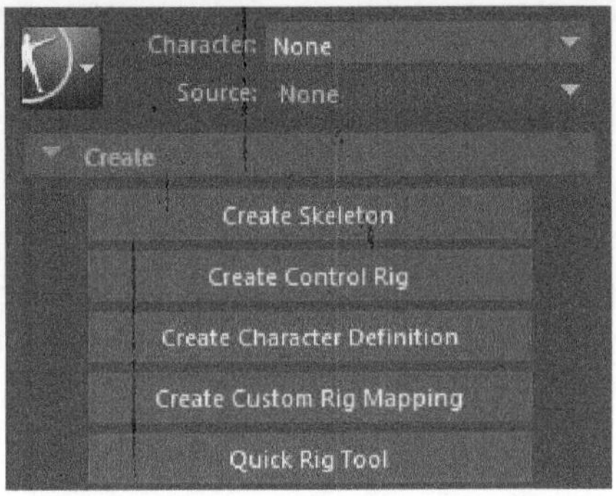

Figure 9-35 *The* ***Character Controls*** *window*

Source Drop-down List

The **Source** drop-down list is used to display information about the types of source that drives the character.

Create Area

The tools in the **Create** area are used to create a skeleton or a rigged character in the viewport.

Import Area

The buttons in the **Import** area are used to import the inbuilt HumanIK, Animation, and Mocap examples from online creative market. To import the humanIK examples, choose the **HumanIK Example** button from the **Import** area; a character will be displayed in the viewport. To import the Mocap examples, choose the **Mocap Example** button; the default browser window will be displayed. Now, click the **Ok** button to save the Mocap examples file in the system drive.

SKINNING AN OBJECT

Skinning is a process that is used to bind the object to the bones or to the skeleton. To do so, create a cylinder in the viewport. Select the cylinder in the viewport; the **Channel Box / Layer Editor** displaying the parameters of cylinder will be displayed. In the **Channel Box / Layer Editor**, set the value of **Subdivisions Height** to **5** and make sure the cylinder is selected in the viewport. Select the **Animation** menuset from the Status Line. Next, choose **Modify > Transform > Freeze Transformations** from the menubar; the transformation of the cylinder is set to zero. Activate the front-Z viewport and press 4 to switch to the wireframe mode. Next, choose **Skeleton > Joints > Create Joints** tool from the menubar and then create the bone structure, as shown in Figure 9-36. Press W to exit the **Create Joints** tool and then select the cylinder from the viewport. Press and hold the SHIFT key and then select the lowest bone from the bone structure; all the bones will be selected. Now, choose **Skin > Bind > Bind Skin** from the menubar; the color of the bones changes in the viewport, indicating that the bones are connected with the objects.

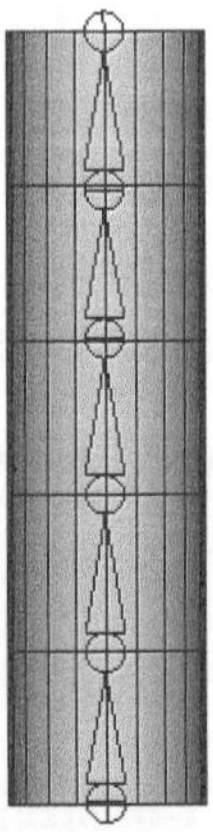

Figure 9-36 *The bone structure created*

Note

It is recommended that you always specify the names of joints so that it becomes easy to work on hierarchy at later stages. To specify the name of a joint, select it; the ***Channel Box / Layer Editor*** *will be displayed. At the top of the* ***Channel Box / Layer Editor****, the name of the corresponding joint will be displayed in the* ***Joint*** *edit box. Change the name as per the hierarchy setup.*

The **Heat Map** binding method uses a heat circulation technique to bind the objects to the bones. To apply this method, select the mesh and the bones, and then choose **Skin > Bind > Bind Skin > Option Box** from the menubar; the **Bind Skin Options** dialog box will be displayed. In this dialog box, choose **Heat Map** from the **Bind method** drop-down list. In this method, the joints that lie inside the mesh act as heat emitters and distribute weights on the surrounding objects. If you bind a skeleton whose end joints lie outside the mesh, the end joints will not receive any weights during binding and will have no influence on the mesh.

Paint Skin Weights Tool

The **Paint Skin Weights** tool is used to increase or decrease the influence of bone on the skin. To do so, select the skinned object from the viewport and choose **Skin > Weight Maps > Paint Skin Weights > Option Box** from the menubar; the **Tool Settings (Paint Skin Weights Tool)** window will be displayed, as shown in Figure 9-37. In the **Influence** area, select the bone whose influence you want to put on the other parts of the object; the influence will be added. Additionally, the area on which the bone has the influence will be displayed in white and the remaining part of the object will be displayed in black.

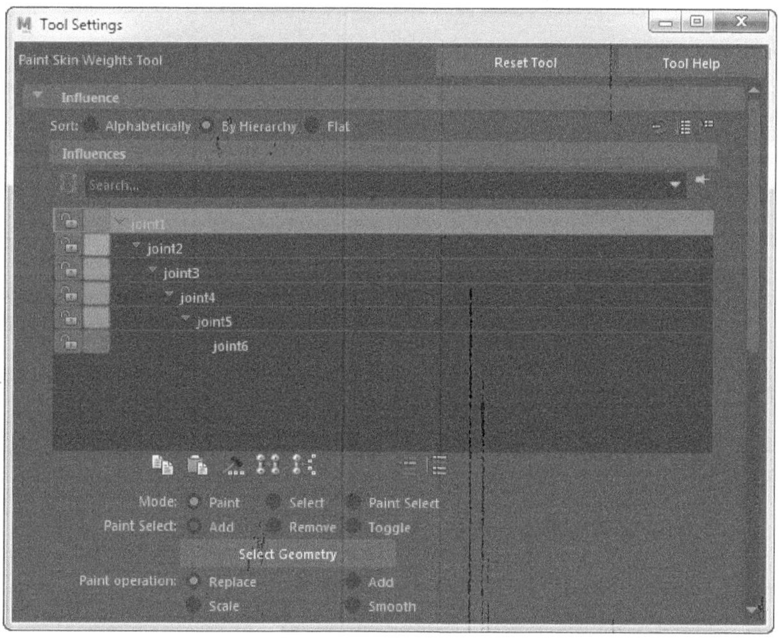

Figure 9-37 *Partial view of the* ***Tool Settings (Paint Skin Weights Tool)*** *window*

Go to Bind Pose

Menubar: Skin > Bind > Go to Bind Pose

The **Go to Bind Pose** tool is defined as a pose in which the skeleton gets bound to the mesh object before the deformations begin. Maya creates a default bind pose node for every skeleton. This bind pose node stores the transformation attributes of joints. To invoke this tool, choose **Skin > Bind > Go to Bind Pose** from the menubar.

MAYA MUSCLE DEFORMER

Maya muscle deformer is a skin deformer, which helps you create quick and easy rigs to create realistic skin deformation. Before you start working with the Maya muscle deformer, you need to activate it. To do so, choose **Menu of items to modify the shelf > Load Shelf** from the Shelf area; the **Load Shelf** window will be displayed, as shown in Figure 9-38. Next, select the **shelf_Muscle.mel** file from the **Load Shelf** dialog box and choose the **Open** button, as shown in Figure 9-39, the tools related to the Maya muscle deformer will be added to the **Muscle** menu as well as to the **Muscle** tab in the **Shelf**. The muscles in Maya are formed by the combination of various muscle objects. These muscle objects are discussed next.

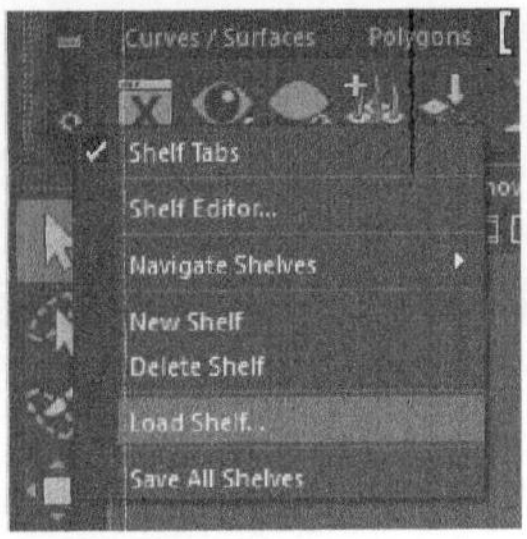

*Figure 9-38 The **Load Shelf** window*

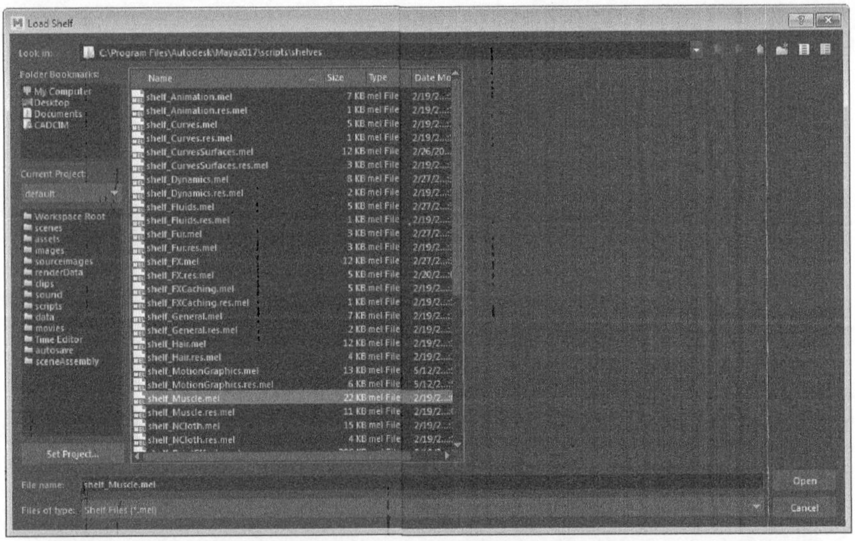

*Figure 9-39 The **Load Shelf** dialog box*

Muscle Objects

The components that together make up a muscle are known as muscle objects. These components are discussed next.

Polygon Bones

A polygon bone is created by converting a polygon mesh into a bone. To do so, select a polygon mesh from the viewport and choose **Deform > Create > Muscle > Muscles / Bones > Convert**

Surface to Muscle/Bone from the menubar; the selected polygon mesh will be converted into a bone. In the **SHAPES** node of the **Channel Box / Layer Editor**, a new muscle object shape node will be created. Figure 9-40 shows the general parameters of a **muscle object shape**.

Capsules

The capsules are similar to the joints in Maya and are used to convert polygon or NURBS objects into muscle objects so that they can be connected to the skin easily. To create a capsule, choose **Deform > Create > Muscle > Muscles/Bones > Make Capsule** from the menubar; a basic capsule object will be created, as shown in Figure 9-41.

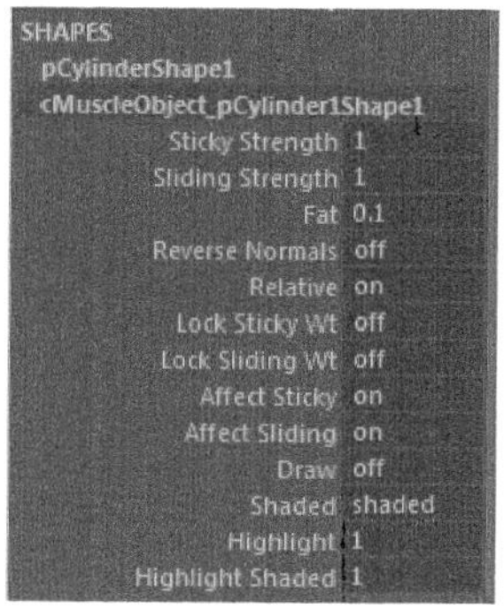

Figure 9-40 *The* ***Muscle Object Shape*** *attributes*

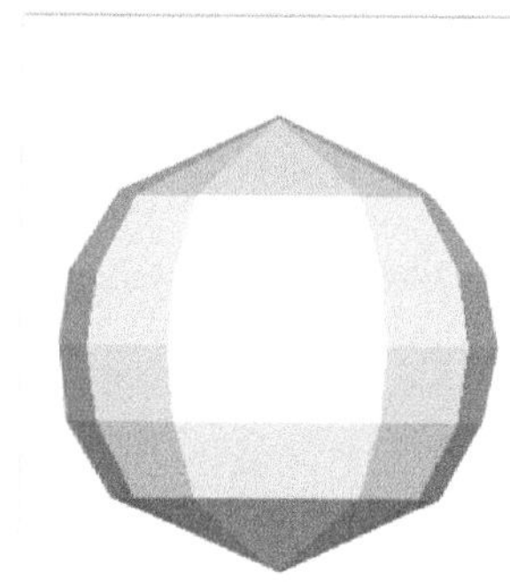

Figure 9-41 *A basic capsule object*

You can also create a capsule with an end locator (the end locator defines the end of a capsule). To do so, choose **Deform > Create > Muscle > Muscles / Bones > Make Capsule with End Locator** from the menubar; a capsule object will be created with an end locator, as shown in Figure 9-42. Select the locator and move it to change the size of the capsule, refer to Figure 9-43. After resizing, you can also select the end locator and spin the capsule on its axis. To add the locator after creating a capsule, select the capsule from the viewport and choose **Deform > Create > Muscle > Muscles / Bones > Add End Locator to Capsule** from the menubar; the locator will be added to the capsule.

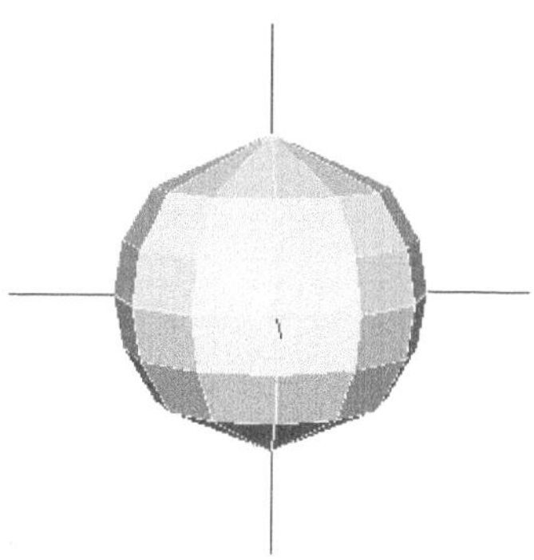

Figure 9-42 *The capsule with an end locator*

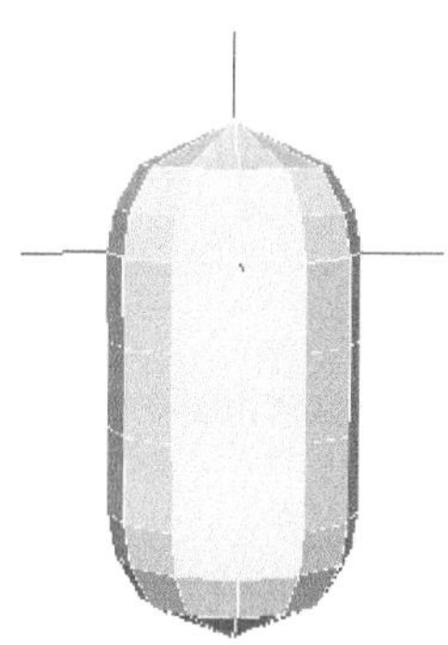

Figure 9-43 *The size of the capsule changes with the movement of locator*

Types of Muscles

In Maya, there are two types of muscles, Muscles and Simple Muscles. These muscle types differ from each other in their respective deforming abilities. The Muscles muscle type is a parametric style NURBS shape that has its own deforming ability, whereas the Simple Muscles type uses the NURBS model with a spline deformer to deform the object.

Muscle Creator

The **Muscle Creator** tool is used to create parametric style NURBS muscles in the viewport. To do so, choose **Deform > Create > Muscle > Muscles / Bones > Muscle Creator** from the menubar; the **Muscle Creator** dialog box will be displayed, as shown in Figure 9-44. Some of the options in this dialog box are discussed next.

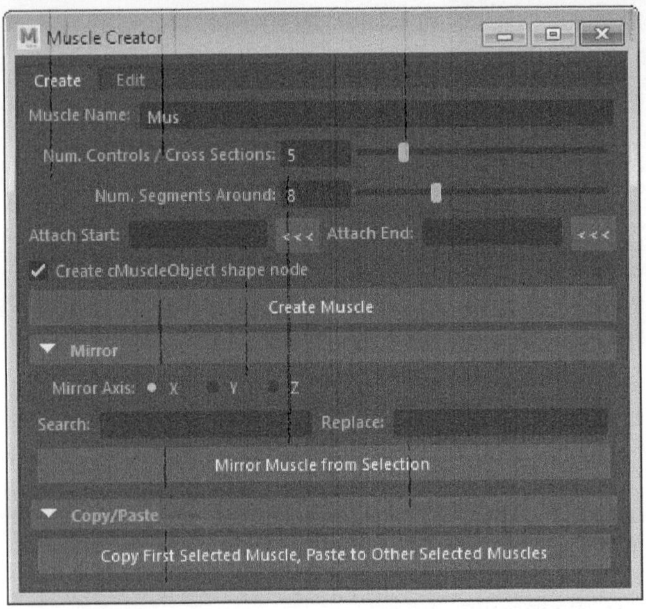

***Figure 9-44** The **Muscle Creator** dialog box*

Create Tab

The options in the **Create** tab are used to define the attributes of the muscle. These options are discussed next.

Muscle Name

The **Muscle Name** attribute is used to assign a name to the new muscle. To do so, enter a name according to the placement of the muscles in this text box.

Num. Controls / Cross Sections

The **Num. Controls / Cross Sections** attribute is used to define the total number of control objects for the muscles and total number of modeling cross-sections existing to create the shape of the muscle.

Num. Segments Around

The **Num. Segments Around** attribute is used to define the number of segments in the muscles.

Attach Start

The **Attach Start** option is used to add an object as the start object of the muscles.

Attach End

The **Attach End** option is used to add an object as the end object of the muscles.

Create cMuscleObject shape node

The **Create cMuscleObject shape node** check box is used to create the muscle object shape node.

Create Muscle

The **Create Muscle** button is used to create a NURBS muscle according to the other options set in this dialog box.

Mirror Area

The options in this area are discussed next.

Mirror Axis: The **Mirror Axis** attribute is used to set the mirror axis of the muscle. You can set the mirror axis by selecting a radio button from this area.

Search/Replace: The **Search/Replace** attribute is used to search the naming conventions and then change the name of the muscles after mirroring. This option helps in preventing duplication of muscle with the same name.

Mirror Muscle from Selection: The **Mirror Muscle from Selection** button is used to create a mirror of the specified muscle according to the other attributes set in the dialog box.

Copy/Paste Area

The option in this area is discussed next.

Copy First Selected Muscle, Paste to Other Selected Muscles: This button is used to copy the attributes of one muscle and paste them on the desired muscle. To do so, select a muscle from the viewport and then choose this button; the attributes of the muscle get copied to the clipboard. Next, select the muscle on which you want to paste these attributes and again choose this button; the attributes get pasted on the new muscle and also their names get interchanged.

SET DRIVEN KEY

The **Set Driven Key** is used to link the attribute of one object to another object. When you set the driven key, you need to specify a driver value and a driven attribute value. In such a case, the value of the driven attribute is locked to the corresponding value of the driver attribute. Therefore, a change in the driver attribute will change the value of the driven attribute as well. Select the **Animation** menuset from the **Menuset** drop-down list. To set a driven key, choose **Key > Set > Set Driven Key > Set** from the menubar; the **Set Driven Key** dialog box will be displayed, as shown in Figure 9-45. Select the object from the viewport that you want to set as the driver and then choose the **Load Driver** button; the name of the object with its attributes will be displayed in the **Driver** area of the **Set Driven Key** dialog box.

Similarly, you can display the attributes of the driven objects in the **Set Driven Key** dialog box. You can also set the attributes of the driver and driven objects by invoking the **Channel Box / Layer Editor**. To do so, select the name of an object (polygonal sphere) from the **Driver** area of the **Set Driven Key** dialog box. Next, select the attribute that you want to set for the selected object; the **Channel Box / Layer Editor** will be displayed. Set the required value for the selected attribute in the **Channel Box / Layer Editor** and choose the **Key** button from the **Set Driven Key** dialog box to set the key. You can also add a new attribute in the **Channel Box / Layer Editor**. To do so, select the object (polygonal sphere) to which you want to add a new attribute in the viewport and then choose **Modify > Attributes > Add Attribute** from the menubar; the **Add Attribute: |pSphere1** dialog box will be displayed, as shown in Figure 9-46.

Figure 9-45 *The **Set Driven Key** dialog box*

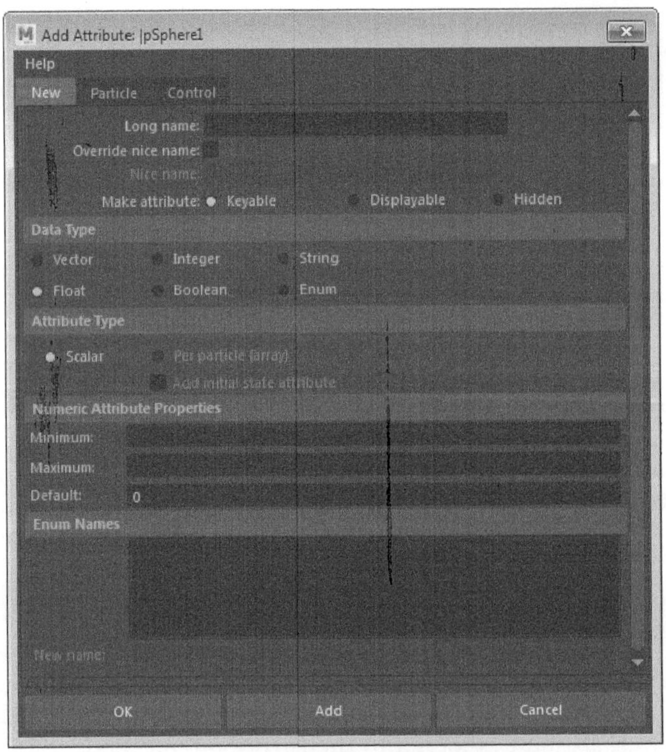

Figure 9-46 *The **Add Attribute** dialog box*

Various options in the **Add Attribute: |pSphere1** dialog box are discussed next.

Long name

The **Long name** attribute is used to specify a name for an attribute, which makes it easier to recognize the functions added to that particular attribute.

Make attribute

The radio buttons corresponding to the **Make attribute** attribute are used to assign different display options to an attribute. The **Keyable** radio button is selected by default. As a result, the attribute is keyable. Select the **Displayable** radio button to make the attribute non-keyable. Select the **Hidden** radio button to hide the attribute.

Data Type Area

The radio buttons in this area are used to set the data types of various attributes. The data type of a programming element refers to the type of data it can hold and store. Different data types in this area are discussed next.

Vector

The **Vector** radio button is used to create a vector attribute consisting of three floating point values.

Float

The **Float** radio button is used to create a floating point attribute. This radio button is selected by default.

Integer

The **Integer** radio button is used to create an integer attribute.

Boolean

The **Boolean** radio button is used to create an attribute that can be toggled.

String

The **String** is an ordered sequence of symbols. The **String** data type radio button is used to create a string attribute that accepts alphanumeric characters as data entries.

Enum

The **Enum** radio button is used to create an attribute that comprises of a drop-down list.

Numeric Attribute Properties Area

The options in this area are used to set the minimum, maximum, and default values that can be entered for a particular attribute in the **Channel Box / Layer Editor**. The **Default** edit box displays the default value for an attribute. In the **Channel Box / Layer Editor**, you can also hide and lock a particular attribute so that the other attributes are not affected when you animate an object. To do so, select the attribute from the **Channel Box / Layer Editor** that you want to hide and lock. Next, press and hold the right mouse button over the attribute and choose the **Lock and Hide Selected** option from the marking menu displayed; the selected attribute will be locked and hidden. There are many attributes in Maya that are not displayed in the **Channel Box / Layer Editor** by default. To display those attributes, choose **Windows > Editors > General Editors > Channel Control** from the menubar; the **Channel Control** dialog box will be displayed, as shown in Figure 9-47.

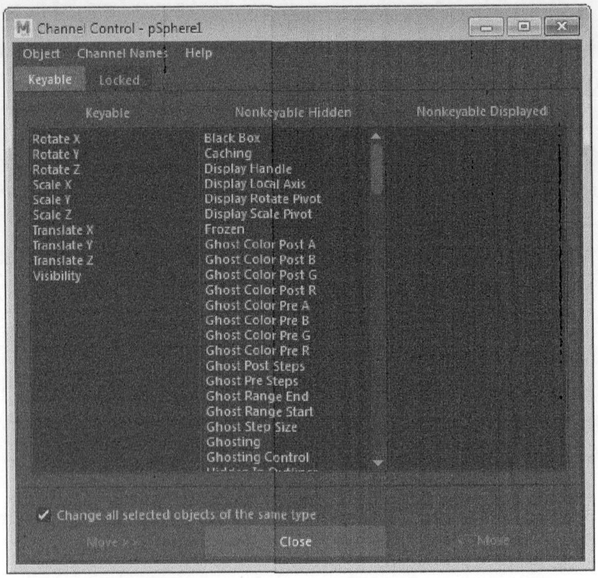

Figure 9-47 *The* ***Channel Control*** *dialog box*

The **Keyable** list box displays the list of attributes that are displayed in the **Channel Box / Layer Editor**, but the **Nonkeyable Hidden** list box lists the attributes that are not displayed and are hidden in the **Channel Box / Layer Editor**. To make the hidden attributes visible, select the attributes from the **Nonkeyable Hidden** list box and choose the **<< Move** button; the selected attributes will move to the **Keyable** list box and will be visible in the **Channel Box / Layer Editor**.

TUTORIALS

Tutorial 1

In this tutorial, you will create the bone structure of a human leg, as shown in Figure 9-48, using **Joint Tool**. **(Expected time: 15 min)**

The following steps are required to complete this tutorial:

a. Create a project folder.
b. Create the bone structure of the leg.
c. Apply IKs to the bone structure.
d. Create the reverse foot setup.
e. Create the pole vector.
f. Save the scene.

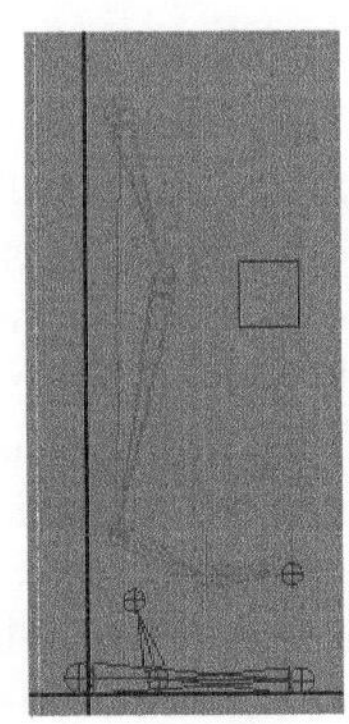

Figure 9-48 *The bone structure of a human leg*

Creating a Project Folder

Create a new project folder with the name *c09_tut1* at *\Documents\maya2017* and then save the file with the name *c09tut1*, as discussed in Tutorial 1 of Chapter 2.

Creating the Bone Structure of Leg

In this section, you will create the bone structure of a human leg.

1. Maximize the side viewport. Select the **Rigging** menuset from the **Menuset** drop-down list in the Status Line. Next, choose **Skeleton > Joints > Create Joints** from the menubar. Next, create the bone structure in the viewport and press the ENTER key, refer to Figure 9-49. (It is recommended that you start the structure from the *Hip* joint).

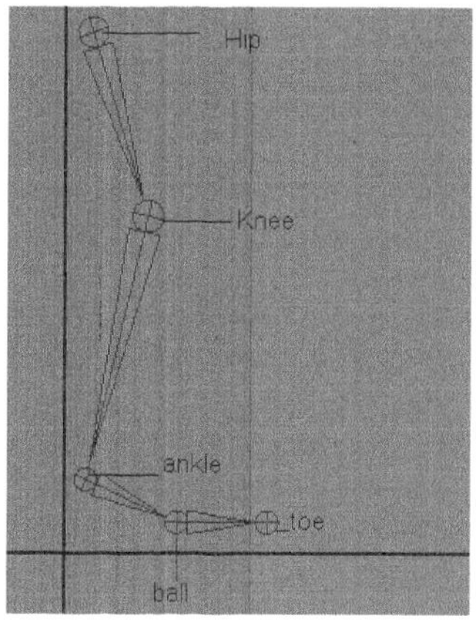

Figure 9-49 *The bone structure*

2. Select the *Hip* joint from the bone structure, refer to Figure 9-49; the entire bone structure is selected. In the **Channel Box / Layer Editor**, click on the default joint name and rename it as ***left_Hipjoint***. Similarly, name other joints as given below:

Joints	Names
Knee	*left_Kneejoint*
Ankle	*left_Anklejoint*
Ball	*left_Balljoint*
Toe	*left_Toejoint*

Note

Naming the joints of a character is very important because it helps you while animating and skinning the character. Use the word 'left' to name the left body joints and 'right' to name the right body joints.

Applying IKs to the Bone Structure

In this section, you will apply IKs to the bone structure.

1. Choose **Skeleton > Ik > Create IK Handle** tool from the menubar.

2. Select the *left_Hipjoint* joint and then the *left_Anklejoint* joint in the viewport; an IK handle is created between these two joints, as shown in Figure 9-50. Rename the IK handle as *ikhandle_ankle* in the **Channel Box / Layer Editor**.

3. Similarly, create other IK handles between the *left_Anklejoint* and *left_Balljoint,* and also between the *left_Balljoint* and *left_Toejoint*, as shown in Figure 9-51. Rename the IK handles as *ikhandle_ball* and *ikhandle_toe*.

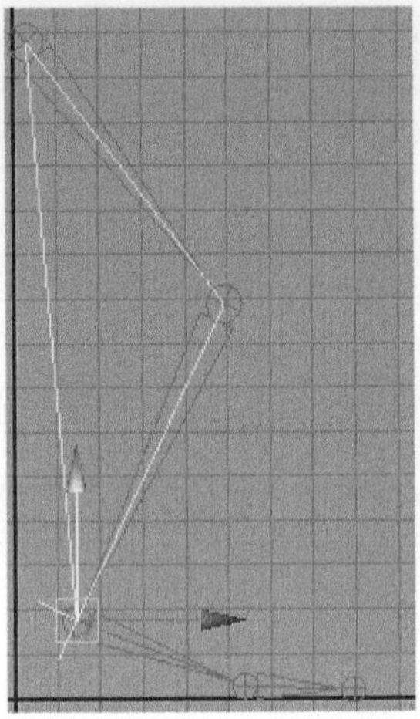

Figure 9-50 *An IK Handle created between joints*

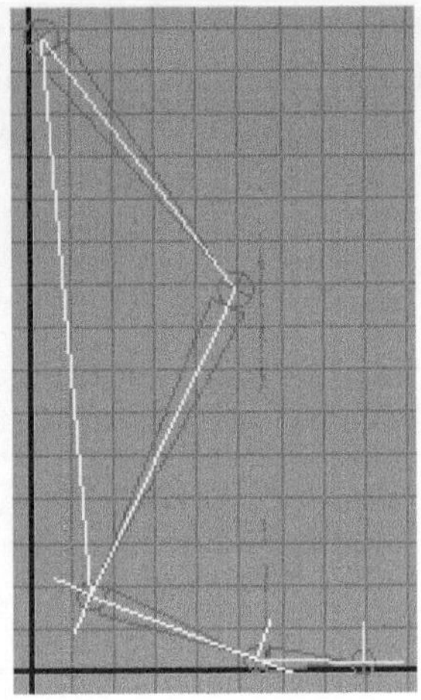

Figure 9-51 *The IK Handles*

> **Tip**
> *To adjust the joints of a bone structure, press and hold the d key and invoke* ***Move Tool****. Once the tool is invoked, you can move the joints to adjust the bone structure. You can also resize the bone structure. To do so, choose* ***Display > Object > Animation > Joint Size*** *from the main menubar; the* ***Joint Display Scale*** *window will be displayed. Now, you can adjust the joint size as required.*

Creating the Reverse Foot Setup

In this section, you need to create the reverse foot setup that will provide control to the movement of the leg.

1. In the side-X viewport, choose **Skeleton > Joints > Create Joints** from the menubar; the **Create Joints** tool is activated. Next, use this tool to create the reverse foot setup, as shown in Figure 9-51. Rename 1, 2, 3, and 4 joints as *rf_leftheeljoint*, *rf_lefttoejoint*, *rf_leftballjoint*, and *rf_leftanklejoint*, respectively, refer to Figure 9-52.

2. Invoke **Move Tool**. Next, select *ikhandle_ankle,* press SHIFT and then select the joint 4, refer to Figure 9-52. Now, press P in the keyboard to make the joint *rf_leftanklejoint* of the reverse foot as parent of *ikhandle_ankle*.

3. Similarly, make the joint *rf_lefttoejoint* as the parent of the *ikhandle_toe* and the joint *rf_leftballjoint* as the parent of the *ikhandle_ball*. Now, hold the reverse foot setup and move the foot as required.

Creating the Pole Vector

In this section, you will create the pole vector to control the movement of the knee joint.

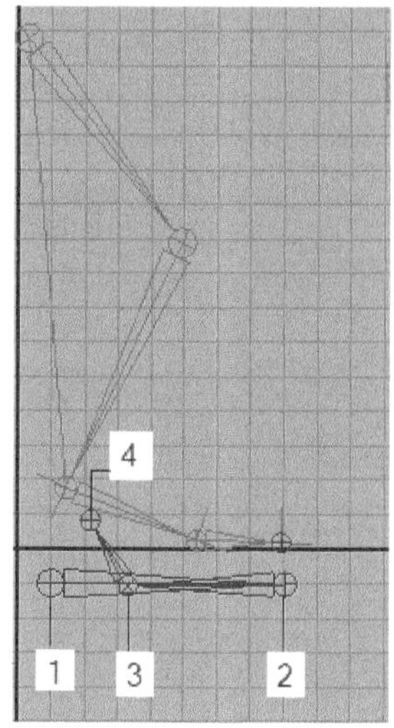

Figure 9-52 *The reverse foot setup*

1. Select *ikhandle_ankle* in the side-X viewport. In the **Attribute Editor**, choose the **ikhandle_ankle** tab and expand the **IK Solver Attributes** area. In this area, select the **Rotate-Plane Solver** option from the **IK-Solver** drop-down list, as shown in Figure 9-53. Next, enter **0**, **1**, **0** in the **Pole Vector** edit boxes.

2. Create the polygon cube in the side-X viewport. Invoke **Move Tool** from the Tool Box and align the cube near the knee in all viewports.

3. Select the polygon cube, press SHIFT, and then select *ikhandle_ankle*. Next, choose **Constrain > Create > Pole Vector** from the menubar; the polygon cube pole vector of the knee is created, as shown in Figure 9-54. Move the cube left and right; the knee joint will move accordingly.

4. Maximize the persp viewport and invoke **Move Tool** from the Tool Box to check the movement of the foot by using IKs and the pole vector.

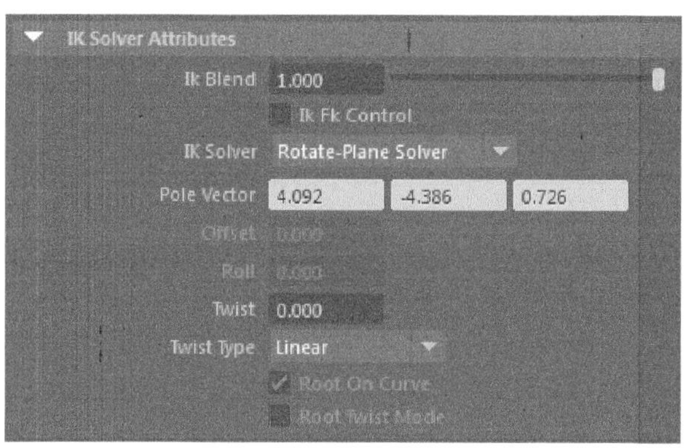

Figure 9-53 *Selecting* ***Rotate-Plane Solver*** *from the* ***IK Solver*** *drop-down list*

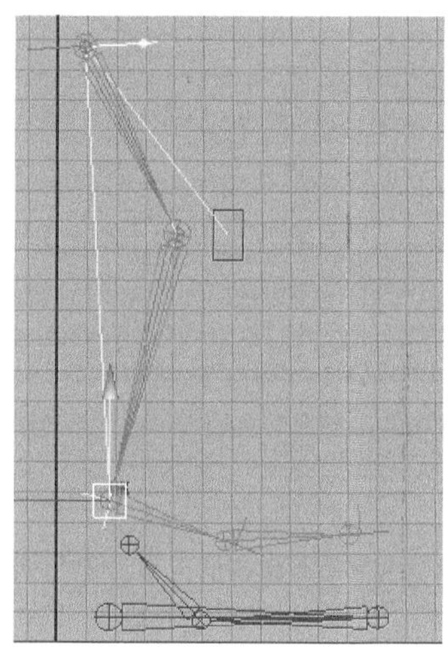

Figure 9-54 *The pole vector constrain*

Saving the Scene

In this section, you need to save the scene that you have created.

1. Choose **File > Save Scene** from the menubar to save the scene.

Tutorial 2

In this tutorial, you will animate a seesaw model by using the **Set Driven Key** tool. The model is shown in Figure 9-55. **(Expected time: 15 min)**

Figure 9-55 A seesaw model

The following steps are required to complete this tutorial:

a. Create a project folder.
b. Download and open the file.
c. Create a driver.
d. Set the driven key.
e. Animate the see-saw model.
f. Save and render the scene.

Creating a Project Folder

Create a new project folder with the name *c09_tut2* at *Documents\maya2017* and then save the file with the name *c09tut2*, as discussed in Tutorial 1 of Chapter 2.

Downloading and Opening the File

In this section, you will download and open the file.

1. Download the *c09_maya_2017_tut.zip* file from *www.cadcim.com*. The path of the file is as follows: *Textbooks > Animation and Visual Effects > Maya > Autodesk Maya 2017: A Comprehensive Guide*.

   Next, extract the contents of the zip file, and save them in the *\Documents* folder.

2. Choose **File > Open Scene** from the menubar; the **Open** dialog box is displayed. In this dialog box, browse to the *c09_maya_2017_tut* folder and select **c09_tut2_start** file from it. Next, choose the **Open** button.

3. Choose **File > Save Scene As** from the menubar; the **Save As** dialog box is displayed. As the project folder is already set, the path *\Documents\maya2017\c09_tut2\scenes* is displayed in the **Look In** drop-down list. Save the file with the name *c09tut2.mb* in this folder.

Creating a Driver

In this section, you need to create a driver for the seesaw model.

1. Maximize the top-Y viewport. Next, choose **Create > Objects > Polygon Primitives > Sphere** from the menubar and create a sphere in this viewport.

2. In the persp viewport, make sure the sphere is selected. In the **Channel Box / Layer Editor**, enter **15** in the **Translate Y** edit box. Also, rename the sphere to ***driver_ball***.

3. Choose **Windows > Editors > Outliner** from the menubar; the **Outliner** window is displayed. Now, select **main_frame** from the **Outliner** window. Press and hold the CTRL key and then select ***driver_ball*** in the **Outliner** window. Next, choose **Modify > Transform > Freeze Transformations** from the menubar; the transformation of the X, Y, and Z axes is set to zero. Close the **Outliner** window and then deselect ***main_frame*** and ***driver_ball*** in the viewport by clicking anywhere in the viewport.

Setting the Driven Key

In this section, you need to set the driven key for the seesaw model.

1. Make sure the **Animation** menuset is selected from the **Menuset** drop-down list in the Status Line. Next, choose **Key > Set > Set Driven Key > Set** from the menubar; the **Set Driven Key** dialog box is displayed. Select **driver_ball** from the viewport and then choose the **Load Driver** button from the **Set Driven Key** dialog box; the **driver_ball** is set as the driver, as shown in Figure 9-56.

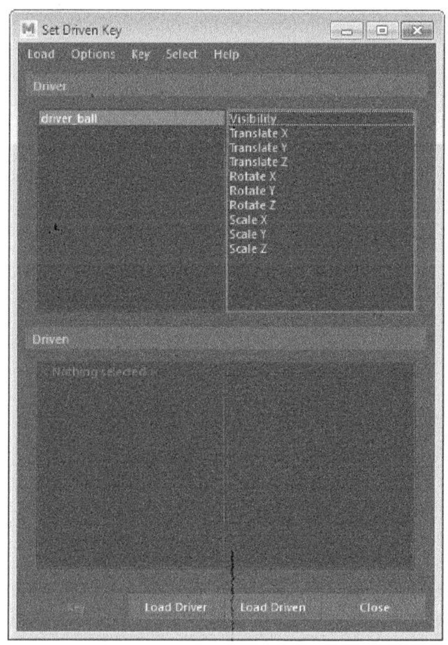

***Figure 9-56** The **Set Driven Key** dialog box*

2. Similarly, select **main_frame** from the viewport and then choose the **Load Driven** button from the **Set Driven Key** dialog box; the **main_frame** is set as driven.

3. In the **Set Driven Key** dialog box, select **driver_ball** and then select the **Translate X** parameter of **driver_ball** in the **Driver** area. Next, select **main_frame** and **Rotate Z** parameters from the **Set Driven Key** dialog box under the **Driven** area. Next, choose the **Key** button; the positions of **driver_ball** and **main_frame** are set.

4. In the **Set Driven Key** dialog box, select **driver_ball**. Next, select the **Translate X** parameter of **driver_ball** in this dialog box and then enter **5** in the **Translate X** parameter in the

Channel Box / Layer Editor. Next, select **main_frame** from the **Set Driven Key** dialog box and then select the **Rotate Z** parameter of **main_frame**. Set **Rotate Z** parameter to **-5** in the **Channel Box / Layer Editor**. Now, choose the **Key** button; the key attributes of **driver_ball** and **main_frame** are set.

5. In the **Set Driven Key** dialog box, select **driver_ball** and then select the **Translate X** parameter of **driver_ball**. Next, set the **Translate X** parameter to **-5** in the **Channel Box / Layer Editor**. Next, select **main_frame**. Next, select the **Rotate Z** parameter of **main_frame** from the **Set Driven Key** dialog box and set **Rotate Z** parameter to **15** in the **Channel Box / Layer Editor**. Choose the **Key** button in the **Set Driven Key** dialog box; a connection is created between **driver_ball** and **main_frame**. Next, close the **Set Driven Key** dialog box.

6. Move **driver_ball** in the viewport toward left and right; the seesaw moves with the movement of the **driver_ball**.

Animating the See-saw Model

In this section, you will animate the see-saw model using the driver ball.

1. Choose the **Animation preferences** button located on the right of the animation playback buttons; the **Preferences** dialog box is displayed. In the **Preferences** dialog box, select **Real-time [24fps]** from the **Playback speed** drop-down list and enter **1** and **48** in the **Animation start/end** edit boxes, respectively. Next, choose the **Save** button to close the dialog box.

2. Select **driver_ball** and move the timeslider to the first frame in the timeline. In the **Channel Box / Layer Editor**, enter **-5** in the **Translate X** edit box and then choose **Key > Set > Set Key** from the menubar; the key is set to the first frame. Alternatively, press S to set the key.

3. Make sure **driver_ball** is selected and move the Time Slider to frame 24. In the **Channel Box / Layer Editor**, enter **5** in the **Translate X** edit box. Choose **Key > Set > Set Key** from the menubar; the **Translate X** value for **driver_ball** is set to the frame 24.

4. Make sure **driver_ball** is selected and move the timeslider to the frame 48. In the **Channel Box / Layer Editor**, enter **-5** in the **Translate X** edit box. Choose **Key > Set > Set Key** from the menubar; the **Translate X** value for **driver_ball** is set to **-5** at the frame 48.

5. Next, choose the **Play forwards** button from the playback control area to preview the animation; the see-saw starts swinging with the movement of ***driver_ball***.

Saving and Rendering the Scene

In this section, you will save the scene that you have created and then render it. You can view the final rendered image sequence of the scene by downloading the *c09_maya_2017_rndr.zip* file from *www.cadcim.com*. The path of the file is as follows: *Textbooks > Animation and Visual Effects > Maya > Autodesk Maya 2017: A Comprehensive Guide.*

1. Choose **File > Save Scene** from the menubar to save the scene.

2. For rendering the scene, refer to Tutorial 1 of Chapter 8.

Tutorial 3

In this tutorial, you will create the model of a palm tree, as shown in Figure 9-57, using the **Bend** deformer. **(Expected time: 30 min)**

Figure 9-57 *The palm tree model*

The following steps are required to complete this tutorial:

a. Create a project folder.
b. Create the trunk.
c. Create leaves.
d. Apply the bend deformer.
e. Save and render the scene.

Creating a Project Folder

Create a new project folder with the name *c09_tut3* at *\Documents\maya2017* and then save the file with the name *c09tut3*, as discussed in Tutorial 1 of Chapter 2.

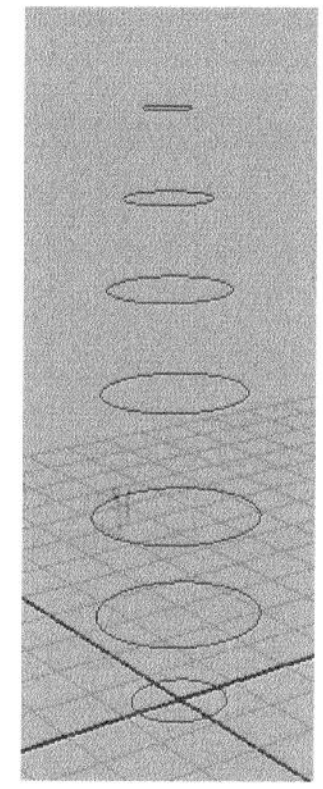

Figure 9-58 *Arrangement of NURBS circles*

Creating the Trunk

In this section, you need to create the trunk of the palm tree using the **Loft** surface method.

1. Maximize the top-Y viewport. Choose **Create > Objects > NURBS Primitives > Circle** from the menubar and create a circle in the top-Y viewport. Press G and then create six more circles of different radii and arrange them at the top of the persp viewport, refer to Figure 9-58.

Note
The G key is used to repeat the last performed action.

2. Select the lowermost circle in the viewport, press and hold the SHIFT key, and then select all circles above it in a sequence. Next, select the **Modeling** menuset from the **Menuset** drop-down list in the Status Line.

3. Choose **Surfaces > Create > Loft** from the menubar; a trunk is created along the selected circles. The trunk of the palm tree is shown in Figure 9-59.

4. Make sure the trunk is selected in the viewport and choose **Modify > Object > Convert > NURBS to Polygons > Option Box** from the menubar; the **Convert NURBS to Polygons Options** dialog box is displayed. Choose **Quads** from the **Type** attribute and **Count** from the **Tessellation method** attribute. Set the required values in this dialog box, as shown in Figure 9-60, and then choose the **Tessellate** button; the NURBS trunk changes to polygons.

5. Make sure the NURBS trunk is selected. Next, select the curves and the surface of the NURBS trunk from the **Outliner** window and then delete them. Next, press and hold the right mouse button over the polygon trunk; a marking menu is displayed. Choose **Vertex** from the marking menu; the vertex selection mode of polygon trunk is activated. Select the topmost vertices of the trunk and select the **Modeling** menuset from the **Menuset** drop-down list in the Status Line. Next, choose **Edit Mesh > Components > Merge To Center** from the menubar; the selected vertices are merged to the center. Next, press and hold the right mouse button over the polygon trunk; a marking menu is displayed. Choose **Object Mode** from the marking menu; the object selection mode of polygon trunk is activated.

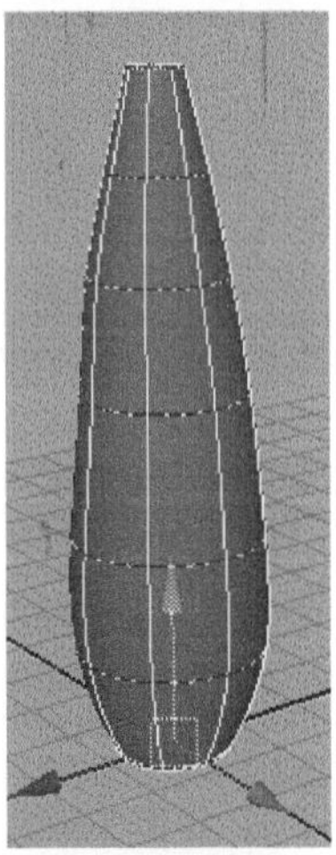

Figure 9-59 The trunk of palm tree

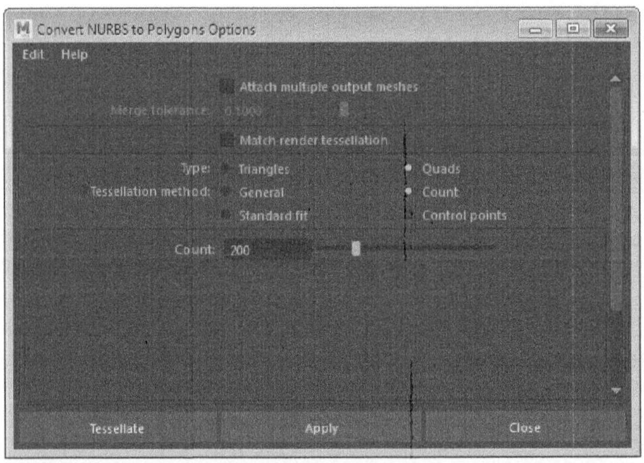

*Figure 9-60 The **Convert NURBS to Polygons Options** dialog box*

Note
The surface and curves used for creating the trunk will not be used in this tutorial.

Creating Leaves

In this section, you need to create the leaves of the palm tree using polygon primitives.

1. Maximize the top-Y viewport and choose **Create > Object > Polygon Primitives > Cone > Option Box** from the menubar; the **Tool Settings (Polygon Cone Tool)** window is displayed in the left in viewport. Enter the following values in the window:

   Radius: **0.2** Height: **40** Height Divisions: **50** Axis: **X**

   Click in the top-Y viewport to create the petiole of the leaf. Next, invoke **Move Tool** from the Tool Box and align the petiole with the trunk, as shown in Figure 9-61. Maximize the front-Z viewport and move the petiole up along the Y-axis.

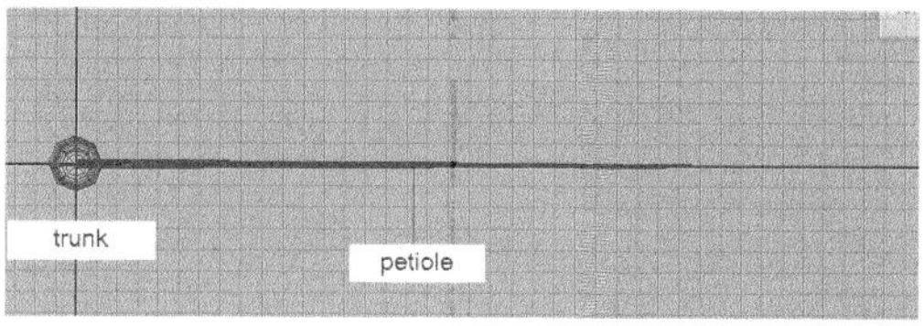

***Figure 9-61** Aligning petiole with the trunk*

2. Maximize the top-Y viewport and choose **Create > Object > Polygon Primitives > Plane > Option Box** from the menubar; the **Tool Settings (Polygon Plane Tool)** window is displayed. Enter the following values for plane in the window:

   Width: **1** Height: **6** Height Divisions: **6**

   Click in the top-Y viewport to create a plane, as shown in Figure 9-62.

3. Press and hold the right mouse button over the plane; a marking menu is displayed. Next, choose **Vertex** from the marking menu; the vertex selection mode is activated. Select vertices and then invoke **Scale Tool** from the Tool Box and adjust the vertices to get the desired shape of the leaf, as shown in Figure 9-63.

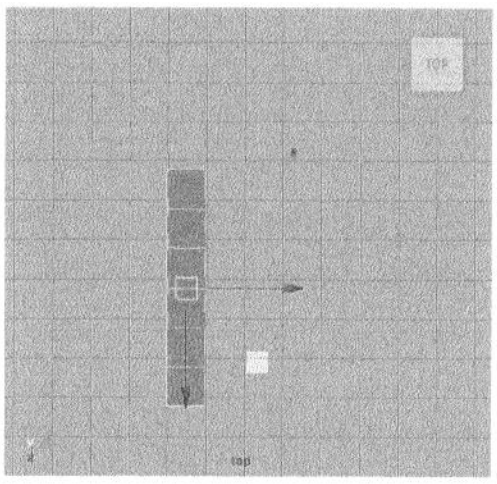

***Figure 9-62** The plane for creating a leaf*

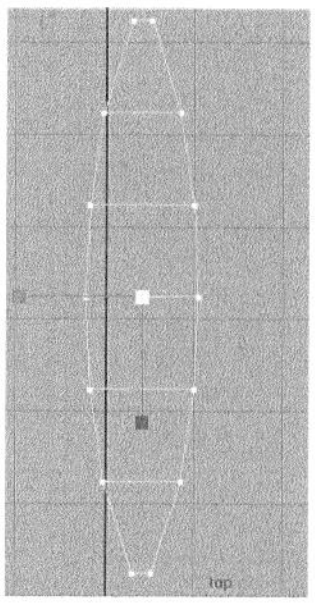

***Figure 9-63** The final shape of the leaf*

4. Press and hold the right mouse button over the plane and then choose **Object Mode** from the marking menu displayed; the object selection mode is activated. Invoke **Move Tool** and press and hold the D key on the keyboard and then set it to the pivot point of the leaf,

as shown in Figure 9-64. Next, adjust the leaf with the petiole, as shown in Figure 9-65. Maximize the front-Z viewport and move the leaf up along the Y-axis.

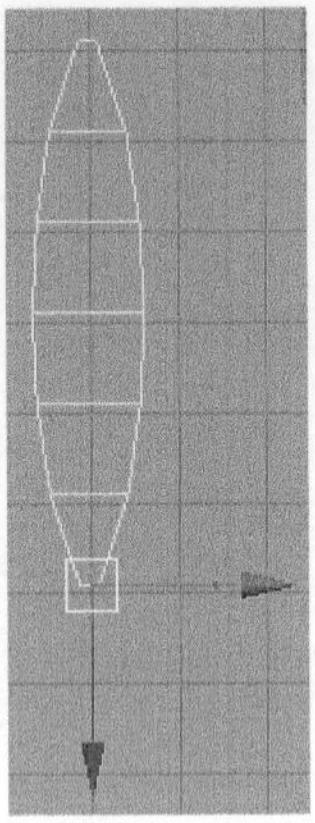

Figure 9-64 *Adjusting the pivot point of the leaf*

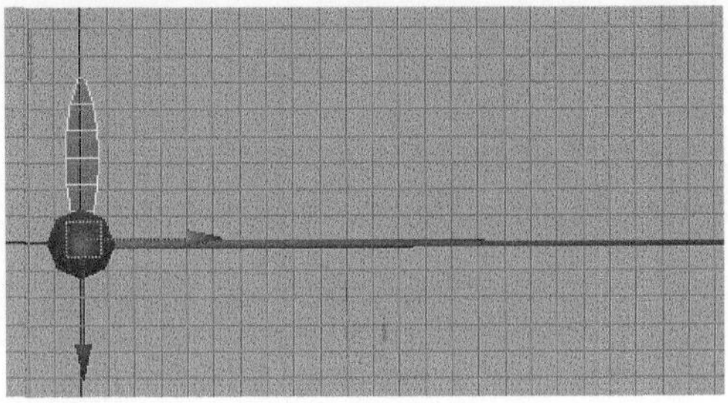

Figure 9-65 *A leaf aligned with the petiole*

5. Maximize the top-Y viewport. Make sure the leaf created is selected in the top-Y viewport and press CTRL+D; a duplicate leaf is created. Move the duplicate leaf to the opposite side of the original leaf. Next, select both the leaves and press SHIFT+D. Now, move the duplicate leaves and then press SHIFT+D multiple times; multiple copies of the leaf are created. Next, arrange the leaves on the petioles, as shown in Figure 9-66.

6. Invoke **Scale Tool** from the Tool Box and scale the leaves individually to get the effect shown in Figure 9-67. Now, choose **Modify > Pivot > Center Pivot** from the menubar; the pivot point is set at the center of the leaf.

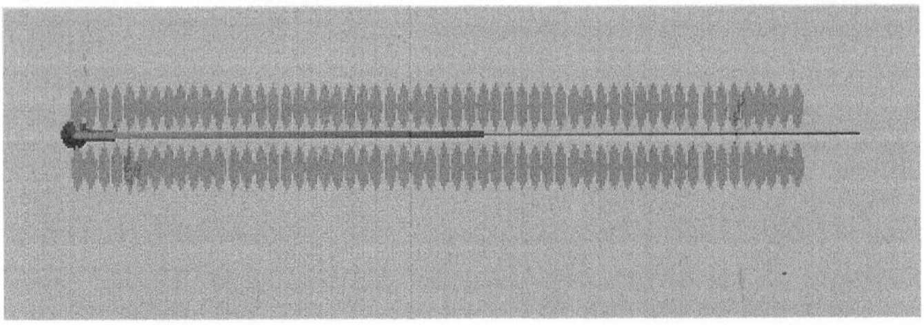

Figure 9-66 *Duplicate leaves aligned with the petiole*

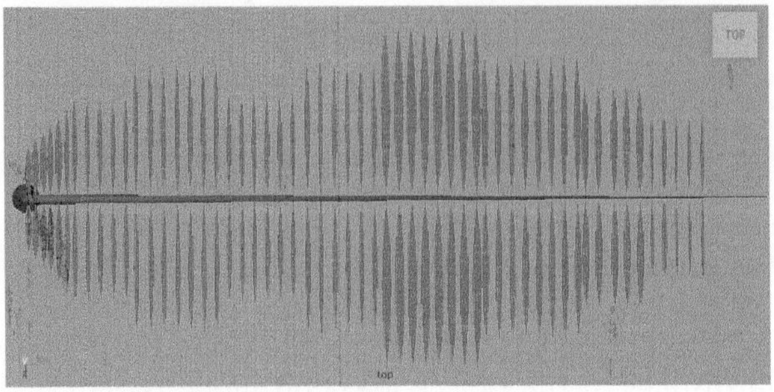

Figure 9-67 *Leaves after scaling*

7. Press and hold the SHIFT key and select all leaves and petioles from the viewport. Next, press CTRL+G to group them.

Applying the Bend Deformer

In this section, you need to apply the **Bend** deformer to leaves to give them a realistic effect.

1. Maximize the persp viewport. Select a leaf from the bunch of leaves and press the up arrow key on the keyboard to select the complete group, as shown in Figure 9-68.

Figure 9-68 *Position of leaves and petiole*

2. Choose the **Rigging** menuset from the Status Line and then choose **Deform > Create > Nonlinear > Bend** from the menubar; the **Bend** deformer is applied to leaves.

3. Make sure the **Bend** deformer is selected. In the **Channel Box / Layer Editor**, set the parameters as follows:

   Rotate X: **90** Rotate Z: **90**

4. Make sure the **Bend** deformer is selected. Press CTRL+A; the **bend1Handle** tab is displayed in the **Attribute Editor**. In the **Attribute Editor**, choose the **bend1** tab and enter **-100** in the **Curvature** edit box; the bend effect is applied, as shown in Figure 9-69.

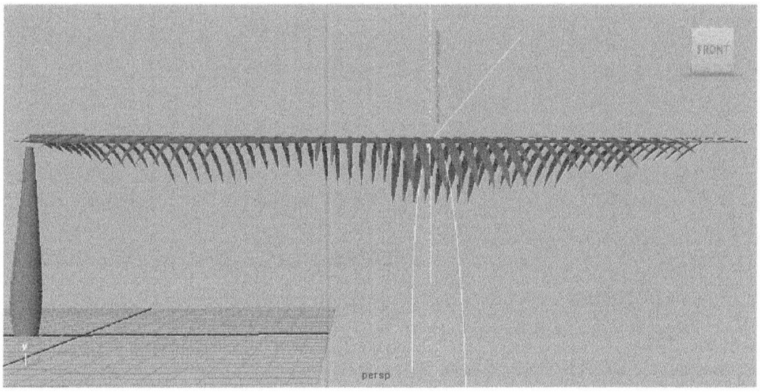

Figure 9-69 *Leaves after applying the **Bend** deformer*

5. Select the leaves and the petiole, as discussed earlier. Choose **Deform > Create > Nonlinear > Bend** from the menubar; the **Bend** deformer is applied to leaves.

6. Make sure the **Bend** deformer is selected. In the **Channel Box / Layer Editor**, enter **90** in the **Rotate Z** edit box.

7. Make sure the **Bend** deformer is selected. Press CTRL+A; the **bend2Handle** tab is displayed in the **Attribute Editor**. In the **Attribute Editor**, choose the **bend2** tab and enter **-50** in the **Curvature** edit box; the bend effect is applied, refer to Figure 9-70.

8. Select all leaves and the petiole and choose **Edit > Delete > Delete > Delete All by Type > History** from the menubar; the history of commands/actions performed on leaves is deleted.

9. Align the leaves with the trunk, as shown in Figure 9-70.

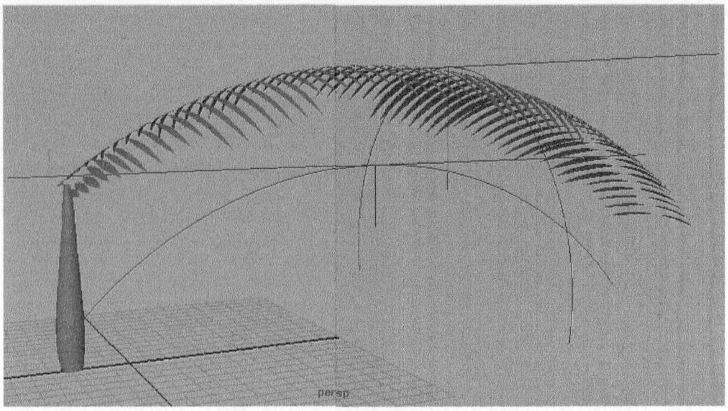

Figure 9-70 *Leaves aligned with the trunk*

10. Create copies of leaves and align them with the trunk to get the final output, as shown in Figure 9-71.

Figure 9-71 *The final output of the palm tree model*

11. Select all leaves and the trunk of the tree from the viewport, and then press CTRL+G; the leaves and trunk are grouped.

Saving and Rendering the Scene

In this section, you will save the scene that you have created and then render it. You can view the final rendered image of the scene by downloading the *c09_maya_2017_rndr.zip* file from *www.cadcim.com*. The path of the file is as follows: *Textbooks > Animation and Visual Effects > Maya > Autodesk Maya 2017: A Comprehensive Guide.*

1. Choose **File > Save Scene** from the menubar to save the scene.

2. Maximize the persp viewport, if it is not already maximized. Choose the **Render the current frame** button from the Status Line; the **Render View** window is displayed. This window shows the final output of the scene, refer to Figure 9-57.

Self-Evaluation Test

Answer the following questions and then compare them to those given at the end of this chapter:

1. Which of the following joints provides free movement to a joint in a skeleton?

   (a) **Hinge joint** (b) **Universal joint**
   (c) **Ball joint** (d) None of these

2. Which of the following deformers is used to modify an object using lattices?

   (a) **Cluster** (b) **Lattice**
   (c) **Flare** (d) **Wrap**

3. __________ is a group of hierarchical structures that provide motion to an object.

4. __________ is the process of binding the skeleton to objects.

5. The __________ deformer is used to deform a particular area of a polygonal mesh.

6. The __________ are used to impose specific limits to objects.

7. The **Pole Vector** constraint is used to move the end of a pole vector based on the movement of the other object it is constrained with. (T/F)

8. The **Flare** deformer is used to taper an object in the X, Y, and Z axes. (T/F)

9. A Muscle is a parametric type of NURBS shape that can be deformed, whereas a Simple Muscle type uses the NURBS model with a sine deformer to deform the object. (T/F)

10. The **Jiggle** deformer is used to shake an object or a part of an object while it is being animated. (T/F)

Review Questions

Answer the following questions:

1. Which of the following deformers is used to morph an object?

   (a) **Cluster** (b) **Blend shape**
   (c) **Lattice** (d) **Flare**

2. Which of the following data types is used to create a vector attribute that has three floating point values?

   (a) **Vector** (b) **Float**
   (c) **Enum** (d) **Integer**

3. The __________ deformer helps you deform high density surface meshes without adjusting vertices manually.

4. The __________ deformer is used to create a rounded deformation on an object.

5. The __________ constrain is used to match the orientation of one object with the other such that the objects are aligned together.

6. The __________ tools are used to alter the geometry of an object.

7. You should avoid changing the number of CVs, vertices, or other lattice points after applying a deformer to an object. (T/F)

8. In inverse kinematics, the object at the bottom of a hierarchy is used to animate the entire chain. (T/F)

9. A constraint is used to restrict the motion of a body to a particular mode while it is animated. (T/F)

10. You can apply the **Blend Shape** deformer only to the objects that have equal number of vertices. (T/F)

EXERCISES

The image sequence of the scenes used in the following exercises can be accessed by downloading the *c09_maya_2017_exr.zip* from *www.cadcim.com*. The path of the file is as follows: *Textbooks > Animation and Visual Effects > Maya > Autodesk Maya 2017: A Comprehensive Guide.*

Exercise 1

Create a simple toy car and then use the **Set Driven Key** method to set keys for the doors of the toy car. **(Expected time: 30 min)**

Exercise 2

Create a pencil stand with a pencil in it. Next, apply texture to the model. Apply the **Lattice** deformer to the pencil. Next, use the keyframe animation technique to make the pencil jump out of the pencil stand, refer Figure 9-72. **(Expected time: 45 min)**

***Figure 9-72** The pencil jumping out of the pencil stand*

Answers to Self-Evaluation Test

1. c, **2.** b, **3.** Skeleton, **4.** Skinning, **5. Cluster**, **6. Constrain**, **7.** T, **8.** T, **9.** F, **10.** T

Chapter 10

Paint Effects

Learning Objectives

After completing this chapter, you will be able to:

- *Use the Content Browser window*
- *Render the paint effect strokes*
- *Use shadow effects*
- *Modify the paint effect brush settings*

INTRODUCTION

In Autodesk Maya, you can create realistic natural objects such as trees, plants, rain, and so on by using paint effects. The paint effects let you paint a scene by using a mouse or a tablet. Different brushes are used to create effects such as rain, thunder, storm, and so on. You can also animate paint effects to create natural motion. All these paint effects and brushes are available in the **Content Browser** window. The **Content Browser** window is discussed next.

WORKING WITH THE Content Browser WINDOW

Menubar: Windows > Editors > General Editors > Content Browser

The **Content Browser** window comprises of preloaded animation clips, default brushes, shader libraries or texture libraries, and so on. To open this window, choose **Windows > Editors > General Editors > Content Browser** from the menubar. The **Content Browser** window is displayed in Figure 10-1. There are various nodes in this window such as **Animation**, **FX**, **Modeling**, **Paint Effects**, and so on. When you choose a particular node, its corresponding nodes will be displayed in the right pane of the **Content Browser** window. For example, when you choose the **Paint Effects** node in the left pane of the **Content Browser** window, various paint stroke nodes will be displayed in the right pane.

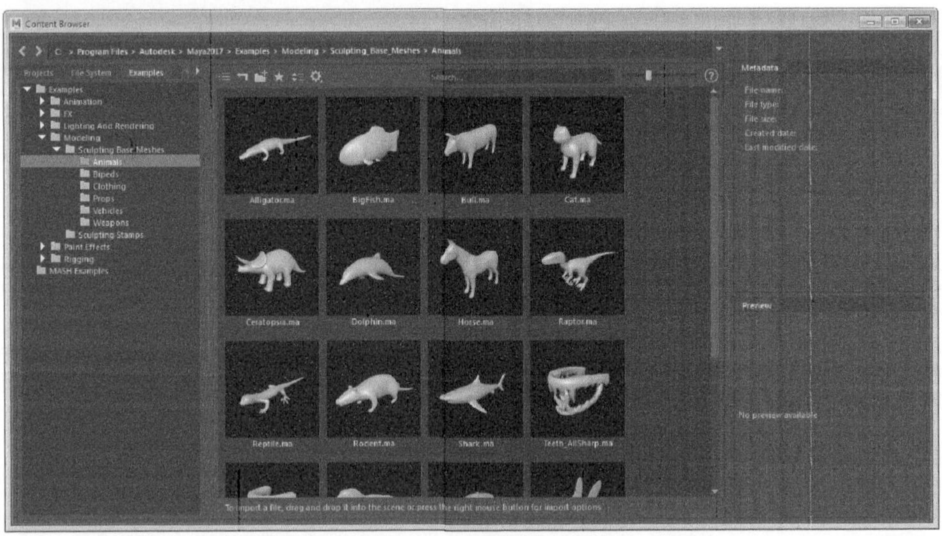

*Figure 10-1 The **Content Browser** window*

Creating Objects

You can create a realistic object such as trees, buildings, and so on using the **Content Browser** window. For example, to create a tree, choose the **Paint Effects > Tree** node at the left pane of the **Content Browser** window; various tree nodes will be displayed in the right pane of the **Content Browser** window. Now, choose the **oakLimb.mel** paint stroke from the displayed options; the shape of the cursor will change into a pencil. Next, activate the top viewport. Press and hold the left mouse button and drag the cursor to create the tree mesh. Next, activate the persp viewport and render the view to get the output shown in Figure 10-2.

Figure 10-2 The rendered image

You can also edit the paint stroke created in the viewport. To do so, select the paint stroke created in the viewport; the name of the selected paint stroke will be displayed in the **INPUTS** area of the **Channel Box / Layer Editor**. Click on the paint stroke name to expand its attributes. You can now modify the selected paint stroke as per your requirement using the attributes in the **Channel Box / Layer Editor**.

You can also draw the paint strokes in the viewport. To do so, choose **Windows > Modeling Editors > Paint Effects** from the menubar; the **Paint Effects** window will be displayed, as shown in Figure 10-3.

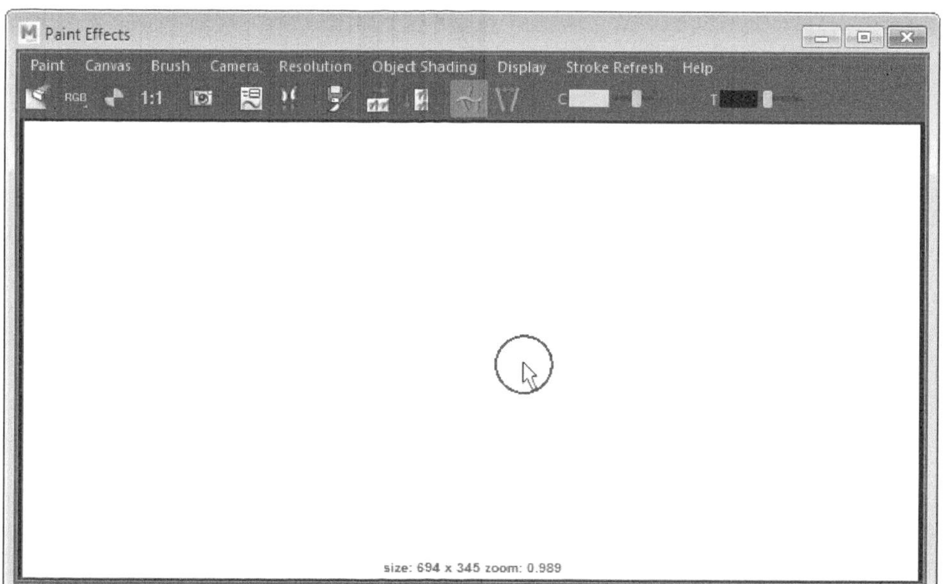

*Figure 10-3 The **Paint Effects** window*

WORKING WITH THE Paint Effects WINDOW

The **Paint Effects** window has its own menubar and toolbar, as shown in Figure 10-4. It consists of menus such as **Paint**, **Canvas**, **Brush**, **Cameras**, and so on, refer to Figure 10-4. The tools in this toolbar of the **Paint Effects** window are used to create different effects by using the paint strokes. To invoke a paint stroke brush, choose the **Get brush** tool from the toolbar, refer to Figure 10-4; the **Content Browser** window will be displayed. Choose the required paint brush stroke from the **Content Browser** window and then paint the stroke in the **Paint Effects** window. You can also edit the attributes of the selected paint brush stroke by using the options in this window. To do so, select the paint stroke from the **Content Browser** window and choose the **Edit template brush** tool from the toolbar; the **Paint Effects Brush Settings** dialog box will be displayed. Alternatively, press CTRL+B to invoke the **Paint Effects Brush Settings** window, as shown in Figure 10-5. Some of the basic options of this window are discussed next.

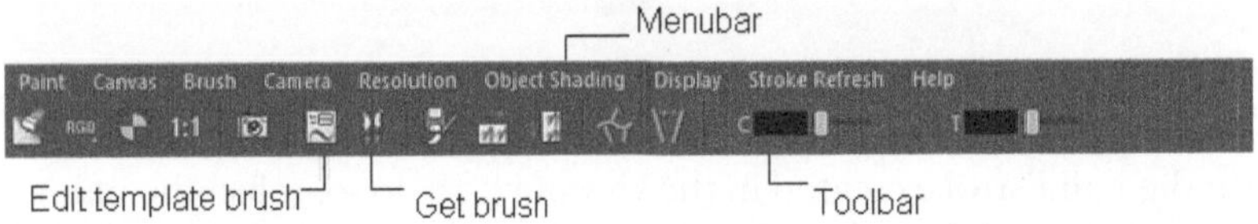

*Figure 10-4 The menubar and toolbar of the **Paint Effects** window*

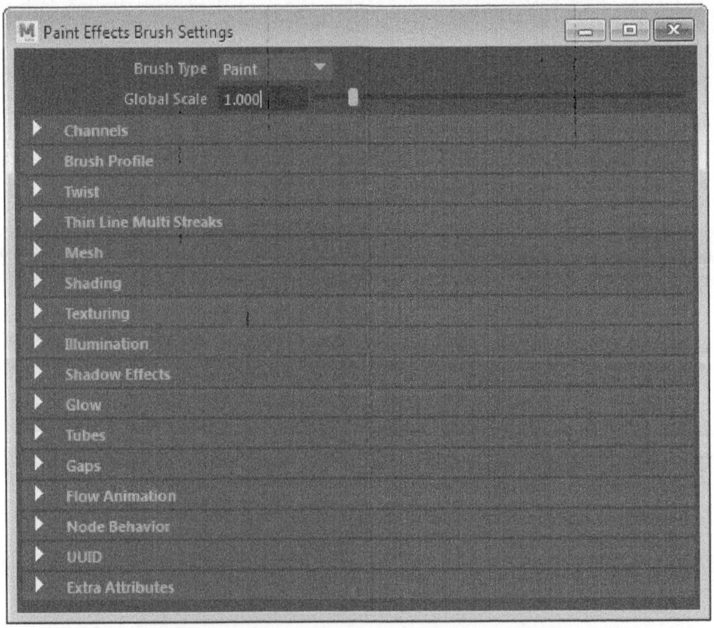

*Figure 10-5 The **Paint Effects Brush Settings** window*

Brush Type

The options in the **Brush Type** drop-down list are used to select the type of brush you want to use. The shape used by the brushes is defined by the brush attributes. The **Paint** brush type applies the paint to stroke path according to the brush attributes you have set. The **Smear** brush type distorts the stroke (paint) already applied to the canvas or scene. If you have enabled fake shadows, the shadows will smear as well. The **Blur** brush type is used to soften the paint already applied to the canvas. The **Erase** brush type removes the paint from the canvas, revealing the color of the canvas. The **ThinLine** brush type allows large numbers of brush stroke quickly than the **Paint** brush type. The **Mesh** brush type is used to create accurate conical geometry with textures that correctly map on the surface.

Global Scale

The **Global Scale** attribute is used to change the value of the brush attributes by a common factor so that you can paint the same stroke in different sizes. When you specify a value for this attribute, the paint effect is scaled uniformly by this value. The default value of this option is 1. Figures 10-6 and 10-7 show an object created by specifying two different values for the **Global Scale** attribute.

Figure 10-6 *Object with the* ***Global Scale*** *value =* ***1***

Figure 10-7 *Object with the* ***Global Scale*** *value =* ***2***

> **Tip**
> *You can interactively specify a value for the* ***Global Scale*** *attribute. To do so, press and hold the left mouse button and then drag to the left or right.*

Channels

Generally, a rendered image consists of three channels: red, green, and blue. These channels represent amount of red, green, and blue colors in the image. Some images may also contain some additional channels such as alpha, mask, and depth. The depth channel is also referred to as Z depth or Z buffer channel. These additional channels are used extensively when artwork is composited in a compositing software such as Fusion or Nuke. By default, paint effects contain three color channels (RGB) and an alpha channel. The attributes in the **Channels** area are used to specify the depth, color, and alpha settings. In the **Paint Effects Brush Settings** window, click on the arrow on the left of the **Channels** area to expand it. On doing so, the **Depth**, **Modify Depth**, **Modify Color**, and **Modify Alpha** check boxes will be displayed. Select the **Depth** check box to create a depth channel. You will notice that brush strokes in the scene appear more natural and realistic. Select the **Modify Depth** check box to paint the depth channel. Select the **Modify Color** and **Modify Alpha** check boxes to paint the color and alpha channels, respectively.

Brush Profile

The attributes in the **Brush Profile** area are used to set the brush settings. On expanding this area, various options will be displayed, as shown in Figure 10-8. Some of these options are discussed next.

Brush Width

The **Brush Width** attribute is used to define the width of the brush. The brush width is defined by the outline of the paint effect generated. Enter a value in the **Brush Width** edit box or move the slider on its right to set the value of the brush width.

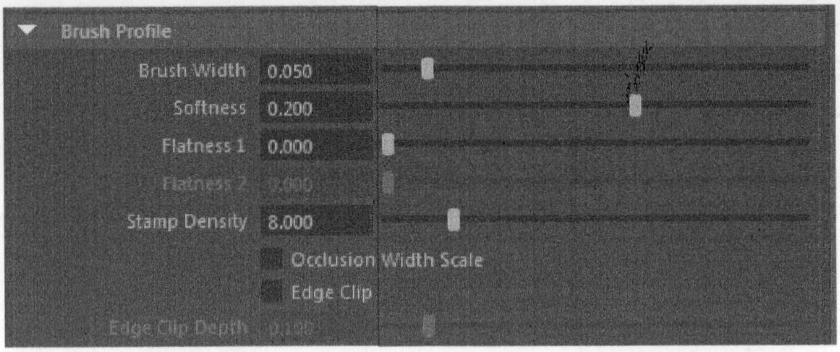

*Figure 10-8 The **Brush Profile** area*

Softness

The **Softness** attribute is used to define the blurriness on the edges of the stroke path. The higher the softness value, the more blurred will be the edges. Refer to Figures 10-9 and 10-10 for variations in the **Softness** value.

*Figure 10-9 Paint stroke with **Softness** = 0*

*Figure 10-10 Paint stroke with **Softness** = 1*

Flatness 1 and Flatness 2

These attributes are used to flatten the paint strokes along the stroke path or to flat each tube at its base and tip. If you are drawing simple strokes, the **Flatness 1** option defines the flatness of the paint strokes along the stroke paths. However, if you are drawing tubes, the **Flatness 1** and **Flatness 2** defines the flatness of each tube at its base and tip. Figures 10-11 and 10-12 show the paint strokes created by using different values of flatness.

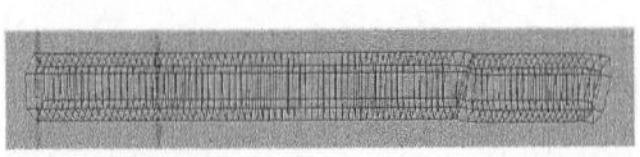

*Figure 10-11 Paint stroke with **Flatness 1** = 0*

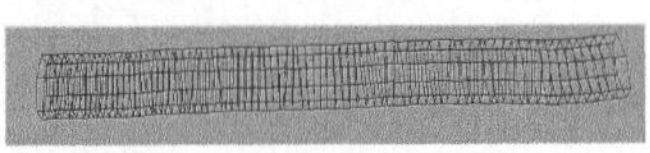

*Figure 10-12 Paint stroke with **Flatness 1** = 0.5*

Stamp Density

When you draw strokes on the canvas, the paint is applied to strokes in overlapping stamps. If a stroke has no tube, the stamps will be applied along the stroke path. However, if a stroke has tubes, the stamps will be applied along the tube path. The **Stamp Density** attribute defines the number of stamps to be applied along the path. The **Stamp Density** attribute is related to the

Brush Width attribute. For example, if you specify a value of 3 for the **Brush Width** attribute and a value of 6 to the **Stamp Density** option, there will be 8 stamps in every 3 units of path.

Occlusion Width Scale

Select this check box if you are using a toon shader. This option reduces the stamp size if foreground objects are overlapping the stamp.

Edge Clip, Edge Clip Depth

Select the **Edge Clip** check box to render 3D strokes as flat 2D strokes. It gives an illusion as if the strokes are directly painted on the texture of a surface. The **Edge Clip Depth** option controls the distance between the surface and a point beyond which the stroke will become visible.

Twist

The attributes in the **Twist** area are used to twist tubes around their own axis as they grow. When you expand the **Twist** area, some more attributes will be displayed, as shown in Figure 10-13. These options are discussed next.

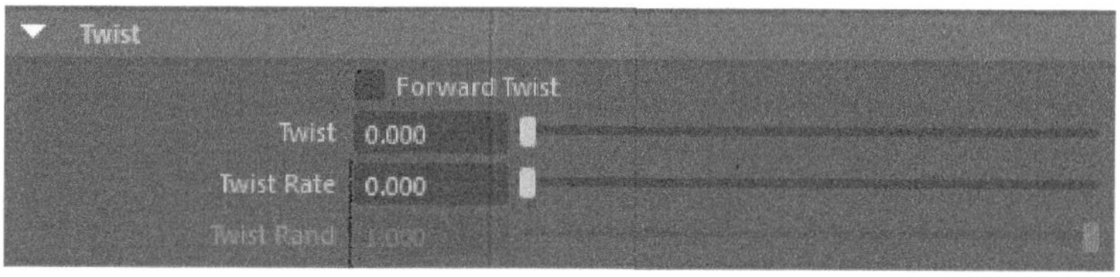

Figure 10-13 *The **Twist** area*

Forward Twist

When this check box is selected, the flat sides of tubes and textures always face the camera.

Twist

The **Twist** attribute defines the initial value of the twist. This attribute is affected by the **Flatness 1** and **Flatness 2** options. Twist is noticeable in the strokes only if the value of the **Flatness 1** and **Flatness 2** options is greater than 0.

Twist Rate

This attribute controls the strength of twist along the length of the strokes. Twist will be only noticeable in the strokes if the **Flatness 1** and **Flatness 2** options' value is greater than 0. Figure 10-14 shows the paint stroke with **Tube Rate** value set to **0** and Figure 10-15 shows the paint stroke with **Tube Rate** value set to **3**.

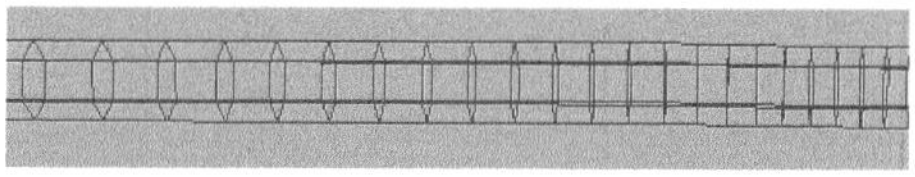

Figure 10-14 *Paint stroke with **Tube Rate = 0***

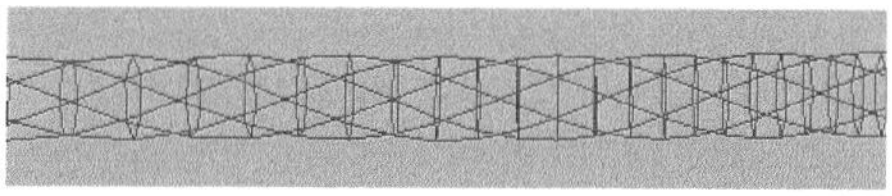

Figure 10-15 *Paint stroke with **Tube Rate = 3***

Twist Rand

This attribute is used to define the randomness applied to the twist.

Mesh

The attributes in the **Mesh** area are used to define the mesh brush. On expanding this area, the **Mesh** area will be displayed, as shown in Figure 10-16. The options in this area are discussed next.

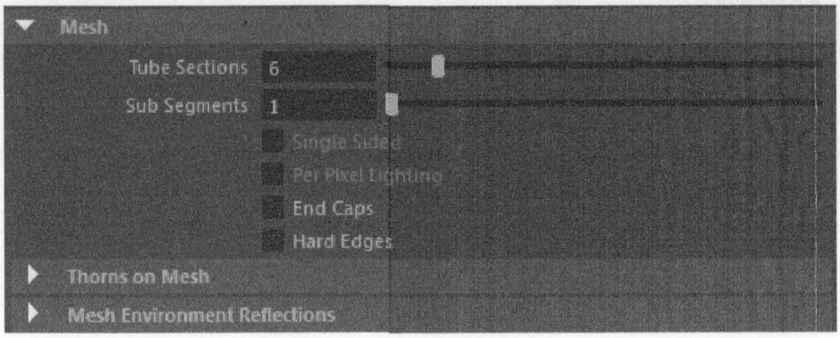

Figure 10-16 The ***Mesh*** *area*

Tube Sections

This attribute is used to define the number of points in the circle which are swept along the tube.

Sub Segments

This attribute is used to set the number of cross-sections per segment of the paint stroke.

Single Sided

This check box is used to cull away the facing triangles of the paint strokes.

Per Pixel Lighting

This check box is used to light up each pixel opposite to the vertices in the paint strokes.

End Caps

This check box is used to add end cap geometry to tubes.

Hard Edges

When this check box is selected, the lighting of the object is affected and the edges around tubes appear hard.

Thorns on Mesh

The attributes in the **Thorns on Mesh** area are used to add thorns on a mesh object. By default, the attributes in this area are inactive. To activate them, select the **Mesh** brush type from the **Brush Type** drop-down list and then expand the **Thorns on Mesh** area. Next, choose the **Branch Thorns** check box to activate the remaining options, refer to Figure 10-17. Note that the thorns are not visible in the viewport. They are visible only at the time of rendering. Figures 10-18 and 10-19 show the paint strokes before and after using the options of the **Thorns on Mesh** area. You can modify the values of density, elevation, length, base width, tip width, specular, and so on for thorns in this area to get the desired result.

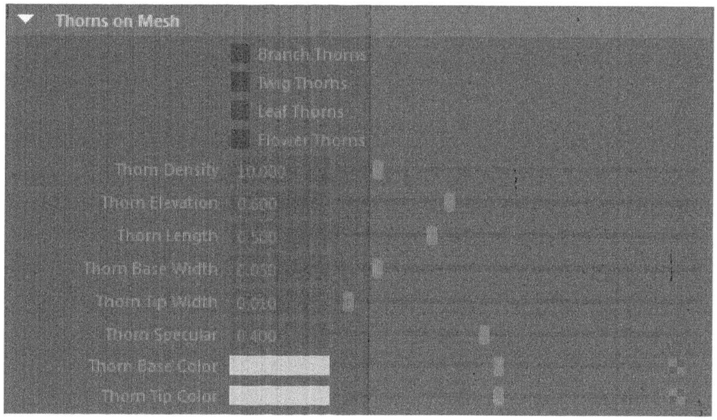

***Figure 10-17** The expanded **Thorns on Mesh** area*

***Figure 10-18** Paint stroke before using the **Thorns on Mesh** attribute*

***Figure 10-19** Paint stroke after using the **Thorns on Mesh** attribute*

Shading

The attributes in the **Shading** area are used to define the shading of the brush strokes. These options will be displayed on expanding this area, as shown in Figure 10-20, and are discussed next.

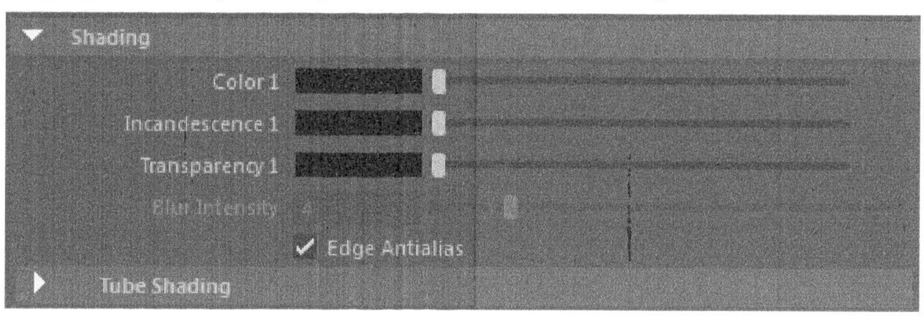

***Figure 10-20** The **Shading** area*

Color 1

Set the **Color 1** attribute to specify the basic color of the paint stroke.

Incandescence 1

The **Incandescence 1** attribute is used to self-illuminate the paint stroke. If you have drawn simple strokes, this attribute controls the glow of the strokes. However, if you have drawn strokes with tubes, this attribute controls the glow of roots of tubes.

Transparency 1

The **Transparency 1** attribute defines the opacity of the paint stroke. If you have drawn simple strokes, this attribute controls the opacity of the strokes. However, if you have drawn strokes with tubes, this attribute controls opacity of the roots of tubes.

Blur Intensity

The **Blur Intensity** attribute is used to apply blurriness to the brush. This attribute will be available only if **Brush Type** is set to **Blur**.

Edge Antialias

By default, the **Edge Antialias** check box is selected. As a result, the edges appear smooth. If you want rough edges, deselect this check box.

Illumination

The attributes in this area are used to change the appearance of the brush strokes by using the lighting, refer to Figure 10-21. Select the **Illuminated** check box to affect the appearance of the stroke. If you clear this check box, no shaded areas or specularity will be visible on the paint strokes even if there are lights in the scene. The **Real Lights** check box will be active only, if you have selected the **Illuminated** check box. When the **Real Lights** check box is selected, the lights in the scene determine the position of shading and specular highlights. If this check box is not selected, a directional paint effects light will be used. You can define its direction by using the **Light Direction** attribute but you cannot change any other attribute of the directional light. Figures 10-22 and 10-23 show an object before and after using the options of the **Illumination** area.

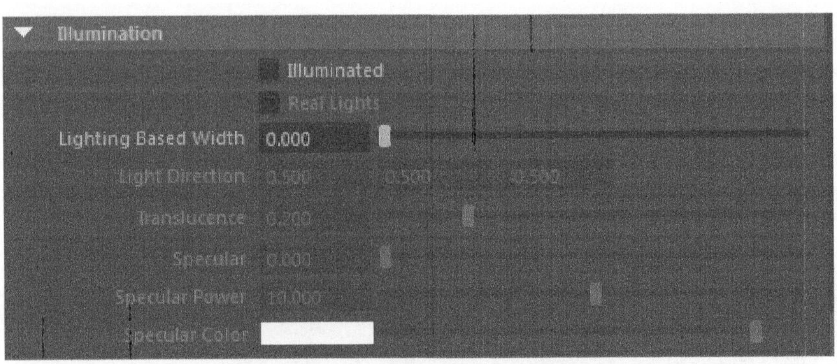

***Figure 10-21** The **Illumination** area*

*Figure 10-22 Paint stroke with the **Illuminated** check box cleared*

*Figure 10-23 Paint stroke with the **Illuminated** check box selected*

Shadow Effects

The attributes in the **Shadow Effects** area are used to apply shadow effect to brush strokes. To apply this effect to brush strokes, expand the **Shadow Effects** area, refer to Figure 10-24, and then adjust the attributes as required to assign the shadow effect to the brush strokes. Some of the attributes in the **Shadow Effects** area are explained next.

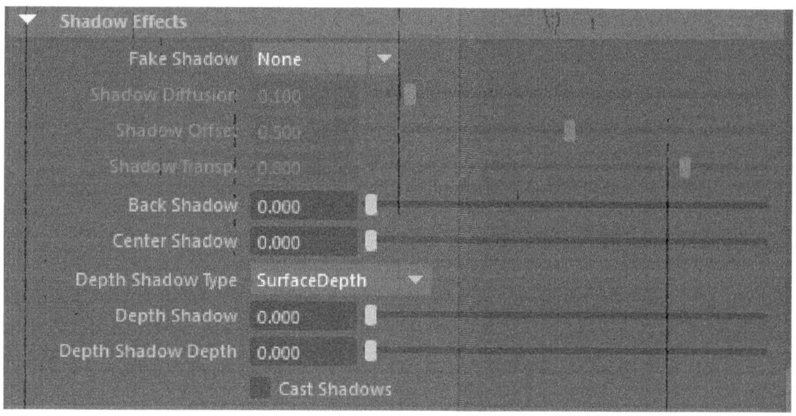

*Figure 10-24 The **Shadow Effects** area*

Fake Shadow

The options in the **Fake Shadow** drop-down list are used to create fake shadows for the brush strokes. It has three options: **None**, **2D Offset**, and **3D Cast**. The **2D Offset** option is used to create a drop shadow like effect. The **3D Cast** option is used to create a flat surface below the stroke and then to cast shadow on that imaginary surface.

Shadow Diffusion

The **Shadow Diffusion** attribute is used to control the softness of fake shadows in a scene, refer to Figures 10-25 and 10-26.

*Figure 10-25 Paint stroke with the **Shadow Diffusion** value = 0*

*Figure 10-26 Paint stroke with the **Shadow Diffusion** value = 1*

Shadow Offset

The **Shadow Offset** attribute is used to control the distance between the shadow and the casting stroke. This attribute is inactive by default. To activate this attribute, select **2D Offset** from the **Fake Shadow** drop-down list. Next, set the offset distance in the **Shadow Offset** edit box or move the slider on its right as required. Figures 10-27 and 10-28 show an object with different shadow offset values.

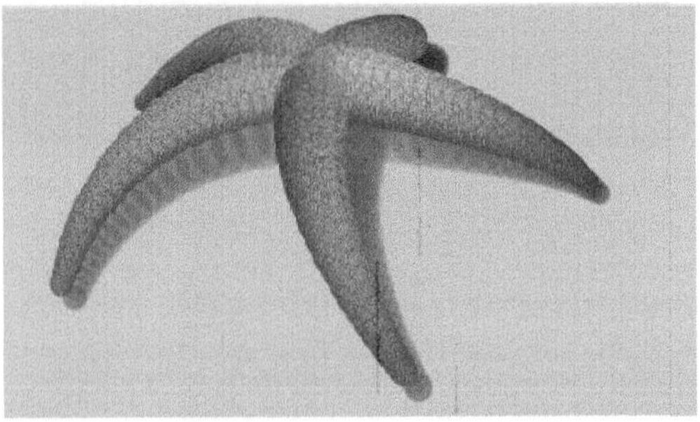

*Figure 10-27 Paint stroke with the **Shadow Offset** value = 0.5*

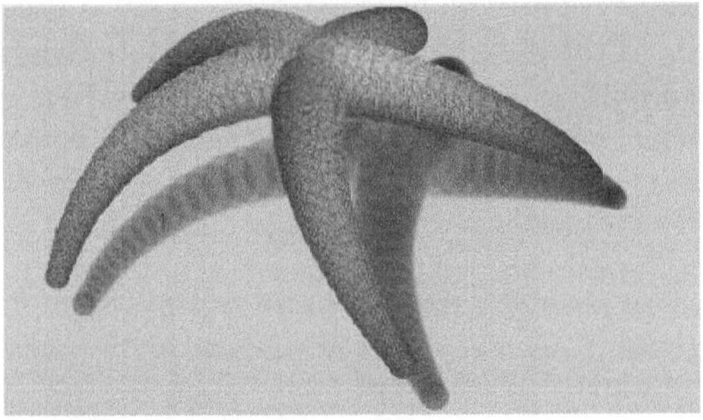

*Figure 10-28 Paint stroke with the **Shadow Offset** value = 1*

Shadow Transp

The **Shadow Transp** attribute is used to specify the value of transparency of the shadow of the paint stroke. Higher the transparency value, lighter will be the shadow effect and vice versa. Figures 10-29 and 10-30 show an object with different values of the **Shadow Transp** attribute.

*Figure 10-29 Paint stroke with the **Shadow Transp** value = 0*

*Figure 10-30 Paint stroke with the **Shadow Transp** value = 0.8*

Glow

The attributes in the **Glow** area used to add standard glow to paint strokes, refer to Figure 10-31. The **Glow** attribute defines the brightness of the glow. Higher the value of the **Glow** option, more will be the glow, as shown in Figures 10-32 and 10-33. The **Glow Color** attribute defines the color of the standard glow. There will be no glow if you set the **Glow Color** attribute to black. The **Glow Spread** attribute controls the halo around the paint strokes. The **Shader Glow** attribute controls the brightness of the shader glow and is more realistic than the standard glow.

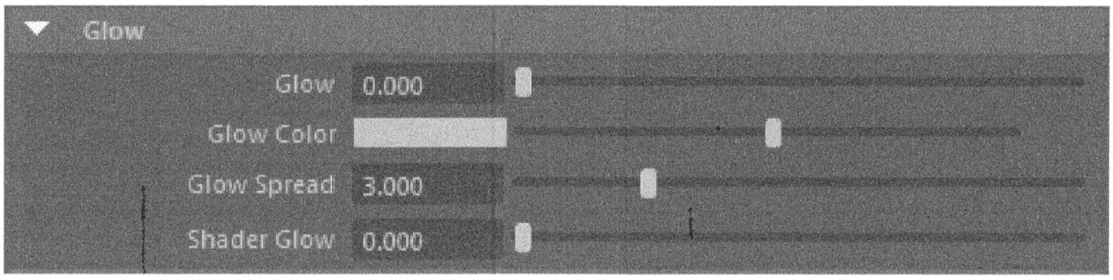

Figure 10-31 *The **Glow** area*

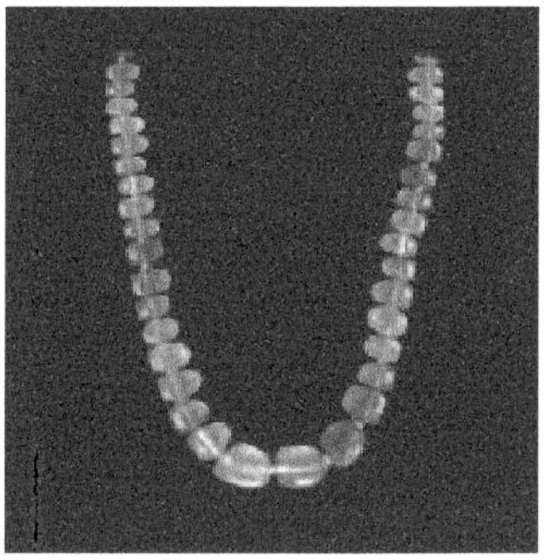

Figure 10-32 *Paint stroke with the **Glow** value = 0*

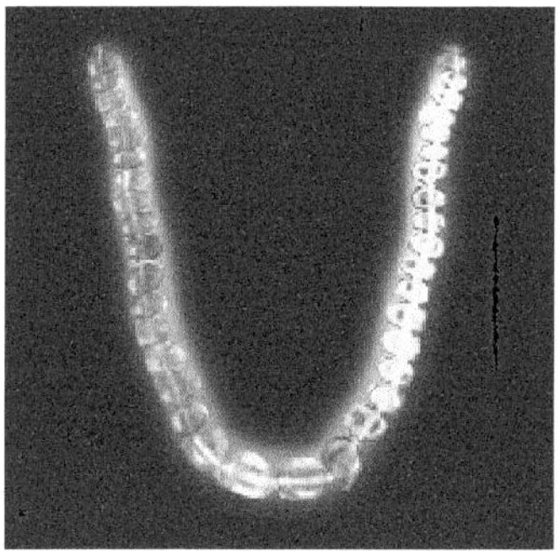

Figure 10-33 *Paint stroke with the **Glow** value = 0.2*

TUTORIALS

Tutorial 1

In this tutorial, you will create a street scene, as shown in Figure 10-34, by using the paint effects. **(Expected time: 20 min)**

The following steps are required to complete this tutorial:

a. Create a project folder.
b. Download the texture file.
c. Create a road for the street scene.
d. Create buildings.
e. Create clouds.
f. Create lights.
g. Save and render the scene.

Figure 10-34 *A street scene*

Creating a Project Folder

Create a new project folder with the name *c10_tut1* at *\Documents\maya2017* and then save the file with the name *c10tut1*, as discussed in Tutorial 1 of Chapter 2.

Downloading the Texture File

In this section, you need to download the texture file.

1. Download the *c10_maya_2017_tut.zip* file from *www.cadcim.com*. The path of the file is as follows: *Textbooks > Animation and Visual Effects > Maya > Autodesk Maya 2017: A Comprehensive Guide.*

2. Extract the contents of the zip file to the *Documents* folder. Open Windows Explorer and then browse to *\Documents\c10_maya_2017_tut*. Next, copy *roadtexture.jpg* to *\Documents\maya2017\c10_tut1\sourceimages.*

Creating a Road for the Street Scene

In this section, you need to create a road for the street scene by using polygon primitives.

1. Maximize the top viewport and choose **Create > Object > Polygon Primitives > Plane** from the menubar. Next, press and hold the left mouse button and drag the cursor to create a plane for the road.

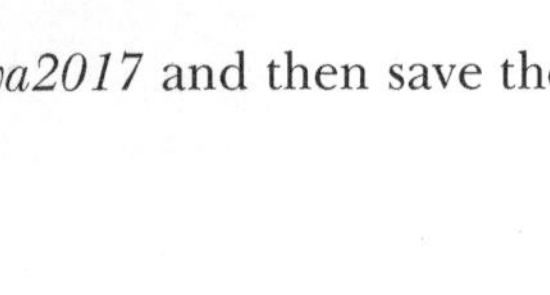

Figure 10-35 Setting the parameters of ***polyPlane1***

2. In the **Channel Box / Layer Editor**, set the parameters of **polyPlane1** in the **INPUTS** area, as shown in Figure 10-35.

3. Choose **Windows > Editors > Rendering Editors > Hypershade** from the menubar; the **Hypershade** window is displayed. Choose **Lambert** from the **Create** area of this window; the **lambert2** shader is created in the Work Area of the **Hypershade** window.

4. Press and hold CTRL and double-click on the **lambert2** shader; the **Rename node** dialog box is displayed. Enter **road** in the **Enter new name** edit box and choose the **OK** button; the shader is renamed to *road*.

5. Select the plane in the viewport and then press and hold the right mouse button over the plane; a marking menu is displayed. Next, choose **Assign Existing Material > road** from the marking menu; the *road* shader is applied to the plane.

6. Click on the *road* shader in the **Hypershade** window; the **road** tab is displayed in the **Property Editor**. In this tab, choose the checker button corresponding to the **Color** attribute in the **Common Material Attributes** area of the **Property Editor**, refer to Figure 10-36; the **Create Render Node** window is displayed. Choose the **File** button from this window; the **File Attributes** area is displayed in the **file1** tab of the **Property Editor**, as shown in Figure 10-40.

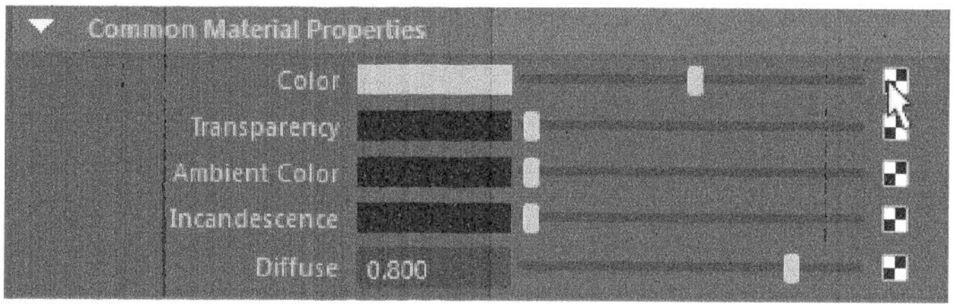

Figure 10-36 *The* ***Common Material Attributes*** *area*

7. Choose the folder icon available on the right of the **Image Name** attribute from the **File Attributes** area, refer to Figure 10-37; the **Open** dialog box is displayed. Next, select the **roadtexture.jpg** and then choose the **Open** button; the texture is applied to the *road*.

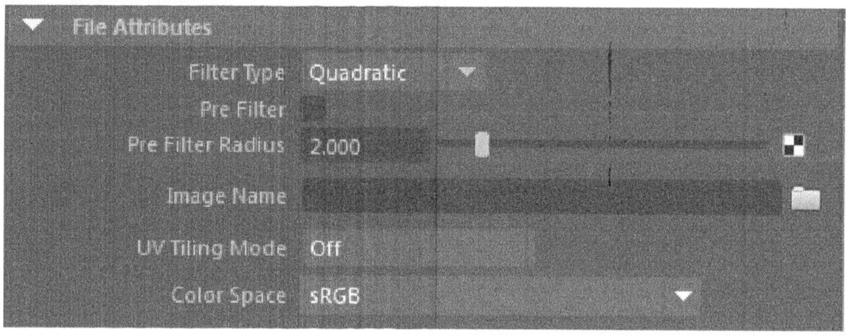

Figure 10-37 *The* ***File Attributes*** *area*

8. Switch to persp viewport and then press 6 to view the texture applied on the road. Make sure the **Modeling** menuset is selected in the **Menuset** drop-down list in the Status Line. Next, select the plane and choose **UV > Modify > Unitize** from the menubar to align the texture on the plane. The plane after applying texture is shown in Figure 10-38.

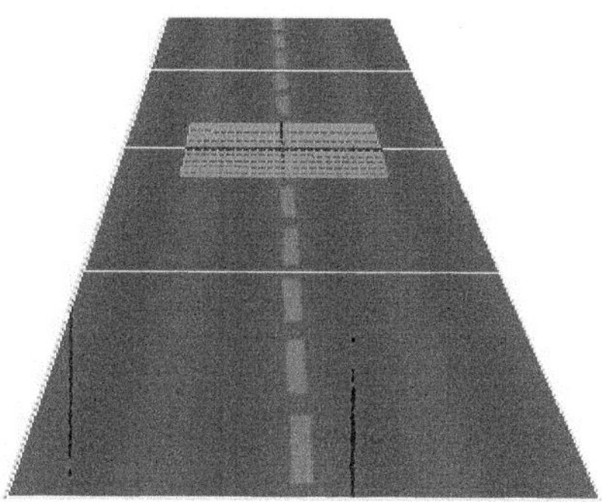

Figure 10-38 *Texture applied on the plane*

9. Choose **Create > Objects > Polygon Primitives > Cube** from the menubar and then create a cube in the viewport. In the **Channel Box / Layer Editor**, set the parameters of **polyCube1** in the **INPUTS** area, as shown in Figure 10-39. Next, duplicate **pCube1** and align both the cubes with the road to get a base for the street using the **Move Tool**, refer to Figure 10-40.

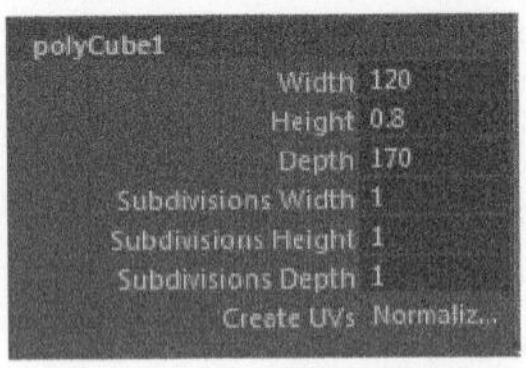

Figure 10-39** Setting the parameters of **polyCube1

***Figure 10-40** The base for the street displayed*

Creating Buildings

In this section, you need to create buildings by using the paint strokes.

1. Choose **Windows > Editors > General Editors > Content Browser** from the menubar; the **Content Browser** window is displayed. Choose the **Paint Effects** node, if it is not already chosen and then select the **cityMesh** folder in the left pane of the **Content Browser** window; the corresponding paint strokes are displayed in the right pane of the **Content Browser** window. Choose the **chicagoTower.mel** paint stroke from the **Content Browser** window, as shown in Figure 10-41. Next, close the **Content Browser** window.

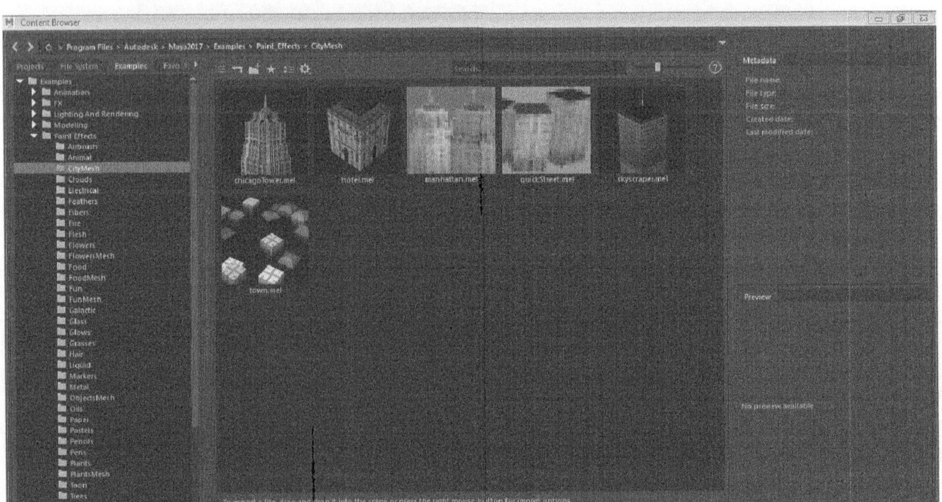

***Figure 10-41** Selecting the **chicagoTower.mel** paint stroke from the **Content Browser** window*

Note

*You can adjust the attributes of the building paint stroke to get different results. Try using different **cityMesh** paint strokes from the **Content Browser** window to create different types of buildings.*

2. Press CTRL+B; the **Paint Effects Brush Settings** window is displayed, as shown in Figure 10-42. Enter **6** in the **Global Scale** edit box of this window to set the brush stroke. Close the **Paint Effect Brush Settings** window.

3. Maximize the top viewport and press 6 to switch to the texture mode. Next, press the left mouse button and drag the cursor; buildings are displayed in the viewport, refer to Figure 10-43.

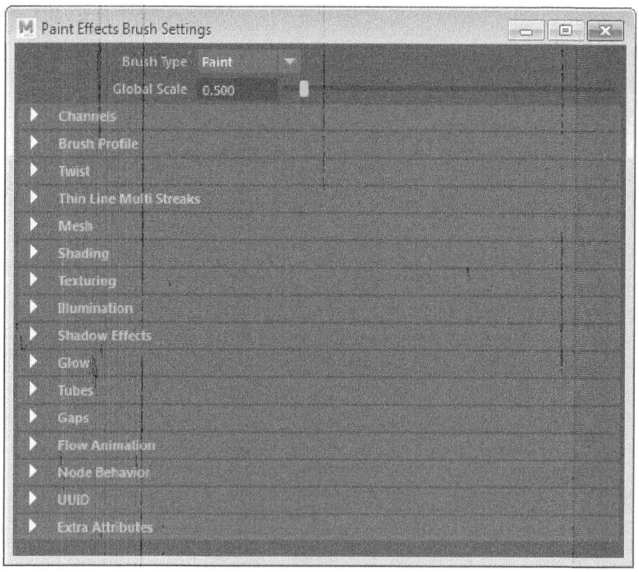

***Figure 10-42** The **Paint Effects Brush Settings** window*

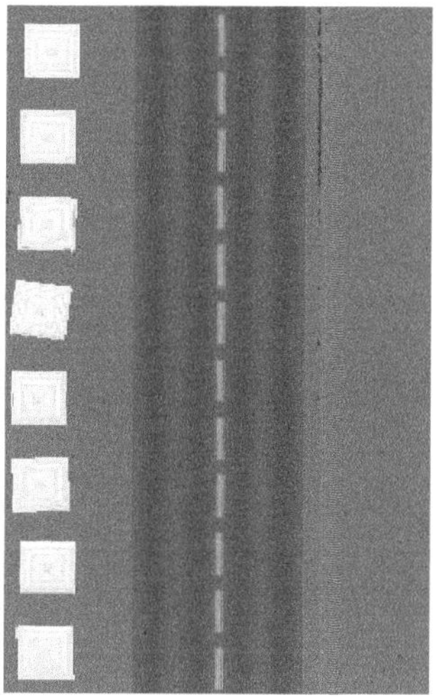

***Figure 10-43** Buildings created*

4. Make sure all building paint strokes are selected in the viewport. Choose **Edit > Duplicate > Duplicate Special > Option Box** from the menubar; the **Duplicate Special Options** dialog box is displayed, as shown in Figure 10-44. In this dialog box, enter **80** in the **x** edit box corresponding to the **Translate** attribute and then choose the **Duplicate Special** button; a duplicate of the building paint stroke is created and aligned to the opposite side of the plane.

5. Maximize the persp viewport. Figure 10-45 shows the building paint stroke created and aligned to the opposite side of the plane.

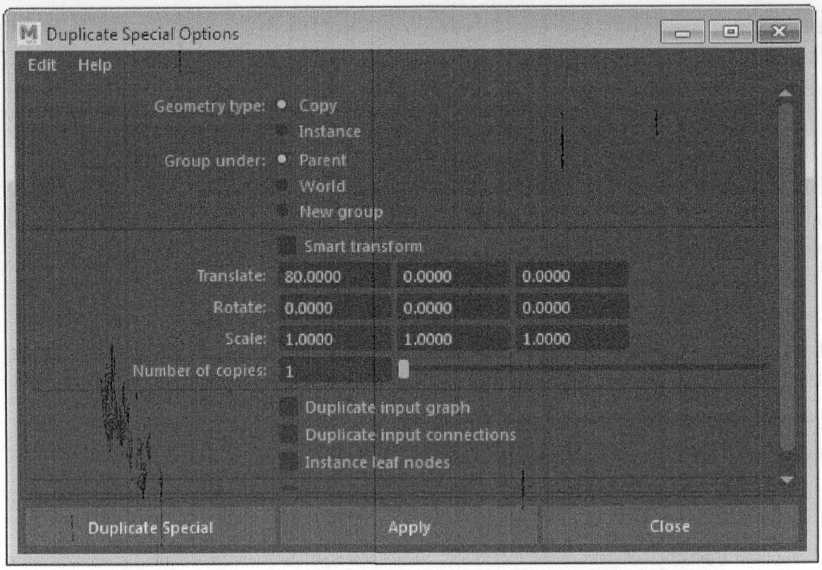

*Figure 10-44 The **Duplicate Special Options** dialog box*

Figure 10-45 Building paint stroke created on the opposite side of the plane

Creating Clouds

In this section, you need to create clouds in the scene by using the paint strokes.

1. Choose **Windows > Editors > Outliner** from the menubar; the **Outliner** window is displayed. Next, select the **persp** camera in the **Outliner** window; various tabs in the **Attribute Editor** are displayed.

2. Make sure the **perspShape** tab is chosen in the **Attribute Editor** and then expand the **Environment** area in it, refer to Figure 10-46. Next, click on the **Background Color** swatch in this tab; the **Color History** palette is displayed. Enter the **HSV** values in the **Color History** palette, as shown in Figure 10-47.

*Figure 10-46 Attributes in the **Environment** area*

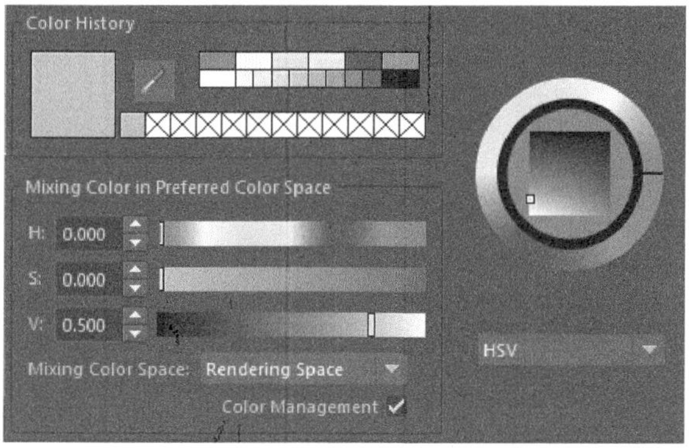

*Figure 10-47 The **Color History** palette*

3. Maximize the top viewport and choose **Windows > Editors > General Editors > Content Browser** from the menubar; the **Content Browser** window is displayed. In the **Paint Effects** node of the **Content Browser** window, select the **cumulusPurple.mel** cloud type from the **clouds** node. Next, in the top viewport, press and hold the B key along with the left mouse button and then drag the cursor to the left or right to increase the brush size. Now, paint the cloud in the top viewport, refer to Figure 10-48.

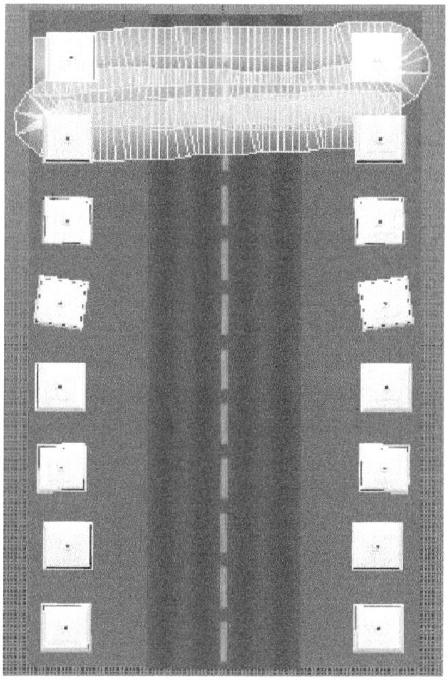

Figure 10-48 Cloud painted in the top viewport

4. In the **Channel Box / Layer Editor**, enter **-85** in the **Translate Z**, **124** in the **Translate Y**, and **-90** in the **Rotate X** edit boxes, respectively. Next, enter **200** in the **Global Scale** edit box in the **INPUTS** area of the **cumulusPurple1** in the **Channel Box / Layer Editor**.

5. Maximize the persp viewport and manually align the clouds paint stroke behind the buildings using **Move Tool**, refer to Figure 10-49.

6. Choose the **Render the current frame** button from the Status Line to render the scene.

Note

You can create more instances of the clouds as per your requirement.

Figure 10-49 Clouds aligned behind the buildings

Creating Lights

In this section, you need to create lights to illuminate the scene.

1. Choose **Create > Objects > Lights > Ambient Light** from the menubar; the ambient light is created. Set the parameters of the light in the **Channel Box / Layer Editor**, as shown in Figure 10-50.

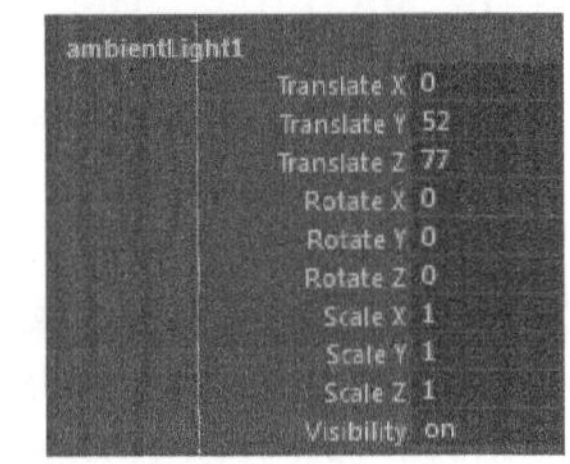

Figure 10-50 *The* ***ambientLight1*** *parameters*

Saving and Rendering the Scene

In this section, you will save the scene that you have created and then render it. You can view the final rendered image of the scene by downloading the ***c10_maya_2017_rndr.zip*** file from ***www.cadcim.com.*** The path of the file is as follows: *Textbooks > Animation and Visual Effects > Maya > Autodesk Maya 2017: A Comprehensive Guide.*

1. Choose **File > Save Scene** from the menubar.

2. Choose **Create > Objects > Cameras > Camera and Aim** from the menubar; the camera is created in the viewport. Invoke the **Outliner** window and expand **camera1_group**. Next, select **camera1_aim** and enter values in the **Channel Box / Layer Editor** for setting the aim of the camera, as shown in Figure 10-51.

3. Select **camera1** from the **Outliner** window. Enter values in the **Channel Box / Layer Editor** for setting the camera position, as shown in Figure 10-52. Next, close the **Outliner** window.

4. In the **Attribute Editor**, make sure the **cameraShape1** tab is chosen. In the **Environment** area of this tab, choose the **Background Color** swatch; the **Color History** palette is displayed. In this palette, enter **1** in the **V** edit box.

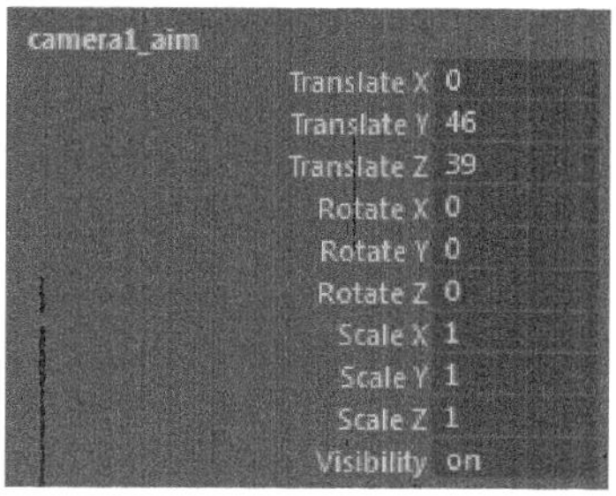

Figure 10-51 The ***camera1_aim*** *parameters*

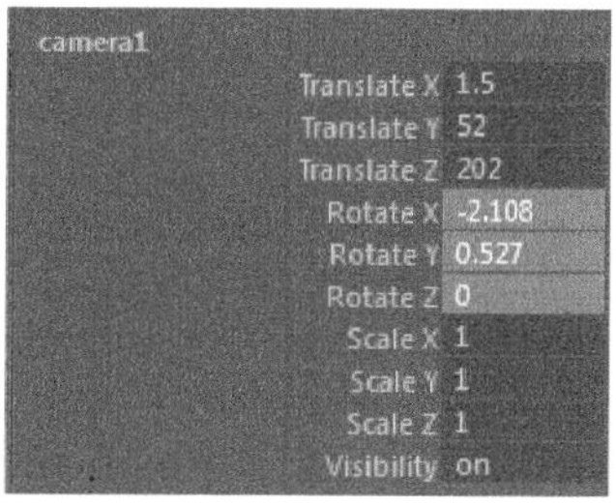

Figure 10-52 The ***camera1*** *parameters*

5. Choose **Panels > Perspective > camera1** from the **Panel** menu; the scene view through the camera is displayed.

6. Choose the **Render the current frame** button from the Status Line to render the scene; the **Render View** window is displayed. This window shows the final output of the scene, refer to Figure 10-53.

Figure 10-53 The final output after rendering

Tutorial 2

In this tutorial, you will create a desert scene, as shown in Figure 10-54, by using the paint strokes. **(Expected time: 30 min)**

The following steps are required to complete this tutorial:

a. Create a project folder.
b. Download the texture file.
c. Create the ground for the desert scene.
d. Create a tree and cactus plants on the plane.
e. Create the camels in the scene.
f. Create the background of the scene.
g. Save and render the scene.

Figure 10-54 A desert scene

Creating a Project Folder

Create a new project folder with the name *c10_tut2* at *\Documents\maya2017* and then save the file with the name *c10tut2*, as discussed in Tutorial 1 of Chapter 2.

Downloading Texture File

In this section, you need to download the texture file.

1. Download the *c10_maya_2017_tut.zip* file from *www.cadcim.com*. The path of the file is as follows: *Textbooks > Animation and Visual Effects > Maya > Autodesk Maya 2017: A Comprehensive Guide*

2. Extract the contents of the zip file to the *Documents* folder. Open Windows Explorer and then browse to *\Documents\c10_maya_2017_tut*. Next, copy *sandbase.jpg, camel.png,* and *sky.jpg* to *\Documents\maya2017\c10_tut2\sourceimages*.

Creating the Ground for the Desert Scene

In this section, you need to create the ground for the desert scene.

1. Maximize the top viewport and choose **Create > Objects > Polygon Primitives > Plane** from the menubar. Now, create a plane in the top viewport. Set the parameters of the plane in the **Channel Box / Layer Editor**, as shown in Figure 10-55.

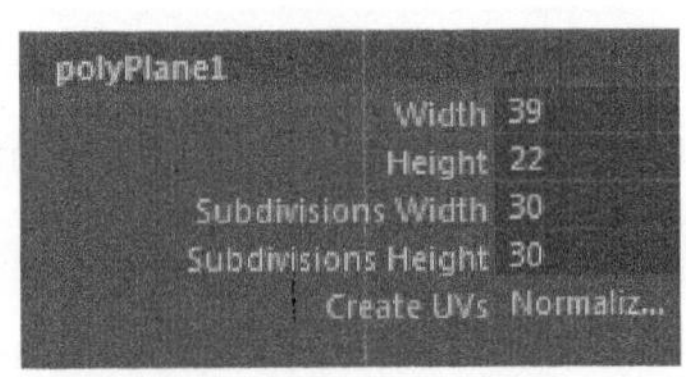

Figure 10-55** Setting the parameters of the plane in the **Channel Box / Layer Editor

2. Make sure the **Modeling** menuset is selected from the **Menuset** drop-down list in the Status Line. Activate the persp viewport and choose **Surfaces > Edit NURBS Surfaces > Sculpt Geometry Tool > Option Box** from the menubar; the **Tool Settings (Sculpt Geometry Tool)** window is displayed.

3. Choose the **Pull** button from the **Sculpt Parameters** area in the **Tool Settings (Sculpt Geometry Tool)** window and sculpt the plane in the **persp** viewport, refer to Figure 10-56.

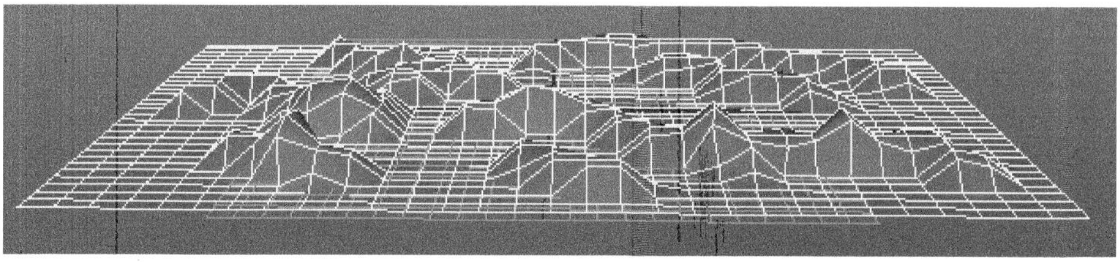

Figure 10-56 The sculpted plane

4. Make sure the plane is selected and then choose **Mesh > Remesh > Smooth** from the menubar to smoothen the edges of the plane.

5. Press and hold the right mouse button on the plane and choose **Assign Favorite Material > Lambert** from the marking menu, as shown in Figure 10-57; the **lambert2** shader is applied to the plane and the **lambert2** tab is displayed in **Attribute Editor**.

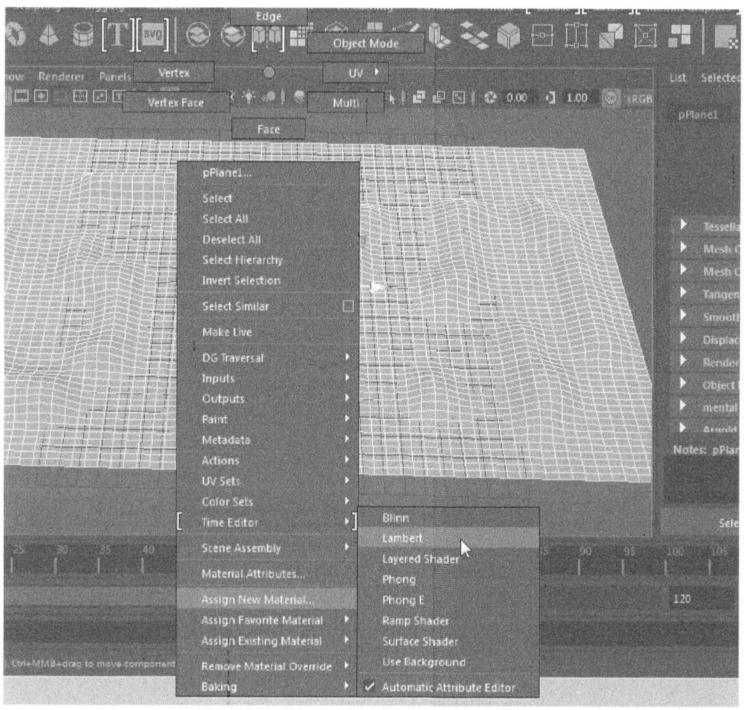

*Figure 10-57 Choosing the **Lambert** option from the marking menu*

6. In the **lambert2** tab, choose the checker button corresponding to the **Color** attribute in the **Common Material Attributes** area; the **Create Render Node** window is displayed. Choose the **File** button from this window; the **File Attributes** area is displayed in the **file1** tab of the **Attribute Editor**.

7. In the **file1** tab, choose the folder icon on the right of the **Image Name** attribute; the **Open** dialog box is displayed. Next, select the **sandbase.jpg** file and then choose the **Open** button. Press 6 to view the texture in the viewport.

8. Select the plane and choose **UV > Create > Automatic** from the menubar. Next, right-click on the plane; a marking menu is displayed. Choose the **Material Attributes** option from the marking menu; the **lambert2** tab is displayed in the **Attribute Editor**. In this tab, click on the arrow on the right side of **Color**. Next, choose the **place2dTexture1** tab and enter **2** in the edit boxes corresponding to the **Repeat UV** attribute. After setting the values, the texture applied to the plane is shown in Figure 10-58.

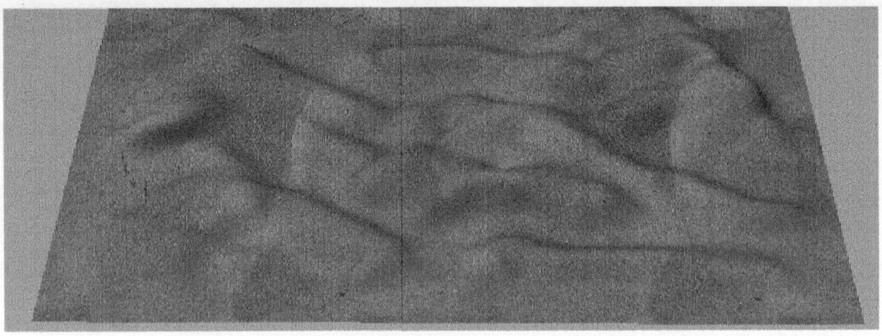

***Figure 10-58** Texture applied on the plane*

Creating a Tree and a Cactus Plants on the Plane

In this section, you need to create a tree and a cactus plants on the plane by using the paint strokes.

1. Choose **Windows > Editors > General Editors > Content Browser** from the menubar; the **Content Browser** window is displayed. Select the **treeBare.mel** paint stroke from the **trees** folder, as shown in Figure 10-59. Next, close the **Content Browser** window. You can increase the size of the paint brush, as required.

***Figure 10-59** Selecting the **treeBare.mel** paint stroke from the **Content Browser** window*

2. In the persp viewport, paint the tree and align the tree with the plane, refer to Figure 10-60.

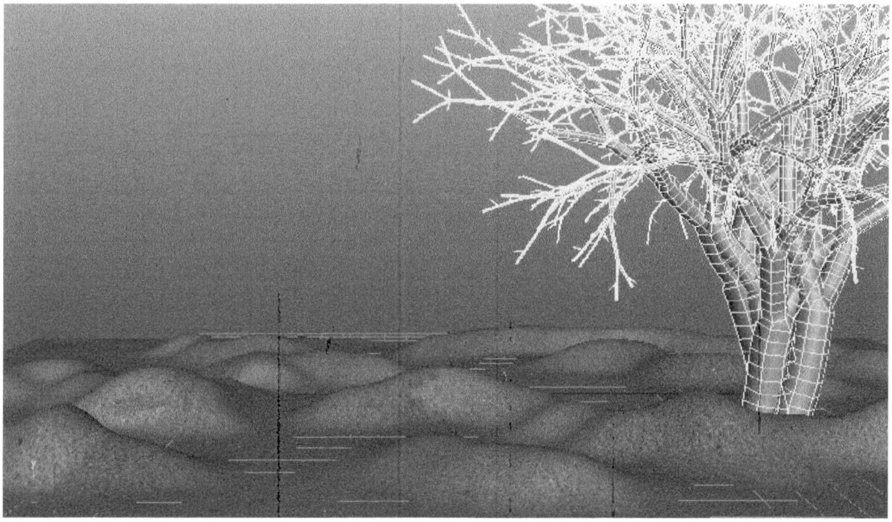

Figure 10-60 *Tree created using the* ***treeBare.mel*** *paint stroke*

3. Similarly, in the **Content Browser** window, select **cactus.mel** from the **Fun** folder, as shown in Figure 10-61. Next, activate the top viewport, paint the cactus plant at different positions on the plane, and then scale them to different sizes.

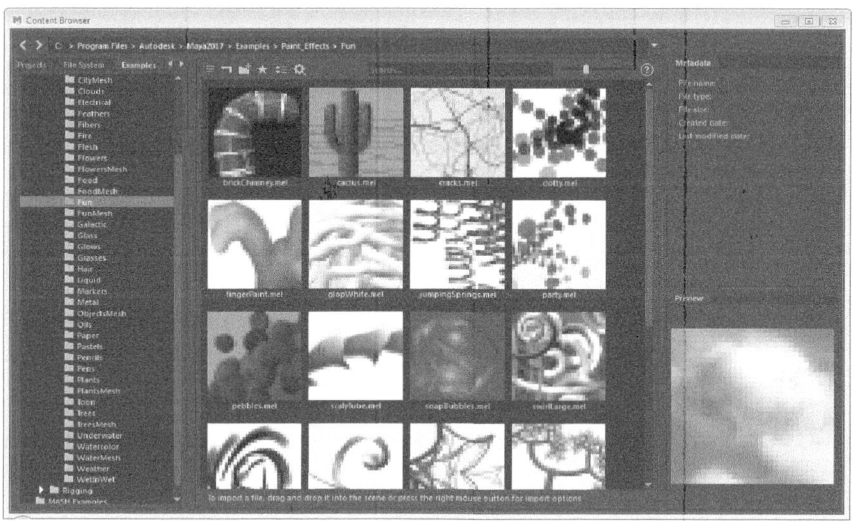

Figure 10-61 *Selecting the* ***cactus.mel*** *paint stroke from the* ***Content Browser*** *window*

Activate the persp viewport to view the scene properly after creating cactus plants using the **cactus.mel** paint stroke, refer to Figure 10-62.

Note

The size of the cactus plant should be proportional to the size of the tree.

*Figure 10-62 Cactus plants created using the **cactus.mel** paint stroke*

Creating Camels in the Scene

In this section, you need to create two planes and assign the alpha map of the camels to the plane.

1. Activate the front viewport. Choose **Create > Objects > Polygon Primitives > Plane** from the menubar and then create a polygon plane in the front viewport.

2. In the **Channel Box / Layer Editor**, set the parameters of the plane in the **INPUTS** area, as shown in Figure 10-63.

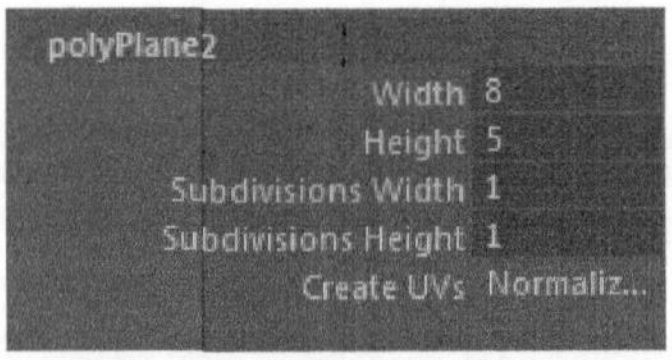

*Figure 10-63 Setting the parameters of the plane in the **Channel Box / Layer Editor***

3. Maximize the persp viewport. Make sure the plane is selected, press and hold the right mouse button on it; a marking menu is displayed. Choose **Assign Favorite Material > Lambert** from the marking menu; the lambert shader is applied to the plane and the **lambert3** tab is displayed in the **Attribute Editor**.

4. In the **Common Material Attributes** area of the **lambert3** tab choose the checker box corresponding to the **Color** attribute; the **Create Render Node** window is displayed. Next, choose the **File** button from this window; the **file2** tab is displayed in the **Attribute Editor**.

5. In the **file2** tab of the **File Attributes** area, choose the folder icon available to the **Image Name** attribute; the **Open** dialog box is displayed. Next, select the **camel.png** and then choose the **Open** button; the image is applied to the plane. Select the new plane and choose **UV > Modify > Unitize** from the menubar to view the camel texture.

6. Make sure the persp viewport is activated. Align the plane in the scene, as shown in Figure 10-64.

Figure 10-64 *The plane adjusted in the scene*

7. Now, select the plane and choose **Edit > Duplicate > Duplicate** from the menubar to create a copy of the plane. Align the duplicated plane in the scene, refer to Figure 10-65.

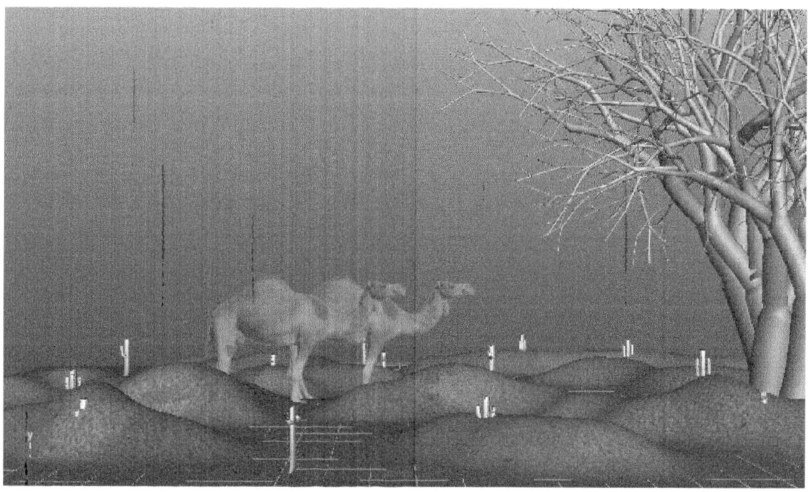

Figure 10-65 *The copy of the plan created and aligned*

Creating the Background of the Scene

In this section, you need to create the background of the scene.

1. Choose **Windows > Editors > Outliner** from the menubar; the **Outliner** window is displayed. Next, select the **persp** camera and close the **Outliner** window; the **perspShape** tab is displayed in the **Attribute Editor**.

2. In the **perspShape** tab, expand the **Environment** area, as shown in Figure 10-66. Next, choose the **Create** button on the right of the **Image Plane** attribute; the **imagePlaneShape1** tab is displayed in the **Attribute Editor**.

Figure 10-66 The ***Environment*** *area*

3. In the **Image Plane Attributes** area of the **imagePlaneShape1** tab, choose the folder icon on the right of the **Image Name** attribute, refer to Figure 10-67; the **Open** dialog box is displayed. Next, select the **sky.jpg** file and then choose the **Open** button.

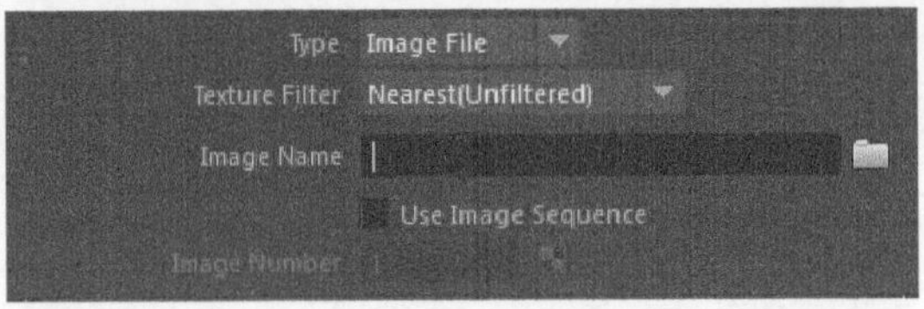

Figure 10-67 The folder icon on the right of the ***Image Name*** *attribute*

4. In the **Placement** area, select **Horizontal** from the **Fit** drop-down list. Next, add lights to the scene, as required.

Saving and Rendering the Scene

In this section, you will save the scene that you have created and then render it. You can view the final rendered image sequence of the scene by downloading the *c10_maya_2017_rndr.zip* file from *www.cadcim.com.* The path of the file is as follows: *Textbooks > Animation and Visual Effects > Maya > Autodesk Maya 2017: A Comprehensive Guide.*

1. Choose **File > Save Scene** from the menubar to save the scene.

2. Maximize the persp viewport, if it is not already maximized. Choose the **Render the current frame** button from the Status Line; the **Render View** window is displayed. This window displays the final output of the scene, refer to Figure 10-68.

Figure 10-68 The final rendered scene

Self-Evaluation Test

Answer the following questions and then compare them to those given at the end of this chapter:

1. Which of the following attributes is used to adjust the density of a paint stroke?

   (a) **Stamp Density** (b) **Flatness**
   (c) **Twist** (d) **Brush Density**

2. Which of the following attributes is used to control the distance between the shadow and the casting stroke?

   (a) **Shadow Offset** (b) **Shadow Diffusion**
   (c) **Shadow Transparency** (d) None of these

3. The __________ attribute is used to define softness on the edges of stroke path.

4. The __________ window comprises preloaded animation clips, brushes, shader libraries, or texture libraries.

5. The __________ attribute is used to set the profile of the brush preset.

6. The __________ attribute is used to twist paint strokes about their own axes.

7. The **Glow** attribute is used to add shadow to paint strokes. (T/F)

8. The **Global Scale** attribute is used to set the size of the brush. (T/F)

9. The **Twist** attribute is used to set the profile for the brush preset. (T/F)

10. The **Thorns on Mesh** attribute is used to apply a glow effect to a mesh object. (T/F)

Review Questions

Answer the following questions:

1. Which of the following attributes is used to control the softness of the shadow?

   (a) **Shadow Diffusion** (b) **Shadow Offset**
   (c) **Shadow Transparency** (d) None of these

2. There are __________ **Brush Types** in the **Paint Effects Brush Settings** window.

3. The attributes in the __________ area are used to affect the appearance of brush strokes by using the lighting.

4. The **Flatness 2** attribute is used to define the flatness of a paint stroke at the base and the tip. (T/F)

5. The **Brush Profile** attribute is used to set the size of a brush. (T/F)

EXERCISES

The rendered output of the models used in the following exercises can be accessed by downloading the *c10_maya_2017_exr.zip* file from *www.cadcim.com*. The path of the file is as follows: *Textbooks > Animation and Visual Effects > Maya > Autodesk Maya 2017: A Comprehensive Guide.*

Exercise 1

Extract the contents of *c10_maya_2017_exr.zip* and then open *c10_exr01_start.mb*. Now, use paint strokes to create an underwater scene around the ant model, as shown in Figure 10-69.

(Expected time: 30 min)

Figure 10-69 *The underwater scene*

Exercise 2

Create the model of a hut, as shown in Figure 10-70. Next, apply texture to it and create a tree on its left side by using the **Content Browser** window, refer to Figure 10-70.

(Expected time: 30 min)

Figure 10-70 The tree created on the left side of a hut model

Exercise 3

Create the model of a flower pot, as shown in Figure 10-71. Next, apply texture to it and use the **Content Browser** window to create flowers in the flower pot. Render the scene to get the final output, as shown in Figure 10-72. **(Expected time: 30 min)**

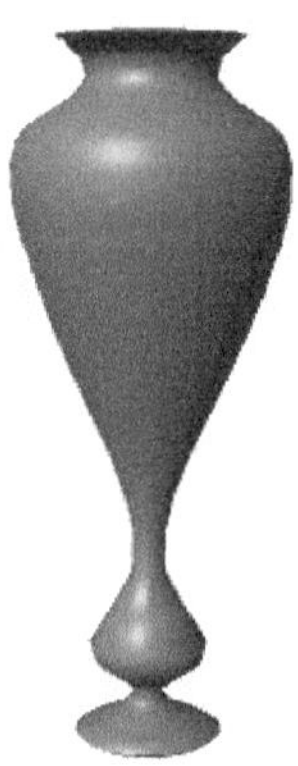

Figure 10-71 The flower pot

Figure 10-72 The rendered flower pot

Answers to Self-Evaluation Test

1. a, **2.** a, **3. Softness**, **4. Content Browser**, **5. Brush Profile**, **6. Twist**, **7.** F, **8.** T, **9.** F, **10.** F

Chapter 11

Rendering

Learning Objectives

After completing this chapter, you will be able to:

- *Use the Render Setup*
- *Understand the basic concepts of rendering*
- *Add caustics to a scene*
- *Understand the basic concepts of Final Gathering and Global Illumination*
- *Add Physical Sun and Sky effect to a scene*
- *Use mental ray and Maya Software renderers*
- *Use Maya Hardware and Maya Vector renderers*

INTRODUCTION

Rendering is the process of generating a 2-dimensional image from a 3-dimensional scene. It is considered as the final stage in 3D production. Rendering helps in visualizing the lighting effects, materials applied, background, and other settings that you set for the scene. In Maya, you can create render layers and render the single layer or multiple layers using the **Render Layer Editor**.

RENDER SETUP

The **Render Setup** window is used to create, edit, and delete layers. It is also used to control the layer bends, collections, and overrides. To open the **Render Setup** window, refer to Figure 11-1, choose the **Launch Render Setup Window** button from the Status Line. The **Render Setup** window is divided into two tabs: **Render Setup** and **Property Editor**. The **Render Setup** window allows you to create layers, collections, and overrides whereas the **Property Editor** allows you to set corresponding values.

> **Tip**
> *If you use the **Rendering - Standard** or **Rendering - Expert** workspaces, the **Render Setup** and **Property Editor** windows are automatically docked for you.*

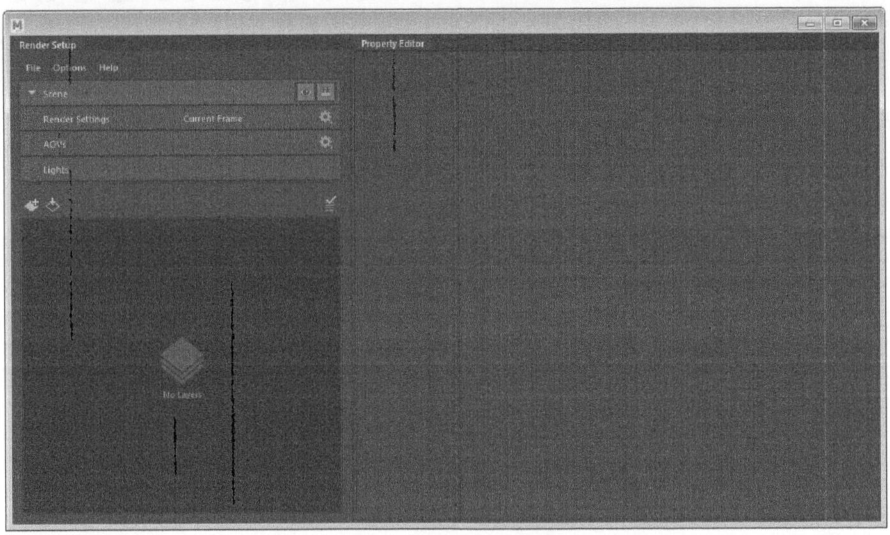

***Figure 11-1** The **Render Setup** window*

In Maya, different types of renderers are used to get the final output of a scene. Some of the most common renderers are discussed next.

MAYA SOFTWARE RENDERER

The **Maya Software** renderer is the default renderer in Maya. It is an advanced, multi-threaded renderer that produces high quality images. This renderer is used to produce effects such as advanced shadows and reflections. It also supports most of the entities in Maya such as particles, fluid effects, and paint effects.

The **Maya Software** renderer has an advanced feature called **IPR** which stands for Interactive Photorealistic Rendering. It is used to preview and make interactive adjustments in the rendered image. It creates a special image file that not only stores the pixel information of an image, but also the data of the surface normals, materials, and objects associated with each of these pixels. Maya updates this information in the **Render View** window as you make changes to the shades or lighting of the scene.

MAYA HARDWARE RENDERER

The **Maya Hardware** renderer is an efficient renderer and it can render depth map shadows. It uses graphics buffers and memory of the computer to generate renders. It also has limitations as it does not render ray trace shadows, reflections, or post-process effects like glow. Particles are rendered using the **Maya Hardware** renderer for the alpha information. If you are rendering a scene for the first time using the **Maya Hardware** renderer, it may take more time. It is so because, the scene is first converted into a data structure, and then it will be calculated by the graphic division of the CPU. The **Maya Hardware** renderer uses the same tessellation settings that are used in the **Maya Software** renderer. Various settings of the **Maya Hardware** renderer are discussed next.

The Maya Hardware Renderer Settings

Choose **Windows > Editors > Rendering Editors > Render Settings** from the menubar; the **Render Settings** window will be displayed. Select **Maya Hardware** from the **Render Using** drop-down list. Next, choose the **Maya Hardware** tab from the **Render Settings** window; the hardware render settings will be displayed, as shown in Figure 11-2.

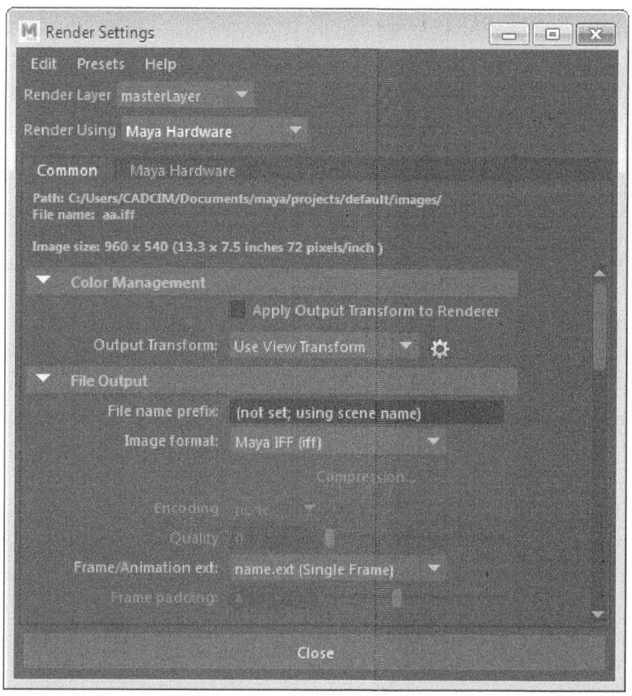

Figure 11-2 The partial view of hardware renderer settings displayed

Quality

The options in the **Quality** area are discussed next.

Presets

The **Presets** drop-down list is used to set the quality of the scene to be rendered. The settings in the rest of the areas depends on the option selected in this drop-down list. These settings directly affect the time taken for rendering a scene. Higher the quality selected in the **Presets** drop-down list, better will be the render quality, but it will take more time in rendering. The **High quality lighting** check box located below the **Presets** drop-down list is used to set a high quality hardware render lighting.

Number Of Samples

The options in the **Number Of Samples** drop-down list are used to select the accurate number of samples per pixel. These samples are used to control the anti-aliasing of objects during rendering.

Frame buffer format

The options in the **Frame buffer format** drop-down list are used to set the video memory for holding the pixels from which the video display is refreshed. You can select the required frame buffer format from this drop-down list. By default, the **Transparent shadow maps** check box located below the drop-down is selected to ensure the usage of transparent shadow maps in your scene.

Transparency sorting

The options in the **Transparency sorting** drop-down list are used to perform sorting before rendering to get better transparency. There are two options in this drop-down list. By default, the **Per object** option is selected and it is used to sort and draw transparent objects from furthest to closest distance with reference to the camera. The **Per polygon** option is used to sort polygons of each object drawn from furthest to closest distance with reference to camera. Therefore, in case of the **Per polygon** option, the scene takes longer time to render as compared to the **Per object** option.

Color resolution

This attribute is used to specify the dimension for map color channels on a material of the baked 2D color image. This image is produced if the **Maya Hardware** renderer is unable to evaluate the shading network. To set the color resolution, you can move the slider located at the right of this attribute or enter a value in the **Color resolution** edit box. The default value of the **Color resolution** is 256 which implies that the baked color image has dimensions of 256 by 256 pixels.

Bump resolution

This attribute is used to specify the dimensions for supported bump maps of the baked 2D color image that is produced only when **Maya Hardware** renderer is unable to evaluate the shading network. To set the resolution, move the slider located at the right of this attribute or enter a value in the **Bump resolution** edit box. The default value of the **Bump resolution** is 512.

Texture compression

The options in the **Texture compression** drop-down list are used to enable or disable the texture compression. When enabled, it reduces the memory usage by 75% at the time of rendering. By default, the **Disabled** option is selected in this drop-down list.

Render Options

The options in the **Render Options** area are discussed next.

Culling

The options in the **Culling** drop-down list are used to select the culling type for the rendering process. By default, the **Per Object** option is selected in this drop-down list. As a result, the settings of the objects that are available in the rendering section of the **Attribute Editor** are used for rendering. Select the **All Double Sided** option from the drop-down list to render both sides of polygons in the scene. Select the **All Single Sided** option to render only those polygons whose normals are facing toward the camera.

Small object culling threshold

This check box is used to remove the objects from rendering that are too small to be seen.

Percent of image size

The **Percent of image size** attribute is used to specify the percentage of image size that the object will occupy on rendering. To set the value of this attribute, either enter a value in the **Percent of image size** edit box or move the slider located on the right of this attribute. This attribute is activated by default. To deactivate it, clear the **Small object culling threshold** check box located above the **Percent of image size** attribute.

Hardware geometry cache

This check box is used to cache the geometry to your video card.

Maximum cache size (MB)

The **Maximum cache size (MB)** attribute is used to control the usage of available memory card which has a maximum limit of 512 MB. The default value for this attribute is 64.

Motion blur

The **Motion blur** check box is used to add the motion blur to an animating object. The **Maya Hardware** renderer achieves blurriness by rendering an object at different positions. These rendered images are then combined into a single image.

Motion blur by frame

The **Motion blur by frame** attribute represents the time range that is blurred. It is used to determine the approximate start and end time of the blur. Also, the software adjusts the time range in accordance with the camera's shutter angle attribute in the **Attribute Editor**. Figure 11-3 shows the rendered image with the motion blur effect.

Number of exposures

The **Number of exposures** attribute is used to specify the number of samples required for creating a smooth motion blur on an animated object.

MAYA VECTOR RENDERER

The **Maya Vector** renderer is used to create unrealistic images such as cartoons, tonal art, wireframe, and so on. Such rendered images can be saved in various formats such as *swf, ai, tiff, svg,* and *eps*.

One of the vector rendered images is shown in Figure 11-4. In this figure, you will notice that the image is more stylized and has more color effects as compared to the images created by using other renderers.

Figure 11-3 *An object with the motion blur effect*

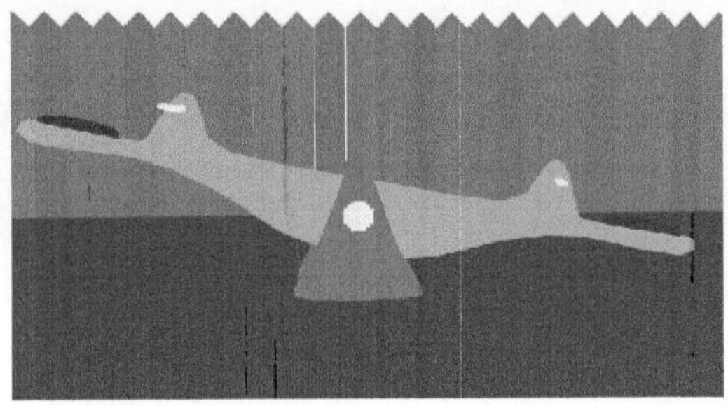

Figure 11-4 *The vector rendered image*

To understand the process of creating effects using the **Maya Vector** renderer better, compare Figure 11-5 with Figure 11-6. In these figures, you will notice that Figure 11-5 is more realistic than the one shown in Figure 11-6. This is because Figure 11-6 displays tonal art effect and such effect is mainly used for creating logos and diagrams.

Figure 11-5 *An image rendered using the* ***Maya Software*** *renderer*

Figure 11-6 *An image rendered using the* ***Maya Vector renderer***

The **Maya Vector** renderer is based on the concept of the RAViX technology. RAViX stands for Rapid Visibility Extension. This technology converts a 3D model into a 2D vector-based image by detecting the lines and vertices that make up a 3D model and then converts them into shaded polygons for recreating the 3D image in a 2D vector format (specifically Adobe Flash SWF and EPS formats). RAViX provides per polygon shading capabilities that are superior to other rendering technologies. Also, the file size created by using this technology is smaller than the other technologies. The **Maya Vector** renderer does not support any light, except the point light. If there is no light in a scene, the vector renderer creates a default light at the camera position during rendering.

The **Maya Vector** renderer cannot render some features such as bump maps, displacement maps, Maya fluid effects, image planes, Maya fur, multiple UVs, Maya Paint Effects, particles, post-render effects, and textures. To render an object with any of these features using the **Maya Vector** renderer, first you need to convert the object into a polygon and then render the object. To convert an object into a polygon, select the object from the viewport and then choose **Modify > Objects > Convert** from the menubar; a cascading menu comprising of all tessellation methods will be displayed. Choose the required option from the cascading menu; the object will be converted into a polygon.

The Maya Vector Renderer Settings

Choose **Windows > Editors > Rendering Editors > Render Settings** from the menubar; the **Render Settings** window will be displayed. In this window, select **Maya Vector** from the **Render Using** drop-down list. Next, choose the **Maya Vector** tab from the **Render Settings** window; the vector renderer settings will be displayed, as shown in Figure 11-7.

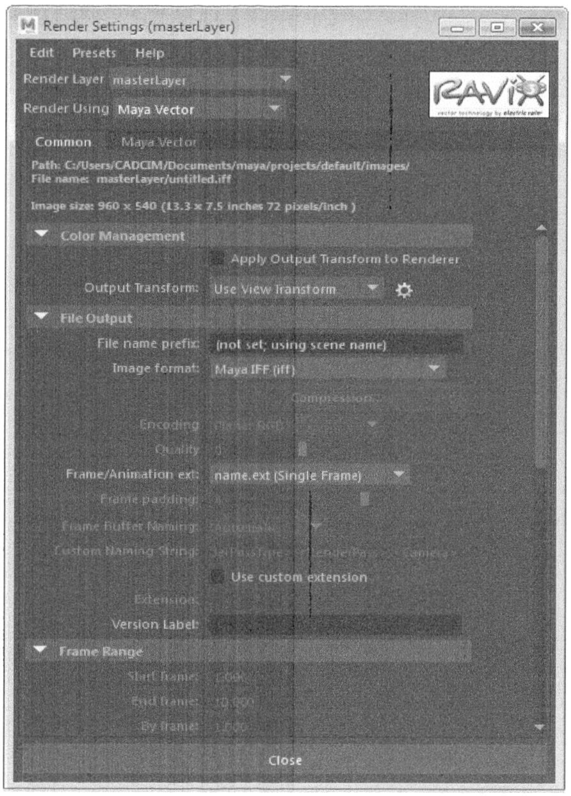

Figure 11-7 *The partial view of vector renderer settings displayed*

If the **Maya Vector** option is not available in the **Render Using** drop-down list, choose **Windows > Editors > Setting/Preferences > Plug-in Manager** from the menubar; the **Plug-in Manager** dialog box will be displayed. Select the **VectorRender.mll** check box, refer to Figure 11-8. Next, choose the **Refresh** button and then the **Close** button; the **Maya Vector** option will be displayed in the **Render Using** drop-down list. Some of the options in the **Maya Vector** tab are discussed next.

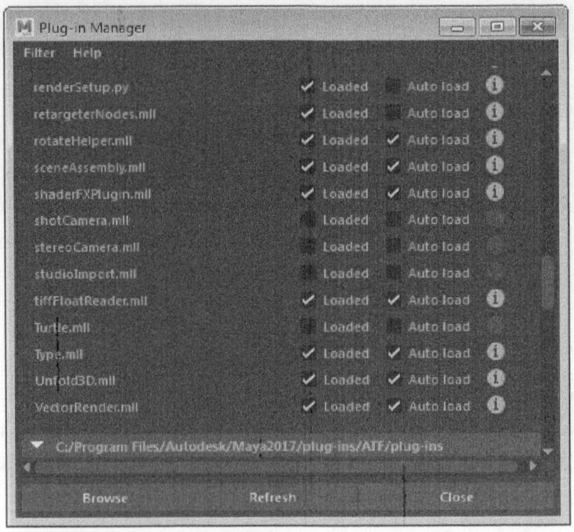

Figure 11-8 The ***vectorRender.mll*** *check box in the* ***Plug-in Manager*** *dialog box*

Image Format Options (maya) Area

By default, there is no option displayed in the **Image Format Options (maya)** area. To display the options, choose the **Common** tab from the **Render Settings** window. Next, select **Macromedia SWF (swf)** or **SVG (svg)** from the **Image format** drop-down list in the **Render Settings** window. Again, choose the **Maya Vector** tab; the options will be displayed in this area in the **Maya Vector** tab, refer to Figure 11-9. You will notice that, on selecting **Macromedia SWF (swf)** from the **Image format** drop-down list, the name of the area changes to the **Image Format Options (swf)**.

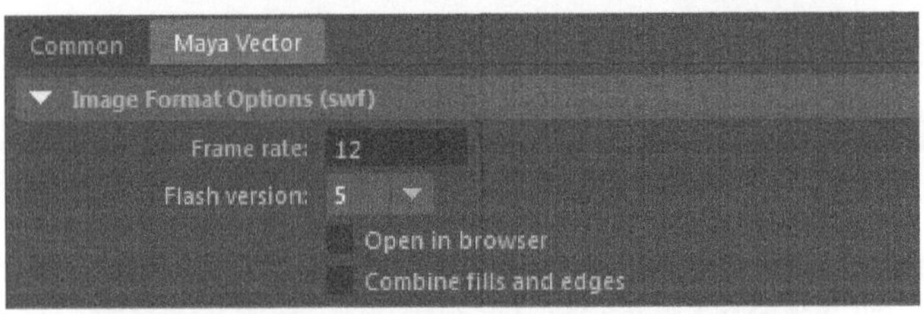

Figure 11-9 The ***Image Format Options (swf)*** *area*

Frame rate

The **Frame rate** attribute is used to specify the number of frames for the animation that will be created on rendering in *swf* or *SVG* file format. The default value for the **Frame rate** attribute is 12.

Flash version

The options in the **Flash version** drop-down list is used to specify the version of the rendered flash player file. The *swf* file can be imported to any flash version. Select the **Open in browser** check box to enable the animation display in the browser after the rendering is completed. Select the **Combine fills and edges** check box to make the outlines and fills of the rendered output as a single object. On selecting this check box, the file size of the rendered output is reduced.

Appearance Options Area

The **Appearance Options** area consists of attributes that control the complexity of the final vector image. These attributes are discussed next.

Curve Tolerance

The **Curve tolerance** attribute is used to set the display of outlines of the rendered image. You can specify the curve tolerance value either by entering a value between 0 and 15 in the **Curve tolerance** attribute or by moving the slider bar located on the right of the attribute. The default value of this attribute is 7.5. If you enter 0 in the edit box, a series of straight line segments, one for each polygon cube, will be created on rendering the final vector image. This results in producing large sized files. But if you enter the value 15 in this edit box, then a series of distorted outlines will be created, thus resulting in smaller sized files. The **Secondary curve fitting** check box is used to control the conversion of line segments into curves. Select this check box to produce better results and smaller file size.

Detail level preset

This drop-down list is used to control the level of detail of the final rendered image. Higher the value selected, more will be the accuracy of the rendered image. By default, **Automatic** is selected in this drop-down list. As a result, the renderer automatically calculates the appropriate level of detail for a scene. Figures 11-10 and 11-11 display two rendered images with **Low** and **High** options, respectively selected from the **Detail level Preset** drop-down list.

Figure 11-10 *Image with the* ***Low*** *option selected*

Figure 11-11 *Image with the* ***High*** *option selected*

Fill Options Area

The options in this area are used to set the type of fill style for the scene being rendered. The options in this area are discussed next.

Fill objects

When you select this check box, the scene is rendered using the different fill styles available in the **Fill Style** area.

Fill Style

The radio buttons in the **Fill Style** area are used to select the style of shading used to fill surfaces in the rendered image.

Single color: The **Single color** radio button is used to fill a surface with a solid color that is based on the material color of the object, as shown in Figure 11-12. As a result, the object will appear flat and there will be no effect of light in it.

Two color: The **Two color** radio button is used to fill a surface of the object with two solid colors that are based on material color and lighting, as shown in Figure 11-13.

*Figure 11-12 Image rendered using the **Single color** fill style*

*Figure 11-13 Image rendered using the **Two color** fill style*

Four color: The **Four color** radio button works similar to the **Two color** fill style. The only difference is that this radio button uses four solid colors to render the scene, as shown in Figure 11-14.

Full color: The **Full color** radio button is used to produce realistic 3D render effects, as shown in Figure 11-15. However, this makes the file size heavier.

*Figure 11-14 Image rendered on applying the **Four color** fill style*

*Figure 11-15 Image rendered on applying the **Full color** fill style*

Average color: The **Average color** radio button is used to shade each face and surface of an image with one solid color, as shown in Figure 11-16.

Area gradient: This radio button is used to fill a surface with one radial gradient that is based on material color and lighting.

Mesh gradient: This radio button is used to fill one linear gradient on each polygon of the surface of the object, depending on the color of the material and lighting used in the scene.

***Figure 11-16** Image rendered on applying the **Average color** fill style*

Show back faces

The **Show back faces** check box is used to render the surfaces with normals facing away from the camera.

Shadows

The **Shadows** check box is used to render the object shadow based on the shadow-casting point lights in the scene. However, shadows increase file size and the render time.

Highlights

The **Highlights** check box is used to render the specularity. This specularity is based on point lights and the shine of the surface material. You can set the level of the highlight either by entering the value in the **Highlight level** edit box or by moving the slider bar located on the right of the edit box.

Reflections

The **Reflections** check box is used to render the surface reflections that are based on the surface material reflectivity. You can set the depth of the reflection either by entering the value in the **Reflection depth** edit box or by moving the slider bar located on the right of the edit box.

Edge Options Area

The options in this area are used to control the visibility of the edges of an object on rendering. Various options in this area are discussed next.

Include Edges

The **Include edges** check box is used to render the surface edges of an object as outlines. Figures 11-17 and 11-18 display the images created before and after selecting the **Include edges** check box, respectively.

Edge weight preset

The options in the **Edge weight preset** drop-down list are used to set the thickness of edges on rendering. To set the thickness of edges, select the required thickness from this drop-down list. Hairline is the default option selected in this drop-down list.

Edge weight

The **Edge weight** attribute is used to add weight/thickness to the edges. To do so, enter the required value in this attribute or move the slider on the right of this option. The default value in the edit box is 0. Figures 11-19 and 11-20 show the rendered images with different

Edge weight values. If you change the value of an edge weight, the corresponding **Edge weight preset** value will also change accordingly.

*Figure 11-17 Rendered image before selecting the **Include edges** check box*

*Figure 11-18 Rendered image after selecting the **Include edges** check box*

*Figure 11-19 Image with the **Edge weight** value = 3*

*Figure 11-20 Image with the **Edge weight** value = 10*

Edge style

The **Edge style** drop-down list is used to render an image having surface edges or polygon edges as outlines. On selecting the **Outlines** option from this drop-down list, the surface edges will be rendered as outlines, as shown in Figure 11-21. On selecting the **Entire Mesh** option, the polygon edges of the object will be rendered as outlines, as shown in Figure 11-22.

Edge color

The **Edge color** attribute is used to change the color of the rendered edges. To do so, choose the color swatch; the **Color History** palette will be displayed. Select a color from this palette to set the color.

Hidden edges

The **Hidden edges** check box is used to display all the hidden edges of an object on being rendered, refer to Figure 11-23. However, it is recommended to avoid using this option because on choosing this option, all the hidden edges are displayed, and you will not get an appropriate view of the rendered image.

*Figure 11-21 Image rendered on selecting the **Outlines** option*

*Figure 11-22 Image rendered on selecting the **Entire Mesh** option*

Edge detail

The **Edge detail** check box is used to render the sharp edges between polygons as outlines. The **Edge detail** check box helps in giving the rendered image a 3D look, as shown in Figure 11-24. To activate this check box, first you need to select the **Outline** option from the **Edge Style** drop-down list. On selecting the **Edge detail** check box, the **Min edge angle** attribute gets activated. This attribute is used to control the edges to be rendered as outlines.

*Figure 11-23 Image displayed after selecting the **Hidden edges** check box*

*Figure 11-24 Image displayed on selecting the **Edge detail** check box*

Outlines at intersections

The **Outlines at intersections** check box is used to show outline along the point where two objects intersect.

Min edge angle

The **Min edge angle** option is used to select the polygon edges which are rendered as outlines when the **Edge Detail** check box is selected.

Render Optimizations Area

The area consists of options that are used to optimize the render image to reduce the file size. The option in this area is discussed next.

Render optimization

The **Render optimization** drop-down list has three options: **Safe**, **Good**, and **Aggressive**. By default, the **Safe** option is selected. It is used to delete the outlines that are visible only on zooming in the scene. Select the **Good** option to remove the sub-pixel geometry, especially in the region of high detail. This is done to reduce the file size. Select the **Aggressive** option to remove excess geometry, sub-pixel geometry, and geometry that is slightly above the single pixel level. This reduces the file size to around 30% of the original file size.

mental ray RENDERER

The **mental ray** renderer is the most preferred renderer in the industry. It generates images of outstanding quality, unsurpassed realism as well as gives scalable performance. The **mental ray** renderer has certain important attributes such as caustics, global illumination, final gathering, and HDRI that provide a realistic look to any scene.

Note

*The **mental ray** plug-in is not installed with the 2017 release of Maya by default. You can download it from the following link: http://www.nvidia.com/object/nvidia-mental-ray-products.html. After installing the plug-in, open Maya and then choose **Windows > Editors > Settings/Preferences > Plug-in Manager** from the menubar; the **Plug-in Manager** window will be displayed. In this widow, select the **Loaded** and **Auto load** checkboxes on the right of the **Mayatomr.mll** option and then choose the **Close** button to close the **Plug-in Manager** window.*

The mental ray options are provided in five tabs in the **Render Setting** window. The **Show Advanced Settings** check box available in **Quality**, **Scene**, and **Configuration** tabs allows the advanced users to fine-tune the reader settings.

The attributes in the **Common** tab of this window are same as those in other types of renderers, discussed earlier. The attributes in the **Scene** tab allow you to perform several actions on a scene such as setting frame buffers, creating render passes, creating image based lighting, and specifying motion blur settings. The attributes in the **Configuration** tab let you specify settings from the **mental ray** renderer. Also, you can specify settings for the interactive rendering, and the GI prototype mode. The attributes in the **Diagnostics** tab allow you to diagnose samples as well as specify the feature and scene overrides. The attributes in the **Quality** tab let you specify the quality settings for the scene. You can also set global illumination and final gathering options from this tab. This tab is discussed next.

Quality Tab

The attributes in the **Quality** tab allow you to set the rendering quality for the scene. The options in this tab are discussed next.

Sampling Area

The options in the **Sampling** area are discussed next.

Overall Quality

This attribute is used to control the rendering quality by increasing or decreasing number of samples per pixel. If there is noise in the scene, you need to increase the sampling to increase the quality. The higher the value specified for this attribute, more is the time taken to render the scene in Maya.

Lighting Quality

This attribute is used to control the lighting quality in the scene. The **mental ray** renderer uses the Light Importance Sampling (LIS) technique to sample the lights. By this technique **mental ray** collects more accurate lighting samples in the scene.

Env Lighting Quality

This attribute is used to control the quality of the environment light. This attribute is available when the environment light is enabled in the scene.

Indirect Diffuse (GI) Mode

The **Indirect Diffuse (GI) Mode** option controls indirect diffuse, reflection and transmission. There are four options in this drop-down list. By default, the **Off** option is selected and it is used to turn off the indirect diffuse effect. The **On (GI Prototype)** option provides indirect diffuse sampling. The **Finalgather** option provides indirect diffuse sampling using the interpolated FG map. The **Finalgather Force** option provides indirect diffuse sampling without using the interpolated FG map.

Indirect Diffuse Quality

This attribute is used to control the number of samples split out for a diffuse interaction with a material.

(MILA) Material Quality

These attributes are used to control the number of samples split out for layering library (MILA) materials with either glossy reflection/refraction or scatter components.

Sample Lock

This attribute is used to control the noise and flickering effect in the still render or a camera sequence.

Volume Sampling

This attribute is used to control the number of samples in Maya volumes.

Filtering Area

The options in the **Filtering** area are discussed next.

Filter

Filters are used to blend samples together to produce smooth results. There are five options available in this drop-down list. By default, the **Box** option is selected and it provides the fastest way to get relatively good result. The **Triangle** option takes more time to process than the **Box** option but gives better results. The **Gauss** option produces the best result but is slowest to render. The **Mitchell** and **Lanczos** options are alternatives to the **Gauss** option and create detailed render image.

Filter Size

This attribute is used to control the size of the pixels used for filtering.

Trace Depth Area

The attributes in the **Trance Depth** area are discussed next.

Diffuse

This attribute works with the **Indirect Diffuse (GI) Mode**. When the **Indirect Diffuse (GI) Mode** is used, it affects the trace depth at which the indirect diffuse sampling is to be used.

Glossy/Specular Reflection

This attribute is used to specify the maximum number of times a ray can be reflected from reflective surfaces.

Glossy/Specular Transmission

This attribute is used to specify the maximum number of times a ray can be reflected through non-opaque surfaces.

Max Trace Depth

This attribute is used to specify the maximum number of times a ray can be reflected and transmitted in a scene.

Geometry Area

The **Displace Motion Factor** attribute in this area is used to control the displacement tessellation quality according to the amount of visual motion, and reduces tessellation density as the objects move faster. This attribute provides an automatic way of adjusting the displacement quality according to the amount of motion for a given object.

Legacy Options Area

The **Legacy Options** area is not displayed by default. To display it, select the **Show Advanced Settings** check box located at the top of the **Quality** tab; the **Legacy Options** area will be displayed. This area contains the legacy settings for the **mental ray** renderer. The commonly used legacy areas are discussed next.

Caustics Area

Caustics are the refraction patterns formed by highly transparent objects such as a glass filled with fluid, as shown in Figure 11-25. They are light patterns formed by focusing the light on a particular object. Each light in Maya supports the **mental ray** renderer. To enable caustics, open the **Render Settings** window by choosing the **Display Render Settings** button on the Status Line. Next, set the **mental ray** renderer type from the **Render Settings** window.

Next, select the **Show Advanced Settings** check-box from the **Quality** tab and then expand the **Legacy Options** area. Now, expand **Caustics** area; various options in this area will be displayed, as shown in Figure 11-26. These options are discussed next.

Caustics: The **Caustics** check box is used to activate the options to set caustics in the **Render Settings** window.

Accuracy: The **Accuracy** attribute is used to set the total number of photons required to set the brightness in a scene. Higher the frequency of photons, more will be the smoothness of the caustics applied to the scene.

Scale: The **Scale** attribute is used to control the effect of indirect illumination on a scene. Choose the white color box on the right of the **Scale** attribute to vary the effect of indirect illumination on the caustics applied to the scene.

Figure 11-25 The caustics effect on a glass

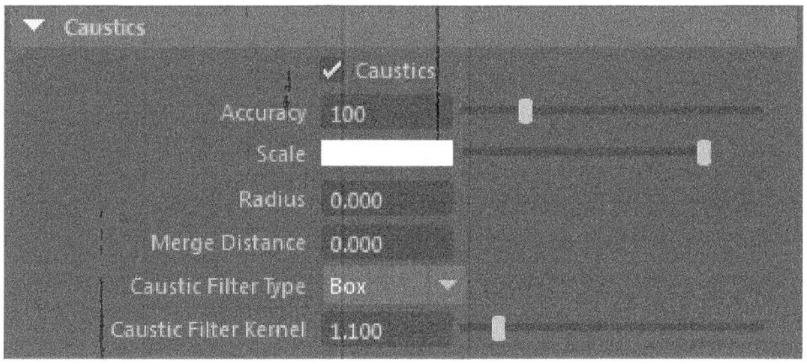

*Figure 11-26 The **Caustics** area*

Radius: The **Radius** attribute is used to set the distance up to which the caustics will be applied.

Merge Distance: The **Merge Distance** attribute is used to merge the photons that come in the specified world space distance.

Caustic Filter Type: The **Caustic Filter Type** drop-down list is used to increase the photon weight by specifying the shape of the caustics created on rendering.

Caustic Filter Kernel: The **Caustic Filter Kernel** attribute is used to smoothen the caustics created while rendering the scene. Higher the value specified for this option, smoother will be the caustics created.

Global Illumination Area

Global illumination is the physical simulation of all lights in a scene. It makes the effect of light more realistic in the scene. The global illumination uses indirect illumination in a scene.

To apply global illumination to a scene, choose **Windows > Editors > Rendering Editors > Render Settings** from the menubar; the **Render Settings** window will be displayed. In this window, select **mental ray** from the **Render Using** drop-down list; the **mental ray** attributes will be displayed in the **Render Settings** window. Now, choose the **Quality** tab from the **Render Settings** window. Next choose, the **Show Advanced Settings** check-box from the **Quality** tab and then expand the **Legacy Options** area. Now, expand the **Global Illumination** area, as shown in Figure 11-27. Various options in this area are discussed next.

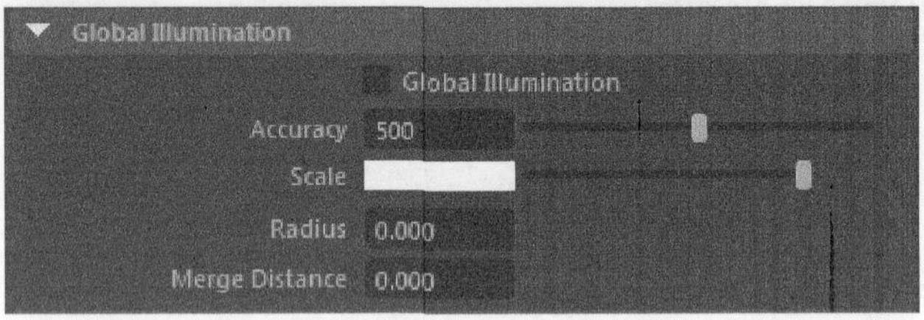

Figure 11-27 *The **Global Illumination** area*

Global Illumination
The **Global Illumination** check box is used to add the global illumination effect to a scene.

Note
The global illumination effect is calculated only for the photon emitting lights. Therefore, before applying global illumination, you need to enable the photon emission to get the desired result.

Accuracy: The **Accuracy** attribute is used to set the number of photons in a scene. The total number of photons in a scene determines the intensity of global illumination in the final output. Higher the number of photons in a scene, more time it will take to render and more will be the smoothness in the scene.

Scale: The **Scale** attribute is used to control the effect of indirect illumination on a scene. Select the white color box on the right of the **Scale** attribute to vary the effect of indirect illumination on the caustics applied to the scene.

Radius: The **Radius** attribute is used to set the distance up to which the global illumination will have its effect on the photons in the scene.

Merge Distance: The **Merge Distance** attribute is used to merge the photons created in the specified world space distance.

Final Gathering Area

The Final Gathering is a rendering option that is used to yield extremely realistic shading effects. You can use this option with global illumination to obtain fine details on rendering. To apply this option, first rays are cast from a light source to a scene. Next, a series of rays is diverted at random angles to calculate the light energy transmitting from the surrounding objects. This light energy is stored in photon maps. The photon maps are used to add the bouncing light effect. This process basically turns every object into a light source. As a result, each object in the scene influences the color of its surroundings, as shown in Figure 11-28.

Figure 11-28 The Final Gathering effect in a scene

To render a scene using the Final Gathering option, choose **Windows > Editors > Rendering Editors > Render Settings** from the menubar; the **Render Settings** window will be displayed. In this window, select **mental ray** from the **Render Using** drop-down list; the **mental ray** attributes will be displayed in the **Render Settings** window. Next, select the **Show Advanced Setting** check box from the **Quality** tab and then expand the **Legacy Options** area. Now, expand the **Final Gathering** area; the parameters in this area will be displayed, as shown in Figure 11-29. Various options in this area are discussed next.

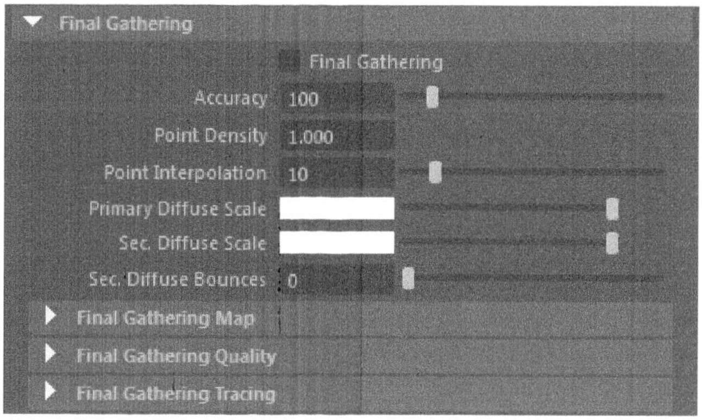

*Figure 11-29 The **Final Gathering** area*

Final Gathering: The **Final Gathering** check box is used to turn the Final Gathering option on/off in the scene.

Accuracy: The **Accuracy** attribute is used to define the number of rays emitted from the sampled rays. Higher the value of this option, better will be the render quality. The default value of this option is 100.

Point Density: The **Point Density** attribute is used to control the total number of Final Gather points to be calculated on rendering. On increasing the value of point density, the rendering time also increases.

Point Interpolation: The **Point Interpolation** attribute is used to define the total number of Final Gather points required for interpolation.

Primary Diffuse Scale: The **Primary Diffuse Scale** attribute is used to control the contribution of Final Gather to the final rendering. To set the intensity, you need to choose the color box on the right of this option and then select the required color.

Sec. Diffuse Scale: The **Sec. Diffuse Scale** attribute is used to control the secondary bouncing to the final render.

Sec. Diffuse Bounces: The **Sec. Diffuse Bounces** attribute is used to set multiple diffuse bounces for the Final Gather effect such that it adds more light and color bleed effect to the final render.

Physical Sun and Sky

The **Physical Sun and Sky** option is used to produce the accurate renders of daylight scenes, as shown in Figure 11-30.

Figure 11-30 *The image with the physical sun and sky effect*

The **Physical Sun and Sky** option uses the **mia_physicalsun** and **mia_physicalsky** shaders. To add the physical sun and sky effect to a scene, choose **Windows > Editors > Rendering Editors > Render Settings** from the menubar; the **Render Settings** window will be displayed. In this window, select **mental ray** from the **Render Using** drop-down list. Next, choose the **Scene** tab and then expand the **Cameras** area. Now, expand the **Environment** area, refer to Figure 11-31; the **Physical Sun and Sky** attribute will be displayed. Next, choose the **Create** button on the right of the **Physical Sun and Sky** attribute; a directional light will be created in the viewport.

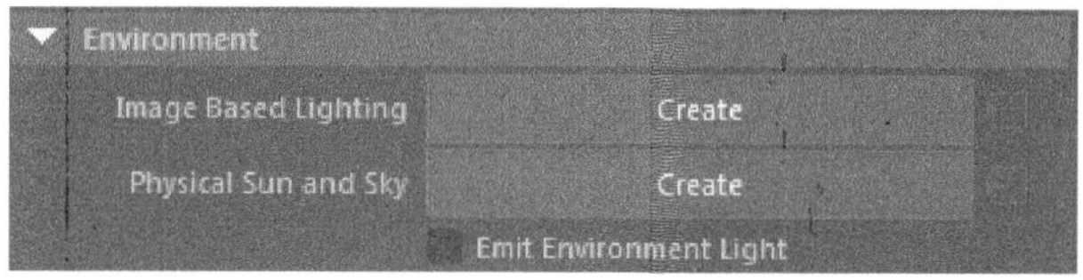

***Figure 11-31** The **Environment** area*

MENTAL RAY SHADERS

The **mental ray** shaders in Maya support all textures and lights. Also, **mental ray** has its own shader library. To set the **mental ray** shaders, first you need to set the default renderer to **mental ray**.

Now, choose the **Display render settings** button from the Status Line; the **Render Settings** window will be displayed. In this window, select **mental ray** from the **Render Using** drop-down list and then choose the **Close** button; the **mental ray** renderer will be set to render the scene. To display various Maya shaders, choose **Windows > Editors > Rendering Editors > Hypershade** from the menubar; the **Hypershade** window will be displayed, as shown in Figure 11-32. The **mental ray** shaders are available on the left of the **Hypershade** window. Alternatively, choose the **Display hypershade window** button from the Status Line to display the **Hypershade** window.

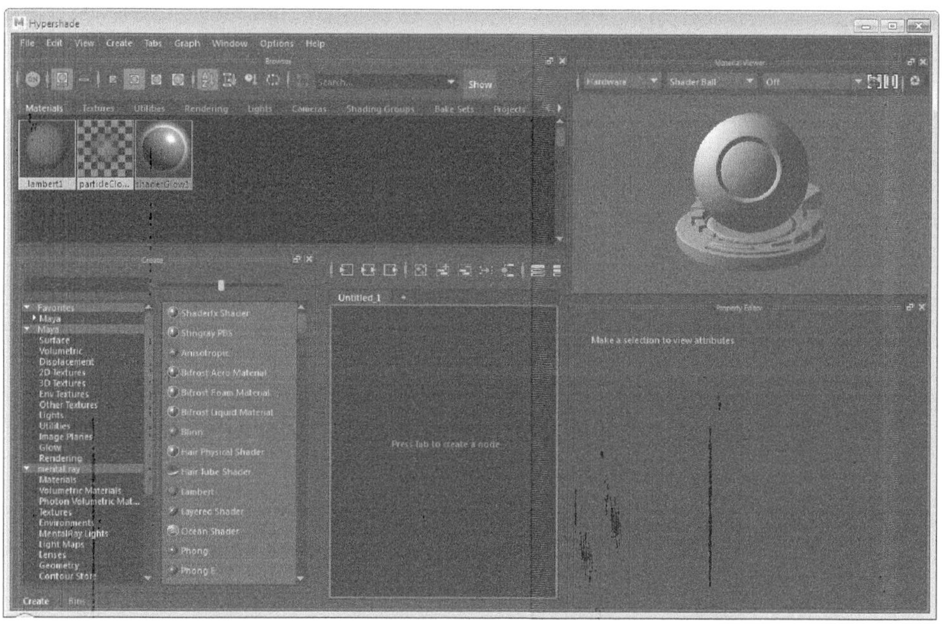

***Figure 11-32** Displaying the **mental ray** shaders in the **Hypershade** window*

You can also load or upload these libraries by choosing **Windows > Editors > Rendering Editors > mental ray > Shader Manager** from the menubar. On doing so, the **mental ray Shader Manager** dialog box will be displayed, as shown in Figure 11-33. Figure 11-34 shows the **mental ray** shaders in the **Create** panel. The **Create** panel has already been discussed in the earlier chapters.

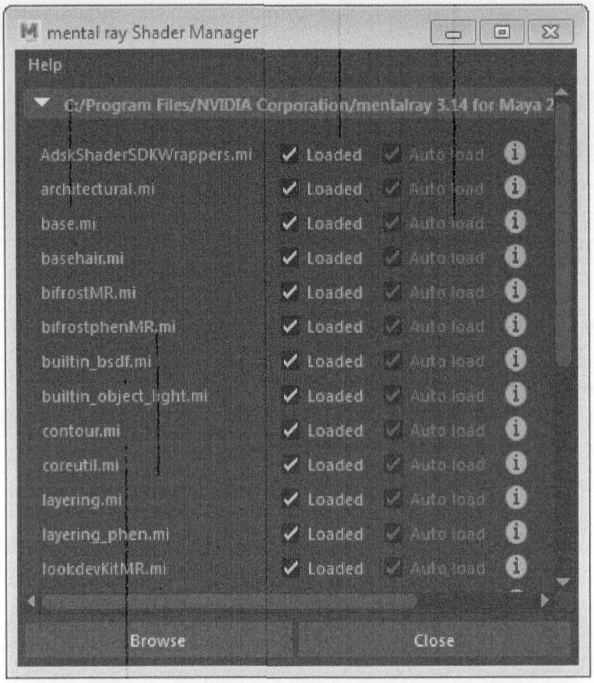

*Figure 11-33 The **mental ray Shader Manager** dialog box*

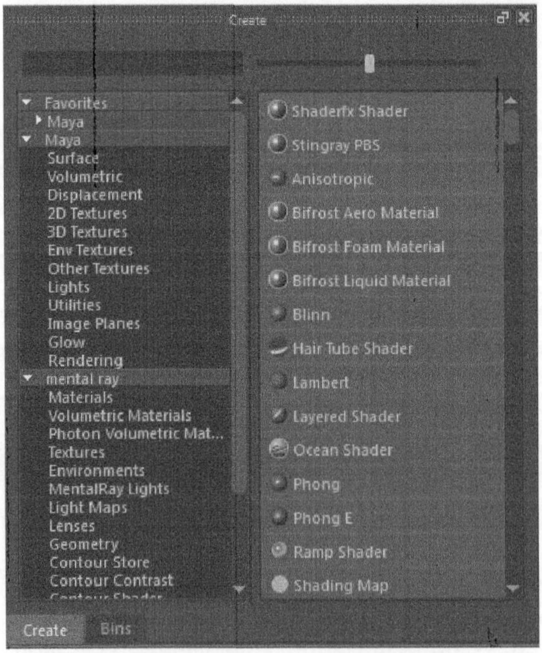

*Figure 11-34 The **Create** panel with **mental ray** shaders*

ARNOLD RENDERER

Arnold is a Maya plug-in introduced in Maya version 2017. It is also known as MtoA. This plug-in allows you to use the Arnold Renderer directly in Maya. Arnold is a cross-platform rendering solution developed by Solid Angle. It is used by prominent studios in the animation, broadcast, and gaming industries across the globe.

The Arnold renderer takes a different approach than the renderers that use biased algorithms such as photon mapping or final gather. Such algorithms cache the data and then re-sample it later. In the process, they take large amount of memory and introduce artifacts such as sampling artifacts. Arnold is an unbiased rendering engine and uses a physically-based Monte Carlo ray/path tracing algorithm. It does not use any caching algorithm thus produces clear and photo-realistic renders.

By default, the Arnold Renderer is active in Maya. If it is not loaded automatically, choose **Windows > Editors > Setting/Preferences > Plug-in Manger**; the **Plug-in Manager** window will be displayed. In this window, select the **Loaded** and **Auto Load** check boxes corresponding to the **mtoa.mll** entry and then choose the **Close** button.

WORKING WITH LIGHTS

You can use regular Maya lights with Arnold. However, the **Ambient** and **Volume** lights are not supported by Arnold. You can create Maya lights from the **Create** menu as well from the **Arnold** menu, refer to Figure 11-35. Arnold also has its own custom lights. Both type of lights are discussed next.

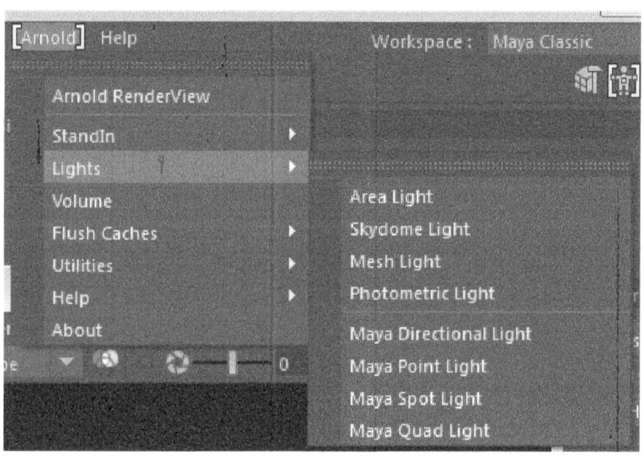

*Figure 11-35 The **Arnold** menu*

Working with Maya Lights

Setup a scene and then choose **Arnold > Lights > Maya Point Light** from the menubar; a Maya point light will be created in the viewport. Adjust the position of the light, refer to Figure 11-36. If you render the render scene, you will see darker output because of the fall of type of the light which is set to quadratic by default. You will know about the decay type later in this section.

You can use **Arnold RenderView** to view the render of the scene. To open it, choose **Arnold RenderView** from the **Arnold** menu.

*Figure 11-36 The position of the **Point Light** in the scene*

When you create a light in Maya, the **Arnold** area appears in the **Attribute Editor**, refer to Figure 11-37, from where you can change Arnold specific attributes of the light. The common light attributes are discussed next.

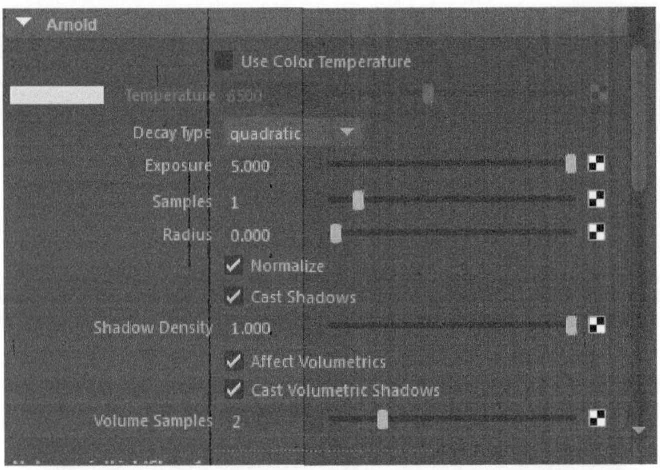

*Figure 11-37 The **Arnold** area in the **Attribute Editor***

Use Color Temperature

When you select this check box, the **Temperature** attribute gets enabled. You can use this attribute to specify the temperature of the light in Kelvins. By default, this attribute is set to **6500K** which is considered as white point. Values greater than 6500K will produce cool colors whereas values less than 6500K will produce warm colors. When you use the temperature for the light, Arnold will override the default color of the light.

Decay Type

By default, quadratic is selected in the **Decay Type** drop-down list, this resembles the real-world decay type and it is recommended that you use it while rendering the scenes for realistic results. The other decay type available is **constant**. On choosing this option, Arnold will disable decay on the light.

Exposure

The value of the **Exposure** attribute behaves like a f-stop value. This value is multiplied with the value of the **Intensity** attribute which is available in the **Point Light Attributes** area of the **Attribute Editor**. The total intensity of the light is calculated using the following formula:

*color * intensity ** $2^{exposure}$

For example, if you set value of the **Intensity** attribute to 1 and value of the **Exposure** attribute to 4, the total intensity of the light will be 16. If you are not comfortable with the **Exposure** settings, you can use the **Intensity** attribute to set the total intensity of the lights. In other words, Intensity=1, and Exposure = 4 is same as Intensity = 16. Figure 11-38 shows the render with the values of the **Intensity** and **Exposure** set to **3** and **5**, respectively. Figure 11-39 shows the render with the values of the **Intensity** and **Exposure** set to **3** and **7**, respectively.

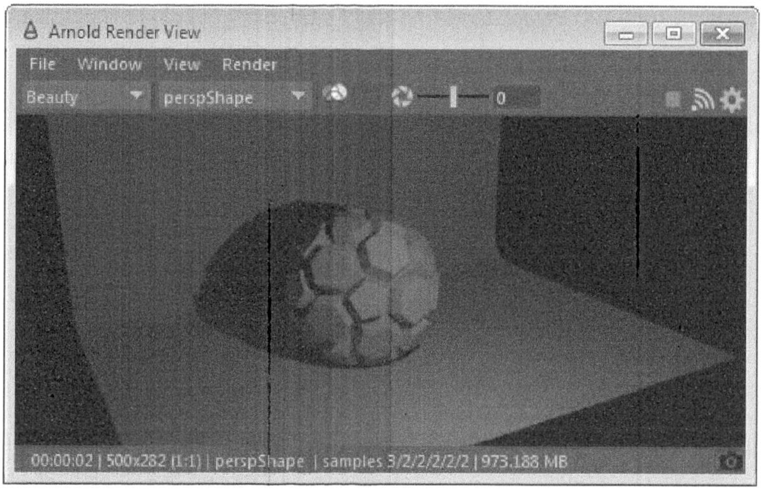

Figure 11-38 *The render with the values of the **Intensity** and **Exposure** set to **3** and **5***

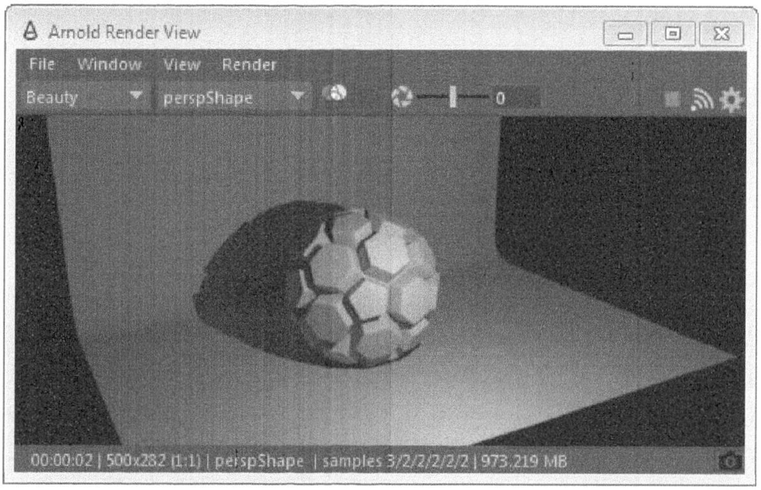

Figure 11-39 *The render with the values of the **Intensity** and **Exposure** set to **3** and **7***

Samples

This attribute controls the quality of noise in the soft shadows and the direct specular highlights. The higher the number of samples, lower the noise will be and longer Arnold will take to render them.

Radius

This attribute controls the area of the spherical surface of the light. If value of the **Radius** attribute is 0, light will behave like a true point light otherwise light source will behave like a spherical light source of the specified radius. Figure 11-40 shows the renders with the values of the **Radius** attribute set to 0 and 5. Higher the value you specify for this attribute, more diffused the shadows will be.

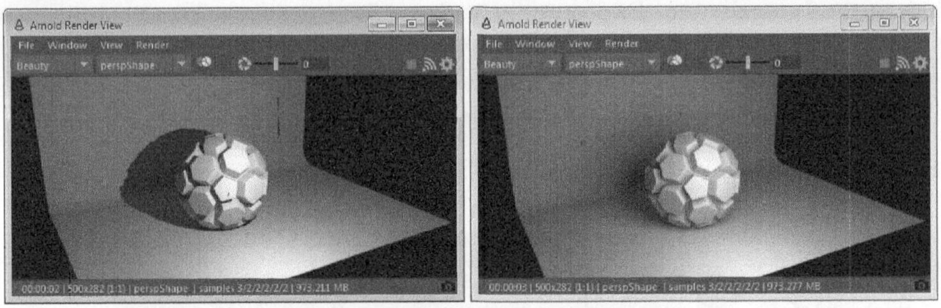

Figure 11-40 *The renders with the values of the* ***Radius*** *attribute set to* ***0*** *and* ***5***

Normalize

Select this check box to change the softness of the shadows by increasing the size of the light. When enabled, changing size of the light does not affect the amount of light being emitted.

Cast Shadows

Select this check box to compute shadows cast in the scene.

Shadow Density

This attribute controls the strength of the shadows.

Affect Volumetrics

On selecting this check box, light affects the atmospheric fog and scattering. The distant lights do not support scattering.

Cast Volumetric Shadows

On selecting this check box, Arnold computes the volumetric samples.

Volume Samples

This attribute is used to set the number of samples to integrate the in-scattering effect from the direct light.

Diffuse, Specular, SSS, and Volume Multipliers

These attributes are used for the per-light scaling of the Diffuse/Specular/SSS/Indirect and Volume components. By default, these attributes are set to 1 and to get accurate results retain default value 1 of these attributes.

Indirect

This attribute controls the energy loss or gain at each ray bounce. For accurate results, you should leave it at its default value 1.

Max Bounces

This attribute controls the number of times energy from the light will be allowed to bounce in the scene. If you set value of this attribute to 0, Arnold will disable the GI for the light. The default value for this attribute is 999. However, in practice you will need a much lower value.

AOV Light Group

AOV stands for Arbitrary Output Variables. AOVs are used to render any arbitrary shading network into different images. You can combine these images using any compositing package to produce the final output. AOVs allow you to fine tune the render of different elements of an image such as shadows, reflections, and so on.

Working with Arnold Lights

Arnold has some built-in custom lights such as **Area Light**, **Skydome Light**, **Mesh Light**, and **Photometric Light**. You can create these lights from the **Arnold** menu. Commonly used lights are discussed next.

Area Light

When you use the regular Maya area light, Arnold considers it a rectangular or quad light source but when you use the Arnold's **Area Light**, you have options for specifying another shape for the light source from the **Light Shape** drop-down list, refer to Figure 11-41. Also, note that the **Intensity** and **Exposure** attributes appear together in the **Attribute Editor**.

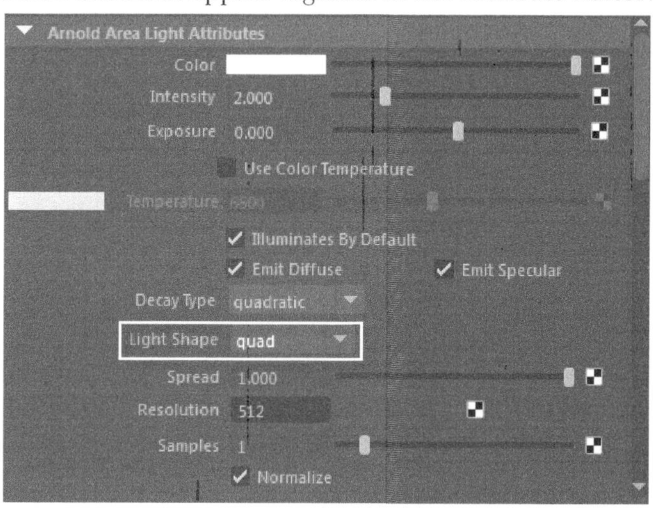

*Figure 11-41 The **Light Shape** drop-down list*

When a shader is connected to an Area Light, Arnold calculates the importance tables for efficient sampling according to the luminance values of the textures. The resolution of the tables is controlled by the **Resolution** attribute. For best result, you should match attribute's value with the resolution of the incoming image.

The **Spread** attribute controls the focus of the light in the direction along the normal. At a value of 1, light will be focussed like a laser beam.

Mesh Light

You can use the **Mesh Light** to create light shapes which are not possible to create from regular shapes such as cylinder or rectangle. To create a mesh light, select a mesh in the viewport and then choose **Arnold > Lights > Mesh Light** from the menubar. To set the attributes of the light, choose the shape node of the mesh in the **Attribute Editor** and then expand the **Arnold** area. Make sure that the **mesh_light** option is selected from the **Arnold Translator** drop-down list.

Photometric Light

This light is used to import and render real-world light distribution files, IES files. An IES file contains the measurement of the light intensity stored in an ASCII file. When you create a photometric light, you can import the file by clicking the folder icon corresponding to the **Photometry File** attribute from the **Photometric Light Attributes** area of the **Attribute** Editor.

STANDARD SHADER

To create any type of material from wood to plastic, from chrome to alluminium, and so on, you can use Arnold's Standard Shader. It is also known as Ai Standard Shader. Once you apply the shader to a mesh, you can control attributes from the **Attribute Editor**. This shader has large number of controls which are grouped under different areas in the **Attribute Editor**. The commonly used groups are discussed next.

Diffuse

The **Color** attribute sets the brightness of the surface when lit directly by a white light source. It defines the percentage of each component of the spectrum which is not absorbed by the surface. The **Weight** attribute defines the weight of the diffuse component. The **Roughness** attribute controls the roughness of the surface. Higher values are suitable for creating material like plaster or sand. The **Backlighting** attribute is used to create a surface as if it is lit from behind by a light source. It is recommended that you use this attribute with single sided geometry as thick objects might not be rendered correctly. If the **Fresnel affects Diffuse** check box is selected, fresnel (viewing angle of the surface) will affect the diffuse component.

Specular

The attributes in this area are used to control the direct and indirect reflections. You can also make the reflections blurry. The **Color** control defines the color of the reflection. You can use this attribute to tint the reflections. The **Weight** attribute controls the brightness of the specular highlights. The **Roughness** attribute controls the glossiness of the specular highlights. The **Anisotropy** attribute reflects and transmits light in a direction that causes the surface to be shiner or rough in a certain direction. The **Rotation** attribute controls the orientation of the anisotropic highlights.

The options in the **Microfacet Distribution** drop-down list allow you to control the shape of the specular highlights. There are two options available: **ggx** and **beckmann**. The default **ggx** option has a sharp peak and a large tail than the **backmaan** option. When the **Fresnel** check box is selected, fresnel will affect the reflection highlights.

Reflection

This is the secondary level of reflection layer. If you want to create perfect reflective surfaces such as mirror, use the attributes available in this area. For other type of reflective surfaces, use the attributes in the **Specular** area.

The **Color** attribute defines the color of the reflection ray. The **Weight** attribute defines the amount of light reflected by the surface. Select the **Fresnel** check box if you want fresnel to affect the reflections. The **Enable Internal Reflections** check box is selected by default. As a result, indirect specular and mirror perfect reflections are calculated.

Refraction

The **Color** and **Weight** attributes defines the color of the refraction and the amount of light passing through the material, respectively. The **IOR** attribute defines the index of refraction of the medium. The **Roughness** attribute defines the blurriness of the refraction. The **Dispersion Abbe Number** attribute defines the abbe number of the material. The default value is 0 which means there will be no dispersion. The typical abbe number for glass and diamonds are in a range of 10 to 70.

The **Fresnel use IOR** check box when selected affects the fresnel reflectance based on the IOR value. The **Transmittance** attribute filters the refraction according to the distance travelled by the ray in a medium. Note that the transmittance color is dependent of the scale of the scene.

The **Opacity** attribute defines the extent to which light is not allowed to travel through a medium. Unlike the **Transparency** attribute, the **Opacity** attribute affects entire shader.

Bump Mapping

The **Bump Mapping** attribute allows you to connect a shader to it. The shader affects the normals of the surface to create the bump effect.

Emission

The attributes in this area allow you to create self-illuminating surfaces. The **Color** attribute defines the emitted light color. The **Scale** attribute defines the amount of emitted light.

Matte

The attributes in this group allow you to create cutouts by rendering the alpha as 0. Select the **Enable Matte** check box to enable the matte effect. The **Matte Color** attribute defines the color of the matte and the **Matte Opacity** attribute defines the opacity of the cutout.

TUTORIAL

Tutorial 1

In this tutorial, you will render the model of a glass using the **mental ray** renderer to get the final output, as shown in Figure 11-42. **(Expected time: 30 min)**

Figure 11-42 The rendered image of a glass using ***mental ray*** *renderer*

The following steps are required to complete this tutorial:

a. Create a project folder.
b. Download and open the file.
c. Apply textures to objects.
d. Add light to the scene.
e. Set the **mental ray** attributes.
f. Save the scene.

Creating a Project Folder

Create a new project folder with the name *c11_tut1* at *\Documents\maya2017*, as discussed in Tutorial 1 of Chapter 2.

Downloading and Opening the File

In this section, you need to download and open the file.

1. Download the *c11_maya_2017_tut.zip* from *www.cadcim.com*. The path of the file is as follows: *Textbooks > Animation and Visual Effects > Maya > Autodesk Maya 2017: A Comprehensive Guide.*

   Next, extract the contents of the zip file to the *Documents* folder.

2. Choose **File > Open Scene** from the menubar; the **Open** dialog box is displayed. In this dialog box, browse to *\Documents\c11_maya_2017_tut* and select **c11_tut1_start.mb** file in it. Choose the **Open** button; the file opens, refer to Figure 11-43.

Figure 11-43 The model of a glass in the scene

3. Now, choose **File > Save Scene As** from the menubar; the **Save As** dialog box is displayed. As the project folder is already set, the path *\Documents\maya2017\c11_tut1\scenes* is already displayed in the **Look In** drop-down list. Save the file with the name *c11tut1.mb*.

Applying Textures to the Objects

In this section, you will apply textures to the objects in the scene.

1. Choose **Windows > Editors > Rendering Editors > Hypershade** from the menubar; the **Hypershade** window is displayed. Choose the **Lambert** shader from the **Create** panel; the **lambert#** shader is created in the **Browser** panel. Press the CTRL key and double-click on the **lambert#** shader in the **Browser** panel; the **Rename node** dialog box is displayed. In this dialog box, enter **box** in the **Enter new name** edit box and choose the **OK** button; the *lambert2* shader is renamed to ***box***.

2. Select the ***box*** in the viewport. Now, press and hold the right mouse button on the *box* shader in the **Browser** panel; a marking menu is displayed. Choose **Assign Material To Selection** from the marking menu; the selected shader is applied to the box.

3. Double-click on the *box* shader in the **Hypershade** window; the **box** tab is displayed in the **Property Editor**. In the **Common Material Properties** area of the **box** tab, set the color of the **Color** attribute to white by moving the slider to the right.

4. Choose the **Phong** shader from the **Create Bar** panel in the **Hypershade** window; the **phong#** shader is created in the **Browser** panel. Rename the **phong#** shader to **glass**, as discussed earlier. Select the glass from the viewport and press and hold the right mouse button on the *glass* shader in the **Hypershade** window; a marking menu is displayed. Choose **Assign Material To Selection** from the marking menu; the *glass* shader is applied to the glass.

5. Click on the *glass* shader in the **Browser** panel; the **glass** tab is displayed in the **Property Editor**. In the **Common Material Properties** area of the **glass** tab, set the color of the **Color** attribute to black by dragging the slider toward left; the color of the glass in the viewport changes to black. Next, click on the **Transparency** color swatch; the **Color History** palette is displayed. Specify the **HSV** values in the palette as given below:

   H: **60** S: **0.0** V: **0.870**

Figure 11-44 The rendered image of the glass

6. Enter **0.1** in the **Diffuse** edit box in the **Common Material Attributes** area of the **glass** tab.

7. In the **Specular Shading** area, set the value of **Cosine Power** to **100** and **Specular Color** to white. Set the **Reflectivity** value to **0.2**.

8. Expand the **Ray Tracing** area in the **glass** tab and select the **Refractions** check box to switch on the refractions. Next, set the value of **Refractive Index** to **1.520** and **Refraction Limit** to **10**. Choose **Render the current frame** button from the Status Line to render the scene. Figure 11-44 shows the rendered image of the glass.

9. Choose the **Phong** shader from the **Create** panel in the **Hypershade** window; the **phong2** shader is created in the **Browser panel**. Rename the **phong2** shader to **water**, as discussed earlier.

10. Make sure the glass is selected in the viewport. In the **Channel Box / Layer Editor**, choose the **Create a new layer** button from the **Display** tab to create a new layer (*layer1*). Next, right-click on the layer1 and choose the **Add Selected Objects** option from the shortcut menu displayed. Double-click on **layer1**; the **Edit Layer** dialog box is displayed. Rename the layer as **glass1** and choose the **Save** button to close it. Similarly, create a new layer for water mesh and rename it as **water1**. Next, hide the glass by choosing the **V** button corresponding to the **glass1** layer in the **Channel Box / Layer Editor**, as shown in Figure 11-45; only the water mesh is displayed in the viewport, as shown in Figure 11-46.

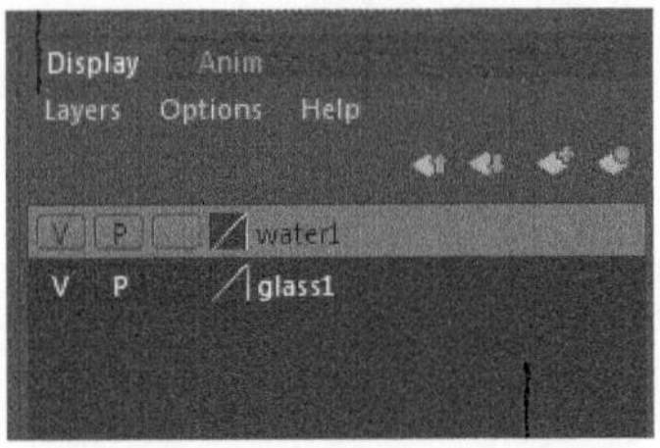

*Figure 11-45 Hiding the **glass1** layer*

Figure 11-46 The water mesh

11. Select the water mesh in the viewport. Next, select the **water** shader from the **Browser** panel of the **Hypershade** window and then press and hold the right mouse button over it; a marking menu is displayed. Choose the **Assign Material To Selection** option from the marking menu; the **water** shader is applied to the water mesh.

12. Double-click on the **water** shader in the **Hypershade** window; the **Property Editor** is displayed with the **water** tab chosen. In the **Common Material Attributes** area of this tab, set the color in the **Color** attribute to black. Next, click on the **Transparency** color swatch; the **Color History** palette is displayed. Set the **HSV** values in the **Color History** palette as follows:

    H: **202** S: **0.5** V: **0.4**

    Make sure the **Diffuse** value is set to **0.8** to adjust the brightness level of the glass.

13. In the **Specular Shading** area in the **Property Editor**, enter **120** in the **Cosine Power** edit box and set the color in the **Specular Color** attribute to white. Also, set the **Reflectivity** value to **0.2** and **Reflected Color** to white.

14. In the **Ray Tracing** area in the **Property Editor**, select the **Refractions** check box. Next, set **Refractive Index** to **1.33** and make sure the **Refraction Limit** is set to **6**.

15. Make the **glass1** layer is visible in the **Layer Editor**, as discussed in the earlier steps. Choose the **Render the current frame** button from the Status Line to render the scene. Figure 11-47 shows the rendered glass and water after applying the raytrace attributes to it.

16. Open the **Hypershade** window and choose the **Lambert** shader from the **Create** panel; the **lambert#** shader is created in the **Browser** panel. Rename the **lambert#** shader to **straw**, as discussed earlier. Select straw from the viewport. Next, press and hold the right mouse button on the **straw** shader in the **Browser** panel of the **Hypershade** window; a marking menu is displayed. Choose **Assign Material To Selection** from the marking menu to apply the shader to the straw in the viewport.

Figure 11-47 *The rendered glass after applying the* ***raytrace*** *attributes*

17. Double-click on the **straw** shader in the **Hypershade** window; the **Property Editor** is displayed with the **straw** tab chosen. In the **Common Material Properties** area of this tab, click on the color swatch of the **Color** attribute; the **Color History** palette is displayed. Enter the following **HSV** values in the **Color History** palette:

    H: **55** S: **0.2** V: **0.9**

Adding Light to the Scene

In this section, you need to add a spot light to the scene.

1. Choose **Create > Objects > Lights > Spot Light** from the menubar; a spot light is created in the viewport. To align the light in the viewport, set the values of the spot light in the **Channel Box / Layer Editor** as follows:

    Translate X: **5** Translate Y: **21** Translate Z: **8**
    Rotate X: **-60** Rotate Y: **35** Rotate Z: **-5**

2. Press CTRL+A and make sure the **spotLightShape1** tab is chosen in the **Attribute Editor**. In the **Spot Light Attributes** area of this tab, set the **Intensity** value to **800** and select **Quadratic** from the **Decay Rate** drop-down list. Set the values for the remaining options as follows:

    Cone Angle: **120** Penumbra Angle: **1** Dropoff: **5**

Setting the mental ray Rendering Attributes

In this section, you need to set the **mental ray** renderer attributes for rendering the scene.

1. Choose **Windows > Editors > Rendering Editors > Render Settings** from the menubar; the **Render Settings** window is displayed. Select **mental ray** from the **Render Using** drop-down list. Next, choose the **Quality** tab and then click on the **Show Advanced Setting** check box. Now, expand the **Legacy Options** area in this window. Now, expand the **Caustics** area, select the **Caustics** check box; the caustics are activated in the scene.

Tip

*If the mental ray renderer is not there in the **Render Using** drop-down list, choose **Windows > Editors > Setting Preferences > Plug-in Manager** from the menubar; the **Plug-in Manager** dialog box is displayed. Select the **Loaded** and **Autoload** check boxes from the **Mayatomr.mll** plug-in to activate the **mental ray** renderer. Choose the **Refresh** button and then the **Close** button from the **Plug-in Manager** dialog box; the **mental ray** renderer is activated in the **Render Settings** window.*

2. Make sure that the light is selected in the viewport. In the **spotLightShape1** tab of the **Attribute Editor**, expand the **mental ray** area and select the **Emit Photons** check box in the **Caustics and Global Illumination** area. Enter **25000** in the **Photon Intensity** edit box and **20000** in the **Caustic Photons** edit box.

3. In the **Render Settings** window, choose the **Quality** tab and expand the **Trace Depth** area. Next, set the values as follows:

   Reflections: **10** Transmission: **10**
   Max Trace Depth: **20**

4. Close the **Render Settings** and **Hypershade** windows.

5. Set the view you want to render. Next, choose **Render the current frame** button from the Status Line; the rendering begins in the **Render View** window. Figure 11-48 shows the final rendered view of the glass. You can view the final rendered image of the model by downloading the *c11_maya_2017_rndr.zip* file from *www.cadcim.com*. The path of the file is as follows: *Textbooks > Animation and Visual Effects > Maya > Autodesk Maya 2017: A Comprehensive Guide*.

***Figure 11-48** The final rendered image of the glass*

Saving the Scene

In this section, you need to save the scene that you have created.

1. Choose **File > Save Scene** from the menubar to save the scene.

Tutorial 2

In this tutorial, you will create a simple studio setup using Arnold lights, as shown in Figure 11-49. **(Expected time: 30 min)**

The following steps are required to complete this tutorial:

a. Create a project folder.
b. Download and open the file.
c. Add lights to the scene.
d. Create material.
e. Save the scene.

*Figure 11-49 The rendered image of a geometry using the **Arnold** renderer*

Creating a Project Folder

Create a new project folder with the name *c11_tut3* at *\Documents\maya2017*, as discussed in Tutorial 1 of Chapter 2.

Downloading and Opening the File

In this section, you need to download and open the file.

1. Download the *c11_maya_2017_tut.zip* from *www.cadcim.com*. The path of the file is as follows: *Textbooks > Animation and Visual Effects > Maya > Autodesk Maya 2017: A Comprehensive Guide.*

   Next, extract the contents of the zip file to the *Documents* folder.

2. Choose **File > Open Scene** from the menubar; the **Open** dialog box is displayed. In this dialog box, browse to *\Documents\c11_maya_2017_tut* and select **c11_tut3_start.mb** file in it. Choose the **Open** button; the file opens.

3. Now, choose **File > Save Scene As** from the menubar; the **Save As** dialog box is displayed. As the project folder is already set, the path *\Documents\maya2017\c11_tut3\scenes* is already displayed in the **Look In** drop-down list. Save the file with the name *c11tut3.mb*.

Adding Lights to the Scene

In this section, you will add Arnold lights to the scene.

1. Choose **Arnold > Lights > Area Light** from the menubar; an area light is added to the scene. Place the light at the left of the geometry, as shown in Figure 11-50. Render the scene; you will notice that the render is dark.

   Next, you will adjust the light's properties.

2. In the **Attribute Editor > aiAreaLightShape1 > Arnold Area Light Attributes** area, enter **4** and **8** in the **Intensity** and **Exposure** edit boxes, respectively. Render the scene. Now the render look brighter, as shown in Figure 11-51.

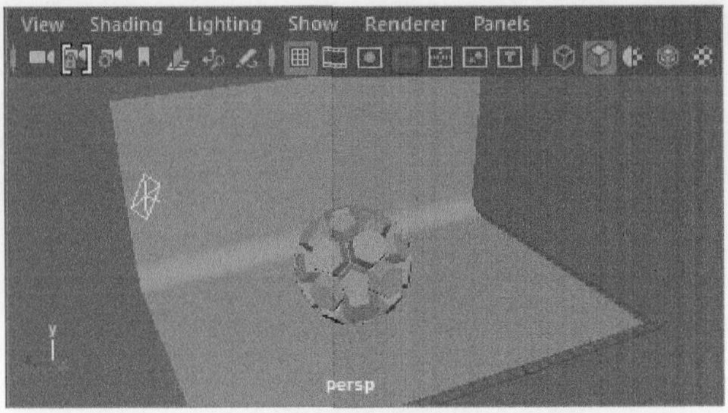

Figure 11-50 The Arnold light placed in the scene

Figure 11-51 The render of the scene

3. Duplicate the light and place it on the right side of the geometry. Again, duplicate the light and place it at the top of the geometry, refer to Figure 11-52.

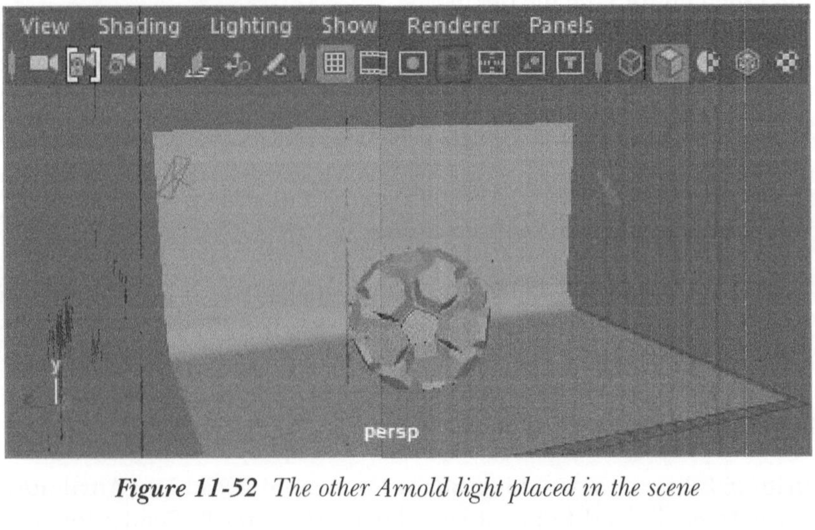

Figure 11-52 The other Arnold light placed in the scene

4. In the **Attribute Editor > aiAreaLightShape1 > Arnold Area Light Attributes** area, enter **3** in the **Samples** edit box. Repeat the process for other two lights.

5. In the **Attribute Editor > aiAreaLightShape1 > Arnold Area Light Attributes** area, select the **Use Color Temperature** check box.

6. In the **Attribute Editor > aiAreaLightShape2 > Arnold Area Light Attributes** area, select the **Use Color Temperature** check box and then enter **4000** in the **Temperature** edit box. Render the scene; notice that the warm and cool temperatures are producing a nice studio light setup.

Creating the Material

In this section, you will create a material for the scene using the **Standard** shader.

1. Right-click on the geometry in the scene and then choose **Assign New Material** from the shortcut menu; the **Assign New Material** window is displayed. In this window, choose **Arnold > Shader > Surface > aiStandard**; the Standard shader is applied to the geometry.

2. In the **Attribute Editor > aiStandard > Diffuse** area, anchor the **Color** slider to extreme left to make the diffuse color black. Enter **0.65** in **Weight** edit box and **0.22** in the **Roughness** edit box.

3. In the **Attribute Editor > aiStandard > Specular** area, enter **0.3**, **0.358** in the **Weight** and **Roughness** edit boxes, respectively. Select the **Fresnel** check box and then enter **0.7** in the **Reflectance at Normal** edit box. Render the scene; you will notice that there is some noise in the specular highlights, refer to Figure 11-53. The noise occurs because of low glossy samples.

Figure 11-53 *The render with noise in the specular highlights*

Next, you will adjust samples.

4. Choose **Display render settings** button on the Status Line; the **Render Settings** window is displayed. In the **Sampling** area of the **Arnold Renderer** tab, enter **4** in the **Glossy** edit box. Render the scene.

Saving the Scene

In this section, you need to save the scene that you have created.

1. Choose **File > Save Scene** from the menubar to save the scene.

Self-Evaluation Test

Answer the following questions and then compare them to those given at the end of this chapter:

1. Which of the following is a refraction pattern formed due to the reflection of light on highly transparent objects?

   (a) Global Illumination (b) Caustics
   (c) Final Gather (d) Raytrace

2. Which of the following options is used to produce the accurate rendering of daylight scenes?

   (a) **Physical sun and sky** (b) **Daylight**
   (c) **Volume light** (d) None of these

3. The__________ renderer generates images with outstanding quality and unsurpassed realism and gives scalable performance.

4. In Maya, the __________ algorithm is used to create photorealistic scenes which results in high computation time.

5. The __________ are the refraction patterns formed by highly transparent objects such as a glass filled with fluid.

6. The __________ plug-in is used to activate the mental ray rendering.

7. In Maya, the mental ray rendering does not support spot lights. (T/F)

8. In Maya, the **Maya Vector** renderer cannot render bump maps, displacement maps, and fluid effects. (T/F)

Review Questions

Answer the following questions:

1. Which of the following rendering options yields extremely realistic shading effects?

   (a) **Caustics** (b) **Final Gather**
   (c) **Global illumination** (d) **Raytracing**

2. Which of the following techniques has a greater dynamic range of values between the light

and colors than any other normal digital imaging techniques?

(a) Global illumination (b) Final Gather
(c) Caustics (d) HDRI

3. The __________ is a process in which the light reflected from one object projects diffuse color on its nearby object or surface.

4. The **Physical Sun and Sky** attribute uses the __________ and __________ shaders.

5. The __________ is a process in which the incident-radiated energy is retained completely by the object.

6. The **Reflection** option in the **Raytrace** area is used to set the maximum number of times a ray can be refracted through a non-opaque object. (T/F)

7. Reflection is a change in the direction of light at the interface between two dissimilar mediums such that the light returns to the medium from where it originated. (T/F)

8. In the **Maya Vector** renderer settings, the **Curve tolerance** edit box in the **Appearance Options** area is used to set the outline of the rendered object. (T/F)

EXERCISES

The rendered output of the scenes used in the following exercises can be accessed by downloading the *c11_maya_2017_exr.zip* file from *www.cadcim.com*. The path of the file is as follows: *Textbooks > Animation and Visual Effects > Maya > Autodesk Maya 2017: A Comprehensive Guide.*

Exercise 1

Create a scene, as shown in Figure 11-54. Apply textures to the scene and then render it using the **mental ray** renderer to get the output shown in Figure 11-55. **(Expected time: 45 min)**

Figure 11-54 *Scene before rendering*

Figure 11-55 Scene after rendering

Exercise 2

Extract the contents of the *c11_maya_2017_exr.zip file*. Open *c11_exr02_start.mb* and then apply textures to it. Next, create a tree on its left using the **Content Browser** window, as shown in Figure 11-56. Next, add lights and render the scene using the **mental ray** renderer to get the output shown in Figure 11-57. **(Expected time: 30 min)**

Figure 11-56 The tree created in the scene

Figure 11-57 The rendered scene

Answers to Self-Evaluation Test

1. b, **2.** a, **3.** **mental ray**, **4.** **Raytrace**, **5.** caustics, **6.** **Mayatomr.mll**, **7.** F, **8.** T

Chapter 12

Particle System

Learning Objectives

After completing this chapter, you will be able to:

- *Create particles*
- *Create emitters*
- *Modify the render attributes of particles*
- *Collide particles*
- *Use the Hardware Renderer*
- *Apply different types of fields and pre-defined effects*

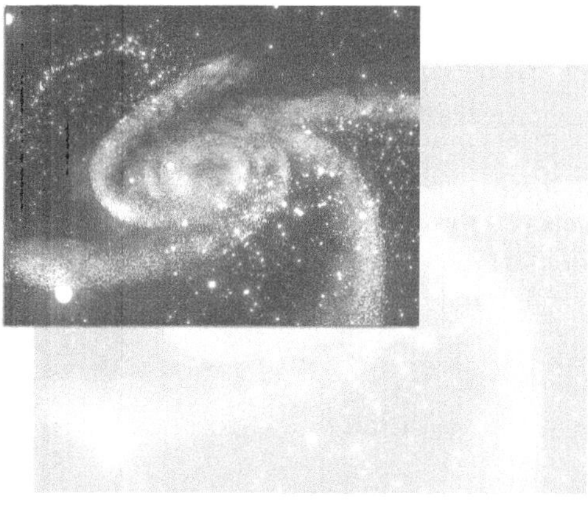

INTRODUCTION

The particle system in Maya is used to create particle-based visual effects in a scene. In this chapter, you will learn to create different effects using particles. Moreover, you will learn about the concept of goal, which is used to control the flow of particles and create predefined particle effects in Maya. You will also learn about the tools used in particle systems.

CREATING PARTICLES

Particles are points in 3D space that can be grouped together to create different effects. To create particles in 3D space, first select the **FX** menuset from the **Menuset** drop-down list in the Status Line. Next, choose **nParticles > Legacy Particles > Particle Tool** from the menubar and click in the viewport; a particle will be created in 3D space. By default, Maya creates one particle on a single click. You can change the default settings of **Particle Tool** using the options in the **Tool Settings (Particle Tool)** window. The options in this window are discussed next.

Tool Settings (Particle Tool) Window

To invoke the **Tool Settings (Particle Tool)** window, choose **nParticles > Legacy Particles > Particle Tool > Option Box** from the menubar; the **Tool Settings (Particle Tool)** window will be displayed, refer to Figure 12-1. Some of the options in this window are discussed next.

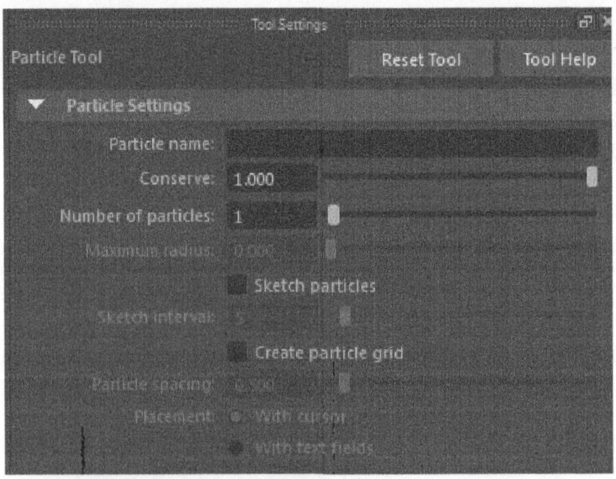

*Figure 12-1 The **Tool Settings (Particle Tool)** window*

Particle name

This attribute is used to specify the name of the particle system. Naming a particle system helps you identify the particle in the **Outliner** window. By default, the name **particle1** is assigned to the particle system created.

Conserve

The **Conserve** attribute is used to control the motion of particles.

Number of particles

The **Number of particles** attribute is used to specify the number of particles to be created in the viewport with a single click. The default value of this attribute is 1. If you specify a value greater than 1 for this attribute, the **Maximum radius** attribute below it will get activated. The

Maximum radius attribute is used to specify a spherical region in which the specified number of particles will be randomly distributed.

Note

If you want to undo the last action performed in the viewport while creating the particles, press the BACKSPACE key. However, you can perform the undo operation till you have not pressed the ENTER key.

Sketch particles

The **Sketch particles** check box is used to sketch a continuous stream of particles. It works similar to the pencil tool used in other 2D software applications. To create a stream of particles, select the **Sketch particles** check box, press and hold the left mouse button in the viewport and drag the mouse to create a particle stream. Press ENTER to create the complete particle system in the viewport. On selecting the **Sketch particles** check box, the **Sketch interval** edit box will be activated. Enter the value in this edit box to specify the spacing between the particles while sketching a continuous stream of particles. Higher the value specified in this edit box, more will be the distance between the particles.

Create particle grid

The **Create particle grid** check box is used to create a grid of particles in the workspace. To create a grid of particles, select this check box and click once in the viewport; a particle is created as the first point of the grid. Next, click at a location that is diagonal to the first point and press ENTER; a grid of particles will be created. On selecting this check box, the **Particle spacing** attribute and the radio buttons in the **Placement** area will be activated. The **Particle spacing** attribute is used to specify the spacing between particles in the particle grid. In the **Placement** area, you can select the **With cursor** radio button to set the particle grid by using the cursor or select the **With text fields** radio button to set the grid coordinates manually.

CREATING EMITTERS

Emitters are the objects that emit particles continuously. Emitters can be used to create various effects such as fireworks, smoke, fire, and so on. To create an emitter, choose **nParticles > Legacy Particles > Create Emitter** from the menubar; the emitter will be created in the viewport, as shown in Figure 12-2. You can change the default settings of an emitter as required. To do so, choose **nParticles > Legacy Particles > Create Emitter > Option Box** from the menubar; the **Emitter Options (Create)** dialog box will be displayed, as shown in Figure 12-3. Various attributes in this dialog box are discussed next.

Figure 12-2 *The emitter created in viewport*

Emitter name

This attribute is used to specify the name of the emitter. Naming an emitter lets you identify the emitter in the **Outliner** window. By default, **emitter1** is displayed as the name of the emitter created.

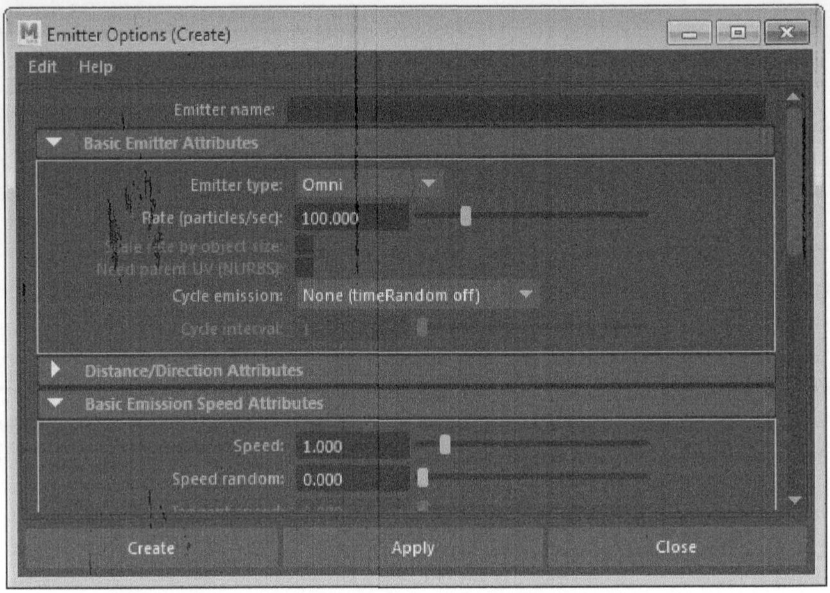

*Figure 12-3 The **Emitter Options (Create)** dialog box*

Basic Emitter Attributes Area

The options in this area are used to set the basic attributes of an emitter, as shown in Figure 12-4. All attributes in the **Basic Emitter Attributes** area are discussed next.

*Figure 12-4 The **Basic Emitter Attributes** area*

Emitter type

The **Emitter type** drop-down list is used to select an emitter type. By default, the **Omni** emitter type is selected from the drop-down list. It is used to emit particles in all directions. Select the **Directional** emitter type from the drop-down list if you want the particles to be emitted only in a particular direction. Select the **Volume** emitter type to emit particles from a closed volume.

Rate (particles/sec)

The **Rate (particles/sec)** attribute is used to set the average rate at which the particles will be emitted per second from an emitter. To set the value for this attribute, enter a value in the edit box or adjust the slider bar. The default value of this attribute is 100.

Scale rate by object size

Select the **Scale rate by object size** check box if you want the particles to be emitted as per the size of the object. By default, this check box is inactive. To activate it, select the **Volume** emitter type from the **Emitter type** drop-down list. Larger the size of the object, more will be the particles emitted.

Need parent UV (NURBS)

This check box is activated for NURBS surface emitters only. On selecting this check box, the **Parent U** and **Parent V** attributes are added to the **particleShape** tab in the **Attribute Editor**.

Cycle emission

The **Cycle emission** drop-down list is used to restart the emission of particles in a random manner. Select the **Frame (timeRandom on)** option from this drop-down list; the **Cycle interval** edit box below this drop-down list will get activated. Enter a value in this edit box to specify the number of frames after which the emission of the particles will restart.

Distance/Direction Attributes Area

The attributes in this area are used to specify distance and direction for particle emission, refer to Figure 12-5. The attributes in this area are discussed next.

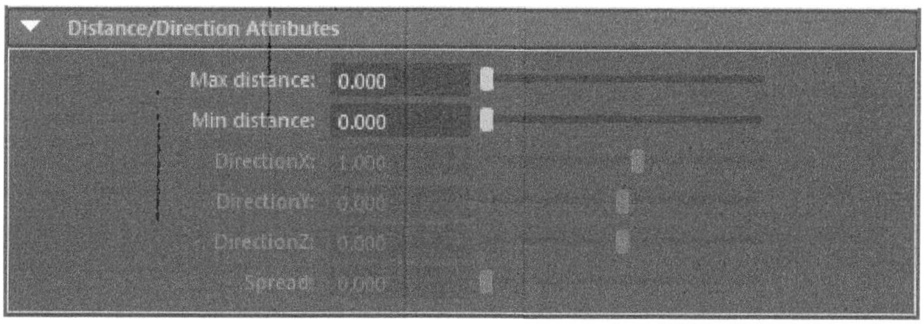

*Figure 12-5 The **Distance/Direction Attributes** area*

Max distance

The **Max distance** attribute is used to set the maximum distance from the emitter from where the emission of particles will occur.

Min distance

The **Min distance** attribute is used to set the minimum distance from the emitter from where the emission of particles will occur. Note that the minimum distance value should always be smaller than the maximum distance value. The **Min distance** and **Max distance** attributes will be activated only when the **Omni** or **Directional** emitter types are selected from the **Emitter type** drop-down list.

DirectionX, DirectionY, and DirectionZ

The **DirectionX**, **DirectionY**, and **DirectionZ** edit boxes are used to set the direction of emission with respect to the position and orientation of the emitter. These attributes will be activated only when the **Directional** and **Volume** emitter types are selected in the **Emitter type** drop-down list.

Spread

The **Spread** attribute is used to set the spread angle for the emission of particles. This attribute will be activated only when the **Directional** emitter type is selected in the **Emitter type** drop-down list.

Basic Emission Speed Attributes Area

The options in this area are used to set the speed attributes for the particles emitted from the emitter, as shown in Figure 12-6. The attributes in this area are discussed next.

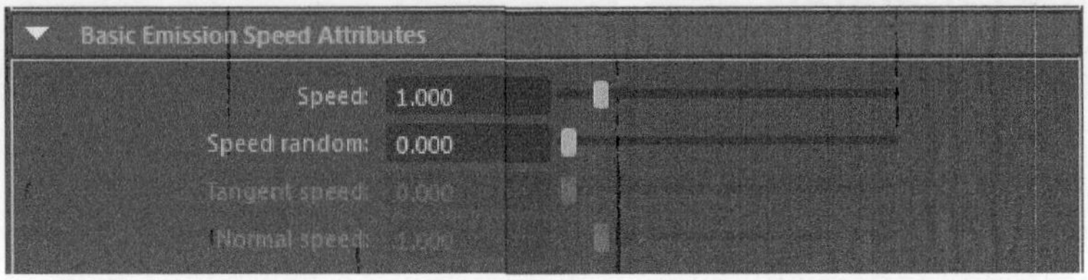

*Figure 12-6 The **Basic Emission Speed Attributes** area*

Speed

The **Speed** attribute is used to determine the speed of the emitted particles. Enter **1** to set the default speed; **0.5** to reduce the speed to half; and **2** to double the speed.

Speed random

The **Speed random** attribute is used to randomize the emission speed.

Tangent speed

The **Tangent speed** attribute is used to set the magnitude of the tangent component of the emission speed for surface and curve emission.

Normal speed

The **Normal speed** attribute is used to set the magnitude of the normal component of the emitted particles.

CREATING GOALS

A goal is used to set the movement of particles in a particular direction. To create a goal, select the particles that you want to be affected by the goal. Next, press and hold the SHIFT key and then select the object that you want to set as goal. Now, choose **nParticles > Create > Goal** from the menubar to set the goal for the selected objects. Play the animation; the movement of the particles will be directed toward the goal. You can set the weight of a goal object to specify the particle attracting power. To do so, choose **nParticles > Create > Goal > Option Box** from the menubar; the **Goal Options** dialog box will be displayed, as shown in Figure 12-7. You can set the **Goal weight** value between 0 and 1. The default value of the **Goal Weight** is 0.5. You can also make a camera act as a goal object.

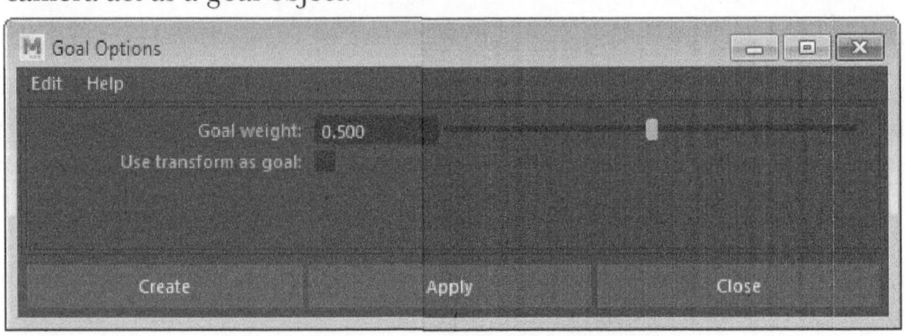

*Figure 12-7 The **Goal Options** dialog box*

COLLIDING PARTICLES

You can make particle objects collide with the polygonal or NURBS surfaces. To do so, select the particles, press SHIFT, and then select the object with which you want the particles to collide. Now, choose **nParticles > Legacy Particles > Make Collide** from the menubar to make the particles collide with the selected object. Play the animation to see the collision effect. You can also make changes in the collision effect. To do so, choose **nParticles > Legacy Particles > Make Collide > Option Box** from the menubar; the **Collision Options** dialog box will be displayed, as shown in Figure 12-8. The attributes of the **Collision Options** dialog box are discussed next.

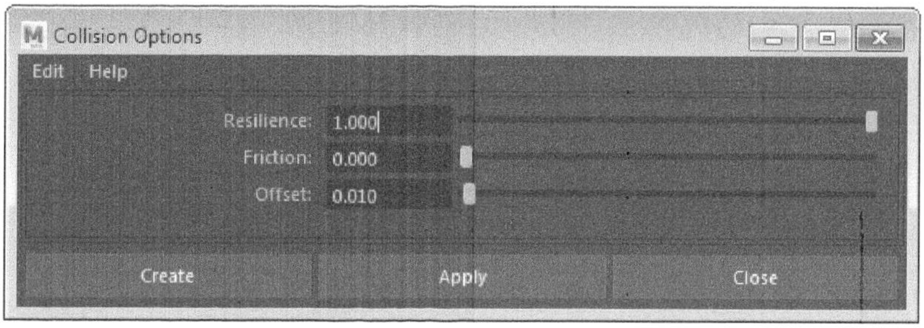

***Figure 12-8** The **Collision Options** dialog box*

Resilience

The **Resilience** attribute is used to set the value upto which the particles will bounce when they collide with a surface. To set this parameter, enter a value in the **Resilience** attribute or adjust the slider bar on its right. Enter **0** for zero bounce and **1** for maximum bounce. The default value of this attribute is 1.

Friction

The **Friction** attribute is used to control the velocity of the colliding particles when they bounce off the collision surface. A value of 0 means that particles are unaffected by friction. A value of 1 makes particles bounce along the normal of the surface. Values between 0 and 1 correspond to natural friction.

Offset

The **Offset** attribute is used to specify the distance between the original streaks of particles and the bounced particles.

RENDERING PARTICLES

In Maya's classic particle system, there are two types of particles: hardware particles and software particles. The hardware particles have various render types such as **MultiPoint**, **MultiStreak**, **Numeric**, **Points**, **Spheres**, **Sprites**, **Streak**, and so on. The software particles have render types such as **Blobby Surface (s/w)**, **Cloud (s/w)**, **Tube (s/w)**, and so on. The hardware particles take less time to render as compared to software particles, but the render output of the software particles is better as compared to the hardware particles. To render hardware particles, you must set up the hardware render buffer. To do so, choose **Windows > Editors > Rendering Editors > Hardware Render Buffer** from the menubar; the **Hardware Render Buffer** window will be displayed, as shown in Figure 12-9. You can also render **Points**, **MultiPoint**, **Spheres**, **Sprites**, **Streak**, and **MultiStreak** particle types using the **mental ray** renderer.

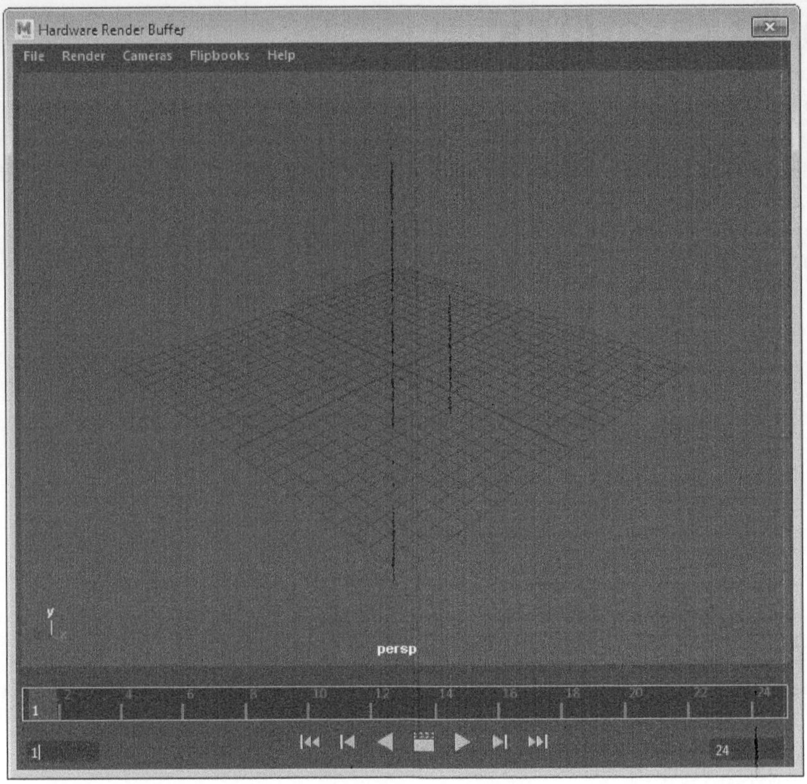

*Figure 12-9 The **Hardware Render Buffer** window*

Note

*The **Maya Hardware** renderer will work only when there is graphic card in your system.*

ANIMATING PARTICLES USING FIELDS

Fields are the physical properties that simulate the motion of natural forces. To access the fields in Maya, select the **FX** menuset from the **Menuset** drop-down list in the Status Line. Next, choose the **Fields/Solvers** menu from the menubar. There are various types of fields available in this menu and they are discussed next.

Air

Menubar: Fields/Solvers > Create > Air

The **Air** field is used to simulate the effect of moving air. To apply the **Air** field, create a grid of particles in the viewport, and then select it. Next, choose **Fields/Solvers > Create > Air > Option Box** from the menubar; the **Air Options** dialog box will be displayed, as shown in Figure 12-10. On choosing the **Wake** button, the options for simulating the movement of air disrupted and pulled along by a moving object are set. On choosing the **Wind** button, the options for simulating the wind are set. On choosing the **Fan** button, the options for simulating the air coming from a fan are set.

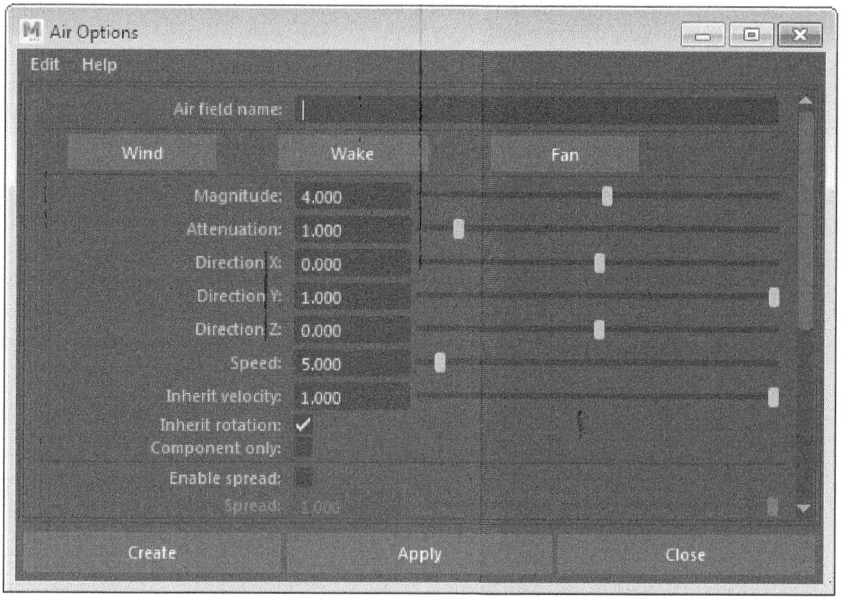

***Figure 12-10** The **Air Options** dialog box*

To apply the wake effect, choose the **Wake** button from the dialog box; the values in the **Air Options** dialog box will be modified. Then, choose the **Create** button. Now, create a poly sphere in the viewport and align it with the particles. Next, animate the sphere from one to another end of the particle grid. Next, choose **Windows > Editors > Outliner** from the menubar; the **Outliner** window will be displayed. Select **airField1** from the **Outliner** window, press and hold the SHIFT key, and then select sphere. Next, choose **Fields/Solvers > Connect > Use Selected as Source** from the menubar to link particles to the sphere. Preview the animation; the particles will move along the movement of the sphere.

Drag

Menubar: Fields/Solvers > Create > Drag

The **Drag** field is used to apply an opposite force on an object that is animated with dynamic motion. For example, you can add this field to the water fountain to control the rise of water. You can change the default settings of the **Drag** field. To do so, choose **Fields/Solvers > Create > Drag > Option Box** from the menubar; the **Drag Options** dialog box will be displayed, as shown in Figure 12-11. Now, change the settings in this dialog box as required.

Gravity

Menubar: Fields/Solvers > Create > Gravity

The **Gravity** field is used to simulate the earth's gravitational force on objects such that they start accelerating in a particular direction. To apply this field, create an emitter in the viewport and select the particles emitted from the emitter. Now, choose **Fields/Solvers > Create > Gravity** from the menubar and preview the animation; the particles will accelerate in the specified direction. You can also set the options of the gravitational force as required. To do so, choose

Fields/Solvers > Create > Gravity > Option Box from the menubar; the **Gravity Options** dialog box will be displayed, as shown in Figure 12-12. Make necessary changes in the dialog box and choose the **Create** button.

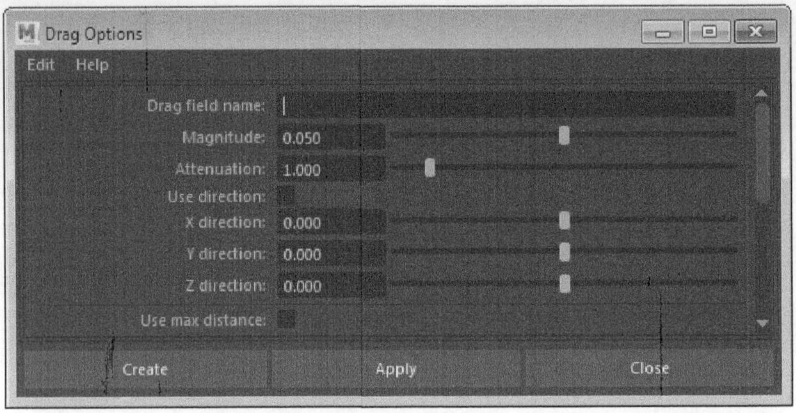

*Figure 12-11 The **Drag Options** dialog box*

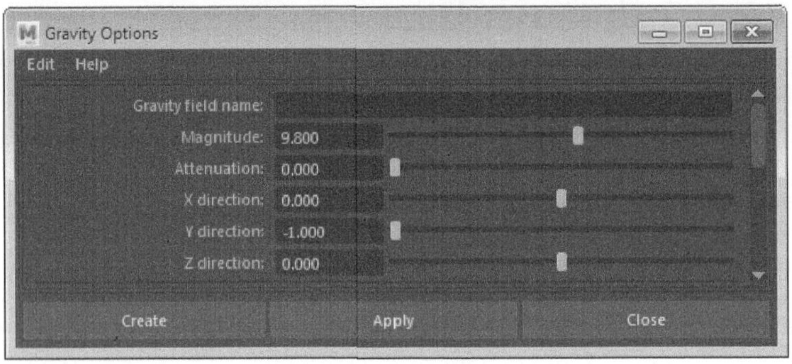

*Figure 12-12 The **Gravity Options** dialog box*

Newton

Menubar:	Fields/Solvers > Create > Newton

The **Newton** field is used to pull objects. Using this field, you can create different types of effects such as planets orbiting around an axis, objects colliding with each other, and so on. This field is based on the principle that the mutually attractive force between any two objects in the universe is proportional to the product of their masses. You can change the default settings of the **Newton** field. To do so, choose **Fields/Solvers > Create > Newton > Option Box** from the menubar; the **Newton Options** dialog box will be displayed, as shown in Figure 12-13. Now, change the settings in this dialog box as required.

Radial

Menubar:	Fields/Solvers > Create > Radial

The **Radial** field is used to attract or repel any object or particle in the viewport. The procedure for applying the **Radial** field is similar to the other fields, as discussed earlier. You can change the default settings of the **Radial** field. To do so, choose **Fields/Solvers > Create > Radial > Option Box** from the menubar; the **Radial Options** dialog box will be displayed, refer to Figure 12-14. You can change the settings in this dialog box as required.

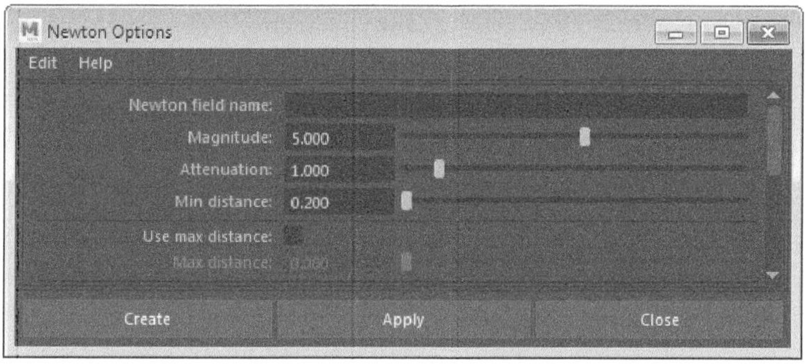

***Figure 12-13** The **Newton Options** dialog box*

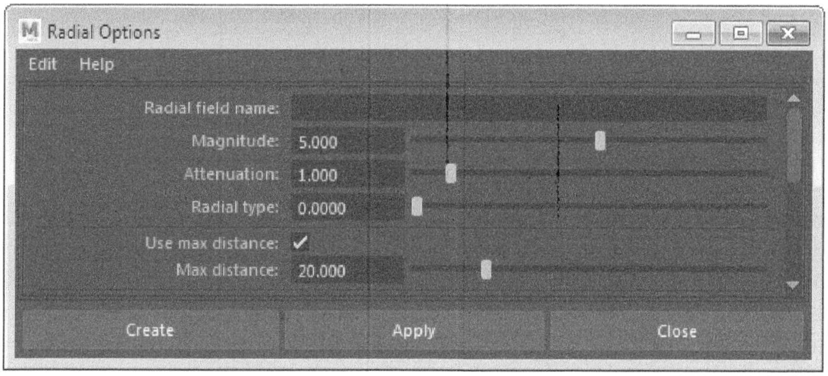

***Figure 12-14** The **Radial Options** dialog box*

Turbulence

Menubar: Fields/Solvers > Create > Turbulence

The **Turbulence** field is used to add irregularity to an object. To apply this field, create a NURBS plane in the viewport and then increase the number of height and width segments of the plane. Select the plane and choose **nParticles > Legacy Particles > Soft Body** from the menubar to convert the plane into a soft body. Again, select the plane from the viewport and choose **Fields/Solvers > Create > Turbulence** from the menubar; the **Turbulence** field will be applied to the plane. Now, play the animation to see the turbulence effect in the viewport. Figure 12-15 shows a plane before applying the **Turbulence** field and Figure 12-16 shows a plane after applying the **Turbulence** field.

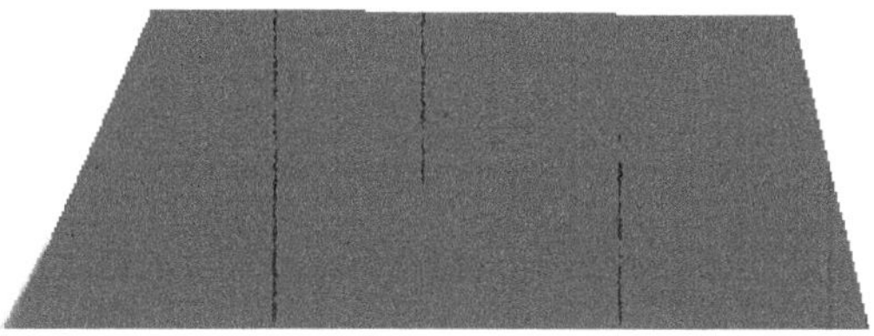

***Figure 12-15** A plane before applying the **Turbulence** field*

***Figure 12-16** A plane after applying the **Turbulence** field*

You can change the default settings of the **Turbulence** field. To do so, choose **Fields/Solvers > Create > Turbulence > Option Box** from the menubar; the **Turbulence Options** dialog box will be displayed, as shown in Figure 12-17. Now, change the settings in this dialog box as required.

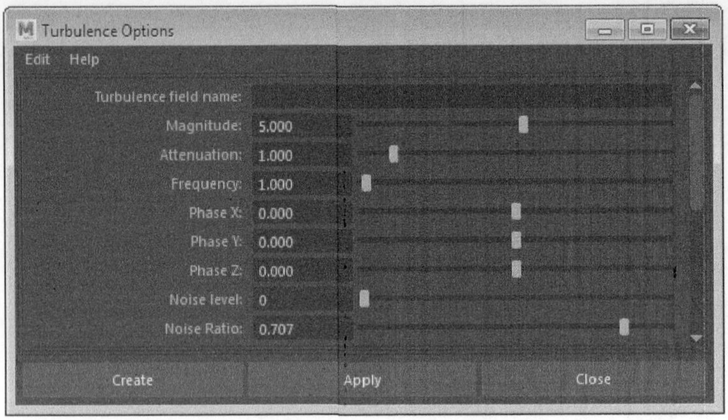

*Figure 12-17 The **Turbulence Options** dialog box*

Uniform

Menubar: Fields/Solvers > Create > Uniform

The **Uniform** field is used to move particles in a uniform direction. To apply this field, create a grid of particles in the viewport. Now, select the particles and choose **Fields/Solvers > Create > Uniform** from the menubar; a uniform field is applied to the selected particles. Preview the animation to check if the particles are moving in one direction. You can change the default settings of the **Uniform** field. To do so, choose **Fields/Solvers > Create > Uniform > Option Box** from the menubar; the **Uniform Options** dialog box will be displayed, refer to Figure 12-18. You can change the settings in this dialog box as required.

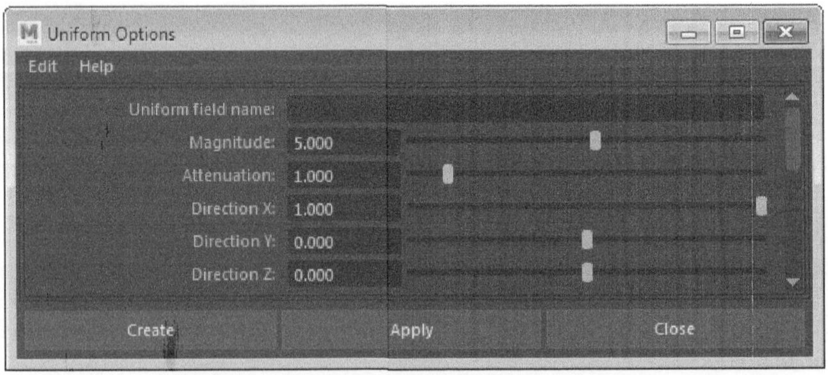

*Figure 12-18 The **Uniform Options** dialog box*

Vortex

Menubar: Fields/Solvers > Create > Vortex

The **Vortex** field is used to pull particles or objects in a circular or spiral path. For example, you can apply this field to create a tornado effect or a universe scene showing several galaxies. To apply this field, create a grid of particles in the viewport. Now, select particles and choose **Fields/**

Solvers > Create > Vortex from the menubar; the field will be applied to the particles. Now, play the animation to view the effect of the **Vortex** field. You can change the default settings of this field. To do so, choose **Fields/Solvers > Create > Vortex > Option Box** from the menubar; the **Vortex Options** dialog box will be displayed, refer to Figure 12-19. You can set values in this dialog box as required.

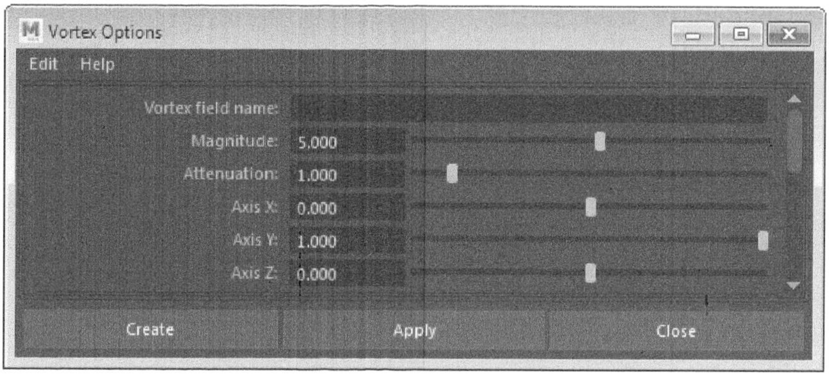

*Figure 12-19 The **Vortex Options** dialog box*

Volume Axis

Menubar: Fields/Solvers > Volume > Volume Axis

The **Volume Axis** field is used to move objects or particles uniformly in all directions, but in a specified volume. The procedure for applying this field is similar to procedures discussed earlier. Like other fields, you can change the default settings of this field as well. To do so, choose **Fields/Solvers > Volume > Volume Axis > Option Box** from the menubar; the **Volume Axis Options** dialog box will be displayed, refer to Figure 12-20. In this dialog box, you can set the values for different attributes as required.

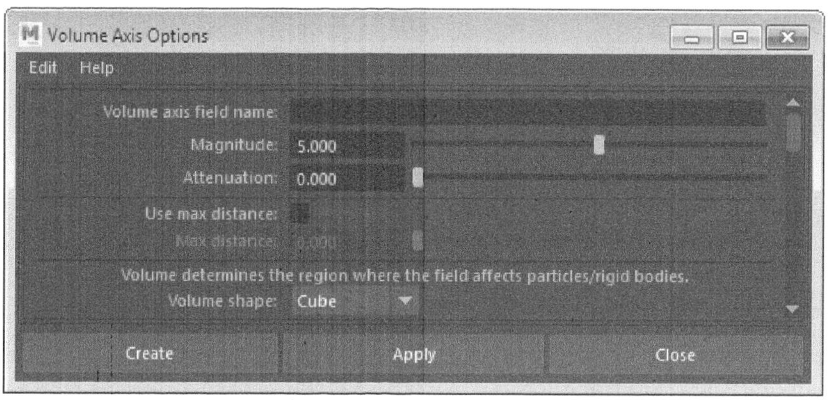

*Figure 12-20 The **Volume Axis Options** dialog box*

Creating Effects

In Maya, there are some in-built scripts that can be used to create different types of complex effects and animations in a scene. To access the effects in Maya, select the **FX** menuset from the **Menuset** drop-down list in the Status Line. Next, choose the **Effects** menu from the menubar. There are various types of effects available in this menu and they are discussed next.

Creating the Fire Effect

Menubar:	Effects > Create > Fire

The **Fire** option is used to create a realistic fire effect in a scene. To emit fire from an object, first convert the object into a polygon and then choose **Effects > Create > Fire** from the menubar. If you want to emit fire from a number of surfaces or objects, select all the objects and choose **Modeling** menuset from the **Menuset** drop-down list in the Status Line. Next, choose **Mesh > Combine > Combine** from the menubar; the objects will get combined. Now, select the combined objects and choose **Effects > Create > Fire** from the menubar. Next, play the animation. The emitted particles will appear as circles in the viewport, as shown in Figure 12-21. Render the scene to get the final output, as shown in Figure 12-22.

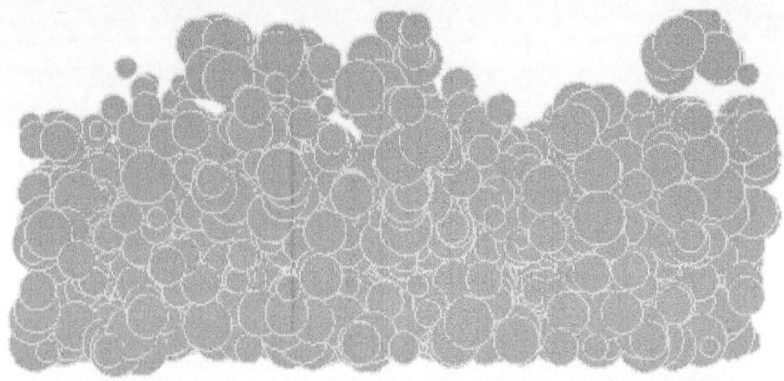

Figure 12-21 *The fire created using the **Fire** option*

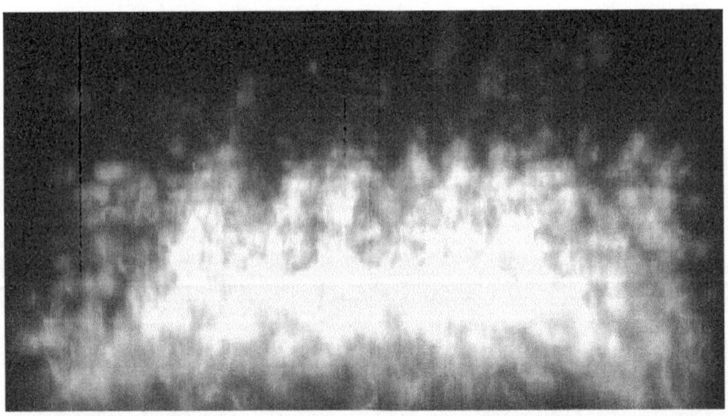

Figure 12-22 *The rendered fire effect*

Creating the Smoke Effect

Menubar:	Effects > Create > Smoke

The **Smoke** option is used to create smoke effect in a scene. You can use this effect to emit smoke from an object or a group of objects. To emit smoke from a group of objects, you first need to combine the objects together and then apply the **Smoke** effect on the combined object. To apply the smoke effect, select the object from the viewport and choose **Effects > Create > Smoke > Option Box** from the menubar; the **Create Smoke Effect Options** dialog box will be displayed, as shown in Figure 12-23. Assign a name in the **Sprite image name** edit box and then choose the **Create** button. Next, preview the animation; the smoke will appear to be coming from the object that you had selected in the viewport, as shown in Figure 12-24.

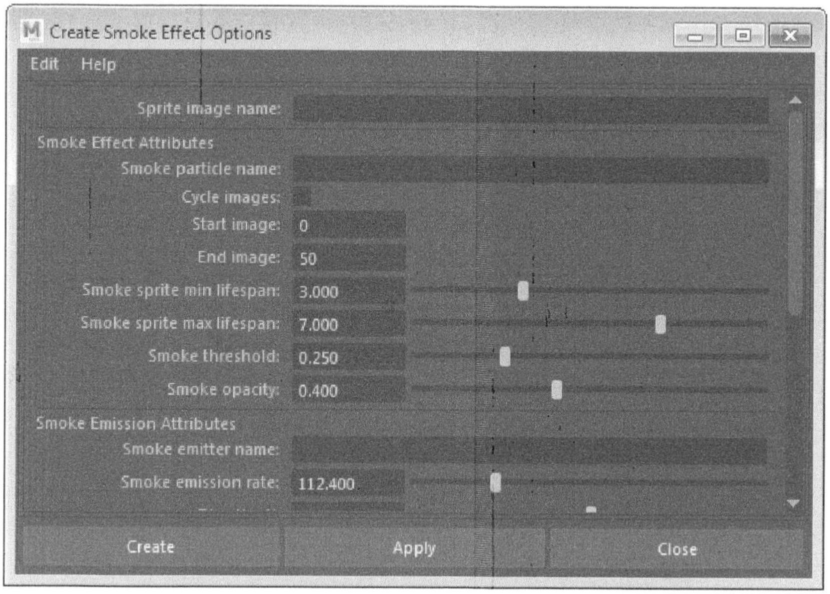

***Figure 12-23** The **Create Smoke Effect Options** dialog box*

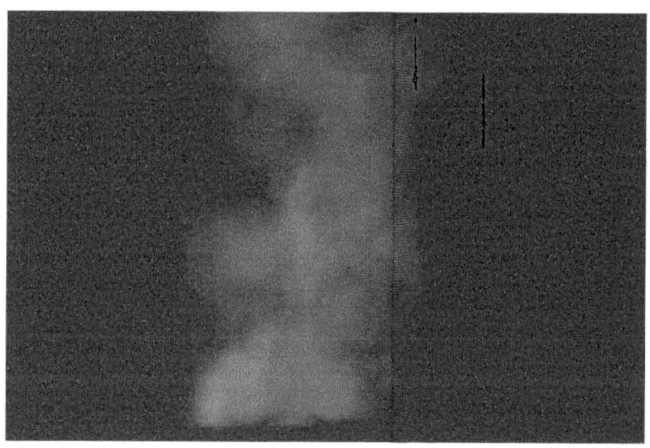

***Figure 12-24** The smoke emitting from an object*

Note

*The **Smoke** effect can only be rendered using the **Maya Hardware** renderer.*

Creating the Fireworks Effect

Menubar: Effects > Create > Fireworks

The **Fireworks** option is used to create fireworks effect in a scene. The fireworks can be rendered using the **Maya Software** renderer. To create this effect, choose **Effects > Create > Fireworks** from the menubar; an emitter will be created in the viewport. Play the animation to see the fireworks effect. Render the fireworks effect to get the result, as shown in Figure 12-25. The particle streaks in fireworks have a pre-applied gravity field. You can set different fireworks options by choosing **Effects > Create > Fireworks > Option Box** from the menubar; the **Create Fireworks Effect Options** dialog box will be displayed, as shown in Figure 12-26. You can set the required values in this dialog box.

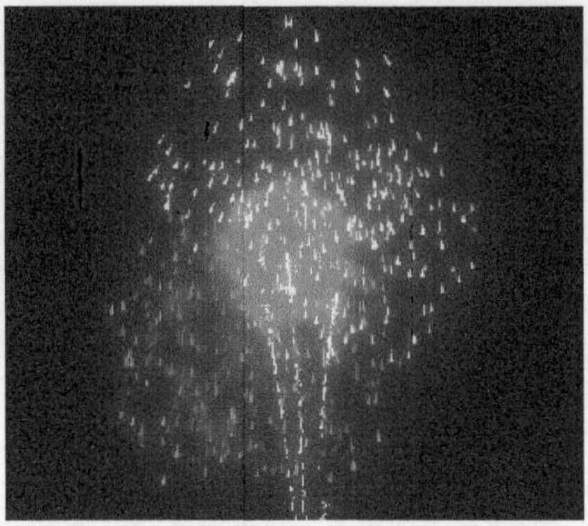

Figure 12-25 The fireworks effect

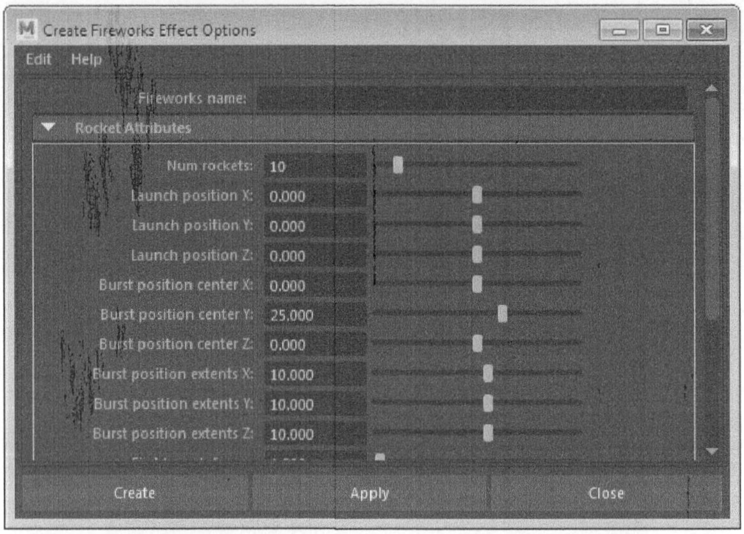

*Figure 12-26 The **Create Fireworks Effect Options** dialog box*

Creating the Lightning Effect

Menubar: Effects > Create > Lightning

The **Lightning** option is used to add lightning effect to a scene. To create the lightning effect, select two objects in the viewport. Next, choose **Effects > Create > Lightning** from the menubar; the lightning bolt will be created between the objects. The lightning bolt is made up of soft body curves with extruded surfaces. Play the animation to view the lightning bolt and render the scene; the lightning effect will be displayed, as shown in Figure 12-27. You can change the default settings of the lightning effect such as color, glow intensity, glow spread, and more using the **Create Lightning Effect Options** dialog box. To invoke this dialog box, choose **Effects > Create > Lightning > Option Box** from the menubar; the **Create Lightning Effect Options** dialog box will be displayed, as shown in Figure 12-28. You can change the attribute values in this dialog box as required.

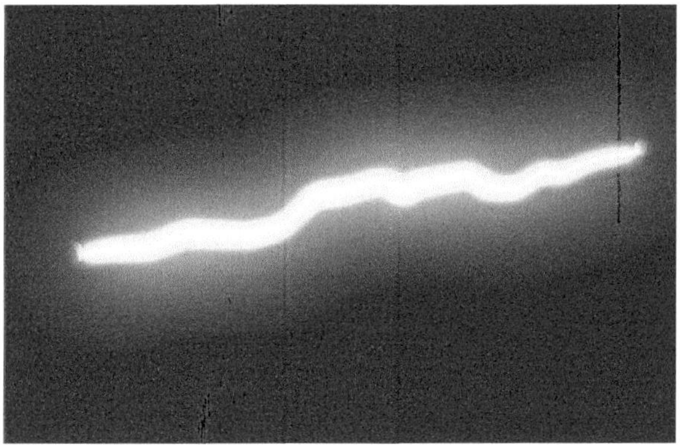

***Figure 12-27** The lightning effect*

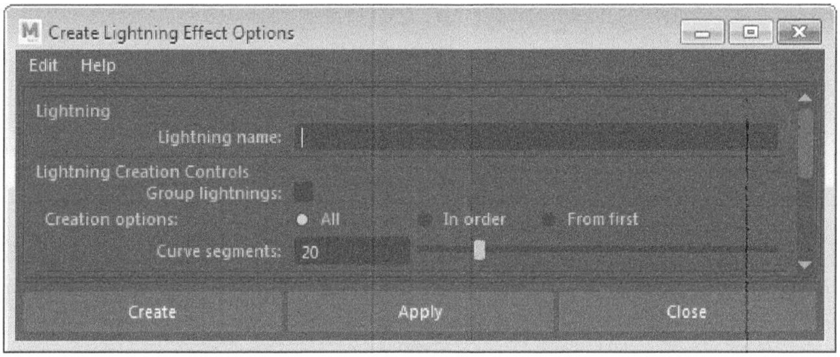

***Figure 12-28** The **Create Lightning Effect Options** dialog box*

Creating the Shatter Effect

Menubar: Effects > Create > Shatter

The **Shatter** option is used to break an object or a surface into pieces. There are three different types of shatters: surface, solid, and crack. Before applying a shatter, you need to specify the shatter type that you want to apply to an object. To break an object into pieces, first create a surface object in the viewport and then choose **Effects > Create > Shatter > Option Box** from the menubar; the **Create Shatter Effect Options** dialog box will be displayed, as shown in Figure 12-29. You can set the attribute values in this dialog box to create the desired shatter effect.

Creating the Curve Flow Effect

Menubar: Effects > Create > Flow > Create Curve Flow

The **Create Curve Flow** option is used to make particles flow along a curve. When you apply this effect, a number of emitters are created along the curve. These emitters control the movement of particles. For example, this effect can be used to create a scene of water flowing from a valley or a waterfall. To create an effect using this option, create a NURBS curve in the viewport. Next, select the curve and choose **Effects > Create > Flow > Create Curve Flow** from the menubar. Now, play the animation to view the effect; a number of flow locators will be created on the curve, as shown in Figure 12-30. Also, the particles will start flowing from the emitter such that they appear to be moving from one end to the other. The flow locators on the curve define the path for the movement of particles. You can also scale the flow locators using **Scale Tool** as required.

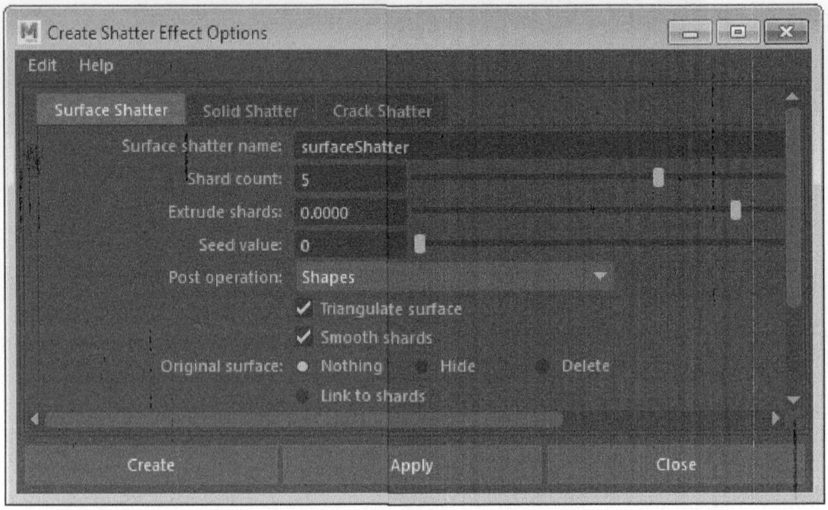

***Figure 12-29** The **Create Shatter Effect Options** dialog box*

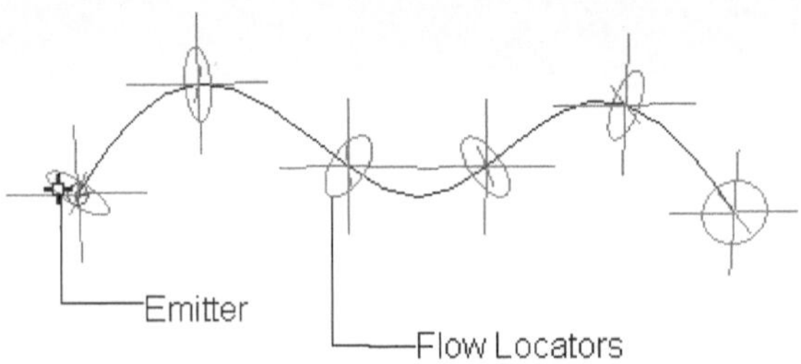

***Figure 12-30** The curve flow*

Creating the Surface Flow Effect

Menubar: Effects > Create > Flow > Create Surface Flow

The **Create Surface Flow** option is used to create particles over a NURBS surface. The flow of particles changes automatically with the change in the NURBS surface. To apply this effect, first create a NURBS surface in the viewport. Next, choose **Effects > Create > Flow > Create Surface Flow** from the menubar; the effect will be applied on the surface. Now, you can play the animation to view the effect.

TUTORIALS

Tutorial 1

In this tutorial, you will use particles to create the effect of water coming out of a pipe, as shown in Figure 12-31. **(Expected time: 30 min)**

Figure 12-31 *The final rendered scene at frame 100*

The following steps are required to complete this tutorial:

a. Create a project folder.
b. Download and open the file.
c. Create an emitter.
d. Set emitter attributes.
e. Create the material for water.
f. Save and render the scene.

Creating a Project Folder

Create a new project folder with the name *c12_tut1* at *\Documents\maya2017* as discussed in Tutorial 1 of Chapter 2.

Downloading and Opening the File

In this section, you need to download and open the file.

1. Download the *c12_maya_2017_tut.zip* file from *www.cadcim.com*. The path of the file is as follows: *Textbooks > Animation and Visual Effects > Maya > Autodesk Maya 2017: A Comprehensive Guide.*

   Extract the contents of the zip file to the *Documents* folder.

2. Choose **File > Open Scene** from the menubar; the **Open** dialog box is displayed. In this dialog box, browse to the location *\Documents\c12_maya_2017_tut* and select **c12_tut1_start.mb** file from it. Next, choose the **Open** button.

3. Now, choose **File > Save Scene As** from the menubar; the **Save As** dialog box is displayed. As the project folder is already set, the path *\Documents\maya2017\c12_tut1\scenes* is displayed in the **Look In** drop-down list. Save the file with the name **c12tut1.mb** in this folder.

Creating the Emitter

In this section, you will create an emitter that will emit particles in your scene.

1. Maximize the persp viewport. Now, select the **FX** menuset from the **Menuset** drop-down list in the Status Line. Choose **nParticles > Legacy Particles > Create Emitter > Option Box** from the menubar; the **Emitter Options (Create)** dialog box is displayed.

2. Enter **water_flow** in the **Emitter name** edit box and select **Volume** from the **Emitter type** drop-down list in the **Basic Emitter Attributes** area.

3. In the **Volume Emitter Attributes** area, select the **Cylinder** option from the **Volume shape** drop-down list. In the **Volume Speed Attributes** area, set the parameters as follows:

   Away from axis: **0** Along axis: **10**

   Now, choose the **Create** button; an emitter is created in the viewport, as shown in Figure 12-32.

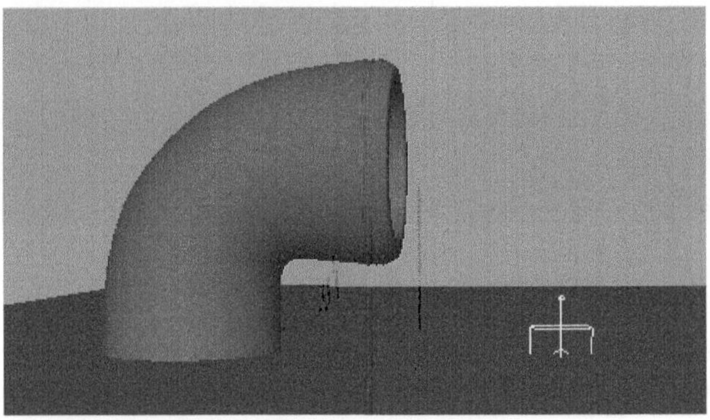

Figure 12-32 *The emitter created in the viewport*

> **Note**
> *The **Along Axis** attribute is used to define the speed of particles. More the value of the **Along Axis** attribute, better will be the movement of particles.*

4. Choose **Modify > Pivot > Center Pivot** from the menubar to set the pivot of the emitter.

5. Align the emitter with the opening of the pipe by using **Scale Tool**, **Move Tool**, and **Rotate Tool**, as shown in Figure 12-33.

Setting Emitter Attributes

In this section, you need to set the attributes of the emitter created in the previous step.

1. Make sure the emitter is selected in the viewport and then invoke the **Attribute Editor**.

2. In the **water_flow1** tab of the **Attribute Editor**, make sure the **Basic Emitter Attributes** area is expanded and set the **Rate (Particles/Sec)** attribute value to **8000**. Next, choose the **Play forwards** button; the particles appear to be emitted from the emitter, as shown in Figure 12-34.

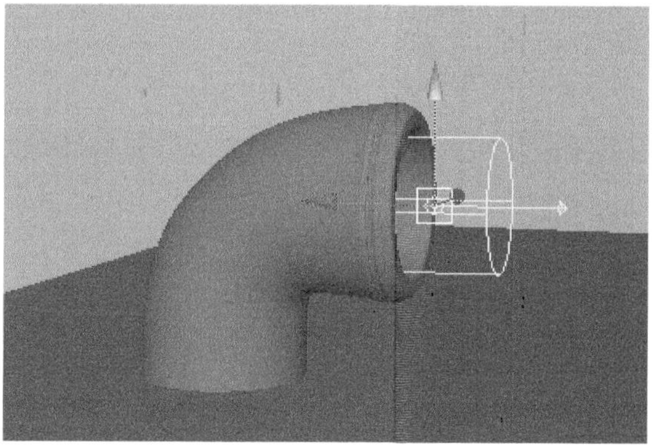

Figure 12-33 *The emitter aligned with the pipe*

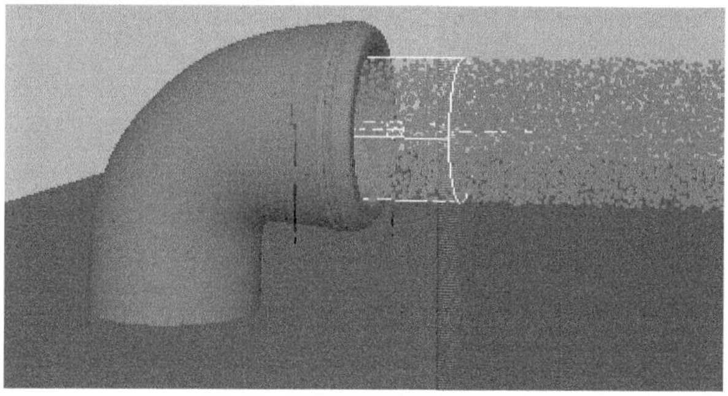

Figure 12-34 *Particles emitted from the emitter*

3. Choose the **particleShape1** tab from the **Attribute Editor**. In the **Lifespan Attributes (see also per-particle tab)** area, select the **Constant** option from the **Lifespan Mode** drop-down list to make the lifespan of the particles constant. Set the value of the **Lifespan** option to **2**.

4. In the **Render Attributes** area, select the **Blobby Surface (s/w)** option from the **Particle Render Type** drop-down list. Next, preview the animation; the shape of the particles in the viewport changes to blobmesh, as shown in Figure 12-35.

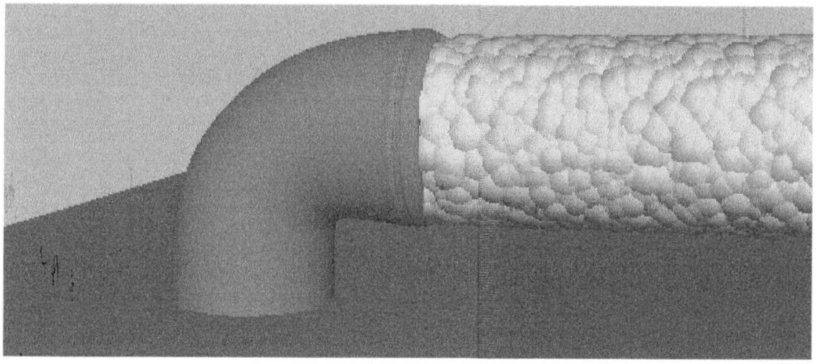

Figure 12-35 *The particle render type set to blobmesh*

5. Choose the **Current Render Type** button from the **Render Attributes** area in the **Attribute Editor**, refer to Figure 12-36; the attributes of the particle render type are displayed.

6. Enter the following values in the **Render Attributes** area:

   Radius: **0.7** Threshold: **1**

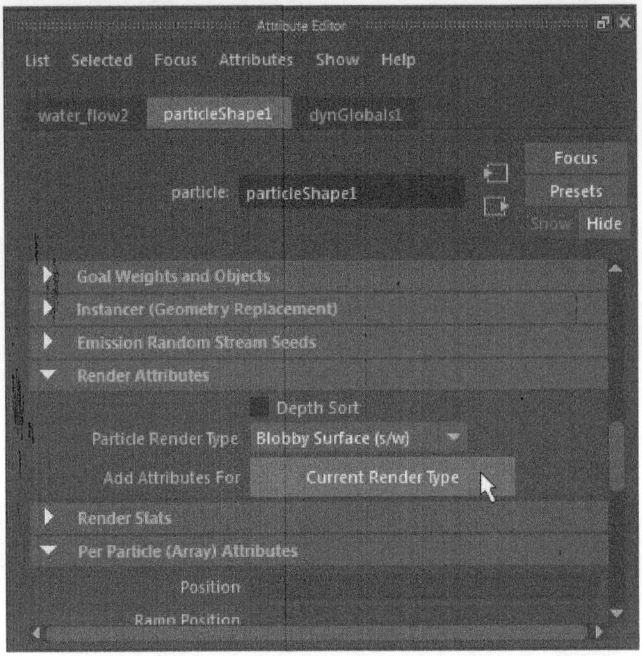

***Figure 12-36** The **Render Attributes** area*

Figure 12-37 shows the particles after modifying the **Radius** and **Threshold** attributes.

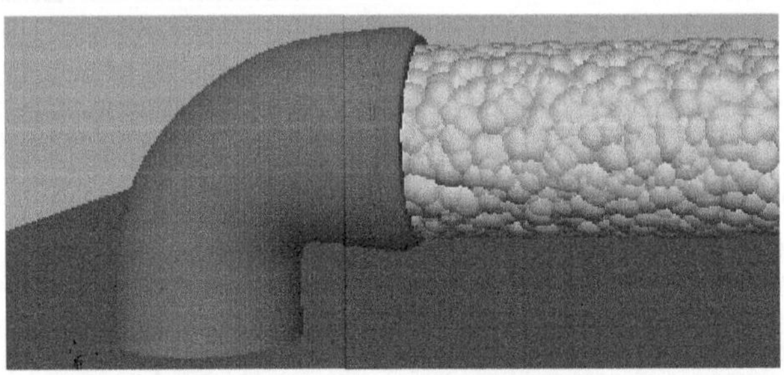

***Figure 12-37** The particles after modifying the **Radius** and **Threshold** attributes*

7. Set the timeline to frame **200** and preview the animation; the particles appear to be crossing the front wall. Select the particles coming out from the emitter, press and hold the SHIFT key, and select the wall. Now, choose **nParticles > Legacy Particles > Make Collide** from the menubar; the particles collide with the wall. Now, preview the animation; the particles do not cross the wall.

8. Select the particles from the viewport and choose **Fields/Solvers > Create > Gravity** from the menubar; the gravity is applied to the particles.

9. Select the particles from the viewport and press CTRL+A; the **Channel Box / Layer Editor** is displayed. Expand the **geoConnector1** node in the **INPUTS** area and set the following values in it:

   Resilience: **0.7** Friction: **0.7**

   Preview the animation to view the flow of particles, as shown in Figure 12-38.

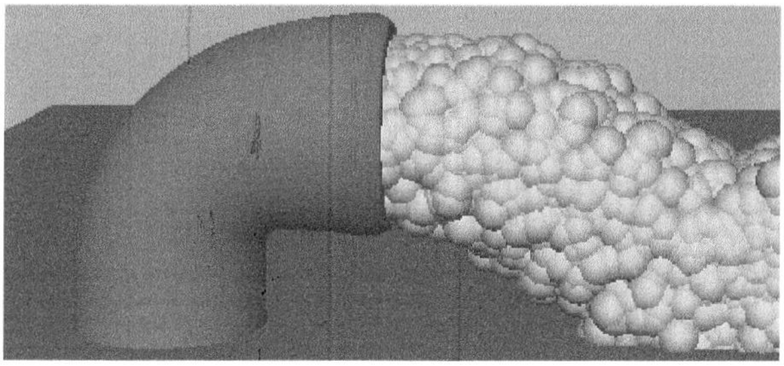

***Figure 12-38** The gravity applied to the particles*

Creating the Material for Water

In this section, you need to create the material for water in the viewport.

1. Choose **Windows > Editors > Rendering Editors > Hypershade** from the menubar; the **Hypershade** window is displayed.

2. Choose the **Blinn** shader from the **Create** panel in the **Hypershade** window; the **blinn1** shader is created in the **Untitled_1** tab. Rename the **blinn1** shader to *water*.

3. Choose the **Utilities** option from the **Create** panel in the **Hypershade** window and then choose **Sampler Info**. Next, choose **Blend Colors** from the **Create** panel; three nodes are created in the **Untitled_1** tab, as shown in Figure 12-39.

4. Press and hold the middle mouse button over the **samplerInfo1** node, and then drag the cursor to the **blendColors1** node; a flyout is displayed. Choose the **Blender** option from the flyout; the **Connection Editor** is displayed, as shown in Figure 12-40.

5. Select the **facingRatio** option from the **Outputs** area and then the **blender** option from the **Inputs** area of the **Connection Editor**. Next, close the **Connection Editor**; the required connection is created between the two attributes.

6. Press and hold the middle mouse button over the **blendColors1** node in the **Untitled_1** tab of the **Hypershade** window and then drag the cursor to the *water* shader; a flyout is displayed. Choose **Transparency > Transparency** option from the flyout; the color attribute of the **blendColors1** node is linked to the transparency attribute of the *water* shader.

7. Click on the **blendColors1** node to display its attributes in the **Property Editor**. In the **blendColors1** tab of the **Property Editor**, set the **Color 1** attribute to light grey (RGB: 128, 128, 128) and the **Color 2** attribute to dark teal (RGB: 74, 74, 80). Make sure that the **RGB, 0 to 255** option is selected in the **Range** drop-down list.

*Figure 12-39 Three nodes created in the **Hypershade** window*

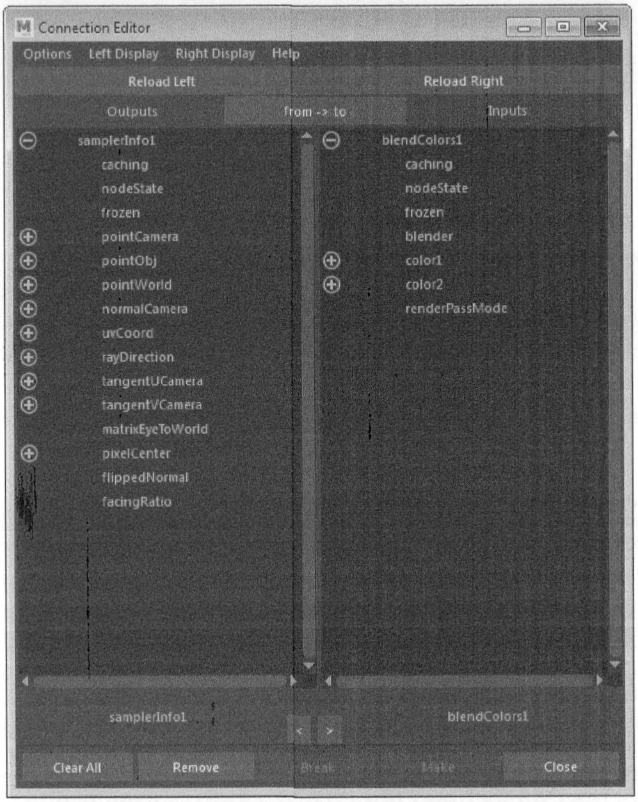

*Figure 12-40 The **Connection Editor***

8. Click on the **water** shader; the **water** tab is displayed in the **Property Editor**. In the **Common Material Attributes** area of this tab, set the **Ambient Color** attribute to bluish green (RGB: 24, 85, 100).

9. In the **Specular Shading** area, assign the 3D texture **Brownian** map to the **Specular Color** attribute, as discussed in the earlier chapters. On doing so, a realistic effect is added to the flow of water.

10. Select the particles in the viewport. Next, press and hold the right mouse button over the *water* shader in the **Hypershade** window; a marking menu is displayed, as shown in

Figure 12-41. Choose the **Assign Material To Selection** option from the marking menu; the **water** shader is applied to the particles.

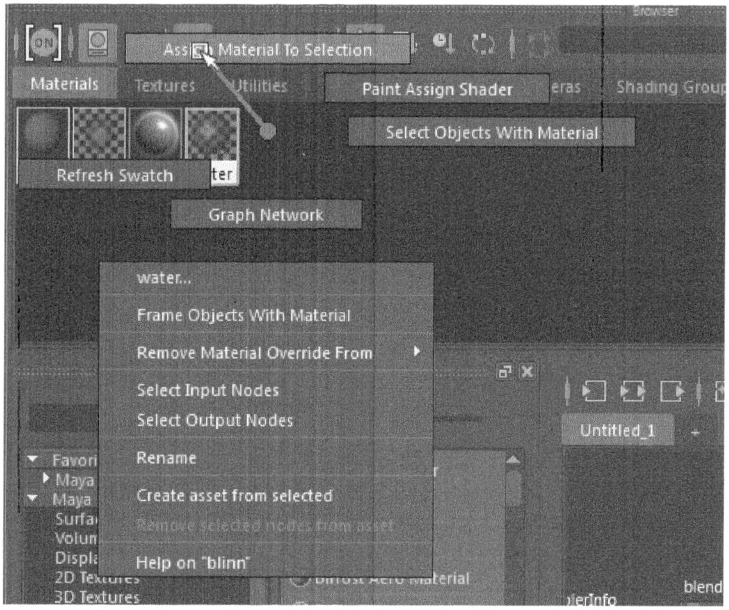

***Figure 12-41** Marking menu*

Saving and Rendering the Scene

In this section, you will save the scene that you have created and then render it. You can view the final rendered image sequence of the scene by downloading the *c12_maya_2017_rndr.zip* file from *www.cadcim.com*. The path of the file is as follows: *Textbooks > Animation and Visual Effects > Maya > Autodesk Maya 2017: A Comprehensive Guide.*

1. Choose **File > Save Scene** from the menubar to save the scene.

2. Maximize the persp viewport. Choose **Panels > Perspective > camera1** from the **Panel** menu; the camera1 view is displayed in the viewport.

3. Choose **Windows > Editors > Settings/Preferences > Plug-in Manager** from the menubar; the **Plug-in Manager** dialog box is displayed. Now, select the **Mayatomr.mll** check box from the **Plug-in Manager** dialog box. Next, invoke the **Render Settings** window and select **mental ray** from the **Render Using** drop-down list in the **Render Settings** window to set the **mental ray** renderer as the current renderer.

4. Choose the **Scene** tab and then choose the **Create** button corresponding to the **Physical Sun and Sky** attribute from the **Environment** area.

5. Choose the **Common** tab from the **Render Settings** window. Now, select **TIFF(tif)** from the **Image format** drop-down list to set the format of the final render. Select **name.#.ext** from the **Frame/Animation ext** drop-down list and enter **3** in the **Frame padding** edit box. In the **Frame Range** area, set the value of **End frame** to **144** and close the window.

6. Select the **Rendering** menuset from the **Menuset** drop-down list in the Status Line. Now, choose **Render > Batch Render** from the menubar to render the animation. The rendered file is saved in the *c12_tut1/images* folder. The final rendered scene at frame 100 is shown in Figure 12-31.

Tutorial 2

In this tutorial, you will use particles to create spiral galaxy, as shown in Figure 12-42.

(Expected time: 30 min)

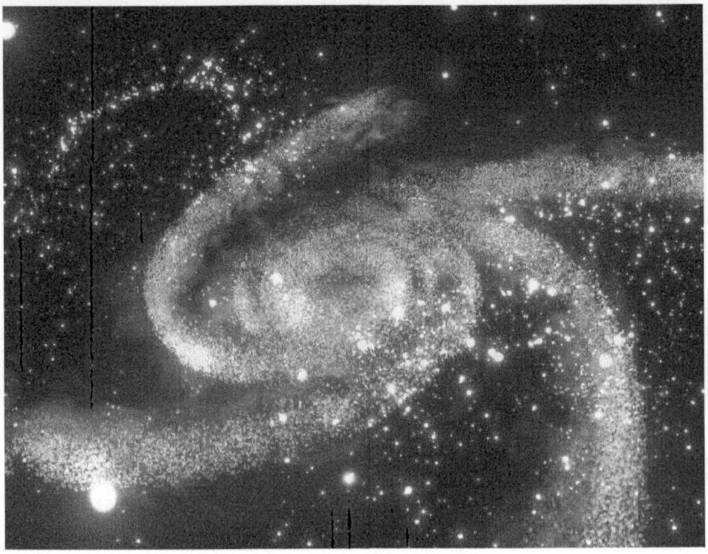

Figure 12-42 *The spiral galaxy*

The following steps are required to complete this tutorial:

a. Create a project folder.
b. Create particles and apply fields on them.
c. Set particle attributes.
d. Save and render the scene.

Creating a Project Folder

Create a new project folder with the name *c12_tut2* at *\Documents\maya2017* and then save the file with the name *c12tut2*, as discussed in Tutorial 1 of Chapter 2.

Creating Particles and Applying Fields on Them

In this section, you will create particles in the viewport and apply field on them.

1. Select the **FX** menuset from the **Menuset** drop-down list in the Status Line and choose **nParticles > Legacy Particles > Particle Tool > Option Box** from the menubar; the **Tool Settings (Particle Tool)** window is displayed on the left of the viewport. Set the following parameters in the **Tool Settings (Particle Tool)** window:

Particle name: **Galaxy** Sketch Particles: **On** Number of particles: **500**
Conserve: **0.9** Maximum radius: **0.5**

2. Drag the cursor in the viewport to create particles such that they form the shape shown in Figure 12-43. Next, press ENTER; the particles are created in the viewport.

Figure 12-43 *Particles created in the top viewport*

3. Make sure the particles are selected in the viewport and choose **Fields/Solvers > Create > Vortex** from the menubar; the field is applied to the particles in the viewport.

4. Choose **Windows > Editors > Setting/Preferences > Preferences** from the menubar; the **Preferences** dialog box is displayed. In this dialog box, choose **Time Slider** from the **Categories** area; the **Time Slider: Animation Time Slider and Playback Preferences** area is displayed at the right in the dialog box.

5. Set the following attribute in the **Time Slider** in the **Preferences** dialog box:

   Playback start/end: **1** to **1000**

   Then, choose the **Save** button.

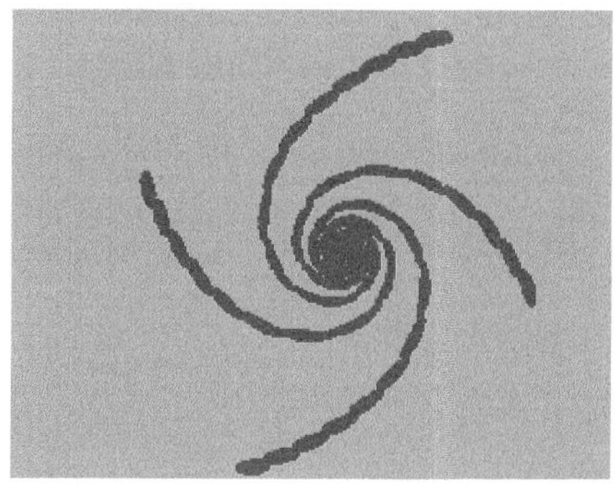

Figure 12-44 *The shape of the particles*

6. Play the animation till the shape of the particles in the viewport changes to the shape shown in Figure 12-44. Pause the animation at that particular frame.

7. Select the particles and choose **Fields/Solvers > Solvers > Initial State > Set for Selected** from the menubar; the shape of the particles at the current frame is set to the initial state. Now, go to the frame **1** and check the shape of the particles. If the shape of the particles does not resemble Figure 12-44, you need to repeat step 6 to get the shape.

8. Activate the persp viewport and make sure the particles are selected. Next, press CTRL+A; the **Channel Box / Layer Editor** is displayed. In this editor, set the Rotate X value to **15**; the particles start rotating about the X axis, as shown in Figure 12-45.

Setting Particle Attributes

In this section, you need to set the attributes of the particles in the viewport.

1. Make sure the particles are selected in the viewport and choose CTRL+A; the **Attribute Editor** is displayed. Choose the **GalaxyShape** tab from the **Attribute Editor**.

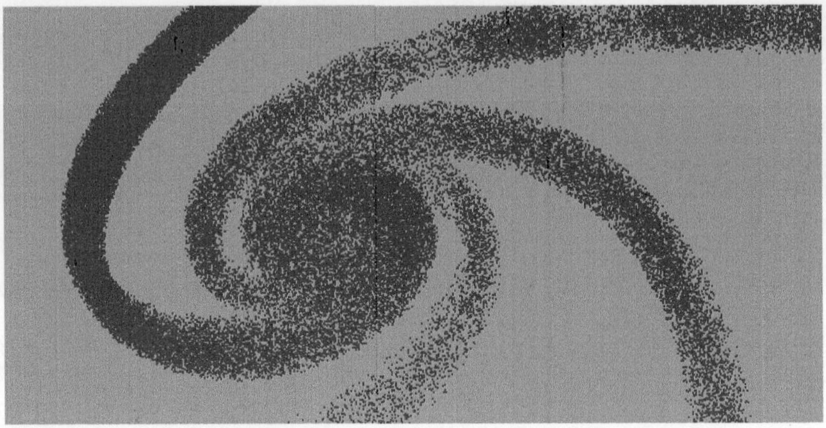

Figure 12-45 The particles rotating about the X axis

2. In the **GalaxyShape1** tab, scroll down to the **Render Attributes** area in the **Attribute Editor** and expand it, if it is not already expanded. Next, set **Particle Render Type** to **Tube (s/w)**; the shape of particles changes. Next, choose the **Current Render Type** button from the **Render Attribute** area.

3. Set the following **Tube (s/w)** render type attributes in the **Render Attributes** area:

   Radius 0: **0.1** Radius 1: **0.1** Tail Size: **0.1**

   Figure 12-46 displays the shape of the particles in the viewport after setting the values in the **Render Attributes** area.

*Figure 12-46 The particle shape changed to the **Tube(s/w)** render type*

4. Choose the **particleCloud1** attribute tab from the **Attribute Editor**. In the **Common Material Attributes** area of this tab, choose the checker button on the right of the **Color** attribute, as shown in Figure 12-47; the **Create Render Node** window is displayed.

5. Choose the **Solid Fractal** button from the **3D Textures** area of the **Create Render Node** window and choose the **Close** button; the **Solid Fractal Attributes** area is displayed in the **solidFractal1** tab in the **Attribute Editor**, as shown in Figure 12-48.

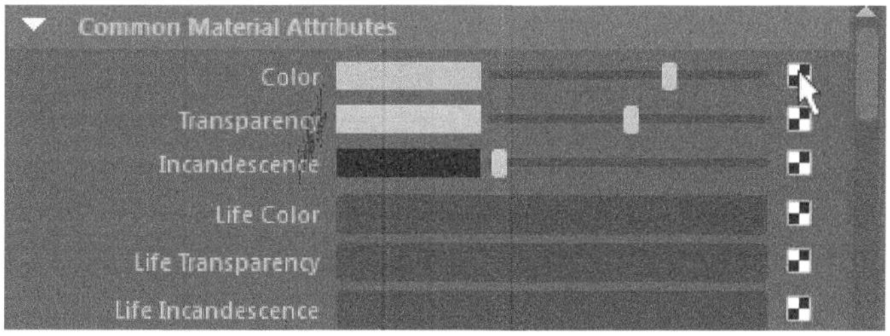

Figure 12-47 *The* ***Common Material Attributes*** *area*

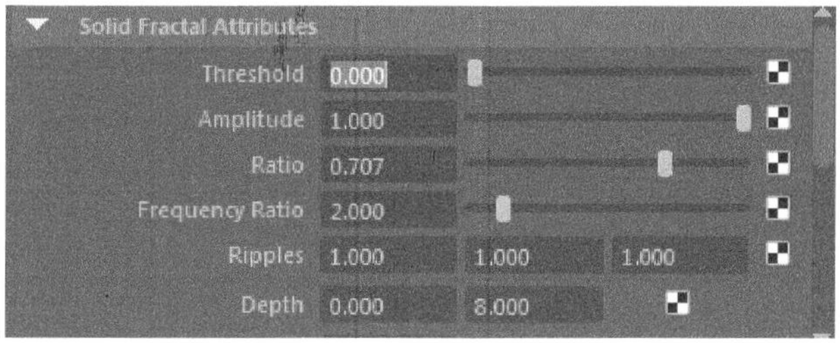

Figure 12-48 *The* ***Solid Fractal Attributes*** *area*

6. In the **Color Balance** area of the **solidFractal1** tab, set the **HSV** values of the attributes as follows:

   Default Color: **22, 0, 0.25** Color Gain: **65, 1, 1**
   Color Offset: **32, 1, 1**

7. Play the animation and stop it at frame 410. Choose the **Render the current frame** button from the Status Line to render the scene. Figure 12-49 displays the render image in the **Render View** window at frame 410.

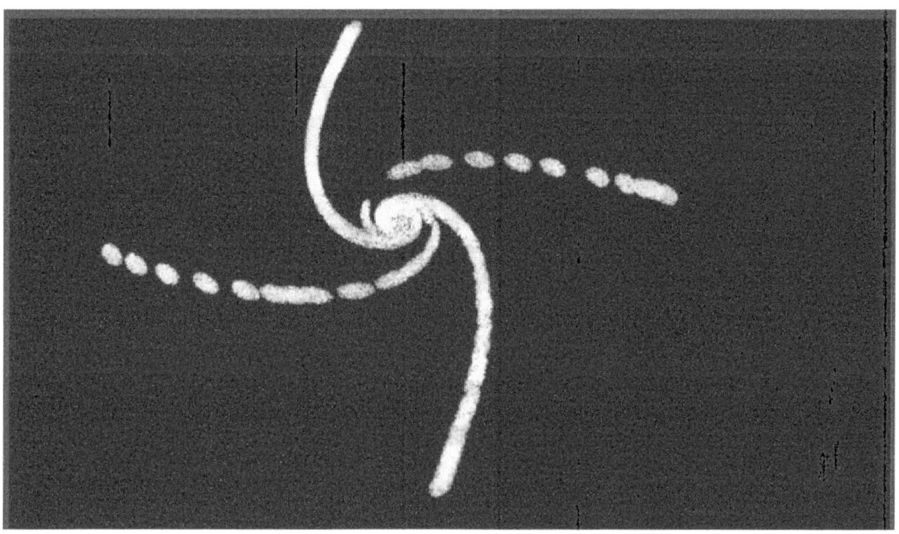

Figure 12-49 *The render in the* ***Render View*** *window at frame 410*

8. Select **Galaxy** from the **Outliner** window; the **Attribute Editor** is displayed with the **Galaxy** tab chosen. In the **Attribute Editor**, make sure the **particleCloud1** tab is chosen and enter **0.1** in the **Glow Intensity** edit box of the **Common Material Attributes** area. Enter **5.0** in the **Density** edit box of the **Transparency** area.

9. Choose the **Render the current frame** button from the Status Line to render the scene; Figure 12-50 displays the rendered scene in the **Render View** window.

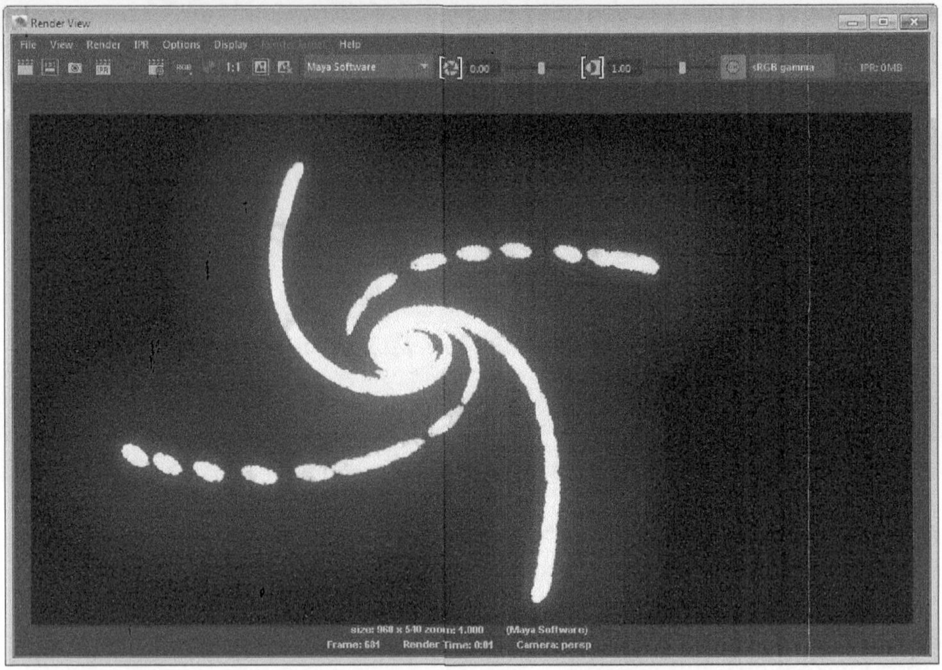

Figure 12-50 *The rendered scene in the* ***Render View*** *window*

10. Make sure the particles are selected in the viewport and then press CTRL+D to create their duplicates. Rotate the duplicated particles about the Y-axis.

11. Choose **Windows > Editors > Rendering Editors > Hypershade** from the menubar; the **Hypershade** window is displayed. In the **Hypershade** window, choose **Volumetric** in the **Maya** area of the **Create** panel and then choose **Particle Cloud**; the **particleCloud2** node is created in the **Untitled_1** tab of the **Hypershade** window.

12. Select **Galaxy1** from the **Outliner** window and then press and hold the right mouse button over the **particleCloud2** shader in the **Hypershade** window; a marking menu is displayed. Choose the **Assign Material To Selection** option from the marking menu; the **particleCloud2** shader is applied to the selected particles.

13. Click on the **particleCloud2** shader in the **Untitled_1** tab of the **Hypershade** window; the **particleCloud2** tab is displayed in the **Property Editor**.

14. In the **Common Material Attributes** area of the **particleCloud2** tab, choose the checker button on the right of the **Color** attributes; the **Create Render Node** window is displayed.

15. Repeat step 5. Next, in the **Color Balance** area of the **solidFractal2** tab, set the **HSV** values of the attributes as follows:

    Default Color: **60, 0, 0.5**   Color Gain: **23, 1, 0.8**
    Color Offset: **23, 1, 0**

    Enter **60** in the **Threshold** edit box in the **Solid Fractal Attributes** area.

16. Make sure **Galaxy1** is selected in the **Outliner** window and the **Galaxy1** tab is displayed in the **Attribute Editor**. In the **particleCloud2** tab, enter **2** in the **Glow Intensity** edit box of the **Common Material Attributes** area. Enter **0.010** in the **Density** edit box of the **Transparency** area.

Saving and Rendering the Scene

In this section, you will save the scene that you have created and then render it. You can view the final rendered image sequence of the scene by downloading the *c12_maya_2017_rndr.zip* file from *www.cadcim.com*. The path of the file is as follows: *Textbooks > Animation and Visual Effects > Maya > Autodesk Maya 2017: A Comprehensive Guide.*

1. Choose **File > Save Scene** from the menubar to save the scene.

2. For rendering the scene, refer to Tutorial 1 of Chapter 8. The final rendered output is shown in Figure 12-51.

> **Tip**
> *You can also enhance the appearance of your scene by applying some paint strokes to it. To do so, choose **Windows > Editors > General Editors > Content Browser** from the menubar; the **Content Browser** window will be displayed. In the **Examples** tab of this window, select **Paint Effects > Galactic** and then apply different paint strokes. The rendered image after adding paint strokes is shown in Figure 12-52.*

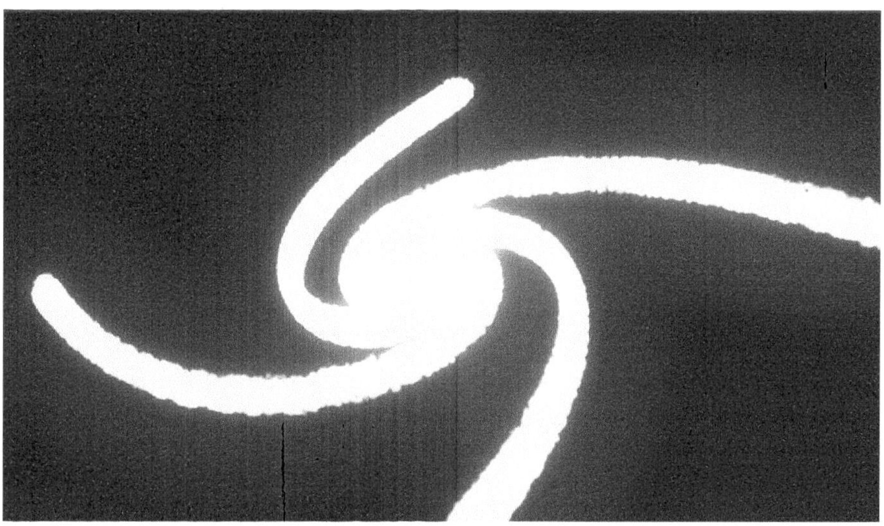

***Figure 12-51** The render in the **Render View** window at frame 360*

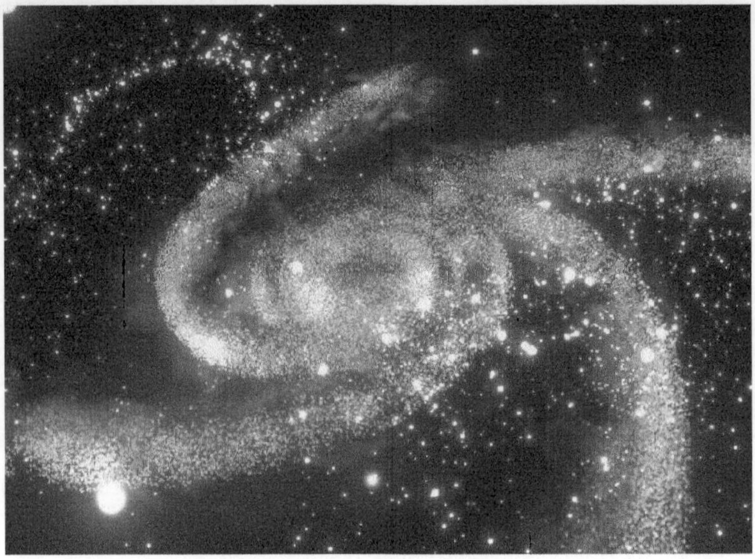

Figure 12-52 The spiral galaxy after adding paint strokes

Self-Evaluation Test

Answer the following questions and then compare them to those given at the end of this chapter:

1. Which of the following attributes is used to sketch a continuous stream of particles?

   (a) **Sketch Particles** (b) **Number of Particles**
   (c) **Grid Particles** (d) None of these

2. Which of the following forces is used to exert opposite force on the object that is animated with dynamic motion?

   (a) **Gravity** (b) **Turbulence**
   (c) **Vortex** (d) **Drag**

3. __________ are physical properties that simulate the motion of natural forces.

4. The particle streaks in fireworks have the __________ field pre-applied to them.

5. The __________ effect is used to break an object or a surface into multiple pieces.

6. The **Create Surface Flow** effect is used to create particles over a __________ surface.

7. The **Uniform** field is used to move a particle in a uniform direction. (T/F)

8. The **Volume Axis** field is used to create a force to move particles around a specific volume. (T/F)

9. The **Turbulence** field is used to add irregularity to an object. (T/F)

10. The **Gravity** field is used to simulate the moving air effect. (T/F)

Review Questions

Answer the following questions:

1. Which of the following fields is based on the principle that the mutually attractive force between any two objects in the universe is proportional to the product of their masses?

   (a) **Gravity** (b) **Newton**
   (c) **Turbulence** (d) **Air**

2. Which of the following fields is used to simulate earth's gravitational force onto the particle system?

   (a) **Gravity** (b) **Turbulence**
   (c) **Newton** (d) **Air**

3. The __________ field is used to move particles uniformly in all directions, but within a specified volume.

4. The __________ effect is used to create lightning between two objects.

5. The smoke effect can only be rendered using the Maya __________ renderer.

6. The lightning effect is used to create lightning on a single object. (T/F)

7. The **Radial** field is used to attract or repel any object or particles. (T/F)

8. A goal is used to set the movement of particles toward a particular direction. (T/F)

9. The **Normal Speed** attribute is used to set the magnitude of the normal component of the emitted particles. (T/F)

10. The **Vortex** field is used to push particles or objects in a circular or spiral path. (T/F)

EXERCISES

The rendered output of the scenes used in the following exercises can be accessed by downloading the *c12_maya_2017_exr.zip* from *www.cadcim.com*. The path of the file is as follows: *Textbooks > Animation and Visual Effects > Maya > Autodesk Maya 2017: A Comprehensive Guide.*

Exercise 1

Create the fireworks effect over a city, as shown in Figure 12-53, using the pre-effects given in the **Visor** window. **(Expected time: 30 min)**

Figure 12-53 *The fireworks effect*

Exercise 2

Create the model of mountains and use the particle system to make the water flow through the mountains, as shown in Figure 12-54. Next, apply textures to the mountains and water to get the rendered output, as shown in Figure 12-55. **(Expected time: 45 min)**

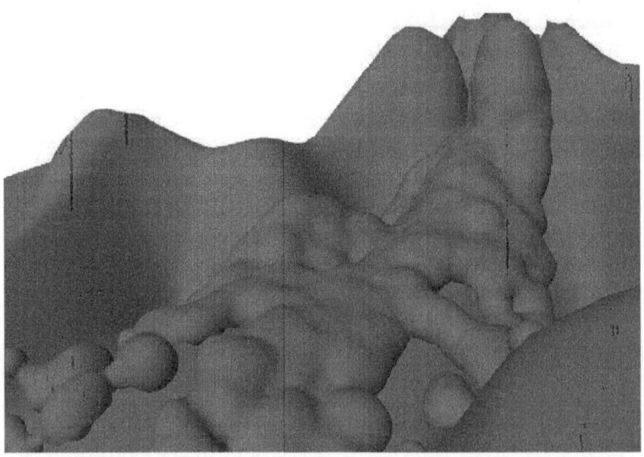

Figure 12-54 *Model of mountains and water*

Figure 12-55 *The scene after rendering*

Exercise 3

Animate the hot air balloons using the **Air** field, as shown in Figure 12-56.

(Expected time: 15 min)

Figure 12-56 *The balloons in the scene*

Exercise 4

Create the scene of a warehouse, as shown in Figure 12-57. Next, apply texture to the scene and then use the curve emitter on the rope to get the rendered output, as shown in Figure 12-58.

(Expected time: 30 min)

Figure 12-57 *The scene of a warehouse*

Figure 12-58 *The scene after rendering*

Answers to Self-Evaluation Test

1. a, **2.** d, **3.** Fields, **4. Gravity**, **5. Create Shatter**, **6. NURBS**, **7.** T, **8.** T, **9.** T, **10.** F

Chapter 13

Introduction to nParticles

Learning Objectives

After completing this chapter, you will be able to:

- *Create nParticles*
- *Collide nParticles with geometry*
- *Simulate liquids*
- *Work with the Maya Nucleus solver*
- *Use the force fields*

INTRODUCTION

The nParticle system in Maya is used to produce a wide variety of visual effects. It uses the Maya Nucleus solver dynamic simulation framework to generate simulations. The nParticles are used to simulate a variety of effects such as liquids, smoke, clouds, spray, and dust. In this chapter, you will learn to create different effects using the nParticles simulations. You will also learn about goals. The goal objects control the motion of the particles. The goal attributes of nDynamics are inherited from Maya classic particles and they are not a part of the Nucleus system.

The nParticles are points in 3D space which can be grouped together to create different effects. These points can be displayed in different styles such as dots, balls, cloud, thick cloud, and water. nParticles use the classic particle render types such as points, streaks, and blobby surfaces. An nParticle object can collide and interact with another nParticle object. The nParticle system allows you to create those effects which you cannot create with standard keyframe animation.

CREATING nParticles

Menubar: nParticles > Create > nParticle Tool

To create nParticles, select the **FX** menuset from the **Menuset** drop-down list in the Status Line, as shown in Figure 13-1. Next, create nParticles in the viewport. You can change the default settings of this tool. To do so, choose **nParticles > Create > nParticle Tool > Option Box** from the menubar, refer to Figure 13-2; the **Tool Settings (Particle Tool)** window will be displayed. Most of the options in this window have already been discussed in Chapter 12. After setting the options in this window as required, create nParticles in the viewport and press ENTER to complete the particle creation process; the attributes corresponding to the nParticle system/ object will be displayed in the **Attribute Editor**. These attributes are discussed next.

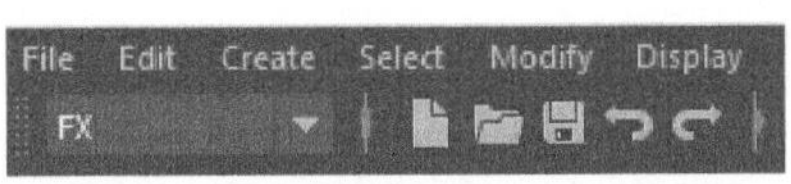

*Figure 13-1 The **FX** menuset selected from the **Menuset** drop-down list in the status line*

*Figure 13-2 Choosing **nParticle Tool** from the menubar*

nParticle ATTRIBUTES

When you create an nParticle system using **nParticle Tool**, various attributes for setting the nParticle object properties will be displayed in the **Attribute Editor**. These attributes determine how the nParticle objects will move and collide with other Nucleus objects. The **Attribute Editor** for nParticles has six tabs: **nParticle1**, **nParticleShape1**, **nucleus1**, **npPointsBlinn**, **time1**, **and particleSamplerInfo1**. The **nParticle1** tab has familiar translate, rotate, and scale attributes for the nParticle object. The **nucleus1** tab contains settings to control forces (such as gravity and wind), ground plane attributes, and time and scale attributes. By default, **nParticleShape1** tab is chosen in the **Attribute Editor**, as shown in Figure 13-3. The attributes in the **nParticleShape1** tab are discussed next.

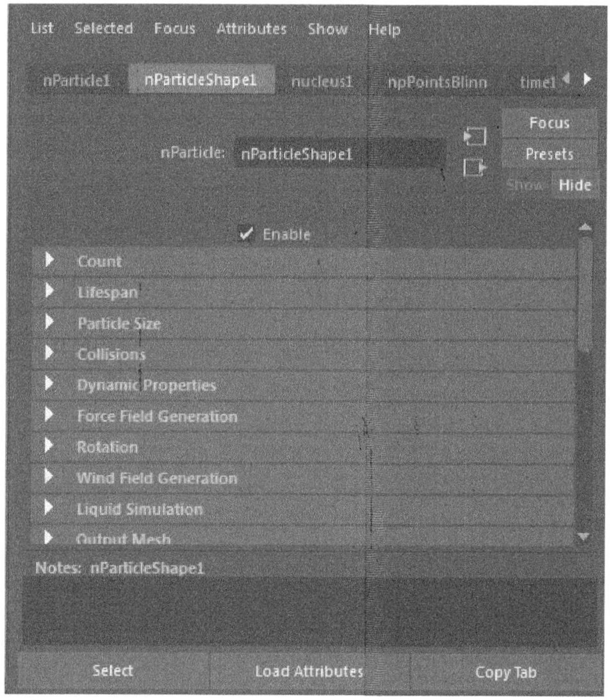

*Figure 13-3 The **nParticleShape1** tab displayed in the **Attribute Editor***

nParticleShape1 Tab

The attributes in this tab are used to specify the settings for the nParticle objects, refer to Figure 13-3. These attributes are discussed next.

Enable

By default, the **Enable** check box is selected. As a result, the nParticle object will be considered a part of the Maya Nucleus solver calculations.

Count Area

This area has two attributes, **Count** and **Total Event Count**. The **Count** attribute displays the total number of nParticles emitted in the scene. The **Total Event Count** attribute displays the total number of collision events.

Lifespan Area

The attributes in the **Lifespan** area are used to determine the life of the selected nParticle object in the viewport, refer to Figure 13-4. Some of the attributes in this area are discussed next.

Lifespan Mode

The options in the **Lifespan Mode** drop-down list are used to specify the lifespan of an nParticle object. By default, the **Live forever** option is selected in this drop-down list, refer to Figure 13-4. This option ensures that the nParticles will live forever unless they are killed by collision events or on volume exit. If you select the **Constant** option from this drop-down list, nParticles will have a constant lifespan and will die at a specified time. On selecting this option, the **Lifespan** edit box will be activated. Enter the required value in this edit box. On selecting the **Random range** option from this drop-down list, nParticles will die randomly. When you select this option, the **Lifespan Random** edit box will be activated. You can assign a value in this edit box to ensure that some nParticles die randomly. The **lifespanPP only** option is used in combination with expressions.

*Figure 13-4 The **Lifespan** area*

Particle Size Area

The attributes in this area are used to specify the size of the nParticles. These attributes are discussed next.

Radius

This attribute is used to specify the radius of the nParticle object in the viewport.

Radius Scale Area

The attributes in this area are used to specify the per-particle radius scale values. Some of the attributes in this area can be specified using the ramps, refer to Figure 13-5. Some of the attributes in this area are explained next.

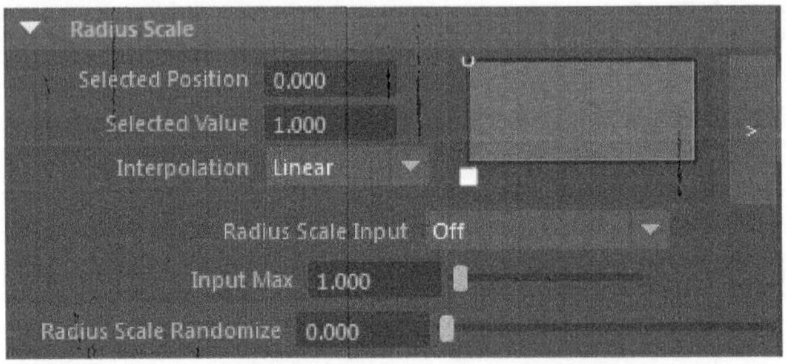

*Figure 13-5 The **Radius Scale** area in the **Attribute Editor***

Selected Position: The **Selected Position** attribute is used to specify the position of the value selected on the ramp.

Selected Value: The **Selected Value** attribute is used to specify the per-particle attribute value of the ramp at the selected position.

Interpolation: The options in this drop-down list are used to control the way the per-particle attribute values blend. The **Linear** option is selected by default in this drop-down list and is used to interpolate per-particle attribute values along a linear curve. This is the most basic type of interpolation. The other types of interpolation are, **None**, **Smooth**, and **Spline**. On selecting the **None** option, the curve between the points will become flat. The **Smooth** option is used to interpolate per-particle attribute values along a bell curve. The **Spline** option is used to interpolate per-particle attribute values along a spline curve.

Radius Scale Input

The options in the **Radius Scale Input** drop-down list determine which attribute will be used to map the **Radius Scale** ramp values. By default, the **Off** option is selected in the **Radius Scale** input drop-down list. As a result, the per-particle radius attributes will be deleted. The other options in drop-down list are discussed next.

Age: On selecting the **Age** option, the per-particle radius will be determined by its age, which will depend on the nParticle's lifespan mode selected in the **Lifespan Mode** drop-down list.

Normalized Age: On selecting the **Normalized Age** option, the radius of the nParticle object will be determined by the normalized age of an nParticle. This option is available only if the **Constant** or **Random range** option is selected in the **Lifespan Mode** drop-down list.

Speed: On selecting the **Speed** option, the per-particle radius values will be calculated by the speed of the nParticle object.

Acceleration: On selecting the **Acceleration** option, the per-particle values will be determined by its acceleration.

Particle ID: On selecting the **Particle ID** option, the value of per-particle object is determined by the nParticle object ID.

Randomized ID: On selecting the **Randomized ID** option, per-particle radius is determined by randomized nParticle ID.

Input Max

This attribute is used to specify the maximum value for the range used by the ramp.

Radius Scale Randomize

This attribute is used to set a random multiplier for per-particle attribute values.

Collisions Area

The attributes in this area are used to specify various collision parameters when nParticles self-collide or collide with other nParticle objects, refer to Figure 13-6. Various attributes in this area are discussed next.

Collide

By default, the **Collide** check box is selected. As a result, the current nParticle objects collide with passive objects, nCloth objects, and other nParticle objects that share the same Nucleus solver and vice versa.

Self Collide

On selecting the **Self Collide** check box, particles emitted from a single source will be allowed to collide with each other.

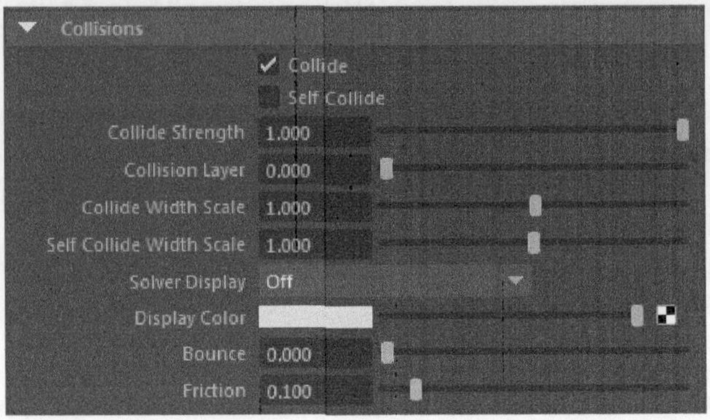

Figure 13-6 Partial view of the ***Collisions*** *area*

Collide Strength

The **Collide Strength** attribute is used to specify the amount of force generated by nParticle objects on collision with each other or with other nParticle objects that share the same Nucleus solver. The default value in this edit box is 1. As a result, nParticle objects fully collide with each other as well as with other nParticle objects. If you enter 0 in this edit box, the collision will not occur.

Collision Layer

This attribute is used to assign an nParticle object to a specific collision layer.

Collide Width Scale

This attribute is used to specify the scale values for collisions between the current nParticle object and other Nucleus objects. The greater the value of this attribute, the farther will be the nParticle objects from each other. The default value of this attribute is 1.

Self Collide Width Scale

This attribute is used to determine a self-collision scale value for the current nParticle object. It allows you to scale the thickness of collision that occurs between particles that are emitted from the same nParticle object. The greater the value, the smoother will be the simulation.

Solver Display

The options in the **Solver Display** drop-down list are used to specify which Maya Nucleus solver information will be displayed in the viewport for the current nParticle object. The options in this drop-down list are discussed next.

Off: This option is selected by default. As a result, no information of Maya Nucleus solver is displayed in the scene.

Collision Thickness: On selecting the **Collision Thickness** option, the collision volumes for the current nParticle object will be displayed in the viewport. It is used to determine the thickness of colliding nParticles.

Self Collision Thickness: On selecting the **Self Collision Thickness** option, the self-collision volumes for current nParticle object will be displayed in the viewport.

Display Color

This attribute is used to specify the color of collision volumes of the nParticle object selected in the viewport.

Note

The display color will be visible in the viewport only when you select the ***Collision Thickness*** *or* ***Self Collision Thickness*** *option from the* ***Solver Display*** *drop-down list.*

Bounce

The **Bounce** attribute is used to specify the way in which the nParticle will bounce off the surface on self collision or with other nParticle objects that share the same Maya Nucleus solver. It depends on the type of the surface on which nParticle bounces off. The default value of this attribute is 0.0.

Friction

This attribute is used to determine the friction of the nParticle objects. It specifies the reaction of nParticle on self collision or its collision with other nParticle objects. The default value of this attribute is 0.0.

Stickiness

The **Stickiness** attribute is used to define the adhering of nParticle objects on self-collision or its collision with other nParticle objects. The default value of this attribute is 0 which implies that the nParticles will not stick to each other.

Max Self Collide Iterations

This attribute is used to display the number of iterations that occur at every step of collision. Increasing the value of this attribute will increase the calculation and slow down the simulation. The default value of this attribute is 4.

Collision Ramps Area

The attributes in this area are used to set collide strength, bounce, friction, and stickiness of nParticle objects. Figure 13-7 shows the partial view of the **Collision Ramps** area.

Collide Strength Scale Area

The attributes in this area are used to determine the strength of the collision. All the options in this area have already been discussed. The **Collide Strength Scale Input** option is explained next.

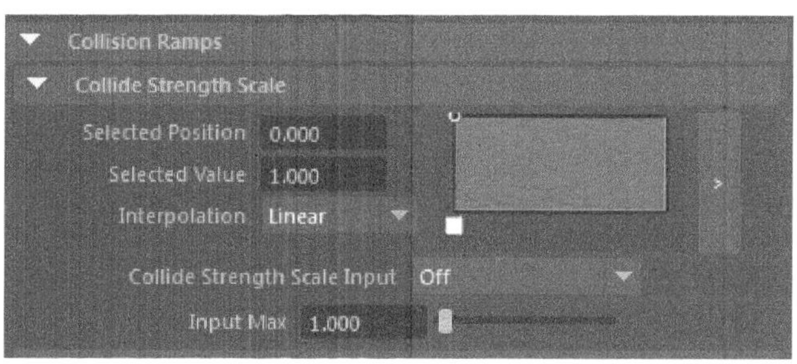

Figure 13-7 *Partial view of the* ***Collision Ramps*** *area*

Collide Strength Scale Input: The options in this drop-down list are used to map the **Collide Strength Scale** ramp values. These are same as those discussed in the **Radius Scale Input** drop-down list. By default, the **Off** option is selected in this drop-down list.

Bounce Scale Area

The attributes in the **Bounce Scale** area are used to control the per-particle bounce scale values, refer to Figure 13-8. Most of the options in this area have been discussed earlier. The **Bounce Scale Input** and **Bounce Randomize** attributes are discussed next.

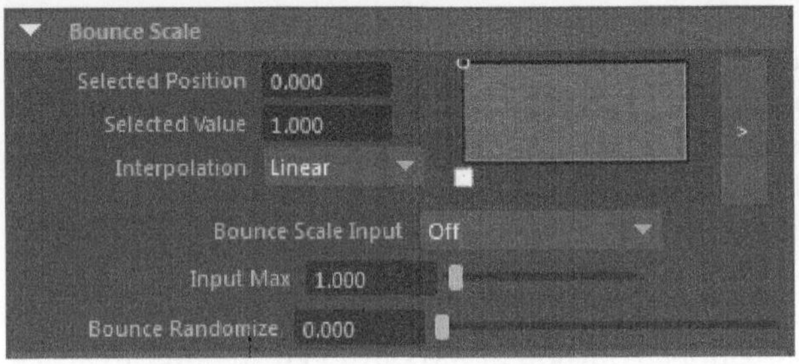

Figure 13-8 The ***Bounce Scale*** *area*

Bounce Scale Input: The options in this drop-down list are used to specify which attribute will be used to map the bounce scale ramp value. Most of the options in this list have already been discussed earlier in the **Radius Scale Input** drop-down list. By default, the **Off** option is selected in the **Bounce Scale Input** drop-down list.

Bounce Randomize: You can set the random multiplier for the per-particle bounce scale values in this edit box. The default value of this attribute is 0.

Friction Scale Area

The attributes in this area are used to determine the per-particle friction scale values, refer to Figure 13-9. Some of the attributes are discussed next.

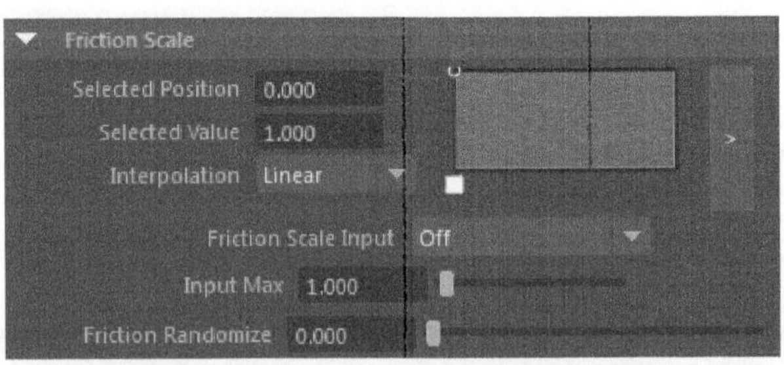

Figure 13-9 The ***Friction Scale*** *area*

Friction Scale Input: The options in this drop-down list are used to determine per-particle friction scale values. By default, the **Off** option is selected in this drop-down list.

Friction Randomize: You can set the random multiplier for per-particle friction scale values in this edit box. The default value in this edit box is 0.

Stickiness Scale Area

The attributes in this area are used to specify the adhering of nParticle objects on self-collision or on collision with other nParticle objects, refer to Figure 13-10. The **Stickiness Scale Input** attribute in this area is discussed next.

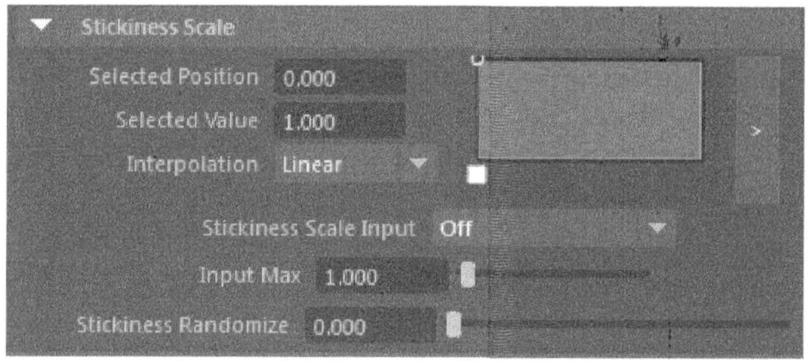

*Figure 13-10 The **Stickiness Scale** area*

Stickiness Scale Input: The options in this drop-down list are used to determine the per-particle object stickiness scale values. By default, the **Off** option is selected in this drop-down list.

Dynamic Properties Area

The **Dynamic Properties** area displays various attributes related to nParticle dynamics, as shown in Figure 13-11. The attributes in this area are discussed next.

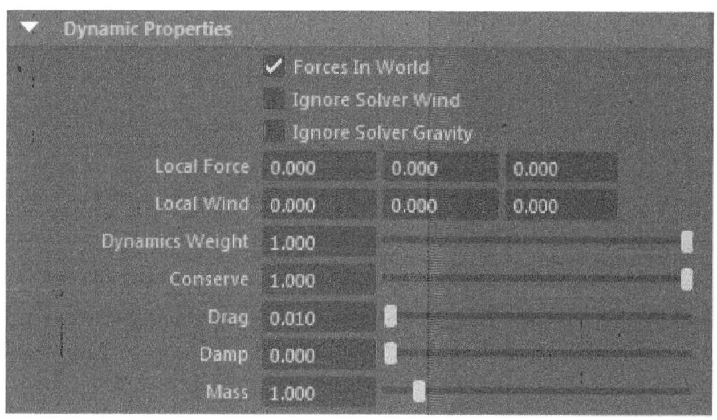

*Figure 13-11 The **Dynamic Properties** area*

Forces In World

On selecting this check box, nParticles will be affected by fields in world space irrespective of the local axis orientation.

Ignore Solver Wind

On selecting this check box, the wind solver will be disabled for the current nParticle object.

Ignore Solver Gravity

On selecting this check box, the gravity solver will be disabled for the current nParticle object.

Local Force
This attribute is used to apply local force similar to gravity on nParticle object without affecting the other Nucleus objects.

Local Wind
This attribute is used to apply local force similar to Nucleus wind on an nParticle object without affecting the other Nucleus objects.

Dynamics Weight
The **Dynamics Weight** attribute is used to control the effect of fields, collisions, springs, and goals connected to the nParticle object.

Conserve
The **Conserve** attribute is used to control the velocity of nParticles retained from frame to frame. The default value of this attribute is 1.

Drag
This attribute is used to specify the amount of drag applied to the selected nParticle object. The default value of this attribute is 0.01.

Damp
This attribute is used to specify the amount of damping on the selected nParticle object. The default value of this attribute is 0.

Mass
This attribute is used to specify the base mass of the selected nParticle object. As a result, the behavior of particle object on self-collision or with other nParticle objects will be affected. The default value of this attribute is 1.

Mass Scale Area
The attributes in this area are used to specify the mass scale values, refer to Figure 13-12. The **Mass Scale Input** and **Mass Scale Randomize** attributes are discussed next.

Mass Scale Input: The options in this drop-down list are used to determine mass scale input of per-particle object.

Mass Scale Randomize: In this drop-down list, you can set the random multiplier for the per-particle mass scale value.

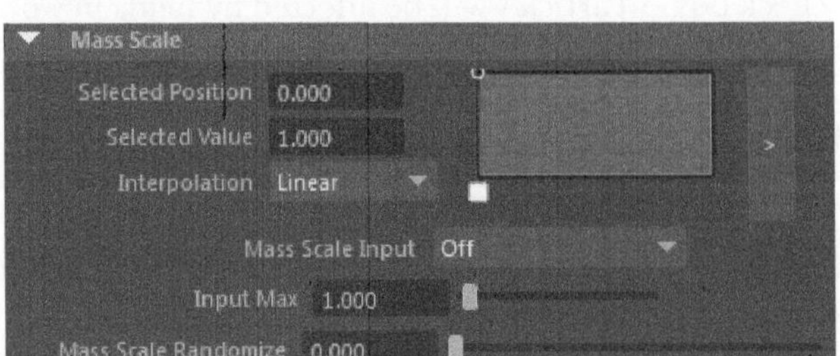

***Figure 13-12** The **Mass Scale** area*

Force Field Generation Area

The attributes in this area are used to generate force that helps in producing positive fields (push) or negative fields (pull) on the selected nParticles from the current nParticle objects sharing the same Nucleus solver. Various attributes in this area are shown in Figure 13-13. These attributes are discussed next.

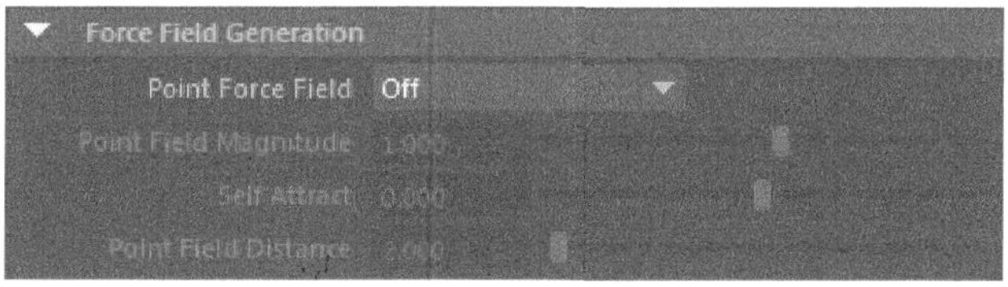

*Figure 13-13 The **Force Field Generation** area*

Point Force Field

The options in this drop-down list are used to control the orientation of the point force field. It has the following options: **Off**, **ThicknessRelative**, and **Worldspace**. By default, the **Off** option is selected. If you select the **ThicknessRelative** or **Worldspace** option in this drop-down list, then the other attributes in this area will be activated. These attributes are discussed next.

Point Field Magnitude: The **Point Field Magnitude** attribute is used to specify the strength of the Point Force Field. The default value of this attribute is 1. This attribute determines whether the selected nParticles will generate positive or negative fields.

Self Attract: This attribute is used to specify the self-attracting strength between the individual particles of an nParticle object. It has both positive (push) and negative (pull) values. The default value of this attribute is 0.

Point Field Distance: This attribute is used to control the distance beyond which Point Force Field will not affect any other particle objects. The default value of this attribute is 2.

Point Field Scale Area

The attributes in this area are inactive by default, refer to Figure 13-14. These options will be activated only when you select the **ThicknessRelative** or **Worldspace** option from the **Point Force Field** drop-down list. It is dependent on the values of the **Point Field Distance** and **Point Field Magnitude** attributes. The attributes in this area are **Selected Position**, **Selected Value**, **Interpolation**, **Point Field Scale Input**, and **Input Max**. The **Point Field Scale Input** drop-down list is explained next.

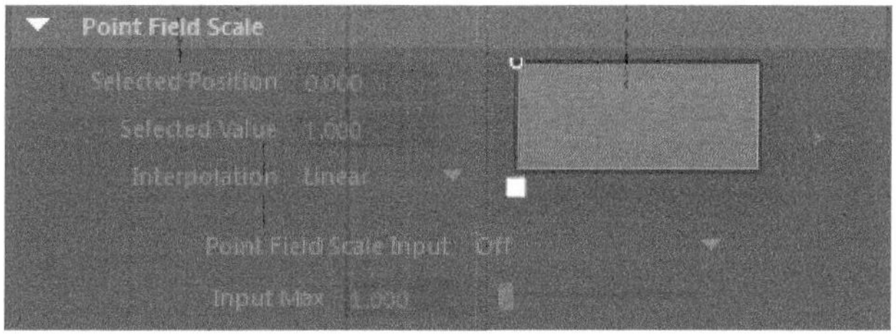

*Figure 13-14 The **Point Field Scale** area*

Point Field Scale Input: The options in this drop-down list are used to determine the attributes that are used to map **Point Field Scale** ramp values.

Point Field Dropoff Area

The options in this area are used to determine the value of Point Field Magnitude drop off when you move away from the nParticle, toward the **Point Field Distance** area. The attributes in this area are shown in Figure 13-15.

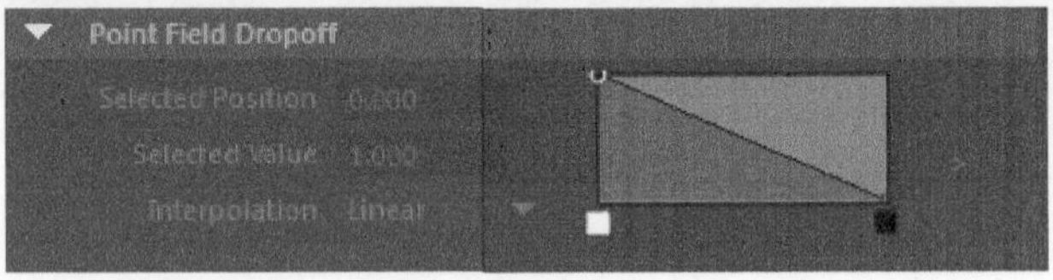

*Figure 13-15 The **Point Field Dropoff** area*

Rotation Area

Rotation is initiated by the friction generated between particles and collision objects. On selecting the **Compute Rotation** check box from the **Rotation** area, the nParticles rotate on a per-particle basis after they collide or self-collide and the **Rotation Friction** and **Rotation Damp** attributes will be enabled, refer to Figure 13-16. The attributes in the **Rotation** area are discussed next.

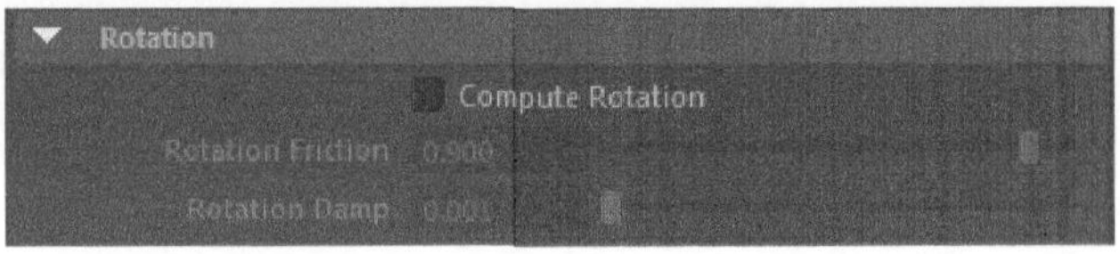

*Figure 13-16 The **Rotation** area*

Rotation Friction

This attribute is used to specify the amount of friction that is applied when nParticles collide with each other or with other nParticle objects. The default value of this attribute is 0.9. The value 0 means no rotation.

Rotation Damp

This attribute is used to specify the amount of damping applied to the nParticle's rotational velocity. On increasing the Rotation Damp value, nParticles rotation slows down after collision or self-collision. The default value of this attribute is 0.001.

Wind Field Generation Area

The attributes in this area are used to define the properties of wind field that produces movement in the nParticles object. Various attributes in this area are shown in Figure 13-17. These attributes are discussed next.

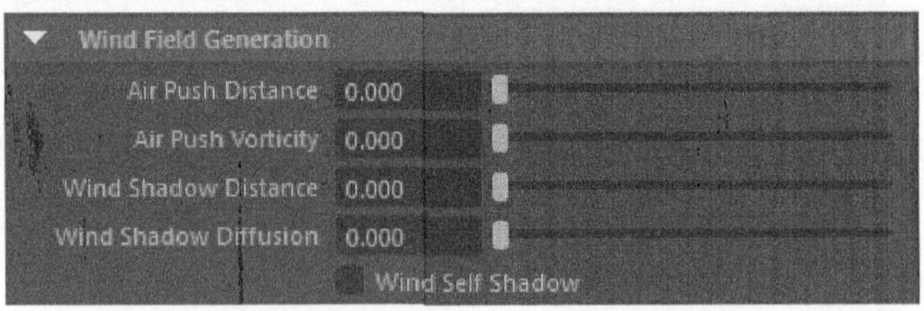

*Figure 13-17 The **Wind Field Generation** area*

Air Push Distance

The **Air Push Distance** attribute directly influences the nParticle system. The default value of this attribute is 0. It means no wind is produced by the motion of the selected nParticles.

Air Push Vorticity

The **Air Push Vorticity** attribute is used to change the direction of wind created by the motion of the current nParticle object. It is used to specify the number of rotations or curls in the flow of wind caused by the current nParticle objects. By default, the value of this attribute is 0. The change in the Air Push Vorticity value affects the nParticle only when the value of the **Air Push Distance** attribute is greater than 0.

Wind Shadow Distance

This attribute is used to obstruct the wind of the nucleus system from the other nParticle system. The default value of this attribute is 0.

Wind Shadow Diffusion

The **Wind Shadow Diffusion** attribute is used to specify the number of curls formed by the wind around the current nParticle object. The default value of this attribute is 0.

Wind Self Shadow

On selecting this check box, the current nParticle object blocks the dynamic wind of its nucleus system from affecting itself.

Liquid Simulation Area

The attributes in the **Liquid Simulation** area are used to generate realistic liquid simulations. It helps the nParticles in simulating the behavior of fluids. These attributes are discussed next.

Enable Liquid Simulation

On selecting this check box, the liquid simulation properties are added to the selected nParticle object, refer to Figure 13-18.

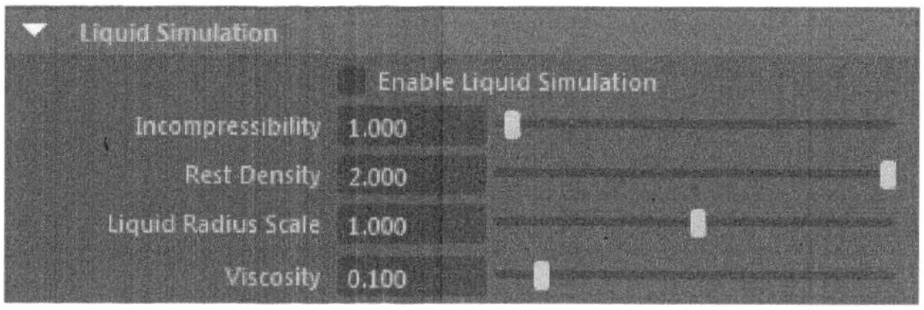

Figure 13-18 *Partial view of the* ***Liquid Simulation*** *area*

Incompressibility

It is used to specify the degree at which the nParticles would resist compression. The default value of this attribute is 1.

Rest Density

This attribute is used to determine the amount of the nParticles in the liquid that overlap each other in the process of settling down when an nParticle object is at rest. The default value of this attribute is 2 implying that only two nParticles will overlap at a point while settling down.

Liquid Radius Scale
This attribute determines the amount of overlapping between the nParticles based on the radius. The default value of this attribute is 1.

Viscosity
The value of this attribute determines the resistance of the fluid to flow. For example, thin fluids such as water have lower viscosity and thick fluids such as honey have higher viscosity. The default value of this attribute is 0.1.

Viscosity Scale Area
The attributes in this area are used to determine the viscosity per-particle. Figure 13-19 displays the **Viscosity Scale** area. The **Surface Tension** attribute in this area is discussed next.

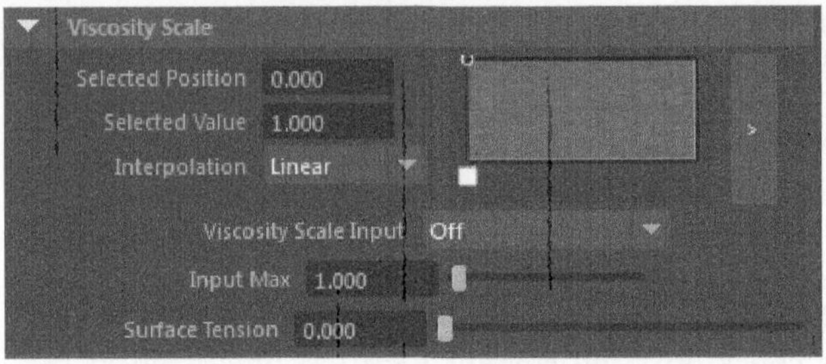

***Figure 13-19** The **Viscosity Scale** area*

Surface Tension
The **Surface Tension** attribute is used to add a realistic effect to the liquid simulation. It is used to specify the amount of surface tension applied to the liquid nParticles. The default value of the **Surface Tension** attribute is 0. Increasing the surface tension value increases the power of molecules to attract each other.

Surface Tension Scale Area
The attributes in the **Surface Tension Scale** area are used to set the ramp for per-particle surface tension values. Figure 13-20 shows various attributes in this area and some of these attributes are discussed next.

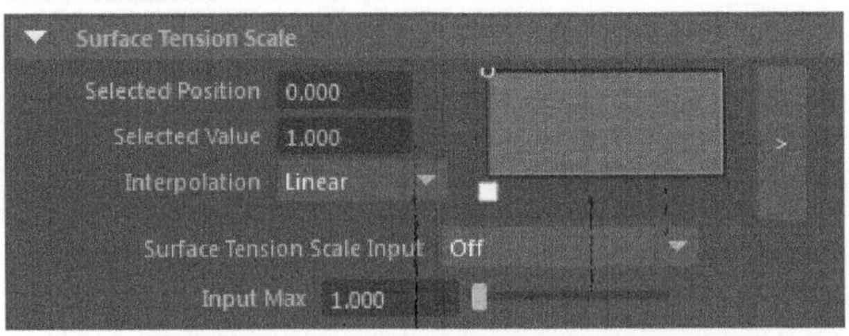

***Figure 13-20** The **Surface Tension Scale** area*

Surface Tension Scale Input
The options in this drop-down list are used to determine the surface tension scale values per nParticle surface.

Input Max

This attribute is used to specify maximum range of Surface Tension Scale values.

Output Mesh Area

The attributes in this area are used to control the characteristics such as size, smoothness, and so on of nParticle objects with blobby surfaces after they are converted into polygon meshes. To convert nParticle objects into polygon meshes, choose **Modify > Objects > Convert > nParticle to Polygons** from the menubar, as shown in Figure 13-21. Once the particles are converted into polygons, they automatically change into mesh and can be seen in the viewport. The attributes in this area are shown in Figure 13-22 and discussed next.

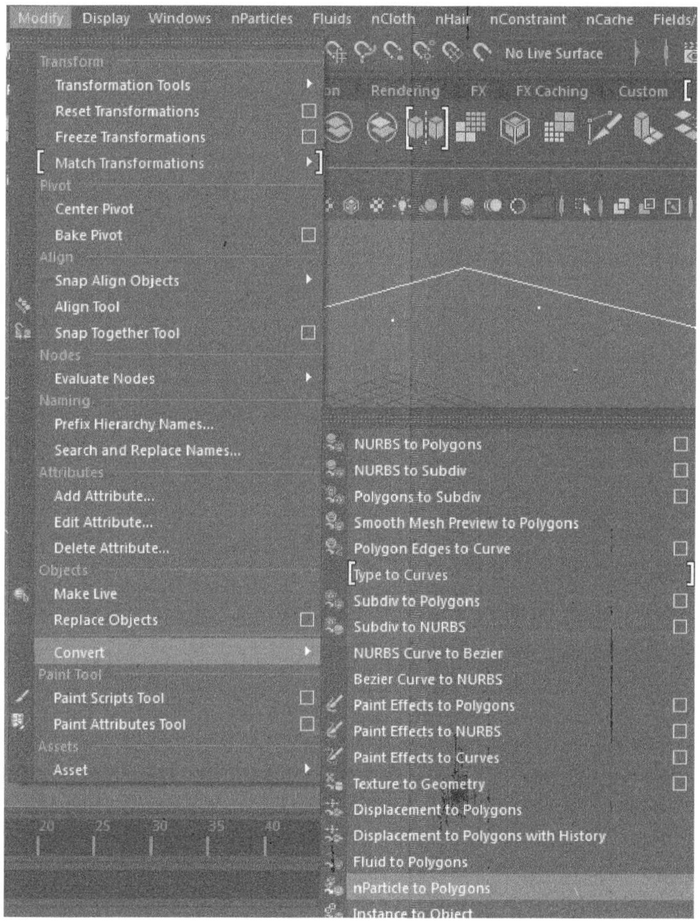

Figure 13-21 Choosing the ***nParticle to Polygons*** *option from the menubar*

Threshold

This attribute is used to determine the smoothness of the surface created by overlapping of blobby surface nParticles. The default value of this attribute is 0.1.

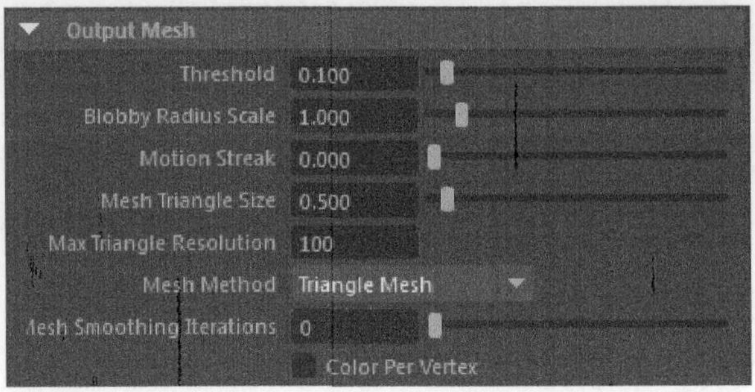

*Figure 13-22 Partial view of the **Output Mesh** area*

Blobby Radius Scale

The **Blobby Radius Scale** attribute is used to specify the extent upto which nParticle radius will be scaled to create blobby surface nParticles. The default value of this attribute is 1.

Motion Streak

This attribute is used to elongate individual nParticles based on their direction. This attribute is very useful for creating motion blur type of effects. Its default value is 0 which specifies that nParticles will be round in shape.

Note

*The **Motion Streak** attribute can only be used when nParticles are converted into polygons.*

Mesh Triangle Size

This attribute is used to specify the size of triangles. The size of triangle is inversely proportional to the resolution of mesh which means a small sized mesh triangle will take more time to render as it has a high resolution.

Max Triangle Resolution

This attribute is used to specify the resolution of volume pixel (voxel) of nParticles. Its default value is 100.

Mesh Method

The options in this drop-down list are used to specify different types of polygon mesh that will be used in producing iso-surface meshes. By default, the **Triangle Mesh** option is selected in this drop-down list. The options in this drop-down list are discussed next.

Triangle Mesh: The **Triangle Mesh** option is used to convert an nParticle into a cube polygon mesh using a high resolution 3D surface algorithm (marching cubes) method. This option is selected by default.

Tetrahedra: The **Tetrahedra** option is used to convert an nParticle into a triangle polygon mesh using the marching tetrahedra method.

Acute Tetrahedra: The **Acute Tetrahedra** option is used to convert an nParticle into a triangle polygon mesh with a slightly higher resolution as compared to the Tetrahedra method.

Quad Mesh: It is used to convert nParticles into quad mesh.

Mesh Smoothing Iterations

This attribute is used to determine the amount of smoothing applied to smoothen the nParticle output mesh. As a result, a smooth topology is created which is uniform in shape. Its default value is 0.

Color Per Vertex

Select this check box to generate color per-vertex data value when you convert an nParticle object to an output mesh. This data is derived from the nParticle object's per-particle color values.

Opacity Per Vertex

Select this check box to generate opacity per-vertex data value when you convert an nParticle object to an output mesh. This data is derived from the nParticle object's per-particle opacity values.

Incandescence Per Vertex

Select this check box to produce incandescence per-particle vertex data when you convert an nParticle object to an output mesh.

Velocity Per Vertex

This attribute is used to produce velocity per-vertex data when you convert an nParticle object to an output mesh. It helps in producing motion blur when mesh is rendered using the **mental ray** renderer.

Uvw Per Vertex

The **Uvw Per Vertex** attribute is used to produce UVW texture coordinates when you convert an nParticle object to a polygon mesh.

Use Gradient Normals

This check box is used to improve the appearance and smoothness of nParticle output mesh. By default, this check box is clear.

Caching Area

The attributes in this area are used to cache the simulation data to local server or hard drive, refer to Figure 13-23. Some of the commonly used attributes in this area are discussed next.

***Figure 13-23** The **Caching** area*

Cacheable Attributes

The options in this drop-down list are used to specify the simulation data when the current nParticle object is cached. The options in this drop-down list are discussed next.

Position: This option is used to cache only particle ID, age, position, and per-particle rotation.

Position And Velocity: This option is used to cache the particle ID, age, position, per-particle rotation, velocity, per-particle angular velocity, and per-particle lifespan of nParticle.

Dynamics and Rendering: This option is used to cache only the mass, per-particle radius, per-particle opacity, per-particle RGB, per-particle incandescence, per-particle spriteNum, per-particle spriteScaleX, and per-particle spriteScaleY.

All: This option is used to cache the entire nParticle attribute data.

Memory Caching (see Dynamics Solvers menu) Area

This area consists of **Cache Data** check box. On selecting this check box, the motion of the nParticle object is saved to the memory.

Emission Attributes Area

The attributes in this area are similar to the options in the **Emitter Options (Emit from Object)** dialog box discussed in Chapter 12, refer to the Figure 13-24.

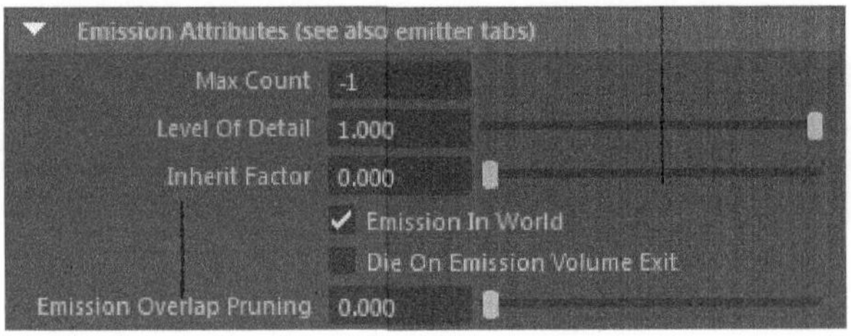

*Figure 13-24 The **Emission Attributes** area*

Max Count

This edit box is used to determine the number of nParticles emitted by the selected object. Its default value is -1.

Level Of Detail

This attribute affects only the emitted particles. It scales the amount of emission to be used for motion testing without having to change emitter values. The default value of this attribute is 1.

Inherit Factor

This attribute is used to define the fraction velocity inherited by emitted nParticles. Its default value is 0. The velocity increases with the increase in its value.

Emission In World

By default, this check box is selected. It is used to let the particle object assume that particles created from emission are in the world space. This makes the particles respond as if they were in the same space as the emitter when they are in some non-identity hierarchy.

Die On Emission Volume Exit

On selecting this check box, nParticles emitted from a volume will die when they will exit that volume.

Emission Overlap Pruning

This attribute is used to determine that new nParticles will be eliminated before they are displayed in the simulation depending on collision with each other or with other nParticle objects.

Emission Random Stream Seeds Area

The attributes in this area are used to create particle systems which operate in the same way and with similar kind of forces, but will look different in terms of placement. If you create two emitters with the positioning of the emitted particles is identical by default. You can make each emitter to emit particles in different random positions by giving each emitted particle object a different value to its **Seed** attribute.

Shading Area

The attributes in this area are used to specify the rendering type for nParticle objects. Figure 13-25 shows various attributes in this area. These attributes are discussed next.

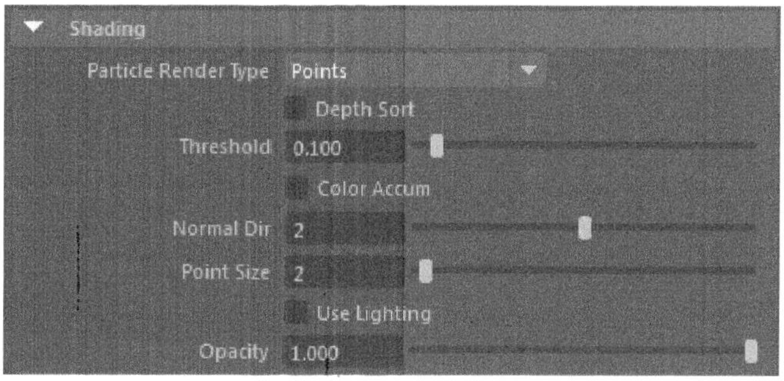

***Figure 13-25** Partial view of the **Shading** area*

Particle Render Type

This attribute displays various types of nParticle render types such as **Multipoint**, **Multistreak**, **Numeric**, **Points**, **Spheres**, and so on. By default, the nParticle objects are in the form of **Points**.

Note

*(s/w) indicates that this form of nParticle will be rendered using the **Maya Software** renderer only.*

Depth Sort

Select this check box to allow depth sorting of particles for rendering.

Threshold

This attribute is used to control the smoothness of the surface created due to overlapping of blobby surface nParticles.

Opacity

It is used to specify the opacity of the nParticle object. The default value of this attribute is 1.

Opacity Scale Area

The attributes in this area are used to set the per-particle opacity scale value. Various attributes in this area are shown in Figure 13-26. These attributes are used to determine opacity scale values per nParticle. Some of the attributes are discussed next.

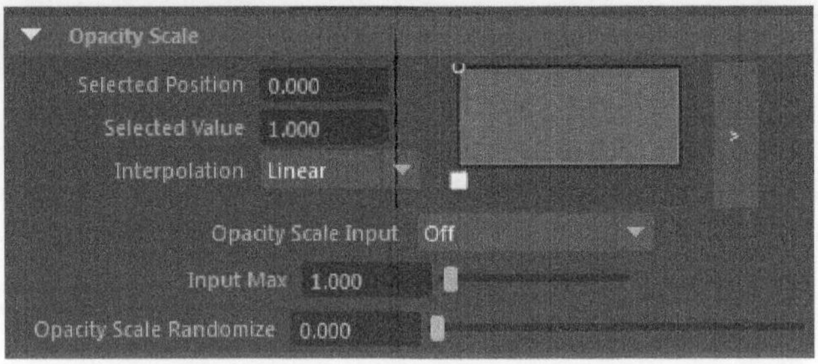

***Figure 13-26** The **Opacity Scale** area*

Input Max: It is used to set the maximum range of opacity scale values.

Opacity Scale Randomize: It is used to set a random multiplier for per-particle opacity value.

Color Area

The attributes in this area are used to determine the color values that can be applied to nParticles. The **Selected Color** attribute displays the color on the ramp at the selected position. The attributes in this area are shown in Figure 13-27.

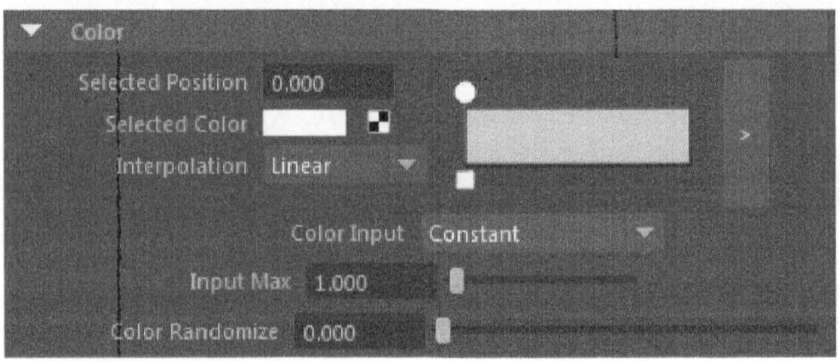

***Figure 13-27** The **Color** area*

Color Input

The options in this drop-down list are used to specify which attribute is used to map the ramp's color values.

Input Max

The **Input Max** attribute is used to set the maximum value for the ramp.

Color Randomize

This attribute is used to set the random multiplier for per-particle color value.

Incandescence Area

This attribute is used to control the intensity of the color of light emitted from the nParticle object due to self-illumination. The **Incandescence** area is shown in Figure 13-28. Some of the attributes in this area are discussed next.

Incandescence Input

The options in this drop-down list are used to specify which attribute is used to map the ramp's color values.

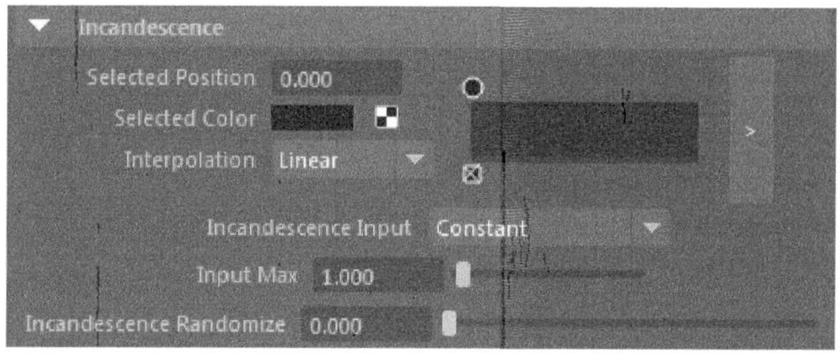

Figure 13-28 The ***Incandescence*** *area*

Input Max

This attribute is used to set the maximum range of Incandescence values.

Incandescence Randomize

This attribute is used to set a random value multiplier for per-particle Incandescence value.

Per Particle (Array) Attributes Area

The attributes in this area are used to set attributes on per-particle basis, refer to Figure 13-29.

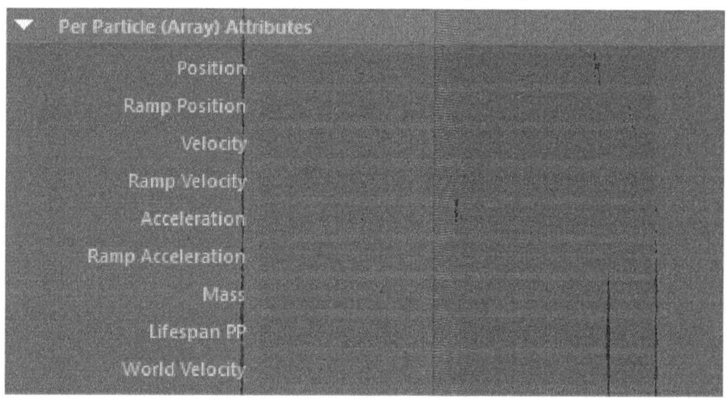

Figure 13-29 Partial view of the ***Per Particle (Array) Attributes*** *area*

Add Dynamic Attributes Area

The attributes in this area are used to add custom attributes to an nParticle object. These attributes can be on per-particle or per-object basis and are generally used to create complex particle effects. Choose the **General** button from this area; the **Add Attribute: nParticleShape1** dialog box will be displayed, as shown in Figure 13-30. Now, you can create custom attributes by using this dialog box.

Goal Weights and Objects Area

The attribute in this area is used to determine the properties of goal objects whose attributes are used to control nParticle simulation.

Goal Smoothness

The **Goal Smoothness** attribute is used to control the smoothness of goal forces. The default value of this attribute is 3. The higher the value of nParticle, the smoother will be the goal forces even if the weight changes.

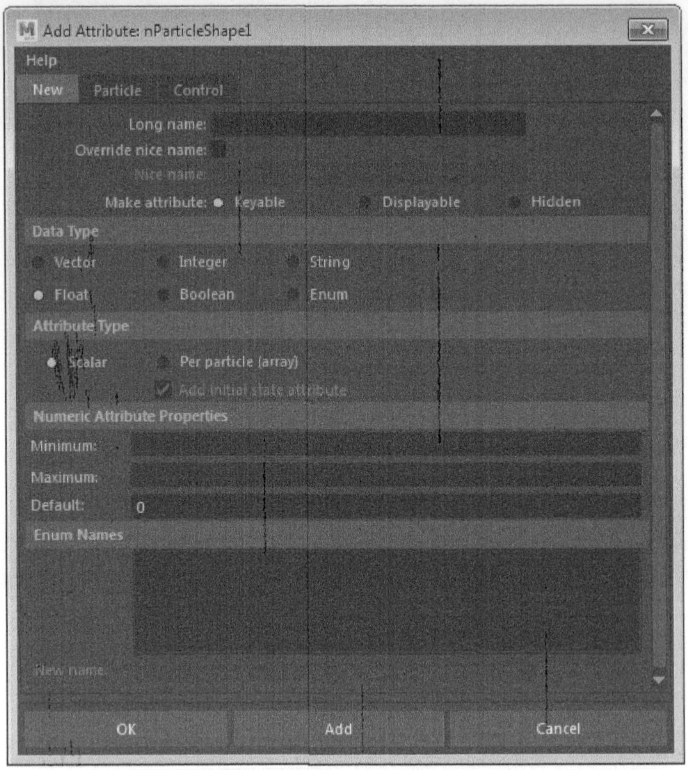

Figure 13-30 The ***Add Attribute: nParticleShape1*** *dialog box*

Instancer (Geometry Replacement) Area

The attributes in the **Instancer (Geometry Replacement)** area are used to change the default settings of the instanced objects. Note that these attributes will not be activated till the selected nParticles are converted into instances. To change the default settings of the instanced objects, choose **nParticles > Create > Instancer** from the menubar, as shown in Figure 13-31.

Figure 13-31 Choosing ***Instancer*** *from the nParticles menu*

On doing so, the attributes in the **Instancer (Geometry Replacement)** area will be activated, as shown in Figure 13-32. Some of the attributes are discussed next.

Instancer Nodes

The options in this drop-down list are used to select the instancer which is connected to the selected instanced objects.

Allow All Data Types

The **Allow All Data Types** check box is used to enable all data types that can be selected for the inputs. By default, this check box is cleared.

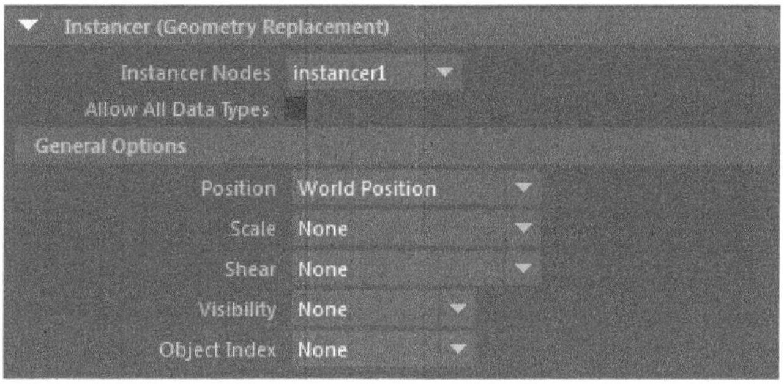

***Figure 13-32** Partial view of the **Instancer (Geometry Replacement)** area*

General Options Area

The attributes in this area are used to set the position, scale, visibility, and so on of the instanced objects. The attributes in this area are discussed next.

Position

The options in the **Position** drop-down list are used to specify the position of instanced objects. By default, the **World Position** option is selected in this drop-down list.

Scale

The options in the **Scale** drop-down list are used to specify the scale of the instanced objects. By default, the **None** option is selected in this drop-down list.

Shear

The options in the **Shear** drop-down list are used to specify the shear of the instanced objects. By default, the **None** option is selected in this drop-down list.

Visibility

The options in the **Visibility** drop-down list are used to determine the visibility of the instanced objects. By default, the **None** option is selected in this drop-down list.

Object Index

The options in the **Object Index** drop-down list are used to specify which object from the constrained object list is instanced for each particle. By default, the **None** option is selected in this drop-down list.

Rotation Options Area

The attributes in this area are used to determine the orientation of the currently instanced objects, refer to Figure 13-33.

Cycle Options Area

The options in this area ensure that particles cycle in a sequential order. To instance the objects, choose **nParticles > Create > Instancer > Option Box** from the menubar; the **Particle Instancer**

Options dialog box will be displayed, as shown in Figure 13-34. Next, select **Sequential** from the **Cycle** drop-down list in this dialog box. Choose **Apply** and then the **Close** button to close the dialog box.

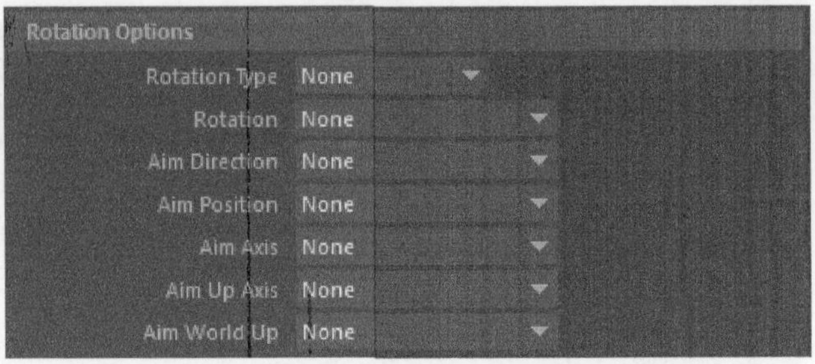

*Figure 13-33 The **Rotation Options** area*

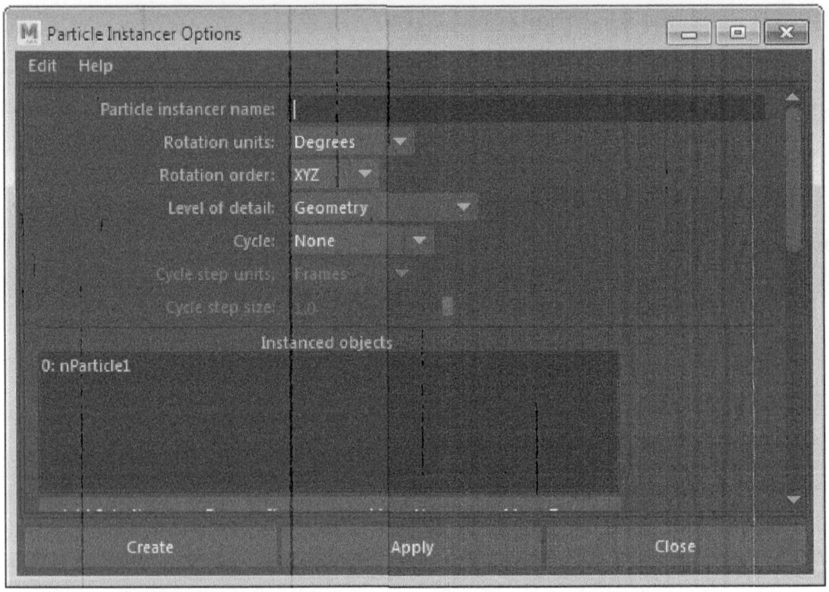

*Figure 13-34 The **Particle Instancer Options** dialog box*

Sprite Attributes Area

The attributes in this area are inactive by default. To activate these attributes, choose **nParticleShape1 > Shading > Particle Render Type > Sprites** from the **Attribute Editor**. The attributes in this area, as shown in Figure 13-35 are discussed next.

Sprite Num

The **Sprite Num** attribute is used to identify any file from stack of files. By default, its value is 1.

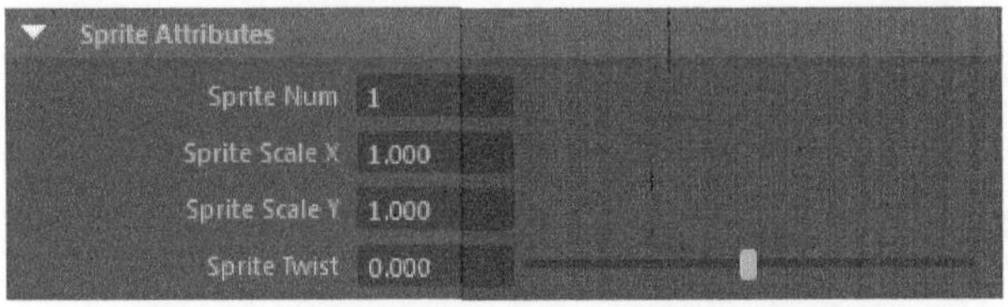

*Figure 13-35 The **Sprites Attributes** area*

Sprite Scale X

The **Sprite Scale X** attribute scales the sprite on the X axis or horizontal line. The default value assigned to this attribute is 1.

Sprite Scale Y

The **Sprite Scale Y** attribute scales the sprite on the Y axis or vertical line. The default value assigned to this attribute is 1.

Sprite Twist

This attribute is used to twist the sprite in X or Y direction. The default value assigned to this attribute is 0.

nucleus1 Tab

This tab consists of attributes that are used to specify gravity wind, ground plane attributes, time scale attributes, and so on. Some of these attributes are discussed next.

Enable

This check box is selected by default. It enables nucleus solver to calculate simulation data which is a part of its nucleus system.

Visibility

By default, this check box is selected. As a result, the location and direction of gravity and wind field is displayed as arrows in the scene.

Gravity and Wind Area

The attributes in this area are used to set the gravity and wind settings for the current Maya Nucleus solver. The attributes in this area are discussed next.

Gravity

This attribute is used to specify the amount of gravity applied to Maya Nucleus solver. The default value of this attribute is 9.8. A value of 0 means no gravity.

Gravity Direction

This attribute is used to specify the direction of gravity applied. By default, the value of this attribute is (0, -1, 0). This indicates that the gravity is applied in downward direction along Y-axis.

Air Density

This attribute is used to specify the air density applied to the nucleus solver. The default value of this attribute is 1. Higher the value, less will be the speed of the nParticle objects falling into space.

Wind Speed

This attribute is used to determine the force and intensity of the wind. A higher value of this attribute indicates a faster wind speed.

Wind Direction
This attribute is used to indicate the direction of the wind. The default value of this attribute is (1,0,0), which means that the wind will move from left to right along the X-axis.

Wind Noise
This attribute is used to specify the level of noise that affects the random falling of nParticle objects on the plane.

Ground Plane Area
The attributes in this area are used to create an imaginary ground plane which acts as a collision object for nParticle. The options in this area are discussed next.

Use Plane
Select this check box to use the plane as an object, which is not visible in the viewport.

Plane Origin
This attribute is used to specify the X, Y, and Z coordinates of the ground plane. The default coordinates of the plane are (0,0,0) which are same as the grid origin coordinates.

Plane Normal
This attribute is used to specify the orientation of the ground plane. The default value of this attribute is (0,1,0).

Plane Bounce
This attribute is used to specify the intensity of the bounce of nParticle objects on the plane. The higher the value, the greater will be the amount of deflective force.

Plane Friction
This attribute is used to specify the amount of friction that is applied when nParticles collide with other nParticle objects. The strength of the plane friction is determined by the type of surface it represents.

Plane Stickiness
This attribute is used to determine the extent to which the nParticles will stick to the ground plane when they collide with it.

Solver Attributes Area
The attributes in the **Solver Attributes** area are used to change the settings of Maya Nucleus solver. These attributes are discussed next.

Substeps
This attribute is used to specify the number of times the Maya Nucleus solver calculates an object's collision per frame. The default value of this attribute is 3.

Max Collision Iterations
This attribute is used to determine the maximum number of collision iterations the nucleus objects can take on colliding with nParticles. The default value of this attribute is 4.

Collision Layer Range
The **Collision Layer Range** attribute is used to set the distance between two objects in order for them to intercollide. The default value of this attribute is 4.

Timing Output
The options in this drop-down list are used to display the time information of the Nucleus in the **Script Editor** in seconds. The three options in this drop-down list are, **None**, **Frame**, and **Subframe**. On selecting **Frame**, the evaluation time in seconds will be displayed at every frame in the **Script Editor**. On selecting **Subframe**, the time for evaluation will be displayed at every substep in the **Script Editor**.

Time Attributes Area
The options in this area are used to edit the timing of the dynamic keyframe animation. These attributes are discussed next.

Start Frame
The **Start Frame** attribute is used to indicate the starting frame at which Maya Nucleus solver starts calculating. This attribute can be modified as per the requirement to start simulation from a specific frame.

Current Time
This attribute is used to specify the speed for all the objects connected to the Maya Nucleus solver. The connection can be broken by right-clicking on it and then choosing **Break Connection** from the shortcut menu displayed, refer to Figure 13-36.

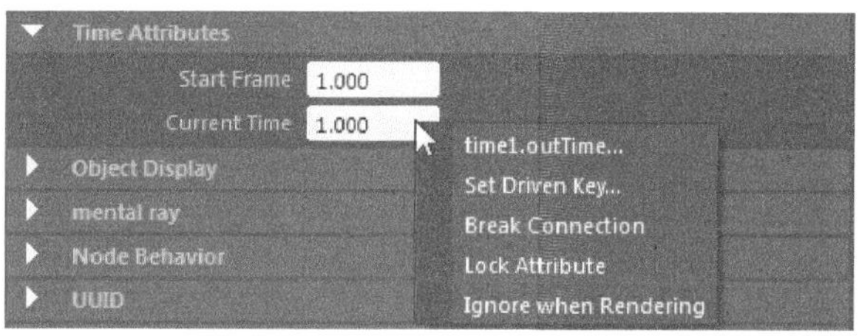

*Figure 13-36 The **Break Connection** option in the shortcut menu*

Node Behavior Area
The attributes in this area help you in saving the simulation data to a server or a local hard drive by caching your nParticle objects or effects.

TUTORIALS

Tutorial 1
In this tutorial, you will create liquid simulation by using nParticles. **(Expected time: 45 min)**

The following steps are required to complete this tutorial:

a. Create the project folder.
b. Download and open the file.
c. Create nParticles.

d. Simulate nParticles.
e. Cache nParticles.
f. Add material to nParticles.
g. Add caustics.
h. Save and render the scene.

Creating the Project Folder

Create a new project folder with the name *c13_tut1* at *\Documents\maya2017*, as discussed in Tutorial 1 of Chapter 2.

Downloading and Opening the File

In this section, you will download and open the file.

1. Download the *c13_maya_2017_tut.zip* file from *www.cadcim.com*. The path of the file is as follows: *Textbooks > Animation and Visual Effects > Maya > Autodesk Maya 2017: A Comprehensive Guide*.

   Extract the content of the zip file to the *Documents* folder.

2. Choose **File > Open Scene** from the menubar; the **Open** dialog box is displayed. In this dialog box, browse to *c13_maya_2017_tut* folder and select **c13_tut1_start.mb** file. Next, choose the **Open** button.

3. Now, choose **File > Save Scene As** from the menubar; the **Save As** dialog box is displayed. Save the file with the name *c13tut1.mb* in this folder.

   As the project folder is already set, the path *\Documents\maya2017\c13_tut1\scenes* is displayed in the **Look In** drop-down list.

Creating nParticles

In this section, you will fill the glass with nParticles.

1. Maximize the front viewport and select the glass, as shown in Figure 13-37. Next, select the **FX** menuset from the **Menuset** drop-down list in the Status Line.

2. Choose **nParticles > Create > Create Option > Water** from the menubar; the nParticles style type changes to **Water**.

3. Choose **nParticles > Create > Fill Object > Option Box** from the menubar; the **Particle Fill Options** dialog box is displayed. In this dialog box, set the following parameters:

   Resolution: **30** Min Y: **0.5** Max Y: **1.0**

   Next, select the **Double Walled** check box.

4. Choose the **Particle Fill** button and then choose the **Close** button; the glass is filled with nParticles, as shown in Figure 13-38.

Figure 13-37 The glass to be selected

Figure 13-38 The glass filled with nParticles

Simulating nParticles

In this section, you will simulate nParticles.

1. Select both the glasses. Choose **nCloth > Create > Create Passive Collider** from the menubar, as shown in Figure 13-39; two rigid bodies **nRigid1** and **nRigid2** are created. These can be seen in the **Outliner** window.

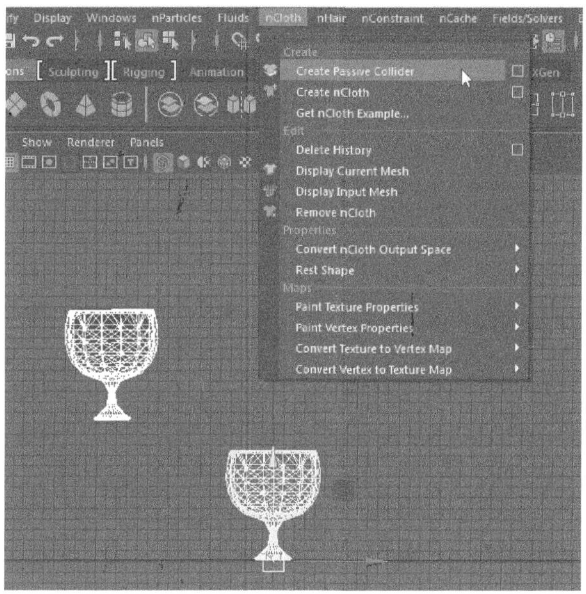

*Figure 13-39 Choosing the **Create Passive Collider** option from the menubar*

2. Play the simulation till all the nParticles settle down. Stop the simulation when the nParticles settle down in the glass.

3. Select the nParticles in the viewport. In the **Attribute Editor**, make sure the **nParticleShape1** tab is chosen. Expand the **Particle Size** area of this tab and enter **0.165** in the **Radius** edit box. Next, expand the **Collisions** area and enter **0.5** in the **Collide Width Scale** edit box.

4. In the **Radius Scale** area, select the **Randomized ID** option from the **Radius Scale Input** drop-down list and enter **0.1** in the **Radius Scale Randomize** edit box. Expand the **Liquid Simulation** area and enter **0.65** in the **Liquid Radius Scale** edit box.

5. Make sure the nParticles are selected. Choose **Fields/Solvers > Solver > Intial State > Set for selected** from the menubar, as shown in Figure 13-40; the current state is set as the initial state.

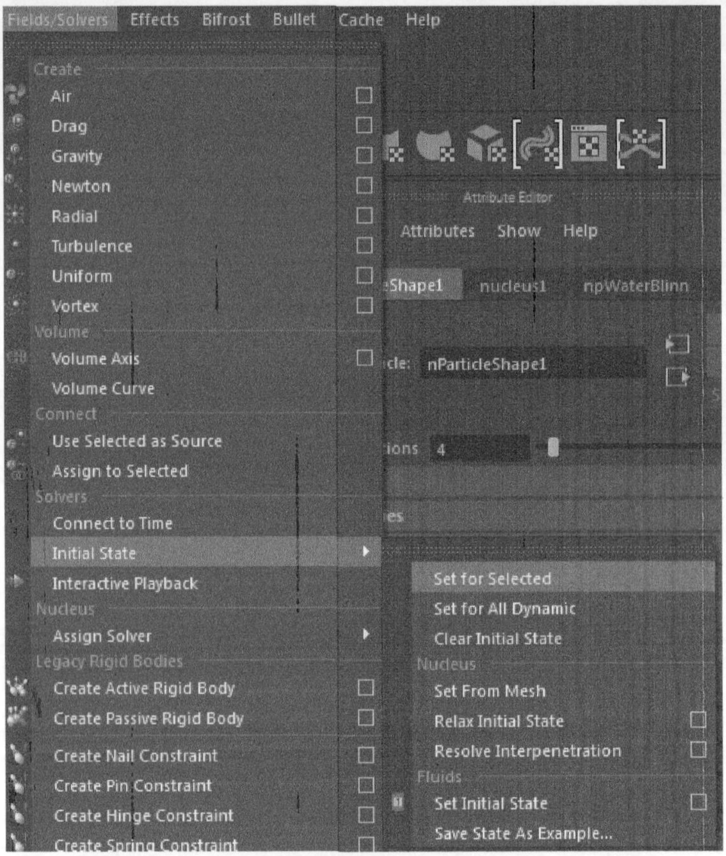

Figure 13-40 *Choosing the* ***Set for Selected*** *option from the menubar*

6. Choose the **nucleus1** tab in the **Attribute Editor**. In the **Ground Plane** area of this tab, select the **Use Plane** check box. Set the value of **Plane Friction** to **0.465**. In the **Solver Attributes** area, enter **20** in the **Substeps** edit box.

7. Select the glass, as shown in Figure 13-41. Place the Time Slider on frame 1 and press the S key. Next, place the Time Slider on frame 30 and enter **-74** in the **Rotate Z** edit box of the **Channel Box / Layer Editor**. Again, press the S key to set the position of glass at frame 30, refer to Figure 13-42.

Figure 13-41 *The glass to be selected*

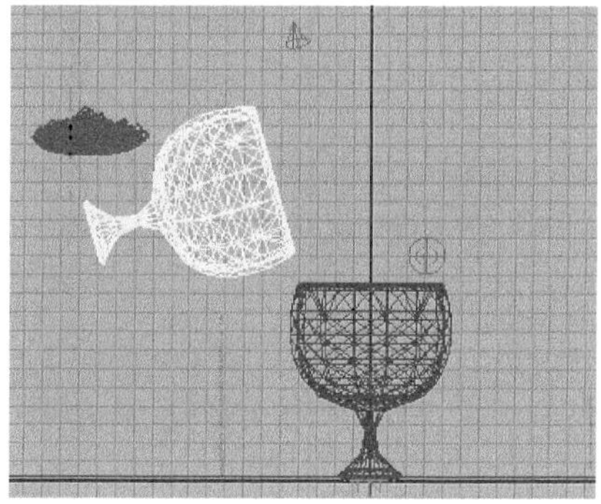

Figure 13-42 *The position of glass at frame 30*

Caching nParticles

In this section, you will cache nParticles.

1. Move the Time Slider at frame 1. Select the nParticles and then choose **nCache > Create > Create New Cache > nObject** from the menubar; the caching begins. Some of the nParticles will flow out of the glass, as shown in Figure 13-43. Also, stop the caching process by pressing ESC.

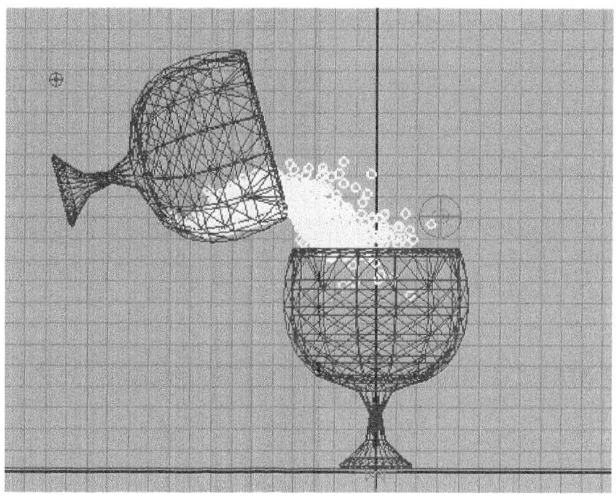

Figure 13-43 *The nParticles flowing out of the glass*

2. Select **nRigid1** in the **Outliner** window; the **nRigidShape1** tab is displayed in the **Attribute Editor**. In this tab, expand the **Force Field Generation** area. Select the **Single Sided** option from the **Force Field** drop-down list, as shown in Figure 13-44.

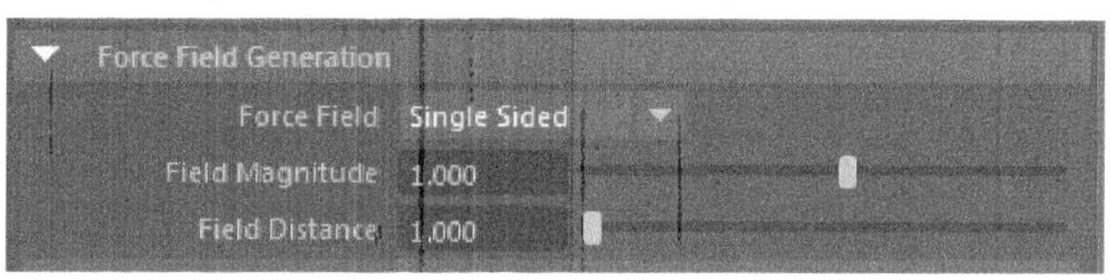

Figure 13-44 *The **Force Field Generation** area*

3. In the **Force Field Generation** area, set the values as follows:

   Field Magnitude: **-4.00** Field Distance: **5**

4. Make sure nParticles are selected in the viewport. In the **Shading** area of the **nparticleShape1** tab of the **Attribute Editor,** set the parameters as follows:

   Threshold: **0.900** Opacity: **0.080**

5. Select the nParticles and make sure the Time Slider is at frame 1. Next, choose **nCache > Create > Replace Caches > nObject** from the menubar; the **Create Cache Warning** message box is displayed. In this message box, choose the **Auto-rename** button; the caching begins.

Adding Material to nParticles

In this section, you will apply materials to the nParticles.

1. Maximize the persp viewport. Make sure nParticles are selected. Choose **Modify > Convert > nParticles to Polygons** from the menubar. You will notice that the nParticles will disappear from the viewport.

2. In the **nparticleShape1** tab of the **Attribute Editor**, expand the **Output Mesh** area and set the parameters as follows:

   Threshold: **0.002** Mesh Triangle Size: **0.200** Motion Streak: **0.3**
   Max triangle Resolution: **500**

3. Make sure the **Triangle Mesh** option is selected in the **Mesh Method** drop-down list. After setting the parameters, mesh is converted into a smoother mesh.

4. Apply the **Blinn** shader using the **Hypershade** window and rename it as **Water**. In the **Water** tab of the **Attribute Editor**, set the parameters as follows:

   Common Material Attributes area

   Color (RGB): **0, 0, 0** Transparency (RGB): **1, 1, 1**

   Specular Shading area

   Eccentricity: **0.618** Specular Roll Off: **0.559** Reflectivity: **0.720**

   In the **Raytrace Options** area, select the **Refractions** check box and then set the following values:

   Refractive Index: **1.50** Refraction Limit: **8**
   Shadow Attenuation: **0.02** Reflection Limit: **3**

Adding Caustics

In this section, you will add caustics.

1. Choose **Windows > Rendering Editors > Render Settings** from the menubar; the **Render Settings** window is displayed. In this window select **mental ray** from the **Render Using** drop-down list, if not already selected, to set the **mental ray** renderer as the current renderer. Choose the **Quality** tab and then expand the **Legacy Options** area in the window. In the **Caustics** area, select the **Caustics** check box; the caustics are applied to the scene. Next, enter **200** in the **Accuracy** edit box.

2. Select the spot light in the viewport. In the **spotLightShape1** tab, expand the **mental ray** area in the **Attribute Editor**; the **Caustic and Global Illumination** area is displayed. In this area, select the **Emit Photons** check box and set the parameters as follows:

   Photon Intensity: **5000** Caustic Photons: **500000**

3. Now, you need to render the scene. For rendering, refer to Tutorial 1 of Chapter 8. The final output after rendering is shown in Figure 13-45.

Saving and Rendering the Scene

In this section, you will save the scene that you have created and then render it. You can view the final rendered image sequence of the scene by downloading the *c13_maya_2017_rndr.zip* file from *www.cadcim.com*. The path of the file is as follows: *Textbooks > Animation and Visual Effects > Maya > Autodesk Maya 2017: A Comprehensive Guide.*

Figure 13-45 *The final output at frame 70*

1. Choose **File > Save Scene** from the menubar to save the scene.

2. For rendering the scene, refer to Tutorial 1 of chapter 8. The final rendered output is shown in Figure 13-45.

Tutorial 2

In this tutorial, you will create the smoke effect by using an emitter object, as shown in Figure 13-46. **(Expected time: 30 min)**

Figure 13-46 *The final output*

The following steps are required to complete this tutorial:

a. Create a project folder.
b. Download and open the file.
c. Create an emitter object.
d. Create a volume axis field.
e. Shade the nParticles.
f. Save and render the scene.

Creating a Project Folder

Create a new project folder with the name *c13_tut2* at *\Documents\maya2017*, as discussed in Tutorial 1 of Chapter 2.

Downloading and Opening the File

In this section, you will download and then open the file.

1. Download the *c13_maya_2017_tut.zip* file from *www.cadcim.com*. The path of the file is as follows: *Textbooks > Animation and Visual Effects > Maya > Autodesk Maya 2017: A Comprehensive Guide.*

   Extract the contents of the zip file to the *Documents* folder.

2. Choose **File > Open Scene** from the menubar; the **Open** dialog box is displayed. In this dialog box, browse to *c13_maya_2017_tut* folder and select the **c13_tut2_start.mb** file. Next, choose the **Open** button.

3. Now, choose **File > Save Scene As** from the menubar; the **Save As** dialog box is displayed. Next, save the file with the name *c13tut2.mb* in this folder.

   As the project folder is already set, the path *\Documents\maya2017\c13_tut2\scenes* is displayed in the **Look In** drop-down list.

4. Extract the *wood.jpg* and *cigarette_texture.jpg* images to the *sourceimages* folder at the location *\Documents\maya2017\c13_tut2*.

Creating an Emitter Object

In this section, you will create an emitter.

1. Select the **FX** menuset from the **Menuset** drop-down list in the menubar. Choose **nParticles > Create Options > Cloud** from the menubar; the nParticles style type changes to **Cloud**.

2. Choose **nParticles > Emit > Create Emitter > Option Box** from the menubar; the **Emitter Options (Create)** dialog box is displayed, as shown in the Figure 13-47.

3. In the **Emitter Options (Create)** dialog box, type **Emitter_sm** in the **Emitter name** edit box and set the following options:

   Emitter type: **Directional** Rate (particles/sec): **120.0**

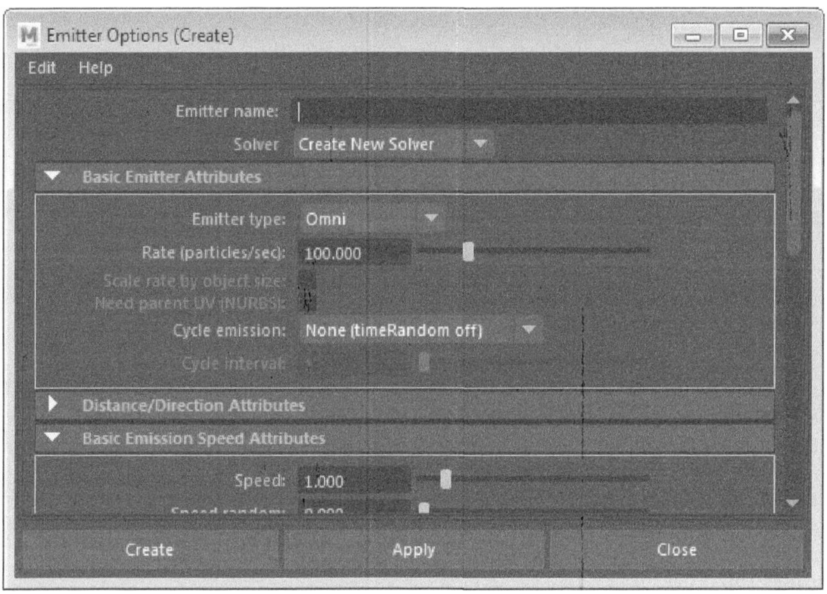

*Figure 13-47 The **Emitter Options (Create)** dialog box*

   In the **Basic Emission Speed Attributes** area, set the following parameters:

   Speed: **2.5** Speed Random: **5**

4. After setting the options, choose the **Create** button; an emitter is displayed in the viewport.

Place the emitter on the tip of the cigarette and play the simulation; the nParticles start flowing along the X axis, refer to Figure 13-48.

Figure 13-48 *The emitter displayed*

5. Select nParticles in the viewport; the **nParticleShape1** tab is displayed in the **Attribute Editor**. In this tab, expand the **Lifespan** area and set the following values:

   Lifespan Mode: **Random range** Lifespan: **15**
   Lifespan Random: **5**

   Expand the **Particle Size** area and enter **0.350** in the **Radius** edit box.

6. In the **Radius Scale** area, add markers to different points on the ramp by using the left mouse button and add value for each marker. The values for different markers are given in Table 13-1:

Table 13-1 *The values for different markers*

Marker	Selected Position	Selected Value
First	0.026	0.140
Second	0.487	0.200
Third	0.783	0.380
Fourth	0.939	0.940

7. Select **Normalized Age** from the **Radius Scale Input** drop-down list and enter **0.250** in the **Radius Scale Randomize** edit box.

8. In the **Dynamics Properties** area, make sure the **Ignore Solver Gravity** check box is cleared and set the following parameters:

   Conserve: **0.450** Drag: **0.190**

9. Make sure the nParticles are selected and choose the **nucleus1** tab in the **Attribute Editor**. In the **Gravity and Wind** area of this tab, enter **0, 1, 0** in the **Wind Direction** edit boxes and **0, 1, 0** in the **Gravity Direction** edit boxes. You will notice that nParticles will start flowing in the upward direction, as shown in Figure 13-49.

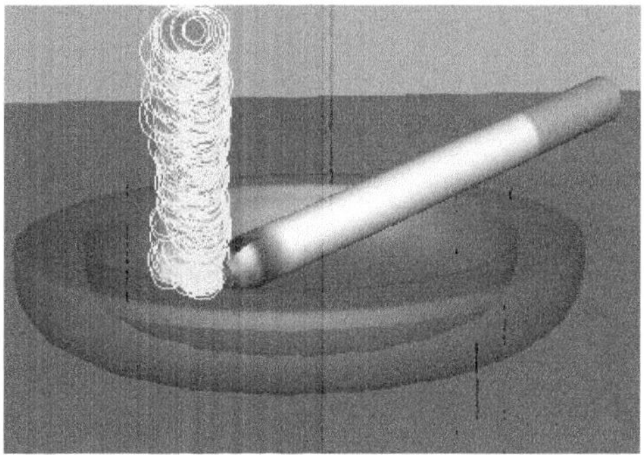

Figure 13-49 *The nParticles moving in the upward direction*

Creating the Volume Axis Field

In this section, you will create a volume axis field for the nParticles.

1. Make sure the nParticles are selected. Next, choose **Fields > Solvers > Volume > Volume Axis > Option Box** from the menubar; the **Volume Axis Options** dialog box is displayed.

2. In the **Volume Axis Options** dialog box, set the values as follows:

Magnitude: **120**	Attenuation: **10**	Away from center: **5**
Directional Speed: **2**	DirectionX: **0**	DirectionY: **1**
Turbulence: **0.700**	Turbulence speed: **0.602**	

3. After setting the above values, choose the **Create** button; the **volumeAxisField1** field is created in the persp viewport. Place it on the ash tray. Play the simulation; the nParticles start flowing upward in curls, as shown in Figure 13-50.

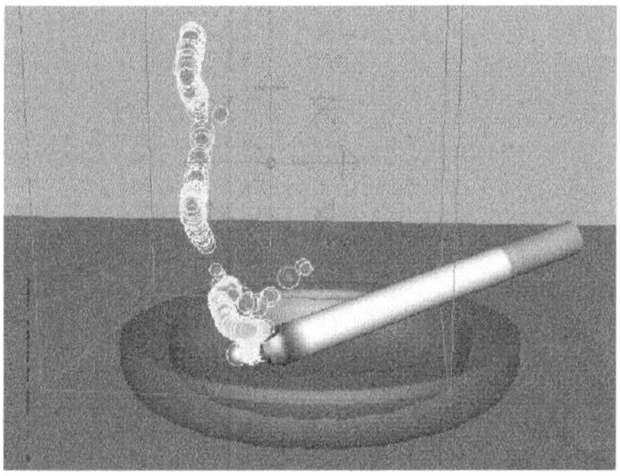

Figure 13-50 *The nParticles flowing upward in curls*

Shading the nParticles

In this section, you will add shades to the nParticles.

1. Select nParticles; the **particleShape1** tab is displayed in the **Attribute Editor**. In the tab, expand the **Shading** area and enter **0.1** in the **Opacity** edit box.

2. In the **Opacity Scale** area, select **Spline** from the **Interpolation** drop-down list and **Normalized Age** from the **Opacity Scale Input** drop-down list.

3. Expand the **Color** area. Next, expand the **Color Palette** ramp by choosing the arrow button next to it, refer to Figure 13-51; the **nParticleShape1.color** window is displayed.

4. In the **nParticleShape1.color** window, select the first marker and click on the **Selected color** swatch. Then, change the color to dark grey (H: **0**, S: **0**, V: **0.341**) and enter **0** in the **Selected**

position edit box. Next, select the second marker and click on the **Selected color** swatch. Then, to change color to light grey (H: **0**, S: **0**, V: **0.671**) and enter **0.521** in the **Selected position** edit box. Create the third marker and click on the **Selected color** swatch. Then, change the color to white and enter **1** in the **Selected position** edit box; the color gradient is set in the **nParticleShape1.color** window. Close the **nParticleShape1.color** window.

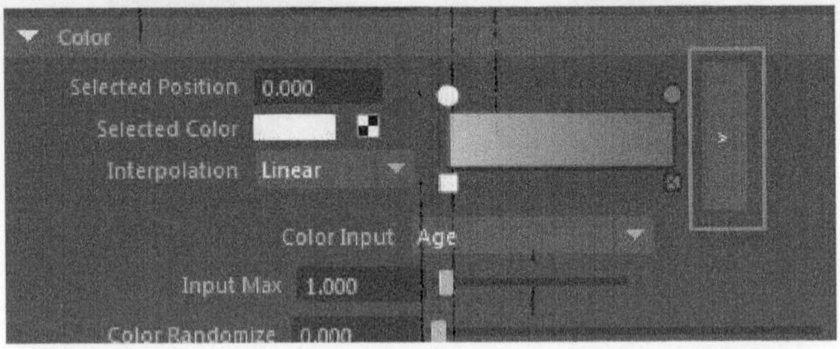

*Figure 13-51 Choosing the arrow button in the **Color** area*

5. In the **Color** area of the **nParticleShape1** tab, enter **0.850** in the **Color Randomize** edit box; the color of the nParticle changes, as shown in Figure 13-52.

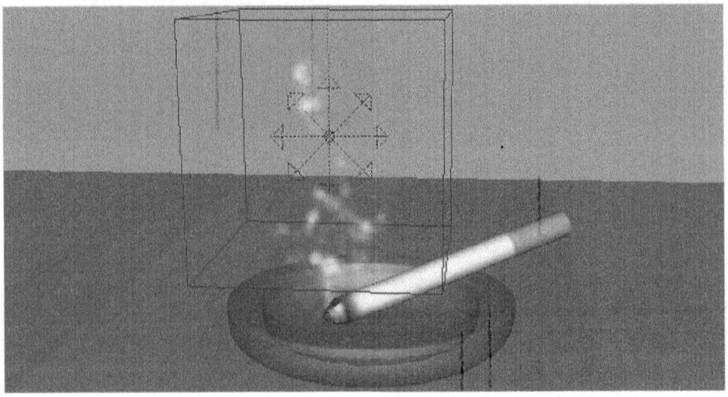

Figure 13-52 The changed color of nParticles

6. Choose the **Animation Preferences** button; the **Preferences** dialog box is displayed. Next, in the **Playback** area of this dialog box, select the **Real-time [24fps]** option from the **Playback speed** drop-down list.

Saving and Rendering the Scene

In this section, you will save the scene that you have created and then render it. You can view the final rendered image sequence of the scene by downloading the *c13_maya_2017_rndr.zip* file from *www.cadcim.com*. The path of the file is as follows: *Textbooks > Animation and Visual Effects > Maya > Autodesk Maya 2017: A Comprehensive Guide.*

1. Choose **File > Save Scene** from the menubar to save the scene.

2. For rendering the scene, refer to Tutorial 1 of chapter 8. The final rendered output is shown in Figure 13-46.

Self-Evaluation Test

Answer the following questions and then compare them to those given at the end of this chapter:

1. Which of the following is the default value of the **Gravity Direction** attribute?

   (a) 1,0,0 (b) 0,0,1
   (c) -1,1,0 (d) 0,-1,0

2. The **Motion streak** option can only be used when nParticles are converted into ________.

3. The default value of the gravity attribute is ________.

4. The ________ attribute is used to control the surface tension during liquid simulation.

5. The ________ attribute displays the total number of particles in an nParticle object.

6. The options in the ________ area are used to define the life of the selected nParticle objects in the viewport.

7. The default value of the **Air Density** attribute is 2. (T/F)

8. There are three types of nParticle styles. (T/F)

9. The **Rest Density** attribute is used to determine the resistance of the fluid to flow. (T/F)

Review Questions

Answer the following questions:

1. Which of the following options is selected by default in the **Interpolation** drop-down list of the **Radius Scale** area?

   (a) **None** (b) **Linear**
   (c) **Spline** (d) **Smooth**

2. The ________ attribute is used to display the amount of damping on the selected nParticle.

3. The ________ attribute is used to define the adhering of nParticle objects on self-collision or on collision with other nParticle objects.

4. The **Bounce Scale** attribute is used to control the ________ scale.

5. The default value of the **Drag** attribute in the **Dynamic Properties** area is ________.

6. The options in the ________ area are used to define the properties of the wind field.

7. The **Air Push Distance** attribute is used to indirectly influence the nParticle system. (T/F)

8. The options in the **Goal Weights and Objects** area are used to determine properties of goal objects. (T/F)

9. The attributes in the **Shading** area are used to modify the appearance of an nParticle object. (T/F)

EXERCISES

The rendered image sequence of the scenes used in the following exercises can be accessed by downloading the *c13_maya_2017_exr.zip* file from *www.cadcim.com*. The path of the file is as follows: *Textbooks > Animation and Visual Effects > Maya > Autodesk Maya 2017: A Comprehensive Guide.*

Exercise 1

Create snowfall in a scene by using nParticles, as shown in Figure 13-53. Apply textures to the snow crystals and then render the scene using the **mental ray** renderer.

(Expected time: 30 min)

Figure 13-53 *The hailstorm effect*

Exercise 2

Create constellation in a scene by using nParticles, as shown in Figure 13-54 and then render the scene. **(Expected time: 30 min)**

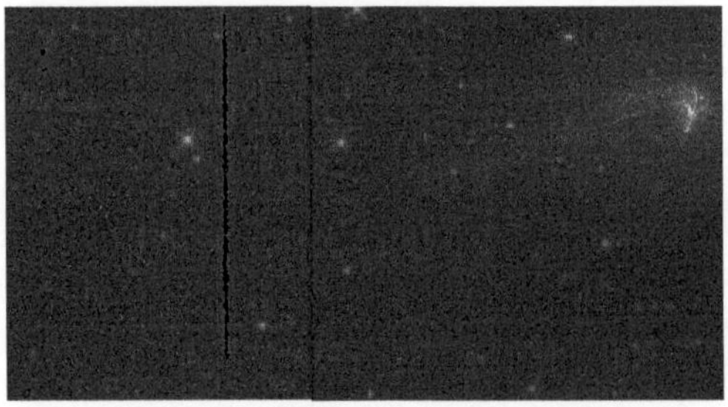

Figure 13-54 *The constellation*

Answers to Self-Evaluation Test

1. d, **2. polygons**, **3.** 9.8, **4. Surface Tension**, **5. Count**, **6. Lifespan**, **7.** F, **8.** F, **9.** F

Chapter 14

Fluids

Learning Objectives

After completing this chapter, you will be able to:

- *Learn about various types of fluids in Maya*
- *Apply the dynamic and non-dynamic fluid effects*
- *Modify the fluid components*
- *Paint in the fluid containers*
- *Add ocean and pond effects to your scene*
- *Connect Maya fields to a container*

INTRODUCTION

In this chapter, you will learn about the fluid effects in Maya. Maya fluids are used to create fluid effects to scene such as running water, explosion, smoke, clouds, and so on. Maya's fluid effects simulation engine is based on Navier-Stokes mathematical equations. It is one of the most complex simulation engines in Maya. In this chapter, you will create various fluid simulations using Maya fluids.

CLASSIFICATION OF FLUID EFFECTS

There are three types of fluid effects in Maya: open water, dynamic, and non-dynamic. These effects are discussed next.

Open Water Fluid Effects

The open water fluid effect is used to make open water fluid surfaces such as oceans, ponds, rivers, and so on. The ocean surfaces are formed using NURBS planes with ocean shader applied to them. To create an ocean, select the **FX** menuset from the **Menuset** drop-down list in the Status Line. Next, choose **Fluids > Create > Ocean > Option Box** from the menubar; the **Create Ocean** dialog box will be displayed, as shown in Figure 14-1.

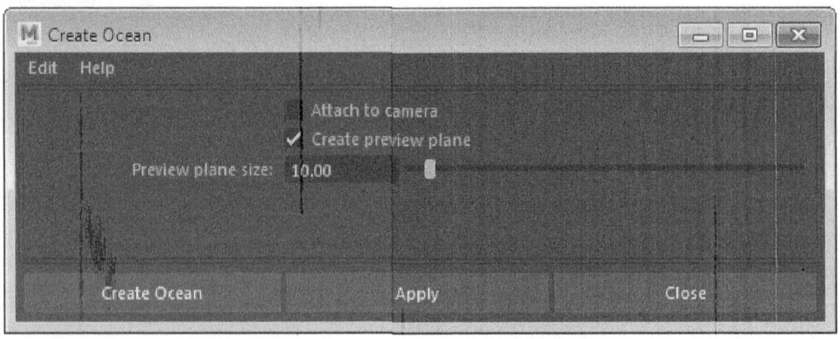

***Figure 14-1** The **Create Ocean** dialog box*

In this dialog box, the **Preview plane size** attribute is used to set the size of the plane that will be used for creating an ocean in the scene. The default value for this attribute is 10. After setting the required value, choose the **Create Ocean** button to create the ocean in the viewport. Next, choose **Render the current frame** button from the Status Line to render the scene. After rendering, the realistic view of the ocean will be displayed, as shown in Figure 14-2.

Dynamic Fluid Effects

The dynamic fluid effect creates the fluids based on the natural law of physics that describes how objects move. In this process, the simulation of the dynamic fluid is calculated on the basis of the Navier-Stokes fluid dynamic equation. To create the dynamic fluid effect, first you need to create a fluid container. In Maya, a fluid container is a rectangular boundary that defines the space in the viewport, where the fluid simulation will be performed. The fluid container is the main component for any dynamic or non-dynamic fluid simulation. When you first create a container, it is empty. To create a fluid effect, you need to modify the container attributes.

Note

For open water effects, you do not require fluid containers.

Figure 14-2 The ocean

In Maya, there are two types of fluid containers, 3D and 2D. To create a 3D fluid container, choose **Fluids > Create > 3D Container** from the menubar; a 3D container will be created in the viewport, as shown in Figure 14-3. Similarly, you can create the 2D container using the **2D Container** option, as shown in Figure 14-4. The fluid containers are formed of grids. Each grid patch in a fluid container is known as voxel (volumetric pixel). Voxel density of the container determines the final output of the fluid particles to be created. You can use the dynamic fluid effects to create effects such as cloud, fire, and so on.

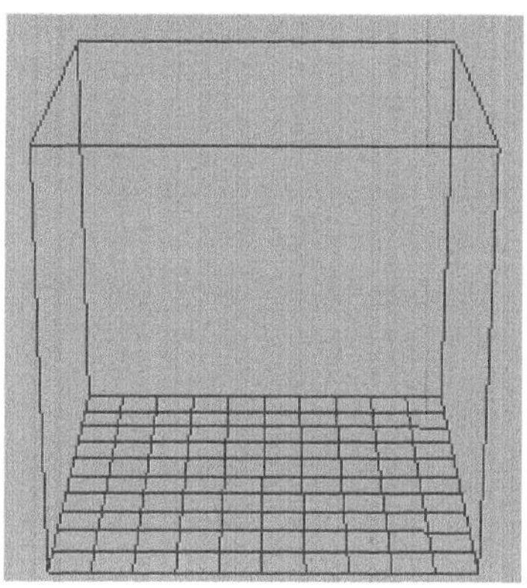

Figure 14-3 The 3D fluid container

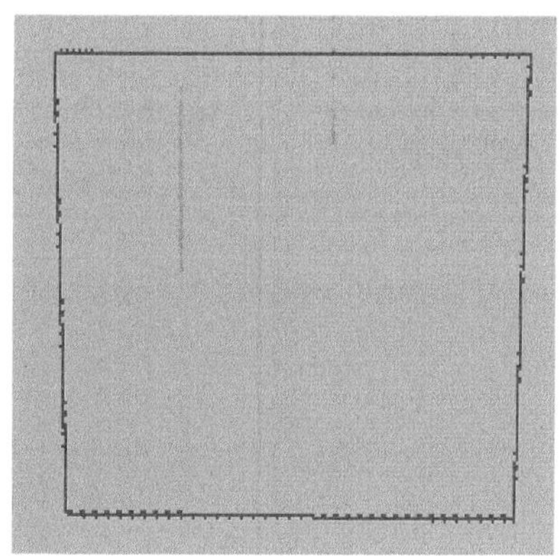

Figure 14-4 The 2D fluid container

Figure 14-5 displays the fire created using the dynamic fluid effect.

Non-Dynamic Fluid Effects

The non-dynamic fluid effects do not behave according to the natural law of fluid dynamics. Instead, the textures and animation are used to simulate the fluid and its motion. In this type of fluid effect, the fluid motion is created by keyframing the texture attributes. Moreover, in this effect, fluid solvers are not used to simulate the fluid motion. As a result, the rendering of the non-dynamic fluid effect is much faster than that of the dynamic fluid effect.

Figure 14-5 Fire or flames created using the dynamic fluid effect

WORKING WITH FLUID CONTAINERS

The fluid simulation in Maya is governed by certain fluid components. The fluid always resides within a container (2D or 3D). Each fluid container is formed of three-dimensional grids, and each unit of a grid comprises of voxels. In other words, a group of voxels combines to form a fluid container. Voxels play a major role in defining the content method of the fluid property. There are two basic ways to define the fluid property in a fluid container; as a preset gradient or as a grid. By specifying the content method to gradient preset, the fluid property can be maintained as constant throughout the container. The gradient preset sets a ramp value between 1 and 0 in a particular axis. By setting the content method to grid, you can place an individual value in each voxel. Therefore, the grid preset can either be defined as static or dynamic. To modify the content method, choose the fluid container in the viewport and open the **Attribute Editor**; the **Contents Method** area will be displayed, as shown in Figure 14-6.

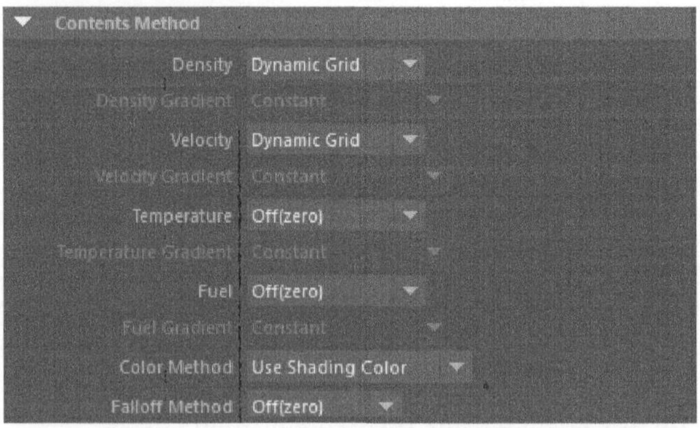

***Figure 14-6** The **Contents Method** area*

During animation, the fluid property value does not change in the static grid, whereas it changes in the case of dynamic grid. This is because the values in each voxel are recalculated at each frame. You can also resize the container and set its resolution. The resolution of the fluid is defined in voxels. Higher resolution produces finer details but also increases the simulation and rendering time. If you scale the container, the voxels in the container also get scaled without changing their contents. To make the container dense and add a finer detail to the fluid simulation, you need to increase its resolution. To do so, select the fluid container and then choose **Fluids > Edit > Edit Fluid Resolution > Option Box** from the menubar; the **Edit Fluid Resolution Options** dialog box will be displayed, as shown in Figure 14-7. Increase the resolution of the container using the options in this dialog box and then choose the **Apply and Close** button. Note that increasing the fluid resolution increases the number of voxels in the fluid container, thus increasing the rendering time.

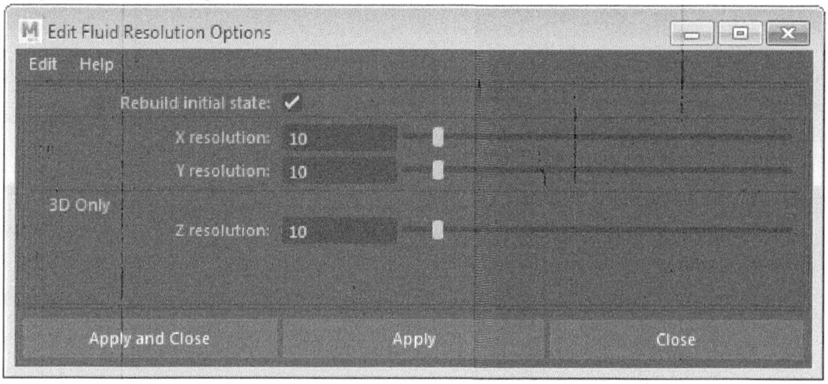

*Figure 14-7 The **Edit Fluid Resolution Options** dialog box*

Attributes of Fluid Container

You can also edit the properties of a 2D or 3D container. To do so, select the 3D container in the viewport and press CTRL+A to open the **Attribute Editor**. By default, the **fluidShape1** tab is chosen in the **Attribute Editor**, as shown in Figure 14-8. The commonly used attributes in this tab are discussed next.

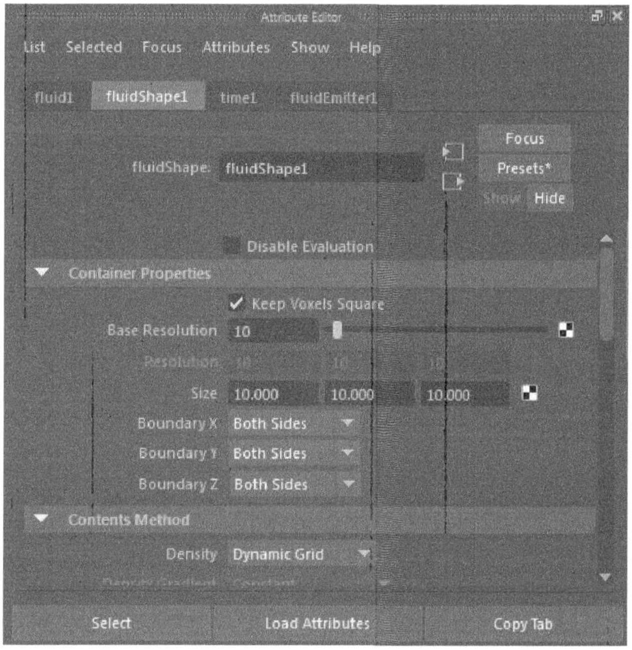

*Figure 14-8 The **fluidshape1** tab chosen in the **Attribute Editor***

Container Properties

The attributes in this area are used to edit the properties of the 2D or 3D container created. These attributes are discussed next.

Keep Voxels Square

This check box is used to set the container's resolution in such a way that the square voxels are maintained or arranged on the basis of the size of the container. By default, this check box is selected.

Base Resolution

This attribute is used to set the X, Y, and Z resolution values of the fluid container. It is activated only when the **Keep Voxels Square** check box is selected.

Resolution

The attribute is used to set the resolution of the fluid containers in voxels. Increasing the resolution will increase the render time.

Size

This attribute is used to set the size of the fluid container in centimeters.

Boundary X, Boundary Y, and Boundary Z

The options in these drop-down lists are used to control the behavior of the fluid when it comes in contact with the boundaries of the container.

Contents Method

The attributes in this area are used to define the method to be used to populate the fluid container. There are four options for defining the fluid property in a fluid container. They are **Off (zero)**, **Static Grid**, **Dynamic Grid**, and **Gradient**. These are discussed next.

Off (zero)

This option is used to set the property value to 0. On selecting this option, the property will have no effect on simulations.

Static Grid

This option is used to create a grid for the property that populates each voxel with specific property values.

Dynamic Grid

This option is used to create a grid for the property that populates each voxel with specific property values for use in any dynamic simulation.

Gradient

This option uses the gradient to populate the fluid container.

Display

The attributes in this area are used to modify the fluid display in the scene. They do not affect the final rendered image.

Shaded Display
The options in this drop-down list are used to define the fluid display in the container when the viewport is in the shaded display mode.

Opacity Preview Gain
This attribute is used to adjust the opacity of the hardware display when the shaded display is not set to **As Render**.

Slices Per Voxel
This attribute is used to define the number of slices displayed per voxel when viewport is in the shaded display mode. It is used only when Maya is in the shaded display mode.

Voxel Quality
The options in this drop-down list are used to define the quality of the voxels in the 3D or 2D container. These options are **Better** and **Faster**.

Boundary Draw
The options in this drop-down list are used to define the way the fluid container is displayed in the viewport. These options are **Bottom**, **Reduced**, **Outline**, and so on.

Numeric Display
The options in this drop-down list are used to define numeric values for the selected property.

Wireframe Display
The options in this drop-down list are used to define the opacity of the property when the viewport is in the wireframe display mode.

Velocity Draw
This check box is used to display the velocity vector for the fluid container.

Draw Arrowheads
This check box is used to display the arrowheads of the velocity vectors.

Velocity Draw Skip
This attribute is used to increase or decrease the number of velocity arrows. By default, the value 1 is displayed for this attribute.

Draw Length
This attribute is used to define the length of velocity vectors.

Dynamic Simulation
The attributes in this area are used to simulate the flow of the fluid. The attributes in this area are discussed next.

Gravity
This attribute is used to simulate the gravitational attraction. By default, its value is 9.8.

Viscosity

This attribute is used to define the resistance of the fluid when it is flowing. Increasing the value of this attribute makes the liquid thicker. Whereas, decreasing its value makes the fluid act like water.

Friction

This attribute is used to define the amount of internal friction used by the solver in the velocity solving.

Damp

This attribute is used to define the dampness of the velocity that tends toward zero at each successive step.

Solver

The options in this drop-down list are used to specify the solver to be used in the fluid simulation. These options are **none**, **Navier-Stokes**, and **Spring Mesh**.

High Detail Solve

The options in this drop-down list are used to add detailing to the solver without increasing the resolution.

Substeps

This attribute is used to define the number of calculations done in simulating fluids per frame.

Solver Quality

It specifies the number of times the solver would perform calculation per frame.

Grid Interpolater

The options in this drop-down list are used to select the interpolation algorithm to be used to retrieve values within the voxel grid.

Start Frame

This attribute is used to set the frame from which the simulation will begin. By default, it is set to 1.

Simulation Rate Scale

This attribute is used to scale the time step used in simulation (emission and solving).

Forward Advection

This check box is used to activate the mass conserving forward prorogation technique. This technique pushes density forward through the grid (voxels). The default solve method uses a backward propagation technique that pulls density into voxels from surrounding voxels.

Conserve Mass

This check box is selected by default. It is used to conserve mass when the density values are updated during solving process.

Use Collisions
This check box is used to collide the fluid with the geometry in the container.

Use Emissions
This check box is used to connect all fluid emitters during simulation.

Use Fields
This check box is used to ensure that Maya ignores all the connected fluid emitters during simulation.

Emit In Substeps
This check box is used to calculate the fluid emission on every substep. It is useful for effects that have high emission speed.

Creating Fluid Containers with Emitter

In Maya, you can create a fluid container with an emitter to simulate the fluid in the container. To do so, choose **Fluids > Create > 3D Container > Option Box** from the menubar; the **Create 3D Container with Emitter Options** dialog box will be displayed, as shown in Figure 14-9.

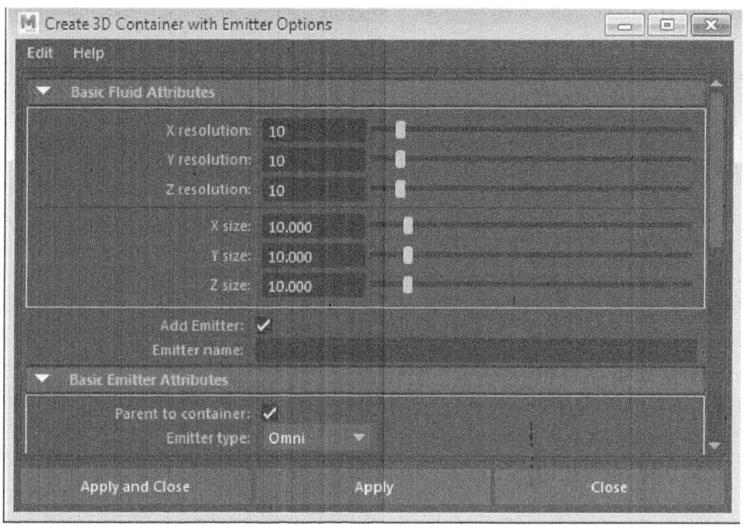

*Figure 14-9 The **Create 3D Container with Emitter Options** dialog box*

Set the required values in the dialog box and then choose the **Apply and Close** button. Similarly, you can create a 2D fluid container with an emitter using the **2D Container** option.

You can also make a surface collide with fluids. To do so, create a 3D container with an emitter in the viewport. Now, create a plane and move it inside the container just above the emitter. Select the plane and the fluid container, and then choose **Fluids > Edit > Make Collide > Option Box** from the menubar; the **Make Collide Options** dialog box will be displayed in the viewport, as shown in Figure 14-10. Increase the value in the **Tessellation factor** attribute and then choose the **Apply and Close** button. The default tessellation factor value is 200. Maya internally converts a NURBS object to polygon before it animates the simulation. The tessellation factor sets the number of polygons created during the conversion. A low tessellation value means that more fluid will appear passing through the geometry. You can increase this value to get the desired smoothness, but it will also increase the simulation time. Now, preview the animation to see the effect of the collision. Figures 14-11 and 14-12 show the difference in the simulation before and after a surface collides with the fluid.

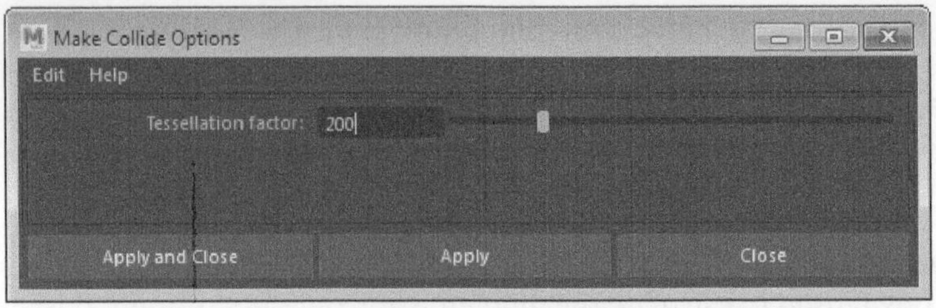

***Figure 14-10** The **Make Collide Options** dialog box*

***Figure 14-11** Fluid simulation before colliding with a geometry*

***Figure 14-12** Fluid simulation after colliding with a geometry*

Painting the Fluid Effects into Containers

In Maya, you can also paint the fluid effect into a container. To do so, first create a 3D fluid container in the viewport. Next, choose **Fluids > Create > Add/Edit Contents > Paints Fluid Tool > Option Box** from the menubar; the **Tool Settings (Paint Fluids Tool)** window will be displayed, as shown in Figure 14-13. The attributes of the **Tool Settings (Paint Fluids Tool)** window are similar to those of the **Tool Settings (Sculpt Geometry Tool)** window. You can adjust the diameter of the paint brush by setting values in the **Radius(U)** and **Radius(L)** edit boxes. To set the radius of the paint fluids tool brush, press and hold the B key along with the middle mouse button, and then drag it in the viewport; the radius of the brush will change accordingly.

FLUID COMPONENTS

The Maya fluid components are used to simulate and render realistic fluid effects. In Maya, there are some pre-defined fluid components, which are discussed next.

Ocean

In Maya, the ocean effect is in-built. However, you can also create an ocean on your own. To create an ocean, choose **Fluids > Create > Ocean > Option Box** from the menubar; the **Create Ocean** dialog box will be displayed, as shown in Figure 14-14. Set a value for the ocean plane size in the **Preview plane size** attribute and then choose the **Create Ocean** button in the dialog box; an ocean will be created in the viewport. You can also add wakes to an ocean. Wakes are fluid containers having a spring mesh solver that adds additional turbulence to the ocean by generating waves and ripples.

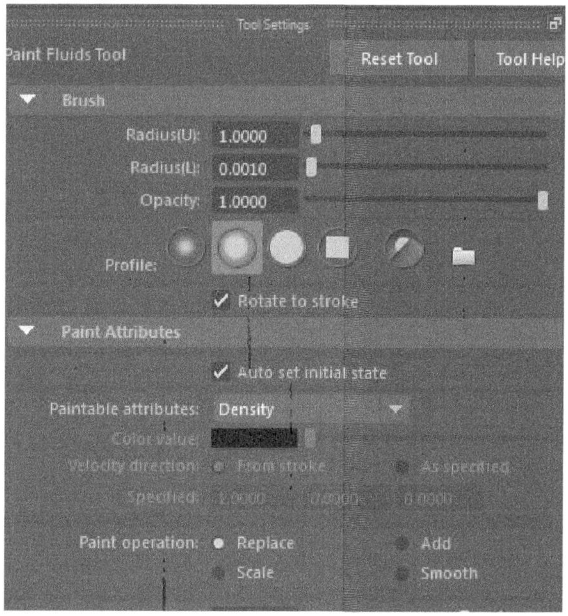

Figure 14-13 Partial view of the ***Tool Settings (Paint Fluids Tool)*** *window*

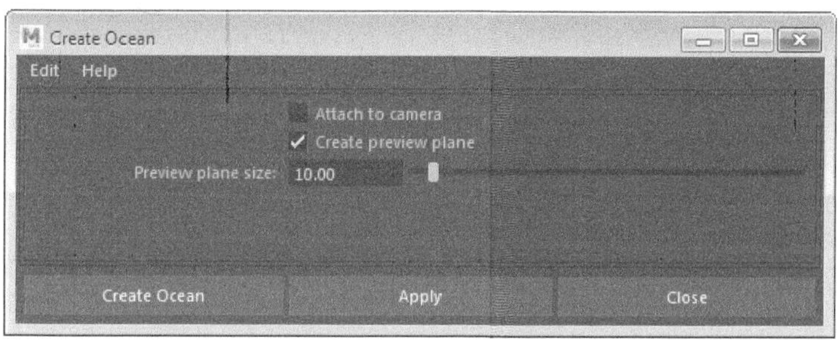

Figure 14-14 The ***Create Ocean*** *dialog box*

To add wakes to an ocean, choose **Fluids > Ocean/Pond > Create Wake > Option Box** from the menubar; the **Create Wake** dialog box will be displayed, as shown in Figure 14-15.

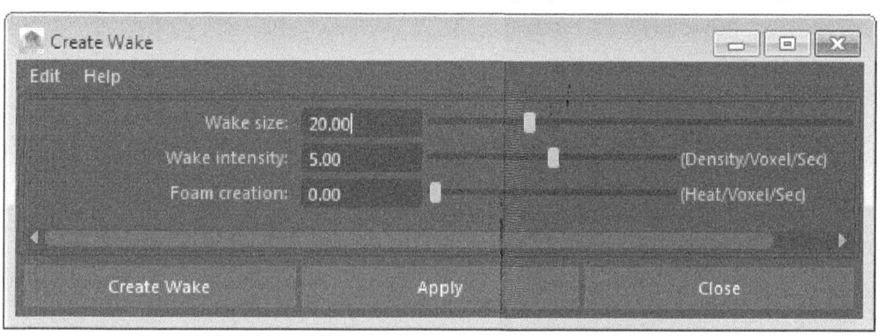

Figure 14-15 The ***Create Wake*** *dialog box*

Choose the **Apply** button from this dialog box; wakes will be created in the ocean, as shown in Figure 14-16.

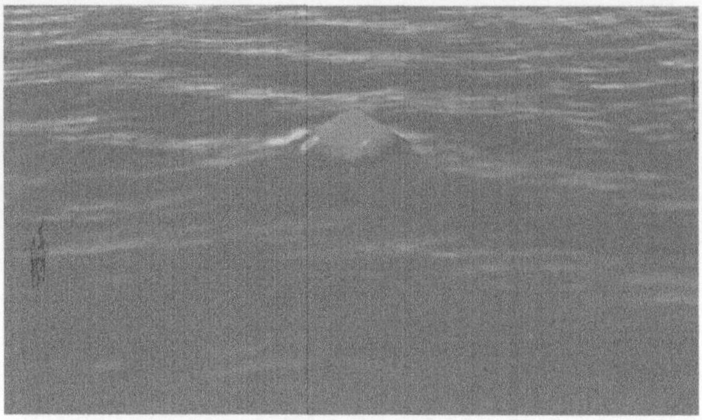

Figure 14-16 *Wakes added to an ocean*

You can also adjust the color, wavelength, foam creation, and other attributes of the ocean in the **Attribute Editor**. To do so, select the ocean plane in the viewport and open the **Attribute Editor**. In the **Attribute Editor**, choose the **oceanShader1** tab; all attributes related to ocean will be displayed. Change the attributes as required.

You can also make the objects float on the surface of an ocean. On doing so, the objects appear to be floating on the surface of the ocean with the waves and ripples. To float the object, select the still object on the ocean. Next, choose **Fluids > Ocean/Pond > Create Boat** from the menubar; a cascading menu will be displayed. The options in this cascading menu allow the selected object to float, refer to Figure 14-17.

Figure 14-17 *An object floating on the surface of the ocean*

Pond

The pond effect is used to create surfaces using a height field and a spring mesh solver so that the resulting surface looks like a pond. The pond fluid effect is also in-built in Maya. To create a pond, choose **Fluids > Create > Pond > Option Box** from the menubar; the **Create Pond** dialog box will be displayed, as shown in Figure 14-18.

Set the attributes of the pond as done in case of the ocean. Also, you can create wakes in the pond, as discussed earlier, refer to Figure 14-19.

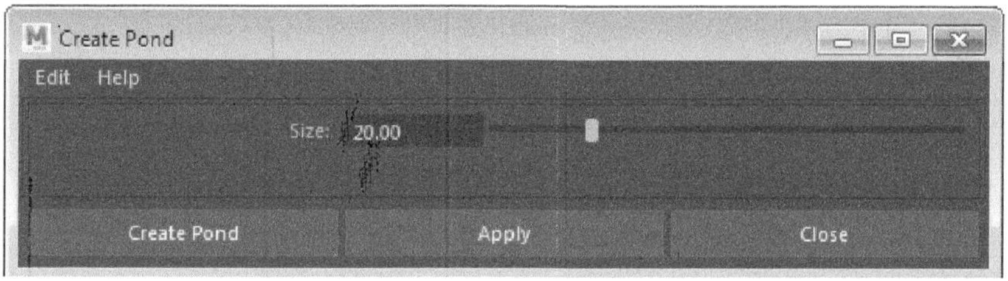

Figure 14-18 *The* ***Create Pond*** *dialog box*

Figure 14-19 *The wakes in the pond*

FLUID EFFECTS

In Maya, there are some in-built fluid effects that are stored in the library. You can select any effect from the library whenever required. To apply an effect, choose **Windows > Editors > General Editors > Content Browser** from the menubar; the **Content Browser** window will be displayed. In this window, choose **Examples > FX > Fluids > Ocean Examples** from the left pane; the fluids nodes are displayed in the right pane of the window, as shown in Figure 14-20.

Next, select the required fluid type from the right pane of the **Content Browser** window; the fluid examples will be displayed in the right pane of the **Content Browser** window. Press and hold the middle mouse button over the required fluid example and drag it in the viewport; the fluid example will be created in the viewport. Render the scene to see the final output. Some of the rendered fluid effects are shown through Figures 14-21 to 14-26.

Figure 14-20 *The* ***Content Browser*** *window*

Figure 14-21 *The cigarette smoke effect*

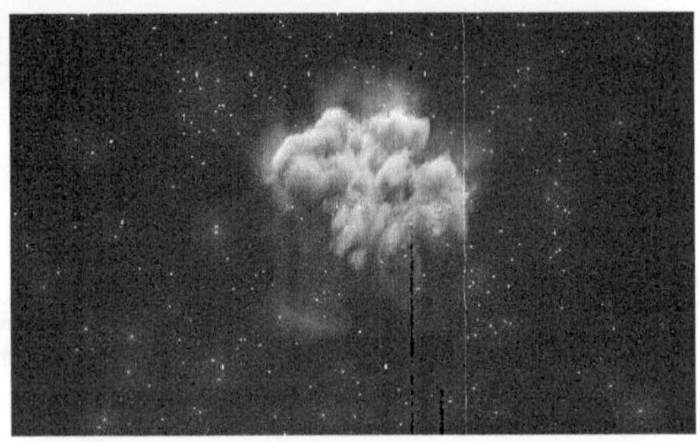

Figure 14-22 *The eagle nebula effect*

Figure 14-23 *The clouds sun effect*

Figure 14-24 *The terrain effect*

Figure 14-25 The underwater caustics effect

Figure 14-26 The giantstorm scene effect

TUTORIALS

Tutorial 1

In this tutorial, you will create the puffy fire explosion effect in a scene, as shown in Figure 14-27, using the 3D fluid container in Maya. **(Expected time: 30 min)**

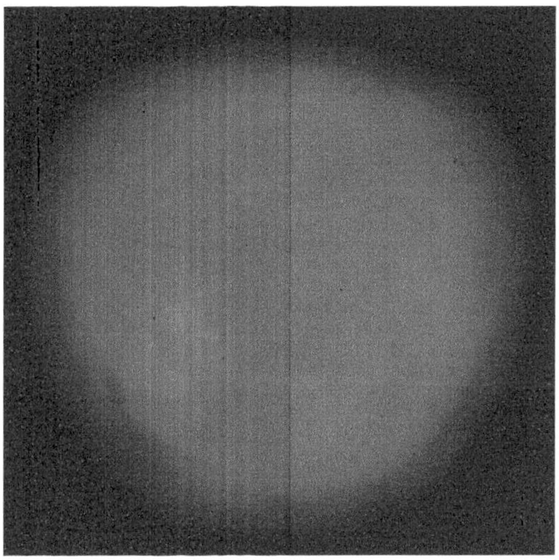

Figure 14-27 The puffy fire explosion

The following steps are required to complete this tutorial:

a. Create a project folder.
b. Create a 3D fluid container.
c. Set the attributes of the 3D fluid container.
d. Set the scene for animation.
e. Save and render the scene.

Creating a Project Folder

Create a new project folder with the name *c14_tut1* at *\Documents\maya2017* and then save the file with the name *c14tut1*, as discussed in Tutorial 1 of Chapter 2.

Creating the 3D Fluid Container

In this section, you will create a 3D fluid container.

1. Select the **FX** menuset from the **Menuset** drop-down list in the Status Line.

2. Choose **Fluids > Create > 3D Container** from the menubar; a 3D fluid container is created in the viewport, as shown in Figure 14-28.

3. Choose **Move Tool** from the Tool Box and align the fluid container to the center of the viewport.

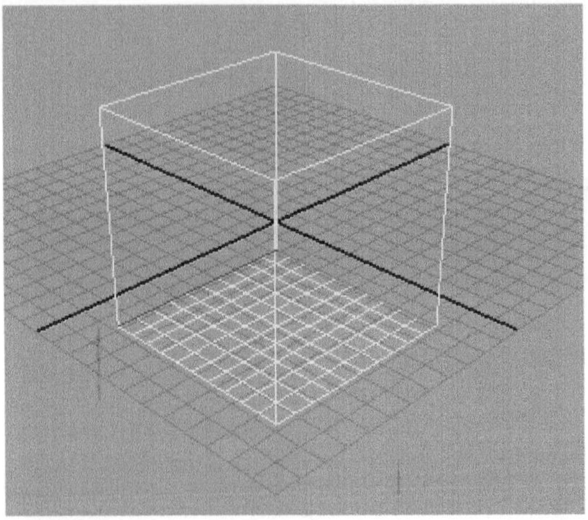

Figure 14-28 The 3D fluid container

Setting the Attributes of the 3D Fluid Container

In this section, you will set the attributes of the container to get the explosion effect.

1. Make sure the 3D fluid container is selected in the viewport and the **fluidShape1** tab is chosen in the **Attribute Editor**.

2. In this tab, expand the **Shading** area. Now, in the **Color** area, set the **Selected Color** to dark gray color (H: **0**, S: **0**, V: **0.231**), refer to Figure 14-29.

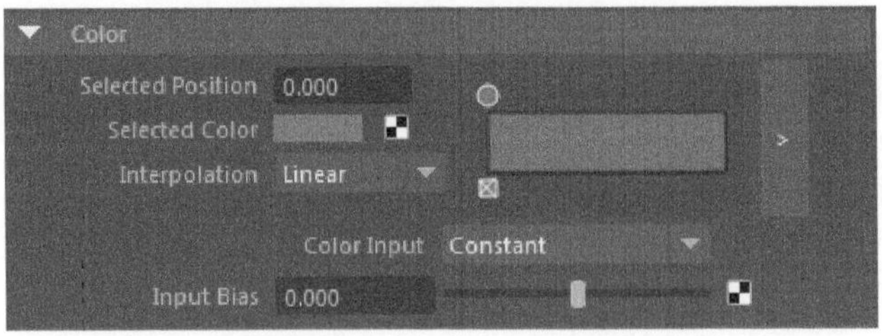

*Figure 14-29 The **Color** area*

3. In the **Opacity** area, set the opacity ramp of fluid, as shown in Figure 14-30. Next, select the **Center Gradient** option from the **Opacity Input** drop-down list and set the **Input Bias** attribute value to **-0.3**.

4. Press 6 in the viewport to view the fluid in the textured mode, refer to Figure 14-31.

5. In the **Incandescence** area, select **Center Gradient** from the **Incandescence Input** drop-down list, refer to Figure 14-32.

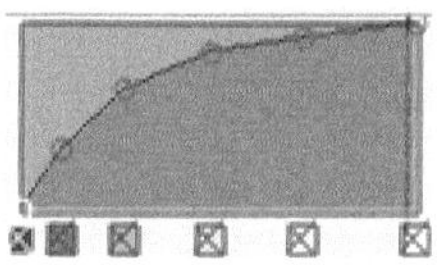

Figure 14-30 *The opacity value graph*

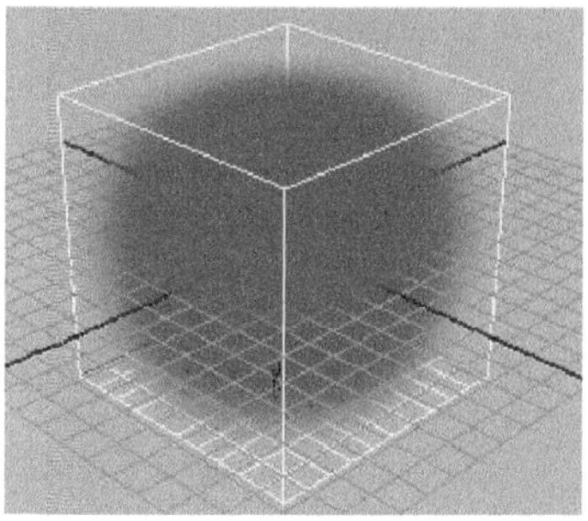

Figure 14-31 *The explosion displayed in the viewport*

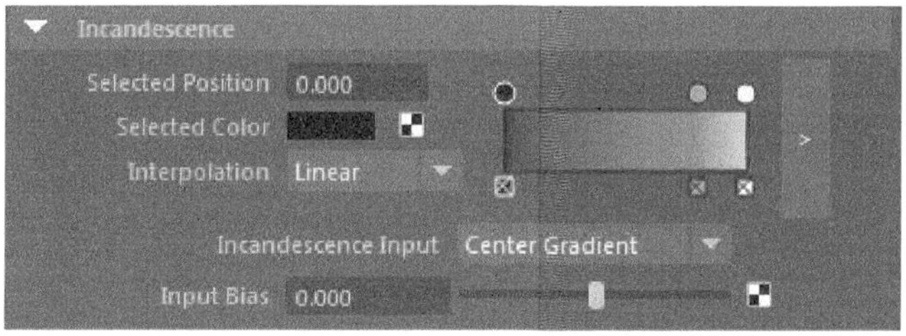

Figure 14-32 *The **Incandescence** area*

6. Expand the **Textures** area and then select the **Texture Color**, **Texture Incandescence**, and **Texture Opacity** check boxes. Next, set the values of the attributes as follows:

   Color Tex Gain: **0.6** Incand Tex Gain: **0.8**
   Depth Max: **4** Frequency: **1.5**
   Implode: **4**

   After setting the attributes in the **Textures** area, the fluid container appears, as shown in Figure 14-33.

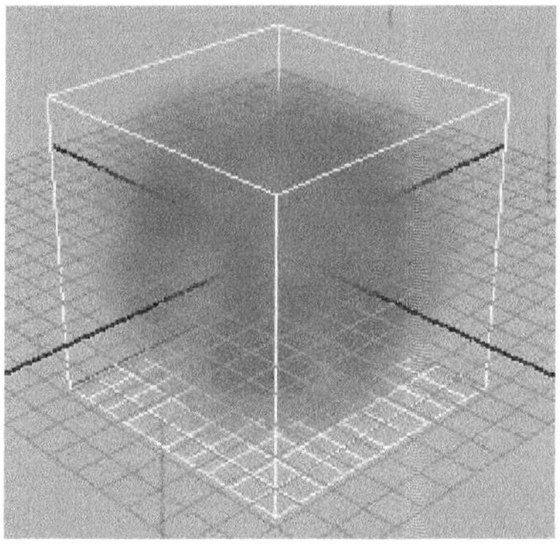

Figure 14-33 *The 3D container after setting the attributes in the **Textures** area*

7. Expand the **Shading Quality** area and then set the values of the attributes as follows:

   Quality: **3** Contrast Tolerance: **0.10**

8. Choose the **Render the current frame** button from the Status Line; the scene is rendered in the **Render View** window. The rendered output of explosion is shown in Figure 14-34.

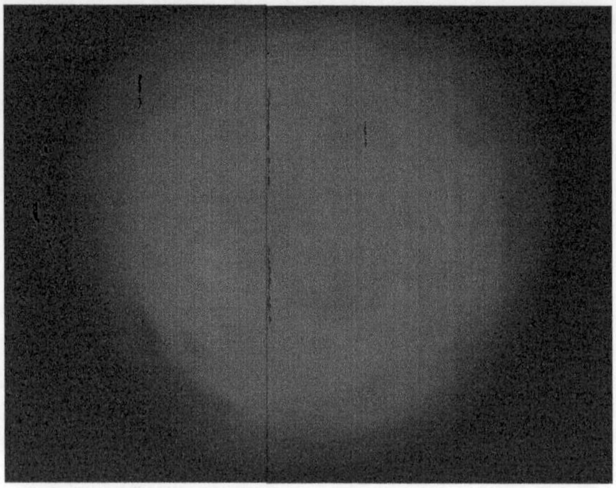

Figure 14-34 *The rendered output of explosion*

Setting the Scene for Animation

In this section, you will animate the explosion effect.

1. Choose **Windows > Editors > Settings/Preferences > Preferences** from the menubar; the **Preferences** dialog box is displayed. Now, select the **Time Slider** category from the **Categories** list; the **Time Slider: Animation Time Slider and Playback Preferences** area is displayed in the right of the dialog box.

2. In this area, set the value in the **Playback start/end** edit boxes to **1** and **200** respectively; the values in the **Animation start/end** edit boxes is updated automatically. Next, choose the **Save** button; the active time segment is set from frame **1** to **200**.

3. Move the Time Slider to frame 1. In the **Incandescence** area of the **fluidShape1** tab and then set the **Input Bias** to **-0.2**. Right-click on the **Input Bias** attribute; a shortcut menu is displayed. Choose the **Set Key** option from the shortcut menu, as shown in Figure 14-35; the key is set at frame 1.

Figure 14-35 *Choosing **Set Key** from the shortcut menu*

4. Move the Time Slider to frame **200** and set the **Input Bias** attribute to **0.5** in the **Incandescence** area. Again, right-click on the **Input Bias** attribute; a shortcut menu is displayed. Choose the **Set Key** option from the shortcut menu to set the key at frame 200.

5. Move the Time Slider to frame 1 and expand the **Opacity** area. In this area, set the **Input Bias** attribute to **-0.676**. Right-click on the **Input Bias** attribute; a shortcut menu is displayed. Now, choose the **Set Key** option from this shortcut menu to set the key at frame 1.

6. Move the slider to frame 72, set the **Input Bias** attribute to **-0.26** in the **Opacity** area. Right-click in the **Input Bias** attribute; a shortcut menu is displayed. Choose the **Set Key** option from the shortcut menu to set the key at frame 72. Similarly, set the **Input Bias** attribute to **0.081** at frame 200 and then add a frame using the **Set Key** option, as done earlier.

Saving and Rendering the Scene

In this section, you will save the scene that you have created and then render it. You can view the final rendered image sequence of the scene by downloading the *c14_maya_2017_rndr.zip* file from *www.cadcim.com*. The path of the file is as follows: *Textbooks > Animation and Visual Effects > Maya > Autodesk Maya 2017: A Comprehensive Guide.*

1. Choose **File > Save Scene** from the menubar to save the scene.

2. For rendering the scene, refer to Tutorial 1 of Chapter 8.

Tutorial 2

In this tutorial, you will create the melting text effect, as shown in Figure 14-36, using the fluid containers. **(Expected time: 30 min)**

The following steps are required to complete this tutorial:

a. Create a project folder.
b. Download the texture file.
c. Create a 2D fluid container.
d. Set attributes and import the image into the container.
e. Set the scene for animation.
f. Save and render the scene.

Figure 14-36 *The melting text effect*

Creating a Project Folder

Create a new project folder with the name *c14_tut2* at *\Documents\maya2017* and then save the file with the name *c14tut2*, as discussed in Tutorial 1 of Chapter 2.

Downloading the Texture File

In this section, you will download the texture file.

1. Download the *c14_maya_2017_tut.zip* file from *www.cadcim.com*. The path of the file is as follows: *Textbooks > Animation and Visual Effects > Maya > Autodesk Maya 2017: A Comprehensive Guide*.

2. Extract the contents of the zip file to the *Documents* folder. Next, copy the *text.png* and *texture.jpg* images to the *sourceimages* folder at the location *\Documents\maya2017\c14_tut2*.

Creating a 2D Fluid Container

In this section, you will create a 2D fluid container.

1. Select the **FX** menuset from the **Menuset** drop-down list in the Status Line.

2. Choose **Fluids > Create > 2D Container** from the menubar; a 2D container is created in the viewport. Invoke **Scale Tool** and scale the fluid container in the front viewport to get the shape, as shown in Figure 14-37.

Figure 14-37 *The scaled 2D fluid container*

3. Choose **Move Tool** from the Tool Box and align the fluid container to the center of the viewport. Now, select the 2D container and open the **Attribute Editor**.

4. Make sure the **fluidShape1** tab is chosen in the **Attribute Editor**. In the **Container Properties** area of this tab, clear the **Keep Voxels Square** check box and enter **400** in the edit boxes corresponding to the **Resolution** attribute.

   Next, select the **None** option from the **Boundary X** and **Boundary Y** drop-down lists; the boundaries of the fluid container are set to **None**.

Setting the Attributes and Importing the Image into the Container

In this section, you will set the attributes of the fluid container and apply the image to the container.

1. Make sure the fluid container is selected in the viewport and choose **Fluids > Create > Add/Edit Contents > Paint Fluids Tool > Option Box** from the menubar; the **Tool Settings (Paint Fluids Tool)** window is displayed.

2. In the **Tool Settings (Paint Fluids Tool)** window, expand the **Import** area in the **Attribute Maps** area of the **Tool Settings (Paint Fluids Tool)** window and then choose the **Import** button from it; the **Import** dialog box is displayed.

3. Select **text.png** from the **Import** dialog box and then choose the **Open** button.

4. Choose **Select Tool** from the Tool Box and press 6 to display the text in the viewport in the shaded mode, if not already displayed, refer to Figure 14-38.

Figure 14-38 *The text visible in the fluid container*

5. Play the animation; the text in the fluid container goes straight in upward direction in the fluid container.

6. Make sure that the fluid container is selected in the viewport. In the **fluidShape1** tab of the **Attribute Editor**, expand the **Dynamic Simulation** area and enter **-10.00** in the **Gravity** edit box and press the ENTER key. Play the simulation; the text moves in the downward direction, as shown in Figure 14-39.

Figure 14-39 *Downward movement of the fluid as the **Gravity** attribute is set to **-10***

7. Make sure the fluid container is selected in the viewport. Next, choose **Fluids > Create > Add/Edit Contents > Paint Fluids Tool > Option Box** from the menubar; the **Tool Settings (Paint Fluids Tool)** window is displayed.

8. In the **Paint Attributes** area of the **Tool Settings (Paint Fluids Tool)** window, select the **Color** option from the **Paintable attributes** drop-down list; the **Cannot paint 'color' on fluidShape1** message box is displayed, as shown in Figure 14-40. Choose the **Set to Dynamic** button; the paint brush is activated in the viewport. Now, you can paint the text in the fluid container.

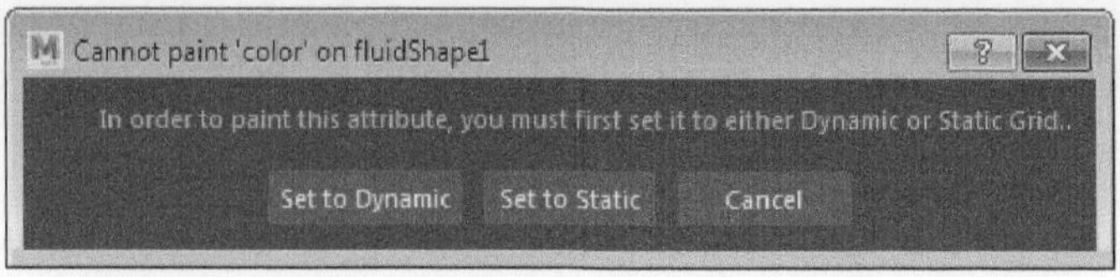

Figure 14-40 The ***Cannot paint 'color' on fluidShape1*** *message box*

9. In the **Attribute Maps** area of the **Tool Settings (Paint Fluids Tool)** window, expand the **Import** area. In the **Import** area, choose the **Import** button; the **Import** dialog box is displayed. Choose **texture.jpg** from the **Import** dialog box and then choose the **Open** button; a color is added to the text in the fluid container, as shown in Figure 14-41. Next, choose **Select Tool** from the Tool Box.

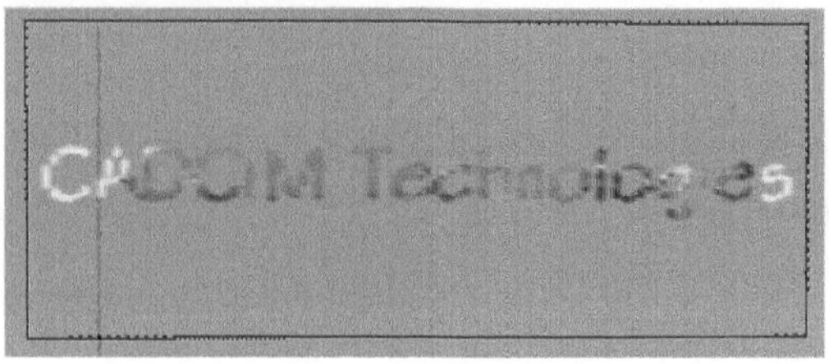

Figure 14-41 *The colored text in the fluid container*

10. Play the animation; the colored text appears to be melting.

Setting the Scene for Animation

In this section, you will set the scene for animation.

1. Choose **Windows > Settings/Preferences > Preferences** from the menubar; the **Preferences** dialog box is displayed. Choose the **Time Slider** category in the **Categories** area of the dialog box; the **Time Slider: Animation Time Slider and Playback Preferences** area is displayed in the right of the **Preferences** dialog box.

2. In this dialog box, set the value in the **Playback start/end** edit boxes to **1** and **100** respectively; the values in the **Animation start/end** edit boxes is updated automatically. Next, choose the **Save** button; the active time segment is set from frame **1** to **100**. Next, preview the animation.

Saving and Rendering the Scene

In this section, you will save the scene that you have created and then render it. You can view the final rendered image sequence of the scene by downloading the *c14_maya_2017_rndr.zip* file from *www.cadcim.com*. The path of the file is as follows: *Textbooks > Animation and Visual Effects > Maya > Autodesk Maya 2017: A Comprehensive Guide*

1. Choose **File > Save Scene** from the menubar to save the scene.

2. For rendering the scene, refer to Tutorial 1 of Chapter 8.

Tutorial 3

In this tutorial, you will create time-lapse effect on clouds in a scene, in a scene, refer to Figure 14-42. **(Expected time: 40 min)**

Figure 14-42 *The time lapse effect on frame 74*

The following steps are required to complete this tutorial:

a. Create a project folder.
b. Create a 3D fluid container.
c. Set the scene for animation.
d. Save and render the scene.

Creating a Project Folder

Create a new project folder with the name *c14_tut3* at *\Documents\maya2017* and then save the file with the name *c14tut3*, as discussed in Tutorial 1 of Chapter 2.

Creating a 3D Fluid Container

In this section, you will create a 3D fluid container in the viewport.

1. Select the **FX** menuset from the **Menuset** drop-down list in the Status Line.

2. Choose **Fluids > Create > 3D Container** from the menubar; a 3D container is created in the viewport. Invoke **Move Tool** from the Tool Box and align the fluid container to the center of the viewport.

3. In the **Attribute Editor**, make sure the **fluidShape1** tab is chosen. In the **Container Properties** area, set the resolution attributes, as shown in Figure 14-43.

4. Expand the **Shading** area in the **fluidShape1** tab. In the **Opacity** area, set the opacity ramp, as shown in Figure 14-44. Select the **Y Gradient** option from the **Opacity Input** drop-down

list. Now, in the **Color** area of the **Shading** area, set the gradient of the **Selected Color** swatch as shown in Figure 14-45. Select the **Y Gradient** option from the **Color Input** drop-down list.

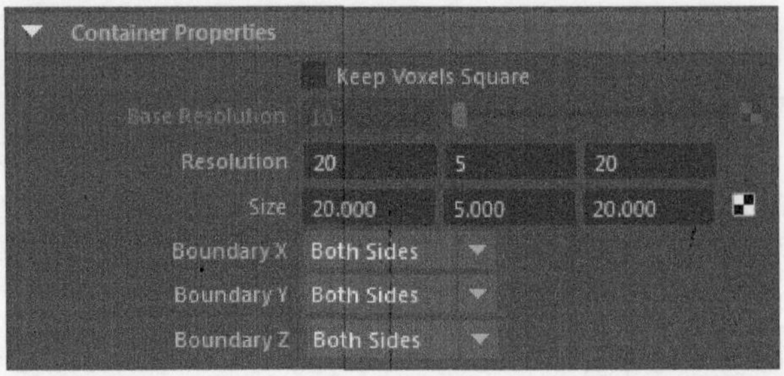

***Figure 14-43** Setting the attributes for the resolution of the container*

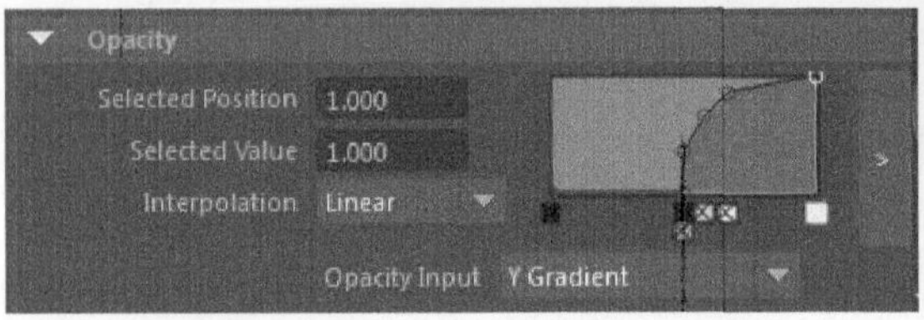

***Figure 14-44** Setting the shading ramp*

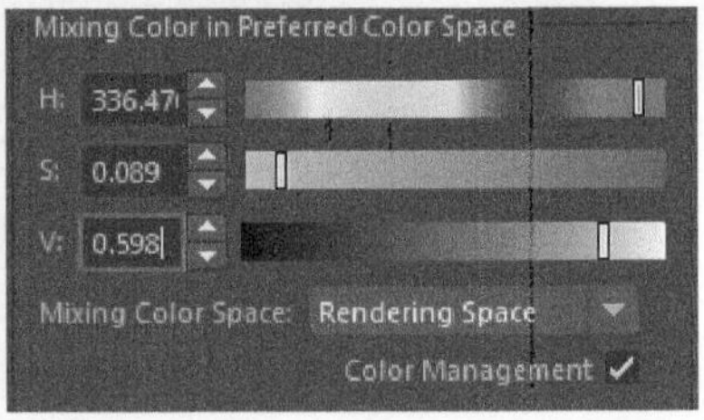

***Figure 14-45** The gradient of the **Selected Color** swatch*

5. In the **Incandescence** area, set the gradient of the **Selected Color** swatch, refer to Figure 14-46. Use the following HSV color values for the Incandescence nodes:

   Node 1: **210.078, 0.529, 0.292** Node 2: **217.09, 0.804, 0.384**
   Node 3: **217.358, 0.765, 0.484**

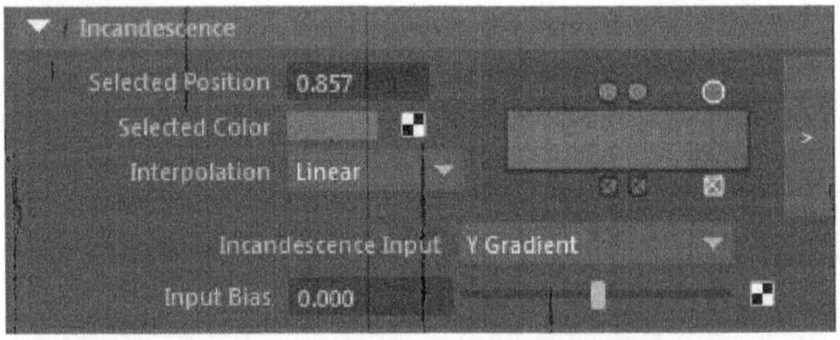

***Figure 14-46** The gradient of the **Selected Color** swatch in the **Incandescence** area*

6. Click in the viewport and press 6; the fluid shape appears in the shaded mode in the viewport.

7. In the **Textures** area, select the **Texture Opacity** check box. Also, select the **Inflection** check box. Next, set the values of the parameters as follows:

   Texture Type: **Perlin Noise** Amplitude: **0.942** Ratio: **0.602**
   Frequency Ratio: **3.752** Depth Max: **4** Frequency: **1**

8. Choose the **Render the current frame** button from the Status Line; the rendered view of the clouds is displayed. You need to zoom in the viewport so that only the clouds are visible not the object.

9. In the **Shading Quality** area, set **Quality** to **3** and then select **smooth** in the **Render Interpolator** drop-down list.

   Now, you will create an expression to create a time lapse effect.

10. In the **Textures** area, right-click in the **Texture Time** attribute; a shortcut menu is displayed. Choose the **Create New Expression** option from the shortcut menu; the **Expression Editor** dialog box is displayed, as shown in Figure 14-47. Next, write the expression **fluidShape1.textureTime=time*0.5** in the **Expression** edit box and choose the **Create** button to create an expression.

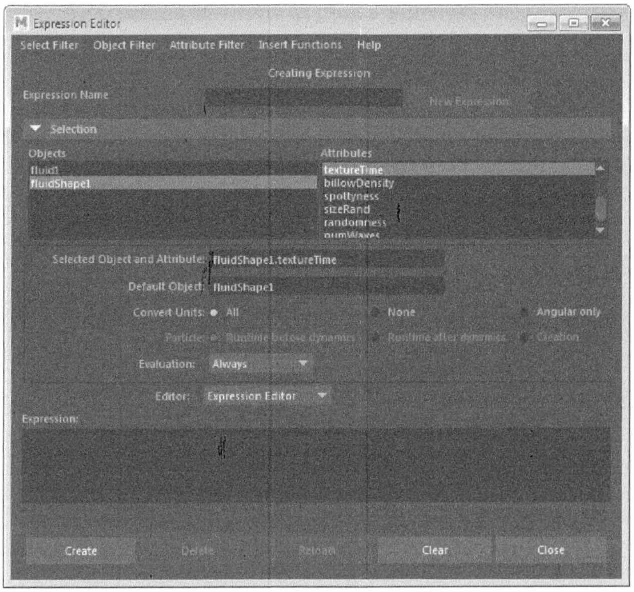

*Figure 14-47 The **Expression Editor** dialog box*

11. Choose the **Close** button from the **Expression Editor** dialog box; the expression is created.

12. Play the animation to view the time-lapse effect.

Setting the Scene for Animation

In this section, you will set the scene for animation.

1. Choose **Windows > Editors > Setting/Preferences > Preferences** from the menubar; the **Preferences** dialog box is displayed. Choose the **Time Slider** category in the **Categories** area of the dialog box; the **Time Slider: Animation Time Slider and Playback Preferences** area is displayed on the right in the **Preferences** dialog box.

2. In this area, set the value in the **Playback start/end** edit boxes to **1** and **200** respectively; the values in the **Animation start/end** edit boxes are updated automatically. Next, choose the **Save** button; the active time segment is set to frame range 1 to 200. Preview the animation.

Saving and Rendering the Scene

In this section, you will save the scene that you have created and then render it. You can view the final rendered image sequence of the scene by downloading the *c14_maya_2017_rndr.zip* file from *www.cadcim.com*. The path of the file is as follows: *Textbooks > Animation and Visual Effects > Maya > Autodesk Maya 2017: A Comprehensive Guide.*

1. Choose **File > Save Scene** from the menubar to save the scene.

2. For rendering the scene, refer to Tutorial 1 of Chapter 8.

Tutorial 4

In this tutorial, you will create an effect using the **Radial** field, as shown in Figure 14-48.

(Expected time: 30 min)

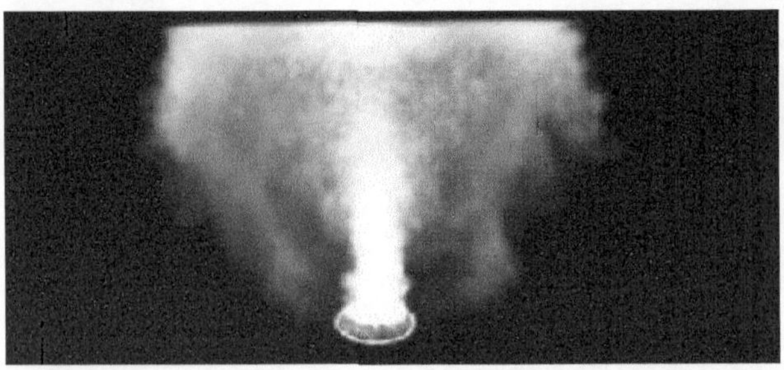

Figure 14-48 The effect created using the ***Radial*** *field*

The following steps are required to complete this tutorial:

a. Create a project folder.
b. Create a 3D fluid container.
c. Set the scene for animation.
d. Save and render the scene.

Creating a Project Folder

Create a new project folder with the name *c14_tut4* at *\Documents\maya2017* and then save the file with the name *c14tut4*, as discussed in Tutorial 1 of Chapter 2.

Creating a 3D Fluid Container

In this section, you will create a 3D fluid container in the viewport.

1. Select the **FX** menuset from the **Menuset** drop-down list in the Status Line.

2. Choose **Fluids > Create > 3D Container** from the menubar; a 3D container is created in the viewport.

3. Choose **Fluids > Edit > Extend Fluid > Option Box** from the menubar; the **Extend Fluid Options** dialog box is displayed. Set the values of the **Extend X by** and **Extend Y by** edit boxes to **10**. Next, choose the **Apply and Close** button; the dialog box is closed.

4. Make sure the **fluidShape1** tab is chosen in the **Attribute Editor**. Next, in the **Container Properties** area, set the values of the parameters, as shown in Figure 14-49.

5. Choose **Create > Objects > Polygon Primitives > Torus** from the menubar. Next, click in the viewport; a torus is created in the viewport. Now, scale it and place it inside the container, as shown in Figure 14-50.

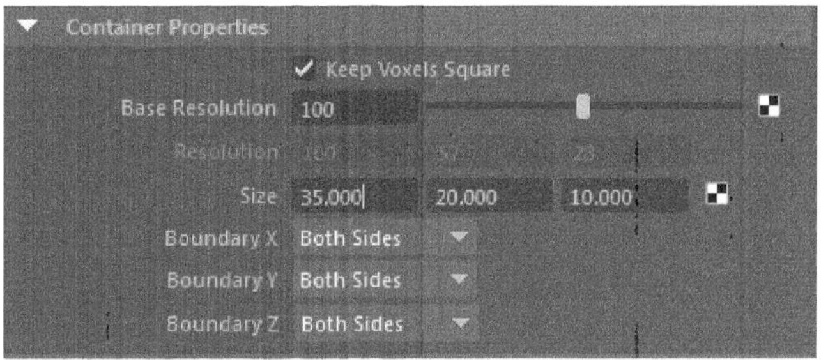

***Figure 14-49** The **Container Properties** area*

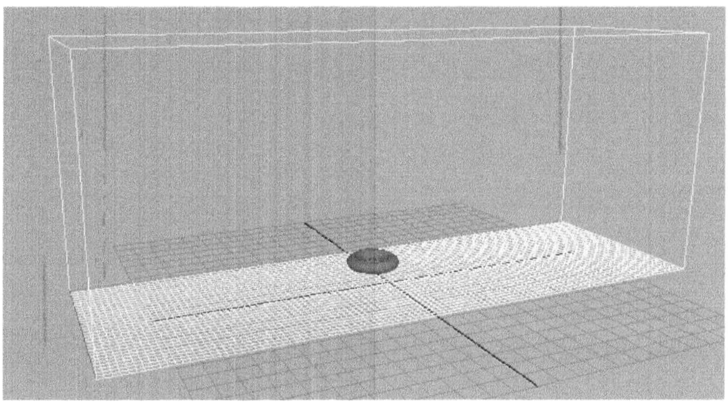

***Figure 14-50** The torus placed inside the container*

6. Select the fluid container in the viewport. Next, press and hold SHIFT and then select the torus in the viewport. Choose **Fluids > Create > Add/Edit Contents > Emit From Object > Option Box** from the menubar; the **Emit from Object Options** dialog box is displayed. Set the following values in the **Emit from Object Options** dialog box:

Density rate: **5** (voxel/sec)	Heat rate: **0** (voxel/sec)	Fuel Rate: **0** (voxel/sec)

Now, choose the **Apply and Close** button.

7. Select the fluid container in the viewport. In the **fluidShape1** tab of the **Attribute Editor**, expand the **Content Details** area. Next, expand the **Density** area and set the following values in it:

Density Scale: **1.2** Buoyancy: **10** Dissipation: **0.01**

8. Expand the **Velocity** area in the **Content Details** area and set the value of **Swirl** to **10**.

9. Make sure the fluid container is selected in the viewport and then choose **Fields/Solvers > Create > Radial** from the menubar. By selecting the fluid container before creating a field, the field and fluid are automatically connected. In the **radialField1** tab of the **Attribute Editor**, expand the **Volume Control Attributes** area. Next, in this area, select **Sphere** from the **Volume Shape** drop-down list.

10. Scale the field icon in the viewport and place it at the center of the container, as shown in Figure 14-51.

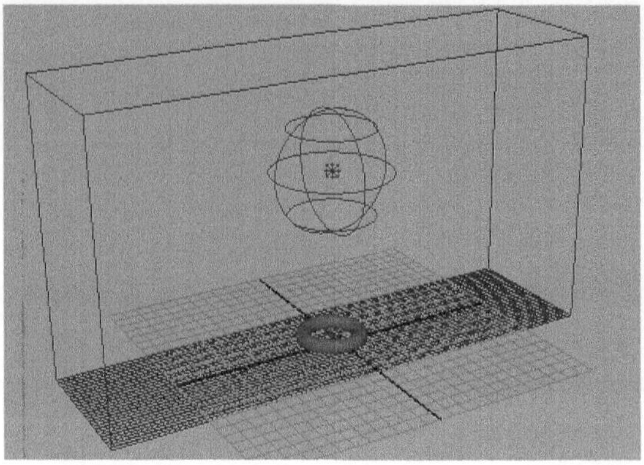

Figure 14-51 *The scaled radial field in the viewport*

11. In the **Radial Field Attributes** area, set the values of the attributes as follows:

Magnitude: **100** Attenuation: **0**

12. Play the simulation.

Setting the Scene for Animation

In this section, you need to set the scene for animation.

1. Choose **Windows > Editors > Settings/Preferences > Preferences** from the menubar; the **Preferences** dialog box is displayed. Choose the **Time Slider** category in the **Categories** area of the dialog box; the **Time Slider: Animation Time Slider and Playback Preferences** area is displayed on the right in the **Preferences** dialog box.

2. In this area, set the value in the **Playback start/end** edit boxes to **1** and **200** respectively; the values in the **Animation start/end** edit boxes are updated automatically. Next, choose the **Save** button; the active time segment is set to frame range 1 to 200. Preview the animation.

Saving and Rendering the Scene

In this section, you will save the scene that you have created and then render it. You can view the final rendered image sequence of the scene by downloading the *c14_maya_2017_rndr.zip* file from *www.cadcim.com*. The path of the file is as follows: *Textbooks > Animation and Visual Effects > Maya > Autodesk Maya 2017: A Comprehensive Guide.*

1. Choose **File > Save Scene** from the menubar to save the scene.

2. For rendering the scene, refer to Tutorial 1 of Chapter 8.

Self-Evaluation Test

Answer the following questions and then compare them to those given at the end of this chapter:

1. Which of the following mathematical equations is used to simulate the fluid effects in Maya?

   (a) Differential equation (b) Algebraic equation
   (c) Functional equation (d) Navier-Stokes equation

2. How many types of fluid effects are available in Maya?

   (a) Two (b) Three
   (c) Four (d) Five

3. The __________ fluid effect does not behave according to the natural law of fluid dynamics.

4. A fluid container is divided into three-dimensional grids, and each unit of a grid is known as __________.

5. The __________ option is used to calculate the fluid emission on every substep.

6. The __________ effect is used to create a surface using a height field and a spring mesh solver.

7. The rendering of a scene with non-dynamic fluid effect is much faster than a scene with dynamic fluid effect. (T/F)

8. You can neither resize nor set the resolution of the fluid containers. (T/F)

9. There are four ways of defining fluid property in a fluid container. (T/F)

10. You cannot paint the fluid effect into a fluid container. (T/F)

Review Questions

Answer the following questions:

1. Which of the following effects is in-built in Maya?

   (a) Ponds (b) Ocean
   (c) Terrain (d) All the above

2. A __________ is a fluid container having a spring mesh solver, which adds additional turbulence to the ocean by generating bubbles and ripples.

3. You can use an emitter to create a fluid container that will simulate fluid in the container. (T/F)

4. You can add wakes only to oceans, not to ponds. (T/F)

5. Increasing the resolution of a fluid container increases the number of voxels in the fluid container, thus increasing the rendering time. (T/F)

6. The **Constant** density gradient method preset is used to maintain the fluid property as constant throughout the container. (T/F)

7. In Maya, you cannot make the objects float on the surface of fluids. (T/F)

EXERCISES

The rendered image sequence of the scene in the following exercises can be accessed by downloading the *c14_maya_2017_exr.zip* file from *www.cadcim.com*. The path of the file is as follows: *Textbooks > Animation and Visual Effects > Maya > Autodesk Maya 2017: A Comprehensive Guide.*

Exercise 1

Create an ocean scene, as shown in Figure 14-52, by using the default effects available in the **Visor** window in Maya. **(Expected time: 30 min)**

Figure 14-52 *The ocean scene*

Exercise 2

Create the 3D models of wood and stone, as shown in Figure 14-53. Next, apply texture to them and add a fluid container to the scene to create fire effect, as shown in Figure 14-54.

(Expected time: 30 min)

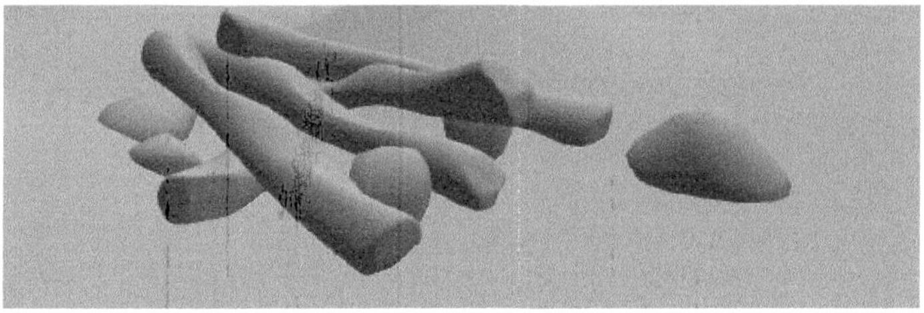

Figure 14-53 *The 3D models of wood and stone*

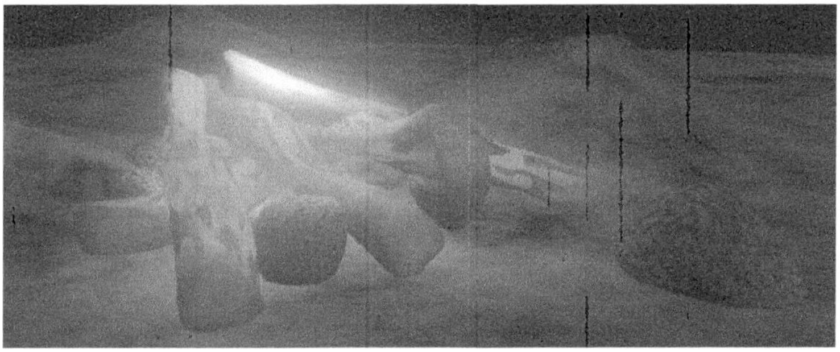

Figure 14-54 *The fire effect in the scene*

Answers to Self-Evaluation Test

1. d, **2.** b, **3.** non-dynamic, **4.** voxel, **5. Emit In Substeps**, **6.** pond, **7.** T, **8.** F, **9.** T, **10.** F

Chapter 15

nHair

Learning Objectives

After completing this chapter, you will be able to:

- *Apply nHair to objects*
- *Simulate nHair*
- *Paint textures on nHair*

INTRODUCTION

In Maya, you can create complex hairstyles such as ponytails, braids, and simulate the natural hair behavior using the nHair. For generating such simulations, you can use the Maya Nucleus technology. You can use nHair to create complex hair simulations such as movement of hair strands with wind, collisions between hair and clothes, hair when swimming underwater, and so on. In this chapter, you will learn to create nHair and simulate it.

nHair

In Maya, you can create nHair system in two ways: by using NURBS curves or Maya Paint Effects. To render the output of nHair Paint Effects, you need to set the renderer to **Maya Software** or convert the Paint Effects nHair to polygons and render them in any renderer. If you want to use any other renderer such as **mental ray**, you need to first convert Paint Effects to polygons.

Creating nHair

You can create nHair on a NURBS or polygon surface in Maya. Select the **FX** menuset from the **Menuset** drop-down list in the Status Line. Select a NURBS or a polygon object in the viewport and choose **nHair > Create > Create Hair** from the menubar; nHair will be created on the selected surface, as shown in Figure 15-1.

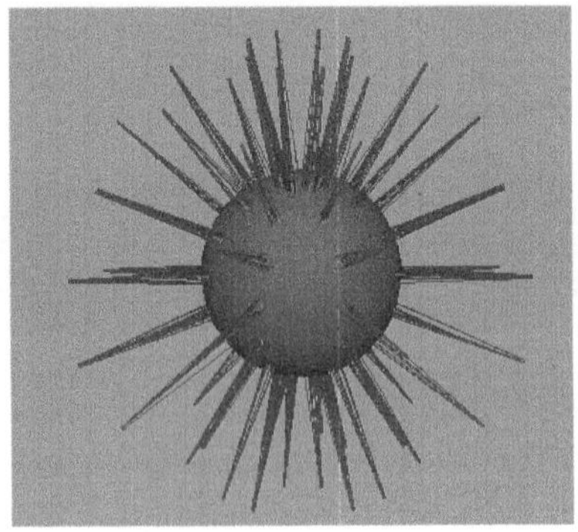

Figure 15-1 *The nHair created on a polygon sphere*

Creating **nHair** on a surface depends on the UV coordinates of the selected surface. Maya allows the user to specify the required number of hair strands that are required to be generated in the U and V directions.

You can define the hair attributes using the **Create Hair Options** dialog box. To do so, choose **nHair > Create > Create Hair > Option Box** from the menubar; the **Create Hair Options** dialog box will be displayed, as shown in Figure 15-2. The options in this dialog box are discussed next.

Output

The options in the **Output** drop-down list are used to define the output of the hair structure created in the viewport. By default, the **Paint Effects** option is selected in this drop-down list. The **Paint Effects** option is used to create nHair paint effects.

In this case, each follicle contains information about the color, shading, and position of the nHair. The **NURBS curves** option is used to create hair follicle in such a manner that each hair follicle contains one NURBS curve defining the position of hair in that follicle. The **Paint Effects and NURBS curve** option is used to display the combined effect of the **Paint Effects** and **NURBS curves** options together.

Create rest curves

The **Create rest curves** check box is used to create a set of rest curves that are straight and normal to the surface of an object.

Collide with mesh

On selecting the **Collide with mesh** check box, nHair collide with the surface of the object on which they are created. The **Grid** radio button located below this check box is used to create hair on the grid of the selected surface. The **At selected surface points/faces** radio button is used to create hair only on the selected vertices or faces.

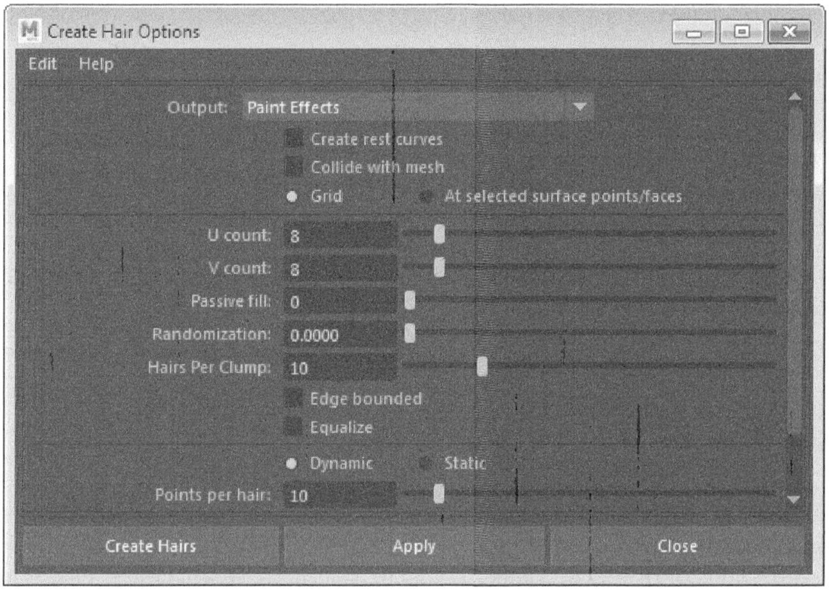

*Figure 15-2 The **Create Hair Options** dialog box*

U count

The **U count** attribute is used to specify the number of follicles to be created along the U direction. To specify the number of follicles, you can either enter a value in the edit box corresponding to this attribute or move the slider to the desired point. The default value for this attribute is 8.

V count

The **V count** attribute is used to specify the number of follicles to be created along the V direction. You can specify the value for this attribute either by entering a value in the edit box or by using the slider bar. The default value for this attribute is 8.

Passive fill

The **Passive fill** attribute is used to specify the number of passive hair curves to be changed into active hair curves. To do so, you can specify a value for this attribute by entering a value or by using the slider bar.

Randomization

The **Randomization** attribute is used to specify the degree of randomization for placing the hair in the U and V directions. The default value for this attribute is 0.

Hairs Per Clump

The **Hairs Per Clump** attribute is used to set the number of hair strands to be rendered for each hair follicle.

Edge bounded

The **Edge bounded** check box is used to create hair follicles along the edge of the U and V directions.

Equalize

The **Equalize** check box is used to equalize hair strands on an uneven surface. On selecting this check box, the uneven mapping between the UV space and the world space is adjusted.

Dynamic

The **Dynamic** radio button is used to create hair strands that respond to the dynamic forces. By default, this radio button is selected.

Static

The **Static** radio button is used to create stationary hair strands. On selecting this radio button, the hair strands do not respond to the dynamic forces.

Points per hair

The **Points per hair** attribute is used to specify the number of points/segments in a hair strand. Increasing the number of points in a hair strand makes the hair smoother. However, for small and stiff hair, less number of points per hair is required. The default value for this attribute is 10.

Length

The **Length** attribute is used to specify the length of hair strands in world space units. To specify the length of hair strands, specify a value for the **Length** attribute or move the slider to its right. The default value of this attribute is 5.

Place hairs into

The options in the **Place hairs into** drop-down list are used to place hair into a new or an existing hair system. By default, the hair is placed in the current **nHair** system.

SIMULATING nHAIR

Hair simulation is used to apply the effect of different external forces on the hair strands. To simulate hair, select a NURBS or a polygon object in the viewport and choose **nHair > Create > Create Hair** from the menubar; nHair will be created on the selected surface. Next, choose **Windows > Editors > Outliner** from the menubar; the **Outliner** window will be displayed. Select **pfxHair1** from the **Outliner** window. Now, choose **nHair > Edit > Display > Current Position** from the menubar; the simulation of hair curves to dynamics with the change in the timeline is updated. Next, select the object from the viewport on which the hair is created. Choose **Fields/Solvers > Solvers > Interactive Playback** from the menubar; the hair will simulate with the change in shape, size, or rotation of the selected object. To observe the change in the behavior of the hair strands in response to the default dynamic forces applied, move the surface and increase the number of frames in the timeline. You can change the behavior of nHair by using the options available in the **hairSystemShape1** and **nucleus1** tabs in the **Attribute Editor**. To do so, select the **pfxHair1** option in the **Outliner** window; the **Attribute Editor** will be displayed on the right of the viewport with the **hairSystemShape1** tab chosen, as shown in Figure 15-3. The attributes in the **hairSystemShape1** tab are discussed next.

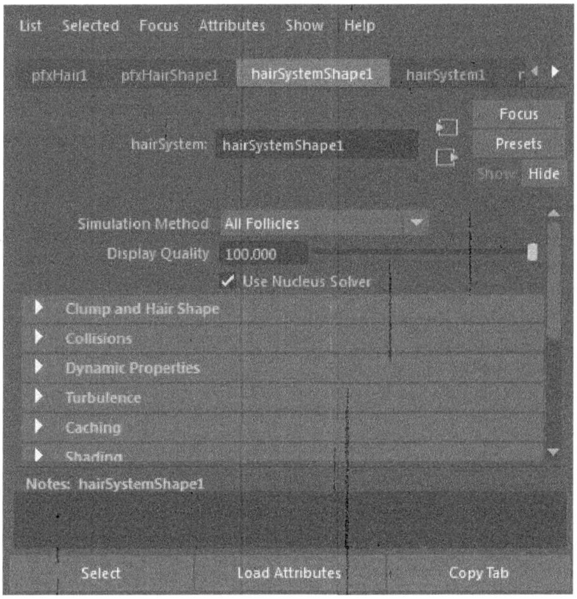

***Figure 15-3** The **Attribute Editor** displayed on choosing the **pfxHair1** node from the **Outliner** window*

hairSystemShape1 Tab

The attributes in this tab are used to specify the properties of the nHair system. The most commonly used attributes are discussed next.

Simulation Method

The options in the **Simulation Method** drop-down list are used to specify whether all the hair strands, dynamic or static, are simulated during the playback of animation. By default, the **All Follicles** option is selected in this drop-down list.

Display Quality

The **Display Quality** attribute is used to specify the percentage of hair to be displayed in clumps.

Use Nucleus Solver

The **Use Nucleus Solver** check box is used to specify whether the hair system will act as a Nucleus object or not. On selecting this check box, the hair system acts as a Nucleus object and is solved by the Nucleus solver. Also, it interacts with other Nucleus objects as well as self-collide. This check box is selected by default.

Clump and Hair Shape Area

The attributes in this area are used to manipulate the shape of the hair, refer to Figure 15-4. The attributes in this area are discussed next.

Hairs Per Clump

The **Hairs Per Clump** attribute is used to set the number of hair strands to be rendered for each follicle. The default value for this attribute is 10.

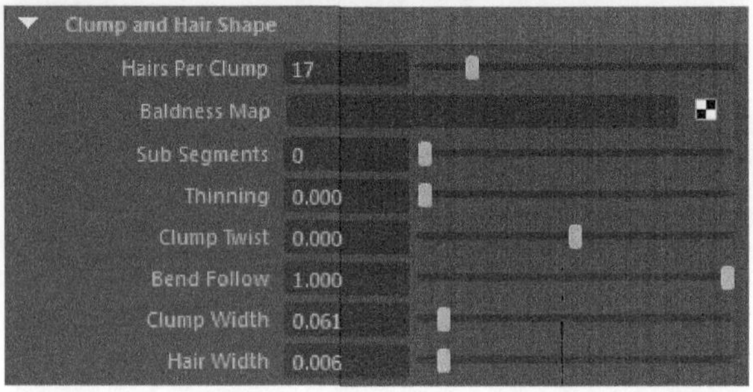

*Figure 15-4 The attributes in the **Clump and Hair Shape** area*

Baldness Map

The **Baldness Map** attribute is used to decrease the hair density by using a 2D texture. You can add a texture by using the checker button next to it.

Sub Segments

The **Sub Segments** attribute is used to smoothen each hair strand at the time of rendering. It provides a finer detail to the hair without affecting the dynamic simulation.

Thinning

The **Thinning** attribute is used to maintain the proportions of short hair by making the hair clumps thinner at the tips.

Clump Twist

The **Clump Twist** attribute is used to rotate the hair clumps about their primary axis.

Bend Follow

The **Bend Follow** attribute is used to specify the amount of the rotation of overall clump will follow the primary hair axis.

Clump Width

The **Clump Width** attribute is used to increase or decrease the width of dynamic hair groups.

Hair Width

The **Hair Width** attribute is used to specify the global width of hair strands.

Clump Width Scale Area

The options in the **Clump Width Scale** area are used to manually adjust the width of the hair clump from its root to tip using a ramp.

Hair Width Scale Area

The options in the **Hair Width Scale** area are used to adjust the width of the overall hair shape manually using a ramp.

Clump Curl Area

The options in the **Clump Curl** area are used to manually create varied curls for hair clumps using a ramp.

Clump Flatness Area

The options in the **Clump Flatness** area are used to manually adjust the varied flatness of the hair clump from root to tip using a ramp.

Clump Interpolation

The **Clump Interpolation** attribute is used to specify the amount of interpolation between the hair clumps. It spreads the tips of hair clumps, thus moving the tips of the hair strands toward the other hair clumps.

Interpolation Range

The **Interpolation Range** attribute is used to specify the maximum distance between the clumps where they still interpolate with each other. The default value for this attribute is 8.

Collisions Area

The attributes in the **Collisions** area are used to control self collisions of hair and collisions between nHair and other nucleus objects, refer to Figure 15-5. The different attributes in this area are discussed next.

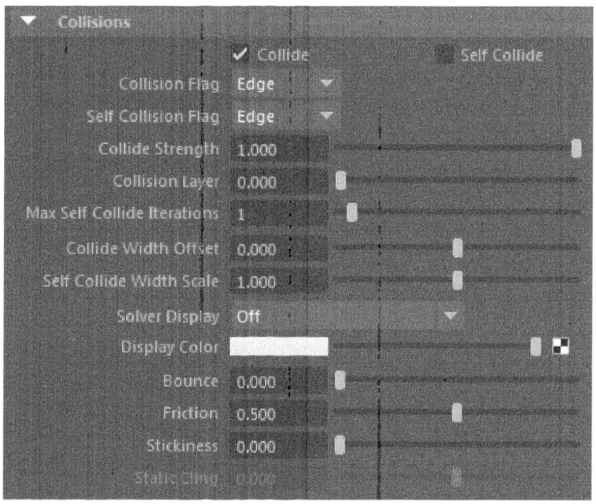

*Figure 15-5 The attributes in the **Collisions** area*

Collide
The **Collide** check box is used to specify whether the nHair will collide with the other nucleus objects or not. This check box is selected by default. On clearing this check box, the nHair will not collide with other nucleus objects.

Self Collide
The **Self Collide** check box is used to collide the hair strands with each other. By default, this check box is cleared.

Collision Flag / Self Collision Flag
The options in the **Collision Flag** drop-down list are used to specify whether the edges or the vertices of the nHair object will collide during collisions with other nucleus objects. The options in the **Self Collision Flag** drop-down list specify whether the edges or vertices of the nHair object collide with each other during self collisions.

Collide Strength
The **Collide Strength** attribute is used to specify the strength of collisions between nHair objects and other nucleus objects. By default, the value for this attribute is set to 1.

Collision Layer
The **Collision Layer** attribute is used to assign a specific collision layer to a selected nHair object. The other nucleus objects will collide with the nHair objects only if they are in the same collision layer or in the layers with higher values.

Max Self Collide Iterations
The **Max Self Collide Iterations** attribute is used to specify the maximum number of iterations in each simulation at the time of self collisions of the nHair objects.

Collide Width Offset
The **Collide Width Offset** attribute is used to create natural hair simulation by preventing the hair strands from penetrating into each other.

Self Collide Width Scale
The **Self Collide Width Scale** attribute is used to adjust the thickness of hair strands and clumps before self collisions.

Solver Display
The **Solver Display** drop-down list displays the information about the Nucleus Solver of the current nHair system used in the viewport. By default, the **Off** option is selected in this drop-down list.

Display Color
The **Display Color** attribute is used to change the color of the hair strand in the viewport. The color of the hair strand will be displayed only when the **Collision Thickness** or **Self Collision Thickness** option is selected in the **Solver Display** drop-down list.

Bounce
The **Bounce** edit box is used to specify the bounciness of the hair strands during self collisions.

Friction

The **Friction** attribute is used to specify the intensity of resistance offered by the nHair object during the collisions.

Stickiness

The **Stickiness** attribute is used to specify the value by which the hair strands will stick to each other during collisions.

Static Cling

The **Static Cling** attribute is used to specify the degree of local attraction between hair strands during self collisions. To activate this attribute, you need to select the **Self Collide** check box in the **Collisions** area.

Dynamic Properties Area

The attributes in this area are used to control the dynamic properties of nHair. The attributes in this area are discussed next.

Start Frame

This attribute is used to specify the frame from which the simulation begins.

Current Time

This attribute is used to specify the current time to be used for the hair solution.

Stretch Resistance

The **Stretch Resistance** attribute is used to specify the resistance that hair offers when they are stretched.

Compression Resistance

The **Compression Resistance** attribute is used to specify the resistance that hair would offer when compressed.

Bend Resistance

The **Bend Resistance** attribute is used to specify the resistance that hair would offer when bended.

Twist Resistance

The **Twist Resistance** attribute is used to specify the resistance that hair would offer when twisted.

Extra Bend Links

The **Extra Bend Links** attribute is used to specify the number of bend links between the vertices of hair strands that are farther from each other.

Rest Length Scale

The **Rest Length Scale** attribute is used to expand or shrink hair strands when no other forces act on the hair.

No Stretch (clip post solve length)

The **No Stretch (clip post solve length)** check box is used to keep the length of hair curves fixed throughout the simulation.

Stiffness Scale

The ramp in the **Stiffness Scale area** is used to control the stiffness of the hair strands.

Start Curve Attract

The attributes in this area are used to specify the intensity of attraction between the hair at current position and the hair at start position. These attributes are used to simulate the behavior of hair with respect to the movement of a character.

Attraction Scale

The ramp in the **Attraction Scale** area is used to reduce the intensity of attraction between the hair at current position and the hair at the start position. This ramp is used to apply varied stiffness in the root and tip of hair strands.

Forces

The attributes in the **Forces** area are used to control the behavior of nHair when external forces are applied to it. These attributes are discussed next.

Mass: The **Mass** attribute is used to control the amount of collision of hair strands with other nucleus objects.

Drag: The **Drag** attribute is used to control the movement of hair strands with respect to hair.

Tangential Drag: The **Tangential Drag** attribute is used to specify the amount of drag along the direction of the hair strands.

Motion Drag: The **Motion Drag** attribute is used to influence the movement of hair strands with respect to hair follicles. It also determines the change in shape of hair caused due to external forces.

Damp: The **Damp** attribute is used to reduce the effect of change in the shape of hair strand while bending and stretching.

Stretch Damp: The **Stretch Damp** attribute is used to increase or decrease the stretching of hair without making it bounce.

Dynamics Weight: This attribute is used to control the influence of external forces on the hair.

Ignore Solver Gravity

The **Ignore Solver Gravity** check box is used to enable or disable the effect of solver's gravity on hair strands.

Ignore Solver Wind

The **Ignore Solver Wind** check box is used to enable or disable the effect of solver's wind on hair strands.

Disable Follicle Anim
This check box is used to enable or disable the calculation of follicle animation on playback. On selecting the **Disable Follicle Anim** check box, the performance of the playback improves.

Turbulence Area
The options in this area are used to control the external disturbance on the hair system caused due to the forces such as drag, gravity, and so on. It consists of three edit boxes that are discussed next.

Intensity
The **Intensity** attribute is used to control the strength of force applied to the hair system.

Frequency
The **Frequency** attribute is used to control the looping of turbulence.

Speed
The **Speed** attribute is used to control the rate at which the turbulence changes with respect to time.

Caching Area
The **Caching** area consists of the **Cacheable Attributes** drop-down list. The options in the drop-down list are used to specify which of the attributes of the nHair system will be processed for caching.

Shading Area
The **Shading** area consists of various attributes that are used to manipulate the color of the hair strands. These attributes are discussed next.

Hair Color
The **Hair Color** attribute is used to specify the base color of hair strands.

Hair Color Scale
The **Hair Color Scale** area is used to specify the variation in the color of hair strands from root to tip. The attributes in this area are discussed next.

Opacity: The **Opacity** attribute is used to control the transparency of hair strands. When the value of this attribute is 0, the hair strands are not visible on rendering.

Translucence: The **Translucence** attribute is used to control the passage of light through hair strands.

Specular Color: The **Specular Color** attribute is used to specify the color of specularity of the hair.

Specular Power: The **Specular Power** attribute is used to adjust the intensity of specularity of the hair.

Cast Shadows: This check box when selected causes hair to cast shadows. It works with depth map only.

Color randomization

The different attributes in this area are used to randomize the color of the hair.

Painting Texture on nHair

In Maya, you can paint textures on the hair. To do so, select **pfxHair1** from the **Outliner** window and then choose **nHair > Create > Paint Hair Textures > Hair Color** from the menubar. Next, choose the **Show/Hide the Tool Settings** button from the Status Line; the **Tool Settings (3D Paint Tool)** window will be displayed, as shown in Figure 15-6. Set the radius of the brush by specifying values in the **Radius (U)** and **Radius (L)** edit boxes in the **Brush** area. Alternatively, press and hold the B key and drag the cursor using the middle mouse button in the viewport to set the radius of the brush. Next, set the color of hair by using the **Color** swatch in the **Color** area. Now, paint on the hair in the viewport to change the color.

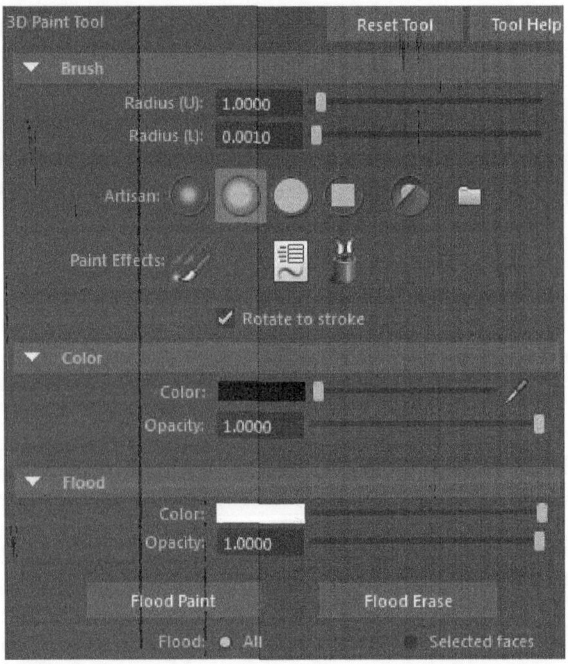

*Figure 15-6 Partial view of the **Tool Settings (3D Paint Tool)** window*

Painting Follicle Attributes

You can paint follicle attributes such as density, hair length, and so on. To do so, choose **nHair > Create > Paint Hair Follicles** from the menubar; the **Paint Hair Follicles Settings** window will be displayed, as shown in Figure 15-7. Set the attributes in this window and then paint the follicle attributes on the surface. You can also change the radius of the brush, as discussed in the previous topic.

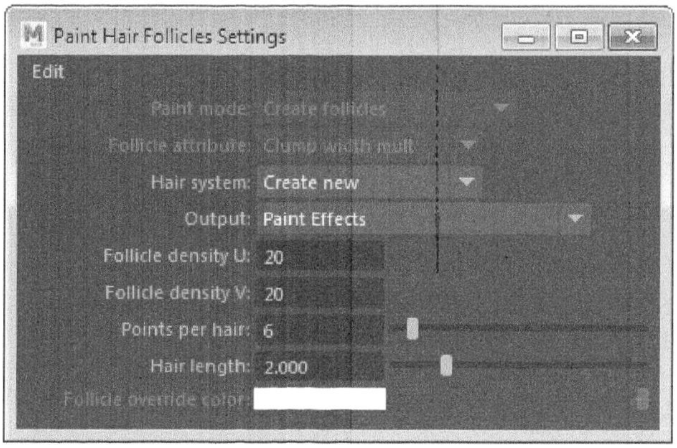

*Figure 15-7 The **Paint Hair Follicles Settings** window*

Styling nHair

In Maya, you can set the hair in different styles using the nHair attributes in the **Attribute Editor** or in the **Channel Box / Layer Editor**. For example, to create a braid using the hair system, you can either use an individual strand or the entire hair. To create a braid, create a hair system and then play the simulation and then stop it on the frame on which the hair stop simulating.

To set the current position of the hair as the start position, set the timeline to **1000** frames and then select **pfxHair1** from the **Outliner** window. Next, choose **nHair > Edit > Set Start Position > From Current** from the menubar. Now, select hair from the viewport and choose **nHair > Create > Convert Selection > To Follicles** from the menubar; the hair follicles will be selected.

Figure 15-8 The braid

Next, open the **Channel Box / Layer Editor** and enter **1** in the **Braid** parameter in the **SHAPES** area; the straight hair will convert into braids. Next, select **hairSystem1** from the **Outliner** window. In **Channel Box / Layer Editor**, set **Clump Width** to **0.6**, **Clump Twist** to **0.5**, **Hairs Per Clump** to **30**, **Thinning** to **0.5**, and **Multi Streaks** to **1** in the **SHAPES** area. Next, render the hair system; the braid will be created, as shown in Figure 15-8.

In Maya, you can also apply various styles to the hair to make them curly, wavy, and so on. To do so, select the hair system and choose **nHair > Edit > Modify Curves** from the menubar; a cascading menu will be displayed. You can choose different options from this cascading menu to set the hair styles.

Applying Shadow to the nHair

You can apply shadow to hair to give them realistic look. To do so, first create a spotlight in the viewport. In the **Attribute Editor**, expand the **Shadows** area and select the **Use Depth Map Shadows** check box in the **Depth Map Shadow** area.

Next, clear the **Use Mid Dist** and **Use Auto Focus** check boxes. Set the value of **Focus** to **150**, **Filter Size** to **2**, and **Bias** to **0.006**. Next, select **pfxHair1** from the **Outliner** window. In the **Attribute Editor**, choose the **hairSystemShape1** tab and then expand the **Shading** area. Make sure the **Cast Shadows** check box is selected. Now, render the scene to view the final result, as shown in Figure 15-9.

Figure 15-9 Braid after applying the shadow

Rendering the nHair

In Maya, you can render the hair by using either the **Maya Software** renderer or the **mental ray** renderer. The **Maya Software** renderer is used only if you have selected paint effects as output while creating the hair. To use the **mental ray** renderer, you need to convert the paint effect strokes into polygons. After converting the paint effect strokes into polygons, choose **Windows > Editors > Rendering Editors > Render Settings** from the menubar; the **Render Settings** window will be displayed. Select the **mental ray** as the active renderer from the **Render Using** drop-down list in the **Render Settings** window. Next, choose the **Diagnostics** tab and expand the **Features Overrides** area in it, if it has not already been expanded; the **Features Overrides** area will be displayed, as shown in Figure 15-10. In this area, make sure the **Render Fur/Hair** check box is selected.

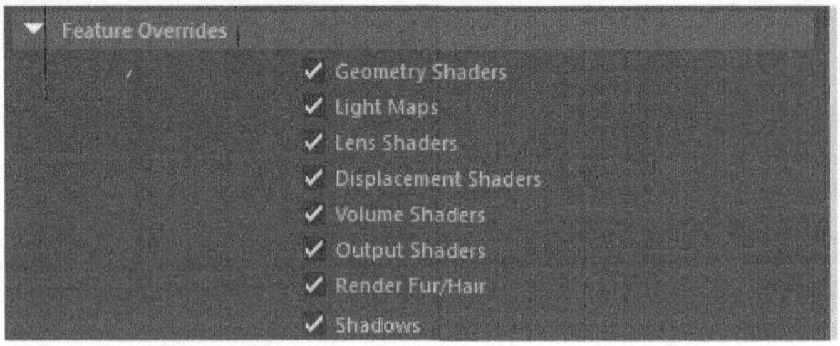

*Figure 15-10 The **Features Overrides** area in the **Render Settings** window*

TUTORIALS

Tutorial 1

In this tutorial, you will create an underwater scene with jellyfish, as shown in Figure 15-11, by using the Maya nHair. **(Expected time: 30 min)**

The following steps are required to complete this tutorial:

a. Create the project folder.
b. Download the texture file.
c. Create the top part of the jellyfish.
d. Create tentacles of jellyfish.
e. Create a plane and add light to the scene.
f. Save and render the scene.

Figure 15-11 The underwater scene

Creating the Project Folder

Create a new project folder with the name *c15_tut1* at *\Documents\maya2017*, as discussed in Tutorial 1 of Chapter 2.

Downloading the Texture File

In this section, you need to download the texture file.

1. Download the *c15_maya_2017_tut.zip* file from *www.cadcim.com*. The path of the file is as follows: *Textbooks > Animation and Visual Effects > Maya > Autodesk Maya 2017: A Comprehensive Guide*

2. Extract *land.jpg* and *texture_light.jpg* to *sourceimages* folder at the location *\Documents\maya2017\c15_tut1*.

Creating the Top Part of the Jellyfish

In this section, you need to create the top part of the jellyfish.

1. Make sure the **Modeling** menuset is selected from the **Menuset** drop-down list in the Status Line.

2. Choose **Create > Polygon Primitives > Sphere** from the menubar to create a sphere in the persp viewport.

3. Maximize the front viewport. Now, press and hold the right mouse button over the sphere; a marking menu is displayed. Choose the **Vertex** option from the marking menu; the vertex selection mode gets activated on the sphere.

4. Select the bottom vertices of the sphere, as shown in Figure 15-12. Next, choose **Edit Mesh Components > Merge Components to Center** from the menubar; the selected vertices merge together at the center, as shown in Figure 15-13.

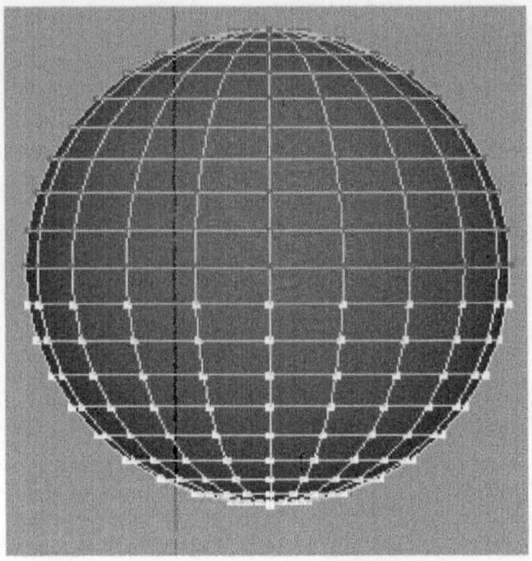

Figure 15-12 *Bottom vertices selected*

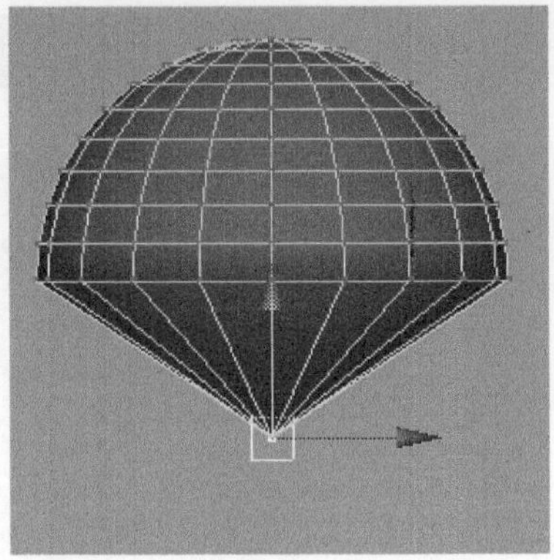

Figure 15-13 *Selected vertices merged at the center*

5. Move the collapsed vertex upward along the Y-axis using **Move Tool**.

6. Choose **View > Predefined Bookmarks > Bottom** from the **Panel** menu; the active viewport changes to the bottom viewport. Make sure the sphere is in the shaded mode.

7. Now, press and hold the right mouse button over the sphere; a marking menu is displayed. Choose the **Edge** option from the marking menu; the edge selection mode gets activated on the sphere.

8. Select the border edge loop of the sphere and then choose **Edit Mesh > Edge > Edit Edge Flow** from the menubar; a new edge loop is created.

9. Choose **Mesh Tools > Tools > Insert Edge Loop Tool** from the menubar; the shape of the cursor is changed. Next, click in between the border and selected edge loop; a loop is created, refer to Figure 15-14.

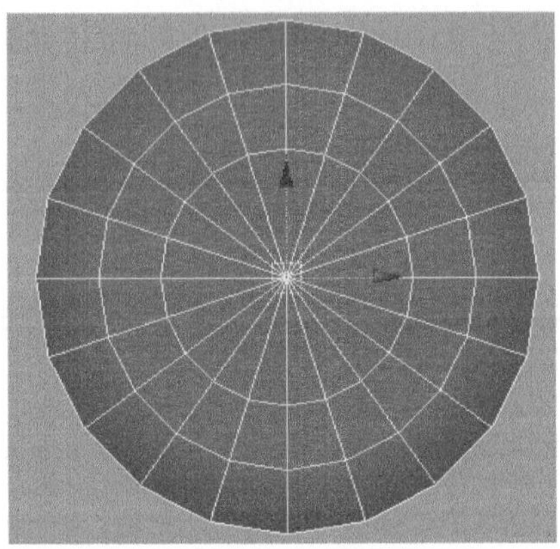

Figure 15-14 *Edge loops created using the **Insert Edge Loop** tool*

10. Press and hold the right mouse button on the sphere in the viewport and choose **Object Mode** from the marking menu displayed. Select the sphere from the viewport and choose **Edit > Duplicate > Duplicate** from the menubar; a duplicate of the sphere is created. Next, invoke the **Move Tool** from the Tool Box and move the duplicate object away from the original sphere.

11. Name the two spheres as **shell_1** and **shell_2**. Invoke **Scale Tool** from the Tool Box and scale the two spheres using the **Scale Tool** such that *shell_1* is bigger than *shell_2*. Again, choose **View > Predefined Bookmarks > Perspective** from the **Panel** menu; the active viewport changes to the persp viewport, as shown in Figure 15-15.

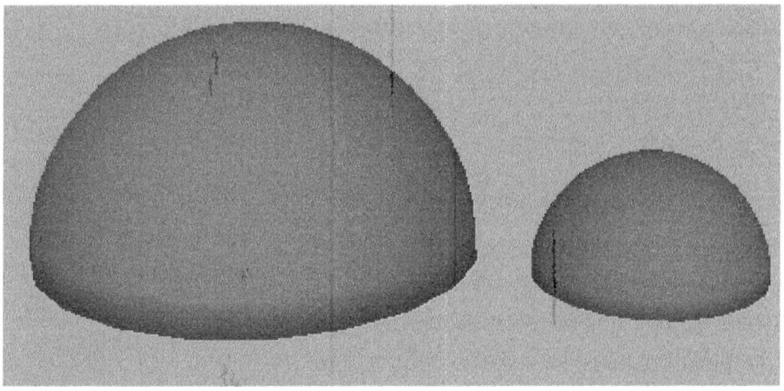

***Figure 15-15** The spheres displayed in the persp viewport*

12. Select *shell_1* and press and hold the right mouse button over *shell_1*; a marking menu is displayed. Choose **Assign New Material** from the marking menu; the **Assign New Material: shell_1** window is displayed. Next, choose **Lambert** from the window; the **lambert2** tab is displayed in the **Attribute Editor**.

13. Rename the **lambert2** shader to **shell_1_color**. Next, in the **Common Material Attributes** area of the **shell_1_color** tab in the **Attribute Editor**, choose the **Color** swatch and then set the **H**, **S**, and **V** values to **212**, **0.7**, and **0.7**, respectively. Next, choose the **Transparency** swatch and then set the **H**, **S**, and **V** values to **212**, **0**, and **0.3**, respectively. Also, set the **Glow Intensity** value to **0.3** in the **Special Effects** area.

14. Select *shell_2* from the viewport and press and hold the right mouse button over it; a marking menu is displayed. Choose **Assign New Material** from the marking menu; the **Assign New Material: shell_2** window is displayed. Next, choose **Lambert** from the window; the **lambert3** tab is displayed in the **Attribute Editor**.

15. Rename the **lambert3** to **shell_2_color**. Next, in the **Common Material Attributes** area of the **shell_2_color** tab in the **Attribute Editor**, choose the **Color** swatch and then set the **H**, **S**, and **V** values to **58**, **0.8**, and **0.5** respectively. Next, choose the **Transparency** swatch and then set the **H**, **S**, and **V** values to **58**, **0.8**, and **0.17**, respectively. Also, set the value of **Glow Intensity** to **0.2** in the **Special Effects** area.

16. Select *shell_2* in the viewport and move it to the center of *shell_1* using **Move Tool**, as shown in Figure 15-16.

***Figure 15-16** Both shells aligned in the viewport*

Creating Tentacles of the Jellyfish

In this section, you need to create the tentacles of jellyfish.

1. Choose **View > Predefined Bookmarks > Bottom** from the **Panel** menu; the active viewport changes to the bottom viewport.

2. Select *shell_1* and then press and hold the right mouse button over it; a marking menu is displayed. Choose **Face** from the marking menu; the face selection mode is activated. Select the outer faces on *shell_1*, as shown in Figure 15-17.

3. Make sure that the faces are selected on the object, refer to Figure 15-17. Select the **FX** menuset from the **Menuset** drop-down list in the Status Line. Choose **nHair > Create > Create Hair > Option Box** from the menubar; the **Create Hair** Options dialog box is displayed.

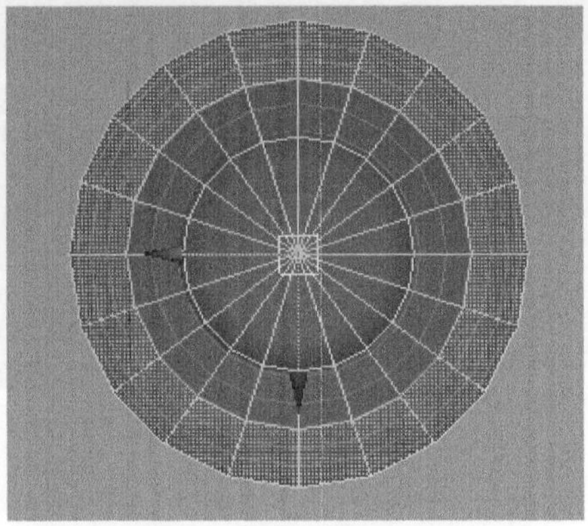

Figure 15-17 The faces selected on shell_1

4. In this dialog box, select the **At selected surface points/faces** radio button and enter **10** in the **Length** edit box. Next, choose the **Create Hairs** button from the dialog box; hair are created on the selected faces. Choose **View > Predefined Bookmarks > Perspective** from the **Panel** menu; the active viewport changes to the persp viewport.

5. Set the timeline to **1000** frames and play the animation. Stop the animation at frame 25. Next, select the hair from the viewport and choose **nHair > Edit > Set Start Position > From Current** from the menubar; the position of the hair at the current frame is set to 1. Figure 15-18 displays the nHair after making the modifications.

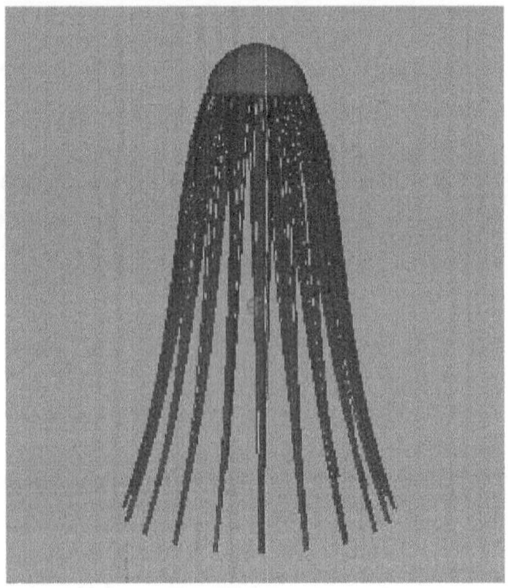

Figure 15-18 The appearance of hair

6. Select *shell_2* and then *shell_1* using CTRL. Next, press P on the keyboard to make *shell_1*, the parent of *shell_2*. Select *shell_1* from the viewport. Next, choose **Fields/Solvers > Solvers > Interactive Playback** from the menubar and move *shell_1* in the viewport; hair starts behaving interactively with the sphere.

7. Stop the simulation and invoke the **Outliner** window. In this window, select **pfxHair1**. Next, choose **Modify > Objects > Convert > Paint Effects to Polygons** from the menubar; the hair changes to polygons.

8. Press and hold the right mouse button over the hair and choose **Material Attributes** from the marking menu; the **hairTubeShader1** tab is displayed in **Attribute Editor**. Select **Lambert** from the **Type** drop-down list; the **Lambert4** tab is displayed in the **Attribute Editor**.

9. Choose the checker button on the right of the **Color** attribute in the **Common Material Attributes** area of the **lambert4** tab; the **Create Render Node** window is displayed. Choose the **Ramp** button from this window; the **ramp1** tab is displayed in the **Attribute Editor**.

10. In the **Ramp Attributes** area of the **ramp1** tab, create four nodes on the ramp and align them, as shown in Figure 15-19. Set the **H**, **S**, and **V** values of the nodes as follows:

Node 1: **218, 0.9, 0.7** Node 2: **200, 0.7, 1**
Node 3: **195, 0.2, 1** Node 4: **0, 0, 1**

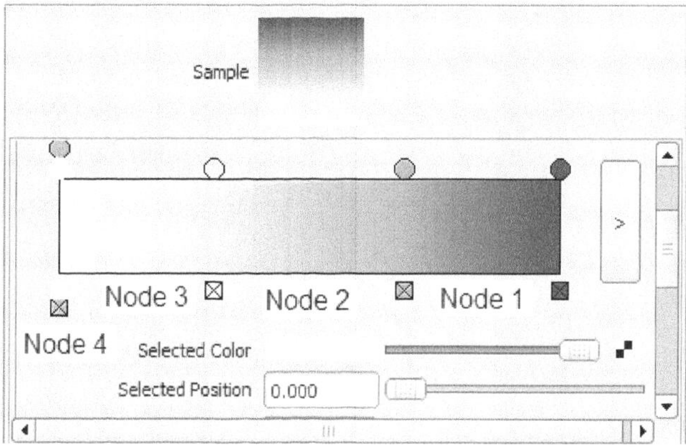

Figure 15-19 *Nodes arranged on the ramp in the* ***Attribute Editor***

11. Select the hair in the viewport, and press and hold the right mouse button over it; a marking menu is displayed. Choose **Material Attributes** from the marking menu; the **lambert4** tab is displayed in the **Attribute Editor**.

12. In the **Special Effects** area of the **lambert4** tab, set the **Glow Intensity** value to **0.3**; the glow is added to the hair.

    The jellyfish is created in the viewport. Next, you need to render the scene to get the output.

13. Choose the **Render the current frame** button from the Status Line; the render view of the jellyfish is displayed in the **Render View** window, as shown in Figure 15-20.

    Next, you need to add more hair to the jellyfish.

14. Make sure the hair is selected in the persp viewport and choose **Display > Hide > Hide Selection** from the menubar; the hair are hidden. Choose **View > Predefined Bookmarks > Bottom** from the **Panel** menu; the active viewport changes to the bottom viewport.

15. Select *shell_2* and press and hold the right mouse button and choose **Face** from the marking menu; the face selection mode of the object is activated. Select the faces at the center, as shown in Figure 15-21.

16. Choose **nHair > Create Hair > Option Box** from the menubar; the **Create Hair** dialog box is displayed. In this dialog box, select the **New hair system** option from the **Place hairs into** drop-down list and then choose the **Create Hairs** button. Select the new hair created and choose **Modify > Convert > Paint Effects to Polygons** from the menubar; the hair changes to polygons.

Figure 15-20 The rendered view of the jellyfish

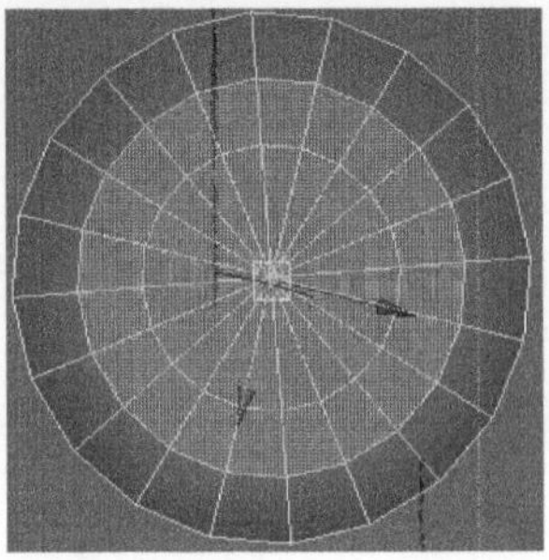

Figure 15-21 The faces at the center

17. Repeat steps 8, 9, 10, and 11, and then set **Glow Intensity** to **0.4** under the **Special Effects** area. Switch to persp viewport and choose **Display > Show > All** from the menubar; the hidden hair are displayed in the viewport.

18. Choose the **Render the current frame** button from the Status Line; the render view of the jelly fish is displayed in the **Render View** window.

Creating a Plane and Adding Light to the Scene

In this section, you need to create a plane and set the spot light and the directional light in the scene.

1. Create a polygonal plane in the viewport. In the **polyPlane1** area of the **INPUTS** node of the **Channel Box / Layer Editor**, set the following values:

   Width: **65** Height: **60**
   Subdivisions Width: **40** Subdivisions Height: **40**

2. Select the **Modeling** menuset from the **Menuset** drop-down list and double-click on **Move Tool** in the Tool Box; the **Tool Settings (Move Tool)** window is displayed. In the **Soft Selection** area of this window, select the **Soft Select** check box.

3. Make sure the plane is selected in the viewport. Press and hold the right mouse button and choose **Vertex** from the marking menu displayed; the vertex selection mode is activated. Select a vertex of the plane; the soft selection falloff is displayed around the selected vertex. Next, drag the manipulator of **Move Tool** in the Y direction; a bump is created on the surface. Similarly, create more bumps to create an uneven surface.

4. Press and hold the right mouse button on the plane and choose **Object Mode** from the marking menu displayed. Make sure the **Move Tool** is activated. Now, align the plane below

the jellyfish. Next, choose **Mesh > Remesh > Smooth** from the menubar; the plane appears smooth, as shown in Figure 15-22. Click on the polygonal plane to switch back to the object mode.

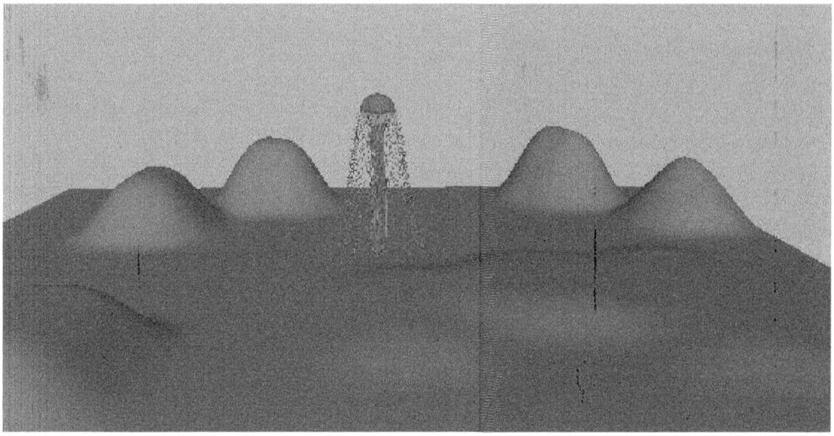

Figure 15-22 *The plane after using the **Smooth** tool*

5. Make sure the plane is selected. Press and hold the right mouse button over the plane and choose **Assign New Material** from the marking menu; the **Assign New Material: pPlane1** window is displayed. Next, choose **Lambert** from the window; the **lambert6** tab is displayed in the **Attribute Editor**.

6. In the **lambert6** tab, choose the checker button next to the **Color** swatch from the **Common Material Attributes** area; the **Create Render Node** window is displayed. Next, choose the **File** button from this window; the **file1** tab is displayed in the **Attribute Editor**.

7. In the **file1** tab, choose the folder icon on the right of the **Image Name** attribute in the **File Attributes** area; the **Open** dialog box is displayed. Next, select the **land.jpg** and then choose the **Open** button; the texture is applied to the plane. Press 6 to view the texture in the viewport, as shown in Figure 15-23.

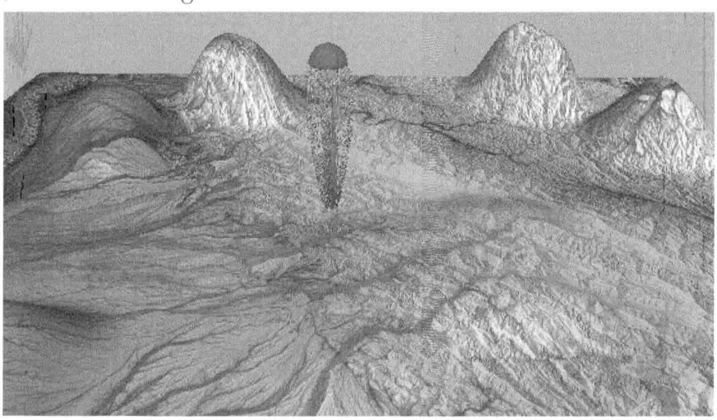

Figure 15-23 *Texture applied on the plane*

8. Activate the front viewport. Choose **Create > Lights > Spot Light** from the menubar; a spot light is created in the viewport.

9. In the **Channel Box / Layer Editor**, enter the following values:

   Translate X: **1.5** Translate Y: **20**
   Translate Z: **26** Rotate X: **-45**
   Rotate Y: **-4** Rotate Z: **0**

   Figure 15-24 displays the light placed in the persp viewport after setting the values in the **Channel Box / Layer Editor**.

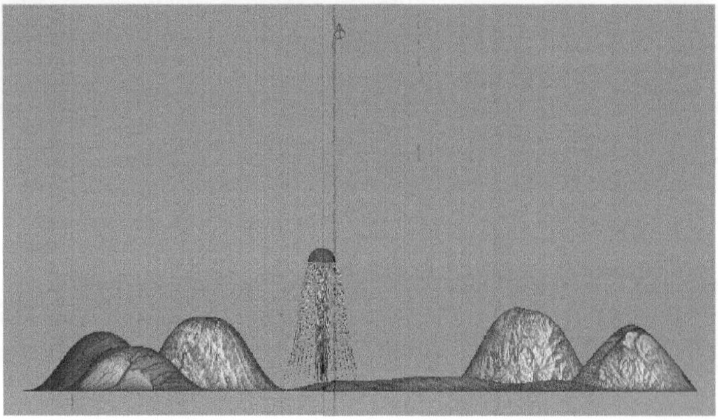

Figure 15-24 *The adjusted spot light*

10. Choose **Display > Show > Light Manipulators** from the menubar; the light manipulators are displayed in the viewport, as shown in Figure 15-25. Select the manipulator ring 10. Next, press and hold the left mouse button over this manipulator ring and move it downward until the ring passes through the polygonal plane in the viewport.

11. Choose **Display > Hide > Light Manipulators** from the menubar to hide the manipulators.

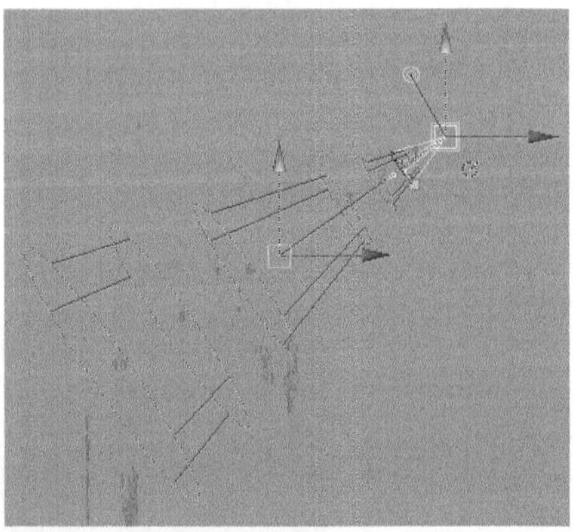

Figure 15-25 *The light manipulators*

Note

You can also set the position of the spot light with respect to the position of the jellyfish in the viewport.

12. Make sure the spot light is selected in the viewport. In the **spotLightShape1** tab of the **Attribute Editor**, choose the checker button on the right of the **Color** attribute in the **Spot Light Attributes** area; the **Create Render Node** window is displayed. In this window, choose the **File** button; the **file2** tab is displayed in the **Attribute Editor**.

13. In the **file2** tab of the **Attribute Editor**, choose the folder icon on the right of the **Image Name** attribute from the **File Attributes**; the **Open** dialog box is displayed. Next, select the **texture_light.jpg** image and choose the **Open** button.

14. Select the spot light; the **spotLightShape1** tab is displayed in the **Attribute Editor**. In this tab, set the **Cone Angle** value to **60** in the **Spot Light Attributes** area. Expand the **Light Effects** area and choose the checker button on the right of the **Light Fog** attribute; the **lightFog1** tab is displayed in the **Attribute Editor** and the fog effect is applied to the light.

15. Choose **Create > Lights > Directional Light** from the menubar; the directional light is created in the viewport.

16. Make sure the directional light is selected in the viewport and enter the following values in the **Channel Box / Layer Editor**:

    Translate X: **0** Translate Y: **9** Translate Z: **1**
    Rotate X: **-90** Rotate Y: **-10** Rotate Z: **58**

17. Choose **Windows > Editors > General Editors > Attribute Editor** from the menubar; the **Attribute Editor** is displayed with the **directionalLightShape1** tab chosen. In the **Directional Light Attributes** area of the **directionalLightShape1** tab, choose the **Color** swatch; the **Color History** palette is displayed. In this palette, set the **H**, **S**, and **V** values to **55**, **0.15**, and **1**, respectively. Also, set the value to **0.5** in the **Intensity** edit box.

18. Create multiple copies of jellyfish and then align them. You can also scale them by using **Scale Tool**.

Saving and Rendering the Scene

In this section, you will save the scene that you have created and then render it. You can view the final rendered image sequence of the scene by downloading the *c15_maya_2017_rndr.zip* file from *www.cadcim.com*. The path of the file is as follows: *Textbooks > Animation and Visual Effects > Maya > Autodesk Maya 2017: A Comprehensive Guide.*

1. Choose **File > Save Scene** from the menubar to save the scene.

2. Maximize the persp viewport, if it is not already maximized. Choose the **Render the current frame** button from the Status Line; the **Render View** window is displayed. This window shows the final output of the scene, refer to Figure 15-26.

> **Tip**
> *You can also enhance the quality of the scene by applying paint strokes to it. To do so, choose* ***Window > Editors > General Editors > Content Browser****; the* ***Content Browser*** *window is displayed. In the* ***Content Browser*** *window, select the* ***bubbles.mel*** *paint stroke from* ***Examples > Paint Effects > Underwater*** *folder and then apply it to the scene. Similarly, apply other paint strokes in the scene to get the output shown in Figure 15-26.*

Figure 15-26 The final rendered scene

Tutorial 2

In this tutorial, you will create a rope and simulate natural movement in it by using Maya nHair.

(Expected time: 20 min)

The following steps are required to complete this tutorial:

a. Create a project folder.
b. Create a NURBS curve and make it dynamic.
c. Set different attributes for the dynamic curve.
d. Save and render the scene.

Creating the Project Folder

Create a new project folder with the name *c15_tut2* at *\Documents\maya2017* and then save the file with the name *c15tut2*, as discussed in Tutorial 1 of Chapter 2.

Creating the NURBS Curve and Making it Dynamic

In this section, you will create a curve for the rope and make it dynamic.

1. Activate the front viewport. Choose **Create > Objects > Curves Tools > EP Curve Tool** from the menubar.

2. In the front viewport, create a profile curve, as shown in Figure 15-27.

3. Select **Modeling** from the **Menuset** drop-down list in the Status Line. Next, make sure the profile curve is selected in the viewport, and choose **Curves > Edit > Rebuild > Option box** from the menubar; the **Rebuild Curve Options** dialog box is displayed. In this dialog box, enter **150** in the **Number of spans** edit box. Next, choose the **Rebuild** button; the spans are added to the curve.

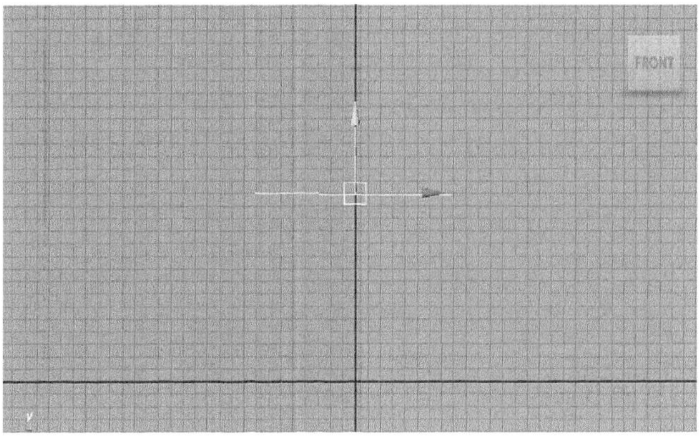

Figure 15-27 *Profile curve for a rope*

4. Choose **FX** from the **Menuset** drop-down list. Make sure that the profile curve is selected in the viewport.

   Next, choose **nHair > Edit > Make Selected Curves Dynamic** from the menubar; the curve is converted into a dynamic hair curve.

5. In the timeline, set the end time of the playback range to **500** and play the animation.

   You will notice that the curve starts bouncing up and down while its two ends remain stationary. Figure 15-28 displays the nHair curve at frame 200.

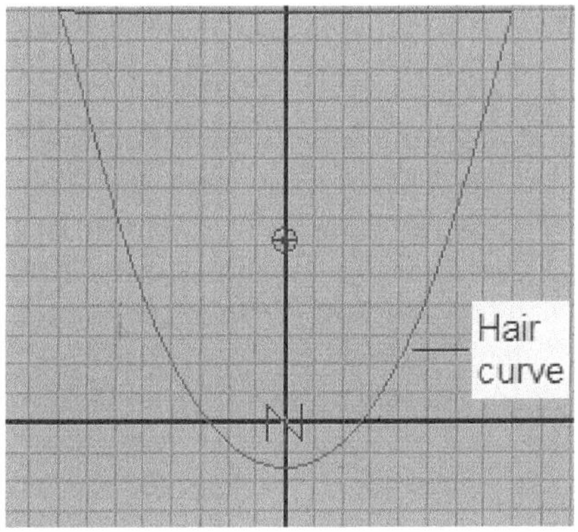

Figure 15-28 *Hair curve at frame 200*

Setting Different Attributes for the Curve

In this section, you will set different attributes for the curve to simulate rope like behavior in it.

1. Select **hairSystem1** from the **Outliner** window and then choose the **nucleus1** tab from the **Attribute Editor**. Select the **Use Plane** check box in the **Ground Plane** area of the **nucleus1** tab. On playing the animation, you will notice that the curve collides with the imaginary grid placed at the origin, refer to Figure 15-29.

2. Choose the **hairSystemShape1** tab from **Attribute Editor**. Select the **Self Collide** check box in the **Collisions** area. Next, enter **2** in the **Collide Width Offset** edit box of the **Collisions** area.

3. Expand the **Dynamic Properties** area of the **hairSystemShape1** tab and enter **20** in the **Stretch Resistance** edit box.

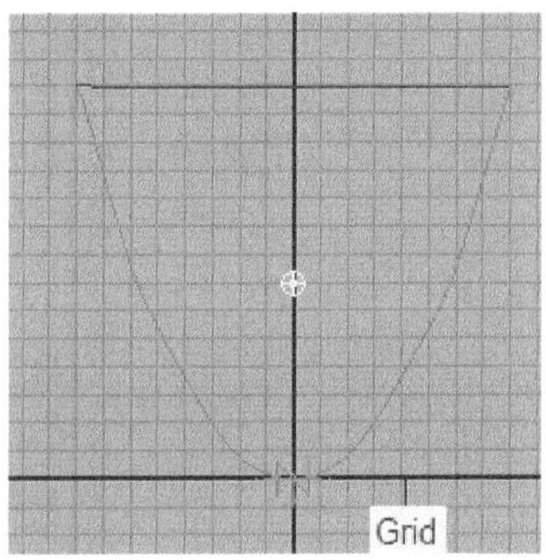

Figure 15-29 *Hair curve colliding with the grid*

4. Invoke the **Outliner** window. Next, expand **hairSystem1Follicles** and then select **follicle1**; the **follicle1**, **follicleShape1**, and **hairSystemShape1** tabs are displayed in the **Attribute Editor**. Choose the **follicleShape1** tab and select the **Tip** option from the **Point Lock** drop-down list in the **Follicle Attributes** area. Activate the persp viewport and play the animation. You will notice that one end of the curve is stationary and the other end is moving, refer to Figure 15-30.

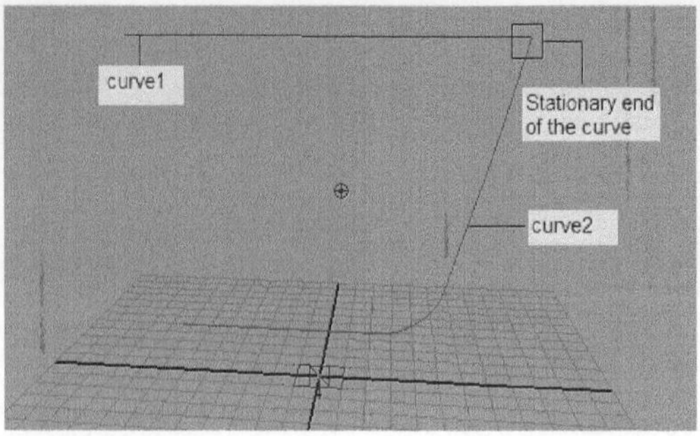

Figure 15-30 *The curve after selecting the **Tip** option*

5. Select the **hairSystem1OutputCurves > curve2** node from the **Outliner** window. Next, select **Modeling** from the **Menuset** drop-down list. Choose **Windows > Editors > General Editors > Content Browser** from the menubar; the **Content Browser** window is displayed. In this window and choose **Examples > Paint Effects > Fibers** from the left pane. Next, choose **rope.mel** from the right pane of the window. Choose **Generate > Paint Effects > Curve Utilities > Attach Brush to Curves** from the menubar; the curve is converted into a rope. Figure 15-31 shows the curve in the persp viewport.

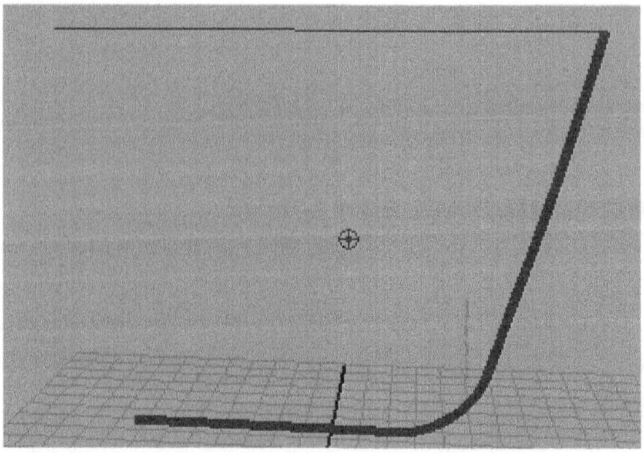

Figure 15-31 *Curve after choosing the **Attach Brush to Curves** option*

6. Play the simulation.

7. Select **FX** from the **Menuset** drop-down list. Next, choose **Fields/Solvers > Solvers > Interactive Playback** from the menubar; the curve starts moving. Using **Move Tool**, move the curve; the curve simulates the behavior of a rope.

Saving and Rendering the Scene

In this section, you will save the scene that you have created and then render it. You can view the final rendered image sequence of the scene by downloading the *c15_maya_2017_rndr.zip* file from *www.cadcim.com*. The path of the file is as follows: *Textbooks > Animation and Visual Effects > Maya > Autodesk Maya 2017: A Comprehensive Guide.*

1. Choose **File > Save Scene** from the menubar to save the scene.

2. For rendering the scene, refer to Tutorial 1 of Chapter 8.

Self-Evaluation Test

Answer the following questions and then compare them to those given at the end of this chapter:

1. Which of the following attributes in the **Attribute Editor** is used to specify the number of hair strands visible in the viewport per paint stroke?

   (a) **Display Quality** (b) **Hairs Per Clump**
   (c) **Static Cling** (d) **Baldness Map**

2. The __________ attribute is used to rotate the hair clumps about their primary axis.

3. The __________ ramp is used to specify the variation in the color of hair strands from root to tip.

4. The __________ drop-down list in the **Attribute Editor** gives you the information about the Nucleus Solver used in the scene view for the current nHair system.

5. The __________ attribute is used to specify the number of passive hair curves to be changed into active hair curves.

6. The **Damp** attribute is used to minimize the oscillation of hair strands. (T/F)

7. The **Bounce** attribute is used to specify the intensity of resistance offered by hair strands during collisions. (T/F)

8. The options in the **Collision Flag** drop-down list are used to specify whether the edges or the vertices of the **nHair** object collide during collisions with other nucleus objects or not. (T/F)

9. The **Twist Resistance** attribute is used to specify the intensity with which the hair strands resist shrinking. (T/F)

Review Questions

Answer the following questions:

1. Which of the following attributes is used to create the natural hair simulation by preventing the hair strands from penetrating into each other?

   (a) **Collision Layer** (b) **Collide Strength**
   (c) **Self Collide Width Scale** (d) **Collide Width Offset**

2. Which of the following attributes is used to expand or shrink hair strands when no other force acts on the hair?

   (a) **Stretch Resistance** (b) **Rest Length Scale**
   (c) **Extra Bend Links** (d) **Stiffness Scale**

3. The __________ option sets the position of the hair at which the simulation stops.

4. The __________ attribute is used to specify the resistance that hair offer when they are stretched.

5. The __________ attribute is used to specify the number of hair strands visible in each clump of hair.

6. The **Friction** attribute is used to specify whether the hair strands will stick to each other during collisions or not. (T/F)

7. The **Baldness Map** attribute is used to maintain the proportion of hair by making the hair clumps thinner at ends. (T/F)

8. The **Clump Interpolation** attribute is used to spread the tips of hair clumps, thus bringing them closer to each other. (T/F)

9. The **Edge bounded** check box is used to create hair strands along the horizontal and vertical edges. (T/F)

EXERCISE

The rendered output of the scene used in the following exercise can be accessed by downloading the *c15_maya_2017_exr.zip* file from *www.cadcim.com*. The path of the file is as follows: *Textbooks > Animation and Visual Effects > Maya > Autodesk Maya 2017: A Comprehensive Guide.*

Exercise 1

Create a beaded curtain using Maya nHair, as shown in Figure 15-32.

(Expected time: 30 min)

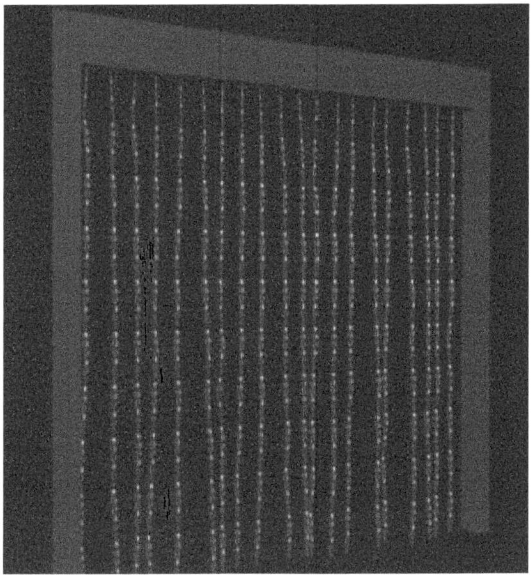

Figure 15-32 *A beaded curtain*

Answers to Self-Evaluation Test

1. a, **2. Clump Twist**, **3. Hair Color Scale**, **4. Solver Display**, **5. Passive fill**, **6.** T, **7.** F, **8.** T, **9.** F

Chapter 16

Bifrost

Learning Objectives

After completing this chapter, you will be able to:

- *Understand the fundamental concept of Bifrost*
- *Create and optimize Bifrost fluids*
- *Add collider to Bifrost fluids*
- *Add mesh to Bifrost particles*

INTRODUCTION

Bifrost is a fluid dynamics engine in Maya used for creating high-quality liquid simulations. It is a procedural frame work based on FLIP solver that can create simulated liquids such as foam, waves, and droplets. In this chapter, you will learn about simulation workflow in Bifrost.

FLIP SOLVER

FLIP (Fluid Implicit Particle) solver stores all the fluid data in each of the particles. It is similar to the particle based dynamic system. If you create waves in Bifrost then it will store all the information of the fluid.

WORKING WITH BIFROST LIQUID

To create a Bifrost simulation, select the **FX** menuset from the **Menuset** drop-down list in the Status Line. Next, choose **Windows > Workspaces** from the menubar; a cascading menu will be displayed. Select the **Bifrost** option from this menu, as shown in Figure 16-1; the **Bifrost** menu will be displayed in menubar, as shown in Figure 16-2. To create Bifrost liquid, first select a polygon object in the viewport and then choose **Bifrost > Create > Liquid** from the menubar; the **bifrostliquid1** node along with other nodes will be displayed in the **Outliner** window, as shown in Figure 16-3. Figures 16-4 and 16-5 show the object before and after creating the Bifrost liquid. Various attributes for modifying the Bifrost liquid will be displayed under different tabs in the **Attribute Editor**. Some of the tabs are discussed next.

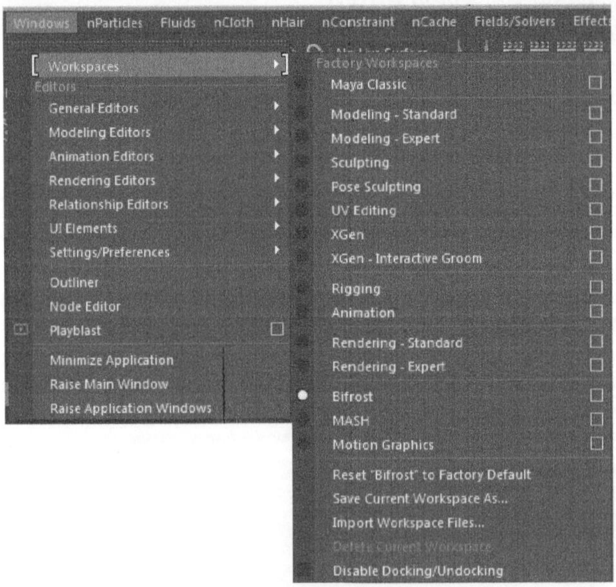

*Figure 16-1 Selecting the **Bifrost** option from the cascading menu*

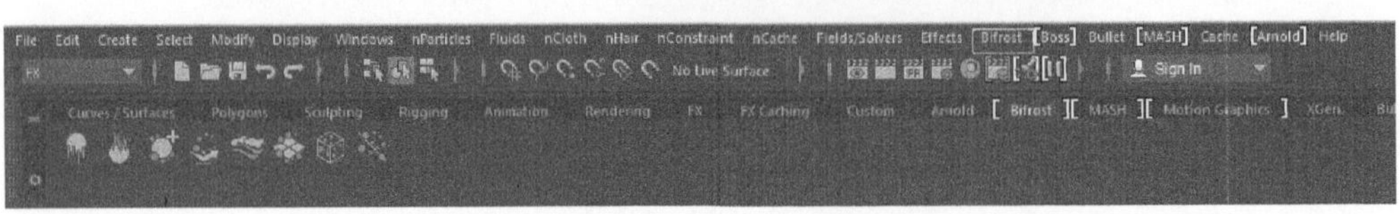

*Figure 16-2 The **Bifrost** menu is displayed in the menubar*

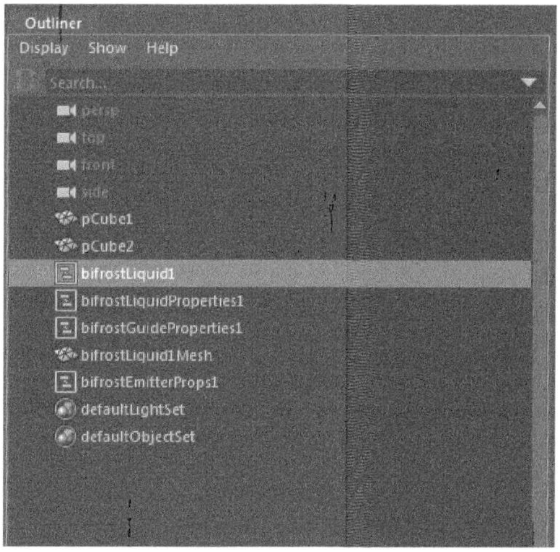

Figure 16-3 *Nodes in the* ***Outliner*** *window*

Figure 16-4 *The object before creating the Bifrost liquid*

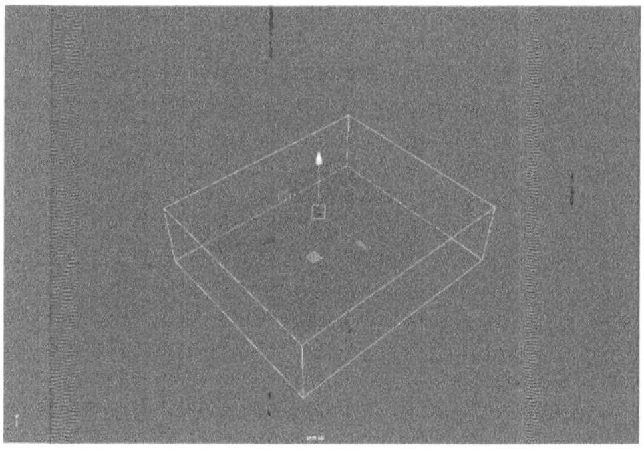

Figure 16-5 *The object after creating the Bifrost liquid*

bifrostLiquidContainer1 Tab

The attributes in this tab are used to specify the settings for controlling simulation, refer to Figure 16-6. These attributes are discussed next.

Container Attributes Area

By default, the **Enable** check box in the **Container Attributes** area is selected. As a result, this node is evaluated. The options in the **Evaluation Type** drop-down list allow you to control how the node will be evaluated. It is recommended that you do not change the default evaluation type.

Simulation Attributes Area

The options in this area are discussed next.

Scratch Cache

The **Scratch Cache** check box in the **Simulation Attributes** area is used to temporarily enable the scratch cache to speed up the playback. By default, this check box is cleared.

Start Frame
The **Start Frame** attribute is used to set the first frame of the simulation.

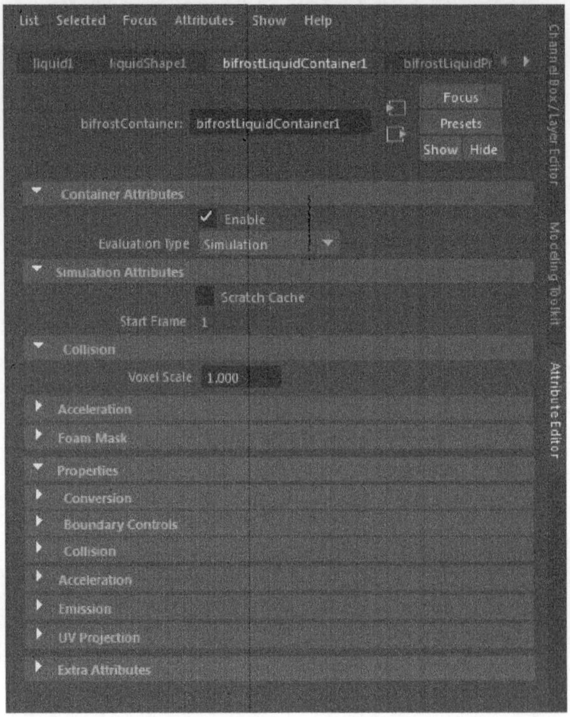

Figure 16-6 *Various attributes of the Bifrost liquid in the* ***Attribute Editor***

Collision, Acceleration, and Foam Mask Areas
All three areas contain an attribute with the name **Voxel Scale**. The value you specify for this attribute acts as a multiplier for the master voxel size. It is used for voxelizing all objects of corresponding type. Large voxel sizes provide low detail which can be used for quick tests and reviews. Small voxel sizes provide high detail and better accuracy for the final output.

liquidShape1 Tab
The attributes in this tab are used to control the render quality, particle size, particle count, and so on, refer to Figure 16-7. Some attributes are discussed next.

Render Area
The options in this area are discussed next.

Render Quality
The **Render Quality** attribute in the **Render** area is used control the render quality of simulation.

Filter
The **Filter** attribute in the **Render** area is used to control the amount of surface smoothing while rendering. Higher values can create smooth quality.

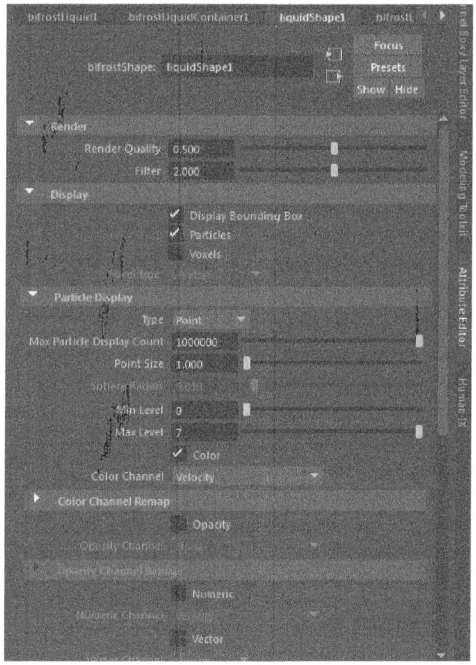

*Figure 16-7 Various attributes of the **liquidShape1** tab in the **Attribute Editor***

Display Area

The check boxes in this area are used to display the shape of particles.

Particle Display Area

The attributes in this area are discussed next.

Type

The options in this drop-down list are used to set the display of liquid.

Max Particle Display Count

The **Max Particle Display Count** attribute is used to set the count of the particles in the viewport.

Point Size

The **Point size** attribute is used to set the size of the particles. You can increase or decrease the size of particles.

WORKING WITH BIFROST AREO

Bifrost Areo is used to create effects like smoke, mist, and other gaseous simulations. To create an Areo simulation, first select one or more objects in the viewport and then choose **Bifrost > Create > Areo** from the menubar, as shown in Figure 16-8; the selected polygon object will get converted to Bifrost Areo object. Also **bifrostAreo1** node along with other nodes will be displayed in the **Outliner** window, as shown in Figure 16-9 and various attributes of the Bifrost

Areo will also get displayed in the **Attribute Editor**, refer to Figure 16-10. The attributes in the **bifrostAreoContainer1** tab are same as that of the **bifrostLiquidContainer1** tab.

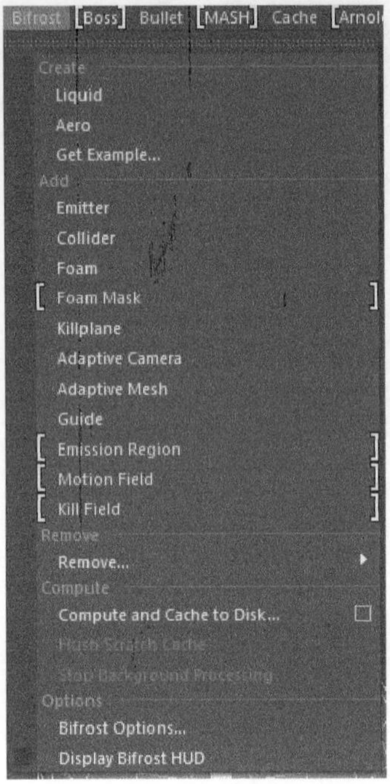

*Figure 16-8 The **Areo** option in the **Bifrost** menu*

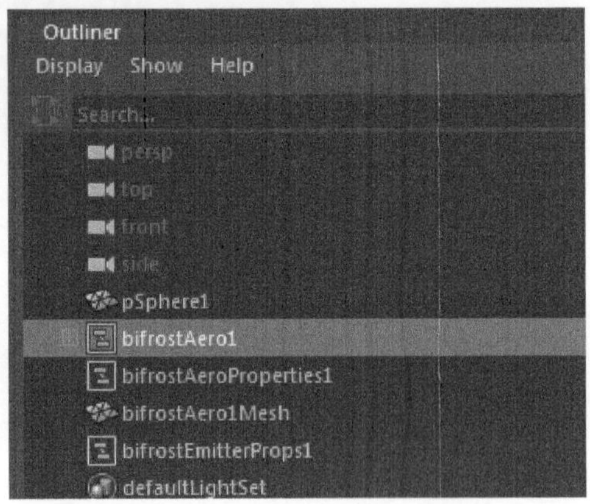

*Figure 16-9 Nodes in the **Outliner** window*

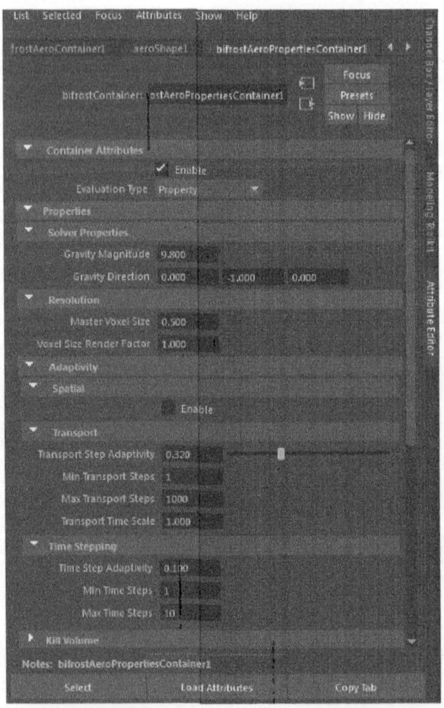

*Figure 16-10 Various attributes of the Bifrost Areo in the **Attribute Editor***

EMITTERS

Emitters are the objects that emit continuous particles in the Bifrost simulation. Emitters can be used to create various effects such as smoke, fire, fireworks, and so on.

Adding Emitters

In order to add an emitter, at least one Bifrost container and at least one mesh must be selected. To add an emitter, create a one or more polygon objects in the viewport. Select existing Bifrost liquid node such as **bifrostLiquid1** from the **Outliner** window and then select the polygon object by using the CTRL key. Next, choose **Bifrost > Add > Emitter** from the menubar; emitter will be added to an existing Bifrost simulation, refer to Figure 16-11.

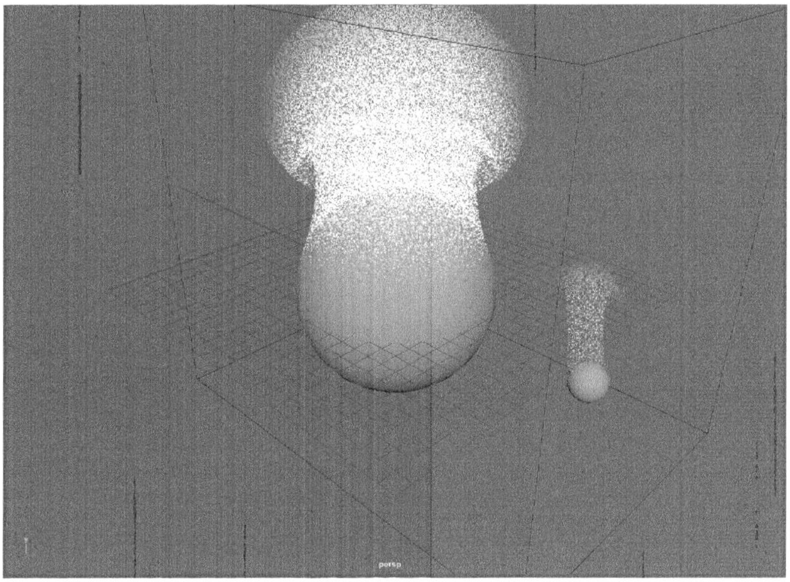

Figure 16-11 *Add emitter to an existing Bifrost simulation*

Removing Emitter

You can also remove an existing emitter from a scene. To remove an emitter, you can select the Bifrost liquid with emitter object from the **Outliner** window and then choose **Bifrost > Remove > Remove > Emitter** from the menubar; the emitter will be removed.

COLLIDERS

Colliders are the obstacles in a Bifrost simulation. You can create a container and use it as a collider that prevents liquid from falling away under gravity. You can also animate them to create waves and splashes.

Adding Colliders

You can create one or more polygon meshes to act as colliders. Select **bifrostLiquid1** and then select the meshes by using the CTRL key from the **Outliner** window. Next, choose **Bifrost > Add > Collider** from the menubar; the meshes will act as colliders, refer to Figure 16-12.

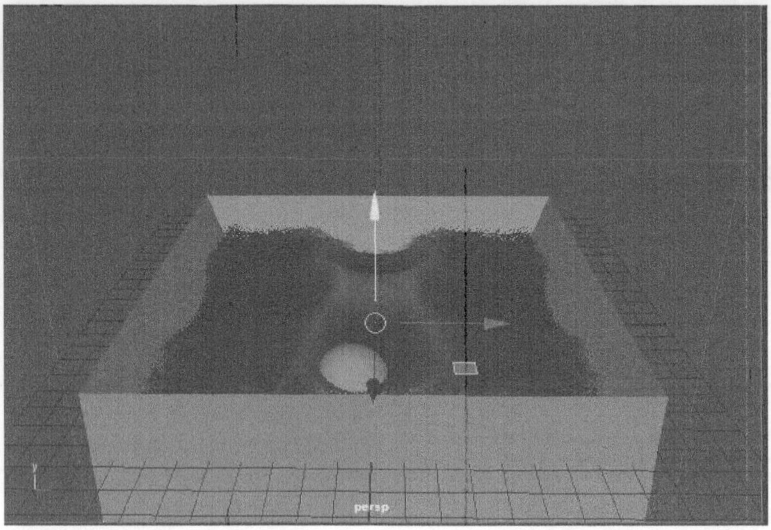

Figure 16-12 The meshes interacting with liquid

Removing Colliders

You can also remove the colliders from the viewport. To remove colliders, select the **bifrostLiquid1** from the **Outliner** window and then select other colliders by using the CTRL key. Next, choose **Bifrost > Remove > Remove > Collider** from the menubar to remove the colliders.

CACHING A SIMULATION TO DISK

You can store cache per frame as files on the system disk. Building cache files helps in speeding up the playback as Maya reads data from stored files instead of recomputing the simulation. Cache files are created for each Bifrost object, liquid, aero, foam, and solids for collision object. The user cache is intended for final simulation, unlike the temporary scratch cache which is meant for scrubbing and playback on the fly.

Flush Scratch Cache

Maya stores the scratch cache in memory and dumps it to temporary files on disk. It is automatically deleted and regenerated when you change the simulation and return to the first frame or you close the scene. If you need to flush out the scratch cache, choose **Bifrost > Compute > Flush Scratch Catch** from the menubar.

Compute and Cache to Disk

This option is used to save the cache files at the desired location. The Bifrost simulation reads the cache files at each frame, instead of recomputing the simulation. To do so, choose **Bifrost > Compute > Compute and Cache to Disk > Option Box** from the menubar; the **Bifrost Compute and Cache Options** dialog box will be displayed, as shown in Figure 16-13. Some of the attributes in this dialog box are discussed next.

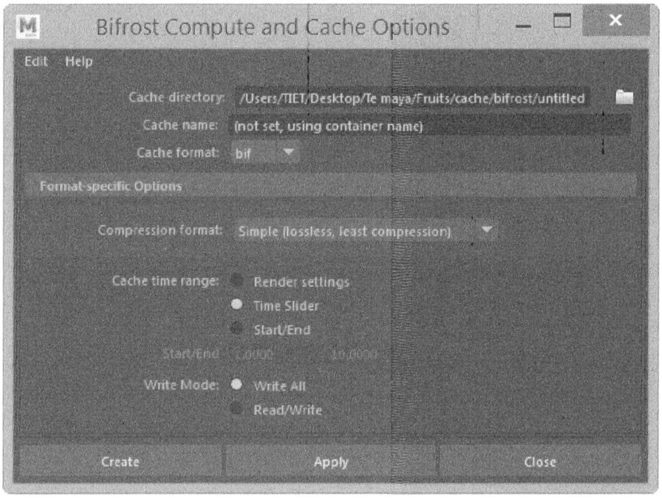

*Figure 16-13 The **Bifrost Compute and Cache Option** dialog box*

Cache directory

The **Cache directory** attribute is used to display the location of the cache files. Click on the folder icon corresponding to the **Cache directory** attribute; the **Set** dialog box will be displayed. Navigate to a location and then choose the **Open** button. The selected path will be displayed in the **Cache directory** field.

Cache name

The **Cache name** attribute is used to specify the directory for storing the cache files associated with the selected Bifrost containers. The cache files for each object are stored in the sub-directory of the directory specified in the **Cache name** attribute.

Cache format

The options in the **Cache format** drop-down list are used to specify the format of the cache file.

Compression format

The options in the **Compression format** drop-down list allow you to set the compression format for the cache files.

Cache time range

The radio buttons corresponding to this attribute are used to specify the time range for creating the cache files

FOAM

The **Foam** option in the **Bifrost** menu is used to create foam from the existing Bifrost liquid. You can use foam to create bubbles and spray effects. To add foam, you can select the Bifrost liquid node from the **Outliner** window and then choose **Bifrost > Add > Foam** from the menubar; the foam will be created and **bifrostFoamProperties1** node will be added to the **Outliner** window.

Remove Foam

To remove the foam, select the Bifrost liquid or foam node from the **Outliner** window and then choose **Bifrost > Remove > Foam** from the menubar.

TUTORIAL

Tutorial 1

In this tutorial, you will create an animation of water pouring into a fruit bowl, as shown in Figure 16-14. **(Expected time: 30 min)**

Figure 16-14 *The final rendered scene*

The following steps are required to complete this tutorial:

a. Create the project folder.
b. Download and open the file.
c. Set the scene for simulation.
d. Create the Bifrost simulation object.
e. Create the collision objects.
f. Refine the simulation.
g. Bake the cache.
h. Generate the mesh.
i. Add material to Bifrost.
j. Adding light to the scene.
k. Save and the render the file.

Creating a Project Folder

Create a new project folder with the name *c16_tut1* at *\Documents\maya2017* and then save the file with the name *c16tut1*, as discussed in Tutorial 1 of Chapter 2.

Downloading and Opening the File

In this section, you need to download and open the file.

1. Download the *c16_maya_2017_tut.zip* file from *www.cadcim.com*. The path of the file is as follows: *Textbooks > Animation and Visual Effects > Maya > Autodesk Maya 2017: A Comprehensive Guide.*

   Extract the contents of the zip file to the *Documents* folder.

2. Choose **File > Open Scene** from the menubar; the **Open** dialog box is displayed. In this dialog box, browse to the location *\Documents\c16_maya_2017_tut* and select **c16_tut1_start.mb** file from it. Next, choose the **Open** button; the scene is displayed in the viewport, as shown in Figure 16-15.

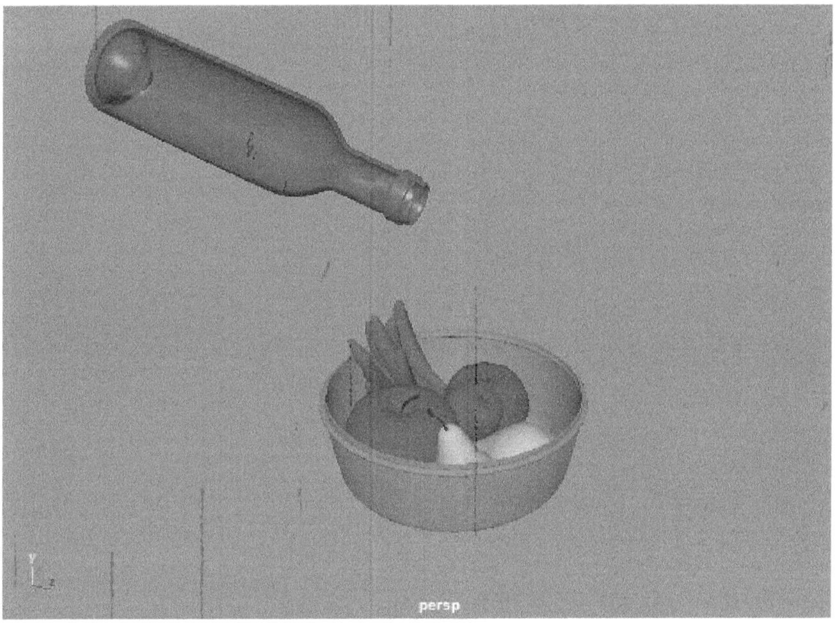

Figure 16-15 *The scene displayed in the viewport*

3. Choose **File > Save Scene As** from the menubar; the **Save As** dialog box is displayed. As the project folder is already set, the path *\Documents\maya2017\c16_tut1\scenes* is displayed in the **Look In** drop-down list. Save the file with the name **c16tut1.mb** in this folder.

Setting the Scene for Simulation

In this section, you will set the scene for animation.

1. Choose **Windows > Editors > Setting/Preferences > Preferences** from the menubar; the **Preferences** dialog box is displayed. Choose the **Time Slider** category in the **Categories** area of the dialog box; the **Time Slider: Animation Time Slider and Playback Preferences** area is displayed on the right in the **Preferences** dialog box.

2. In this area, set the value in the **Playback start/end** edit boxes to **1** and **120** respectively; the values in the **Animation start/end** edit boxes are updated automatically. Next, choose the **Save** button; the active time segment is set to a frame range of 1 to 120.

Creating the Bifrost Simulation

In this section, you will create the polygon mesh and then convert it into Bifrost liquid simulation.

1. Choose **Create > Polygon Primitives > Cylinder** from the menubar; a cylinder is displayed in the viewport, refer to Figure 16-16. Rename the cylinder to **liquid**.

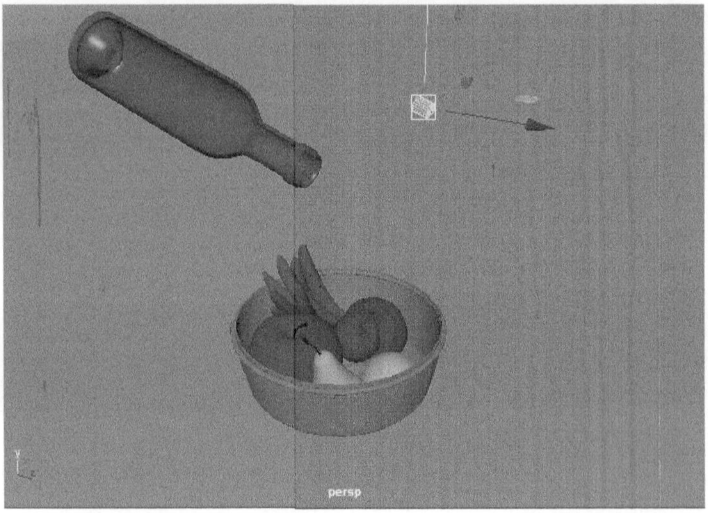

Figure 16-16 *The cylinder is created in the viewport*

2. Drag the *liquid* object and place it on the neck of the bottle. Adjust the scale of the object so that it fits inside the inner geometry of the bottle. Make sure the object is not touching the inner walls of the neck, refer to Figure 16-17.

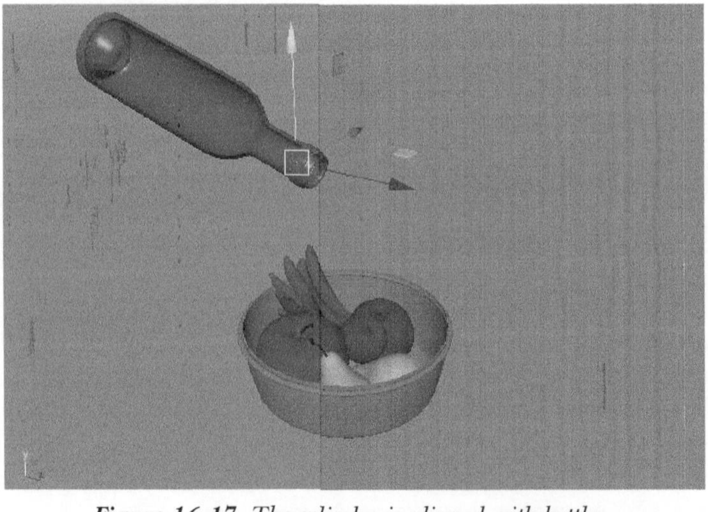

Figure 16-17 *The cylinder is aligned with bottle*

3. Select the **FX** menuset from the **Menuset** drop-down list in the Status Line.

4. Choose **Window > Workspace > Bifrost** from the menubar; the **Bifrost** menu is displayed in menubar.

5. Make sure the *liquid* object is selected. Next, choose **Bifrost > Create > Liquid** from the menubar; the *liquid* object is converted into bifrost liquid and **bifrostliquid1** along with other nodes is displayed in the **Outliner** window.

6. Choose the **Play forwards** button from the Timeline. Notice that the liquid is dropping straight from the bottle, as shown in Figure 16-18.

Figure 16-18 *The liquid dropping straight from the bottle*

Creating the Collision Objects

In this section, you will collide the particles to objects.

1. Make sure **bifrostliquid1** selected in the **Outliner** window. Next, select *bottle* by using the CTRL key. Now, choose **Bifrost > Add > Collider** from the menubar; the *bottle* is converted into a collider object. Press the play button from the Timeline bar; the simulation starts and bottle starts deflecting the particles.

2. Make sure **bifrostliquid 1** selected in the Outliner window. Select all the fruits with the basket using the SHIFT key. Next, choose **Bifrost > Add > Collider** from the menubar; all the objects are converted into collider objects. Now, play the simulation. Figure 16-19 shows the renderd image of the simulation.

Refining the Simulation

In this section, you will refine the simulation by setting the attributes.

1. Make sure **bifrostLiquid1** is selected in the **Outliner** window. In the **Attribute Editor**, choose the **liquidShape1**tab; the attributes of this tab are displayed. Expand the **Particle Display** area and then enter **3** in the **Point Size** attribute, as shown in Figure 16-20.

The **Point Size** attribute is used to set the size of Bifrost liquid.

Figure 16-19 *The rendered image of Bifrost simulation*

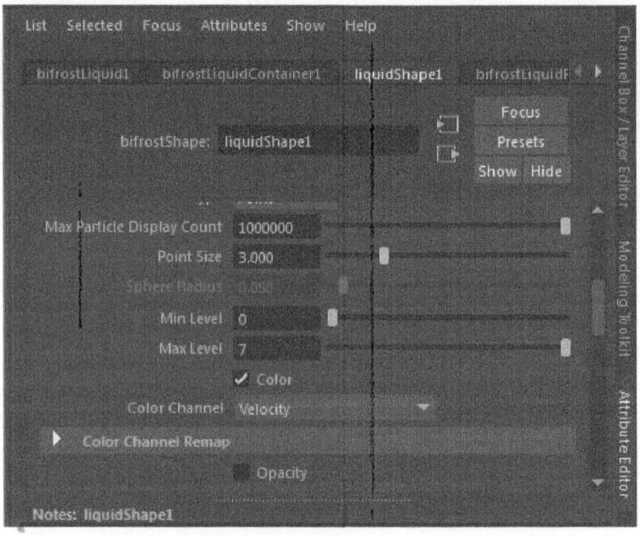

Figure 16-20 *The* ***Point Size*** *attribute in the* ***liquidShape1*** *tab*

2. In the **Attribute Editor**, choose the **bifrostliquidPropertiesContainer1** tab; the attributes of this tab are displayed. Expand the **Resolution** area and then enter **0.1** in the **Master Voxel Size** attribute.

   The **Master Voxel Size** parameter is used to set the size of the voxels in metre.

3. Play the simulation. Notice that the strength of Bifrost liquid is increased, as shown in Figure 16-21.

Figure 16-21 Bifrost liquid after setting the strength

Baking the Cache

In this section, you will bake the cached data and also set the output location to save.

1. Choose **Bifrost > Compute > Compute and Cache to Disk > Option Box** from the menubar; the **Bifrost Compute and Cache Options** dialog box is displayed.

2. Click on the folder icon corresponding to the **Cache directory** attribute; the **Set** dialog box is displayed. Next, select the directory from the listing. The name of the directory is displayed in the **Directory** text box, as shown in Figure 16-22. Choose the **Open** button; the location is set and the dialog box is closed.

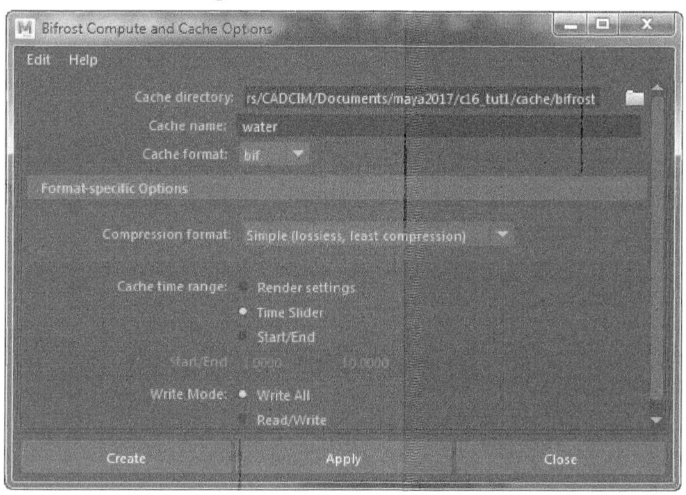

Figure 16-22 Setting the location for cache

3. In the **Bifrost Compute and Cache Options** dialog box, enter **water** in the **Cache name** text box. Next, choose the **Create** button; a file sequence containing simulation data is created. Also, the Time Line is displayed in blue color, as shown in Figure 16-23.

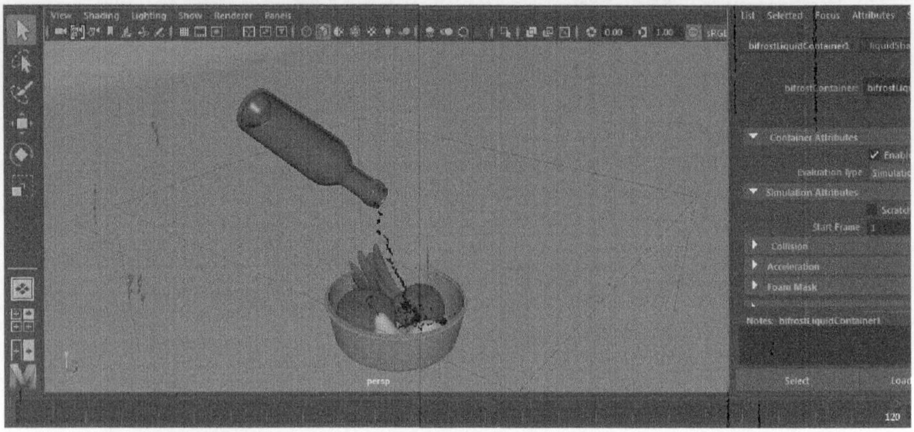

Figure 16-23 *The Time Line is displayed in blue color*

Generating the Mesh

In this section, you will generate the mesh.

1. Make sure the **bifrostLiquid1** node is selected in the **Outliner** window. In the **Attribute Editor**, choose the **liquidShape1** tab; the attributes of this tab are displayed. Expand the **Display** area and then clear the **Particles** check box, refer to Figure 16-24.

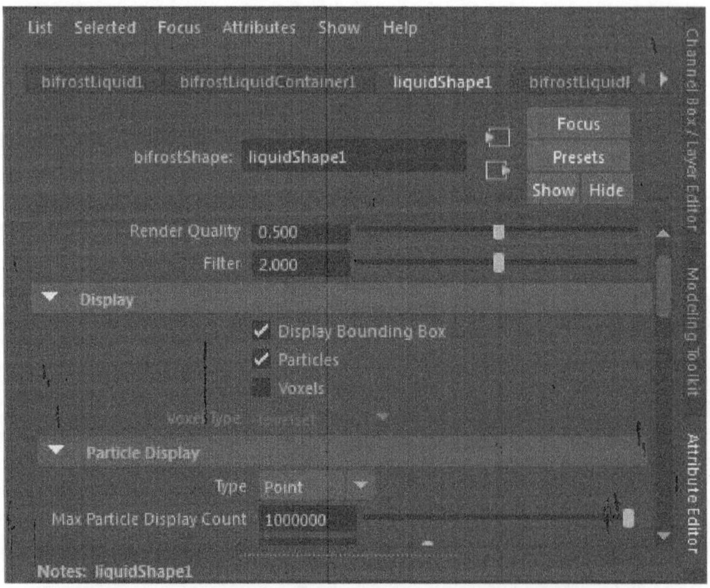

Figure 16-24 *The* ***Particles*** *check box in the* ***Display*** *area*

2. Make sure the **liquidShape1** tab is chosen. Next, expand the **Bifrost Meshing** area; the attributes of this are displayed. Now, select the **Enable** check box, as shown in Figure 16-25. Notice that mesh is generated in the viewport, as shown in Figure 16-26.

   The **Enable** check box is used to activate the mesh properties.

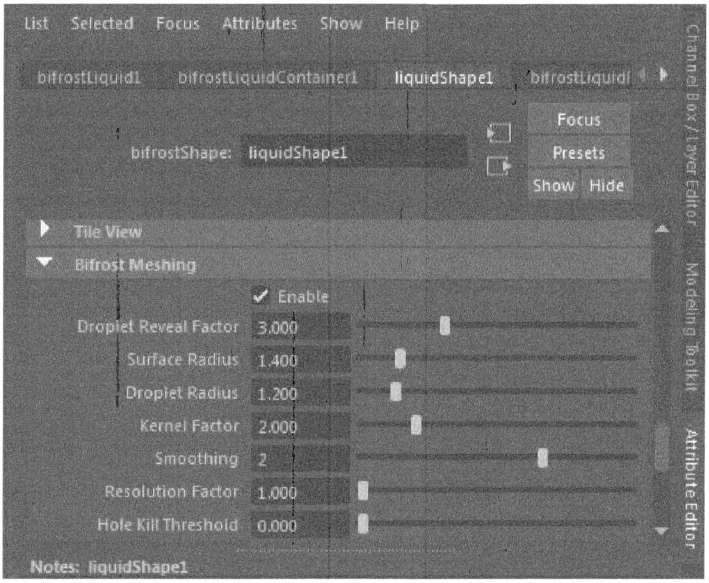

***Figure 16-25** The **Enable** check box is selected*

***Figure 16-26** The mesh is created*

3. Select the **liquid** object from the **Outliner** window. Next, press CTRL+ H. Notice that the selected object gets hidden from the viewport.

Adding Material to Bifrost Mesh

In this section, you will apply materials to the Bifrost mesh.

1. Maximize the persp viewport. Select **bifrostLiquidMesh** from the **Outliner** window.

2. Right-click on the Bifrost mesh in the viewport and then choose **Assign New Material** from the shortcut menu; the **Assign New Material** window is displayed. In this window, choose **Arnold > Shader > aiStandard**; the **aiStandard1** tab is displayed in the **Attribute Editor**.

3. In **Attribute Editor > aiStandard1 > Diffuse** area, enter **0** in the **Weight** edit box. Also, adjust the **Color** slider to its extreme left.

4. In **Attribute Editor > aiStandard1 > Specular** area, enter **1** in the **Weight** edit box and **0** in the **Roughness** edit box. Also, adjust the **Color** slider the extreme left.

5. In **Attribute Editor > aiStandard1 > Refraction** area, enter **1** in the **Weight** edit box. Also, enter **1.33** in the **IOR** field and **0.968** in the **Roughness** field.

6. Click on the color swatch and then choose light blue color. Render the scene; you will notice that there is some noise in the liquid render. To fix it, you need to increase the glossy and refraction samples.

7. Choose the **Display render settings** tool from the Status Line; the **Render Settings** dialog is displayed. In the **Arnold Renderer** tab, enter **3**, **4**, and **4** in the **Diffuse**, **Glossy**, and **Refraction** edit boxes, respectively. Render the scene.

Adding Light to the Scene

In this section, you will add a light to the scene.

1. Choose **Create > Light > Point Light** from the menubar; a point light is added to the scene. Now, place the lights above and in the front of the geometries in the scene and align them properly, refer to Figure 16-27. Render the scene; you will notice dark render.

   Now, you need to adjust the exposure settings.

2. In the **Attribute Editor > pointLightShape1 > Arnold** area, enter **12**, **3**, and **1** in the **Exposure**, **Samples**, and **Radius** edit boxes, respectively. Render the scene.

3. Choose **Arnold > Lights > Area Light** from the menubar to add an area light to the scene. Place the light as shown in Figure 16-28.

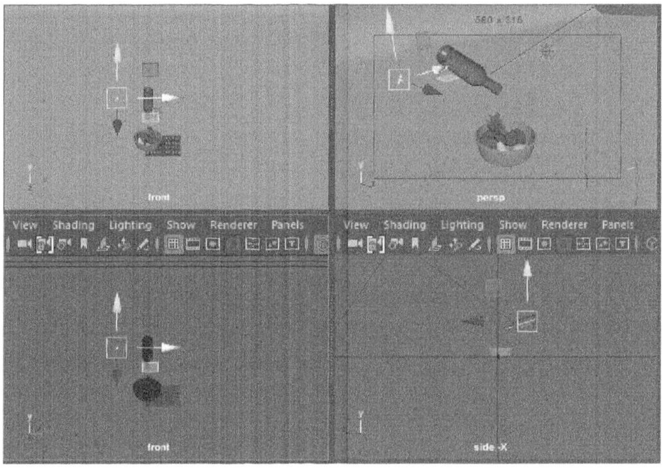

Figure 16-27 *Aligned area light*

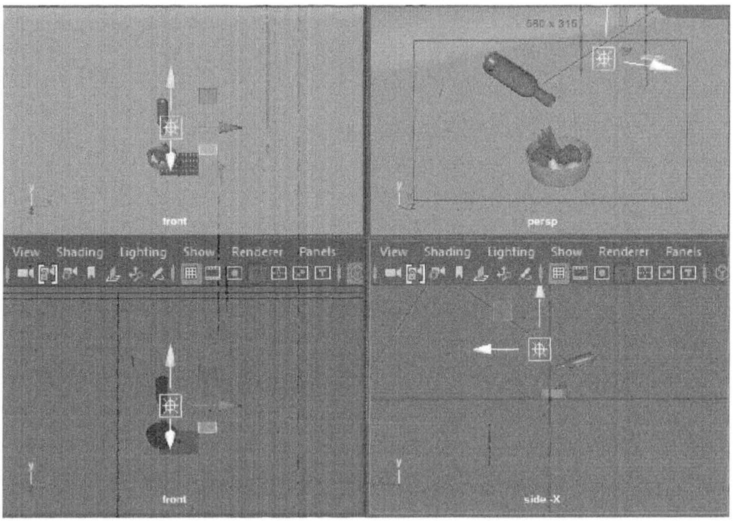

Figure 16-28 *Aligned point light*

4. In **Attribute Editor > aiAreaLightShape1 > Arnold Area Light Attributes** area, enter **10** in the **Exposure** edit box and **3** in the **Samples** edit box. Render the scene.

Saving and Rendering the Scene

In this section, you will save the scene that you have created and then render it. You can view the final rendered image sequence of the scene by downloading the *c16_maya_2017_rndr.zip* file from *www.cadcim.com*. The path of the file is as follows: *Textbooks > Animation and Visual Effects > Maya > Autodesk Maya 2017: A Comprehensive Guide.*

1. Choose **File > Save Scene** from the menubar to save the scene.

2. Maximize the persp viewport if it is not already maximized.

3. Choose the **Display render settings** tool from the Status Line; the **Render Settings** window is displayed. Enter **bifrost-simulation** in the **File name prefix** text box in the **File Output** area.

4. Select **jpeg** from the **Image format** drop-down list. Next, select **name.#.ext** from the **Frame/ Animation ext** drop-down list.

5. In the **Frame Range** area of the **Render Settings** window, enter **100** in the **End Frame** edit box.

6. Select the **Rendering** menuset from the **Menuset** drop-down list in the Status Line. Next, choose **Render > Batch Render > Batch Render** from the menubar; the rendering starts.

   You can view the rendering progress by choosing the **Script Editor** button from the Command Line.

Self-Evaluation Test

Answer the following questions and then compare them to those given at the end of this chapter:

1. Which of the following options in the **Bifrost** menu is used to scratch cache in memory and dump it to the temporary files in the disk?

   (a) **Scratch** (b) **Liquid**
   (c) **Foam** (d) **None of these**

2. The __________ solver stores all the fluid data in each particle.

3. The __________ attribute in the **Render** area is used to control the render quality of simulation.

4. The __________ attribute in the **Render** area is used to control the amount of surface smoothing while rendering.

Review Questions

Answer the following questions:

1. Which of the following options in the **Bifrost** menu is used to create Bifrost simulation?

   (a) **Areo** (b) **Liquid**
   (c) **Foam** (d) **None of these**

2. Which of the following attributes is used to increase the size of the particles?

   (a) **Point Size** (b) **Min Level**
   (c) **Master Voxel Size** (d) **Voxel Size**

3. The __________ check box in the **Simulation Attributes** area is used the scratch cache to speed up the playback.

4. The **Start Frame** attribute is used to set the first frame of simulation. (T/F)

EXERCISE

The rendered output of the scene used in the following exercise can be accessed by downloading the *c16_maya_2017_exr.zip* file from *www.cadcim.com*. The path of the file is as follows: *Textbooks > Animation and Visual Effects > Maya > Autodesk Maya 2017: A Comprehensive Guide.*

Exercise 1

Create honey simulation by using Bifrost, as shown in Figure 16-29.

(Expected time: 30 min)

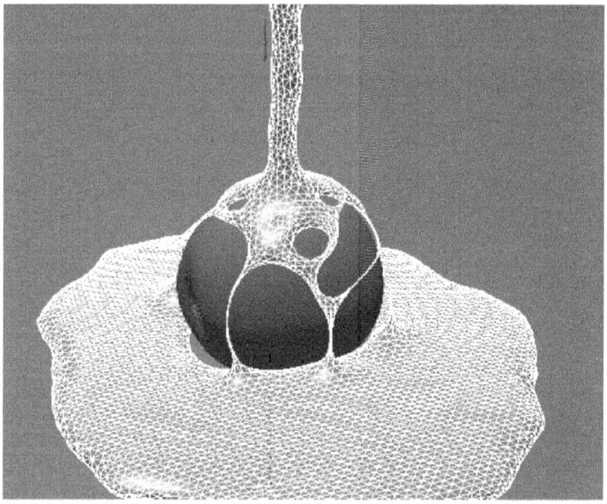

Figure 16-29 *Honey simulation by using Bifrost*

Answers to Self-Evaluation Test

1. a, **2.** FLIP, **3. Render Quality**, **4. Filter**

Chapter 17

Bullet Physics

Learning Objectives

After completing this chapter, you will be able to:

- *Work with rigid and soft bodies*
- *Create a soft body*
- *Create constraints*

INTRODUCTION

In Maya, you can create realistic, dynamic and kinematic simulations using Bullet Physics engine. The Maya Bullet Physics simulation plug-in of the Bullet Physics engine is built from the Bullet physics library. This plug-in is automatically installed when you install Maya 2017 on your system.

By default, the **Bullet** plug-in is not loaded in Maya. You need to load it from the **Plug-in Manager**. To do so, choose **Windows > Editors > Settings/Preferences > Plug-in Manager** from the menubar; the **Plug-in Manager** will be displayed. Select the check box next to the **bullet.mll** option and then select the **Loaded** and **Auto load** check boxes available on the right of **bullet.mll** option. When you select the **Auto load** check box, the **Bullet** plug-in will be loaded automatically every time you start Maya.

BULLET OBJECTS

The **Bullet** plug-in consists of a collection of objects that have built-in dynamic simulations. All these objects can be accessed by using the options available in the **Bullet** menu from the menubar. The **Bullet** menu will be displayed when you choose **FX** from the **Menuset** drop-down list.

On choosing the **Bullet** menu, a list of options will be displayed, refer to Figure 17-1. The most commonly used options in this menu are discussed next.

*Figure 17-1 The **Bullet** menu*

Creating Active Rigid Body

The **Active Rigid Body** option is used to create an active rigid body or to convert a 3D object into an active rigid body. To convert a 3D object into an active rigid body, select the object in the viewport, and then choose **Bullet > Create > Active Rigid Body** from the menubar. Now, choose the **Play forwards** button from the playback controls area. You will notice that the object moves downward.

To set creation options for an active rigid body, choose **Bullet > Create > Active Rigid Body > Option Box** from the menubar; the **Create Rigid Body Options** dialog box will be displayed, as shown in Figure 17-2. This dialog box consists of different options that are used to set the properties of the rigid body.

After setting the required options in this dialog box, choose the **Apply and Close** button; a rigid body will be created in the viewport. After creating the rigid body, you can modify its different attributes by using the **Attribute Editor**. To do so, select the rigid body and press CTRL+A to display the **Attribute Editor**, if not already displayed.

Next, choose the **bulletRigidBodyShape#** tab from the **Attribute Editor**; the attributes will be displayed. These attributes are discussed next.

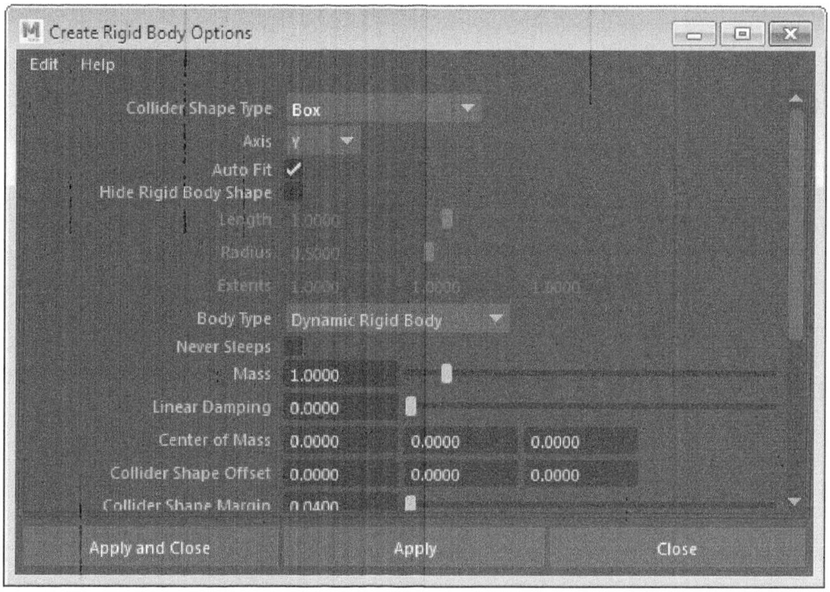

*Figure 17-2 The **Create Rigid Body Options** dialog box*

Rigid Body Properties Area

The **Rigid Body Properties** area consists of attributes that are used to set the different behavioral properties of a rigid body during dynamic simulations, refer to Figure 17-3. All these attributes are discussed next.

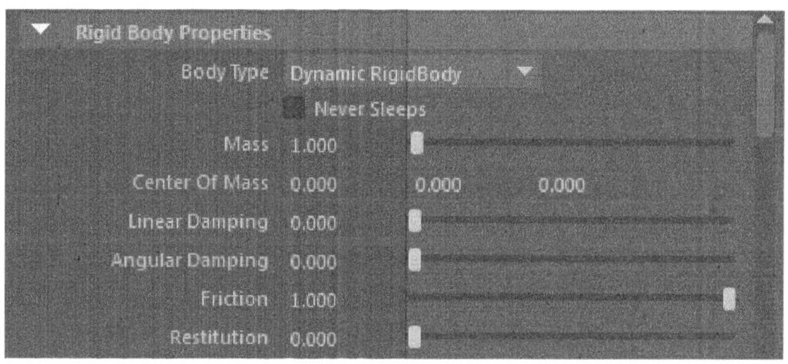

*Figure 17-3 The **Rigid Body Properties** area*

Body Type

The options in the **Body Type** drop-down list are used to specify the type of rigid body. This drop-down list consists of three options. These options are discussed next.

Static Body: This option is used to convert an active body into a stationary body.

Kinematic RigidBody: This option is used to convert a stationary body into a kinematic body.

Dynamic RigidBody: This option is used to convert a stationary body into a dynamic body.

Never Sleeps
The **Never Sleeps** check box when selected, makes the rigid body participate in the dynamic simulation. This check box is cleared by default.

Mass
The **Mass** attribute is used to control the movement of the rigid body with respect to its weight. For example, if the mass of a rigid body is set to 0, then it will not move, as it gets converted into kinematic rigid body.

Center of Mass
The **Center of Mass** attribute is used to determine the location of the rigid body.

Linear Damping
The **Linear Damping** attribute defines a clamp value that is applied to the linear velocity when calculating the rolling friction. This attribute applies damping so that the objects can come to the rest.

Angular Damping
The **Angular Damping** attribute is used to define a clamp value that is applied to the angular velocity of the object.

Friction
The **Friction** attribute is used to control the amount of resistance offered by the rigid body when it collides with other objects.

Restitution
The **Restitution** attribute is used to control the bounciness of the rigid body. If the value of restitution is set to 0, the rigid body will not bounce.

Initial Conditions Area
The **Initial Conditions** area, refer to Figure 17-4, consists of the attributes that are applied to the rigid body when the Bullet solver starts simulating. These attributes are discussed next.

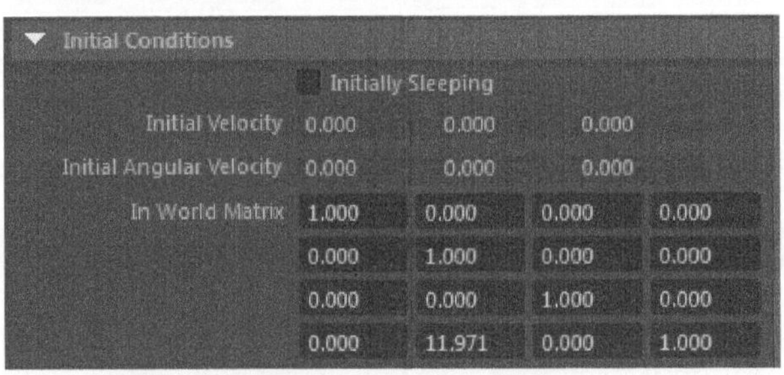

Figure 17-4 *The* ***Initial Conditions*** *area*

Initially Sleeping
The **Initially Sleeping** check box is used to specify whether the dynamic rigid body would start in a deactivated state or not. On selecting this check box, the dynamic rigid body will not move unless it is hit by another rigid body.

Initial Velocity

The **Initial Velocity** attribute is used to set the initial speed and direction of the rigid body.

Initial Angular Velocity

The **Initial Angular Velocity** attribute is used to set the rate of change of angular position of a rigid body when it rotates.

In World Matrix

The **In World Matrix** attribute is used to specify the initial position of the rigid body in world system coordinates.

Forces/Impulses Area

The **Forces/Impulses** area consists of attributes, refer to Figure 17-5, that are used to control the forces that act on the rigid body. These attributes are discussed next.

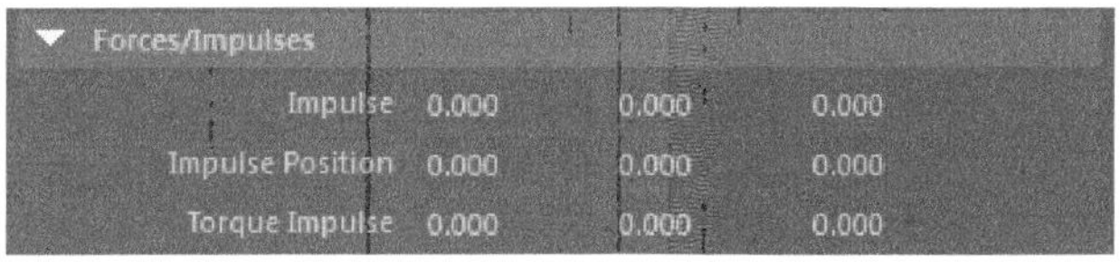

*Figure 17-5 The **Forces/Impulses** area*

Impulse

The **Impulse** attribute is used to specify the force acting on a rigid body on each frame of simulation.

Impulse Position

The **Impulse Position** attribute is used to specify the position at which the impulse force is applied on the rigid body with respect to time.

Torque Impulse

The **Torque Impulse** attribute is used to specify the rotational impulse force acting on the rigid body with respect to time.

Collider Properties Area

The **Collider Properties** area, as shown in Figure 17-6, consists of different attributes that are used to specify the shape and dimensions of the rigid body during collisions. These attributes are discussed next.

Collider Shape Type

The options in the **Collider Shape Type** drop-down list are used to specify the shape of the rigid body which collides with other objects. By default, the **box** option is selected in this drop-down list.

Input Mesh

The **Input Mesh** attribute displays the name of the 3D object that has been converted into an active rigid body.

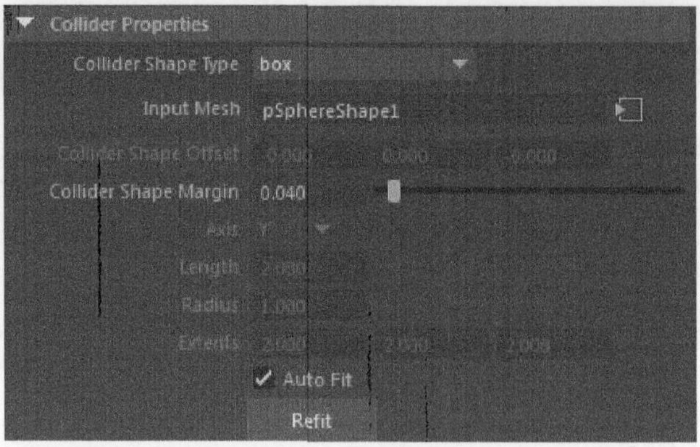

*Figure 17-6 The **Collider Properties** area*

Collider Shape Offset

The **Collider Shape Offset** attribute is used to specify the offset value between the collider shape and the object.

Collider Shape Margin

The **Collider Shape Margin** attribute is used to specify the size of the gap between rigid objects for them to collide.

Axis

The **Axis** drop-down list is used to specify the axis of the collider shape. By default, this drop-down list is inactive. It is activated only when the **cylinder** or **capsule** option is selected from the **Collider Shape Type** drop-down list and the **Auto Fit** check box is cleared.

Length

The **Length** attribute is used to specify the length of the cylinder or capsule collider shapes. By default, this drop-down list is inactive. It can be activated only when the **cylinder** or **capsule** option is selected from the **Collider Shape Type** drop-down list and the **Auto Fit** check box is cleared.

Radius

The **Radius** attribute is used to specify the radius of the cylinder, capsule, or sphere collider shape.

Extents

The **Extents** attribute is used to specify the length, width, and height of the box collider shape.

Auto Fit

The **Auto Fit** check box is used to automatically set the axis, length, radius, and extents when a rigid body is first created on an object. By default, this check box is selected.

Refit

The **Refit** button is used to perform one time auto-fit on the existing rigid body.

Collision Filters Area

The check boxes in this area are used to specify whether the rigid body will collide with other objects or not. You can select the check boxes from this area as per your requirement for selective collisions. By default, the **DefaultFilter** check boxes are selected in this area, refer to Figure 17-7.

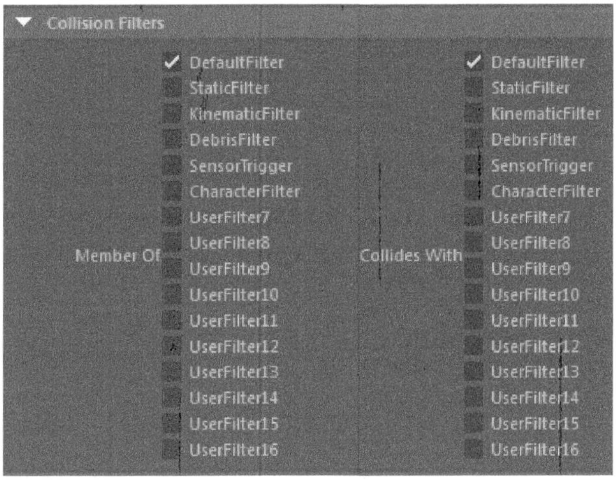

*Figure 17-7 The **Collision Filters** area*

Dynamics System Area

The attributes in this area are used to access the solver node that helps in controlling various attributes such as wind, gravity, and so on. To access the solver node, click on the arrow on the right of the **Solver** attribute; different areas will be displayed in the **bulletSolverShape#** tab, as shown in Figure 17-8. The different areas in this tab are discussed next.

Solver Properties Area

The **Solver Properties** area consists of different attributes that help in controlling the properties of a bullet solver. The bullet solver acts as the main object in all dynamic simulations. It calculates the different attributes related to dynamic simulations and uses the current state of a rigid body to calculate its next state. The different attributes in this area are discussed next.

Enable Simulation: The **Enable Simulation** check box is used to enable the simulation. On clearing this check box, no simulation will take place. This check box is selected by default.

Start Time: The **Start Time** attribute is used to set the frame from where the dynamic simulation will begin. The default value of this attribute is 1.

Split Impulse: The **Split Impulse** check box lets you separate the interpenetrating objects at the start of the simulation.

Solver Acceleration: The options in the **Solver Acceleration** drop-down list are used to accelerate the simulation. The **solver acceleration** attribute only affects the soft bodies not the rigid bodies.

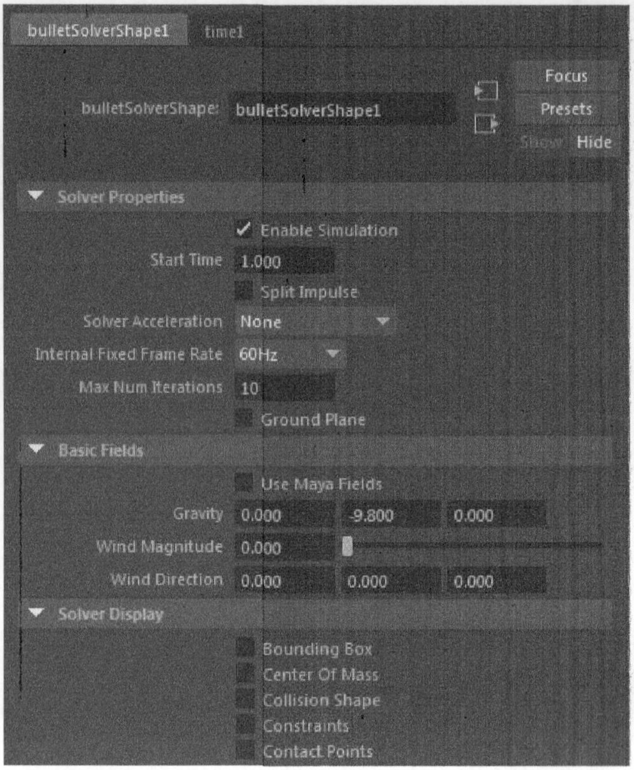

Figure 17-8 Different attributes under the ***bulletSolverShape#*** *tab*

Internal Fixed Frame Rate: The **Internal Fixed Frame Rate** drop-down list consists of different values that are used to set the rate at which the dynamic simulation will take place.

Max Num Iterations: The **Max Num Iterations** attribute is used to specify the time interval between two adjacent frames during simulation.

Ground Plane: Select the **Ground Plane** check box to set the Maya view plane as floor for the objects that you are simulating.

Basic Fields Area

The attributes in this area are used to control attributes such as gravity, intensity, or the direction of the wind flow during the simulation.

Solver Display Area

The check boxes in this area are used to set the display options for the rigid sets and the **Glue** constraint.

Creating Passive Rigid Bodies

The **Passive Rigid Body** option is used to create a new passive rigid body or to convert a 3D object into a passive rigid body. A passive rigid body is an object that does not move during simulation. To create a passive rigid body, choose **Bullet > Create > Passive Rigid Body > Option Box** from the menubar; the **Create Rigid Body Options** dialog box will be displayed. This dialog box consists of different attributes that are used to set the properties of the passive rigid body. After specifying the required attributes in this dialog box, choose the **Apply and Close** button; a passive rigid body will be created in the viewport. You can also convert a 3D mesh into a passive rigid body. To do so, select the 3D mesh in the viewport and then choose **Bullet > Create > Passive Rigid Body** from the menubar. After creating a passive rigid body, you can modify its different attributes by using the **bulletRigidBodyShape#** tab in the **Attribute Editor**.

Creating Soft Bodies

The **Soft Body** option is used to create a new soft body or to convert a 3D object into a soft body. A soft body is an object whose shape gets deformed during simulation. It is created using the polygon objects. To create a soft body, select the polygon object in the viewport and then choose **Bullet > Create > Soft Body > Option Box** from the menubar; the **Create Soft Body Options** dialog box will be displayed, as shown in Figure 17-9.

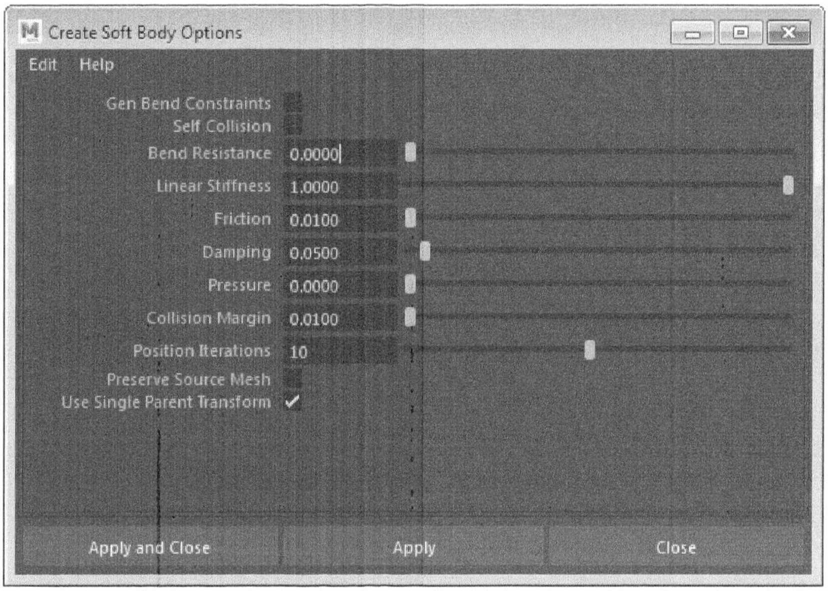

*Figure 17-9 The **Create Soft Body Options** dialog box*

This dialog box consists of different options that are used to set the properties of the soft body. These options are discussed next.

Gen Bend Constraints

The **Gen Bend Constraints** check box is used to control the bending of the joints at each vertex of the soft body during simulation.

Self Collision

The **Self Collision** check box is used to control the collisions occurring between different parts of the same soft body such that they do not penetrate into each other.

Bend Resistance

The **Bend Resistance** option is used to control the resistance offered by different parts of the soft body while bending. By default, the value of this attribute is set to 0.

Linear Stiffness
The **Linear Stiffness** attribute is used to control the amount of stretching in the soft body.

Friction
The **Friction** attribute is used to control the amount of resistance offered by the soft body when it collides with other objects.

Damping
The attribute controls the damping factor applied to the overall motion of the soft body.

Pressure
The **Pressure** attribute is used to control the volume of a soft body. On increasing the value of **Pressure** attribute, the volume of the soft body will also increase.

Collision Margin
The **Collision Margin** option is used to set a boundary between the soft body and other objects during collisions between them.

Position Iterations
The **Position Iterations** option is used to specify the number of iterations that will occur in the solver with respect to the position of the soft body.

Preserve Source Mesh
Select the **Preserve Source Mesh** check box to maintain the source mesh at the start point of the solver.

Use Single Parent Transform
By default, this check box is selected. It reuses the source transform and adds a new cloth shape instead of creating a new transform node and output mesh shape.

Rigid Body Constraint
The **Rigid Body Constraint** option is used to restrict the movement of a rigid body. The movement of a rigid body can be constrained to a particular position in a scene or to other rigid bodies. To apply a constraint to a rigid body, select the rigid bodies and then choose **Bullet > Create > Rigid Body Constraint > Option Box** from the menubar; the **Create Rigid Body Constraint Options** dialog box will be displayed, as shown in Figure 17-10.

In this dialog box, there are different types of constraints that can be applied to a rigid body. These constraints can be selected from the **Constraint Type** drop-down list in the **Create Rigid Body Constraint Options** dialog box. These constraints are discussed next.

Point
The **Point** constraint is used to restrict the movement of two rigid bodies in such a way that the pivot points of these bodies match in the world space. On playing the simulation, the movement of the bodies will be limited around the pivot point. You can limit the translation so that the

pivot points between the two rigid bodies match in the world space. You can use this constraint to create effects such as chain link.

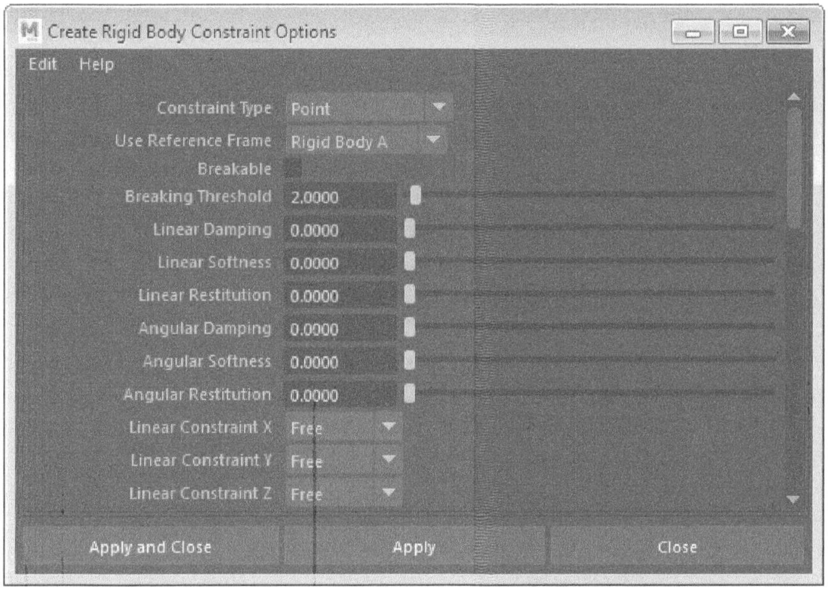

*Figure 17-10 The **Create Rigid Body Constraint Options** dialog box*

Hinge

The **Hinge** constraint is used to restrict the movement of a rigid body in such a way that the body can only rotate around the Z axis of the constraint point. This constraint can be used to simulate the effect of a door attached to a hinge.

SpringHinge

The **SpringHinge** constraint is used to restrict the movement of a rigid body in such a way that the body appears to be connected to a spring like shaft.

Slider

The **Slider** constraint allows the rigid body to rotate and move along the Z axis of the constraint point at the same time.

ConeTwist

The **ConeTwist** constraint is used to simulate the effect of the limbs by adding cone and twist axis limits. The X axis serves as a twist axis.

SixDOF

The term **SixDOF** constraint stands for Six Degrees of Freedom. This constraint is used to imitate different constraints in such a way that the first three axes represent the linear movement of the rigid bodies and the other three axes represent the rotation of the rigid bodies. Each axis can be locked, freed, or limited. By default, all the six axes are unlocked.

SpringSixDOF

The **SpringSixDOF** constraint is similar to the **SixDOF** constraint with the only difference that **SpringSixDOF** constraint includes the addition of springs for each of the degrees of freedom.

Soft Body Anchor

The **Soft Body Anchor** option is used to hold the portion of a soft body at a particular position while the rest of the body moves during simulation. This option can be used to create different simulations, such as a cloth hanging on a hook. You can anchor the soft body to a rigid body. However, if you do not create a rigid body, a rigid body anchor will be created automatically. To create a soft body anchor, create a plane with 30 height and width subdivisions and convert it into a soft body. Next, choose **Create > Construction Aid > Locator** from the menubar; a locator will be created in the viewport. Select a vertex of the plane that you want to act as an anchor and make sure that the locator lies on the selected vertex. With both the vertex and the locator selected, choose **Bullet > Create > Soft Body Anchor** from the menubar. Now, play the simulation. You will notice that the selected vertex on the soft body will remain fixed, while rest of the body will move downward, refer to Figure 17-11.

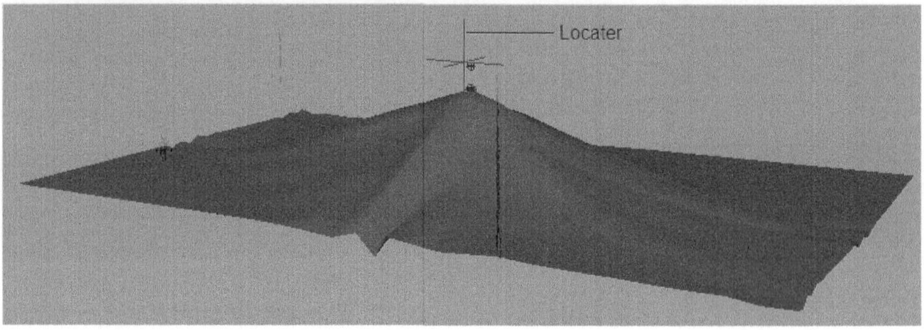

***Figure 17-11** The soft body during simulation*

Soft Body Vertex Properties

The **Soft Body Vertex Properties** option is used to set the attributes of the vertices of a soft body. To set the attributes of the vertices of the soft body, choose **Bullet > Edit > Soft Body Vertex Properties** from the menubar; a cascading menu will be displayed, as shown in Figure 17-12. The options in this cascading menu are discussed next.

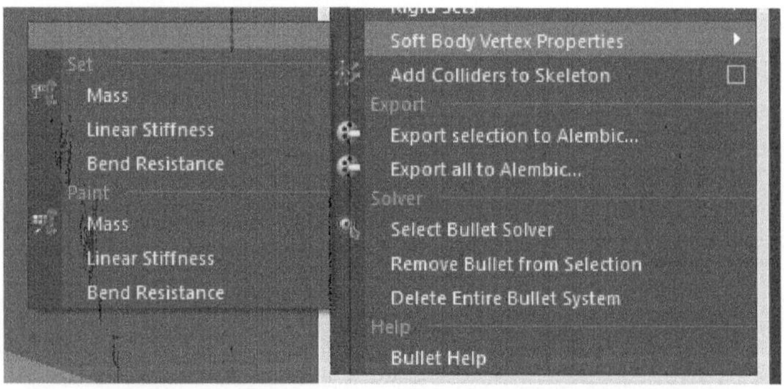

***Figure 17-12** Cascading menu displayed on choosing the **Soft Body Vertex Properties** option*

Mass
The **Mass** option is used to lock the position of a vertex at a particular position.

Linear Stiffness
The **Linear Stiffness** option is used to specify the stretching value of a vertex.

Bend Resistance
The **Bend Resistance** option is used to specify the value of the resistance caused by the vertices on bending.

TUTORIAL

Tutorial 1

In this tutorial, you will create simulation of colliding bowling pins, as shown in Figure 17-13.

(Expected time: 20 min)

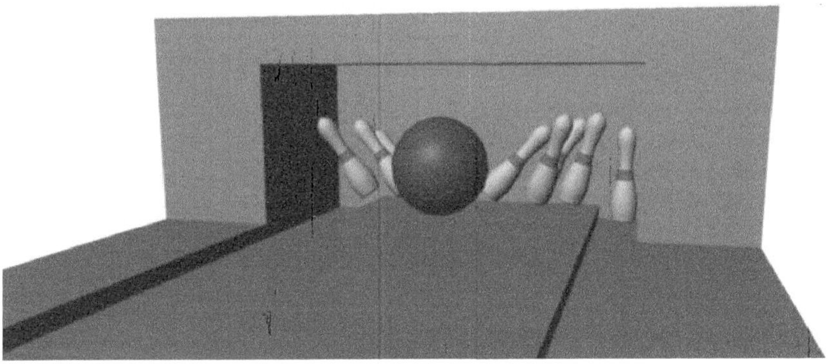

Figure 17-13 Bowling pins after collision

The following steps are required to complete this tutorial:

a. Create a project folder.
b. Download and open the file.
c. Convert objects into rigid bodies.
d. Set attributes of different rigid bodies.
e. Modify the playback settings.
f. Save and render the scene.

Creating the Project Folder
Create a new project folder with the name *c17_tut1* at *\Documents\maya2017*, as discussed in Tutorial 1 of Chapter 2.

Downloading and Opening the File
In this section, you will download the scene file.

1. Download the *c17_maya_2017_tut.zip* file from *www.cadcim.com*. The path of the file is as follows: *Textbooks > Animation and Visual Effects > Maya > Autodesk Maya 2017: A Comprehensive Guide.*

   Extract the contents of the zip file and save them in the *Documents* folder.

2. Choose **File > Open Scene** from the menubar; the **Open** dialog box is displayed. In this dialog box, browse to *c17_maya_2017_tut* folder and select **c17_tut1_start.mb** file. Next, choose the **Open** button; the *c17_tut1_start.mb* file is displayed. Figure 17-14 shows the bowling pins and ball in the scene.

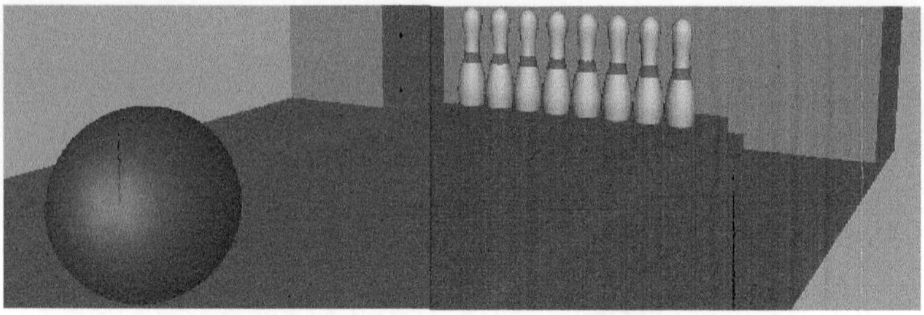

Figure 17-14 *Bowling pins and the ball*

3. Choose **File > Save Scene As** from the menubar; the **Save As** dialog box is displayed. As the project folder is already set, the path *\Documents\maya2017\c17_tut1\scenes* is displayed in the **Look In** drop-down list. Save the file with the name *c17tut1.mb* in this folder.

Converting Objects into Rigid Bodies

In this section, you will convert the objects into rigid bodies.

1. Select **bowling_alley** from the **Outliner** window. Next, choose **Bullet > Create > Passive Rigid Body** from the menubar; the bowling alley is converted into a passive rigid body and now it is going to remain stationary throughout the simulation.

2. Make sure that the *bowling_alley* is selected in the viewport. Also, make sure the **bulletRigidBodyShape1** tab is chosen in the **Attribute Editor**. In the **Collider Properties** area of this tab, select **mesh (static only)** from the **Collider Shape Type** drop-down list and then choose the **Refit** button.

3. Select **bowling_ball** from the **Outliner** window. Choose **Bullet > Create > Active Rigid Body** from the menubar; the bowling ball is converted into an active rigid body.

4. Similarly, select **bowling_pin1**, **bowling_pin2**, **bowling_pin3**, **bowling_pin4**, **bowling_pin5**, **bowling_pin6**, **bowling_pin7**, and **bowling_pin8** from the **Outliner** window, and convert them into active rigid bodies, as done in the previous step.

Set Attributes of Different Rigid Bodies

In this section, you will set the different attributes of the bowling pins and bowling ball.

1. Select the **bowling_ball** in the viewport. In the **Attribute Editor**, choose the **bulletRigidBodyShape2** tab. Now, in the **Rigid Body Properties** area, set the attributes as shown in Figure 17-15.

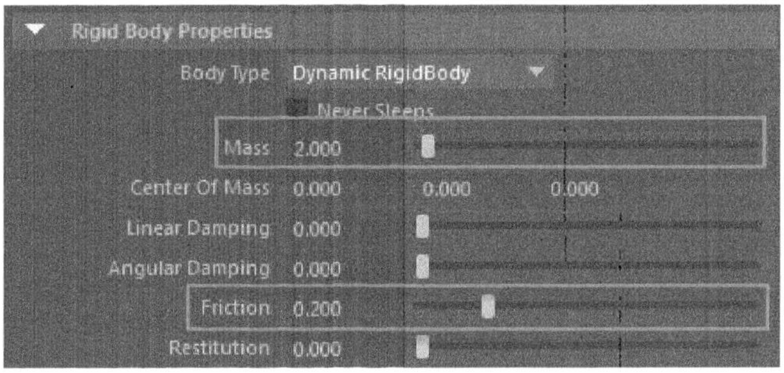

***Figure 17-15** Setting the attributes in the **Rigid Body Properties** area*

2. Make sure that the *bowling_ball* is selected in the viewport. Expand the **Initial Conditions** area of the **bulletRigidBodyShape2** tab and enter **-40** in the Z axis edit box corresponding to the **Initial Velocity** attribute, refer to Figure 17-16. Expand the **Forces/Impulses** area and enter **-0.2** in the Z axis edit box corresponding to the **Impulse** attribute, refer to Figure 17-16.

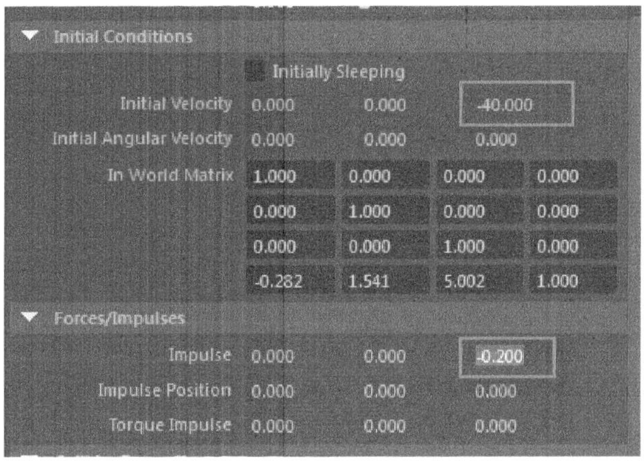

Figure 17-16** Setting the values of **Initial Velocity** and **Impulse

3. Expand the **Collider Properties** area and then select the **hull** option from the **Collider Shape Type** drop-down list. Select **bowling_pin1** from the **Outliner** window. Next, in the **bulletRigidBodyShape3** tab of the **Attribute Editor**, select the **Initially Sleeping** check box in the **Initial Conditions** area. Now, in the **Collider Properties** area, select cylinder from the **Collider Shape Type** drop-down list.

4. In the **Rigid Body Properties** area, set **Mass** to **2** for all bowling pins.

5. Repeat the procedure followed in step 3 to set the attributes for the rest of the bowling pins.

Modifying the Playback Settings

In this section, you will modify the playback settings for animation.

1. Set the end time to **125** in the timeline.

2. Choose the **Animation preferences** button from the right of the **Auto keyframe toggle** button; the **Preferences** dialog box is displayed. In this dialog box, select the **Real-time [24 fps]** option from the **Playback speed** drop-down list in the **Playback** area. Next, choose the **Save** button.

3. Choose the **Play forwards** button to preview the simulation.

Saving and Rendering the Scene

In this section, you will save the scene that you have created and then render it. You can also view the final rendered image sequence of the scene by downloading the *c17_maya_2017_rndr.zip* file from *www.cadcim.com*. The path of the file is as follows: *Textbooks > Animation and Visual Effects > Maya > Autodesk Maya 2017: A Comprehensive Guide.*

1. Choose **File > Save Scene** from the menubar. For rendering the scene, refer to Tutorial 1 of Chapter 8. The final output of the scene at frame 9 is shown in Figure 17-17.

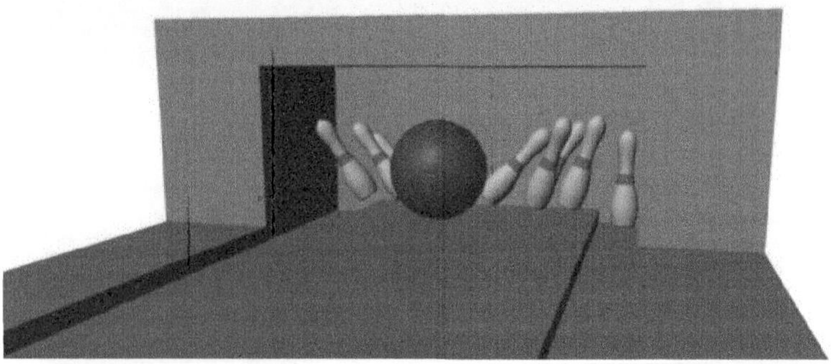

***Figure 17-17** The final output*

Self-Evaluation Test

Answer the following questions and then compare them to those given at the end of this chapter:

1. Which of the following attributes is used to control the distance between a rigid body and the point where the constraint is applied?

   (a) **Angular Damping** (b) **Restitution**
   (c) **Linear Damping** (d) **Axis**

2. Which of the following attributes is used to specify the force acting on a rigid body in different axes with respect to time?

   (a) **Impulse** (b) **In World Matrix**
   (c) **Center of Mass** (d) **Mass**

3. The __________ tool is used to set the attributes of the vertices of a soft body.

4. The __________ attribute is used to specify the rotational impulse force acting on a rigid body with respect to time.

5. The rigid body will not bounce if the value of restitution in the **Rigid Body Properties** area is set to __________.

6. The __________ option is used to set the initial speed and direction of a rigid body.

7. The **Linear Stiffness** attribute is used to lock the position of a vertex of a soft body at a particular position. (T/F)

8. The **Split Impulse** option is used to control the movement of a rigid body at its initial position by preventing it from diving. (T/F)

9. The **Impulse Position** attribute is used to specify the position at which the **Impulse** force will be applied on a rigid body. (T/F)

Review Questions

Answer the following questions:

1. Which of the following options is used to specify the length, width, and height of the collider shape?

   (a) **Radius** (b) **Extents**
   (c) **Axis** (d) **Length**

2. The __________ option is used to keep the polygon object intact and simulate only the soft body that is created from it.

3. The __________ tool is used to set the attributes of the vertices of a soft body.

4. The __________ constraint is used to restrict the movement of a rigid body in such a way that the body appears to be connected to a spring like shaft.

5. The __________ rigid body can be manually animated during the simulation but it does not have an in-built dynamic simulation.

6. The term **SixDOF** stands for __________.

7. The **Damping** option is used to hold the portion of a soft body at a particular position while the rest of the body moves during the simulation. (T/F)

8. The **Axis** drop-down list is activated only when the **Cylinder** or **Capsule** option is selected from the **Collider Shape Type** drop-down list. (T/F)

Answers to Self-Evaluation Test

1. c, **2.** a, **3. Soft Body Vertex Properties**, **4. Torque Impulse**, **5.** 0, **6. Initial Velocity**, **7.** F, **8.** T, **9.** T

Index

D

E

F

G

H

O

P

R

S

W

Z

Other Titles of Interest - BPB/TICKOO SERIES

Publications by BPB/TICKOO SERIES

The following is the list of some of the publications by BPB/TICKOO series:

3ds Max Textbooks

- Autodesk 3ds Max 2017: A Comprehensive Guide, 17th Edition
- Autodesk 3ds Max 2017 for Beginners: A Tutorial Approach, 17th Edition

MAXON CINEMA 4D Textbook

- MAXON CINEMA 4D R18 Studio: A Tutorial Approach, 5th Edition

Pixologic ZBrush 4R7 Textbook

- Pixologic ZBrush 4R7: A Comprehensive Guide, 2nd Edition

Programming Textbooks

- Introduction to C++ Programming, 2nd Edition
- Learning Oracle 12c: A PL/SQL Approach, 2nd Edition
- Introduction to Java Programming, 2nd Edition

Autodesk Revit Architecture Textbook

- Exploring Autodesk Revit 2017 for Architecture, 13th Edition

RISA-3D Textbook

- Exploring RISA-3D 14.0

Bentley STAAD.Pro Textbook

- Exploring Bentley STAAD.Pro V8i (SELECTseries 6)

AutoCAD Civil 3D Textbook

- Exploring AutoCAD Civil 3D 2017, 7th Edition

AutoCAD Map 3D Textbook

- Exploring AutoCAD Map 3D 2017, 7th Edition

Autodesk Navisworks Textbook

- Exploring Autodesk Navisworks 2017, 4th Edition

Oracle Primavera Textbook

- Exploring Oracle Primavera P6 v8.4

AutoCAD Raster Design Textbook
- Exploring AutoCAD Raster Design 2017

Autodesk Inventor Textbook
- Autodesk Inventor 2017 for Designers, 17th Edition

AutoCAD MEP Textbook
- AutoCAD MEP 2016 for Designers, 3rd Edition

NX Textbook
- NX 11.0 for Designers, 10th Edition

NX Nastran Textbook
- NX Nastran 9.0 for Designers

SolidWorks Textbook
- SOLIDWORKS 2017 for Designers, 15th Edition

Creo Parametric Textbook
- PTC Creo Parametric 3.0 for Designers, 3rd Edition

Autodesk Alias Textbook
- Learning Autodesk Alias Design 2016, 5th Edition

AutoCAD Electrical Textbook
- AutoCAD Electrical 2017 for Electrical Control Designers, 8th Edition

CATIA Textbook
- CATIA V5-6R2016 for Designers, 14th Edition

Solid Edge Textbook
- Solid Edge ST9 for Designers, 14th Edition

AutoCAD LT Textbook
- AutoCAD LT 2017 for Designers, 12th Edition

CAD/CAM/CIM/GIS/ANIMATION/CIVIL BOOKS

by **Prof. Sham Tickoo** (Purdue University, USA and Autodesk Authorised Author)

NX Nastran 9
For Designers
ISBN 978-93-8655-122-1
Price: ₹ 899/-

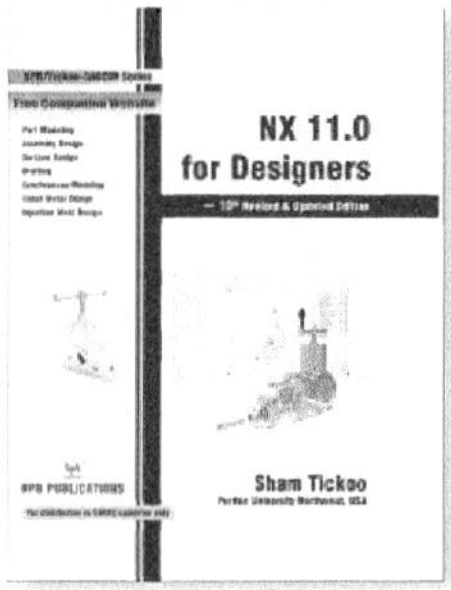

NX 11
for Designers
ISBN 978-93-8655-124-5
Price: ₹ 1099/-

Mold Design
Using NX 11
ISBN 978-93-8728-406-7
Price: ₹ 599/-

Siemens NX 12.0
for Designers
ISBN 978-93-8728-407-4
Price: ₹ 1099/-

Autodesk Inventor Professional 2019
For Designers
ISBN 978-93-8817-629-3
Price: ₹ 1299/-

Autodesk Inventor Professional 2018
For Designers
ISBN 978-93-8655-164-1
Price: ₹ 1199/-

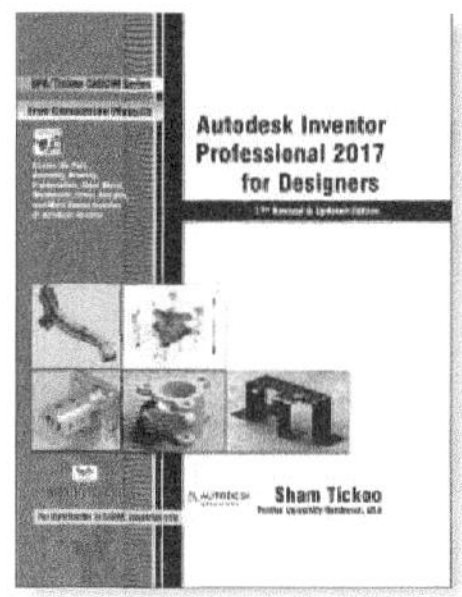

Autodesk Inventor Professional 2017
For Designers
ISBN 978-93-8655-126-9
Price: ₹ 1299/-

Autodesk FUSION 360
A Tutorial Approach
ISBN 978-93-8728-441-8
Price: ₹ 599/-

Solid Edge ST 10
For Designers
ISBN 978-93-8728-410-4
Price: ₹ 1099/-

Solid Edge ST 9
For Designers
ISBN 978-93-8655-120-7
Price: ₹ 1099/-

Solid Works 2017
For Designers
ISBN 978-93-8655-121-4
Price: ₹ 1299/-

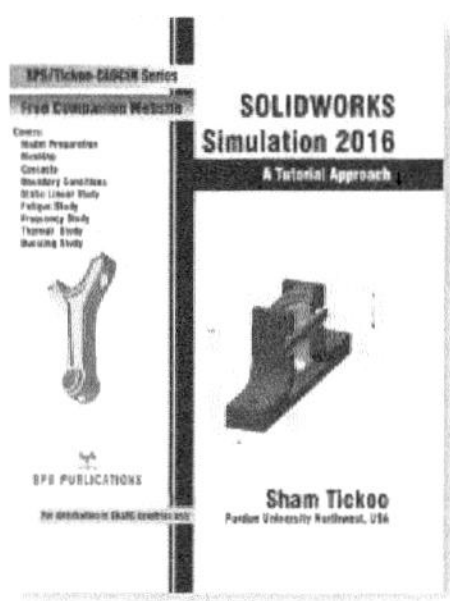

Solid Works Simulation 2016
A Tutorial Approach
ISBN 978-93-8655-175-7
Price: ₹ 499/-

Available on **www.bpbonline.com** and all leading book stores.

bpb PUBLICATIONS | #1 Publisher of Computer Books | 62 Years of Excellence | OVER 90 Million Books Sold Worldwide

CAD/CAM/CIM/GIS/ANIMATION/CIVIL BOOKS

by **Prof. Sham Tickoo** (Purdue University, USA and Autodesk Authorised Author)

Solid Works 2018
For Designers
ISBN 978-93-8728-409-8
Price: ₹ 1299/-

Solid Works Simulation 2018
For Designers
ISBN 978-93-8728-411-1
Price: ₹ 599/-

Solid Works 2018
A Tutorial Approach
ISBN 978-93-8817-631-6
Price: ₹ 799/-

Learning Solid Works 2018
A Project Based Approach
ISBN 978-93-8817-632-3
Price: ₹ 699/-

Exploring AutoCAD Civil 3D 2017
ISBN 978-93-8655-102-3
Price: ₹ 999/-

Exploring AutoCAD Civil 3D 2018
ISBN 978-93-8728-413-5
Price: ₹ 999/-

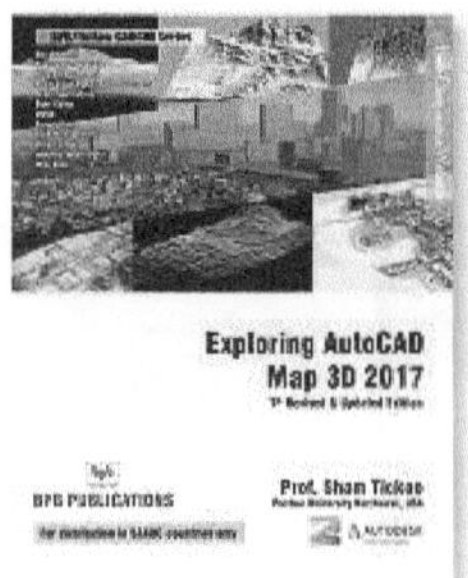

Exploring AutoCAD Map 3D 2017
ISBN 978-93-8655-103-0
Price: ₹ 875/-

Exploring AutoCAD Map 3D 2018
ISBN 978-93-8655-166-5
Price: ₹ 799/-

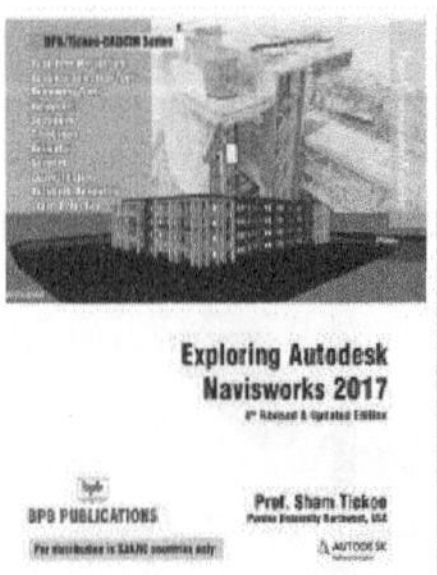

Exploring Autodesk
Navisworks 2017
ISBN 978-93-8655-104-7
Price: ₹ 699/-

Exploring Oracle
Primavera P6 R8.4
ISBN 978-93-8655-105-4
Price: ₹ 599/-

Exploring Autodesk
Revit 2017
For Architecture
ISBN 978-93-8655-106-1
Price: ₹ 999/-

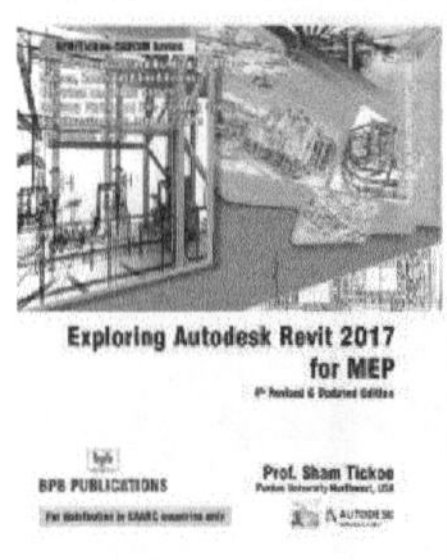

Exploring Autodesk
Revit 2017
For MEP
ISBN 978-93-8655-107-8
Price: ₹ 799/-

Available on **www.bpbonline.com** and all leading book stores.

---

bpb PUBLICATIONS | #1 Publisher of Computer Books | 62 Years of Excellence | OVER 90 Million Books Sold Worldwide